# COMMERCIAL REPORTS

# AREA STUDIES SERIES

EDITORIAL DIRECTOR   Professor J J O'Meara
RESEARCH UNIT DIRECTOR   T F Turley
ASSISTANT DIRECTOR   S Cashman

CHIEF EDITORIAL ADVISERS

P Ford
*Professor Emeritus, Southampton University*
Mrs G Ford

SPECIAL EDITORIAL CONSULTANT FOR
THE UNITED STATES PAPERS

H C Allen
*Commonwealth Fund Professor of American History, University College, London*
*Director of the London University Institute of United States Studies*

RESEARCH EDITORS
Johann A Norstedt
Marilyn Evers Norstedt

*This Series is published with the active co-operation of*
SOUTHAMPTON UNIVERSITY

IRISH UNIVERSITY PRESS AREA STUDIES SERIES

BRITISH PARLIAMENTARY PAPERS

UNITED STATES OF AMERICA

36

Embassy and consular
commercial reports
1892-93

IRISH UNIVERSITY PRESS
*Shannon Ireland*

## PUBLISHER'S NOTE

The documents in this series are selected from the nineteenth-century British House of Commons *sessional and command papers*. All of the original papers relating to the United States of America are included with the exception of two kinds of very brief and unimportant papers. Omitted are (1) random statistical trade returns which are included in the larger and complete yearly trade figures and (2) returns relating to postal services, which are irregularly presented, of tangential USA relevance, and easily available in other sources.

The original documents have been reproduced by photo-lithography and are unabridged even to the extent of retaining the first printers' imprints. Imperfections in the original printing are sometimes unavoidably reproduced.

This reprint is an enlargement from the original octavo format.

© 1971 Irish University Press Shannon Ireland
*Microfilm, microfiche and other forms of micro-publishing*
© *Irish University Microforms Shannon Ireland*

ISBN 0 7165 1536 9

*Printed and published by*
Irish University Press Shannon Ireland
DUBLIN   CORK   BELFAST   LONDON   NEW YORK
T M MacGlinchey *Publisher*   Robert Hogg *Printer*

# Contents

IUP Page Number

*For ease of reference IUP editors have assigned a continuous pagination which appears on the top outer margin of each page.*

**Commercial Reports**

F.O. annual series no. 964: report on Philadelphia, 1890
1892 [C.6550–26] LXXXIV . . . . . . . 9

F.O. annual series no. 986: report on New Orleans, 1891
1892 [C.6550–48] LXXXIV . . . . . . . 37

F.O. annual series no. 987: report on the agriculture of
New Orleans, 1891
1892 [C.6550–49] LXXXIV . . . . . . . 55

F.O. annual series no. 989: report on Galveston, 1891
1892 [C.6550–51] LXXXV . . . . . . . 161

F.O. annual series no. 994: report on Pensacola, 1891
1892 [C.6550–56] LXXXV . . . . . . . 183

F.O. annual series no. 1001: report on Baltimore, 1891
1892 [C.6550–63] LXXXV . . . . . . . 195

F.O. annual series no. 1015: report on Boston, 1891
1892 [C.6550–77] LXXXV . . . . . . . 215

F.O. annual series no. 1072: report on Charleston, 1891
1892 [C.6550–134] LXXXV . . . . . . . 227

F.O. annual series no. 1078: report on Philadelphia, 1891
1892 [C.6812–3] LXXXV . . . . . . . 267

F.O. annual series no. 1080: report on New York, 1891
1892 [C.6812–5] LXXXV . . . . . . . 303

F.O. annual series no. 1081: report on the agriculture of the
San Francisco district, 1891
1892 [C.6812–6] LXXXV . . . . . . . 331

F.O. annual series no. 1086: report on San Francisco, 1891
1892 [C.6812–11] LXXXV . . . . . . . 349

F.O. annual series no. 1103: report on Chicago, 1891
1892 [C.6812–28] LXXXV . . . . . . . 411

F.O. annual series no. 1157: report on the foreign commerce
of the United States, 1892
1893 [C.6855–44] XCVII . . . . . . . 467

F.O. annual series no. 1164: report on Galveston, 1892
1893 [C.6855–51] XCVII . . . . . . . 493

F.O. annual series no. 1176: report on Baltimore, 1892
1893 [C.6855–63] XCVII . . . . . . . 515

F.O. annual series no. 1181: report on Boston, 1892
1893 [C.6855–68] XCVII . . . . . . . 537

F.O. annual series no. 1203: report on Charleston, 1892
1893 [C.6855–90] XCVII . . . . . . . 549

F.O. annual series no. 1205: report on New Orleans, 1892
1893 [C.6855–92] XCVII . . . . . . . 593

F.O. annual series no. 1233: report on Chicago, 1892
1893 [C.6855–120] XCVII . . . . . . . 635

As most commercial reports are extracted from larger papers, the reader should note that a particular report may lack a proper title page.

# FOREIGN OFFICE.
# 1891.
# ANNUAL SERIES.

## N⁰· 964.

## DIPLOMATIC AND CONSULAR REPORTS ON TRADE AND FINANCE.

# UNITED STATES.

### REPORT FOR THE YEAR 1890
ON THE
### TRADE OF THE CONSULAR DISTRICT OF PHILADELPHIA.

REFERENCE TO PREVIOUS REPORT, Annual Series No. 731.

*Issued during the Recess and Presented to both Houses of Parliament by Command of Her Majesty.*

LONDON:
PRINTED FOR HER MAJESTY'S STATIONERY OFFICE,
BY HARRISON AND SONS, ST. MARTIN'S LANE,
PRINTERS IN ORDINARY TO HER MAJESTY.

And to be purchased, either directly or through any Bookseller, from
EYRE & SPOTTISWOODE, EAST HARDING STREET, FLEET STREET, E.C., and
32, ABINGDON STREET, WESTMINSTER, S.W.; or
JOHN MENZIES & Co., 12, HANOVER STREET, EDINBURGH, and
90, WEST NILE STREET, GLASGOW; or
HODGES, FIGGIS, & Co., 104, GRAFTON STREET, DUBLIN.

1891.
*Price Twopence.*

[C. 6550—26.]

## New Series of Reports.

Reports of the Annual Series have been issued from Her Majesty's Diplomatic and Consular Officers at the following places, and may be obtained from the sources indicated on the title-page:—

| No. | | Price. | No. | | Price. |
|---|---|---|---|---|---|
| 842. | Calais | 1d. | 903. | Bengazi | 1d. |
| 843. | Boston | 1d. | 904. | Tahiti | ½d. |
| 844. | Bordeaux | 2½d. | 905. | Chinkiang | 1d. |
| 845. | Charleston | 1½d. | 906. | San Francisco | 3d. |
| 846. | Manila | 5d. | 907. | Brindisi | 2d. |
| 847. | Madeira | ½d. | 908. | Beyrout | 1d. |
| 848. | Paris | 2d. | 909. | Noumea | ½d. |
| 849. | Tripoli | ½d. | 910. | San Francisco | 1d. |
| 850. | Swatow | 1d. | 911. | New York | 1½d. |
| 851. | Saigon | ½d. | 912. | Caracas | 1½d. |
| 852. | Vienna | 1½d. | 913. | Greytown | ½d. |
| 853. | Algiers | 2d. | 914. | Corunna | 2d. |
| 854. | Algiers | 1d. | 915. | Christiania | 5½d. |
| 855. | Mozambique | 8d. | 916. | Callao | 1d. |
| 856. | Antwerp | 1½d. | 917. | Macao | 1d. |
| 857. | Mogador | 2d. | 918. | Söul | 1d. |
| 858. | Ichang | ½d. | 919. | Dunkirk | 1d. |
| 859. | Calais | 8½d. | 920. | Tamsui | 1d. |
| 860. | Riga | 2d. | 921. | Bussorah | ½d. |
| 861. | San José | 1d. | 922. | Yokohama | 3½d. |
| 862. | Genoa | 1½d. | 923. | Bilbao | 1½d. |
| 863. | Warsaw | 1d. | 924. | Barcelona | 2½d. |
| 864. | Wuhu | 1d. | 925. | Netherlands India | 1d. |
| 865. | Marseilles | 1d. | 926. | Chefoo | 1d. |
| 866. | Syra | 1d. | 927. | Buenos Ayres | ½d. |
| 867. | Jeddah | ½d. | 928. | Santo Domingo | ½d. |
| 868. | Savannah | ½d. | 929. | Constantinople | ½d. |
| 869. | Suakin | ½d. | 930. | Erzeroum | 1½d. |
| 870. | Berlin | 1d. | 931. | Gothenburg | 2d. |
| 871. | Batoum | 1½d. | 932. | Tunis | 1d. |
| 872. | Rosario | ½d. | 933. | New York | 1d. |
| 873. | Buenos Ayres | ½d. | 934. | Nagasaki | 1d. |
| 874. | Mogador | 1d. | 935. | Hakodate | 1½d. |
| 875. | Tainan | 6½d. | 936. | Sofia | 3d. |
| 876. | Pakhoi | 1d. | 937. | Frankfort | 2d. |
| 877. | Odessa | 2½d. | 938. | Bangkok | 9d. |
| 878. | Trebizond | 1½d. | 939. | Berne | 1½d. |
| 879. | Mollendo | ½d. | 940. | The Hague | 1½d. |
| 880. | Kiukiang | 1d. | 941. | Christiania | 1d. |
| 881. | Antananarivo | 1d. | 942. | Christiania | ½d. |
| 882. | Stettin | 2½d. | 943. | Brunei | 1½d. |
| 883. | Fiume | 1½d. | 944. | Alexandria | 1½d. |
| 884. | Batavia | 1d. | 945. | Therapia | ½d. |
| 885. | Samoa | ½d. | 946. | Bushire | 1½d. |
| 886. | Cherbourg | 1d. | 947. | Tokio | 2½d. |
| 887. | Cagliari | 1d. | 948. | Stockholm | 2d. |
| 888. | Hankow | 1½d. | 949. | Palermo | 2½d. |
| 889. | Vienna | 1½d. | 950. | St. Petersburg | 2½d. |
| 890. | Amoy | 1d. | 951. | Quito | ½d. |
| 891. | Adrianople | ½d. | 952. | Rio de Janeiro | 2d. |
| 892. | Chicago | 2½d. | 953. | Naples | 2d. |
| 893. | Brest | 1d. | 954. | Amsterdam | 1d. |
| 894. | Smyrna | 1d. | 955. | Tangier | 2d. |
| 895. | Cadiz | 1d. | 956. | Paramaribo | 1d. |
| 896. | Aleppo | 1d. | 957. | Teneriffe | 1d. |
| 897. | Foochow | 1d. | 958. | Athens | 2d. |
| 898. | Kiungchow | 1d. | 959. | Odessa | 1d. |
| 899. | The Hague | 1½d. | 960. | Copenhagen | 9d. |
| 900. | Nice | 1½d. | 961. | Tokio | 1d. |
| 901. | Nantes | 1½d. | 962. | Salonica | 1½d. |
| 902. | Port-au-Prince | 1½d. | 963. | Stettin | 3½d. |

# No. 964.

*Reference to previous Report, Annual Series No 731.*

## UNITED STATES.

### PHILADELPHIA.

*Consul Clipperton to the Marquis of Salisbury.*

My Lord,            *Philadelphia, September* 15, 1891.

I HAVE the honour to enclose herewith a Report on the Trade and Commerce of Philadelphia during the year 1890.

I have, &c.

(Signed)     ROBT. CHAS. CLIPPERTON.

---

*Report on the Trade, Commerce, and Manufactures of the Consular District of Pennsylvania, Ohio, Indiana, and Michigan.*

Introductory.

This Consular district, including four of the most important States of the Union for industrial and agricultural products, as well as mineral deposits and railway enterprises, has continued to enjoy a steady prosperity equal to, if not surpassing, any other section of the United States. Finances at times have met with temporary shocks, only to return, however, to a normal condition in a short time. The past winter was much colder than several previous ones, and that gave vigour to the former stagnant coal trade and the woollen industries. Railways and mining of anthracite and bituminous coals and slate have largely prospered. The building trades have steadily kept pace, wages holding their own and no upheavals of extensive strikes. The iron and steel trade has enjoyed continuous activity, and, on the whole, the year 1890 has expired with few disasters and numerous evidences of increased prosperity.

The labour market has not experienced, to any extent, the former year's predictions of evil in the way of depression and strikes. The contest for eight hours per day at the same wages has gained some ground, but it is not by any means universal, and is being opposed by capitalists and operators with vigour during the present year. The McKinley Bill has, as yet,

The labour market.

(1198)

had no effect on the labour market. There are reasons for this, the foremost one being that during the latter stages of the contest in Congress, and when the eventual passage of the Bill was assured, foreign houses flooded this country with manufactured goods. Every warehouse in the country was filled up with imported goods from England, France, Germany, and other countries. This enormous stock has to be disposed of before the American manufacturers can avail themselves of the "shut out" principle of the McKinley Bill. This holds good, no doubt, till about the present time, and the increased manufacturing by the American mills, which will inevitably follow, is not likely to affect wages to any perceptible extent until later on. After that, competitive enterprises are likely to loom up so rapidly as to cause the prices of labour, both skilled and unskilled, to return to a normal condition of manufactures and the wages resultant thereon, is the uncertainty of the next national elections. Should the Democratic party return to Federal power, a change in the tariff laws will be anticipated as likely to occur within a year or two. Were it not for this uncertainty, English manufacturing plants or branches thereof would have been removed from Bradford, Leeds, Birmingham, and elsewhere to this country, and have taken their part in the flux of industrial competition that is inevitably to take place at no late date.

In the woollen mills, on what are known as Bradford work stuff goods, as well as the mills on other fabrics, the pay of the employés runs as follows:—

|  | Hours per Week. | Currency. |  | Sterling. |  |
|---|---|---|---|---|---|
|  |  | Dol. | Dol. | £ s. d. | £ s. d. |
| Men | 60 | 12 to | 14 | 2 9 5 to | 2 16 8 |
| Boys over 16 years | 60 | 7 | 10 | 1 8 10 | 2 1 2 |
| „ under „ | 60 | 2 | 4 | 0 8 4 | 0 16 0 |
| Women | 60 | 7 | 10 | 1 8 10 | 2 1 2 |
| Girls | 60 | 3 | 7 | 0 12 4 | 1 8 10 |

There must be 60 hours of labour per week, but the Saturday half-holiday is obtained by working overtime during the week.

In the early part of this year (1891) there have broken out some heavy strikes in the coal regions, and some bloodshed caused by encounters between union and non-union men. The Governor of Pennsylvania ordered a number of militia companies to proceed to the scenes of rioting, and order was soon restored. The miners are returning to work by degrees, having failed in their efforts for eight hours and against a reduction of wages. In the Connelsville region great suffering was felt among the miners, many families living chiefly on the charity of farmers. About 120,000 men went out on this strike. The coke drawers refused to accept a reduction of 10 per cent.

## PHILADELPHIA.

The employment of large numbers of Italians, Poles, and Hungarians has caused much discontent. The immigration of this foreign element is on the verge of creating serious complications, and meetings of the different associations have been held with a view to checking it. There appears to be no sympathy with this tide of immigration in any section of the community, and it is predicted that more stringent and restrictive laws will be enacted by the next national Congress.

Several trades have recently gone out on strike either for higher wages, against a reduction of wages, or for the eight hours a day without a reduction of wages. All the chief centres of the country have been more or less affected. According to the latest returns there are now from 5,000 to 6,000 railway miners of the Pittsburgh district out, pending an agreement on the new scale of wages; but they are about to return. At Hocking and Sandy Creek Valley, Ohio, the miners to the number of 11,500 are out, pending an adjustment of the wages' question, but they are expected to return in a few days. In Iowa 10,000 coal miners are out, the wages' question being the grievance. At Pittsburgh, Pennsylvania, 3,600 men of the building trades are out on the eight hours' and present wages' question. These men include 1,800 carpenters, 700 stone masons, and 700 bricklayers. In New York, Brooklyn, and Jersey City 4,000 housesmiths have struck for eight hours. Some firms have conceded the demands, and the men expect to win. In New York and vicinity 1,200 painters have gone out for an advance of $2\frac{1}{2}d.$ per hour. About 600 have gained their demands. In Indiana there are 3,000 block coal and bituminous miners out, pending the settlement of a new scale of wages. In Illinois 3,000 coal miners have struck for eight hours and a weekly pay day. In West Virginia 1,000 coal miners have struck on the wages' scale question. At Chicago 1,700 cigar makers have struck for a new scale of wages. At St. Louis a large number of mechanics, say 1,000, are out. These figures aggregate 15,200 men, which, added to the 120,000 in the Connelsville district above referred to, make a total of 135,200 men. The Connelsville men and the coke operators in the Westmoreland district, however, are gradually returning to work, and virtually admit the strikes in those sections to be failures. These coal and coke oven strikes cannot succeed, and the men will perceive that in future they will do better to lead themselves, instead of blindly following professional leaders. These men must be paid whether working or idle by the working men, and the latter can pay them more easily and support themselves by working than by remaining idle.

The mortality returns for Philadelphia in 1890 were:—

|  | Number. |
|---|---|
| Specific diseases | 20,154 |
| Old age | 817 |
| Violence | 761 |

Vital statistics.

(1198)

## UNITED STATES.

**Small-pox.**

Typhoid fever was and is prevalent, especially in the suburban districts. On the other hand, small-pox has virtually been exterminated. But four cases, and no deaths, occurred. The history of this formerly dreaded disease, so far as Philadelphia is concerned, is interesting.

In the years following the deaths and population were:—

| Year. | Population. | Deaths from Small-pox. |
|---|---|---|
| | Number. | Number. |
| 1807 | 111,210 | 32 |
| 1824 | 137,097 | 325 |
| 1830 | 188,797 | 86 |
| 1850 | 408,762 | 40 |
| 1872 | 674,022 | 2,585 |
| 1881 | 846,980 | 1,336 |
| 1890 | 1,044,894 | .. |

In the early part of the year 1872, there not being a single case of small pox in the city, an immigrant landed from shipboard having the incipient germs of the disease in his system, and he escaped the medical examination. Proceeding at once to the residence of an acquaintance and sleeping two nights, he left for another section of the city. In the family of the first stopping place he left the disease with them, and also the adjacent neighbourhood. He changed his abode from district to district, remaining but a short time in each, and his trail was followed by the march of the dreaded disease. He was not discovered, and it is supposed that he eventually left the city for the West. Two thousand five hundred and eighty-five deaths were the result of his visit to Philadelphia.

**Influenza epidemic.**

This complaint, "la grippe," was and continues to be epidemic again throughout this Consular district. In fact, it prevails in all sections of the Union. Notably in this city, Pittsburgh, Cincinnatti, Cleveland, and other cities, the disease has been, indirectly, very fatal, and the medical profession appear to be unable to suppress the serious results that follow in a great number of the cases. There have been no statistical figures collated, and it is not likely that there will be, as it seems difficult, if not impossible, to attribute many of the sudden deaths as the immediate results of "la grippe."

The course of this complaint seems to have been accurately traced from St. Petersburgh, in 1889; thence to Berlin; thence to London and Paris, and in December of the same year the first cases were in New York. From that sea-port it ran westward, traversing half the continent. Returning eastward again it embraced Philadelphia with virulence. This course carries out the general rule that influenza passes from east to west. Late in December, 1889, the hospitals of Philadelphia were crowded with cases. The symptoms of the attack varied greatly, with, however, a general resemblance. Fever, aching of the bones, especially the joints, without swelling, severe irritative cough, with little inflammation of the air-passages, and great general depression. The deaths resulting directly were not many, as but 123 were recorded, but its complications were extremely fatal. Pneumonia, heart disease, and other diseases of the heart and lungs were credited with an altogether unusual number of deaths during and immediately after the epidemic. The effect was marked on the general death rate, children and old persons especially succumbing. Neither cholera or small-pox has ever ravaged Philadelphia with such universality, and only yellow fever of half a century ago counted as many victims as did this insidious influenza.

Consumption continues to head the list, and appears to be the most destructive of all maladies of the present age. In Philadelphia alone there are not less than 10,000 cases, and the annual death rate 3,000.

Very many of these unfortunate victims are without means to secure proper treatment, and are compelled to continue the hard struggle for bread, which aggravates the disease, leading steadily on to an untimely end. The large majority of consumptives are adults who should be bread-winners and not burdens on their families. It is also now generally conceded by physicians that the disease is a slow but almost sure source of contagion, and a constant peril to all around the afflicted person. In view of this it is under consideration by philanthropists that a public hospital for the treatment of consumptives only would be a most praiseworthy undertaking by the charitable. While hospitals for the treatment of consumptives abound in European cities, there are none in Philadelphia, and perhaps none in any city of the Union. There are semi-private institutions on a limited scale in the city, but the patients are expected to pay for board and lodging. But no public hospital for the treatment of consumptives such as the six celebrated ones in different sections of London, and it is said to be a reproach that a city like Philadelphia with its long medical traditions and its devotion to hospital work—unsurpassed by any community in the world—that a public consumptive hospital does not exist. Steps, however, are now being taken by a number of benevolent and wealthy citizens to found an hospital for the exclusive treatment of consumptive patients. The ablest medical skill has taken an interest in the project, tending their time and professional services gratuitously. It can be stated that this beneficent charity is assured, and a fund of 40,000*l*. will soon be raised to construct and equip the "Rush Hospital."

Notwithstanding the efforts of the temperance portion of the citizens of Pennsylvania, an abatement in the manufacture and sale, with their attendant evils, of malt and spirituous liquors, appears to be as far distant as ever. The practical working of the "Brooks Bill" and the careful scrutiny of the judges empowered to grant wholesale and retail licenses, seems to be virtually a failure. Sundry amendments to the present law are before the State Legislature, but even if the best of them should be enacted, it is a mooted question if they will check the evils

*Liquor traffic and high license.*

(1198)

that inevitably result from the present system of dealing in intoxicating beverages.

The first few months after the passage of the "Brooks Bill" there was undoubtedly a decrease in crime, and a decided falling-off in the commitments to prison for sundry of the minor grades of crime; but it was not long before ingenious means of evading the law cropped out, and the evils of the liquor question "were found to be more numerous and more serious than before the efforts to abate them were made by the law. The present system of the License Courts is to as evenly distribute the licensed places as possible, and not to disturb those saloons formerly licensed, and who have managed to keep up a semblance of a peaceable and good reputation. Still, ingenious means soon cropped out by which the law was evaded, and a number of grog shops were conducted secretly, especially on Sundays. Under a decision of the Supreme Court of Pennsylvania, all applications for wholesale license were granted if no formal remonstrance was filed. Hence a large number of licenses were issued to ostensible wholesale dealers, who used the privilege for the purpose of evading the restrictions of the Brooks law, selling spirits to the amount of one quart for immediate consumption. To this fact the Law and Order Society ascribe the increase in number of arrests for drunkenness and disorderly conduct in 1890 over that of 1889. The commitments were:—Males, 9,876; females, 1,428; total, 11,304.

The number of licenses issued in Philadelphia, 1,173.

*Fraudulent investment companies.* Within the past year an extraordinary greed for making money without giving a due equivalent in mental or physical labour has seized a large class of the less intelligent people in this country.

Since laws of the United States recently enacted have been in active force against using the mails for the circulation of tempting lottery schemes, new "financial" concerns have sprung up—and almost daily continue to spring up—in divers sectional centres of the country. They are known as the "Beneficial Order of Earnest Workers," "Fraternal Societies Company," "Order of the Golden Grail," "Operative Indemnity Union," "People's Five Year Benefit Commercial Endowment Order," "The Advance Beneficial Order," as well as by a score of other high-sounding titles, and are emblazoned by gorgeous prospectuses, alike fascinating to the unwary and tempting to those in the race for wealth.

So far as this city is concerned the boldest and most apparent in fraudulent manipulation of these companies receive their patronage from the mill and factory employés—men, women, and children. The agents fall upon the operatives like a plague, and with their glittering promises and plausible arguments succeed in entrapping large numbers. These people are hard working and make very small wages, and it is hoped that by the persistent attacks of the newspapers upon such nefarious schemes that their eyes will be opened and their money saved.

A single instance cited is sufficient to explain this system of fraudulent banking, and attention is called to it in order that the

English reading public may know of its baneful effects in this country.

One of the latest and boldest schemes is to agree to pay 20*l*. in cash to each member in four months from the date of his certificate of membership, the dues payable not to exceed 4*s*. per week. A sick or accident benefit is also offered after 60 days' membership. Such benefits, however, are not paid to the member, but are held as payment of dues, so that in reality there is no such thing as a sick benefit in the concern. The estimated total cost of this "certificate" for 20*l*. is just 6*l*., 1*l*. of which must be paid on initiation, 16*s*. as expense dues, 16*s*. as a contribution to the relief fund, and 3*l*. 8*s*. as dues payable weekly for 17 consecutive weeks. The sick benefit of 4*s*. per week—which is never paid—is only to be claimed by members who are unable to follow their employment, and who are under the care of a physician. This is one of the schemes used to get rid of members whose certificates are about maturing, for the rule is that all dues shall be paid in advance, under a penalty of 2*s*. If they are not paid within the following week the member is suspended until all arrears are paid, and the certificate does not mature until four months after reinstatement. Each member of the order is compelled to bring into the order, within two weeks from the date of his certificate, two good and reliable members, and failing to comply with this law will cause the unlucky member to lose 10*l*. from his certificate value. Astonishing as it may appear, it is nevertheless true that thousands of people are continually duped by such bare-faced representations.

Another system is to induce members to take bonds for 200*l*. each, who can, on payment of a small stipulated monthly sum, and a little effort to obtain new members for 200*l*. bonds each, receive payment of their bonds within the space of one year. For instance, upon obtaining 35 new subscribers, who remain in good standing six months, a holder of a 200*l*. bond is promised payment of that sum in one year. The scheme appears to be that it takes 35 new members to pay off one old member in one year. In other words, the society offers an enormous commission to the person securing 35 customers who will agree to pay in for six months. By this system the members agree to stand by each other for mutual protection—that is, not to stand by each other, for there would be no profit in that, but to lean on and cling to 35 outside parties for support, and these 35 outside parties, when they become inside parties, are to lean on 1,225 other outside parties. There is no help inside; it appears to be all outside, and therefore the outside is the only safe side.

Some of the States have dealt effectively with these so-called "investment companies" by imposing fines on any person acting as their agent or soliciting subscriptions for them. One State (Vermont) imposes a fine of 200*l*., and the Inspector of Finance has published a list of over 100 of these swindling concerns, all promising a very large return upon a small monthly payment. The investors ought to know, and many of them doubtless do know, that all that they may receive beyond the current rate of interest on their loans must come wrongfully out of the pockets of other people. Very little, if any, however, of the money left with the managers of these concerns is put out at interest. It goes out nearly as fast as it is taken in in exorbitant salaries, liberal extensive advertising, and in payments to the first investors.

It is a notable fact that the members and activity of these fraudulent concerns have vastly increased since the suppression of the lotteries. In this the gambling propensity has found a new means of employment. Though authorised by the laws of Pennsylvania, these alleged " investment fund " institutions, with their false and alluring promises, are more demoralising in their influence and far less honestly conducted than were the lotteries that have been so sternly placed under the ban of the law. In the lotteries every number placed in the wheel had an equal, though small, chance of drawing a prize for its holder. In the " investment fund " schemes of robbing Peter to pay Paul, the first comers may receive considerably more than the amount of their investment, but the crowd that follows in the rear will find nothing left. It is this gambling chance, with the promise of speedy and large returns for a small risk, and with the certainty that many of the investors are to be defrauded, which makes these concerns so attractive to multitudes of deluded persons.

With ostentatious morality Pennsylvania and other States have vigorously suppressed every form of lottery gambling, including the chances for prizes at church festivals. The State has taken by the collar the manipulators of the " sweat cloth " and the " thimble riggers " at county fairs, the keepers of roulette tables, and the faro dealers. But it grants great chartered privileges to alleged " investment " companies which flaunt their false prospectuses in the face of the public, and whose schemes have been mathematically proven to be fraudulent. It is creditable to the journalists of the country that they have, almost without exception, condemned these mushroom and fraudulent financial schemes. There is no jugglery in true finance.

Building associations. How different are the principles on which building and loan associations are so successfully managed in Philadelphia. What infinite good these societies have done for the industrial classes, and largely aided in making the city truly a " city of homes." Their system is simple and legitimate, ensuring a fair and equitable return for the investors or shareholders, when managed by upright and capable officers, which is the case with rare exceptions. Each share represents 40*l*., and the holder thereof is entitled to a loan of that sum on giving satisfactory security and the payment of 4*s*. per month on the share and 4*s*. per month as interest on the loan at 6 per cent. per annum. Thus a shareholder having, say, 15 shares, would be entitled to a loan of 600*l*., with which he could build for himself and family a home worth that sum, and his monthly payments would be but slightly over the rental of such a property. In about 10 years all his dues and interests would be paid up, and his property, in absolute freehold, would be in his unencumbered possession. A small premium is paid by the borrowers when there is a number of competitors for loans, and these premiums become the profits of the association, which are shared by all stockholders, borrowers or non-borrowers. This system is devoid of all intricacies and delusive promises, and is readily understood by all ordinarily intelligent people.

After years of contention the Congress of the United States have passed an International Copyright Law, and at last English authors will have a fair showing in this country. Heretofore English literature has been published in this country at the bare cost of printing, and that in a very careless and cheap form. All the contemporary English authors of the present generation have had the fruits of their brain seized and put out over here in cheap editions, which flooded the country from news' stands and railway stations.

English authors will be enabled to copyright their works in this country, and, of course, vice versâ for Americans. Publishers of the higher grades of books will be content, as they feel that quite as large returns will follow the sale of a limited edition of an expensive novel as a large sale of a cheap one.

American authors will also profit by a falling-off in the popularity of foreign writers, as their works will necessarily be placed on a much higher financial shelf.

It is doubtless true that had this law been on the statute books in the days of Scott, Dickens, and Thackeray, the great boon of these authors to the public taste, morals, and manners would not have had one-tenth of its usefulness, as not a twentieth portion of the number of their works would have been sold.

It is granted that the new law will improve things for authors and producers of literature throughout the world, but the effect to publishing houses in general cannot be told until a few years of experience have been had.

The law is not retrospective, and will only affect the works of present living authors. It is also a matter of reciprocity, only protecting authors of those countries where American authors receive the same privileges. The special feature in the publication of the work or book to be protected is that it must be printed and made in this country.

During the year ending June 30, 1890, 24,490 immigrants arrived at this port, 21 of whom were workaways, and 75 stowaways. The male sex predominated, and the age ranging from 15 years to 40 years, claimed two-thirds of the total number landed. Ireland sent the greatest number, 5,342; then England, 4,497; with Germany, 3,607; Sweden and Norway sent 2,783. After these nationalities come a class not so desirable, viz. :— Poland, 1,604; Russia, 981; Hungary, 268; Italy, 95.

During the six months from July 1 to December 31, 1890, the arrivals were 10,699, of which there were, English, 2,023; Irish, 1,835; Scotch, 384; Welsh, 13; German, 2,107; Russian, 704; Polish, 824; Hungary, 391; Sweden, Norway, Belgium, and Denmark, 1,263; Austria, 208. Citizens of the United States returning are not included.

## UNITED STATES.

It is quite probable that the immigration laws will be made still more stringent by the next Congress, with a view to restrict the landing of so many of the lowest order of Huns, Poles, and Sicilians, who bring with them habits and evil propensities that are held to be very objectionable and dangerous by the Anglo-Saxon race.

*Population.* The population of the United States, as per census of 1890, was 62,480,540. The States of this Consular district showed:—Pennsylvania, 5,248,574; Ohio, 3,666,719; Indiana, 2,189,030; and Michigan, 2,089,792; being an increase for the decade of 24·47 per cent. These figures do not include the white persons and the Indians on the Indian reservations and the territory of Alaska. The population in 1880 was 50,155,783, and in 1870 it was 38,558,371.

*Shipping and navigation.* The shipping at the port of Philadelphia has increased from that of the year 1888, when it fell off, and the following tables show the ascendancy of the British flag over all the other nationalities combined. The arrivals of American and all foreign vessels, as per returns from the United States custom-house, for 1890 were:—

ENTERED—SAIL.

| Nationality. | With Cargo. Number of Vessels. | Tons. | In Ballast. Number of Vessels. | Tons. | Total. Number of Vessels. | Tons. |
|---|---|---|---|---|---|---|
| Austrian | 6 | 3,242 | 3 | 2,768 | 9 | 6,010 |
| British | 130 | 76,000 | 17 | 23,031 | 147 | 99,031 |
| Dutch | 2 | 1,537 | ... | ... | 2 | 1,537 |
| French | 3 | 1,993 | 2 | 2,458 | 5 | 4,451 |
| German | 17 | 17,074 | 1 | 1,584 | 18 | 18,658 |
| Italian | 51 | 31,114 | 14 | 9,469 | 65 | 40,583 |
| Norwegian | 39 | 25,896 | 6 | 4,818 | 45 | 30,714 |
| Portuguese | 10 | 3,685 | 1 | 430 | 11 | 4,115 |
| Russian | 2 | 1,381 | ... | ... | 2 | 1,381 |
| Spanish | 4 | 2,371 | ... | ... | 4 | 2,371 |
| Swedish | 2 | 831 | ... | ... | 2 | 831 |
| Total | 266 | 165,124 | 44 | 44,558 | 310 | 209,682 |

STEAM.

| Nationality. | With Cargo. Number of Vessels. | Tons. | In Ballast. Number of Vessels. | Tons. | Total. Number of Vessels. | Tons. |
|---|---|---|---|---|---|---|
| Belgian | 18 | 41,265 | 3 | 4,623 | 21 | 45,888 |
| British | 527 | 747,028 | 59 | 86,602 | 586 | 833,630 |
| French | ... | ... | 5 | 5,837 | 5 | 5,837 |
| German | 14 | 22,282 | 22 | 43,304 | 36 | 65,586 |
| Italian | 3 | 4,844 | ... | ... | 3 | 4,844 |
| Mexican | 1 | 215 | 1 | 151 | 2 | 366 |
| Norwegian | 96 | 56,992 | ... | ... | 96 | 56,992 |
| Portuguese | 1 | 1,896 | ... | ... | 1 | 1,896 |
| Russian | ... | ... | 2 | 4,456 | 2 | 4,456 |
| Spanish | 7 | 11,288 | ... | ... | 7 | 11,288 |
| Swedish | 2 | 1,628 | ... | ... | 2 | 1,628 |
| Total | 669 | 887,438 | 92 | 144,973 | 761 | 1,032,411 |
| „ sail and steam | ... | ... | ... | ... | 1,071 | 1,242,093 |

## PHILADELPHIA.

### AMERICAN.

|  | Number of Vessels. | Tonnage. | Number of Vessels. | Tonnage. |
|---|---|---|---|---|
| Sailing— | | | | |
| With cargo | 305 | 154,364 | } 307 | 157,365 |
| In ballast | 2 | 3,001 | | |
| Steam— | | | | |
| With cargo | 49 | 56,110 | } 51 | 56,243 |
| In ballast | 2 | 133 | | |
| Total sailing and steam | .. | .. | 358 | 213,608 |

### CLEARED—SAIL.

| Nationality. | With Cargo. |  | In Ballast. |  | Total. |  |
|---|---|---|---|---|---|---|
| | Number of Vessels. | Tons. | Number of Vessels. | Tons. | Number of Vessels. | Tons. |
| Austrian | 9 | 5,941 | ... | .. | 9 | 5,941 |
| British | 109 | 80,343 | 12 | 5,918 | 121 | 86,261 |
| Dutch | 1 | 435 | ... | ... | 1 | 435 |
| French | 5 | 4,451 | ... | ... | 5 | 4,451 |
| German | 19 | 20,088 | ... | ... | 19 | 20,088 |
| Italian | 78 | 48,485 | ... | ... | 78 | 48,485 |
| Norwegian | 44 | 30,774 | ... | ... | 44 | 30,774 |
| Portuguese | 10 | 3,783 | ... | ... | 10 | 3,783 |
| Russian | 1 | 1,129 | ... | ... | 1 | 1,129 |
| Spanish | 3 | 1,802 | ... | ... | 3 | 1,802 |
| Swedish | 2 | 1,088 | ... | ... | 2 | 1,088 |
| Total | 281 | 198,319 | 12 | 5,918 | 293 | 204,237 |

### STEAM.

| Nationality. | With Cargo. |  | In Ballast. |  | Total. |  |
|---|---|---|---|---|---|---|
| | Number of Vessels. | Tons. | Number of Vessels. | Tons. | Number of Vessels. | Tons. |
| Belgian | 22 | 48,058 | ... | ... | 22 | 48,058 |
| British | 387 | 555,516 | 40 | 35,231 | 427 | 590,747 |
| French | 5 | 5,837 | ... | ... | 5 | 5,837 |
| German | 35 | 64,178 | ... | ... | 35 | 64,178 |
| Italian | 3 | 4,844 | ... | .. | 3 | 4,844 |
| Mexican | ... | ... | 2 | 184 | 2 | 184 |
| Norwegian | 35 | 27,361 | 49 | 23,461 | 84 | 50,822 |
| Russian | 3 | 5,067 | ... | ... | 3 | 5,067 |
| Spanish | 1 | 1,556 | ... | ... | 1 | 1,556 |
| Swedish | ... | ... | 1 | 814 | 1 | 814 |
| Total | 491 | 712,417 | 92 | 59,690 | 583 | 772,107 |
| ,, sail and steam | ... | ... | ... | ... | 876 | 976,344 |

## UNITED STATES.

AMERICAN.

|  | Number of Vessels. | Tonnage. | Number of Vessels. | Tonnage. |
|---|---|---|---|---|
| Sailing— | | | | |
|   With cargo | 181 | 100,578 | } 183 | 102,349 |
|   In ballast | 2 | 1,771 | | |
| Steam— | | | | |
|   With cargo | 29 | 44,364 | } 46 | 50,338 |
|   In ballast | 17 | 5,974 | | |
| Total sailing and steam | .. | .. | 229 | 152,687 |

The figures reported by the customs officer fall short 71 ships, and 82,280 tons, so far as the arrivals of British ships are concerned. This discrepancy between the Consular and the custom-house registers is explained by the fact that the tables are made out at the custom-house as from foreign ports, while the Consular include entrances from all parts of the world, the United States included.

The actual Consular registration figures:—Entrances, 804, tonnage, 1,014.941; clearances, 818, tonnage, 1,028,176.

*Steamship communication with Philadelphia.*
There are six regular lines of steamships now trading with this port, and are the Earn Line, Red Star, Allan, American, Atlantic, Transport, and North Atlantic. The coastwise lines of steamers are the Winsor's, Ericssons, Clyde, and Ocean, with a good fleet to each line.

## PHILADELPHIA.

TABLE showing the Total Number and Tonnage of all Sea-going Vessels for all Countries of the World in 1889.

| Countries. | Number of Vessels. | Tonnage. |
|---|---|---|
| United Kingdom | 9,167 | 10,241,856 |
| Colonies | 2,904 | 1,355,250 |
| United States of America | 3,272 | 1,823,882 |
| Norway | 3,369 | 1,584,355 |
| Germany | 1,876 | 1,569,311 |
| France | 1,380 | 1,045,102 |
| Italy | 1,555 | 816,567 |
| Spain | 883 | 534,811 |
| Sweden | 1,470 | 475,964 |
| Russia | 1,181 | 427,335 |
| Netherlands | 544 | 378,784 |
| Greece | 971 | 307,640 |
| Denmark | 808 | 280,065 |
| Austria | 368 | 269,648 |
| Turkey | 907 | 229,777 |
| Japan | 289 | 171,554 |
| Brazil | 506 | 149,066 |
| Belgium | 85 | 110,571 |
| Chile | 152 | 102,391 |
| Portugal | 216 | 91,202 |
| China | 41 | 45,840 |
| Argentine | 126 | 43,142 |
| Hawaii | 27 | 19,405 |
| Uruguay | 31 | 12,014 |
| Peru | 37 | 11,048 |
| Mexico | 32 | 11,041 |
| Zanzibar | 6 | 4,723 |
| Hayti | 13 | 4,390 |
| Siam | 10 | 4,163 |
| Venezuela | 13 | 3,758 |
| Montenegro | 17 | 3,282 |
| Sarawak | 7 | 2,616 |
| Bolivia | 3 | 2,302 |
| Roumania | 5 | 936 |
| Persia | 1 | 838 |
| Costa Rica | 3 | 816 |
| Columbia | 2 | 444 |
| Other countries | 21 | 15,762 |
| Total | 32,298 | 22,151,651 |

For several years there has been a continuous decrease in the number of vessels afloat, and this feature is again apparent, there being 364 fewer vessels existing at the end of the year 1889 than there were at the close of the previous year. While, however, the number of vessels has decreased, the aggregate tonnage has abnormally increased by 1,102,947 tons. Evidently larger types of vessels continue to take the place of those which disappear by losses and breaking up, &c.

The receipts of merchandise at this port during the year 1890 were as follows:— *Trade and Commerce*

Flour, 2,164,422 barrels; wheat, 1,644,582 bushels; corn (maize), 17,949,350 bushels; rye, 98,425 bushels; oats, 4,522,670 bushels; barley, 1,056,300 bushels; malt, 203,600 bushels; oatmeal, 4,019 barrels; corn meal, 1,915 barrels; clover, 8,732 bags; timothy, 6,976 bags; flax, 343,671 bushels; feed, 10,770 bushels; hay, 67,183 tons; oilcake, 9,171 bags; high wines, 22,435 barrels; whisky, 61,420 barrels; tobacco (leaf), 40,438 packages; tobacco (manufactured), 88,678 packages; pork, 4,164 barrels; beef, 14,349 barrels; hams, 55,360 barrels; ham, 39,357 pieces; shoulders, 79,111 pieces; sides, 606 pieces; lard, 23,405 barrels; butter, 208,099 packages; eggs, 375,477 packages; wool, 134,937 bales; cotton, 75,644 bales; lumber, 237,090,000 feet; petroleum (crude), 1,256,761 barrels; petroleum (refined), 493,470 barrels.

**Imports and exports.**

The port of Philadelphia has made steady progress during the year as will be seen by the following table of imports and exports. They are given in detail in order to show the countries trading with this section of the United States. The last three months' importations of the following tables were under the celebrated high tariff Act of Congress, known as the "McKinley Bill" of October 1, 1890. There was not a falling-off of any consequence in the imports during the short time the Bill has been in operation, and it is predicted that before any disastrous results arise the McKinley Bill will be repealed, or so materially cut of its oppressive sections as to bring the tariff back to its former normal condition of protective duties and cumbrous customs machinery.

The customs officers have made the import tables in two sections, one of nine months under the old tariff, and the other of three months under the new tariff or "McKinley Bill," and they are so returned in this report. The falling-off of imports during the last three months amounted to 575,200*l.*, as compared with any three of the previous nine months.

The following is a summary statement of the value of goods imported direct from foreign countries to the port of Philadelphia, for the nine months ending September 30, 1890, under the tariff Act of March 3, 1883 :—

## PHILADELPHIA.

| Countries. | Free. | Dutiable. | American. | Foreign. | Totals. |
|---|---|---|---|---|---|
|  | Dollars. | Dollars. | Dollars. | Dollars. | Dollars. |
| Argentine Republic | 61,500 | 1,159 | ... | 62,659 | 62,659 |
| Austria | 9,720 | 253,611 | 1,740 | 261,591 | 263,331 |
| Belgium | 99,283 | 342,201 | ... | 441,484 | 441,484 |
| Brazil | 186 | 655,966 | 94,805 | 561,347 | 656,152 |
| Costa Rica | 15,884 | ... | 5,680 | 10,204 | 15,884 |
| Guatemala | 13,700 | ... | ... | 13,700 | 13,700 |
| Honduras | 9,781 | ... | ... | 9,781 | 9,781 |
| Nicaragua | 119,618 | ... | 4,347 | 115,271 | 119,618 |
| Chile | 123,967 | ... | 80,681 | 43,286 | 123,967 |
| China | 328 | 10,284 | ... | 10,612 | 10,612 |
| Denmark | ... | 2,116 | ... | 2,116 | 2,116 |
| Danish West Indies | ... | 12,342 | 12,342 | ... | 12,342 |
| Greenland | 60,490 | ... | ... | 60,490 | 60,490 |
| France | 224,912 | 1,806,717 | 36,051 | 1,995,578 | 2,031,629 |
| French Guiana | 14,225 | ... | 12,325 | 1,900 | 14,225 |
| ,, possessions in Africa | 45,415 | 163,860 | 7,243 | 202,032 | 209,275 |
| Germany | 367,702 | 6,070,671 | 13,570 | 6,424,803 | 6,438,373 |
| England | 1,449,757 | 9,768,753 | 2,262,323 | 8,956,187 | 11,218,510 |
| Scotland | 29,070 | 780,159 | 29,995 | 779,234 | 809,229 |
| Ireland | 730 | 135,265 | 16,897 | 119,098 | 135,995 |
| Nova Scotia | 5,647 | 4,024 | 3,320 | 6,361 | 9,681 |
| Ontario | ... | 15,805 | 15,805 | ... | 15,805 |
| British West Indies | 552,157 | 1,669,938 | 290,093 | 1,932,002 | 2,222,095 |
| ,, Guiana | ... | 2,140,387 | 593,742 | 1,546,645 | 2,140,387 |
| ,, Honduras | 7,875 | ... | ... | 7,875 | 7,875 |
| ,, East Indies | 180,462 | 408,992 | 16,971 | 572,483 | 589,454 |
| Hong Kong | 1,336 | 1,413 | ... | 2,749 | 2,749 |
| British possessions in Africa | 20,734 | ... | ... | 20,734 | 20,734 |
| Australia | 514 | ... | ... | 514 | 514 |
| Greece | ... | 52,680 | ... | 52,680 | 52,680 |
| Hayti | 70,988 | ... | 20,721 | 50,267 | 70,988 |
| Italy | 315,375 | 876,389 | 8,644 | 1,183,100 | 1,191,764 |
| Japan | ... | 5,451 | ... | 5,451 | 5,451 |
| Liberia | 3,818 | ... | ... | 3,818 | 3,818 |
| Mexico | 12,966 | 3,469 | 12,966 | 3,469 | 16,435 |
| Netherlands | 20,018 | 48,278 | ... | 68,296 | 68,296 |
| Dutch East Indies | 8,988 | 456,630 | ... | 465,618 | 465,618 |
| Portugal | 169,898 | 26,531 | 582 | 195,847 | 196,429 |
| Madeira Islands | ... | 671 | ... | 671 | 671 |
| Russia on the Baltic | 37,021 | 80,883 | ... | 117,904 | 117,904 |
| ,, Black Sea | ... | 8,943 | ... | 8,943 | 8,943 |
| Spain | 42,709 | 632,370 | 15,116 | 659,963 | 675,079 |
| Cuba | 144,387 | 11,570,054 | 5,216,894 | 6,497,547 | 11,714,441 |
| Porto Rico | 239 | 259,743 | 27,482 | 232,500 | 259,982 |
| Philippine Islands | ... | 590,902 | 116,318 | 474,584 | 590,902 |
| Sweden and Norway | 125 | 50,850 | ... | 50,975 | 50,975 |
| Switzerland | 14,346 | 316,931 | 2,372 | 328,905 | 331,277 |
| Turkey in Europe | 1,302 | 40,745 | ... | 42,047 | 42,047 |
| ,, Asia | 1,489 | 269,389 | 55,397 | 215,481 | 270,878 |
| ,, Africa | 53,496 | 5,391 | 215 | 58,672 | 58,887 |
| United States of Colombia | 67,885 | ... | 20,000 | 47,885 | 67,885 |
| Uruguay | 50,942 | 560 | 15,188 | 36,314 | 51,502 |
| Arabia and Persia | 3,243 | ... | ... | 3,243 | 3,243 |
| Total | 4,434,238 | 39,540,523 | 9,009,845 | 34,964,916 | 43,974,761 |

The following is a summary statement of the values of goods imported direct from foreign countries to the port of Philadelphia, for the three months ending December 31, 1890, under the tariff Act of October 1, 1890:—

| Countries. | Free. | Dutiable. | American. | Foreign. | Totals. |
|---|---|---|---|---|---|
| | Dollars. | Dollars. | Dollars. | Dollars. | Dollars. |
| Austria | 18,182 | 347,197 | 1,151 | 364,228 | 365,379 |
| Belgium | 28,690 | 82,912 | ... | 111,602 | 111,602 |
| Brazil | 15 | 504,808 | 48,103 | 456,720 | 504,823 |
| Nicaragua | 45,114 | ... | ... | 45,114 | 45,114 |
| Chile | 27,703 | ... | ... | 27,703 | 27,703 |
| China | 419 | 936 | ... | 1,355 | 1,355 |
| Greenland | 34,915 | ... | 2,181 | 32,734 | 34,915 |
| France | 38,692 | 654,727 | 67,915 | 625,504 | 693,419 |
| French Guiana | 5,724 | ... | ... | 5,724 | 5,724 |
| ,, possessions in Africa | 35,756 | 10,234 | ... | 45,990 | 45,990 |
| Germany | 163,927 | 1,594,224 | 4,179 | 1,753,972 | 1,758,151 |
| England | 681,523 | 3,085,641 | 717,699 | 3,049,465 | 3,767,164 |
| Scotland | 4,924 | 296,033 | 8,508 | 292,449 | 300,957 |
| Ireland | 8,295 | 46,207 | 19,469 | 35,033 | 54,502 |
| Nova Scotia | 3,450 | 12,272 | 2,400 | 13,322 | 15,722 |
| Ontario | 10,694 | 14,070 | 24,764 | ... | 24,764 |
| British West Indies | 130,207 | 37,573 | 12,572 | 155,208 | 167,780 |
| ,, Guiana | 2,700 | 738,531 | 57,112 | 684,119 | 741,231 |
| ,, East Indies | 83,801 | 775 | 886 | 83,690 | 84,576 |
| Hong-Kong | 561 | 987 | 1,548 | ... | 1,548 |
| British possessions in Africa | 15,455 | 1,296 | ... | 16,751 | 16,751 |
| Australia | 1,015 | ... | ... | 1,015 | 1,015 |
| Greece | ... | 10,126 | ... | 10,126 | 10,126 |
| Hayti | 9,891 | ... | 4,510 | 5,381 | 9,891 |
| Italy | 47,894 | 138,574 | 3,587 | 182,881 | 186,468 |
| Japan | ... | 492 | ... | 492 | 492 |
| Mexico | 2,191 | 1,651 | 820 | 3,022 | 3,842 |
| Netherlands | 7,143 | 15,864 | ... | 23,007 | 23,007 |
| Dutch East Indies | ... | 1,117,391 | ... | 1,117,391 | 1,117,391 |
| Portugal | 16,000 | 1,107 | 389 | 16,718 | 17,107 |
| Russia on the Baltic | 12,837 | 44,706 | .. | 57,543 | 57,543 |
| ,, Black Sea | ... | 14,458 | ... | 14,458 | 14,458 |
| Spain | 15,386 | 186,509 | 2,753 | 199,142 | 201,895 |
| Cuba | 51,937 | 647,676 | 175,765 | 523,848 | 699,613 |
| Porto Rico | ... | 71,245 | ... | 71,245 | 71,245 |
| Philippine Islands | ... | 426,100 | ... | 426,100 | 426,100 |
| Sweden and Norway | 4,507 | 37,980 | ... | 42,487 | 42,487 |
| Switzerland | 3,741 | 157,980 | 2,965 | 158,756 | 161,721 |
| Turkey in Europe | 20,431 | 15,386 | 799 | 35,018 | 35,817 |
| ,, Asia | 95,634 | 73,014 | 37,834 | 130,814 | 168,648 |
| ,, Africa | ... | 2,563 | ... | 2,563 | 2,563 |
| United States of Colombia | 49,873 | .. | ... | 49,853 | 49,873 |
| Uruguay | 11,638 | ... | ... | 11,638 | 11,638 |
| Morocco | 140 | ... | ... | 140 | 140 |
| Total | 1,691,005 | 10,391,245 | 1,197,909 | 10,884,341 | 12,082,250 |

| | Free of Duty. | Subject to Duty. | American Vessels. | Foreign Vessels. | Totals. |
|---|---|---|---|---|---|
| | Dollars. | Dollars. | Dollars. | Dollars. | Dollars. |
| For 9 months | 4,434,238 | 39,540,523 | 9,009,845 | 34,964,916 | 43,974,761 |
| ,, 3 ,, | 1,691,005 | 10,391,245 | 1,197,909 | 10,884,341 | 12,082,250 |
| Totals | 6,125,243 | 49,931,778 | 10,207,754 | 45,849,257 | 56,057,011 |
| Equivalent in sterling | 1,260,338*l*. 1*s*. 4*d*. | 10,274,028*l*. 7*s*. 11*d*. | 2,100,360*l*. 18*s*. 2*d*. | 9,454,579*l*. 12*s*. 8*d*. | |

The exports from Philadelphia for 1890 are officially reported to have been 7,100,000*l*.

**A trades guild.**

Another commercial organisation is in the act of formation. Its object will be an extension of the market for Philadelphian merchandise, better manufacturing facilities and uniform privileges for transportation by railways. Heretofore the trade of Philadelphia has been checked rather than encouraged by the railway transportation, notably that of the Pennsylvania Railroad, and the interests of her merchants have been set aside for those of New York and Chicago.

## PHILADELPHIA.

The sugar refineries of Philadelphia and the importation of raw sugars, cane and beetroot, have become a marked feature of the port. The import duty is to be taken off all sugars over 16 Dutch Standard, April, 1891. The refiners can continue making the sugars and have them bonded till that date. If they sell before, the duty must be paid. As soon as the McKinley Bill passed Congress, the refineries which had closed were again set in motion, and their products are bonded as stated. The refineries turn out immense quantities, some as high as 2,200,000 lbs., or 7,000 barrels per day.

Sugar.

The great increase in this country of steel ingots and direct castings during the past decade is surprising. The production for the whole country aggregates 4,466,926 tons of (2,000 lbs.), a percentage of 290, or 3,321,215 tons over the production of the year 1880, at which steel was made in but 14 States of the Union, while 19 are engaged in the industry at the present time. The production of Bessemer steel rails shows a remarkable growth, increasing from 741,475 tons in 1880 to 2,036,654 tons in 1890.

Iron and stee

A few steel works produce blisten, cemented and other miscellaneous steel, but the quantity made annually is small and is not included in the following figures:—

| Kinds of Steel (Ingots or Direct Castings). | Tons of 2,000 lbs. | |
| --- | --- | --- |
| | 1880. | 1890.* |
| Bessemer steel | 985,208 | 3,788,572 |
| Open-hearth | 84,302 | 504,351 |
| Crucible | 76,201 | 85,536 |
| Clapp-Griffiths steel | .. | 83,963 |
| Robert Bessemer ,, | .. | 4,504 |
| Total | 1,145,711 | 4,466,926 |

\* Table for the year ending June 30, 1890.

Pennsylvania is the leading producer of steel in the United States, turning out 62 per cent. of the total production in 1890. Illinois and Ohio (the latter State of this Consular district) were second and third in rank. From 1880 to 1890 the increase in production in Pennsylvania was 324 per cent.; in Illinois 241 per cent; and in Ohio, 314 per cent. In Pennsylvania the number of steel works in 1890 was 79, and the production of all kinds, 2,768,253 tons; in Illinois, 14 works, and production 868,250 tons; Ohio, 18 works, turning out 446,808 tons; Michigan, two works, with a production of 5,600 tons; and Indiana, six works, and 1,350 tons production.

The production of Bessemer steel in the United States during the year 1890 was 3,877,039 tons, including steel made by the

Bessemer steel.

(1198)

Clapp-Griffiths and Robert Bessemer processes, which is an increase of 294 per cent. over the production of 1880.

The works numbered 11 in 1880, and 53 in 1890. Pennsylvania produced in 1890, Bessemer steel ingots or direct castings 2,297,726 tons of (2,000 lbs.), and 1,377,119 tons of Bessemer steel rails. The demand for steel in forms other in rails, occasioned the remarkable growth of this industry during the last decade. The competition in the manufacture of Bessemer steel rails has obliged many of the rail mills to turn their attention to the production of steel for other uses than rails, as their production is at the present time only profitable at those mills which are favourably located for the supply of cheap raw materials, and are run in at the latest improved methods of manufacture. While the demand for steel rails has shown a remarkable growth, thereby forcing a practical discontinuance of the manufacture of iron rails, there has also been a rapidly increasing use of steel for nails, bars, wire, and other miscellaneous forms. In 1880 over 75 per cent. of the ingots produced was converted into rails, while in 1890, only 53 per cent. of the production went into rails.

**Open-hearth and crucible steel.** The output of open-hearth steel, of ingots, or direct castings in Pennsylvania for 1890 was 406,292 tons, and of crucible steel, 64,235 tons of (2,000 lbs.); Ohio turned out 61,232 tons of open-hearth, but no crucible; Michigan produced 2,000 tons of crucible, but no open-hearth; and Indiana produced 1,000 tons of open-hearth, and 350 tons crucible steel; making the output for the whole Consular district 66,585 tons of crucible, and 468,524 tons of open-hearth. The crucible steel industry has shown slow progress during the past 10 years. For the whole country the mills were 36 in number in 1880, and had increased only to 47 in 1890. For purposes requiring special grades of steel the product of the crucible process will be always in demand, but the high cost of manufacture prevents it in many instances from successfully competing in price with the other processes.

**The basic process.** The first basic steel made in America was produced experimentally in Pennsylvania six years ago in a Bessemer converter. Its production for purposes of commerce dates from 1888, since when the manufacture has continued. 16 furnaces will soon be in full operation for the manufacture of this product in Pennsylvania, being of a combination of the Bessemer and open-hearth processes. The basic process is applicable to either the Bessemer or open hearth, and its use in this country in connection with the open-hearth furnace is promising of successful results, and the indications now are that the growth of the basic industry in the United States will be large and rapid. The total production during 1890 in the United States was 62,173 tons, nearly all of it being made by the basic open-hearth method, but a small part being produced by the duplex process, a combination of the Bessemer and open-hearth methods.

For 1891 combinations of the heavier steel railmakers are

predicted with a view to squeezing out the smaller manufacturers and enhancing the profits of the few mills that would be left in the industry. In 1880 there were ten different companies, now there are but six. In the intervening period nine others were formed, but they passed out of existence or were abolished. No one of the six companies is powerful enough to absorb all the others, but the business is so centralised as to make the formation of a "Trust" an easy matter whenever it is so desired by the manufacturers.

Iron.
The year 1890 was the year of greatest production in the American iron trade, with the exception of the last two months, which showed a falling-off in the demand for pig-iron, steel rails, and all other iron and steel products. Stacks of pig-iron accumulated, and many furnaces were blown out, while the rail mills have been working far under their capacity. At this writing (April, 1891) the demand for pig-iron has not improved, and the prices are somewhat lower; but the railway companies have commenced to buy steel rails, and the market is tending towards better prices.

The demand for pig-iron, hitherto unprecedented, was healthily caused by a demand for Bessemer steel first, and then for open-hearth steel for bridges, ships, and buildings and machinery purposes. The railway rolling stock required large quantities, and the new naval cruisers made heavy demands.

The consumption of pig-iron in the United States for 1890 was 18,000,000 gross tons: and the coke used there for Connelsville, 6,221,518 net tons; Pocahontas flat top coke, 433,319 net tons.

In all the States the production of pig-iron was 9,202,703 gross tons, being 1,599,061 more tons than in the previous year of 1889. The production of Spiegeleisen and ferru-manganese was 149,162 net tons. The production of Bessemer ingots was 3,688,871 gross tons.

The importation of all kinds of iron and steel in 1880 was 16,552,132$l$. 2$s$. which fell to 8,647,683$l$. 10$s$. in 1890. The quantity imported in 1890 was 665,678 gross tons. The exports of all kinds, except agricultural implements, were 5,555,583$l$. 3$s$. Agricultural implements exported amounted to 671,809$l$. 12$s$. The importation of tin plate for the whole country was, in 1889, 331,311 gross tons, worth 4,470,515$l$. 15$s$., and in 1890 329,346 gross tons, worth 4,870,402$l$. 15$s$. In 20 years 3,622,750 gross tons were imported, valued at 63,236,914$l$. 8$s$.

Railways.
There were built in the United States 6,334 miles of new track in 1890, as compared with 5,756 in 1889, being an increase of 588 miles. In 1887 the construction figured 12,985 miles. In locomotive building the output of the year has never been exceeded. Fourteen firms built 2,213 locomotives.

There is no doubt that railway companies, notably the Pennsylvania Railroad, continue to discriminate in the rates of passenger and freight traffic against the port of Philadelphia and in favour of New York. Great railroad improvements are about to be commenced in Philadelphia. A line, known as the "Belt Line," will encircle the entire city on the two river fronts, having sufficient space to accommodate all the railway and steamship traffic to and from the port. The Philadelphia and Reading Railroad will have an elevated track into the heart of the city, and the Baltimore and Ohio will increase their interests and facilities to a great extent. The islands in the middle of the Delaware River in front of the city are being taken away at a cost of millions of dollars, and the stream deepened and the docks widened so as to accommodate the largest shipping.

*Anthracite and bituminous coal. Anthracite.*

The coal trade in 1889 was depressed by a very heavy output of hard, or anthracite, coal of the previous year, and of a series of mild winters. The latter cause was equally applicable to a depression of the market for soft, or bituminous, coal. Large stocks were carried over by producers, dealers, and consumers, which it was necessary to exhaust before any heavy operations in mining could safely be recommenced. For the year 1890, however, matters were changed for the better, so far as anthracite was concerned, due to quite legitimate causes; the increased consumption of the domestic sizes owing to the colder temperature of the latter part of the year, and an increased use of the steam sizes owing to the scant supply of bituminous. This improvement was measurably prospective, and it is expected that the trade will reap the main benefit in the year 1891.

The Philadelphia and Reading Railroad Company is the most important factor in this industry, and its managers are at the present time developing plans that will enable the Company to command increased traffic, and lead to a higher position in the production and carrying of coals of their immense mining possessions.

In anthracite coal the smaller sizes, as the "nut" and "pea," are in increased use, and the demand for these small sizes is considerably in excess of the supply. The only size that is weak and in excess of the supply is the "broken," or large size.

The hard coal is slowly taking the place of the soft or bituminous coals; many of the ocean steamers are using it, and the smaller sizes are creeping into the factories and mills. For 1891 it is expected trade will be called for the north-western section of the county, but it will be a spasmodic trade, from hand to mouth, as it were, and be subject to a number of annoyances in the matter of prices. Travelling men report but little coal in stock in that section of the county, and that there is a decided aversion on the part of dealers to buying beyond their actual daily needs.

*Trade growth.*

The growth of this great mineral production in the United States is rapid. It doubled between the years 1860 and 1870, and more than doubled between 1870 and 1880, and again more than doubled between 1880 and 1890. This extraordinary increase each decade cannot be accepted as likely to continue every ten years. If it were to do so, by the year 1900 the production would be over 300,000,000 tons or more than the production of the whole world.

The output of anthracite in the State of Pennsylvania for the years following was :—

| Region. | 1887. | 1888. | 1889. | 1890. |
|---|---|---|---|---|
|  | Tons. | Tons. | Tons. | Tons. |
| Wyoming | 19,684,929 | 21,852,365 | 18,647,925 | 18,657,694 |
| Lehigh | 4,347,061 | 5,639,236 | 6,285,420 | 6,329,658 |
| Schuylkill | 10,609,028 | 10,654,116 | 10,474,364 | 10,867,821 |
| Total | 34,641,017 | 38,145,718 | 35,407,710 | 35,865,174 |

The increase of 1890 over 1889 was some 447,000 tons, the greater of which occurred in the month of December. For the year 1891 the output, as estimated by dealers, will not be less than 37,000,000 tons. This amount will be quite sufficient on the basis of a legitimate business, where a profit is expected by the producer on each ton of coal sent out. The trade will be confined very largely to the supplying of what is known as the domestic fuel of the country, as there are many places where soft coal is sold so cheaply as to bar out the anthracite. The suspension of mining, during periods aggregating about one-third of the year, was due mainly to the inability of the market to absorb a larger product.

TABLE showing the Shipments of Anthracite Coal since 1820 from the Pennsylvania Regions.

| Years. | Schuylkill Region. Long Tons. | Per cent. | Lehigh Region. Long Tons. | Per cent. | Wyoming Region. Long Tons. | Per cent. | Total. Long Tons. |
|---|---|---|---|---|---|---|---|
| From 1820 to 1859 inclusive | 44,049,622 | 52·54 | 17,755,009 | 21·18 | 22,031,210 | 26·28 | 83,835,841 |
| 1860 ,, 1869 ,, | 44,769,022 | 41·80 | 20,035,073 | 18·71 | 42,288,823 | 39·49 | 107,092,918 |
| 1870 ,, 1879 ,, | 68,237,040 | 34·87 | 35,683,152 | 18·23 | 91,794,184 | 46·90 | 195,714,376 |
| 1880 ,, 1889 ,, | 96,428,369 | 30·56 | 55,016,850 | 17·44 | 164,077,794 | 52·00 | 315,523,013 |
| Total | 253,484,053 | 36·10 | 128,490,084 | 18·30 | 320,192,011 | 45·60 | 702,166,148 |

PHILADELPHIA.

The distribution of anthracite for 1889 was :—

| Sections. | Long Tons. | Per cent. |
|---|---|---|
| Pennsylvania, New York, and New Jersey | 22,314,331 | 63·02 |
| New England States | 5,407,357 | 15·27 |
| Western States | 4,922,076 | 13·90 |
| Southern States | 1,613,120 | 4·56 |
| Pacific Coast | 20,900 | 0·06 |
| Canada | 1,094,736 | 3·09 |
| Foreign | 35,190 | 0·10 |
| Total | 35,407,710 | 100·00 |

The prices of anthracite at the mines of the Lehigh and Schuylkill regions are quoted :—

|  | s. d. |
|---|---|
| Lump | 9 11 |
| Broken and egg | 9 11 |
| Stove | 10 6 |
| Chestnut | 9 4 |
| Pea | 5 2 |
| Buckwheat | 3 1 |

The Philadelphia and Reading Railroad Company prices, f.o.b. at Port Richmond (Delaware River at Philadelphia) are :—

|  | Broken. | Egg. | Stove. | Chestnut. | Pea. |
|---|---|---|---|---|---|
|  | s. d. | £ s. d. | £ s. d. | £ s. d. | s. d. |
| Hard white ash | 15 0 | 0 16 3 | 0 16 8 | 0 15 3 | 9 4 |
| Free " " | 15 5 | 0 15 5 | 0 16 8 | 0 15 3 | 9 4 |
| N. Franklin white ash | 16 8 | 0 16 8 | 0 16 8 | 0 14 10 | .. |
| Shamoki | 16 3 | 0 16 3 | 0 17 8 | 0 15 3 | .. |
| Schuylkill red ash | 16 3 | 0 16 3 | 0 17 8 | 0 16 1 | .. |
| Larberry | 16 3 | 1 0 2 | 0 17 8 | 0 16 1 | .. |
| Lykas valley | 19 2 | .. | 1 0 2 | 1 0 2 | .. |
| Hard white ash and steamboat | 15 10 | .. | .. | .. | .. |

The number of persons employed during the year, including superintendents, engineers, and clerical force, was 125,229, including boys, say 25 per cent. of the whole force.

The total amount paid in wages to all classes was 8,055,992*l.* 11*s.* 11*d.* In these figures are the wages paid to the boys, who earn from 4*s.* to 6*s.* per week, making the average earnings per capita 64*l.* 5*s.* per annum. The total number of establishments, or " breakers," equipped for the preparation and shipment of coal was 342, nineteen of which were idle during the year. Besides these there were 49 small diggings and washeries supplying local trade. There were also 18 new establishments

24    UNITED STATES.

in course of construction. The largest actual shipment during any year in the trade's history was in 1888, being 38,145,178 tons (of 2,240 lbs.).

In the Consular report for 1889 mention was made of the slack, or culm, which is left after the coal has been sent through the breakers. This culm is lying about in huge piles, and in some places where the mines have been worked out. A small breaker or "separator" is now coming into use for the purpose of separating the "pea" and "chestnut" sizes of coal contained in the great piles of culm. It is estimated that at one worked out mine property alone nearly 1,000,000 tons of culm is lying unused, about 20 per cent. of it being marketable coal.

Bituminous. The bituminous or soft coal market continues in good shape, and a large trade is predicted at the Eastern points for 1891. It is evident that there is not to be any particular cessation of work at the mines on which the seaboard interests are dependent for supplies. In some few instances, however, a sentiment prevails among the miners that local cessation of mining will be resorted to by the operators in order that the production be kept down as low as possible to offset expected strike throughout the mining regions for eight hours labour. The miners fear that it is the intention of the operators to keep them as poor as possible in the Lackawanna and Wyoming Valleys. Some coal train crews in the former coal carrying valley have been laid off, and other companies are slowly falling in the line of reduction.

The production for the year in the whole United States now aggregates 100,000,000 tons annually, and the demand has kept up to this enormous supply. There has been no particularly increased price realised for this variety of fuel, but it is granted that values are stronger than they were a twelvemonth ago, and some advance is expected in 1891. The "pool system" or association of the operators of Pennsylvania, Virginia, West Virginia, and Maryland continued sending the product to seaboard under regulations and restrictions respecting the output and the prices. In some few instances these regulations were broken; and, as a consequence, when the autumn rush came, some contractors were obliged to buy coal in the open market at a higher rate than they were receiving, in order to fill their contracts. This association sent into competitive markets some 7,000,000 tons. The production of bituminous coal in Pennsylvania was:—

|      | Tons. |
|------|-------|
| 1888 | 33,000,000 |
| 1889 | 32,000,000 |
| 1890 | 34,000,000 |

The prices at the mines range from 4s. 5d. to 4s. 10d. per ton, and for the year 1891 they are likely to be slightly better.

Wages for 1891 will be as follows:—Indiana, screened coal, 3s. 6d. per ton; run of mine, 2s. 9d.; and cannel, 3s. 4d.; Ohio and Pennsylvania (Central Pennsylvania)—2s. 1d.; Monongahela River, 4s. 2d. for screened coal, and 2s. 11d. for run of mine; Western Pennsylvania, 3s. 9d. for screened coal, and 2s. 11d. for run of mine; Kocking Valley, 3s. 4d. for screened coal, and 2s. 6d. for run of mine.

The figures below are authentic, and fairly represent so many gross tons in the calendar years named; while the returns from certain States are made by mine inspectors and others for fiscal years, and in net tons, there is always a large amount of coal used by the local industries, the mining population, railroads in the districts, country banks for farmers' use, small mines that are not under the mine inspectors' regulations, and, in fact, there is a vast amount of supply coal that never gets into the returns. In the item of anthracite the shipments of commercial coal are given:— *Coal produced in the United States and territories.*

| States. | 1887. | 1890. |
|---|---|---|
|  | Tons. | Tons. |
| Alabama | 3,000,000 | 4,200,000 |
| Arkansas | 200,000 | 500,000 |
| California | 100,000 | 90,000 |
| Colorado | 1,791,735 | 3,000,000 |
| Dakota | 60,000 | 100,000 |
| Georgia | 200,000 | 225,000 |
| Illinois | 10,500,000 | 13,000,000 |
| Indiana | 3,217,711 | 3,500,000 |
| Indian territory | 500,000 | 700,000 |
| Iowa | 4,014,490 | 4,200,000 |
| Kansas | 1,850,000 | 2,600,000 |
| Kentucky | 2,000,000 | 2,600,000 |
| Maryland | 2,926,785 | 3,631,185 |
| Michigan | 50,000 | 60,000 |
| Missouri | 3,500,000 | 3,750,000 |
| Montana | 20,000 | 150,000 |
| New Mexico | 400,000 | 800,000 |
| Ohio | 11,000,000 | 12,250,000 |
| Oregon | 125,000 | 75,000 |
| Penn. { Anthracite | 34,641,017 | 35,865,174 |
| Penn. { Bituminous | 30,000,000 | 34,000,000 |
| Tennessee | 2,100,000 | 2,900,000 |
| Texas | 150,000 | 300,000 |
| Utah | 200,000 | 361,000 |
| Virginia | 1,500,000 | 2,250,000 |
| Washington | 700,000 | 1,500,000 |
| West Virginia | 4,400,000 | 5,424,904 |
| Wyoming | 1,000,000 | 2,000,000 |
| Total | 120,146,738 | 140,032,263 |

In the line of slate deposits running from Maine to Georgia, Pennsylvania is the most important State; thence come Vermont, Maine, New York, Maryland, and Virginia. Outside of these States the operations are of limited extent, and in the case of Arkansas, California, and Utah of very recent date. *Slate.*

As the initial operations of slate quarrying are those of stripping and excavating, preliminary to actual output, some time must necessarily elapse before any returns for labour are realised. This explains why the expenses incurred in Arkansas, California, and Utah exceed the value of the output in those States.

The production in Pennsylvania was 1,729,163 squares; the number of quarries 104; number of squares of roofing slate, 474,602; total value of roofing slate, 336,820*l.*; total value of slate for other purposes, 77,125*l.* 15*s.*; total value of all slate produced, 413,945*l.* 15*s.*; total wages paid for entire product, 264,100*l.* 15*s.*; all other expenses in addition to wages, 89,127*l.*; total expenses of producing entire amount of slate, 353,227*l.* 15*s.*

The next largest producing State is Maine, with four quarries only, which produced 43,500 squares of roofing slate at a valuation of 43,000*l.*

The total production of slate in the United States was as follows:—

|  | £ | s. |
|---|---|---|
| Value in land | 1,446,613 | 2 |
| „ buildings and fixtures | 104,635 | 5 |
| „ tools, live stock, machinery, and supplies on hand.. | 242,580 | 0 |

Mining casualties.

The casualties in the mining districts have been disastrous during the past year. The chief cause of the fatal calamities that have happened was a negligence on the part of the miners in the use of safety lamps, and other precautionary measures by the proprietors. The number of fatal casualties has been large.

LONDON:
Printed for Her Majesty's Stationery Office
By HARRISON AND SONS,
Printers in Ordinary to Her Majesty.
(75 10 | 91—H & S 1198)

# FOREIGN OFFICE.
## 1892.
## ANNUAL SERIES.

### No. 986.

### DIPLOMATIC AND CONSULAR REPORTS ON TRADE AND FINANCE.

# UNITED STATES.

### REPORT FOR THE YEAR 1891
#### ON THE
### TRADE OF THE CONSULAR DISTRICT OF NEW ORLEANS.

REFERENCE TO PREVIOUS REPORT, Annual Series No. 833.

*Presented to both Houses of Parliament by Command of Her Majesty,*
*FEBRUARY, 1892.*

LONDON:
PRINTED FOR HER MAJESTY'S STATIONERY OFFICE,
BY HARRISON AND SONS, ST. MARTIN'S LANE,
PRINTERS IN ORDINARY TO HER MAJESTY.

And to be purchased, either directly or through any Bookseller, from
EYRE & SPOTTISWOODE, EAST HARDING STREET, FLEET STREET, E.C., and
32, ABINGDON STREET, WESTMINSTER, S.W.; or
JOHN MENZIES & Co., 12, HANOVER STREET, EDINBURGH, and
90, WEST NILE STREET, GLASGOW; or
HODGES, FIGGIS, & Co., 104, GRAFTON STREET, DUBLIN.

1892.

[C. 6550—48.] *Price Three Halfpence.*

# New Series of Reports.

Reports of the Annual Series have been issued from Her Majesty's Diplomatic and Consular Officers at the following places, and may be obtained from the sources indicated on the title-page:—

| No. | | Price. | No. | | Price. |
|---|---|---|---|---|---|
| 868. | Savannah | ½d. | 927. | Buenos Ayres | ½d. |
| 869. | Suakin | ½d. | 928. | Santo Domingo | ½d. |
| 870. | Berlin | 1d. | 929. | Constantinople | ½d. |
| 871. | Batoum | 1½d. | 930. | Erzeroum | 1½d. |
| 872. | Rosario | ½d. | 931. | Gothenburg | 2d. |
| 873. | Buenos Ayres | ½d. | 932. | Tunis | 1d. |
| 874. | Mogador | 1d. | 933. | New York | 1d. |
| 875. | Tainan | 6½d. | 934. | Nagasaki | 1d. |
| 876. | Pakhoi | 1d. | 935. | Hakodate | 1½d. |
| 877. | Odessa | 2½d. | 936. | Sofia | 3d. |
| 878. | Trebizond | 1½d. | 937. | Frankfort | 2d. |
| 879. | Mollendo | ½d. | 938. | Bangkok | 9d. |
| 880. | Kiukiang | 1d. | 939. | Berne | 1½d. |
| 881. | Antananarivo | 1d. | 940. | The Hague | 1½d. |
| 882. | Stettin | 2½d. | 941. | Christiania | 1d. |
| 883. | Fiume | 1½d. | 942. | Christiania | ½d. |
| 884. | Batavia | 1d. | 943. | Brunei | 1½d. |
| 885. | Samoa | ½d. | 944. | Alexandria | 1½d. |
| 886. | Cherbourg | 1d. | 945. | Therapia | ½d. |
| 887. | Cagliari | 1d. | 946. | Bushire | 1½d. |
| 888. | Hankow | 1½d. | 947. | Tokio | 2½d. |
| 889. | Vienna | 1½d. | 948. | Stockholm | 2d. |
| 890. | Amoy | 1d. | 949. | Palermo | 2½d. |
| 891. | Adrianople | ½d. | 950. | St. Petersburg | 2½d. |
| 892. | Chicago | 2½d. | 951. | Quito | ½d. |
| 893. | Brest | 1d. | 952. | Rio de Janeiro | 2d. |
| 894. | Smyrna | 1d. | 953. | Naples | 2d. |
| 895. | Cadiz | 1d. | 954. | Amsterdam | 1d. |
| 896. | Aleppo | 1d. | 955. | Tangier | 2d. |
| 897. | Foochow | 1d. | 956. | Paramaribo | 1d. |
| 898. | Kiungchow | 1d. | 957. | Teneriffe | 1d. |
| 899. | The Hague | 1½d. | 958. | Athens | 2d. |
| 900. | Nice | 1½d. | 959. | Odessa | 1d. |
| 901. | Nantes | 1½d. | 960. | Copenhagen | 9d. |
| 902. | Port-au-Prince | 1½d. | 961. | Tokio | 1d. |
| 903. | Bengazi | 1d. | 962. | Salonica | 1½d. |
| 904. | Tahiti | ½d. | 963. | Stettin | 3½d. |
| 905. | Chinkiang | 1d. | 964. | Philadelphia | 2d. |
| 906. | San Francisco | 3d. | 965. | Mexico | 2d. |
| 907. | Brindisi | 2d. | 966. | Malaga | 2½d. |
| 908. | Beyrout | 1d. | 967. | Berne | 1d. |
| 909. | Noumea | ½d. | 968. | Puerto Rico | ½d. |
| 910. | San Francisco | 1d. | 969. | Buda-Pesth | 1d. |
| 911. | New York | 1½d. | 970. | Bogotá | 1d. |
| 912. | Caracas | 1½d. | 971. | Panama | 1½d. |
| 913. | Greytown | ½d. | 972. | Munich | 2d. |
| 914. | Corunna | 2d. | 973. | Copenhagen | 4d. |
| 915. | Christiania | 5½d. | 974. | Guatemala | 1d. |
| 916. | Callao | 1d. | 975. | Munich | 2d. |
| 917. | Macao | 1d. | 976. | Meshed | 1½d. |
| 918. | Söul | 1d. | 977. | Para | ½d. |
| 919. | Dunkirk | 1d. | 978. | Florence | 1d. |
| 920. | Tamsui | 1d. | 979. | The Hague | 1½d. |
| 921. | Bussorah | ½d. | 980. | Patras | 1d. |
| 922. | Yokohama | 3½d. | 981. | Paris | 1½d. |
| 923. | Bilbao | 1½d. | 982. | Zanzibar | 2½d. |
| 924. | Barcelona | 2½d. | 983. | Buenos Ayres | ½d. |
| 925. | Netherlands India | 1d. | 984. | Copenhagen | 1d. |
| 926. | Chefoo | 1d. | 985. | Stuttgart | 1d. |

# No. 986.

*Reference to previous Report, Annual Series No 833.*

## UNITED STATES.

### NEW ORLEANS.

*Consul de Fonblanque to the Marquis of Salisbury.*

My Lord,                   *New Orleans, January* 26, 1892.

I HAVE the honour to enclose herewith my Annual Trade Report for the year 1891, and that from Vice-Consul Barnewall at Mobile.

        I have, &c.
      (Signed)     A. de G. de FONBLANQUE.

---

*Annual Trade Report for* 1891.

ABSTRACT of Contents.

| | PAGE |
|---|---|
| The cotton crop | 1 |
| Cotton bales (size and condition) | 2 |
|    „ country, ginning of | 2 |
|    „ limiting production of | 3 |
|    „ fires in | 4 |
| Sugar bounty | 4 |
| McKinley tariff, present effects of | 4 |
| Cereals | 6 |
| Cotton seed products | 6 |
| Railroad projects | 6 |
| Immigration | 7 |
|    „ legal decisions respecting | 7 |
| Lottery projects | 7 |
| Strikes | 8 |
| Public works | 8 |
| Annex A.—Statement of principal exports in British ships | 9 |
|    „ B.—Movements of British and foreign shipping | 9 |
|    „ C.—Canadian banking system | 10 |

### The Cotton Crop.

The prosperity of New Orleans is much less dependent on the cotton crop of the Southern States than it used to be even a few

*The cotton crop.*

(1232)

years ago, but still the business done in this respect is an important factor in assessing the general results of the year. It is now estimated that the crop of 1891–2 will not fall much short of its extraordinary predecessor, and it is bringing even lower prices. This is disastrous to the producers, but the Cotton Exchange is able to report as follows:—

*Cotton exchange report.*

"The cotton trade of New Orleans has experienced one of the most prosperous seasons witnessed for years past; or, in the words of one of the leading committees, we have handled more cotton at our wharves and depots, and in our warehouses, than ever before but once in the history of the trade; our contract business has increased 30 per cent., and the roll of the Exchange is now more numerous than for several years past. As a matter of fact, New Orleans has forged ahead into the front ranks of the progressive cities of the country, and, notwithstanding the financial stringency which during the earlier part of the past season so seriously affected many leading trade centres, we have controlled an increased trade and enlarged the territory of our operations.

*Operations in cotton.*

"Upwards of 1,500,000 bales of cotton have been sold by our members on the spot and 'to arrive,' not including considerable quantities controlled by them in the interior, which form a part of the transit; and our future department has covered operations amounting in all to 10,000,000 bales."

*Good financial position.*

With all this great volume of trade, involving interests perhaps exceeding 100,000,000 dol., the business has proceeded smoothly, with no interruptions, and a freedom from financial embarrassments that is remarkable.

*Better condition of bales.*

A noteworthy feature of the season's operations, pointed out by the Supervision Committee, is that, as a general rule, cotton shipped from this port has been in much better order than for some years past, and fewer claims than usual have been brought for damages. This applies, however, to cottons actually handled by our local trade, the "through cottons," as stated by the chief supervisor, "showing no improvement, a great deal of it having been wet and rusty, with ragged bagging."

*Size of bales.*

One cause of this may be the unwieldy size to which the country-made cotton bale has grown. It has been steadily growing for years, the explanation being very simple—that the railroads and steamboat companies generally carry a bale for the same price, whether it weighs 450 lbs. or 600 lbs., and the baling and packing costs no more. Commencing with 400 lbs. the bale has steadily increased in weight, until now it has for some years past averaged over 500 lbs. The increase has been steady up to the present time, but so far this year we have dropped behind the previous one, our bales averaging only 511·36 lbs., as against 513·26 lbs., a loss of nearly 2 lbs. Louisiana shows the heaviest decline, 7·25 lbs. per bale; Alabama, 6 lbs.; Georgia, 5·85 lbs., and Tennessee, 5 lbs., the other States making a slight increase.

*Country gins.* The trouble has been that the country gins at which the cotton is first baled and compressed cannot afford the expensive mahinery necessary to bring the bales down to the proper size.

In time, no doubt, we will have more powerful presses established throughout the country, so that the cotton can be compressed at them, and not have to be shipped to the seaboard for this purpose. As a matter of fact, a large number of new presses have been established in the large interior towns, and a great many bales of cotton now come through ready for immediate shipment, but the great majority of them are still the old-fashioned big bale, which has to undergo a second treatment before it is ready for export.

The "Atlanta Constitution" believes that a plan has finally been discovered that will obviate this difficulty in the recent invention of a Texan, which enables the ginner to make a bale as small as that turned out by the powerful compresses, and of greater density and at less expense than the plantation bale is made. This does away with the big compresses at one stroke. It is estimated that the invention will save directly to the planter from 1 dol. to 2 dol. 50 c. per bale, and to the South from 7,000,000 dol. to 20,000,000 dol. a year. The process, which is simple in principle, compresses the cotton as it is ginned by passing it between rollers and making it into a web, which is laid layer upon layer in the bale. The air and elasticity are thus eliminated in large part before the pressure is exerted on the bulk. The process makes a bale of uniform size and of a density of 25 lb. to the cubic foot. It requires no more power than is used in making the plantation bale, hence the cost, as a matter of fact, is less. The cotton farmer does not share in the prosperity of those who have marketed his crops. The large amount of cotton produced and the low prices which necessarily followed from the inordinate supply, have caused considerable discussion as to the feasibility of limiting the acreage to be planted. *Improved compressing.*

The Atlanta Cotton Congress suggested that the acreage be reduced so as to assure a crop of not over 7,000,000 bales, and proposes that each of the cotton States should hold a Convention and adopt resolutions to that effect. That a maximum crop of 7,000,000 would be profitable to the South is admitted by all It would cost less to produce, and it would return the same amount as an 8,500,000 bale crop; but it is out of question that resolutions will ever accomplish anything of this kind. The lesson the cotton planter is receiving now will have far more effect. He has found cotton so low during the last two years that he has made little profit from it, and in some cases he has actually lost money; and this experience will go further to cure him of the "all-cotton idea" than a thousand Conventions. The American belief in the efficacy of resolutions is great, but they will scarcely have the effect of reducing the cotton acreage if the farmers think the staple will bring a good price. This is a matter in which experience is the best teacher, and it is now teaching the southern farmers a salutary lesson. *Limiting production cotton.*

(1232)

## UNITED STATES.

### Fires in Cotton.

**Fires in cotton.** I regret to say that fires in cotton, both on the levee and on board ships whilst loading, during the voyage and at their ports of discharge, have again become disastrously frequent. In some cases (notably that of the ss. "Chollerton") they were criminally set, but all others are, in my opinion, due to the absence of proper protection for bales stored on the levees or carried in railway cars. I do not like to repeat what I have so often written in detail on this subject, but cannot change my opinion that the safe arrival of any cotton cargo (in the circumstances under which it is loaded here) is due to good luck only.

### Bounty on Sugar.

**The sugar bounty.** The arrangements made for assessing this bounty have worked smoothly, considering the complexity of the work, and that this is the first year in which it has been performed; but there has been some delay in payments which (as the bounty practically represents profits) has inconvenienced smaller producers. The amount of bounty to be paid for the year ending June 30, 1892, will, it is estimated, be as follows: on cane sugar, 8,912,500 dol.; on beet sugar, 500,000 dol.; sorghum sugar, 40,000 dol.; maple sugar, 176,250 dol.; total, 9,628,750 dol. This country is a large consumer of sugar, the people using more per capita than those of any other country except that of England. **Consumption of sugar.** In the last fiscal year we imported 3,483,442,325 lbs. of sugar, of the value of 105,661,431 dol., and produced 512,261,530 lbs.

The amount of sugar produced in the United States is about one-eighth of the amount consumed. Already the political atmosphere is full of portents indicating stormy weather for the sugar planters, and if the Republican party be successful in 1893 it is not unlikely that their bounty will be swept away.

### McKinley Tariff.

**McKinley tariff.** Owing to the large importations which were made in anticipation of this measure, the statistics published by its advocates are unreliable. Another year, at least, must pass before its effects can be realised. One result recognisable at present is that Nottingham lace goods, and the lighter woollen fabrics of Bradford, are practically excluded from this market in which they formerly had a ready and remunerative sale. Bobinet, used extensively in the south for mosquito "bars," but uncalled for in the north, have escaped nominal taxation, and comes in at 35 per cent. as "cotton goods not expressly named." There is, therefore, still a market for it. **Present results of.** I quote the following from a local paper on the increased cost of living:—

"Prices of dry goods and household articles in September,

1891, as compared with prices for September, 1890, before the new Law was passed: street gloves, men's, September, 1890, were 1 dol. 50 c., in September, 1891, 1 dol. 75 c.; common laced curtains were advanced by the McKinley Tariff between those dates from 2 dol. per pair to 2 dol. 40 c., the cheaper sort from 37½ c. per pair to 45 c.; furniture, mohair, average quality, was advanced from 2 dol. 50 c. a yard to 3 dol. a yard; plushes from 2 dol. 50 c. per yard to 3 dol. 50 c. per yard; plush garments were advanced from 20 dol. to 25 dol.; flannel wrappers from 5 dol. to 5 dol. 50 c. per yard; French jersey waists from 10 dol. to 13 dol.; staple pearl buttons from 9 dol. per gross to 14 dol. per gross; pearl buttons from 75 c. per dozen to 1 dol. 17 c. per dozen; common broadcloth from 1 dol. 25 c. per yard to 1 dol. 50 c. per yard; black diagonals from 2 dol. 50 c. per yard to 3 dol. per yard; corduroy pants goods from 75 c. per yard to 1 dol. per yard; combs from 15 c. each to 21 c. each; tooth brushes from 15 c. each to 20 c. each. Increased cost of living.

"In underwear the advances caused by the protectionist Act will doubtless cause many struggling families to suffer injury to health during the coming winter, since they will have to put up with inferior stuffs. Real woollen ware is placed by the Act beyond the means of many persons; ladies' and men's Cartwrights, cotton and wool, have been advanced from 2 dol. 25 c. to 2 dol. 75 c. each; cotton balbriggan from 1 dol. to 1 dol. 25 c.; men's domestic underwear have been advanced 1 dol. per dozen; corsets of the commonest kind have been advanced 30 per cent.; common scissors have been advanced from 50 c. per pair to 62 c. per pair; shears from 50 c. to 75 c. per pair; pocket knives from 50 c. each to 62 c. each; domestic blankets from 2 dol. 10 c. to 2 dol. 25 c.; mohair braid from 50 c. per yard to 67 c. per yard; men's Derby hats from 1 dol. 75 c. each to 2 dol. each; hammocks from 1 dol. 50 c. to 1 dol. 75 c.; woollen shirts from 2 dol. 12 c. to 2 dol. 37 c.; neckties of a certain grade from 50 c. to 75 c.; beaded edging from 62 c. per yard to 75 c. per yard; common cotton laces from 20 c. per yard to 25 c. per yard; curtain muslin from 20 c. per yard to 25 c. per yard; serge coat linings from 50 c. per yard to 55 c. per yard; Scotch cheviots from 25 c. per yard to 37½ c. per yard; percale from 25 c. to 27½ c. *Advance in warm clothing.*

"Glassware has been forced up likewise. Common tumblers have had their retail price advanced since September, 1890, as much as 12 per cent.; jelly tumblers, 10 per cent.; white lamp shades, 15 per cent.; bowls, 16 per cent.; preserve dishes, from 17 per cent. to 20 per cent.; two-quart pitchers, 14 per cent.; coffee cups and saucers, from 5 per cent. to 12 per cent. Common window glass has had its price advanced from 1 dol. 62 c. per box to 2 dol. 25 c. per box; ground glass from 6 dol. 75 c. per 100 ft. to 13 dol. 80 c. per 100 ft.; greenhouse and farmers' double seconds from 2 dol. 70 c. to 3 dol. 50 c." *Glassware.*

*Imports and Exports.*

Annex A. contains a statement of the principal exports in *Exports.*
(1232)

British ships, and compared with 1891 shows an increase and decrease in the most important articles (cereals and cotton) as follows:—

**Increase in wheat.**

| Articles. |  |  |  |  |  | Increase. | Decrease. |
|---|---|---|---|---|---|---|---|
| Cotton | .. | .. | .. | Bales | .. | 220,175 | .. |
| Corn | .. | .. | .. | Bushels | .. | .. | 9,458,836 |
| ,, | .. | .. | .. | Sacks | .. | .. | 51,668 |
| Wheat | .. | .. | .. | Bushels | .. | 7,976,569 | .. |
| ,, | .. | .. | .. | Sacks | .. | 1,101 | .. |

## Cotton Seed Products.

**Cotton seed products.**

I have received many enquiries from British firms as to these, and hitherto have had to reply that their sale is governed by a close "trust" or combination. There are now indications that this is considerably shaken and may break up.

**Prospects of New Orleans as a grain port.**

A low state of the Mississippi River prevented the arrival of a great deal of grain, and this is rather fortunate as existing facilities for "handling" it might have proved insufficient and produced a bad effect on future business. I have seen so many grand schemes for the amelioration of New Orleans (from the outside) break down, that I must offer the latest on this subject with reserve. It is said that Mr. Jay Gould intends to make this port the outlet for north-western grain. His plan, as announced by himself, is to complete a line from Fort Smith to a junction with the Cotton Belt Railroad, giving him over these roads and the Texas and Pacific a direct line from Kansas City to New Orleans. It would then be an easy matter for him to make the same rates on grain from all points in Kansas to New Orleans as to Chicago, as these two cities are almost the same distance from the grain fields. At Chicago the wheat would still be almost as far from the seaboard as ever, and have over 1,000 miles journey to New York to make. At New Orleans it could be put at once upon shipboard and sent at a minimum cost to Europe.

The whole matter is very easily and simply arranged, and a man like Jay Gould, backed by one of the biggest railroad lines in the country, could put it in operation in a few weeks. The grain was drifting to New Orleans naturally before he proposed his plan. Now, if he should take hold of the matter, no obstructions or hindrances can stand in the way. With its great advantages, New Orleans was certain of becoming in time a far greater commercial city than it is to-day; with Jay Gould's influence and railroad behind it, that commercial supremacy will come sooner than we imagined.

**Grain elevators to be erected.**

It is announced that large elevators will be erected here in time for next season. This scheme presents no drawbacks, because the old prejudice against the shipment of grain from

New Orleans on account of (alleged) beating is thoroughly exploded.

## Phosphates.

Several British steamers have gone hence to Tampa and Charlotte Harbour (Florida) to load phosphates, and returned to fill up with cotton. The bed of Lake Okechobee, near the place last named, is said to be very rich in this material. Good freights have been obtained, but expenses are high, as ships have to enter at Tampa or Key West. *Phosphates.*

Annex B. contains the movements of British and foreign shipping during the year 1891. From this it will appear that the British entries were 440 vessels (steam and sail) against 455 in 1890, but the tonnage of the lesser number exceeded that of the greater by 43,666 tons. In the early part of the present year business was slack, but the unprecedented number of 68 steamers arrived during the month of November. *Foreign and British shipping.*

## Immigration.

Some of the most vexatious features of the Act of Congress on this subject which came into force on April 1 (as attempted to be enforced here) have been eliminated by decisions of the United States Circuit Court in the cases of ex Stanley (habeas corpus) and United States v. Sandrey, which decide that persons originally stowaways put bonâ fide on the articles of a ship cannot be considered as alien immigrations or paupers. *Immigration.* *Legal decisions.*

## Financial.

Annex C. contains some interesting comments on the Canadian system of banking. *Canadian banking.*

In a recent number of the Board of Trade journal was published an extract from a report of my Belgian colleague commenting favourably on the fact that Mississippi was the only North American State which had no debt. This financial position was brought about by repudiation of 7,000,000 of bonds in 1841, and was confirmed by the new Constitution framed two years ago. *Mississippi debt.*

A proposition made by the Louisiana State Lottery to obtain a renewal of its charter has already had the effect of breaking-up the Democratic party into three bitterly opposed factions, and is likely to cause much excitement in the election which will take place in April next. *Louisiana State lottery.*

The Lottery Company offer an annual subsidy as follows:—

| | Dollars. |
|---|---|
| For public schools | 350,000 |
| levees | 350,000 |
| public charities | 150,000 |
| pensions to Confederate soldiers | 50,000 |
| city improvement, drainage, paving, &c. | 100,000 |
| the general fund | 250,000 |
| Total | 1,250,000 |

*Proposed subsidy of.*

That this money is badly wanted and cannot be obtained by extra taxation is certain. Whether the continuance for 20 years of a corrupting institution is not too heavy a price to pay for the proffered relief, is a question which divides many conscientious persons and arouses fanaticism on both sides.

The Lottery Company is recognised by the Constitution of the State, and the proposed extension of its charter will come up as a constitutional amendment to be voted upon at the next general election.

## Strikes.

*Strikes.*

There has been no strike of any moment during the past twelve months. An attempt to raise the rates for "handling" cotton may be expected at the commencement of every season, but, fortunately for all concerned, the draymen (of cotton) did not succeed in a short-lived combination to drive their business away from the port.

## Public Works.

*Public works.*

My report on this head, I am sorry to say, must be a negative one, with the exception of the paving of some few miles of "dirt" street with Rosetta gravel, nothing has been done in the way of public improvements. The drainage of the city (or rather the lack of it) remains as it was. After a sharp shower our main street becomes a chain of ponds, which frequently overflow into the neighbouring shops. The "dirt" streets become like the gateway of a ploughed field through which a large cart has passed in an open season. If two-thirds of the wharves resist the next high water I shall be surprised. Their approaches are as bad as ever, and no attempt has been made to provide labour-saving appliances.

*Little improvement in.*

Two commissions have recommended New Orleans as the site of a navy and dockyard, but nothing has been done to carry out the work.

*Paid fire brigade.*

Following the example of all cities of her size, New Orleans has organised her volunteer fire companies into a paid department.

## Annex A.—Return of Principal Exports carried in British Ships during the Year 1891.

| Articles. | | Quantity. |
|---|---|---|
| Cotton | Bales | 1,414,790 |
| " seed | Sacks | 4,646 |
| " " oil | Barrels | 25,416 |
| " " " cakes | Sacks | 204,883 |
| " " meal | " | 379,198 |
| " " soap stock | Barrels | 23,178 |
| Corn | Bushels | 1,359,648 |
| " | Sacks | 20,775 |
| Wheat | Bushels | 8,789,269 |
| " | Sacks | 7,741 |
| Flour | " | 23,872 |
| Tobacco | Hogsheads | 2,759 |
| " | Cases | 196 |
| Staves | Pieces | 1,219,425 |
| Timber | Feet | 93,518 |
| " | Logs and pieces | 38,904 |
| Lumber | Feet | 938,323 |
| " | Logs and pieces | 21,890 |
| Lead | Bars and pigs | 139,279 |
| Copper ore | Sacks | 9,969 |
| Silver " | " | 3,360 |
| Rice polish | " | 13,294 |
| " bran | " | 9,255 |
| Molasses | Barrels | 4,466 |
| Tallow | Tierces | 1,845 |
| Lard | " | 700 |
| Cattle | Head | 711 |
| Tanning root | Sacks | 5,197 |
| Hay | Bales | 150 |
| Coffee | Sacks | 300 |
| Rice | " | 100 |
| Phosphate rock | Tons | 1,200 |
| Coal | Hogsheads | 92 |
| Bricks | | 15,000 |
| Moss | Bales | 30 |
| Boat oars | | 3,996 |
| Prawns | Cases | 1,275 |

## Annex B.—Return of all Shipping at the Port of New Orleans in the Year 1891.

ENTERED.

| Nationality. | Sailing. Number of Vessels. | Tons. | Steam. Number of Vessels. | Tons. | Total. Number of Vessels. | Tons. |
|---|---|---|---|---|---|---|
| British | 14 | 2,254 | 426 | 625,900 | 440 | 628,154 |
| American* | 36 | 13,185 | 200 | 115,373 | 236 | 128,558 |
| Italian | 29 | 13,437 | 21 | 13,712 | 50 | 27,149 |
| Spanish | 13 | 8,657 | 75 | 129,150 | 88 | 137,807 |
| Norwegian and Swedish | 7 | 6,806 | 68 | 34,442 | 75 | 41,248 |
| German | 9 | 9,805 | 25 | 45,430 | 34 | 55,235 |
| French | 3 | 1,590 | 16 | 42,602 | 19 | 44,192 |
| Austrian | 2 | 1,362 | ... | ... | 2 | 1,362 |
| Mexican | 3 | 515 | 3 | 1,461 | 6 | 1,976 |
| Total | 116 | 57,611 | 834 | 1,008,070 | 959 | 1,065,681 |
| " for the year preceding | ... | ... | ... | ... | 907 | 971,024 |

## UNITED STATES.

CLEARED.

| Nationality. | Sailing. Number of Vessels. | Sailing. Tons. | Steam. Number of Vessels. | Steam. Tons. | Total. Number of Vessels. | Total. Tons. |
|---|---|---|---|---|---|---|
| British | 16 | 4,588 | 411 | 597,218 | 427 | 601,806 |
| American* | 20 | 6,525 | 179 | 101,347 | 199 | 107,872 |
| Italian | 25 | 10,843 | 23 | 16,713 | 48 | 27,556 |
| Spanish | 15 | 10,103 | 75 | 133,328 | 90 | 143,431 |
| Norwegian and Swedish | 5 | 5,245 | 67 | 34,000 | 72 | 39,245 |
| German | 8 | 8,538 | 24 | 42,861 | 32 | 51,399 |
| French | 3 | 1,590 | 15 | 39,940 | 18 | 41,530 |
| Austrian | 2 | 1,362 | ... | ... | 2 | 1,362 |
| Mexican | 3 | 515 | 3 | 1,461 | 6 | 1,976 |
| Total | 97 | 49,309 | 797 | 966,868 | 894 | 1,016,177 |
| ,, for the year preceding | ... | ... | ... | ... | 973 | 913,482 |

\* This is exclusive of coasting ships.

### Annex C.—CANADIAN Banking.

This country is practically at sea on the currency question. Whether the outcome will be collision and disaster no one can say. At such times it is wise to consult the experiences of other nations, and we have only to turn to Canada to find a country allied to us physically, geographically, and in many other ways, and yet with a bank and currency system which has given her a circulating medium fully meeting all the requirements of every season, both as to elasticity and safety—in fact, with one of the best currency systems in the world.

The experiences with continental currency, and more recently with State bank issues during the period of wild-cat banking, have planted a prejudice in the minds of the American people against any kind of bank note issues that are not specially secured. Nevertheless, we find in Canada a currency not so secure, and yet absolutely sound.

The growth of the Canadian system was slow and sure, rising step by step from a specially-secured circulation like that of our national bank notes to the present broad and scientific method. During this growth Canadian financiers had at first much of the same fanatical element to contend with that we are accustomed to in this country. There was, however, no concession to wild or compromising schemes, and the advance was from good to better.

To-day the Bank Act, comprising 100 clauses, thoroughly regulates the system. In addition to many wise general provisions, the note issues are specially cared for. No bank can issue notes with less capital than 250,000 dol. paid up. The notes are a first lien upon all assets of the bank, above every other claim. Stock-holders are doubly liable. There is, in addition, a guarantee fund, contributed to by all banks. Notes of broken banks bear interest at 6 per cent. until redeemed. There is no taxation upon circulation.

"Bank notes are sent in daily for redemption, like cheques. It is for the benefit of each bank to keep as many of its own notes out as possible. Hence it will send in daily for redemption all notes of other banks which it takes in.

"Each bank has agencies for the redemption of its notes in all the principal cities from one end of the broad domain to the other, making all notes par everywhere. The result, in a word, is this: every dollar in the Canadian bank notes has over 9 dol. on the average, and 5 dol. at the lowest, in security at the back of it to make it good.

"Canadian notes are thus five to nine times as strong as national bank notes. The branch system of banking in Canada distributes the idle money gathered in one part of the dominion to all points where enterprise can use it, and makes note issues profitable.

"As to elasticity, the Canadians never know what it is to go through an American money squeeze in the autumn. It has never been necessary to issue more than about 60 per cent. of the amount of bank notes authorised by law. Panics for fear of stringency are thus unknown.

"Every thinking banker knows that our own currency system is inadequate, unsatisfactory, and dangerous. It is time for reconstruction by the most skilled economic wisdom which we can call to our aid. In such a time a deliberate consideration of the better systems in operation should do some good. I have endeavoured to show how scientific and completely filling all the requirements of the community is the Canadian bank and note system now in successful operation in a country very near us, under conditions largely resembling our own, its arteries stretching over vast country and carrying the life-blood of commerce to hamlet and town and metropolis, building up a great prosperity among the sturdy people of our sister nation, Canada."

---

## Mobile, Alabama.

### Abstract of Contents.

| | Page |
|---|---|
| Exports | 12 |
| „ cotton | 12 |
| „ lumber | 12 |
| „ general | 12 |
| Naval stores | 13 |
| Annex A.—Imports | 14 |
| „ B.—Exports | 14 |
| „ C.— „ value of | 15 |
| „ D.—Shipping | 15 |
| „ E.—Depth of harbour channel | 16 |

Mr. Vice-Consul Barnewall reports as follows:—

Commercial year commencing September 1, 1890, and ending August 31, 1891.

## UNITED STATES.

**Cotton receipts, prices.**

Receipts, 311,673 bales, valued at 13,779,063 dol., against 261,957 bales, valued at 13,341,013 dol. 67 c., receipts of the year previous; average price per bale 44 dol. 21 c., against 51 dol. 31 c.; and average price per pound 8 dol. 78 c., against 10 dol. 19 c. the year previous.

**Exports—Cotton.**

There has been an increase in the direct exports to Liverpool of 7,865 bales, and an increase to other points of 30,846 bales.

**Timber shipments, value, &c.**

The following statement gives the timber trade of Mobile, including the exports and the amounts towed to the islands. Total hewn and sawn, 4,521,798 cubic feet, against 5,392,000 cubic feet the year previous.

The value of foreign shipments show the average value of hewn to be $13\frac{1}{2}$ c. per cubic foot, against 14 c. last year; sawn shows an average of 13 c. per cubic foot, against $13\frac{1}{2}$ c. last year.

Total exports of foreign hewn and sawn, 3,592,924 cubic feet, valued at 478,251 dol. 4 c., against 3,814,987 cubic feet, valued at 522,998 dol. 9 c., the year previous.

**Lumber.**

The lumber trade of the past 12 months, which was fair, was not as satisfactory or as large as last season, owing in part to low prices and the financial situation in some parts of the world.

During the past commercial year about 59,000,000 feet were shipped from Mobile by vessels and railroads, against 65,000,000 feet last year, but if we add to the lumber the timber shipments, we will have a direct trade of 102,000,000 feet, against 111,000,000 feet the year previous; then if we add to the above the amount towed to Horn and Ship Islands, local consumption, river trade, &c., the trade of Mobile for the 12 months ending August 31 will be about 122,000,000 feet, valued at 1,415,000 dol., against 136,000,000 feet last year.

## NEW ORLEANS.

**Exports, foreign.**

| Country. | 1890-91. Quantity. | Value. | 1889-90. Quantity. | Value. |
|---|---|---|---|---|
| | Feet. | Dol. c. | Feet. | Dol. c. |
| Exports, foreign— | | | | |
| Great Britain | 2,641,023 | .. | 4,493,256 | .. |
| Ireland | 275,818 | .. | 454,347 | .. |
| France | 308,981 | .. | 147,905 | .. |
| Germany | 526,126 | .. | 262,296 | .. |
| Holland | 1,254,987 | .. | 91,416 | .. |
| Spain | 924,980 | .. | 395,404 | .. |
| Rio Janeiro | 1,675,064 | .. | 6,558,957 | .. |
| River Plate | 2,314,200 | .. | 1,314,141 | .. |
| Mexico | 3,204,968 | .. | 1,081,359 | .. |
| Aspinwall | 429,926 | .. | .. | .. |
| Cuba | 10,400,886 | .. | 11,817,871 | .. |
| Jamaica | 1,388,244 | .. | 735,335 | .. |
| Trinidad | 797,383 | .. | 608,028 | .. |
| Africa | 472,464 | .. | 295,154 | .. |
| Various | 4,570,105 | .. | 2,155,962 | .. |
| Total | 31,185,155 | 385,051 75 | 30,411,431 | 385,006 83 |
| Exports, coastwise, &c.— | | | | |
| New York | 12,638,547 | .. | 19,558,506 | .. |
| Philadelphia | .. | .. | 242,933 | .. |
| Boston | 4,568,833 | .. | 840,493 | .. |
| Providence | 221,000 | .. | 239,634 | .. |
| New Haven | .. | .. | 1,207,369 | .. |
| Wilmington, D.I. | 1,680,864 | .. | .. | .. |
| Various | 598,406 | .. | 378,944 | .. |
| Total | 19,707,650 | .. | 22,467,879 | .. |
| ,, shipments foreign and coastwise | 50,892,805 | .. | 52,879,310 | .. |

**Exports coastwise, &c.**

The exports, foreign, are nearly 1,000,000 feet larger than last year, and the shipments coastwise nearly 3,000,000 feet less than last year. Besides those places mentioned in detail, there have been shipments made to Barbadoes, Hayti, Italy, New South Wales, and many other places which appear in various, and the statement also shows that the exports to Cuba and New York continued very large. Compared with last year the exports show an increase of 331,000 feet to Rio Janeiro, 2,118,000 feet to the Continent, 2,123,000 feet to Mexico, 650,000 feet to Jamaica, and 3,729,000 feet to Boston. The principal decreases were 2,031,000 feet to the United Kingdom, 4,245,000 feet to the River Plate, 1,417,000 feet to Cuba, and 6,920,000 feet to New York.

The trade of the past year was fair but not satisfactory.

Receipts, resin, 89,672 barrels; turpentine, 21,686 barrels; total value, 535,689 dol.; against resin 93,906 barrels, and turpentine 21,092 barrels, value 556,399 dol. the year previous.

The vegetable trade continues to grow in importance, but

**Naval stores. Receipts—Resin, turpentine, &c.**

**Vegetables.**

owing to an unusual cold spell on April 6 last the yield was not as large as last year.

The value of the crop of Mobile county, as a whole, is less than last year, and the estimated value for the past year of 357,000 dol. is 101,000 dol. less than last year, while the value of the shipments from Mobile, including Prichards and Cox's stations on Mobile-Ohio Railroad, is 76,000 dol. less than last year.

*Staves, prices.* Prices ruled steady, and the average price of the foreign shipments is 146 dol. per million, against 135 dol. 50 c. last year.

*Shipments.* The shipments of foreign pipestaves were 68,168, valued at 8,345 dol., against 475,245, valued at 53,612 dol., the year previous.

*Real estate.* There has been a steady and growing demand for realty, and the sales amount to double that of the preceding year.

Annex A.—RETURN of Principal Articles of Export from Mobile during the Years 1890–91 and 1889–90.

| Articles. | | 1890–91. | | 1889–90. | |
|---|---|---|---|---|---|
| | | Quantity. | Value. | Quantity. | Value. |
| | | | £ s. d. | | £ s. d. |
| Cotton | Bales | 299,852 | 2,761,761 17 2 | 261,141 | 2,800,211 3 7 |
| Timber | Cub. feet | 3,592,924 | 99,635 12 8 | 3,893,916 | 110,931 3 2 |
| Lumber | Feet | 50,892,805 | 125,382 9 7 | 52,879,310 | 132,212 15 8 |
| Staves | Millions | 68,168 | 1,738 10 10 | 475,245 | 11,169 4 2 |
| Shingles | Thousands | 895,100 | 896 13 5 | 757,950 | 655 0 0 |
| Merchandise | ... | ... | 1,969 15 2 | ... | 5,405 9 8 |
| Vegetables | ... | ... | 74,391 0 10 | ... | 95,430 4 2 |
| Total | ... | ... | 3,065,775 19 8 | ... | 3,156,015 0 5 |

N.B.—1*l.* sterling valued at 4 dol. 80 c.

Annex B.—RETURN of Principal Articles of Import to Mobile during the Years 1890–91 and 1889–90.

| Articles. | | 1890–91. | | 1889–90. | |
|---|---|---|---|---|---|
| | | Quantity. | Value. | Quantity. | Value. |
| | | | £ s. d. | | £ s. d. |
| Bagging | Pieces | 20,973 | ... | 21,554 | ... |
| Iron ties | Bundles | 32,315 | ... | 19,707 | ... |
| Bacon | Hhds. | 15,705 | ... | 15,835 | ... |
| Cotton | Bales | 311,673 | 2,870,638 2 6 | 261,957 | 2,800,211 3 7 |
| Coffee | Sacks | 12,633 | ... | 15,746 | ... |
| Corn | ,, | 426,525 | ... | 441,347 | ... |
| Flour | Barrels | 154,341 | ... | 142,536 | ... |
| Fertilisers | Sacks | 286,898 | ... | 195,597 | ... |
| Hay | Bales | 72,731 | ... | 75,016 | ... |
| Lard | Tierces | 5,361 | ... | 5,222 | ... |
| Molasses | Barrels | 2,251 | ... | 2,748 | ... |
| Oats | Sacks | 85,737 | ... | 132,338 | ... |
| Potatoes | Barrels | 16,341 | ... | 17,691 | ... |
| Pork | ,, | 1,520 | ... | 916 | ... |
| Rice | ,, | 6,333 | ... | 6,092 | ... |
| Salt | Sacks | 16,212 | ... | 18,067 | ... |
| Soap | Boxes | 19,835 | ... | 22,603 | ... |
| Sugar | Barrels | 14,561 | ... | 17,010 | ... |
| Tobacco | Boxes | 25,796 | ... | 28,290 | ... |
| Whiskey | Barrels | 6,923 | ... | 7,366 | ... |
| Coal | Tons | 53,042 | ... | 40,647 | ... |
| Wool | Lbs. | 973,100 | 47,641 7 1 | 639,300 | 31,965 0 0 |

I cannot enumerate articles imported from foreign countries, nor give the value of above enumerated articles, with the exception of cotton and wool.

Annex C.—TABLE showing the Total Value of all Articles Exported from Mobile and Imported to Mobile from and to Foreign Countries during the Years 1889–90 and 1890–91.

EXPORTS.

|         | £       | s. | d. |
|---------|---------|----|----|
| 1889-90 | 702,229 | 7  | 4  |
| 1890-91 | 670,638 | 5  | 2  |

IMPORTS.

|         | £      | s. | d. |
|---------|--------|----|----|
| 1889-90 | 20,880 | 4  | 2  |
| 1890-91 | 18,164 | 15 | 10 |

I have no means of dividing the above exports as to countries except as regards cotton included in above.

|                         | £       | s. | d. |
|-------------------------|---------|----|----|
| Great Britain, 1889-90  | 478,775 | 14 | 11 |
| „            1890-91    | 484,965 | 5  | 7  |

Annex D.—RETURN of all Shipping at the Port of Mobile in the Year 1891.

ENTERED.

| Nationality. | Sailing. Number of Vessels. | Sailing. Tons. | Steam. Number of Vessels. | Steam. Tons. | Total. Number of Vessels. | Total. Tons. |
|---|---|---|---|---|---|---|
| British | 54 | 23,767 | 6 | 9,268 | 60 | 33,035 |
| Norwegian | 41 | 39,352 | 7 | 2,846 | 48 | 42,171 |
| American | 57 | 19,957 | ... | ... | 57 | 19,957 |
| Spanish | 4 | 1,779 | ... | ... | 4 | 1,779 |
| Italian | 2 | 993 | ... | ... | 2 | 993 |
| Russian | 7 | 4,708 | ... | ... | 7 | 4,708 |
| German | 4 | 3,237 | ... | ... | 4 | 3,237 |
| French | 1 | 622 | ... | ... | 1 | 622 |
| Swedish | 1 | 1,174 | ... | ... | 1 | 1,174 |
| Dutch | 2 | 1,848 | ... | ... | 2 | 1,848 |
| Argentine Republic | 1 | 1,178 | ... | ... | 1 | 1,178 |
| Total | 174 | 98,588 | 13 | 12,114 | 187 | 110,702 |
| Coastwise | ... | ... | ... | ... | 146 | 80,163 |
| Grand total | ... | ... | ... | ... | 333 | 190,865 |
| Total for the year preceding | ... | ... | ... | ... | 352 | 221,073 |

(1232)

## UNITED STATES.

**CLEARED.**

| Nationality. | Sailing. Number of Vessels. | Sailing. Tons. | Steam. Number of Vessels. | Steam. Tons. | Total. Number of Vessels. | Total. Tons. |
|---|---|---|---|---|---|---|
| British | 52 | 18,598 | 10 | 14,074 | 62 | 32,672 |
| American | 69 | 24,099 | ... | ... | 69 | 24,099 |
| Norwegian | 37 | 33,213 | 7 | 2,846 | 44 | 36,059 |
| German | 4 | 2,613 | ... | ... | 4 | 2,613 |
| French | 1 | 622 | ... | ... | 1 | 622 |
| Spanish | 3 | 1,260 | 3 | 4,595 | 6 | 5,855 |
| Italian | 3 | 1,266 | ... | ... | 3 | 1,266 |
| Russian | 5 | 3,442 | ... | ... | 5 | 3,442 |
| Hondurian | 1 | 88 | ... | ... | 1 | 88 |
| Swedish | 1 | 1,174 | ... | ... | 1 | 1,174 |
| Dutch | 2 | 1,325 | ... | ... | 2 | 1,325 |
| Argentine Republic | 1 | 1,178 | ... | ... | 1 | 1,178 |
| Total | 179 | 88,878 | 20 | 21,515 | 199 | 110,393 |
| Coastwise | ... | ... | ... | ... | 120 | 62,651 |
| Grand total | ... | ... | ... | ... | 319 | 173,044 |
| Total for the year preceding | ... | ... | ... | ... | 303 | 171,763 |

Annex E.—CONDITION of Dredge at Channel of Mobile Harbour, August 1, 1891.

| Mean Low Water, Minimum Central Depth. | Mobile River, Length. | Mobile Bay, Length. |
|---|---|---|
| Feet. | Feet. | Feet. |
| 23 and over | 10,910 | 48,836 |
| 22 to 23 | 975 | 2,208 |
| 21   22 | 1,570 | 1,900 |
| 20   21 | 2,000 | 17,167 |
| 19   20 | 2,380 | 24,888 |
| 18   19 | 4,810 | 29,437 |
| 17   18 | 2,695 | 10,512 |
| 16   17 | 150 | 7,730 |
| 15   16 | .. | .. |

Length of the whole channel from mouth of Chickasaboyne Creek to 23 feet curve in lower Mobile Bay is 31·85 miles.

LONDON:
Printed for Her Majesty's Stationery Office,
By HARRISON AND SONS,
Printers in Ordinary to Her Majesty.

(75   2 | 92—H & S   1232)

# FOREIGN OFFICE.
## 1892.
### ANNUAL SERIES.

---

### No. 987.
### DIPLOMATIC AND CONSULAR REPORTS ON TRADE AND FINANCE.

---

# UNITED STATES.

---

### REPORT FOR THE YEAR 1891
ON THE
### AGRICULTURE OF THE CONSULAR DISTRICT OF NEW ORLEANS.

---

REFERENCE TO PREVIOUS REPORT, Annual Series No. 827.

---

*Presented to both Houses of Parliament by Command of Her Majesty,*
*MARCH, 1892.*

---

LONDON:
**PRINTED FOR HER MAJESTY'S STATIONERY OFFICE,**
BY HARRISON AND SONS, ST. MARTIN'S LANE,
PRINTERS IN ORDINARY TO HER MAJESTY.

And to be purchased, either directly or through any Bookseller, from
EYRE & SPOTTISWOODE, EAST HARDING STREET, FLEET STREET, E.C., and
32, ABINGDON STREET, WESTMINSTER, S.W.; or
JOHN MENZIES & Co., 12, HANOVER STREET, EDINBURGH, and
90, WEST NILE STREET, GLASGOW; or
HODGES, FIGGIS, & Co., 104, GRAFTON STREET, DUBLIN.

1892.
*Price Tenpence.*

[C 6550 49.]

# New Series of Reports.

Reports of the Annual Series have been issued from Her Majesty's Diplomatic and Consular Officers at the following places, and may be obtained from the sources indicated on the title-page:—

| No. | | Price. | No. | | Price. |
|---|---|---|---|---|---|
| 865. | Marseilles | 1d. | 926. | Chefoo | 1d. |
| 866. | Syra | 1d. | 927. | Buenos Ayres | ½d. |
| 867. | Jeddah | ½d. | 928. | Santo Domingo | ½d. |
| 868. | Savannah | ½d. | 929. | Constantinople | ½d. |
| 869. | Suakin | ½d. | 930. | Erzeroum | 1½d. |
| 870. | Berlin | 1d. | 931. | Gothenburg | 2d. |
| 871. | Batoum | 1½d. | 932. | Tunis | 1d. |
| 872. | Rosario | ½d. | 933. | New York | 1d. |
| 873. | Buenos Ayres | ½d. | 934. | Nagasaki | 1d. |
| 874. | Mogador | 1d. | 935. | Hakodate | 1½d. |
| 875. | Tainan | 6½d. | 936. | Sofia | 3d. |
| 876. | Pakhoi | 1d. | 937. | Frankfort | 2d. |
| 877. | Odessa | 2½d. | 938. | Bangkok | 9d. |
| 878. | Trebizond | 1½d. | 939. | Berne | 1½d. |
| 879. | Mollendo | ½d. | 940. | The Hague | 1½d. |
| 880. | Kiukiang | 1d. | 941. | Christiania | 1d. |
| 881. | Antananarivo | 1d. | 942. | Christiania | ½d. |
| 882. | Stettin | 2½d. | 943. | Brunei | 1½d. |
| 883. | Fiume | 1½d. | 944. | Alexandria | 1½d. |
| 884. | Batavia | 1d. | 945. | Therapia | ½d. |
| 885. | Samoa | ½d. | 946. | Bushire | 1½d. |
| 886. | Cherbourg | 1d. | 947. | Tokio | 2d. |
| 887. | Cagliari | 1d. | 948. | Stockholm | 2d. |
| 888. | Hankow | 1½d. | 949. | Palermo | 2½d. |
| 889. | Vienna | 1½d. | 950. | St. Petersburg | 2½d. |
| 890. | Amoy | 1d. | 951. | Quito | ½d. |
| 891. | Adrianople | ½d. | 952. | Rio de Janeiro | 2d. |
| 892. | Chicago | 2½d. | 953. | Naples | 2d. |
| 893. | Brest | 1d. | 954. | Amsterdam | 1d. |
| 894. | Smyrna | 1d. | 955. | Tangier | 2d. |
| 895. | Cadiz | 1d. | 956. | Paramaribo | 1d. |
| 896. | Aleppo | 1d. | 957. | Teneriffe | 1d. |
| 897. | Foochow | 1d. | 958. | Athens | 2d. |
| 898. | Kiungchow | 1d. | 959. | Odessa | 1d. |
| 899. | The Hague | 1½d. | 960. | Copenhagen | 9d. |
| 900. | Nice | 1½d. | 961. | Tokio | 1d. |
| 901. | Nantes | 1½d. | 962. | Salonica | 1½d. |
| 902. | Port-au-Prince | 1½d. | 963. | Stettin | 3½d. |
| 903. | Bengazi | 1d. | 964. | Philadelphia | 2d. |
| 904. | Tahiti | ½d. | 965. | Mexico | 2d. |
| 905. | Chinkiang | 1d. | 966. | Malaga | 2½d. |
| 906. | San Francisco | 3d. | 967. | Berne | 1d. |
| 907. | Brindisi | 2d. | 968. | Puerto-Rico | ½d. |
| 908. | Beyrout | 1d. | 969. | Buda-Pesth | 1d. |
| 909. | Noumea | ½d. | 970. | Bogotá | 1d. |
| 910. | San Francisco | 1d. | 971. | Panama | 1½d. |
| 911. | New York | 1½d. | 972. | Munich | 2d. |
| 912. | Caracas | 1½d. | 973. | Copenhagen | 4d. |
| 913. | Greytown | ½d. | 974. | Guatemala | 1d. |
| 914. | Corunna | 2d. | 975. | Munich | 2d. |
| 915. | Christiania | 5½d. | 976. | Meshed | 1½d. |
| 916. | Callao | 1d. | 977. | Para | ½d. |
| 917. | Macao | 1d. | 978. | Florence | 1d. |
| 918. | Söul | 1d. | 979. | The Hague | 1½d. |
| 919. | Dunkirk | 1d. | 980. | Patras | ½d. |
| 920. | Tamsui | 1d. | 981. | Paris | 1½d. |
| 921. | Bussorah | ½d. | 982. | Zanzibar | 2½d. |
| 922. | Yokohama | 3½d. | 983. | Buenos Ayres | ½d. |
| 923. | Bilbao | 1½d. | 984. | Copenhagen | 1d. |
| 924. | Barcelona | 2½d. | 985. | Stuttgart | 1d. |
| 925. | Netherlands-India | 1d. | 986. | New Orleans | 1½d. |

# No. 987.

*Reference to previous Report, Annual Series No. 827.*

## UNITED STATES.

### NEW ORLEANS.

*Consul de Fonblanque to the Marquis of Salisbury.*

My Lord,   New Orleans, January 26, 1892.

I HAVE the honour to enclose herewith my Annual Agricultural Report for the year 1891, that from Vice-Consul Barnewall at Mobile, and that from Mr. Vice-Consul Howe of Pensacola.

I have, &c.
(Signed)   A. de G. de FONBLANQUE.

---

*Report on Agriculture for the Year* 1891.

ABSTRACT of Contents.

|  | PAGE |
|---|---|
| General condition of the farmer | 1 |
| Excess of cotton | 2 |
| Ocala platform | 2 |
| Sugar | 3 |
| Cereals | 3 |
| Hints to colonial farmers | 3 |
| Strawberries | 3 |
| Work for fruit trees | 4 |
| Fersimmons | 4 |
| Grapes | 4 |
| Pruning | 5 |
| Annex A.—Statement of cereals grown in consular district in 1891 | 7 |
| „  B.—Sugar bulletins, Nos. 5, 6, and 11 | 8 |
| „  C.—General experiments, No. 7 | 79 |

Notwithstanding the large amount of farm products exported from the United States, the farmer is not in a prosperous condition throughout the country; and in these Southern States his is a decidedly bad case. With no capital (generally speaking) to fall back upon he is embarrassed by mortgages, and is seldom out of debt to his factor or merchant. There are very few, if any,

*General condition of the farmer.*

(1233)

*One crop men.* all round farmers in this district. There are all cotton men, all sugar men, all rice men, who rely on their one crop and buy salted meat for their family and hands, and hay and oats for their stock. A farmer who makes his land yield all the necessaries it can supply is yet to be found. The cost of transportation (for which the railroads are blamed) is one cause given for this depression, and the injurious effect charged against the system of selling products for future delivery (strictly called "Futures") is another. Upon the first question I am unable to express an opinion, except that the railroads do not flourish at their present rates. On the second, I think that, situated as he is, the farmer is not injured by "futures," as he cannot hold his produce and wait for a good market because he has to gather and ship it in haste to meet the claims of his factor.

*Effect of "futures."*

*Limiting production of cotton.* Never before in my experience of 20 years has there been so much cotton stored for shipment in New Orleans, and the price is the lowest ever quoted. As a remedy against the repetition of such congestion it is proposed to limit the acreage to be planted with this staple, and some observations on this head will be found in my trade report.*

This is the text of the much discussed "Ocala platform," which the Farmers' Alliance have adopted—

1. (*a*) We demand the abolition of national banks.

*"Ocala platform."* (*b*) We demand that the Government shall establish sub-treasuries or depositories in the several States, which shall loan money direct to the people at a low rate of interest, not to exceed 2 per cent. per annum, on non-perishable farm products and also upon real estate, with proper limitations upon the quantity of land and amount of money.

(*c*) We demand that the amount of the circulating medium be speedily increased to not less than 50 dol. per capita.

2. We demand that Congress shall pass such laws as will effectually prevent the dealing in futures of all agricultural and mechanical production; providing a stringent system of procedure in trials that will secure the prompt conviction, and imposing such penalties as shall secure the most perfect compliance with the law.

3. We condemn the Silver Bill recently passed by Congress, and demand in lieu thereof the free and unlimited coinage of silver.

4. We demand the passage of laws prohibiting alien ownership of land, and that Congress take prompt action to devise some plan to obtain all lands now owned by aliens and foreign syndicates; and that all lands now held by railroads be reclaimed by the Government and held for actual settlers only.

5. Believing in the doctrine of equal rights to all and special privileges to none, we demand—

(*a*) That our national legislation shall be so framed in the future as not to build up one industry at the expense of another.

(*b*) We further demand a removal of the existing heavy tariff tax from the necessities of life that the poor of our land must have.

* No. 986 Annual Series.

NEW ORLEANS.

(c) We further demand a just and equitable system of graduated tax on income.

(d) We believe that the money of the country should be kept as much as possible in the hands of the people, and hence we demand that all national and State revenues shall be limited to the necessary expenses of the Government economically and honestly administered.

6. We demand the most rigid, honest, and just State and national Government control and supervision of the means of public communication and transportation, and if this control and supervision does not remove the abuse now existing, we demand the Government ownership of such means of communication and transportation.

7. We demand that the Congress of the United States submit an amendment for the constitution providing for the election of United States Senators by direct vote of the people of each State.

Sugar Bulletins Nos. 5, 6, 7, and 11 of the Sugar Experimental Station at Audubon Park are enclosed. No. 5 is of interest to small planters. *Sugar.*

Annex A. contains an account of cereals grown in this district in 1891. *Cereals.*

The British agriculturist has nothing to learn from his brethren in the States composing this consular district, on the contrary there is much that the latter can be taught. Even the truck farmer (market gardener) does not make the most of his land, and purchases much that he ought to produce for his own wants. But I will offer some hints that may be worthy of attention in colonies where the soil and climate may be similar to ours. *Hints to colonial farmers.*

There are two distinct ways of renewing strawberry plantations: the one which is generally preferred and adopted being simply transplanting, and the other some form of self-renewal by the agency of runners. An objection to the latter is the continued occupation of the same piece of ground, the fertility being partly exhausted by the previous growth. This objection may be in a great degree remedied by copious and skilful manuring, and if the soil has been found by trial to be especially benefited by some particular fertiliser, the plant will be so improved by an addition of it to the barn manure. A mode adopted by a cultivator in Canada, and reported to a fruit growers' meeting, was found to have some particular advantages. The rows were not 4 feet apart, and when renewing was desired the old rows were rolled over and not ploughed up, and the trench thus formed was filled with fine manure, the old plants sending their runners over it and taking strong hold. The next season the old row was cut out, and the new plants given entire possession. Another mode is to plough the ground, which has become densely filled with strawberry plants, leaving a strip 6 inches wide of the old plants, which will form a narrow matted row and filling the shallow furrows with fine old manure. All the runners but two are cut off immediately after the gathering of the crop. These two set each a new plant. The middle row, *Strawberries*

(1233)

after fruiting, may be cut out. Still another mode we have used where we have a few rare plants to be removed to another place in the same garden. Square cavities are made with the spade in regular rows, and then the plants are lifted, with a mass of earth on them, and placed in position in the new bed. This work may be done any time in the year, when the ground is not frozen. We have had ripe berries in this way 6 weeks after early spring planting. Caution is necessary in adopting this mode on adhesive or heavy soils, not to press it with the spade with such firmness as to make it compact, solid, or adhesive.

Large and highly profitable crops have been produced at Ponchatoula in Louisiana.

Wash for fruit trees. According to the experiments made at the Ohio Experiment Station, the addition of lime to arsenites tends to prevent injury to the foliage of fruit trees when they are applied in quantities which would burn the leaves when used without it. London purple, as is well-known, does more harm to the foliage than Paris green; and in the experiments made with 1 lb. of London purple to 100 gallons of water, which is at least twice as strong as safety permits, the leaves were badly corroded; but the addition of half a peck of fresh slaked lime to the 100 gallons prevented any injury.

Persimmons. The persimmon is a fruit resembling our medlar, only with a crab-apple flavour which, however, is reduced by cultivation.

Among the interesting papers read before the Florida Horticultural Society was one by Robert A. Mills upon grafting the Japan persimmon. The following is his method: My choice of all the processes for propagating the kaki is root grafting on native persimmon stock, and if possible where the native tree comes up, and best sizes are from ½ inch to 1½ inches in diameter at the crown. It is not a serious objection if they stand within 1 foot from each other, or the roots can readily be transplanted in grove form, and when the leaves are off and at the end of the following year root grafted. Grafts will grow if put in from November until the leaf buds begin to swell on the native persimmon. Kakis "leave out" in this portion of Florida later than the native trees. The grafting is so simple a process that even a novice may succeed with very little previous experience. After selecting the stick to be grafted it is cut or sawn off at the ground or below the surface if the "stock" is long enough to allow splitting and inserting the graft. The graft should be cut wedge-shape, the slopes about three-fourths of an inch long leaving more bark on the (to be) split "stock." Then place a piece of old cloth or paper over the top of the stock and heap damp earth on it, just covering the top of the graft. Grafting wax is not required.

Grapes. The late Casper Wild, who grew grapes with much success and profit within the limits of the City of New Orleans, used the arbour system exclusively. The posts were planted in the soil to a height of 5½ feet to 6 feet, and were about 12 feet apart. Wooden strips 2 inches by 3 inches ran one way, which were kept from decay by a coating of cold tar. Wires were stretched cross-wise, and the whole structure was strong and substantial. The merits of this style of training was: the clusters hung below, not coming in contact with the wood and foliage, and there is less danger from rot. They were more free from injury by birds, and the space underneath being fully shaded neither grass or weeds were troublesome.

Mr. Wild also utilised his vineyard as a poultry yard, thus saved the expense of fertilising, which was done by his fowls. The product of the small area, some 2½ acres, justified Mr. Wild in recommending his method above all others.

The main disadvantage of this system was the difficulty experienced in pruning. The operator is compelled to work overhead, which is a neck-breaking and tiresome process.

Vines may be planted about the dwelling with great pleasure and profit, both for shade and for fruit; but care should be exercised and not set them too near, for they should be planted at least 12 feet away from the house or building.

This will give room for the right preparation of the beds, which should be raised slightly above the surrounding surface and well fertilised. The beds proper should be at least 6 feet wide. The posts long enough to reach the desired height should be braced by wooden strips, both top and bottom, and also by pieces long enough to extend from the top of each post to the building, where it should be well secured. The immediate spaces should be filled with No. 12 galvanised iron wire, as directed for the construction of an upright trellis, nailed about 3 feet apart. A tree of this description, constructed with good material, will, if properly made, last for ten years without repair, and the product of a half-dozen or more vines will furnish an ample supply of fruit for any family.

Of pruning fruit trees an authority writes:—No operation requires greater foresight than the operation of pruning. We must have a definite object in view, and no branch should be removed for whose removal a good reason cannot be given. The reasons which may justify pruning are: (1) the removal of dead or dying branches; (2) thinning; (3) helping the growth of one part of a tree by removing another part. Pruning for the first-named reason is a simple matter, which requires no particular skill or knowledge; pruning for thinning cannot be done properly without a knowledge of plant life; cutting out one part in order to assist another part requires simply good judgment. *Pruning.*

A few well-developed branches are of more value a number of times than many which are crowded together without light and air. If possible the removal of large, healthy limbs should be avoided. The injury is, of course, in proportion to the amount of loss of leaf surface and the size of the wound. Whether to remove a limb or not is a question to be answered in the affirmative only when the benefits expected from the pruning are larger than the necessary injury. Knife and thumb are better pruning tools than saw and axe. Every blow of an axe or push of the saw in the removal of large limbs is a threat at the tree's life and vitality. By lessening the leaf's surface we lessen the digestive apparatus, and consequently the absorption of food.

In transplanting nursery-grown trees in orchard we should cut back the top to make them correspond with the size of the roots. Such trees often have very little root. The best time for pruning trees in orchard is soon after the leaves have fallen. Pruning in spring involves a greater check to the tree, and pruning after growth has commenced is still more injurious. There is no particular objection to pruning in winter, when the trees are frozen, except the discomfort of the pruner. Pruning may be done after the formation of dormant buds in summer, as any damage at that time is quickly repaired. When the wounds are large the injury is lessened by coating them with clay paint or coating wax. Judicious pruning gives us the means of thickening growth, or elongating it and making it more open and spreading. Root pruning can be resorted to for the purpose of checking rank growth in a tree of bearing age, thus hastening its fruitfulness, but, on the whole, Professor Taft did not deem it advisable to resort to such violent means.

The cause of many failures in apple-growing may be found in the bare stems 6 feet or 8 feet high to the lowest branches. Low-headed trees are usually preferable.

In a general way, pruning should be done frequently with knife and thumb.

**Nut culture. Pecans.** A full-bearing pecan* tree near this city is worth from 25 dol. to 50 dol. a year. The pecan is generally propagated from seed, that being the easiest and surest method of obtaining a stand. In growing this nut it must be fully understood that the seed does not always produce its like, unless gathered from a grove that produces the large variety or from a tree sufficiently isolated from other inferior kinds.

For planting purposes nothing but the large, soft (or so-called paper shell) kinds should be chosen. These must be from the new crop, used when as fresh as possible, or packed for future in moist sand or leaf mould.

The best soil for a pecan grove will be a creek or river bottom. An occasional overflow does not harm the young tree, provided it does not cover it up entirely, or does not remain too long.

In setting out a seedling orchard it is always advisable to give them plenty of room. 70 feet to 75 feet is none too close when the soil is low and rich, or 50 feet on poorer up-lands.

**Forming pecan orchard.** The land set aside for the orchard must be both hog and cattle-proof, until the trees are large and strong enough to escape injury from stock. When the time arrives for planting a stake may be driven where the tree is to remain permanently, and from two to three nuts placed near the stake about $2\frac{1}{2}$ inches to 3 inches below the surface, and a mould of forest leaves or leaf mould applied, which will prevent the seed from drying out. This may be raked aside the following spring. If the seed has been properly selected

* Pronounced "pecaun."

and preserved nearly all will grow. The extra plants, with the nut attached, may be carefully transplanted, either into the nursery or used in extending the orchard.

However careful be the cultivation and large the crop of fruit, it will be unprofitable unless well and carefully packed for market. The following quotation is in point. Every year some of o r growers and green fruit packers have to be retaught by experiencing heavy losses, the very important question of packing their fruit carefully. Thousands and thousands of dollars' worth of fruit is yearly thrown away both in the local and eastern markets, because proper care was not exercised in handling before shipment. From the time the fruit is plucked from the tree it should be handled as carefully as if each was an egg. The slightest bruise, scratch, over-ripeness, or accumulation of moisture is a detriment, and may cause several dollars' loss.

It pays better to hire careful painstaking labourers at 1 dol. 50 c. and 1 dol. 75 c. per day than slovenly, don't-care workmen at 1 dol. It is the most expensive sort of economy to try to handle and pack fruit under shade trees or improvised cotton shelter. It is essential for fruit to be kept cool and dry if it is expected to keep.

Substantial packing sheds, with a good circulation of air, should be provided in abundance. The fruit is 100 per cent. better for being so handled, and the employés are better satisfied and do far better work.

It is the height of folly to take a lot of boxed fruit that has been standing on the railroad platform in the blazing sun for hours, and pack it into a car. It is at that time in the worst possible condition for shipment, and is a most fruitful source of loss to the owner. If the railroad company cannot be induced to provide sufficient sheds for the protection of the fruit, build them yourself. Sheds are not necessarily expensive, and may save a community thousands of dollars in a single season. There is one thing that fruit packers are getting too careful about—it is putting all of the big specimens on the top. This is wrong. The habit of facing with average fruit is not to be depreciated, but facing with fruit better than the average is a deliberate attempt to fool the public, and the public is getting very tired of the practice. It may help to sell the boxes to the consumer, but the consumer is disgusted, and will never buy another box of the same stripe if he can help it. He feels a keen sense of having been swindled, and is not slow to resent it.

ANNEX A.

| State. | Wheat. | Corn. | Oats. |
| --- | --- | --- | --- |
|  | Bushels. | Bushels. | Bushels. |
| Alabama | 2,251,000 | 32,245,000 | 5,188,000 |
| Arkansas | 2,236,000 | 29,665,000 | 4,945,000 |
| Florida |  | 5,460,000 | 1,589,000 |
| Louisiana |  | 18,725,000 | 634,000 |
| Mississippi | 433,000 | 24,685,000 | 3,747,000 |

Annex B.—REPORT on Sugar Making on a Small Scale at the North Louisiana Experiment Station.

This article is intended to give the simplest rudiments of sugar making for the guidance of small farmers who grow only patches of sugar-cane, and make sugar, syrup, and molasses for home consumption or local use.

To make a refined sugar upon an extensive profitable basis, there are required many hundred acres of cane, and a most costly sugar house, consisting of ponderous mills or a diffusion plant clarifier, tanks, filter presses, multiple effects, vacuum pan, mixer, centrifugals, sugar waggons, powerful engines, and enormous boilers. To make sugar on the small scale about to be described there are required only a horse mill, evaporator, and a few boxes capable of holding cane juice—an outfit varying in cost from 50 dol. to 300 dol.

There is also given herein the results of the experiments made at the North Louisiana Experiment Station, Calhoun, La., in growing cane and making sugar. These results were so satisfactory as to justify the prediction heretofore made by the author, that sugar-cane could be grown successfully everywhere in Louisiana, and in the southern parts of the Gulf States. To aid in the development of this prophecy a minute and detailed description of the processes of cane and sorghum growing and manufacture is hereby given.

The first step towards sugar making is the growing of sugar-cane or sorghum. The latter is planted from seed, and, up to date, of the large number of varieties used, none have surpassed the Link's Hybrid, a variety originated by Mr. Ephraim Link, Greenville, Tenn. This is planted either in the drill (and thinned when up to one stalk every 4 inches), or dropped at intervals of 8 inches to 10 inches), and two stalks left to each hill. Its after cultivation is like that given to corn. Sorghum should be cut just as soon as the seed is ripe. In making sugar or syrup from sorghum it should be treated as sugar-cane, but it should be borne in mind that the juices of the former are much more impure, and, therefore, much more difficult to granulate and purge than those from the sugar-cane.

### Preserving Cane for Seed.

Preserving cane for seed.

The question of greatest importance to a sugar planter is the preservation of cane for seed during the winter.

Cane must be planted in the fall, or must be preserved carefully in windrows or "mats" through the winter for spring planting. Upon high, well-drained soils, fall-planting may be practised with success. It should be borne in mind, however, that fall-planted cane should be covered from 3 inches or 4 inches deep with well-pulverised earth. It is customary in the sugar district to run a heavy roller over it, after planting, to firmly press the soil against the cane. Cane may be lost from either wet or dry rot. The former will occur when too much moisture exists in the soil, and the latter when too little. In open, cloddy land, especially during a dry fall and winter, dry rot sometimes occurs despite precautions against it. It is never safe to plant cane in the fall upon low and undrained soils, nor in cloddy, dry lands (unless seasonable rains prevail). When fall-planting is not done the seed must be preserved for the spring. In south Louisiana this is now almost universally done in windrows. The cane with all its adherent leaves and trash is cut at the ground and thrown into the open furrow between the rows, the tops covering the butts in such a manner that when the windrow is completed nothing but the leaves of the cane are visible. Two four-horse turn-ploughs, one right-handed the other left-handed, throw furrows over this windrow, completely covering it. Hoes follow, filling in the inequalities of the soil. The quarter drains are carefully opened, and the windrow is completed. When planting begins in the spring the same ploughs now remove the dirt, and by the aid of mattocks or picks the cane is withdrawn from the row. Vertical mats are found in low, wet grounds, but upon high lands horizontal ones are best. These are made by digging out the soil to the depth of one or two feet, and in this pit the cane is placed so that the tops will everywhere cover and protect he stalks. After filling to the proper height dirt is thrown over the ntire pile. In the spring the pile is broken down and cane planted.

## *Planting Cane.*

In planting the sugar-cane one continuous stalk (and two, if the land be very fertile) should be deposited in an open furrow and securely covered. In the fall this covering should be several inches thick, and the land should be well drained. Early in the spring the extra soil used in covering should be removed in order to secure early germination, for the sooner the cane starts in the spring the greater the maturity in the fall, and, therefore, the richer in sugar. After the germination of cane there is a period of apparent rest, when the young sprout undergoes a multiplication several times by "tillers" or "succours." This process of tillering being over, the cane, the season being favourable, grows with great rapidity. During tillering the harrow or plough should be used only to stir the soil, and with great care. When growth ensues the work of cultivation should be rapid and thorough, to be completed by a "lay by" when the cane has reached a size which will effectually shade the ground and prevent the growth of weeds or grass.

*Planting cane.*

## *Varieties.*

There are two varieties of cane generally planted throughout the south, viz.: Purple or violet cane, and the red ribbon or striped cane. Both are superior canes. The green cane, sometimes found in the hills, is unworthy of extensive cultivation. Of the 76 foreign varieties now introduced at the Sugar Experi-

*Varieties.*

ment Station, one seems pre-eminently adapted to higher latitudes on account of its extreme hardiness. It grows and thrives without much attention, ratoons and stools well, and withstands considerable cold. It is now on trial in Kansas and North Louisiana. It is, however, a hard cane, and has not so high a sugar content as the purple or ribbon cane. It is also difficult to clean it for the mill. But its merits recommend it to all those who live outside of the true sugar-cane belt. This cane is called the Japanese or Zwinga, and is white cane of good length, but small in diameter.

## Cultivation and Fertilisation.

**Cultivation and fertilisation.**

That cultivation found best for corn will generally suit sugar cane and sorghum. Both crops require thorough drainage. The conditions necessary for growing successfully these crops may be summarised as follows:—Thorough and deep preparation of the soil, cultivation rapid and as shallow as the soil will permit, and a "lay by" when the growth shades the ground. Rows varying from 5 feet to 7 feet are now usually adopted. The fertiliser for cane should contain enough nitrogenous matter to insure a large growth by September. An excess should be avoided as detrimental to large sugar content. Phosphoric acid in a soluble form is everywhere beneficial to cane, while potash may be demanded upon light sandy soils.

Experiments have shown that the limits of profit in the use of fertilisers are between 24 lbs. and 48 lbs. of nitrogen and 40 lbs. to 80 lbs. of phosphoric acid.

These ingredients are cheaply furnished in the forms of cotton seed, or cotton-seed meal and acid phosphate.

The following mixture per acre has been found very efficient under cane, viz.: 600 lbs. of cotton-seed meal, 300 lbs. of acid phosphate.

Instead of this meal, cotton-seed may be used at the rate of three to one of the meal (circa).

The above may seem excessive to many, but may be reduced at will, but with favourable seasons, on soils in good tilth, all of the above will be utilised. Crops of 30 tons to 35 tons of cane per acre are frequently obtained in South Louisiana, and may be secured elsewhere.

## Harvesting the Cane.

**Harvesting the cane.**

When the cane is ready to be harvested the cane knife should be used. The fodder is stripped from the cane by a projection on the back of the knife. After removing the fodder the cane is topped; up into the white joints if only syrup is desired, but in the upper red joint if sugar is to be made. After topping the cane is seized with the left hand and severed at the ground with a strong blow, and thrown upon the heap row (every third row), from which all the trash has been removed. The carts now drive between the heap rows, and load from both sides. Sugar waggons and carts specially designed to empty their loads are used by sugar planters. Dump carts, or tumbrels with sideboards, will be found useful in handling cane on a small scale. Reaching the sugar house, the operation of sugar making begins. It is worthy of remark here that all leaves and sheaths should, as far as practicable, be removed from the cane before entering the mill.

*Manufacture.*

**Manufacture.**

The outfit for sugar or syrup making on a small scale consists of a horse mill and evaporator, with boxes and barrels to be used as juice tanks, sulphur machine, coolers, &c. These will be described in detail.

The horse mill must be erected in a substantial manner. The feed roller should be left slightly open to receive the cane, while the bagasse roller should be made to touch everywhere the main roller in order to secure good extraction. The rollers should be tightened every morning, and only when the bagasse comes out in short, dry pieces should the operation of squeezing be considered satisfactory. It pulls the team heavier, but a much larger percentage of juice is obtained. In this way as much as 70 per cent. of the weight of the cane will be procured as juice, while the bagasse, coming from the mill simply pressed, not broken, means often not over 50 per cent. extraction. It is useless to grow the sugar and throw it away in the bagasse. Underneath the mill should be placed a tight box, of a capacity of not less than 15 gallons to 20 gallons. Over this box, and directly under the spout of the mill should be a metallic strainer to intercept all broken fragments of cane, since the latter are very objectionable in sugar making.

On the side of this box, and about 3 inches or 4 inches from the bottom, an inch pipe should be inserted, which leads to the top of the sulphur box. In the latter the juice is sulphured. This box may be made in many forms.

A cheap and effective machine is herewith given, which may be made by any carpenter.

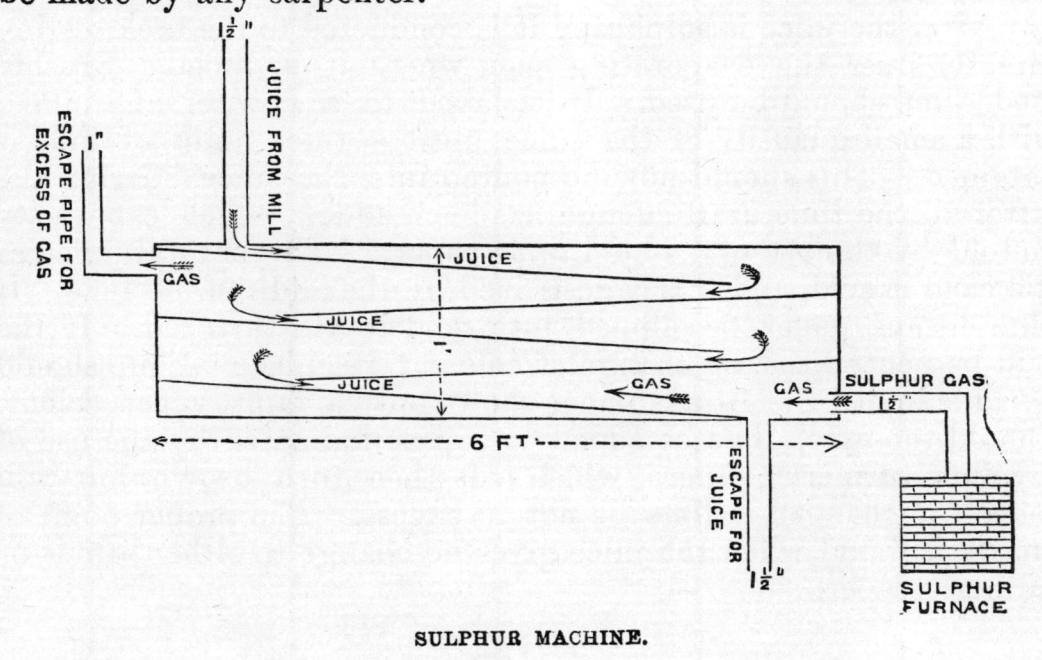

SULPHUR MACHINE.

It is made of thoroughly dried lumber and water-tight. The size of the box will largely depend upon the amount of juice to be sulphured. For a one-horse mill, $1 \times 2 \times 6$ feet, with four or five shelves, will be ample size. A very small brick furnace, three bricks high and two wide each way, with an opening sufficiently large in front to receive a small iron cup, in which the sulphur is burned, is connected with the sulphur machine by a $1\frac{1}{2}$-inch pipe on the side of the box, near the bottom. The fumes of sulphur arise in the box and ascend in the opposite direction of the fall of the juice, and finally any excess escapes the chimney on the upper part of the machine. The shelves down which the juice flows may be much narrower than the box. In this case they must be supported, and must have narrow strips on each side to restrain the juice on the shelf. The juice entering at the top of the box meets with the fumes of sulphur all along its passage, and before escaping becomes charged with this gas.

The object is to retard the flow of the juice through the box, and during its passage to cause it to absorb as much of the fumes of sulphur (sulphur dioxide) as possible.

### Objects of Sulphur.

**Objects of sulphur.**

The objects of sulphuring is threefold: First, it disinfects; second, it bleaches; and third, it assists in defecation. By sulphuring, the juice, already acid, becomes more so, and must be treated with lime (neutralised) before heating to avoid inversion, *i.e.*, a conversion of sugar into molasses.

Instead of the fumes of sulphur, the bi-sulphite of lime, prepared largely by Mr. H. Bonnabel, of New Orleans, may be used with similar results.

This sulphite is placed in the box which receives the juice from the mill at the rate of about 1 quart to every 50 gallons. It should be added to the juice as soon as it begins to run from the mill, so as to have as much time as possible to act upon the impurities.

After the juice is sulphured it is conducted to the tank resting directly over the evaporating pan, where it is limed. Freshly made lime should be used. It is slaked to a powder and mixed with a small quantity of the juice until a thick milk of lime is obtained. This should now be poured into the juice, stirring the latter all the time until enough has been added, which can easily be told by the use of "blue litmus paper." The natural juice of the cane is acid, and this is destroyed by the addition of lime. If blue litmus paper be dipped into acid it will turn red. If the acid be neutralised, no change of colour takes place. Lime should be added until the litmus paper shows only a faint violet colour. Should too much lime be added it will be indicated by the use of "yellow turmeric paper," which will then turn brown, but will remain unchanged if lime be not in excess. The proper point of liming is found when the juice gives no change to either litmus or turmeric paper.

After liming the juice should be permitted to settle, so as to remove all the precipitate produced by the lime and sulphur. Through a valve placed just above the bottom of the settling tank, the clear juice is drawn into the pan, and the process of cooking begins.

Every evaporating pan should consist of three or more separate compartments. In an open kettle sugar house there are four large kettles, known respectively as "the grand," "the flambeau," "the sirop," and "the batterie." The juice is emptied into the grand, where the scums are removed, then into the flambeau, where it is brushed or cleaned; then into the sirop, where it is thoroughly cleaned, and then into the batterie, where it is cooked to sugar. In the small evaporators the flambeau is discarded, and we have three compartments representing the grand, the sirop, and the batterie.

The juice is taken into the grand, where the heat coagulates the scums. The latter are removed by means of a strainer on a long handle. After removing all the scums this juice is transferred to the sirop, where, on account of the increased heat of the furnace and the density of the juice, an ebullition is obtained, which permits of brushing off any floating particles of dust or scums (with a small wooden paddle) back into the grand. Here the juice is thoroughly cleaned and concentrated. When it has reached the density of thin syrup—say 20° or 25° Baume—the latter is transferred to the batterie, where it is cooked to a density of 40° to 42° Baume, or until the thermometer shows a boiling point of 238° to 242° Fahr. When this point is reached it is emptied into a cooler, which may be a water-tight, square box, or even the half of a molasses barrel. When the cooler is full it is generally stirred to induce graining. Usually in 24 hours the "masse cuite" (for such this is called in French) is hard and solid, due to the granulation of the sugar. It is then cut out of the cooler with a sharp spade, all lumps mashed and "potted."

On a large scale the potting is done in hogsheads. It can as easily be done in barrels or kegs. The process of potting consists in taking a barrel or keg and boring three holes equi-distant from each other in the bottom with an inch augur. Into these holes are inserted stalks of cane, with their ends bevelled so as to form an outlet for the molasses. They are often peeled on opposite sides so as to furnish channels for the escape of the molasses. Having adjusted the canes in the barrel, it is placed over a large water-tight box, or over half a molasses barrel, and filled with the "masse cuite" from the cooler. The molasses escapes down the cane and out of the barrel into a box or tub below. In a week or so there will be a barrel of sugar and considerable quantity of molasses (not syrup). Instead of a barrel a strong osnaburg sack suspended over a tub may be used to advantage. The molasses will keep for a long time, and is more valuable than syrup, which can never be relied on if made from rich cane.

## 14 UNITED STATES.

### Instruments and Apparatus.

**Instruments and apparatus.**

The Baume hydrometer mentioned above can be obtained in New Orleans at Claudel and Co., I. L. Lyons and Co., and elsewhere, and costs 75 c. This hydrometer is graduated from 0° to 50°, and may be used for either juice, syrup, or "masse cuite." In making syrup this hydrometer should show 34° to 36°.

The rude sorghum pans now so extensively used are so constructed that the juice is kept flowing continuously in the pan and syrup out of it, without any gates or partitions to separate into compartments. Such pans could be easily remedied by a tinsmith, or even by a farmer himself. It is always best to have at least three compartments, without communication with each other, necessitating the dipping of the juice from one to the other. Even in those pans where gates are provided these should be securely fastened before beginning to cook. A small leak will invariably interfere with successful work.

The small mills are made by the Chattanooga Plough Company, Chattanooga, Tenn., and several houses in Atlanta, Ga., the Blymer Company, of Cincinnati, the Geo. L. Squire Manufacturing Company, of Buffalo, N.Y., and other places. The same houses also make evaporators. Mr. W. J. Sharp, of Baton Rouge, La., makes an evaporating pan which is very highly recommended. It has been successfully used by scores of small sugar planters in Louisiana. It can be obtained of any size and capacity.

There are no safe or reliable preventives of syrups turning to sugar. Cutting the cane up in the green joints, the addition of sour oranges or even acids during boiling are the methods adopted to accomplish this purpose. If the cane be rich in sugar the first two will not prevent granulation. If the latter be used the resulting compound could hardly be called syrup. In re-boiling syrups, milk of lime should first be added, so as to remove all the acidity, and then boiled to the proper density.

### Results of Experiments at North Louisiana Experiment Station, Calhoun, La.

**Results of experiments.**

In the fall of 1888 a few hundred stalks of purple cane were purchased and planted. Only a partial stand was obtained, and a light tonnage made. This cane was used to plant the crop of 1890. A portion was planted in the fall, and the rest, after being successfully matted, was planted in the spring. The stubble left in 1889 was covered first with trash and then with two furrows of a two-horse plough. In the spring it was uncovered. An excellent stand was secured. The fall plant came up early, and a part of it gave a large tonnage. The spring plant came up late, and on account of a prolonged drought in July and August, never attained a large size. The ground upon which this cane was grown is perhaps the poorest in North Louisiana, and has been in cultivation for over 75 years. It was well prepared and laid off in 5-feet rows, and planted a single running stalk. It was fertilised with a mixture of cotton seed meal and acid phosphate.

The small sugar house contained a Victor mill (one house), a Cook's evaporator, a sulphur machine (like the one already described), two juice tanks, six or eight coolers, and several sugar and molasses barrels. With this outfit the results given below were obtained. The following results are the chemical:—

### Analyses of Juices.

| Date. | | Kind of Cane. | Degrees Baume. | Degrees Brix. | Sucrose. | Glucose. | Glucose Ratio. | Purity Co-efficient. |
|---|---|---|---|---|---|---|---|---|
| October | 27 | Stubble | 9·5 | 16·9 | 13·8 | 1·26 | 9·13 | 81·06 |
| ,, | 28 | ,, | 9·8 | 17·3 | 13·9 | 1·19 | 8·56 | 80·34 |
| ,, | 29 | ,, | 9·7 | 17·2 | 14·0 | 1·16 | 8·28 | 81·38 |
| ,, | 30 | Fall plant | 8·8 | 15·5 | 12·6 | 1·94 | 15·38 | 81·35 |
| ,, | 31 | ,, | 8·9 | 15·7 | 12·7 | 1·96 | 15·43 | 80·89 |
| November | 1 | ,, | 8·9 | 15·7 | 12·7 | 1·95 | 15·35 | 80·89 |
| ,, | 2 | Japanese | 7·6 | 13·4 | 9·9 | 3·20 | 32·32 | 73·88 |
| ,, | 4 | Spring plant | 8·4 | 14·9 | 11·9 | 1·80 | 15·12 | 79·86 |
| ,, | 5 | ,, | 8·5 | 15·0 | 12·3 | 1·74 | 14·14 | 82·00 |

|  | Per Cent. |
|---|---|
| Stubble cane gave an extraction of | 69·36 |
| Fall plant cane gave an extraction of | 75·24 |
| Japanese cane gave an extraction of | 66·74 |
| Spring plant cane gave an extraction of | 60·19 |

The above differences in extraction were accomplished by experiments in tightening the rollers.

When the bagasse roller was jammed against the large roller and cane carefully fed, over 75 per cent. of the weight of the cane was obtained in juice.

Again, the fall plant cane consisted of large stalks, and were thus better squeezed. The smaller stalks of the spring plant, with the rollers slightly opened, gave as low as 60 per cent. extraction.

The stubble cane yielded 15·6 tons per acre.

The fall plant cane yielded 16·6 tons per acre, though much of it went over 20 tons.

The spring plant cane gave only about 8 tons per acre.

The Japanese cane gave about 10 tons per acre.

|  |  |  | Lbs. |
|---|---|---|---|
| There were ground of | stubble cane | | 11,155 |
| ,, | ,, | fall plant | 15,678 |
| ,, | ,, | Japanese | 1,010 |
| ,, | ,, | spring plant | 8,526 |
|  | Total cane | | 36,369 |
|  | Or tons | | 18·19 |

(1233)

## UNITED STATES.

The sugar and molasses from each run could not be separated, so only the aggregate of each can be given:—

|  | Lbs. | Gallons. |
|---|---|---|
| Total sugar made | 2,400 | .. |
| „ molasses made | 1,920 | .. |
| „ „ „ | .. | 160 |
| Sugar per ton of cane | 132·08 | .. |
| Molasses „ „ | 105·50 | .. |
| „ „ „ | .. | 8·79 |
| Sugar per acre | 1,600 | .. |
| Molasses per acre | 1,280 | .. |
| „ „ | .. | 106·6 |

The molasses have been sold for 35 c. per gallon. The sugar is worth on the Sugar Exchange in New Orleans, 3½ c. per lb. at this date—at retail in the city 5 c. per lb.

No special effort was made to grow the cane, or to manufacture it. It was grown upon the poorest land and manufactured with inexpensive machinery. What has been done by the station can be accomplished by any farmer in the State. Upon good land, well fertilised and with inexpensive machinery, sugar, molasses, and syrup may be made in abundant quantities for local use, and with a surplus for market.

### FIELD EXPERIMENTS WITH SUGAR CANE AT AUDUBON PARK.

*Weather report.* The station has kept an accurate weather record and diary since March 1, 1886. The following is a condensed record of each year's rainfall and temperature:—

# NEW ORLEANS.

**CONDENSED** Weather Record of Sugar Experiment Station from March 1, 1886, to January 1, 1890.

| Month. | Average temperature. | Maximum temperature. | Minimum temperature. | Rainfall. |
|---|---|---|---|---|
| | Degrees. | Degrees. | Degrees. | Inches. |
| **1886.** | | | | |
| March | 63·00 | 80·00 | 37·00 | 9·13 |
| April | 69·00 | 87·00 | 41·00 | 7·32 |
| May | 76·00 | 93·00 | 57·00 | 3·59 |
| June | 83·00 | 97·00 | 69·00 | 11·05 |
| July | 83·00 | 95·00 | 68·00 | 3·25 |
| August | 84·00 | 96·00 | 66·00 | 4·18 |
| September | 80·00 | 91·00 | 59·00 | 5·24 |
| October | 73·00 | 87·00 | 39·00 | 1·00 |
| November | 66·00 | 75·00 | 33·00 | 5·55 |
| December | 65·00 | 79·00 | 26·00 | 2·75 |
| **1887.** | | | | |
| January | 57·00 | 82·00 | 22·00 | 3·31 |
| February | 65·04 | 80·00 | 30·00 | 5·23 |
| March | 58·02 | 81·00 | 40·00 | 3·27 |
| April | 71·07 | 89·00 | 57·00 | 2·21 |
| May | 78·00 | 94·00 | 59·00 | 6·56 |
| June | 84·00 | 94·00 | 62·00 | 10·35 |
| July | 84·00 | 97·00 | 68·00 | 7·86 |
| August | 82·05 | 95·00 | 69·00 | 6·07 |
| September | 79·00 | 92·00 | 56·00 | 3·03 |
| October | 69·05 | 86·00 | 40·00 | 6·39 |
| November | 60·00 | 80·00 | 30·00 | 0·11 |
| December | 54·06 | 77·00 | 30·00 | 7·14 |
| **1888.** | | | | |
| January | 56·06 | 77·00 | 30·00 | 3·77 |
| February | 59·08 | 76·00 | 37·00 | 9·08 |
| March | 59·00 | 78·00 | 36·00 | 5·79 |
| April | 73·04 | 85·00 | 54·00 | 0·91 |
| May | 76·07 | 92·00 | 54·00 | 11·77 |
| June | 79·08 | 92·00 | 65·00 | 8·69 |
| July | 82·00 | 98·00 | 71·00 | 5·49 |
| August | 81·02 | 95·00 | 70·00 | 15·08 |
| September | 77·03 | 89·00 | 57·00 | 3·29 |
| October | 70·06 | 85·00 | 53·00 | 3·04 |
| November | 62·04 | 84·00 | 34·00 | 2·05 |
| December | 63·06 | 71·00 | 27·00 | 4·12 |
| **1889.** | | | | |
| January | 54·00 | 71·00 | 34·00 | 8·03 |
| February | 55·00 | 75·00 | 31·00 | 3·21 |
| March | 63·06 | 79·00 | 40·00 | 2·38 |
| April | 72·00 | 86·00 | 47·00 | 3·28 |
| May | 78·01 | 91·01 | 48·00 | 0·76 |
| June | 82·03 | 96·00 | 57·00 | 9·43 |
| July | 85·06 | 92·00 | 68·00 | 7·15 |
| August | 81·00 | 90·00 | 66·00 | 5·74 |
| September | 79·01 | 91·00 | 51·00 | 5·03 |
| October | 68·01 | 86·00 | 51·00 | .. |
| November | 58·09 | 82·00 | 30·00 | .. |
| December | 63·00 | 80·00 | 45·00 | 0·43 |

(1233)

## UNITED STATES.

### Summary of Meteorological Observations made at Audubon Park during the Year 1890.

| Name of Month. | Monthly Mean Temperature. | Mean Maximum Temperature. | Mean Maximum Temperature. | Highest Temperature. | Date of Occurrence. | Lowest Temperature. | Date of Occurrence. | Monthly Range of Temperature. | Rainfall in Inches. | Number of Cloudless Days. | Number of Partly Cloudy Days. | Number of Cloudy Days. | Prevailing Direction of Wind. |
|---|---|---|---|---|---|---|---|---|---|---|---|---|---|
| January | 61·08 | 72·00 | 44·03 | 80·0 | 7 and 12 | 32·0 | 17 | 48·0 | 1·00 | 4 | 25 | 2 | North |
| February | 62·03 | 71·08 | 50·00 | 81·0 | 26 | 36·0 | 10 | 45·0 | 3·10 | 2 | 23 | 3 | South |
| March | 60·07 | 69·01 | 51·00 | 79·5 | 31 | 27·0 | 2 | 52·5 | 1·98 | 5 | 23 | 3 | South |
| April | 69·07 | 78·03 | 60·00 | 84·5 | 14 | 42·0 | 11 | 42·5 | 3·27 | 4 | 21 | 5 | South |
| May | 74·07 | 82·08 | 65·00 | 87·5 | 29 | 56·0 | 9 | 31·5 | 10·71 | 4 | 23 | 4 | South |
| June | 87·08 | 89·00 | 72·01 | 94·0 | 29 | 68·0 | 23 | 25·5 | 4·15 | 1 | 25 | 4 | South |
| July | 81·07 | 89·08 | 73·03 | 95·0 | 5 and 6 | 69·0 | 9 and 27 | 26·0 | 7·30 | 1 | 3 | 27 | South |
| August | 79·08 | 87·09 | 71·09 | 92·5 | 26 | 67·0 | 11 | 25·6 | 7·75 | 0 | 30 | 1 | S.W. |
| September | 76·03 | 84·09 | 68·09 | 90·0 | 19 | 56·5 | 30 | 33·5 | 4·56 | 2 | 25 | 3 | North |
| October | 67·45 | 73·04 | 56·09 | 87·0 | 12 | 38·0 | 31 | 49·0 | 4·41 | 7 | 22 | 2 | North |
| November | 61·07 | 71·12 | 52·45 | 82·0 | 16 | 39·0 | 4 | 43·0 | 0·87 | 8 | 20 | 2 | North |
| December | 55·03 | 63·08 | 42·02 | 78·0 | 7 | 33·0 | 19 | 45·0 | 3·55 | 12 | 17 | 2 | North |

In the following table is presented the four years in a comparative form, and it may be useful in determining some of the factors which go toward solving the problem of good crop years.

The winter of 1886 was very severe, destroying much of the seed and stubble; the spring was late and cold, and good stands of cane were not obtained until May. The subsequent seasons were fair, and where good stands prevailed the crop was medium.

The winter of 1887 was mild and conducive to excellent seed cane; the spring was moderately dry and warm; followed by a warm and wet summer grading into a cool dry autumn; conditions favourable to heavy tonnage.

The winter of 1888 was fairly propitious, but the spring was excessively wet, preventing the proper cultivation of the cane. The wet weather extended to July, causing a serious postponement or abandonment of the regular "lay-by" of cane. These rains were succeeded by a dry, cool fall, giving us light tonnage, but heavy sugar yield, due more to the low glucose content than excess of sugar in cane.

The year 1889 will always be remembered as the year of drouth. The rainfall for the year was only 46 inches, and this fell mostly in the winter and summer, giving us a spring and fall of unexampled dryness—a dryness which had been prolonged into the winter of 1890, and up to this time has scarcely been broken.

The year 1890 will be memorable for the enormous crop produced. It was ushered in amidst a drouth lapsing from 1889, with mild, fair weather in January and February, giving an early germination and growth to both plant and stubble cane—both to be cut down by an unusual frost early in March; followed by a propitious spring, with an abundant rainfall in May, preceding enough dry weather in June to permit a careful "lay-by" of the crop. Copious showers, at no time excessive, prevailing through July, August, September, and October, which, together with an abundance of sunshine and a continuance of warm weather, all conspired to give us the largest tonnage perhaps ever known in our history. The season was favourable throughout to the growth of cane, and hence the large crop was harvested in a very immature condition. Neither the temperature nor rainfall has been excessive, but well distributed throughout the season, extending well into the fall.

Taking the table and the seasons, we find that a dry, warm winter followed by a moderately dry spring, and this in time succeeded by a hot, wet summer, are conditions favourable to maximum growth of cane. It seems, too, that a dry, cool autumn, beginning early in September, is necessary to produce a large sugar content.

After the cane is laid by, frequent showers of considerable intensity appear highly beneficial.

The following is the comparative weather statement for the five years:—

(1233)

|  | Average temperature. | Maximum temperature. | Minimum temperature. | Rainfall. |
|---|---|---|---|---|
|  | Degrees. | Degrees. | Degrees. | Inches. |
| 1887 | 70·03 | 97·0 | 22 | 62·43 |
| 1888 | 69·03 | 98·0 | 27 | 75·33 |
| 1889 | 70·01 | 96·0 | 30 | 45·98 |
| 1890 | 69·98 | 95·0 | 27 | 52·65 |
| Spring months, 1886 | 69·03 | 93·0 | 37 | 20·04 |
| ,, ,, 1887 | 69·03 | 94·0 | 40 | 12·04 |
| ,, ,, 1888 | 69·07 | 92·0 | 36 | 18·47 |
| ,, ,, 1889 | 71·02 | 91·0 | 40 | 6·42 |
| ,, ,, 1890 | 68·04 | 87·5 | 27 | 15·96 |
| Summer months, 1886 | 83·03 | 97·0 | 66 | 18·93 |
| ,, ,, 1887 | 83·05 | 97·0 | 62 | 24·91 |
| ,, ,, 1888 | 81·00 | 98·0 | 65 | 29·98 |
| ,, ,, 1889 | 82·09 | 96·0 | 57 | 22·32 |
| ,, ,, 1890 | 83·01 | 95·0 | 67 | 19·20 |
| Fall months, 1886 | 73·01 | 87·0 | 33 | 11·79 |
| ,, ,, 1887 | 69·05 | 92·0 | 30 | 9·80 |
| ,, ,, 1888 | 70·01 | 89·0 | 35 | 9·19 |
| ,, ,, 1889 | 68·07 | 91·0 | 34 | 5·30 |
| ,, ,, 1890 | 74·05 | 92·5 | 38 | 9·87 |
| Winter months, 1887 | 59·00 | 82·0 | 22 | 15·68 |
| ,, ,, 1888 | 56·06 | 77·0 | 27 | 17·69 |
| ,, ,, 1889 | 57·03 | 82·0 | 31 | 11·94 |
| ,, ,, 1890 | 62·05 | 81·0 | 45 | 4·53 |

**Field experiments.**  Field experiments have this year been confined to the following:—
1. Physiological questions.
2. Varieties best adapted to Louisiana.
3. Manurial requirements of cane.

*Physiological Questions.*

In this plat were conducted experiments to test the following questions:—
1. What distance apart shall we give our cane rows?
2. What part of the cane is best to plant?
3. What amount of seed is required for best results?
4. Does cutting the cane injure it?
5. Is stubble or plant cane best for seed?

This plat was planted October 30 and October 31, and November 4 and November 5, 1889, in rows 6 feet apart, except in first series of questions. Each row received 17 lbs. of a fertiliser specially prepared for this plat. It was cultivated in the usual way, and laid by June 26 and June 27.

To determine the first question:

*What distance apart shall Cane Rows be?*

Rows were laid off 3 feet, 4 feet, 5 feet, 6 feet, 7 feet, and 8 feet, and three rows taken for each experiment. These rows were exactly one-half acre in length. They were planted with our home striped or ribbon cane, using three running stalks. It germinated well in January, was cut down by the cold in March, but soon recovered. On May 17 all the stalks on each experiment were carefully counted, and at harvest every stalk was again counted and the cane weighed. Each experiment was carefully worked up in the sugar house and careful analyses of the juices made in the laboratory.

Below are appended the results:—

## UNITED STATES.

### EXPERIMENTS in Different Widths of Rows in Plant Cane for 1890.

| Kind of Experiment. | Number of Stalks, May 17. | Number of Stalks Harvested. | Weight of Cane in Lbs. | Average Weight of a Stalk. | Number of Stalks per Acre. | Tons per Acre. | Analyses of Juice. ||||| 
|---|---|---|---|---|---|---|---|---|---|---|---|
| | | | | | | | Total Solids. | Sucrose. | Glucose. | Glucose Ratio. | Purity Co-efficient. |
| 3 rows, 3 feet wide | 1,177 | 555 | 1,848 | 3·33 | 25,900 | 43·12 | 13·0 | 10·00 | 1·67 | 16·7 | 76·9 |
| 3 ,, 4 ,, | 1,156 | 784 | 2,408 | 3·10 | 27,440 | 42·14 | 12·5 | 9·30 | 1·69 | 18·1 | 74·4 |
| 3 ,, 5 ,, | 1,292 | 917 | 3,034 | 3·31 | 25,976 | 42·47 | 13·5 | 10·45 | 1·61 | 15·4 | 77·4 |
| 3 ,, 6 ,, | 1,207 | 1,095 | 3,300 | 3·01 | 25,550 | 38·50 | 13·3 | 10·20 | 1·67 | 16·3 | 76·6 |
| 3 ,, 7 ,, | 1,396 | 1,308 | 3,766 | 2·88 | 26,160 | 37·66 | 13·3 | 10·00 | 1·47 | 14·7 | 75·1 |
| 3 ,, 8 ,, | 1,382 | 1,420 | 4,244 | 2·98 | 24,850 | 37·13 | 12·8 | 9·60 | 1·48 | 15·3 | 75·0 |

A study of the above reveals the fact that in favourable seasons many stalks after attaining considerable size perish by over-crowding. This was quite apparent at harvest in the 3-feet rows and 4-feet rows by the frequent occurrence of perfectly dead stalks several feet long. The above table also tells the tale of destruction in a most convincing manner.

The 3-feet and 4-feet rows were prostrated by the blow of August 18, and never afterwards recovered. The rest of the plat was but slightly injured. This prostration caused many stalks to die. Since then these experiments have not had a fair showing with the plat. The results are similar to those obtained previously, though in diminished quantities. The 3-feet rows have given the largest yield and the heaviest stalk, followed closely by the 5-feet rows and 4-feet rows. The increase of the 3-feet rows over the 8-feet rows is barely 6 tons—about enough to cover the increased seed required to plant the former, while the 5-feet rows give an increase sufficient to cover the increased seed and very fair profit besides (over 3 tons per acre).

It may be remarked that the 3-feet rows and 4-feet rows received no cultivation after April 14, the cultivator used for the rest of the crop being too wide for these rows.

The above experiments are not so impressive in their results as those of previous years, yet they plainly declare in favour of narrowing our rows. Any planter is safe in adopting 5-feet rows, and upon these the two-horse cultivators can be successfully used.

*What part of the Cane is best to plant?*

is the second question in the physiological plat. To answer this, selected stalks of cane were cut into two and three parts, *i.e.*, tops and butts, and tops, middles and butts. Each were planted separately and three rows taken for each experiment. The ribbon cane was used for seed. The following are the results:—

## UNITED STATES.

### Experiments in Planting Different Parts of the Cane.

| Kind Planted. | Number of Stalks, May 17. | Number of Stalks Harvested. | Weight of Cane in Lbs. | Average Weight of a Stalk. | Tons per Acre. | Total Solids. | Sucrose. | Glucose. | Glucose Ratio. | Purity Co-efficient. |
|---|---|---|---|---|---|---|---|---|---|---|
| 3 rows, upper half | 1,451 | 1,364 | 3,866 | 2·83 | 45·10 | 12·3 | 9·30 | 1·67 | 17·9 | 75·8 |
| ,, lower half | 1,403 | 1,211 | 3,686 | 3·04 | 43·00 | 12·7 | 9·60 | 1·64 | 17·0 | 75·5 |
| ,, upper third | 1,379 | 1,065 | 3,018 | 2·83 | 35·21 | 12·4 | 9·50 | 1·72 | 17·1 | 76·6 |
| ,, middle third | 1,184 | 1,281 | 3,328 | 2·60 | 38·82 | 12·3 | 9·00 | 1·89 | 21·0 | 73·0 |
| ,, lower third | 1,487 | 1,309 | 3,514 | 2·68 | 41·02 | 12·3 | 9·15 | 1·67 | 18·2 | 68·8 |

(Analyses of Juice columns: Total Solids, Sucrose, Glucose, Glucose Ratio, Purity Co-efficient.)

The experiment in the upper thirds of the cane is from some cause behind the others. An old road formerly crossed the plat, and perhaps this may in part account for the loss of stalks between May and December.

Enough is shown, however, in the above to confirm previous deductions that the upper part of the cane was the equal, if not the superior, to any other portion for seed. Some day when the agriculture of cane shall be disconnected from the manufacture, the upper thirds of all canes will be planted and the rest at an increased price will go to the central factory. The third and fourth questions are combined in our experiments. The question

*What number of stalks shall be planted?*

is duplicated in cut and uncut canes. Fortunately, last year the cane was straight and could be planted without using the knife. This year, a repetition of this experiment is denied by the intense crookedness of the cane. In the first series the entire cane was planted "uncut," and in the second it was cut into lengths of 12 inches to 18 inches. Purple cane was used for seed. The following are the results:—

EXPERIMENTS in Planting Different Numbers of Stalks Uncut and Cut.

| How Planted. | Number of Stalks, May 17. | Number of Stalks Harvested. | Weight of cane in Lbs. | Average Weight of a Stalk. | Number of Stalks per Acre. | Tons per Acre. | Total Solids. | Sucrose. | Glucose. | Glucose Ratio. | Purity Co-efficient. |
|---|---|---|---|---|---|---|---|---|---|---|---|
| 1 stalk uncut | 749 | 1,065 | 3,260 | 3·06 | 24,840 | 38·01 | 13·2 | 9·20 | 1·62 | 17·6 | 69·7 |
| 1 ,, cut .. | 641 | 1,180 | 3,248 | 2·80 | 27,580 | 37·87 | 12·4 | 9·00 | 1·56 | 17·3 | 72·5 |
| 2 stalks uncut | 809 | 1,200 | 3,698 | 3·08 | 28,000 | 43·14 | 13·4 | 9·90 | 1·56 | 15·7 | 73·8 |
| 2 ,, cut .. | 775 | 1,180 | 3,208 | 2·72 | 27,580 | 31·42 | 12·2 | 8·65 | 1·57 | 18·0 | 70·9 |
| 3 ,, uncut | 1,378 | 1,257 | 3,722 | 2·91 | 29,330 | 43·42 | 13·4 | 10·05 | 1·43 | 14·2 | 75·0 |
| 3 ,, cut .. | 997 | 1,240 | 3,080 | 2·48 | 28,910 | 35·93 | 13·3 | 9·90 | 1·51 | 15·2 | 74·4 |
| 4 ,, uncut | 1,511 | 1,282 | 3,900 | 3·04 | 29,890 | 45·50 | 13·4 | 9·50 | 1·71 | 18·0 | 70·8 |
| 4 ,, cut .. | 1,279 | 1,324 | 3,676 | 2·70 | 30,870 | 42·91 | 13·6 | 9·75 | 1·71 | 17·5 | 71·6 |

Analyses of Juice.

To plant an acre, one stalk continuously, there are required about 2 tons of cane, 4 tons for 2 stalks, 6 tons for 3 stalks, and 8 tons for 4 stalks. Remembering this, it will be seen from the above that there has been no profit in planting 4 stalks or even 3 stalks. As heretofore announced, with good cane 2 stalks are sufficient to insure the largest returns. Upon good lands 1 stalk uncut may give excellent returns. The second question, judging from the results of this year, are most positively assured. In every instance the uncut has given a larger tonnage, with a larger stalk than the cut, and in all but one a larger sugar content. In the spring the uncut showed a superior height over the cut, and this superiority was visibly maintained up to the prostration of the cane in September.

Judging from these experiments, cutting cane should be avoided as far as possible, and the knife used only to secure horizontal positions for the cane.

### *Which is best for Seed, Plant or Stubble Cane?*

The last series in the physiological plat seeks to solve the merits of plant and stubble for seed. Selected plant cane was used on the first experiment; selected first year stubble on the second; ordinary second year stubble on the third; and small third year stubble coming from planting made the year the station was established near Kenner. These were planted under the same conditions, but in the spring it was found necessary to extend a ditch through this part of the plat to drain other plats nearer the river. It passed through the first year stubble, eliminating two rows and leaving only one, and this at a good distance from the ditch. The results of this experiment are based on one row, and are probably too high. The following are the results:—

## UNITED STATES.

### Which is the Best Seed, Plant or Stubble Cane?

| Kind of Cane. | Number of Stalks, May 17. | Number of Stalks Harvested. | Weight of Cane in Lbs. | Average Weight of a Stalk. | Number of Stalks per Acre. | Tons per Acre. | Analyses of Juice. ||||| 
|---|---|---|---|---|---|---|---|---|---|---|---|
| | | | | | | | Total Solids. | Sucrose. | Glucose. | Glucose Ratio. | Purity Co-efficient. |
| Plant | 1,552 | 1,842 | 3,417 | 2·54 | 31,290 | 39·86 | 14·5 | 11·00 | 1·47 | 13·3 | 75·8 |
| First year stubble | 1,029 | 1,449 | 4,248 | 2·93 | 33,810 | 49·56 | 15·0 | 11·55 | 1·35 | 11·6 | 77·0 |
| Second ,, ,, | 1,030 | 1,281 | 3,345 | 2·61 | 33,390 | 39·02 | 13·6 | 10·20 | 1·56 | 15·2 | 75·0 |
| Third ,, ,, | 1,296 | 1,207 | 3,105 | 2·49 | 28,210 | 35·23 | 13·3 | 10·05 | 1·67 | 16·6 | 74·7 |

The above confirm previous results that stubble cane is the equal if not the superior of plant cane for seed.

Perhaps this may be accounted for by closely studying the history of cane planting. For years cane has been propagated by planting the tops of stubble cane, and may not this custom have superinduced in the cane a stronger vitality in the tops over the butts and in the stubble over the plant? May not Darwin's doctrine of "selection" and "inherited habit" fully account for the fact, if indeed it may yet be called a fact?

*Varieties of cane.* The number of really distinct varieties of cane are believed to be few, yet under different environments, such as soil, climate, latitude, &c., these few varieties have given origin to a large number of sub-varieties—the latter in many instances differing from each other by such slight variations that almost a botanical examination is necessary to establish the difference. The station has received over 100 so-called varieties from different parts of the world, and of these nearly 70 have been successfully grown. For nearly 3 years the station has watched with pleasure the growth and development of these varieties. Several curious facts have been established.

1. The facility with which a variety changes its apparent characteristics under changed conditions of soil and climate. When a foreign variety is received it is carefully examined, and its characteristic features noted in a record book. At the harvest each season another similar but more extended record is made. A comparison of these records alone would fail to identify most of the varieties under cultivation here. This is notably the case with white canes—all having a tendency here to assume more or less a coloured appearance. This is partially accounted for by the difference in maturity between the foreign cane received and its progeny here.

2. The tendency of most varieties to redden in colour, particularly when stripped of their leaves and on the sunny side of the stalk. Once, early in October, samples of every variety were carefully cut and minutely examined. The peculiar characteristics of each kind recorded. At the same time a few standing stalks of each variety were carefully stripped of the lower leaves and left till December fully exposed to the weather and sun. Their properties were again recorded. In many instances the most apparent properties, such as colour, prominence of eyes, &c., had completely changed. The change of colour is always towards red.

3. Frequently canes, when first received of widely different characteristics, have, by constant cultivation, gradually gravitated towards each other in general appearance, and to-day it is quite difficult to distinguish between them. This is particularly the case with the lighter coloured varieties.

4. The gradual diminution in size and increase of sugar content of almost every variety while undergoing acclimation.

5. The power of resisting the prostrating effects of the storms so usual here in the fall, and which frequently injure seriously our

home grown or acclimated varieties. This property may be greatly modified or perhaps eliminated by acclimation.

6. The impossibility of determining the value of a cane by a few years of cultivation here. This is rendered more apparent each year, several canes which were very unpromising the first year or two are by acclimation yearly improving, and may ultimately be useful and vice versâ.

The station is growing the many varieties now on hand with a two-fold object. (1) Affording a variety adapted to our wants and (2) of ultimately properly classifying the varieties and eliminating all closely related sub-varieties. Unfortunately for the botany of cane, the nomenclature of varieties is execrable. There are no specific names, common in all countries. The same cane is known in different countries by different names, frequently the latter being only local. Hence on receipt of a foreign variety its name gives no indication of its presence already in our collection. A few instances of this will illustrate the trouble and confusion which local names sometimes give. The station has been cultivating the Lahaina (called after the island of this name in Hawaii, on which it was first cultivated after its introduction there by Captain Pardon Edwards) for several years and has studied carefully its merits. For a long time the botanical gardens and stations had alluded favourably to a variety called "Keni Keni." This variety after much effort was secured from the Director of Botanical Gardens in Jamaica, and successfully grown the past year. With great surprise it was found to be identical in every respect to the Lahaina, which it had already grown in quantity. Another instance, a large red cane, with a small black stripe, came to it, a few years since from the east, under the name of "Cavengerie." The following year the same cane came from the west under the name of Attamattie. In a collection received from the botanical garden of Jamaica last year is a cane strongly resembling the two above in every respect under the name of "Po-a-ole." The name of a cane, therefore, gives no clue to its true variety.

Of the foreign varieties tried several are unworthy of extensive propagation, some are improving yearly under our cultivation, and may ultimately become useful by thorough acclimation, while a few are full of promise. There are some who believe it useless to attempt to acclimate foreign varieties, and think that energy is better expended in improving the purple and striped varieties already well domiciled. While every effort should be made to accomplish the latter, the former, too, is certainly worthy of persistent trial. There is no record of the introduction and trial in this State of any large quantity of foreign canes in the past. The small creole cane, now deemed everywhere unworthy of cultivation, was once the chief variety in this State. The purple and the striped supplanted this. Were they selected, after a long competitive trial with a great number of varieties, on account of their special adaptation to our soil and climate, or were they simply introduced by chance and became the canes of this country simply because they were found superior to their predecessors? It is unwise to conclude, without exhaustive trial, that we have the best varieties of cane known.

It may be worthy of remark that these two canes are grown extensively only in Louisiana and Java. In Java our purple is known under the name of Teboe Cheviron (dark violet), which there takes 12 months to mature. It is often called Black Java, and this is so identical with our purple cane that the station has stopped its separate propagation. The striped cane is grown there under the name of Batavian Striped, and this variety here is so nearly identical with our striped and with the Mexican striped that its separate cultivation hereafter will be abandoned. Private advices from Java tell us of a cane cultivated there to a limited extent which tassels in 8 months; it is called Teboe Borneo, and is highly recommended for this country. The sample sent us was dead beyond resurrection, and no effort has been made in the last few years to obtain cane from Java on account of the "sereh" disease there prevailing.

In this paper will be given, first, a catalogue of the canes under cultivation, with a short description of each, and second, analyses of their juices, with tonnage per acre of those which have been under cultivation long enough to secure the necessary quantity for experimental tests.

The canes are divided into three classes on the colour line only. The first includes all canes of a white, yellow, or greenish colour; the second all striped varieties; and the third all solid colours other than those given in class one.

No. 1. "Beltran" cane, called also "Panache," presented to the station by Mr. R. Beltran, of New Orleans, and by him cultivated extensively. Stalk long and medium size, colour green, yellow, or white, with black bloom adhering just above nodes; eyes flat and not prominent; stubbles well. A very fine cane. *First class—white, green, or yellow colour.*

No. 2. "La Pice." Said to have been introduced by Mr. Burgundy La Pice, of St. James parish, from ———'s. With similar characteristics to No. 1.

No. 3. "Tibboo Merd." Came from Manilla Islands and is a most excellent variety of cane. In colour, size, and black bloom (cerosin or Invertens Taylorri) closely resembling Nos. 1 and 2, but with prominent, plump, round sharp eyes. Stubbles well. Leaves broad and spreading.

No. 4. "La Sassier;" obtained from Mr. Henry Le Sassier, New Orleans. Almost identical with Nos. 1 and 2 and perhaps from same origin.

No. 5. "Bourbon;" from Trinidad. When received in a mature state the stalk was yellow; under cultivation here it has a greenish white colour, more or less tinged with rose where stalk is exposed. Large, plump, and pointed eyes, stalks large, leaves light green and not very broad; greatly changed by cultivation here.

No. 6. "Crystallina;" originally from Tahiti, sent dy Dr.

(1233)

Alvarez Reynoso, of Cuba, from his private collection. A green cane with yellowish spots. Some black bloom, with upper immature joints slightly pink. Small pale green leaves. No beard. Stalks long and medium size. Eyes medium size and pointed, and very similar to No. 5.

No. 7. "Green Cane;" came from United States consul at Havana and by him called "green." It closely resembles No. 6.

No. 8. "Yellow Cane;" same source as No. 7. Stalks medium size. Yellow colour, with rose tint at the node, and resembles closely Otaheite No. 9.

No. 9. "Blanca d' Otaheite," as its name imports, originally from Tahiti, sent by Dr. Alvarez Reynoso. Yellow colour. Leaf sheaths full of beard. Stalks medium. Leaves broad and rather adherent. Eyes round, plump, and small. Like No. 8.

No. 10. "Portier," originally from Mauritius, sent by Dr. Alvarez Reynoso. Stalks large and of medium height. Leaves pale green, small, few, and open. Colour greenish, and changing to yellow in maturing. Has not stubbled well. Resembles Lahaina No. 12.

No. 11. "Loucier" (spelt also Losier), originally from Mauritius, sent by Dr. Alvarez Reynoso. A vigorous grower. Suckers very well. Stalks greenish yellow, with rose tints. Large; leaves abundant. Greener than No. 10, and sheaths full of bristles. Eyes full, medium size, and pointed.

No. 12. "Lahaina," from Hawaiian Islands, where it is extensively cultivated. Colour green, changing to yellow in maturing. Leaves small, pale green, and flared. Maturing nearly to the top. Long jointed. Black bloom. Upper portion of joint frequently larger than lower. Has not stubbled well with us. Stalks large. Tonnage heavy. Originally from Marquesas Islands.

No. 13. "Caledonia Queen," from Queensland. Colour bright apple-green, without bloom. Stalks large, but medium height. Light green leaves. Very promising.

No. 14. "Creole Cane." This cane formerly extensively cultivated in this State. Worthy of a place only in a botanical collection. Well known to the older planters.

No. 15. "Papuha," native of Hawaiian Island. Stalks large and tall. Greenish yellow, with faintly red narrow stripes. Suckers well, and so far stubbles well.

No. 16. "Uwala," native of Hawaiian Islands; stalks large and tall; colour green, with white spots near node, turning red when exposed to the sun; leaves abundant; a vigorous grower; suckers and stubbles well; pith of the cane yellow.

No. 17. "Kokea," a native of ——— Islands. Stalks medium and tall, green, with red stripes scarcely perceptible; a very promising cane.

No. 18. "Bamboo," originally from Mauritius; sent to station by Dr. Reynoso; stalks medium, amber coloured, with occasional rose tint; enlarged nodes (hence its name), and very large and projecting eyes; leaves adherent; suckers enormously, and stubbles well. A very promising cane.

No. 19. "Rose Bamboo," a native of Queensland: an enormous cane, stalks frequently weighing 8 lbs. to 10 lbs., with slightly enlarged nodes, joints more or less rose coloured; tall, straight cane, and promising; leaves large, long sheathed, and easily removed.

No. 20. "Keni Keni," originally from Marquesas. Received from botanical gardens, Jamaica, and is identical with Lahaina; called Keni Keni (10 c.) because it used to be sold in the streets of Honolulu for this sum.

No. 21. "Vulu Vulu," received from botanical gardens, Jamaica; stalks large, greenish yellow, otherwise very similar to No. 20; a promising cane.

No. 22. "China," received from botanical gardens, Jamaica; stalks large, green; suckers well, and very similar to No. 20; a promising cane.

No. 23. "Salangore," received from botanical gardens, Jamaica; stalks large, dirty white colour; leaves, light green; a cane highly prized in some countries.

No. 24. "Elephant (Green)," received from botanical gardens, Jamaica; stalks very large and vigorous; colour, greenish yellow; leaves darker than Salangore; apparently a good cane.

No. 25. "Lakoua," received from botanical gardens, Jamaica; large canes, well suckered; colour, yellow, tinged with red when exposed; leaves, dark green; a promising cane.

No. 26. "Cuban," received from botanical gardens, Jamaica; small green canes; suckers heavily; long joints; leaves, light green; in size and appearance not promising here.

No. 27. "Sacuri," received from botanical gardens, Jamaica; arge stalks and heavier leaves, otherwise resembles No. 26; from analysis of juice, a most promising cane.

No. 28. "Japanese or Zwenga," imported by General Le Duc, Commissioner of Agriculture, from Japan. This cane was obtained from Soniat Brothers, Tchoupitoulas Plantation. Its chief merit is its extreme hardiness, growing upon ditch banks without cultivation. May be useful in higher latitudes. It is a small, tall, white cane, very hard, and low in sugar; stools and rattoons well.

No. 29. "Soniat," a few canes found in Messrs. Soniat's field, and called by them bastard canes. Had the lower joints purple, and upper joints white. They were planted first as whole canes, and second cut into pieces, the purple joints in one row, and the white joints in another. Three and perhaps four distinct varieties, so far as outward appearances, have been obtained. The white variety has been named "Soniat," and will be fully described after further trial.

No. 30. "Malay," received from botanical gardens, Jamaica; stalks large, stools well; amber with green streaks, leaves large and abundant and dark green; a beautiful cane, standing upright in row.

Second class—striped canes

(1233)

No. 31. "Brisbane," received from botanical gardens, Jamaica; in every respect like No. 30.

No. 32. "Green Rose Ribbon," received from botanical gardens, Jamaica. Characteristics like No. 30.

No. 33. "Red Ribbon," received from director of botanical gardens, Jamaica. It is identical with our common striped or ribbon cane, though not yet fully acclimated.

No. 34. "Mexican Striped," received from Mexico, and identical in every respect with our common striped cane, so much so that the separate growth has been discontinued.

No. 35. "Batavian Striped," originally from Tahiti, and hence often called Otaheite Striped. Received from United States Consul at Guadaloupe. For two years after this cane was received it was small, and low in sugar content. Last year it developed into a fine cane, identical in every respect with our common striped No. 36.

No. 36. "Cypremort Striped," received originally from Mr. Jules Burguieres, of St. Mary, a few large, fine stalks, and have since been separately planted. Is a choice selection of our striped or ribbon cane, and are pale yellowish green canes, with reddish-purple stripes of more or less width, often almost obliterated.

No. 37. "Tsimbic," received from botanical gardens, Jamaica. Large cane. Colour yellow, with reddish-purple stripes. Leaves narrow and medium green. A very attractive cane.

No. 38. "Ysaquia," received from botanical gardens, Jamaica. Canes medium. Colour brown, with whitish stripes. Otherwise closely resembles No. 37.

No. 39. "Vituahaula," received from botanical gardens, Jamaica. Our cane is striped with red and green, while our original description calls for a light purple colour. Fears are entertained that this variety has been mixed with the next.

No. 40. "Horne," received from botanical gardens, Jamaica; canes medium; greenish, with reddish stripes. Worthy of future trial.

No. 41. "Ainakea," or Dark Rose Bourbon, originally from Mauritius; received here from Honolulu. Stalks large, colour green, with bright red stripes of varying widths; foliage bright green; strongly appressed to the upright stalks, with an occasional leaf striped with purple; its size and general appearance attractive.

No. 42. "Kanio," or Light Rose Bourbon, originally from Mauritius; same source as No. 41; stalks smaller than No. 41, of apple green, with yellow and red stripes; leaves a darker green than No. 41; not promising.

No. 43. "Akilolo" (light striped); indigenous in Hawaiian Islands; a beautiful cane, stalks large, intensely green, with deep reddish purple stripes of varying widths; leaves medium green, moderately open top, pith slightly yellow; apparently an attractive cane.

No. 44. "Alkilolo" (dark striped); indigenous in Hawaiian

Islands, in colour, foliage and general appearance like No. 45, but much smaller in size.

No. 45. "Manulete," indigenous in Hawaiian Island; stalks large and tall; colour, dark reddish-purple, with stripes of varying width of lighter purple; foliage deep green; midribs red, with sheaths more or less purplish; upright in growth, with adherent leaves; a promising cane.

No. 46. "Cavengerie," originally from Queensland; received from Dr. Alvarez Reynoso, Havana; stalks large and tall; dark red, with faintly black stripes; closely adherent top; leaves more or less variegated with white stripes; very productive suckers, and stubbles well; tonnage very large. Its only defect is its low sugar content, which improves with acclimation.

No. 47. "Attanattie," originally from Queensland; received from Honolulu; identical with Cavengerie, No. 46.

No. 48. "Po-a-ole," a red cane with narrow black stripes; strongly like Cavengerie, No. 46; received from director botanical gardens, Jamaica.

No. 49. "Nicholls." This name has been assigned to the striped variety, developed from the experiments given under No. 29. It is named in honour of the present Governor of Louisiana, F. T. Nicholls. At present there seems to be two varieties of this striped, a light and dark.

No. 50. "Norman," from botanical gardens, Jamaica; stalks small, numerous, and erect, of light purple colour; leaves pale green, with light purplish vein down the centre of each. Suckers well. *Third class—solid colours other than No. 1.*

No. 51. "Grand Savanne," from botanical gardens, Jamaica; stalks small, very numerous, erect, light purple. Leaves dark green and broad. Suckers enormously.

No. 52. "Naga," from botanical gardens, Jamaica. Stalks small but numerous. Colour deep purple—nearly black. Leaves moderately heavy, but narrow. Is highly recommended as a forage plant. This cane and Nos. 51 and 50 belong to a peculiar type of cane, of which the Japanese is a familiar example. They are not promising as sugar plants, save, possibly, in higher latitudes, where their resistance to cold may outweigh their sugar defects.

No. 53. "Java Light," from botanical gardens, Jamaica; stalks small; colour light purple; leaves heavy; not a promising cane.

No. 54. "Java, Black," received from Antigua. Stalks medium; colour dark purple; leaves of a dark green. Identical in appearance with our darkest purple canes. Our home grown purple canes often present every shade of purple. After a cultivation of several years this cane has the same characteristics.

No. 55. "Hope," received from botanical gardens, Jamaica. Stalks medium, of light purple, and resembles closely No. 53, except the joints are longer.

No. 56. "Breheret," received from botanical gardens, Jamaica. Stalks medium, reddish purple; short thick joints covered with a thin coating of cerosin; upper part of sheath with a row of harmless bristles; a promising cane.

No. 57. "Marabal," received from botanical gardens, Jamaica; stalks large, joints long; otherwise like No. 56 in every respect; a cane full of promise.

No. 58. "Elephant, Purple." This is an enormous cane, light purple colour; received from Mr. Edward Drouet, of New Orleans; introduced by Mr. Eugene A. Duchamp, of St. Martinsville, in 1875; is a curiosity worthy of a place in a botanical garden.

No. 59. "Cuapa," received from botanical gardens, Jamaica; stalks small, short jointed; colour nearly black; without bloom; very much like Ohia.

No. 60. "Liguanea," received from botanical gardens, Jamaica; stalks medium, longer joints than No. 59; otherwise eaxctly alike.

No. 61. "Ohia," indigenous to Hawaiian Islands; stalks medium; colour a pale brown, turning quickly blackish brown when leaves are removed; without bloom; leaves intensely green, adherent closely to stalk; midrib of sheaths of leaves purplish.

No. 62. "Honuaula," indigenous to Hawaiian Islands; stalks larger than No. 61; otherwise general appearance is same; a cane of promise.

No. 63. "Papaa," indigenous to Hawaiian Islands; smaller than No. 61, otherwise exactly alike; has little or no promise.

No. 64. "Bird." This is the name assigned to the purple variety developed by the experiment given under No. 29. The colour of this cane is quite different from our common purple cane. It has been named in honour of Major T. J. Bird, our late commissioner of agriculture.

The following varieties were lost in transplanting :—

No. 65, Tourkoury; No. 66, Batramie; No. 67, Waphendnow; No. 68, Hillii; No. 69, Bouronappa; No. 70, Pine; No. 71, Bourow; No. 72, Nain; No. 73, Queensland.

All of the varieties, except those received from the botanical gardens of Jamaica, were grown in sufficient quantity to be worked up in the sugar house. Those received from Jamaica were all used for seed except a few stalks which were submitted to analysis. They were harvested, planted, and analysed October 10 and 11. This was very early in the season for even plant cane of our home-grown varieties to give high results; therefore, due allowance must be made for some of these seemingly extraordinarily low results. Again experience has shown that single-stalk analyses are far from being true indices of plats or fields of cane. Some of these canes are full of promise, while others, from their growth, general appearance and nalytical results, are unworthy of further cultivation save in a botanical collection. These canes were received in August, 1889, and planted in the horticultural hall under glass, where they remained until April, when they were transplanted to the field. In transplanting, each sucker was carefully removed from its mother stalk and planted separately about 2 feet apart. At harvest each plant had produced a clump of many stalks, the number varying greatly with the variety. No effort was made this year to determine the tonnage per acre. Enough land has been planted to accomplish this purpose next season. A table of analyses is herewith given.

These canes were weighed and put twice through a small three-roller hand mill, and percentage of extraction of each variety carefully determined. The new canes from bud variations and the Japanese were likewise treated and are also given for comparison.

Analyses of canes obtained from the Jamaica botanical gardens and grown for the first time upon the grounds of the Louisiana Sugar Experiment Station, New Orleans:

| Number of Cane. | Name of Variety. | Per Cent. of Juice Extracted. | Total Solids. | Sucrose. | Glucose. | Solids not Sugar. |
|---|---|---|---|---|---|---|
| 20 | Keni Keni | 75·3 | 13·16 | 8·9 | 3·23 | 1·03 |
| 21 | Vulu Vulu | 76·7 | 10·10 | 4·0 | 4·75 | 1·35 |
| 22 | China | 74·3 | 11·46 | 6·1 | 4·00 | 1·36 |
| 23 | Salangore | 75·0 | 11·49 | 6·8 | 3·23 | 1·46 |
| 24 | Elephant, green | 70·4 | 12·56 | 8·7 | 2·78 | 1·08 |
| 25 | Lakoua | 68·0 | 11·67 | 8·0 | 2·22 | 1·45 |
| 26 | Cuban | 69·0 | 12·43 | 8·4 | 2·94 | 1·49 |
| 27 | Sacuri | 70·0 | 14·91 | 11·2 | 2·04 | 1·67 |
| 30 | Malay | 73·8 | 9·04 | 3·2 | 4·17 | 1·67 |
| 31 | Brisbane | 74·4 | 11·43 | 6·8 | 3·70 | 0·93 |
| 32 | Green Rose Ribbon | 71·3 | 9·74 | 3·8 | 4·35 | 1·59 |
| 33 | Red Ribbon | 70·2 | 12·30 | 8·3 | 2·44 | 1·56 |
| 37 | Tsimbic | 70·1 | 11·83 | 6·8 | 4·00 | 1·03 |
| 38 | Ysaquia | 72·8 | 8·79 | 2·5 | 4·54 | 1·75 |
| 39 | Vituahaula | 75·1 | 11·75 | 6·7 | 4·35 | 0·70 |
| 40 | Horne | 72·8 | 11·54 | 6·9 | 3·12 | 1·52 |
| 48 | Po-a-ole | 74·3 | 9·87 | 4·4 | 4·00 | 1·47 |
| 50 | Norman | 69·2 | 10·70 | 6·0 | 4·17 | 0·53 |
| 51 | Grand Savanne | 68·4 | 10·60 | 5·3 | 4·76 | 0·54 |
| 52 | Naga | 66·6 | 12·85 | 7·3 | 4·34 | 1·21 |
| 53 | Java Light | 72·6 | 13·60 | 9·3 | 3·12 | 1·18 |
| 55 | Hope | 72·2 | 10·40 | 7·5 | 2·48 | 0·42 |
| 56 | Breheret | 74·3 | 9·50 | 4·4 | 4·17 | 0·93 |
| 57 | Marabal | 75·0 | 12·80 | 7·1 | 3·23 | 2·47 |
| 59 | Cuapa | 69·2 | 12·43 | 8·2 | 2·78 | 1·45 |
| 60 | Liguanea | 68·6 | 11·65 | 6·7 | 3·85 | 1·10 |
| 29 | Soniat | 74·1 | 12·20 | 7·9 | 2·44 | 1·86 |
| 49 | Nicholls | 72·8 | 12·80 | 9·5 | 2·12 | 1·18 |
| 64 | Bird | 72·6 | 13·20 | 9·9 | 2·43 | 0·87 |
| 28 | Japanese | 58·1 | 10·16 | 2·5 | 5·00 | 2·06 |
| 58 | Elephant, dark | 70·4 | 12·56 | 8·7 | 2·78 | 1·08 |

In the above, the red ribbon, identical in every way with that grown here generally, is lower in sucrose than many others. From this, one would infer that in acclimation the other canes would probably do as well, if not better than this variety has already done by constant cultivation here.

The remaining varieties were grown in sufficient quantities to work up in the sugar house and determine the tonnage per acre. However, with a few of these varieties, not enough seed was available to plant continuously as is usual. The stalks were cut up into pieces of about 1 foot in length, and these were dropped along in the row so as to fill out a given area assigned to that variety. The rows were all 6 feet apart and one-half acre long. Both plant and stubble canes were used for seed, on separate but adjoining plats. Our plan of operation was as follows:—If possible, 50 select canes from the stubble of each variety were used to plant a row one-half acre along, and 25 select canes from plant cane to a row of same length. These numbers were used whenever possible, but many of our varieties were not obtainable in such quantities; therefore, whatever was accessible was planted, so as to have equal areas of all of these varieties under cultivation. Since equal numbers of canes of different varieties varied greatly in weight and length, very unequal quantities were used in planting. Therefore, the stands were very unequal. A table is given, showing the number of stalks to a row, the kind of cane used, the yield per acre and chemical analysis of the juice, with the percentage of extraction as determined by a small hand, three-roller mill, running the cane through twice. There is also given the aggregate of six of the best sucrose plat results in each of our home-grown canes, purple and striped, for comparison. All of the canes grown upon this station this year have been remarkably low in sucrose and high in glucose, and when these foreign varieties are compared with our home canes grown by their side, some of them appear very promising both from tonnage and sugar contents. The following are the results:—

YIELD and Analyses of Varieties of Cane Grown on Sugar Experiment Station, New Orleans, 1890—Harvested December 9-11.

| Station Number. | Name of the Variety. | Kind of Cane Planted. | Stalks per Row used in Planting. | Yield in Tons per Acre. | Per Cent. of Extraction. | Total Solids. | Sucrose. | Glucose. | Solids not Sugar. |
|---|---|---|---|---|---|---|---|---|---|
| 1 | Beltran | Stubble | 50 | 51·45 | 63·08 | 15·30 | 12·10 | 0·98 | 2·22 |
|  | " | Plant | 25 | 40·74 | 70·03 | 13·00 | 9·60 | 1·28 | 2·12 |
| 2 | La Pice | Stubble | 50 | 45·78 | 72·05 | 13·40 | 9·90 | 1·15 | 2·35 |
|  | " | Plant | 25 | 37·38 | 68·04 | 12·80 | 9·10 | 1·51 | 2·19 |
| 3 | Tibboo Merd | Stubble | 50 | 51·14 | 70·02 | 13·30 | 9·75 | 1·50 | 2·05 |
|  | " | Plant | 25 | 38·37 | 71·02 | 12·20 | 8·40 | 1·67 | 2·13 |
| 4 | Le Sassier | Stubble | 50 | 33·81 | 70·00 | 12·00 | 8·70 | 1·52 | 1·78 |
|  | " | Plant | 25 | 32·65 | 71·01 | 12·90 | 9·20 | 1·33 | 2·37 |
| 5 | Bourbon | Stubble | 50 | 48·09 | 73·90 | 13·10 | 9·90 | 1·61 | 1·59 |
|  | " | Plant | 25 | 41·89 | 73·10 | 13·80 | 9·50 | 1·72 | 2·58 |
| 6 | Crystallina | Stubble | 50 | 45·67 | 71·30 | 12·80 | 8·50 | 1·79 | 2·57 |
|  | " | Plant | 25 | 35·91 | 71·00 | 12·20 | 8·00 | 1·67 | 2·53 |
| 7 | Green | Stubble | 50 | 47·98 | 71·20 | 14·10 | 10·10 | 1·47 | 2·53 |
|  | " | Plant | 25 | 38·64 | 71·40 | 12·40 | 8·20 | 1·72 | 2·48 |
| 8 | Yellow | Stubble | 50 | 43·78 | 70·40 | 13·00 | 8·10 | 2·00 | 2·90 |
|  | " | Plant | 25 | 37·64 | 72·70 | 12·90 | 7·90 | 2·80 | 2·20 |
| 9 | Otaheite | Stubble | 50 | 50·29 | 72·40 | 13·20 | 8·20 | 2·32 | 2·78 |
|  | " | Plant | 25 | 44·32 | 77·50 | 13·80 | 8·60 | 2·51 | 2·69 |
| 10 | Portier | Stubble | 50 | 52·39 | 77·00 | 13·10 | 8·60 | 2·50 | 2·00 |
|  | " | Plant | 25 | 48·68 | 75·80 | 13·10 | 7·80 | 2·52 | 2·78 |
| 11 | Loucier | Stubble | 50 | 44·20 | 71·10 | 13·80 | 7·70 | 2·63 | 3·47 |
|  | " | Plant | 25 | 40·11 | 72·00 | 13·00 | 7·80 | 2·38 | 2·82 |
| 12 | Lahaina | Stubble | 25 | 58·23 | 77·50 | 12·00 | 8·70 | 2·07 | 1·23 |
|  | " | Plant | 12 | 20·11 | 9·80 | 13·50 | 7·30 | 2·27 | 3·93 |
| 13 | Caledonia Queen | Plant | 25 | 47·78 | 75·80 | 12·40 | 7·50 | 2·17 | 2·73 |

YIELD and Analyses of Varieties of Cane Grown on Sugar Experiment Station, New Orleans, 1890—Harvested December 9-11—continued.

| Station Number. | Name of the Variety. | Kind of Cane Planted. | Stalks per Row used in Planting. | Yield in Tons per Acre. | Per Cent. of Extraction. | Total Solids. | Sucrose. | Glucose. | Solids not Sugar. |
|---|---|---|---|---|---|---|---|---|---|
| 13 | Caledonia Queen | Stubble | 8 | 30·14 | 77·30 | 13·10 | 8·40 | 2·08 | 2·62 |
| 14 | Creole | " | 50 | 26·88 | 73·50 | 11·40 | 6·90 | 1·56 | 2·94 |
| 15 | " | Plant | 25 | 14·91 | 74·10 | 10·00 | 5·50 | 1·47 | 3·03 |
| 15 | Papuha | " | 25 | 46·57 | 68·40 | 15·20 | 11·10 | 1·00 | 3·10 |
| 16 | " | Stubble | 18 | 58·91 | 74·60 | 12·90 | 8·90 | 1·23 | 2·75 |
| 16 | Uwala | Plant | 25 | 34·96 | 71·20 | 9·70 | 4·20 | 2·00 | 3·30 |
| 17 | " | Stubble | 39 | 57·75 | 75·10 | 12·80 | 7·80 | 1·72 | 3·28 |
| 17 | Kokea | Plant | 25 | 60·79 | 72·90 | 12·60 | 8·90 | 1·56 | 2·14 |
| 18 | " | Stubble | 30 | 37·48 | 73·80 | 12·70 | 8·50 | 2·50 | 1·70 |
| 18 | Bamboo | " | 50 | 60·27 | 77·30 | 13·60 | 9·20 | 2·17 | 2·28 |
| 19 | " | Plant | 25 | 49·81 | 66·70 | 13·80 | 9·00 | 2·27 | 2·23 |
| 19 | Rose Bamboo | " | 25 | 41·26 | 72·70 | 13·56 | 8·00 | 2·38 | 3·12 |
| 34 | " | Stubble | 8 | 29·61 | 74·60 | 14·20 | 8·70 | 2·50 | 3·00 |
| 34 | Mexican striped | Plant | 25 | 37·68 | 72·20 | 13·30 | 10·00 | 1·67 | 1·68 |
| 35 | Cypremort striped | " | 25 | 38·50 | 68·40 | 13·30 | 10·20 | 1·47 | 1·63 |
| 36 | Batavian striped | " | 10 | 23·76 | 73·30 | 13·50 | 8·00 | 2·17 | 3·33 |
| 41 | " | " | 25 | 33·60 | 72·40 | 13·08 | 8·50 | 2·70 | 2·00 |
| 41 | Ainakea | Stubble | 25 | 46·62 | 73·30 | 13·00 | 7·80 | 2·43 | 2·77 |
| 42 | " | Plant | 25 | 57·12 | 75·00 | 13·30 | 7·80 | 2·78 | 2·72 |
| 42 | Kaino | Stubble | 19 | 47·09 | 77·00 | 13·10 | 7·60 | 2·79 | 2·71 |
| 43 | " | Plant | 25 | 47·32 | 73·10 | 12·70 | 7·50 | 2·77 | 2·43 |
| 43 | Alkilolo (light) | Stubble | 4 | ... | 72·80 | 11·50 | 6·10 | 2·94 | 2·46 |
| 44 | " | Plant | 25 | 40·18 | 75·60 | 12·70 | 7·70 | 2·63 | 2·37 |
| 44 | Alkilolo (dark) | Stubble | 23 | 31·36 | 72·20 | 12·70 | 7·50 | 2·48 | 2·72 |
| 45 | " | Plant | 25 | 63·28 | 73·10 | 12·70 | 7·40 | 2·63 | 2·67 |
| 45 | Manulete | | | | | | | | |

YIELD and Analyses of Varieties of Cane Grown on Sugar Experiment Station, New Orleans, 1890—Harvested December 9-11—continued.

NEW ORLEANS.

| Station Number. | Name of the Variety. | Kind of Cane Planted. | Stalks per Row used in Planting. | Yield in Tons per Acre. | Per Cent. of Extraction. | Total Solids. | Sucrose. | Glucose. | Solids not Sugar. |
|---|---|---|---|---|---|---|---|---|---|
| 45 | Manulete | Stubble | 25 | 35·42 | 73·20 | 11·80 | 6·00 | 2·63 | 3·17 |
| 46 | Cavengerie | ,, | 50 | 64·96 | 75·70 | 12·30 | 7·50 | 2·78 | 2·02 |
|    | ,, | Plant | 25 | 47·48 | 75·20 | 11·50 | 6·10 | 2·77 | 2·63 |
| 47 | Attanattie | ,, | 25 | 63·62 | 75·30 | 11·60 | 6·50 | 2·94 | 2·16 |
|    | ,, | Stubble | 61* | 54·60 | 71·20 | 11·50 | 6·40 | 2·78 | 2·32 |
| 54 | Java Black | Plant | 25 | 39·86 | 65·20 | 14·50 | 11·00 | 1·47 | 2·02 |
| 61 | Ohia | ,, | 25 | 37·30 | 70·90 | 10·40 | 4·80 | 2·27 | 3·33 |
|    | ,, | Stubble | 10 |  | 69·00 | 13·20 | 7·90 | 2·63 | 2·67 |
| 62 | Honuaula | Plant | 25 | 49·70 | 73·50 | 12·60 | 7·30 | 2·70 | 2·60 |
|    | ,, | Stubble | 12 |  | 72·70 | 11·20 | 5·80 | 2·50 | 2·90 |
| 63 | Papaa | Plant | 25 | 50·26 | 77·20 | 12·10 | 6·90 | 2·87 | 2·33 |
|    | ,, | Stubble | 11 |  | 77·20 | 13·20 | 8·20 | 2·86 | 1·96 |
|    | 6 best experiments purple cane | Plant | .. | 42·01 | 70·10 | 13·90 | 10·34 | 1·58 | 2·08 |
|    | ,, ,, ribbon cane | ,, | .. | 40·17 | 72·20 | 13·10 | 10·05 | 1·61 | 1·44 |

* Most of the canes were very small.

## UNITED STATES.

Several of the above canes have been grown here for over two years, the rest for three. Analyses have been frequently made of them all. An inspection of these show conclusively that the sucrose content is gradually increasing and encourages the hope that some of them will soon become valuable additions to the sugar industry of this State. Surely with the large number under cultivation, of almost every conceivable shade of colour, from the deepest purple to the lightest green, of different sizes and habits of growth, some few of them should be found adapted to our wants. Several of them continue the habits acquired in the tropics of growing into large, straight, and tall canes, and at the same time are gradually increasing in sugar. Could the tonnage obtained this year with a few of them be maintained and the sucrose be augmented to that contained in our common canes, it would profit the sugar industry more than the enactments of the most liberal tariff laws. The station will continue its efforts at acclimating these canes, fully impressed with the belief that its purposes will be ultimately attained.

All of these canes were diffused in quantities sufficient to thoroughly test them by this process. The larger and softer canes offered some obstacles to the comminutor at first, but this was soon remedied. With our common canes the knives projected only one-sixteenth of an inch. By placing them one-eighth of an inch they took the cane well, gave a fine chip, which was easily diffused.

Several of the above canes were grown at Baton Rouge and at Calhoun. At both of these places growth was greatly diminished and the sugar contents in many instances enhanced.

These analyses were made early in November of these canes and are herewith presented.

An examination and comparison of the tables will show to some extent the relative value of each variety upon the different soils of the State.

ANALYSES of Varieties of Cane Grown on State Experiment Station, Baton Rouge, La, 1890.

| Variety. | Per Cent Extraction. | Total Solids. | Sucrose. | Glucose. | Solids not Sugars. | Purity Co-efficient. | Glucose Ratio. |
|---|---|---|---|---|---|---|---|
| Purple | 65·79 | 15·0 | 12·1 | 2·65 | 0·25 | 80·66 | 21·90 |
| Striped Mexican | 64·78 | 16·0 | 12·4 | 2·00 | 1·60 | 77·50 | 16·13 |
| Rose Bamboo | 66·34 | 12·8 | 9·9 | 2·77 | 0·13 | 79·34 | 27·98 |
| Hanuala | 64·20 | 12·4 | 7·4 | 2·94 | 2·06 | 57·67 | 39·73 |
| Ohia | 70·43 | 13·1 | 8·1 | 4·07 | 0·93 | 61·83 | 50·24 |
| Papaa | 70·77 | 12·6 | 7·3 | 4·24 | 1·06 | 57·86 | 58·08 |
| Otaheite | 74·12 | 14·4 | 8·7 | 4·24 | 1·46 | 60·41 | 48·73 |
| Kokea | 72·28 | 13·5 | 9·5 | 3·41 | 0·59 | 70·37 | 35·89 |
| Lahaina | 75·99 | 13·3 | 8·7 | 3·65 | 0·95 | 65·41 | 41·95 |
| Akieola | 70·81 | 13·8 | 7·8 | 5·04 | 0·96 | 56·52 | 64·61 |
| Ainakea | 72·40 | 12·4 | 7·4 | 4·66 | 0·34 | 59·68 | 62·97 |
| Crystallina | 71·75 | 16·5 | 12·9 | 3·21 | 0·39 | 78·18 | 24·88 |
| Yellow | 70·04 | 14·1 | 9·3 | 3·12 | 1·68 | 65·96 | 33·55 |
| Kanio | 69·53 | 9·9 | 3·0 | 5·70 | 1·20 | 30·30 | 190·00 |
| Cavengerie | 70·64 | 11·0 | 6·0 | 4·07 | 0·93 | 54·54 | 67·83 |
| Loucier, No. 1 | 70·30 | 14·0 | 8·7 | 4·68 | 0·62 | 62·14 | 53·79 |
| Green | 69·90 | 14·0 | 9·0 | 3·03 | 1·97 | 64·28 | 33·55 |
| Bourbon | 68·75 | 14·5 | 11·3 | 2·04 | 1·16 | 77·93 | 18·05 |
| Black Java | 70·64 | 15·5 | 12·9 | 1·73 | 0·87 | 83·23 | 13·41 |
| Portier | 70·08 | 13·4 | 9·1 | 2·69 | 1·61 | 67·91 | 29·56 |
| Blanca d' Otaheite | 75·68 | 13·5 | 8·5 | 4·08 | 0·92 | 62·96 | 48·00 |
| Loucier, No. 2 | 62·00 | 12·5 | 7·6 | 3·92 | 0·98 | 60·80 | 51·58 |
| Japanese | 54·30 | 15·1 | 9·0 | 3·29 | 2·81 | 59·00 | 36·00 |

ANALYSES of Varieties of Cane Grown on the North Louisiana Experiment Station, Calhoun, La.

| Number of Experiment. | Name of Variety. | Total Solids. | Sucrose. | Glucose. | Purityy Co-efficient. | Glucose Ratio. |
|---|---|---|---|---|---|---|
| 1 | Japanese | 13·04 | 9·09 | 3·00 | 70·85 | 30·07 |
| 2 | Bourbon | 15·90 | 14·49 | 0·93 | 90·50 | 6·11 |
| 3 | La Pice | 15·60 | 14·20 | 1·05 | 91·05 | 7·39 |
| 4 | Crystallin | 15·13 | 13·20 | 1·28 | 87·24 | 9·84 |
| 5 | Blanca d' Otaheite | 14·87 | 11·40 | 1·67 | 76·66 | 14·64 |
| 6 | Portier | 15·09 | 12·50 | 1·21 | 82·83 | 9·68 |
| 7 | Loucier | 13·47 | 9·80 | 1·85 | 73·49 | 18·87 |
| 8 | Cavengerie | 14·47 | 10·30 | 1·55 | 71·17 | 15·04 |
| 9 | Creole | 13·29 | 8·90 | 1·64 | 67·06 | 18·42 |
| 10 | Panache | 16·24 | 13·50 | 1·11 | 83·12 | 8·22 |
| 11 | Rose Bamboo | 15·30 | 12·60 | 1·84 | 82·36 | 14·60 |
| 12 | Lahaina | 14·50 | 11·70 | 1·56 | 80·69 | 13·34 |
| 13 | Tibboo Merd | 15·50 | 13·10 | 1·11 | 85·51 | 8·47 |
| 14 | Kokea | 13·60 | 10·90 | 2·00 | 80·04 | 18·35 |
| 15 | Manulete | 13·70 | 11·60 | 1·82 | 84·61 | 15·68 |
| 16 | Uwala | 14·80 | 12·20 | 1·56 | 82·43 | 12·79 |
| 17 | Alkilolo | 14·80 | 12·40 | 1·60 | 83·78 | 12·90 |
| 18 | Papaa | 14·00 | 11·50 | 1·66 | 82·14 | 14·43 |
| 19 | Honuaula | 13·60 | 10·90 | 1·84 | 80·44 | 18·35 |
| 20 | Attamattie | 14·00 | 11·10 | 1·80 | 79·28 | 16·21 |
| 21 | Ohia | 13·20 | 11·00 | 1·95 | 83·33 | 17·72 |
| 22 | Purple | 15·90 | 14·49 | 0·95 | 90·50 | 6·11 |

**Manurial requirements of sugar cane.**

Before giving the results of an extensive series of experiments with fertilisers, it is perhaps best to give the accepted views of the action of the chief ingredients which go to make up these wares.

Commercial fertilisers consist chiefly of one or more of the following ingredients: Nitrogen (ammonia), phosphoric acid and potash. By intelligent planters and farmers the question is frequently asked: Under what conditions can we most profitably increase the returns from our soil by the use of commercial fertilisers? When, where, and what kinds should we use? The first two questions are easily answered. The last is very difficult to decide, especially for the growth of sugar cane on our lands. Fertilisers should be used whenever crops are grown which do not attain their maximum production on account of a deficiency in the soil of one or more of the above ingredients. But the deficiency of plant food is not always the cause of small returns. Water, so essential to all crops and needed in great abundance by some, is frequently in this climate productive of great harm. A drought may call for artificial irrigation, and excess of rainfall for drainage (open or tile). Want of porosity, so common in black clay lands, seriously impedes root development.

Some soils bake or cake after every hard rain, and thus work disaster to the plant. A great defect with many sugar lands in this State is the impermeability of surface water, forming unless high ridges with deeply ploughed middles prevent stagnant water at or near the surface, which brings disaster and sometimes death to a rapidly developing plant. Occasionally land may be deficient and in its absence the increased difficulty of the plant absorbing a sufficiency of food. Humus, so essential to every soil in this climate, is frequently badly needed.

Climatic conditions of a purely local character may temporarily prevail, such as alterations of temperature—hot, parching winds, as in south-western Kansas, often destroying a crop in a few days. It may, therefore, be asserted that whenever a soil from a physical, chemical, or climatic defect, forbids the growth of large crops, even when well supplied with fertilising ingredients, then the application of commercial fertilisers is a waste. The amelioration of its environments is now more needed by the plant than manures. Better seek a remedy in irrigation, drainage, deep ploughing, better cultivation, harrowing, hoeing, incorporation of vegetable matter, &c. After these ameliorating conditions are established, then, and not till then, should liberal manuring be practised. It should be borne in mind by the planters that every improvement in the quality of the soil increases its capacity for absorbing large quantities of manure and the transmutation into maximum crops. Heavy plant growth and excellent soil culture mean an enormous conversion of plant food into crops. Where the largest crops are producible there will be the heaviest demand for manures. Hence rich soils can successfully appropriate heavy applications of fertilisers, while poor soils must be fed with great care. Perfect all the other conditions of heavy plant growth, and then there will be demand for commercial fertilisers, not a demand to appease hunger, but one to "fatten." In fattening our domestic animals, we first perfect all the conditions of digestion, and then give them all they will eat—not what they need. Our object is to transform a larger amount of plant food into fat and muscle within the animal's frame than is required for its maintenance, and this we accomplish by a carefully compounded ration known to be both digestible and palatable. In successful stock breeding, we first select animals known to possess intensive powers of converting plant food into fat, and then supply them with the specially prepared food in great abundance. So, too, in farming, whenever practicable plants of known capacity for absorbing fertilisers should be cultivated, and then these plants should be stimulated to a most intensive assimilation of plant food by the application of suitable manures. While the better class of soils always respond more liberally to fertilisers than poorer ones, still the latter under favourable conditions often yield remarkable results. Great care is needed to see that the favourable conditions are fully attained, and unless they are very unsatisfactory results too frequently follow the use of commercial fertilisers. Sometimes the use of fertilisers overcomes the unfavourable surroundings. They cause a larger and deeper root development in early growth, and thus enable the plant to withstand a subsequent drought. They frequently cause an early shading of the ground, thus preventing surface hardening, and enable the sugar planter to give an early "lay by" to his crop.

These brief remarks will show that fertilisers can be successfully used on both fertile and poor soils.

To this assertion every sugar planter is ready to ask: What

forms of fertiliser shall we use to attain a maximum crop of cane, containing a maximum amount of sugar, and in what quantities, and when shall we apply them? After five years of patient investigation upon poor and rich soils, with every kind of fertiliser accessible, the station must answer that this question as to sugar cane has not yet been satisfactorily solved, and its solution compared with other crops is fraught with great difficulties.

It can grow maximum crops of cane, but it has not yet succeeded in putting maximum sugar content in them. In fact, it is almost ready to exclaim! Can it be done? Is not excessive tonnage incompatible with large sucrose content? The question is yet an open one, and some day may be solved. It is quite easy to tell which one of the three ingredients is needed by our soils to grow large crops of cane. Both phosphoric acid and nitrogen seem to be needed, while potash in any form gives no increased returns. That our soils abound in potash is shown by field experiments with potash, by their chemical composition, and the abundant growth of a certain class of plants which are large potash consumers, viz., cow peas, white clover, &c.

Nitrogen, the most costly ingredient of fertilisers, must be applied with care, since an excess may cause an abnormal development of the plant and a very low sugar content, and any residues not used by the crop may be lost by leaching during the winter.

Fortunately there are two unfailing sources of this element to the sugar planter—first, cow peas turned under a crop which has recently been shown beyond further cavil to have enormous capacity of abstracting and appropriating this element from the air, and second, cotton seed meal, a contribution from the neighbouring cotton fields. The cotton seed meal also contains goodly percentages of phosphoric acid and potash. This substance, however, should never be used alone, unless the soil gives unmistakeable evidence of an abundance of mineral food. On account of its leaching properties, nitrogen should never be applied until just before it is needed by the plant, and every attempt at storing away a surplus of this ingredient in the soil is uneconomical and irrational. It is estimated that at best, plants can utilise only 2 pounds out of every 3 pounds given to the soil.

The agricultural properties of phosphoric acid are almost the reverse of those of nitrogen. It can be stored away in the soil, remaining almost in the same place in which it is deposited. It does not leach. Indeed, a surplus of phosphoric acid in a soil is needed to produce, under average conditions, the maximum crops. Too large a surplus is, however, not economical or rational, and may, perhaps, sometimes be injurious. This is particularly true of the soluble phosphates. It is now conceded by every one that strong applications of phosphoric acid hasten the maturity of plants, especially when the latter are not supplied with a surplus of nitrogen. This is particularly the case with cotton. The plant becomes yellow early in the season and prematurely ripens its fruit and dies. This fertiliser has been used to extend the cotton crop northward, and frequently serves the hill planter in forcing his crop to maturity before the cotton and boll worms accumulate in sufficient quantities to destroy it. This ingredient is said to have a quickening effect on all the vital functions of the plant—causes it to prematurely ripen and die. The ripening process is but a cessation of activity in the manufacture of vegetation material, and the transference of these ready-made products through the leaves and stalks to the fruit. The presence of a surplus of nitrogen prevents or rather retards this cessation of activities, and the plants remain green a much longer time. An excess of phosphoric acid frequently causes an excessive early plant production, requiring a correspondingly large amount of nitrogen, and the latter, unless in large quantities, is soon exhausted, and a nitrogen starvation ensues, and the plant prematurely dies. Hence, in poor soils, this application of excessive quantities of soluble phosphates to cotton frequently diminishes the yields. The cotton "burns up." The plant is starving for nitrogen, and the hot, dry weather, usual in summer, is more injurious to a starving plant, than to one well fed. The cotton, under heavy doses of phosphates, exhibits an early, luxuriant development, which is sustained as long as the limited supply of nitrogen lasts. When this is exhausted, it starves to death. An application of nitrogen, as soon as the plant shows signs of decay, will often resuscitate it.

Potash is far more abundantly found in soils than either of the other ingredients discussed, and few soils in Louisiana need as yet this ingredient in manures to grow any crop. Where needed, it can be cheaply supplied with some of the German salts, either the crude form of kainite or the refined products sulphate and muriate. They perform their best results when applied some time before the growing of the crop, which they are intended to benefit. Kainite contains much common salt, and the latter has a binding effect on the soil, and enhances its power of retaining moisture. On very light soils an application of kainite is frequently beneficial from this effect, even when the soil contains an abundance of potash. On stiff, heavy soils, per contra, it may be detrimental. To that class of plants known as nitrogen gatherers (cow peas, clovers, &c.) potash is of great importance, and the luxuriant growth of these crops upon a soil unmanured, is the best index that it holds an abundance of potash.

With the above facts fully established, it would seem on first glance to be an easy task to determine a fertiliser, which would give a large tonnage with high sucrose percentage. A little reflection may, however, dispel this allusion; if not, the review of a number of carefully conducted experiments will surely dissipate it. A large crop of cane can certainly be made by the application of fertilisers, whenever the other conditions of heavy crop growth are perfect, but will this large crop of cane be rich in sugar? Rarely. One would suppose, from analogous results with other crops, that excessive quantities of soluble phosphates would prematurely ripen cane and give it a large sugar content.

Perhaps so; but then our large tonnage is eliminated. Our sugar cane, under the most favourable circumstances, grows only about eight months, and, with the varieties we cultivate, this is just now about two-thirds as long as they ought to grow. In tropical countries they are rarely harvested under 12 months, and frequently longer. Therefore, the power of prematurely ripening them here is relative, not absolute, and when any condition interposes to stop the activities of growth it must be done at the expense of the size of the crop. The manures suitable for heavy tonnage will rarely give maximum sugar content, and vice versâ. Seasons favourable to enormous field results seldom give satisfactory yields per ton in the sugar house. It is, however, known that excessive quantities of nitrogen frequently give "very green cane," whose juices annoy greatly the sugar maker. Therefore manures containing nitrogen should be mixed with phosphates, in order to prevent this injury. But then this mixture in quantities will give a large tonnage. A large tonnage means nearly always a long period of growth to the cane. A long period of growth here means immaturity, and immaturity is antagonistic to high sugar content. It now seems improbable to combine excessive tonnage and high sucrage. A high sucrage with low tonnage, or high tonnage with low sucrage, appear now as the horns of the sugar planter's dilemma. Each individual planter must exercise his own judgment in selecting the horn he will pursue.

In the excellent report recently issued by Professor J. R. Bovell of the results obtained on the experiment fields in Barbados, and received since the above was written, is found, on page 28, the following among his conclusions:—

"No. 8. No information has yet been obtained with regard to increasing the richness of the canes, either by the manures, or by growing them from portions of the cane rich in sugar."

If in Barbados, where cane reaches perfect maturity, and even bears true seed, no means has yet been found whereby the sucrose content can be increased, surely we can hardly hope to accomplish such a desirable end here where our cane never fully matures.

Perhaps out of the large number of foreign varieties of cane under cultivation, one or more may be found of higher sucrose content, and with equal or higher tonnage than the canes we now cultivate. This seems at present our last hope of increasing the sugar in our canes.

This was the first year's experiments at the Sugar Experiment Station. Prior to our occupancy it was a part of Audubon Park, and had not been in cultivation for years. It had grown annually the native grasses (chiefly the deep-rooted paspulums), which were sometimes cropped for hay, but more frequently left upon the ground to decompose. By this treatment the soil had become so heavily charged with organic matter as to give but little recompense to the application of nitrogenous manures.

(1233)

This long rest had doubtless served to accumulate on the surface soil an increased quantity of mineral matters in a readily available form. In short, this soil had every physical and chemical condition of new ground, and subsequent results have shown similar action.

Plats 3a, 3b, and 3c were devoted to manurial questions. The first to potash, the second to phosphoric acid, and the third to nitrogen. The questions asked are:—(1) Do these soils need each of these ingredients to grow a maximum crop of cane? (2) If so, in what forms shall these ingredients be used? (3) In what quantities per acre? The potash has been used under the forms of kainite (12 per cent. of potash), sulphate of potash (50 per cent.), muriate of potash (50 per cent.), ashes of cotton seed hull (20 per cent.), and nitrate of potash (46 per cent.). The phosphoric acid has been used as dissolved bone-black (14 per cent. soluble), acid phosphate (14 per cent. soluble), bone-black (24 per cent. insoluble), and bone-meal (24 per cent. insoluble), South Carolina floats and Thomas slag were to have been used, but failed to reach us in time.

The nitrogen was furnished in the form of cotton-seed meal, (7 per cent. nitrogen), dried blood (12 per cent.), sulphate of ammonia (21 per cent.), nitrate of soda (14 per cent.), tankage (6 per cent.), and fish scrap (6 per cent.).

In using the above, such quantities of each were taken as to represent equal quantities of nitrogen and potash and soluble phosphoric acid. In the insoluble phosphates the same number of pounds were used as with the soluble, since the cost was about the same. The substances were also used in one and two rations. Nitrogen was used at the rate of 24 lbs. (one ration) and 48 lbs. (two rations) per acre; soluble phosphoric acid, 36 lbs. (one ration), and 72 lbs. (two rations); and potash, 25 lbs. (one ration), and 50 lbs. (two rations). In experimenting with any one ingredient, of course, all of the others were present in excess.

The following was the cultivation of all the plats planted October, 1889:— Off-barred and scraped, January 20; again off-barred, February 27; further scraped, March 1. Pulverised middles with disc harrow; fertilised and middles split out, April 16. After that cultivation was done with Mallon's improved cultivator, laying by June 27. The cane was harvested November 10 to December 1. All of the cane was cut down by the frost March 3.

*Plat 3A, potassic manures.*

In this plat nitrogen and phosphoric acid are the constants and potash the variable. The first was used at the rate of 48 lbs. per acre, the second 72 lbs., while the third 25 lbs. and 50 lbs. in the various forms. In this plat there are two experiments without manure, and two without potash. The expression nitrogen phosphate is used in the table as an abbreviation of 48 lbs. nitrogen and 72 lbs. soluble phosphoric acid. The word nitrogen carries with it the quantity used, 24 lbs. The nitrogen was furnished this plat under the forms of nitrate of soda and dried blood, and the phosphoric acid as acid phosphate. Ashes of cotton seed hulls are used alone, with nitrogen, and with nitrogen phosphates.

The following are the field and laboratory results:—

## NEW ORLEANS.

### Plat 3a.—POTASSIC MANURES—Results.

| Number of the Experiment. | Fertilisers Used per Acre. | Yield per Acre in Tons. | Analyses of Juice. ||||||
|---|---|---|---|---|---|---|---|---|
| | | | Total Solids. Brix. | Sucrose. | Glucose. | Solids, not Sugar. | Glucose Ratio. | Purity Co-efficient. |
| 1 | 210 lbs. kainite | 43·86 | 12·9 | 10·00 | 1·85 | 1·05 | 18·53 | 77·50 |
| 2 | 210 ,, and nitrogen phosphate | 40·08 | 12·2 | 9·20 | 2·00 | 1·00 | 21·30 | 75·40 |
| 3 | 420 ,, ,, ,, | 39·74 | 14·1 | 11·20 | 2·00 | 0·90 | 17·90 | 79·40 |
| 4 | Nitrogen phosphate | 35·52 | 13·1 | 9·10 | 1·92 | 2·08 | 21·09 | 69·40 |
| 5 | 50 lbs. sulphate potash | 37·69 | ·· | 9·60 | 1·92 | ·· | 20·00 | ·· |
| 6 | 50 ,, ,, and nitrogen phosphate | 38·45 | 12·6 | 9·10 | 1·92 | 1·58 | 21·09 | 72·20 |
| 7 | 100 lbs. sulphate potash and nitrogen phosphate | 39·78 | 13·10 | 9·10 | 2·17 | 1·83 | 23·84 | 69·40 |
| 8 | No manure | 37·94 | 11·70 | 9·15 | 1·79 | 0·76 | 19·60 | 78·20 |
| 9 | 50 lbs. muriate potash | 35·91 | 11·50 | 8·60 | 1·79 | 1·11 | 20·80 | 74·80 |
| 10 | 50 ,, ,, and nitrogen phosphate | 37·56 | ·· | 8·90 | 1·76 | ·· | ·· | ·· |
| 11 | 100 lbs. muriate potash and nitrogen phosphate | 36·59 | 12·60 | 9·55 | 1·61 | 1·44 | 16·90 | 75·80 |
| 12 | Nitrogen phosphate | 37·78 | 12·90 | 8·80 | ·· | ·· | 18·20 | 68·20 |
| 13 | 200 lbs. ashes cotton hulls | 38·71 | 12·60 | 9·15 | 1·67 | 1·78 | 18·20 | 68·20 |
| 14 | 200 ,, ,, ,, and nitrogen | 40·76 | 13·10 | 9·70 | 2·00 | 1·40 | 20·60 | 74·04 |
| 15 | 200 ,, ,, ,, phosphate | 40·46 | 13·50 | 9·00 | 2·00 | 1·90 | 20·80 | 71·10 |
| 16 | No manure | 37·05 | 13·50 | 9·40 | 1·92 | 2·18 | 20·40 | 69·60 |
| 17 | 108 lbs. nitrate potash and nitrogen phosphate | 41·21 | ·· | 10·35 | 1·56 | ·· | 15·00 | ·· |

Plat 4A, phosphoric acid manures.

In this plat the nitrogen and potash were the constants, and the phosphoric acid the variable. The nitrogen was furnished in the form of sulphate of ammonia, and the potash as sulphate, both highly desirable forms. There are experiments also with gypsum, to see how far this necessary ingredient of every soluble phosphate is accountable for the good effects of the latter. The nitrogen is supplied at the rate of 48 lbs. per acre, and the potash 50 lbs. Basic mixture then means 230 lbs. sulphate of ammonia, and 100 lbs. sulphate of potash. The soluble phosphoric acid is supplied at the rate of 36 lbs. (one ration), and 72 lbs. (two rations) per acre. The same number of pounds of insoluble phosphates are used as with the soluble phosphates.

The following are the field and laboratory results:—

## Plat 4A.—Phosphoric Acid Manures—Results.

### NEW ORLEANS.

| Number of the Experiment. | Fertilisers Used per Acre. | Yield per Acre in Tons. | Total Solids. Brix. | Sucrose. | Glucose. | Solids, not Sugar. | Glucose Ratio. | Purity Co-efficient. |
|---|---|---|---|---|---|---|---|---|
| 1 | 258 lbs. dissolved bone black | 48·89 | 13·5 | 10·35 | 1·61 | 1·54 | 15·6 | 76·60 |
| 2 | 258 ,, ,, and basal mixture | 38·64 | 12·6 | 8·90 | 1·85 | 1·85 | 20·8 | 70·60 |
| 3 | 516 lbs. dissolved bone black and basal mixture | 40·11 | 13·2 | 9·25 | 1·79 | 1·98 | 19·3 | 70·00 |
| 4 | Basal mixture | 39·22 | 12·6 | 8·80 | 1·92 | 1·88 | 21·8 | 71·60 |
| 5 | 258 lbs. acid phosphate | 38·87 | 13·7 | 9·50 | 1·47 | 2·73 | 15·4 | 69·34 |
| 6 | 258 ,, ,, and basal mixture | 39·90 | 12·5 | 8·70 | 1·25 | 2·55 | 14·3 | 69·60 |
| 7 | 516 ,, ,, ,, ,, | 40·85 | 14·4 | 9·60 | 1·56 | 3·24 | 16·2 | 66·66 |
| 8 | No manure | 38·36 | 14·4 | 9·60 | 1·61 | 3·19 | 16·7 | 66·66 |
| 9 | 516 lbs. bone black | 38·17 | 13·5 | 9·30 | 1·85 | 2·35 | 19·8 | 68·80 |
| 10 | 516 ,, ,, and basal mixture | 38·89 | 13·5 | 9·20 | 2·00 | 2·30 | 21·7 | 68·10 |
| 11 | 516 ,, meal ,, ,, ,, | 39·20 | 13·9 | 9·70 | 1·89 | 2·33 | 19·4 | 69·71 |
| 12 | 516 ,, ,, and 100 lbs. sulphate potash | 37·89 | 14·6 | 9·80 | 1·92 | 2·88 | 19·5 | 67·10 |
| 13 | 516 lbs. bone meal and basal mixture | 37·46 | 14·5 | 10·30 | 1·79 | 1·96 | 17·3 | 71·40 |
| 14 | Basal mixture | 35·90 | 13·7 | 9·80 | 1·85 | 2·05 | 19·4 | 71·60 |
| 15 | 258 lbs. gypsum | 37·80 | 13·9 | 9·40 | 1·85 | 2·65 | 19·6 | 67·40 |
| 16 | 258 ,, ,, and basal mixture | 36·40 | 14·6 | 10·40 | 1·67 | 2·53 | 16·0 | 71·20 |
| 17 | No manure | 38·50 | 14·2 | 10·10 | 1·85 | 2·25 | 18·3 | 71·10 |
| 18 | 516 lbs. gypsum | 36·05 | 13·7 | 9·90 | 1·56 | 2·24 | 15·6 | 72·30 |
| 19 | 516 ,, ,, and basal mixture | 35·70 | 13·3 | 9·65 | 1·67 | 1·98 | 17·4 | 72·50 |

(1233)

Plat 5A, nitrogenous manures.

The phosphoric acid and potash are the constants in this plat, with nitrogen as the variable. Acid phosphate (14 per cent. soluble) furnished the phosphoric acid, while, as in plat 4a, sulphate of potash supplies the potash. Soluble phosphoric acid is used at the rate of 72 lbs. per acre, and potash 50 lbs. Mixed minerals mean, then, 576 lbs. acid phosphate, and 100 lbs. sulphate of potash per acre. The nitrogen is used at the rate of 24 lbs. (one ration), and 48 lbs. (two rations) per acre.

The following are the field and laboratory results:—

## NEW ORLEANS.

### Plat 5A.—NITROGEN Manures—Results.

| Number of the Experiment. | Fertilisers Used per Acre. | Yield per Acre in Tons. | Total Solids. Brix. | Sucrose. | Glucose. | Solids, not Sugar. | Glucose Ratio. | Purity Co-efficient. |
|---|---|---|---|---|---|---|---|---|
| 1 | 350 lbs. cotton-seed meal | 40·46 | 14·6 | 10·7 | 1·59 | 2·31 | 14·8 | 73·2 |
| 2 | 350 ,, ,, and mixed minerals | 39·98 | 12·6 | 8·9 | 1·61 | 2·09 | 18·0 | 70·6 |
| 3 | 700 lbs. cotton-seed meal and mixed minerals | 42·91 | 13·3 | 9·0 | 1·92 | 2·38 | 21·3 | 67·6 |
| 4 | Mixed minerals | 36·33 | 13·3 | 9·1 | 1·85 | 2·38 | 20·3 | 69·1 |
| 5 | 200 lbs. dried blood | 35·43 | 13·0 | 8·5 | 1·92 | 2·58 | 22·5 | 65·3 |
| 6 | 200 ,, ,, and mixed minerals | 35·91 | 13·1 | 9·2 | 1·85 | 2·05 | 20·1 | 70·2 |
| 7 | 400 ,, ,, ,, | 37·80 | 13·5 | 9·9 | 1·85 | 1·75 | 17·8 | 73·3 |
| 8 | No manure | 36·47 | 13·5 | 9·75 | 1·85 | 1·90 | 18·9 | 72·2 |
| 9 | 115 lbs. sulphate of ammonia | 38·99 | 13·5 | 9·80 | 1·85 | 1·85 | 18·5 | 72·7 |
| 10 | 115 ,, ,, ,, and mixed minerals | 37·94 | 12·6 | 8·70 | 2·08 | 1·82 | 23·9 | 69·0 |
| 11 | 230 lbs. sulphate of ammonia and mixed minerals | 40·46 | 13·5 | 9·50 | 1·85 | 2·15 | 19·4 | 70·3 |
| 12 | Mixed minerals | 40·74 | 13·5 | 9·55 | 1·79 | 2·16 | 18·7 | 70·7 |
| 13 | 160 lbs. nitrate soda | 39·36 | 13·5 | 9·50 | 1·85 | 2·15 | 19·4 | 70·3 |
| 14 | 160 ,, ,, and mixed minerals | 39·01 | 13·7 | 10·30 | 1·85 | 1·55 | 17·9 | 72·9 |
| 15 | 320 ,, ,, ,, | 37·59 | 14·2 | 10·55 | 1·79 | 1·86 | 16·8 | 74·2 |
| 16 | No manure | 36·30 | 14·5 | 11·00 | 1·61 | 1·89 | 14·6 | 76·3 |
| 17 | 400 lbs. tankage | 37·17 | 13·6 | 10·40 | 1·67 | 1·53 | 16·0 | 76·4 |
| 18 | 400 ,, ,, and 100 lbs. sulphate potash | 38·48 | 13·2 | 10·00 | 1·61 | 1·59 | 16·1 | 75·7 |
| 19 | 400 lbs. tankage and mixed minerals | 39·20 | 13·0 | 9·65 | 1·67 | 1·68 | 17·3 | 74·2 |
| 20 | 400 lbs. fish scrap and mixed minerals | 45·99 | 14·4 | 11·45 | 1·43 | 1·52 | 12·5 | 79·6 |

(1233)

The above experiments cover nearly every possible formula by which the various brands of commercial fertilisers are manipulated. Every raw material available has been secured, and their combinations represent in quality, if not in proportion in which they are mixed, many of the standard fertilisers sold on our markets. The experiments just given have failed to give the information desired. From a scientific standpoint they are failures. No deductions of even a probable character can be drawn from them. There are many reasons for their failure.

1. The newness, or rather freshness, of the soil, as hitherto explained, which induced on all of the experiments, even where no fertiliser was applied, a most extraordinary growth.

2. These plats had to be levelled before occupying them with the cane, thus exposing in places the subsoil, and making many inequalities in the plats.

3. Early in the fall all of the cane was severely prostrated by a storm, and in its prostrate state assumed a new growth, which continued until harvest.

4. The unusually favourable season, which has everywhere given the largest tonnage ever known before in this State, with a generally low sucrose content.

This unusually large crop has been productive of no positive scientific benefit, and the experiments must be repeated another year.

The station is indebted to the Standard Guano and Chemical Company and Planters' Fertiliser Company, both of New Orleans, for the fertilisers used in above experiments.

---

REPORT OF OPERATIONS FOR THE YEAR 1890-91 IN THE SUGAR HOUSE AND LABORATORY OF THE SUGAR EXPERIMENT STATION.

Since our last report of work performed in the sugar house, the station has been removed from near Kenner to Audubon Park, New Orleans. An iron sugar house, 40 feet by 100 feet, with numerous openings for ventilation, had recently been erected for the reception of the machinery from Kenner. This house, being much larger than our old sugar house, permitted the re-arrangement of the machinery and its adjustment in such a manner as experience had determined best suited to our wants. Mr. John Paul Baldwin was placed in charge of its erection, and so well was his work performed that little or no difficulty was experienced during the entire campaign.

In the boiler house, 30 feet by 60 feet, 20 feet from the sugar house, are two boilers of sufficient size to furnish an abundant supply of steam for all the operations of the sugar house. The sugar house completed may be thus summarised:— The cane is conveyed by a carrier to an ensilage cutter, with four knives 14 inches in length, and there cut into pieces of

¾ inch to 1 inch in length, and elevated by another carrier to a fan and shaker, when all the leaves, trash and dust are removed. This cutter and its carriers were made by the E. W. Ross Company, of Springfield, O., and by them donated to the station. The gearings of the carriers were not sufficiently strong for the heavy work which it was sometimes found necessary for the cutter to perform. This was especially true in handling some of the large foreign cane, this year worked for the first time. Otherwise the entire apparatus worked well, and replacing the linked belts with larger ones will, it is thought, give entire satisfaction in future work. The fan is entirely similar to those used for cleaning wheat, rice, &c. Six paddles were arranged for in the construction of the machine, but in practice it was found that four were sufficient to perform the required work. The shaker was this year changed from a horizontal to a vertical motion, and gave good results. The ensilaged chips, cleaned by the fan and shaker, were dropped into a box, from which an endless screw conveyed them to a comminutor. The latter is an invention of Mr. M. A. Swenson, and was made and presented to the station by the Fort Scott Foundry Company, Fort Scott, Kan.

The comminutor had eight knives, and when not overfed did excellent work. Its capacity was, however, not as great as the ensilage cutter, and great care had to be exercised in feeding the latter, so as to prevent an overfeed and choking of the former. From the comminutor the chips were elevated on a trough by small drags attached at regular intervals to an endless link belt chain. From openings in this trough, over each cell, the chips are conveyed to the battery. The diffusion battery consists of 14 cells, each 47 inches by 28 inches, and holding 13·56 cubic feet. It is a double line battery, and has a maximum capacity of 2 tons of cane per hour. Diffusion batteries are located in a straight line, in a double line, or in a circle. The number of cells used are from 9 to 16. It has been shown by a local experiment that 9 to 10 cells, when properly worked, are abundant for good work. (See Bulletin 23, pp. 349–50, of this station.) Sometimes double-line batteries are worked as two batteries. This method gives increased time for diffusion.

*Explanation of Diffusion Battery.*

A diffusor is an iron cylindrical cell, made to close tightly at the bottom and top, and supplied with pipes below and above. Nine or more of these cells are connected and called a battery. Believing that the diffusion battery will ultimately be the chief, and perhaps the only method of extracting juice from the cane, and that at present the chief objection to its use may be found in the ignorance of properly working it, it has been deemed proper to here insert several diagrams, by which the battery and its proper working may be easily understood.

PLATE I.

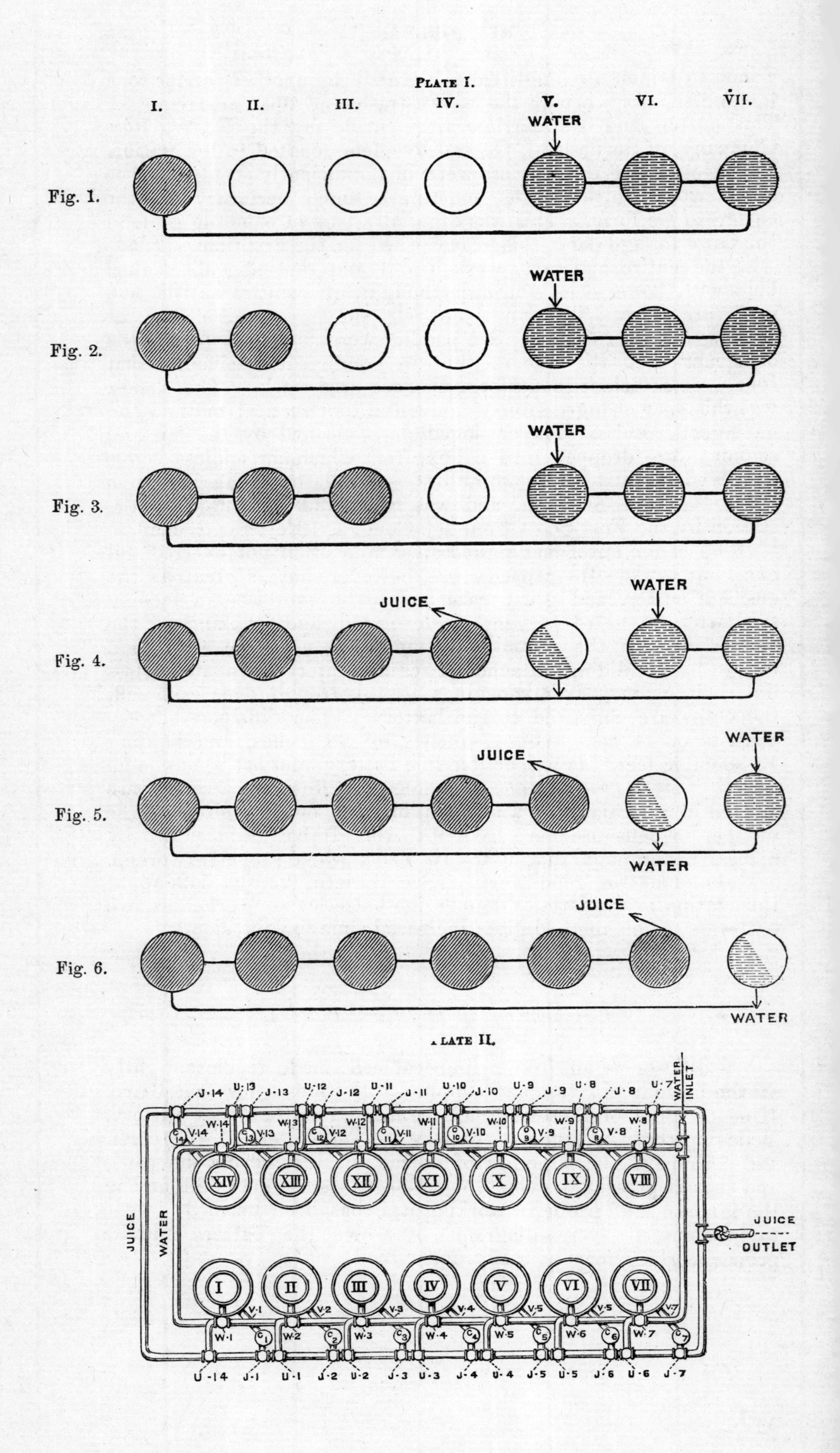

Fig. 1.    I.    II.    III.    IV.    V. WATER    VI.    VII.

Fig. 2.    WATER

Fig. 3.    WATER

Fig. 4.    JUICE    WATER

Fig. 5.    JUICE    WATER / WATER

Fig. 6.    JUICE    WATER

PLATE II.

In Plate I. is seen a single battery of seven cells, in the actual conditions which obtain from the filling of first cell till the battery gets in regular working order. The arrow shows the water entering, and finally the juice departing to the measuring tank or weighing machine. Figure 1 shows the condition of battery when first cell is filled with chips. Figure 2 when two cells are filled. Figure 3 when three cells are filled, &c. The horizontal shading means filled with water; the diagonal lines, chips, and the rest are empty.

Plate II. gives a plan of our battery, with its cells, calorisators, pipes and valves. The cells are numbered from I. to XIV.; the water valves, w to w14; the juice valves, J to J14; the valves connecting the cells, U to U14; the calorisators or heaters, C to C14; and the pipes connecting the cells and heaters, V to v14.

In the beginning of work the last three or four cells on the battery are filled with water and heated before being drawn on to the chips in the first cells.

In our sugar house a large heater, disconnected from the battery, aids in heating the water in its passage from the water tank in the roof of the house to the battery.

*Process of Working the Battery.*

As soon as the machinery is in motion and the chips begin to fall into cell No. 1, the last three or four cells are filled slowly with water, heating it in its passage with the calorisators. The water comes from the water tank directly through the big heater, and then through tube W and valve w12 into diffuser XII. from above; passes v12 to c12, and ascends the heater, through N12, over w13, into cell XIII., then on through v13, c13, over J13, through N13, over w14, into cell XIV., thence into v14 and c14, travels the short distance from J14 to J1 in the juice pipes, and runs into c1 from above, passes v1 and ascends into cell I. from below, upwards through the first chips. As soon as the fluid has reached cell I. the diffuser is closed, the air cock opened and kept opened until the water begins to come through, when it is closed.

While water is entering cell I., which should be done slowly to permit of its being heated "in transitu" through the heaters, cell II. is being filled with chips. When filled, the water entering c14 passes over J14 through U14, over w1 into cell I. from above, driving the juice through v1, c1, J1, J2, c2, and v2 into cell II. This process is repeated until you wish to draw juice from the battery. Suppose it is desired to draw the juice from cell IV. The juice now goes from c14 over J14, through U14 over w1, through I.; v1, c1 over J1, through U1 over w2, through II.; v2, c2 over J2, through U2 over w3, through III.; v3, c3, J3, J4, c4, v4, and ascends into cell IV. through the fresh chips. As soon as all air is expelled from this cell, the valves from c3 are changed. The juice now rising in c3 goes over J3 through U3 over w4, through IV., v4, c4, J4, and leaves the battery at J to enter the measuring tank or juice weigher.

This work is continued until sugar work is reached. From now on in our work one cell is being emptied while the other is being filled with chips. Before emptying a cell the entire water in the battery is driven forward, one cell by applying air pressure to the cell to be emptied. In this way the chips are released of much of their superabundant moisture. Before emptying a cell it is completely isolated from the rest of the battery. As a general rule, the juice should enter every cell from above, except the one just filled with chips, and this invariably from below to drive out the air and prevent the accumulation of foam and steam in the cell. The temperature is controlled by the valves leading from steam pipe to calorisators.

### *Requisites for Good Diffusion.*

1. Fineness of chips. To obtain this the knives must be kept sharp, and must project beyond the cylinder as little as possible to perform good work. With our common canes a projection of one-sixteenth of an inch gave a most excellent chip with rapid work, while many of the larger foreign canes, on account of their softness, could not be comminuted at all with this projection. To perform good work the knives had to be given a projection of at least one-eighth of an inch. The solidity of the canes determine the projection of the knives, and to a large extent the size of the chip. It may be assured that the finer the chip, "ceteris paribus," the better it diffuses.

2. Heat is essential to excellent work. How far a high heat may influence other extractive matter detrimental to crystalisation and good clarification is a question yet to be definitely solved. For a high extraction of sugar by diffusion, heat as high as can be obtained is requisite.

3. With the above conditions secured, the time of diffusion can be greatly diminished. With a coarse chip and low heat, even a long diffusion fails to accomplish complete extraction. Time, then, is an important essential of diffusion.

### *Baldwin's Juice Weigher.*

From the battery the juice was discharged directly into the "juice weigher." This juice weigher was adjusted to weigh 365 lbs. of juice, and direct tests of the machine, made 17 different times, showed variations from 364 lbs. to 367 lbs., with an average of 365½ lbs. This juice weigher performed its part excellently in the early part of the season, as was shown by constant checks, and measurements, and weighings. Three weeks of constant use, however, without attention, caused an accumulation of viscous matter on the sleeve, which prevented it from turning readily, and thus delayed or hindered the automatic discharge and readjustment of the machine. As soon as the irregularity was discovered and its causes located, the entire machine was cleansed and again put to practical work, with the same excellent results.

This machine, like every other now in use in our sugar houses, must be kept in first-class order in order to obtain the best results. I am informed by the patentee that the machine had been further improved, with the probability of entirely overcoming the present apparent defects. This machine is also arranged to take a fair sample of each discharge. This was tried, with very unsatisfactory results. The hole, through which the small sample was discharged, frequently became more or less closed, causing very unequal discharges.

On a large scale, in a sugar house working fairly uniform canes, the difficulty we experienced would hardly have been appreciated. But in an experimental sugar house, where in one experiment the discharges consisted of both the regular juice and the washings of the battery, such unequal discharges must vitiate the accuracy of the aggregation of samples. This defect, it is believed, can and will be easily remedied.

This machine has great merit, and when perfected, as is believed it will be very soon, will constitute one of the most valuable additions to a modern sugar house, enabling one to exercise with comparative chemical ease a control over the juice and syrup.

### Clarifiers.

The juice was next pumped to the clarifiers, and there heated with chemicals for clarification. Connected with this clarifier was a sulphur machine by which a clarifier could be sulphured to any desirable extent. Arrangements are being made by which the scums from the clarifier can be sent directly to the diffusion battery or through a Pusey and Jones' filter press. The latter was the course adopted in our experimental work, since an unknown quantity of juice with each return to the battery entered the chemical problem which the daily experiment attempted to solve.

### Double Effect.

The juice from the clarifier was concentrated to syrup in an upright double effect of 400 square feet of heating surface. This double effect has, by the ordinary methods of running it, occasioned great loss by entrainment and overflow. It has been found that by lowering the juice in each effect that the loss diminished, until it was practically nil, when the tubes were kept about half full. The following method of working proved so successful that it will hereafter be followed:—In starting the effects, juice is drawn in until the tubes are about half covered; then steam is turned on, and the juice kept at this constant level. Looking in through the lower glasses, two curves can be seen, the juices rising from the tubes and falling down the "downtake." The quantity evaporated was also largely increased.

### Strike Pan.

The syrup thus made was sent to the strike pan of same size as one of the effects. Here it was cooked to grain, with little or no mechanical loss during the season. The "masse cuite" was taken to a mixer, and from it taken to a Hepworth's centrifugal, where it was purged of its molasses. The latter was cooked to string, and put into cars, and stored in the hot-room.

Besides the above complete outfit a small miniature equipment, consisting of a clarifier, an open evaporator, a very small strike pan and a hand centrifugal, was frequently used for making preliminary experiments with various chemicals, &c.

With this outfit the campaign of 1890 was begun on November 11. 15 distinct runs were made, analysing the fresh and diffusion chips, the diffusion juices before and after clarification, the syrup, sugar, and molasses; and weighing the cane, diffusion juice, syrup, sugar, and molasses. Every check possible was adopted to determine mechanical or chemical loss, and later, the merits of different kinds of clarification. The question of diffusion was also studied, and every effort made to determine its merits. It is deemed best for the public to divide our work up and present it under different heads. The question first to be considered is diffusion.

### Diffusion.

Before giving the results it would be well to state how this work was controlled. The fresh chips going to the battery were pressed in a small but powerful 3-roller hand mill, giving about 55 per cent. extraction of juice. This juice was carefully analysed for total solids, sucrose, glucose, solids, not sugar, and sometimes for ash and albuminoids. At the same time the fibre in the fresh chips was frequently determined and the total juice calculated. The entire juice was assumed to be of same composition as that extracted (a fact not yet proven, however). The exhausted chips were treated in a similar way, and the percentage of sucrose, fibre, and water determined. There was always a small amount of wash water lost on opening the doors of the battery to empty the chips. This was several times analysed, and results showed it to be always lower in sugar than the chips from which it fell. It is therefore assumed that much of the waste water came from spaces between the chips, while the juice extracted from the diffusion chips was a mixture of this wash water and mixture of juice and water contained in the cells. The latter being richer in sugar, caused the mill juice to be correspondingly higher.

By taking these results as data, the problem of extraction is easily calculated for each run, as follows:—

| Description. | Date. | Fibre. | Extraction per Cent. On Cane. | Extraction per Cent. On Sugar in Cane. | Dilution on Normal Juice. | Minimum Sucrose in Chips. |
|---|---|---|---|---|---|---|
| 1st run | Nov. 11 | 8·05 | 86·09 | 93·58 | 150·92 | ·65 |
| 2nd ,, | ,, 13 | 7·43 | 87·55 | 94·58 | 136·39 | ·50 |
| 3rd ,, | ,, 16 | 8·23 | 87·67 | 95·15 | 128·88 | ·50 |
| 4th ,, | ,, 18 | 8·67 | 85·95 | 94·12 | 141·73 | ·55 |
| 5th ,, | ,, 21 | 8·00 | 86·91 | 94·47 | 145·64 | ·50 |
| 6th ,, | ,, 24 | 8·00 | 88·32 | 96·00 | 137·00 | ·40 |
| 7th ,, | ,, 27 | 8·00 | 86·57 | 94·10 | 145·00 | ·62 |
| 8th ,, | ,, 29 | 8·00 | 87·74 | 95·40 | 152·00 | ·45 |
| 9th ,, | Dec. 1 | 8·00 | 88·30 | 96·10 | 131·00 | ·40 |
| 10th ,, | ,, 3 | 9·27 | 83·00 | 95·80 | 147·00 | ·45 |
| 11th ,, | ,, 5 | 9·00 | 89·10 | 98·00 | 144·00 | ·20 |
| 12th ,, | ,, 8 | 9·00 | 87·26 | 95·90 | 149·00 | ·40 |

The above dilution is calculated on the strength of the diffusion and mill juice. In the experiments, amounts of juice, varying from the weight of the chips in each cell, up to the weight of water added to each cell, were drawn off, and results showed that the extraction depended also upon conditions other than dilution, viz., density of chips in cell, fineness of chips, heat of battery and time of diffusion. In Run No. 11, when extraction reached the maximum of the season the chips were fine, the heat good, dilution large. Besides all these the time of diffusing each cell was unnecessarily long, caused by the delay incident to the clarification process followed that day. It may here be remarked that the exhausted chips contained an average for the season of 13 per cent. fibre. In winding up a run and emptying a battery a considerable loss of sucrose is inevitable. The following plan was found by experiment to give the least loss with the least dilution. The battery is first emptied completely with air and then six rearmost cells are filled again slowly with hot water and driven entirely through the battery. In this way the sucrose left over in the last cell rarely ever exceeds 2 per cent.

### Methods of Clarification—Lime only.

Runs Nos. 1 and 2 were made by simply adding milk of lime to neutrality in each cell of the battery. In 1888 the addition of lime to the cell gave a clarification which permitted the sending of the juice directly from the battery to the double effect. Not so this year. In spite of every effort the clarifier had to be used. The juice in 1888 had a sucrage of 13 per cent. with glucage of 0·9 per cent., while the average of all the runs this year show less than 10 per cent. sucrose, and over 1·5 per cent. glucose. The clarification, on account of the green cane, had to be completed in the clarifier. The following are the laboratory notes of each run:—

*First Run.—Five Tons Cane.*

| Description. | Total Solids. | Sucrose. | Glucose. | Glucose Ratio. | Purity Co-efficient. | Fibre. |
|---|---|---|---|---|---|---|
| Mill juices | 13·07 | 10·13 | 1·95 | 19·23 | 77·39 | 8·05 |
| Diffusion juices | 8·66 | 6·65 | 1·32 | 18·95 | 77·37 | ... |
| Syrup | 34·08 | 25·90 | 5·25 | 20·27 | 76·00 | ... |
| Sugar | ... | 95·60 | 0·96 | ... | ... | ... |
| Molasses | 79·09 | 40·00* | 25·00 | ... | ... | ... |

\* Double polarisation, 42·15 per cent.

Yield of chemically pure sugar as firsts, 124 lbs. per ton. No seconds made, the molasses being used for experimental purposes. The extraction was 86 per cent on the cane, or 174 lbs. sugar per ton. Of this amount 71 per cent. was secured as first sugars.

*Second Run.—Seven Tons of Cane used.*

| Description. | Total Solids. | Sucrose. | Glucose. | Glucose Ratio. | Purity Co-efficient. | Fibre. |
|---|---|---|---|---|---|---|
| Mill juices | 12·93 | 9·23 | ... | ... | 71·38 | 7·43 |
| Diffusion juices | 9·48 | 6·80 | 1·46 | 21·40 | 71·79 | ... |
| Syrup | 44·31 | 31·90 | 6·86 | 21·50 | 72·05 | ... |
| Sugar | ... | 96·50 | 0·80 | ... | ... | ... |
| Molasses | 81·30 | 38·00* | 25·00 | ... | ... | ... |

\* Double polarisation, 40·64 per cent.

Yield of chemically pure sugar as firsts, 116 lbs. per ton. No seconds made. Extraction, 87·55 per cent., or 162 lbs. of sugar per ton. Of this amount 72 per cent. was secured as first sugars.

*Lime and Bisulphite of Lime used as Reagents.—Third Run.— Eight Tons of Cane used.*

Milk of lime was added in slight excess in diffusion cells to the chips. The juice slightly alkaline was received in a settling tank, into which was emptied 2 gallons of bisulphite of lime to every 350 gallons of juice. This rendered the settled juice slightly acid, which was carefully neutralised in the clarifier. A pretty juice was made.

The following are the laboratory results:—

## NEW ORLEANS.

| Description. | Total Solids. | Sucrose. | Glucose. | Glucose Ratio. | Purity Co-efficient. | Fibre. |
|---|---|---|---|---|---|---|
| Mill juices | 12·18 | 9·00 | 1·77 | 19·66 | 73·89 | 8·23 |
| Diffusion juices | 9·32 | 6·99 | 1·19 | 17·09 | 75·00 | ... |
| Syrup | ... | 28·10 | 5·10 | 18·00 | ... | ... |
| First sugars | ... | 94·65 | 1·39 | ... | ... | ... |

Yield of chemically pure sugar as firsts, 99 lbs. per ton; of seconds, 12 lbs.; total, 111 lbs., or 70 per cent. sucrose extracted in the juice. Extraction of juice was 87·67 per cent. of the cane.

*Fourth Run.—Nine and One-Half Tons Cane used.*

Clarification same as above, with following results:—

| Description. | Total Solids. | Sucrose. | Glucose. | Glucose Ratio. | Purity Co-efficient. | Fibre. |
|---|---|---|---|---|---|---|
| Mill juices | 13·3 | 9·68 | 1·82 | 18·80 | 72·78 | 8·67 |
| Diffusion juices | ... | 6·83 | 1·19 | 17·42 | ... | ... |
| Syrup | 43·2 | 30·95 | 5·71 | 18·40 | 71·64 | ... |

Yield of chemically pure sugar as firsts, 128 lbs. per ton; of seconds, 9 lbs.; total, 137 lbs., or 82 per cent. of total sugar extracted. Extraction of juice was 85·95 per cent. on the cane.

*Fifth Run.—Twelve Tons of Cane used.*

Clarification same as above, with following results:—

| Description. | Total Solids. | Sucrose. | Glucose. | Glucose Ratio. | Purity Co-efficient. | Fibre. |
|---|---|---|---|---|---|---|
| Mill juices | 13·6 | 9·19 | 1·63 | 17·79 | 67·57 | 8·00 |
| Diffusion juices | ... | 6·31 | 1·03 | 16·40 | ... | ... |
| Syrup | 51·0 | 36·40 | 6·65 | 18·27 | 71·37 | ... |

Yield of chemically pure sugar as firsts, 101 lbs. per ton; of seconds, 13 lbs.; total, 114 lbs., or 73 per cent. of sugar extracted in the juice. Extraction of juice was 86·91 per cent. of the cane.

The use of bisulphite in the manner described above gave a pretty juice, which was easily cleaned and worked. Its chief objections are the large quantities necessary for good results and the amount of sulphite and sulphate of lime which enter into the juice and are finally left in the molasses. The exact action of these salts upon the crystallisation of sugar is as yet not clearly known, but they are believed to be mellassigenic. The bisulphite used in the above experiments was kindly donated by

(1233)

## UNITED STATES.

Mr. H. Bonnabel, 29, Bienville Street, New Orleans, who manufactures it on a large scale.

*Lime and Acid Phosphate of Calcium.*

Three runs, Nos. 6, 12, and 13 were made with these as agents, the "modus operandi" being as follows: The milk of lime was added to alkalinity in the diffusion cells, and the acid phosphate of calcium to the juice in the settling tank or clarifier, and clarification completed in the clarifier.

*Run No. 6.—Nine and One-Half Tons Cane were used.*

In this run the acid phosphate was used to slight acidity, there being required 3 quarts to every 350 gallons of juice. The chemical results show that it was left acid, since inversion took place from raw juice to "masse cuite."

The following are the results:—

| Description. | Total Solids. | Sucrose. | Glucose. | Glucose Ratio. | Purity Co-efficient. | Fibre. |
|---|---|---|---|---|---|---|
| Mill juices | 13·95 | 9·685 | 1·88 | 19·51 | 69·45 | 8·00 |
| Diffusion juices | ... | 7·060 | 1·27 | 17·90 | ... | ... |
| Clarified ,, | ... | 6·74 | 1·36 | 20·10 | ... | ... |
| Syrup | 42·97 | 30·95 | 6·67 | 21·70 | 69·70 | ... |

The yield of chemically pure sugar was per ton of cane, firsts, 131 lbs.; seconds, 12 lbs.; total, 143 lbs., or 83 per cent. of sugar extracted in the juice. Extraction of juice was 88·32 per cent. of the cane.

*Run No. 13.*

In this run 14 field experiments, aggregating 13 tons, and covering nine varieties of cane, were used. It is quite difficult to give the exact average of the mill juices, or the average extraction, since it was impossible to determine fibre in every variety. The mill juices had about 9·53 per cent. sucrose. The following were carefully determined:—

| Description. | Sucrose. | Glucose. | Glucose Ratio. |
|---|---|---|---|
| Diffusion juices | 7·47 | 1·03 | 13·7 |
| Clarified ,, | 7·29 | 0·97 | 13·2 |
| Syrups | 38·90 | 5·25 | 13·5 |

There were 2,080 lbs. of sugar in the syrup worked. Of this amount 1,685 lbs. of chemically pure sugar was extracted as first sugar, or 81 per cent. of the total contained in the syrup. The sugar was simply dried in the centrifugal without water and polarised 93 degrees.

The acid phosphate was used in the above experiment to as near neutrality on the acid side as could be done by the proceases now generally used.

### Run No. 14.

This run was even more complicated than No. 13. 36 varieties of cane contributed to make up the 12½ tons used in this trial, and where separate determination of each mill juice was made, the varying weights and extraction of each tend to make accurate determination of the average mill juice an impossibility. It was somewhere between 8 per cent. and 9 per cent. The acid phosphate was again used here to slight excess. The following are partial results of laboratory:—

| Description. | Total Solids. | Sucrose. | Glucose. | Glucose Ratio. | Purity Co-efficient. |
|---|---|---|---|---|---|
| Diffusion juices | .. | 6·4 | 1·39 | 21·7 | .. |
| Clarified ,, | .. | 6·5 | 1·42 | 21·8 | .. |
| Syrups | 57·3 | 33·4 | 7·69 | 23·0 | 65·1 |

There were in the syrups sent to this pan 1,700 lbs. of sugar, of this amount 1,187 lbs. being secured as firsts, or 71 per cent. of total. A very fair yield considering the low purity and excessive glucose of the syrup.

The acid phosphate of calcium used in the above experiments was kindly donated by the Provident Chemical Works, of St. Louis, and was a liquid of 20 degrees Baume density.

### Lime and Sulphur as Reagents.

Milk of lime was added in excess in the diffusion cells, and the alkaline diffusion juices treated with fumes of sulphur in the clarifier.

Runs Nos. 7 and 8 were made with these reagents.

### Run No. 7.—Eleven Tons of Cane used for this Trial.

The alkaline juices were made slightly acid with sulphur, with the following results:—

| Description. | Total Solids. | Sucrose. | Glucose. | Glucose Ratio. | Purity Co-efficient. | Fibre. |
|---|---|---|---|---|---|---|
| Mill juices | 13·84 | 9·88 | 1·68 | 7·1 | 71·2 | 8·00 |
| Diffusion juices | ... | 6·80 | 1·02 | 15·0 | ... | ... |
| Clarified ,, | ... | 6·90 | 1·12 | 16·2 | ... | ... |
| Syrup | 48·01 | 35·20 | 6·25 | 17·7 | ... | ... |

(1233)

The yield of chemically pure first sugar was 126 lbs. per ton; of seconds, 13 lbs.; total, 139 lbs., or 82 per cent. of sugar extracted in the juice. Extraction of juice was 86·57 per cent. of the cane.

*Run No. 8.*

11 tons of cane used in this trial. The juice treated as No. 7, with the following results:—

| Description. | Total Solids. | Sucrose. | Glucose. | Glucose Ratio. | Purity ent. | Fibre. |
|---|---|---|---|---|---|---|
| Mill juices | 13·31 | 9·32 | 1·87 | 19·9 | 7·01 | 8·05 |
| Diffusion juices | ... | 5·90 | 1·14 | 19·5 | ... | ... |
| Clarified ,, | ... | 6·10 | 1·19 | 19·5 | ... | ... |
| Syrup ,, | 47·10 | 33·00 | 7·10 | 21·51 | ... | ... |

The yield of chemically pure first sugar was 122 lbs. per ton. No seconds obtained, even after nine months. This is 75 per cent. of the sugar in the juice. Extraction of juice was 87·74 per cent. of the cane.

*Wilcox's Albumen Process.*

Three runs were made with this process, in accordance with instructions given by the patentee, to Mr. B. Remmers, his agent, who assisted in executing the work.

The following instructions were given in writing:—

First process: Run the sulphured juice into the defecator; into another vessel for every pound of juice in the defecator put 3½ grains of dried albumen. Add sufficient water to this to put it thoroughly in solution. Add the contents of this vessel to the defecator. Mix well and turn on steam. When the juice is about 190° Fahr. shut off steam and commence to add milk of lime until the juice shows perfectly neutral. When the neutral point is reached turn on steam again, and blanket off the scums. Shut off steam and add enough sulphurous acid to raise the acid point of the juice, so that it shows slight acid on litmus paper. Allow juice to settle one hour, and draw off the clean liquor and boil to sugar.

Second process: Run the sulphured juice into the defecator as before, turn on steam and blanket. When the scum has been taken off, shut off steam and pour into the hot juice the albumen solution in same proportion as before, and mix thoroughly. Let stand 5 minutes or 10 minutes, then add milk of lime to neutrality, boil for a few minutes, shut off steam, bring back to acid point as before and settle. The only point gained by this way is the heavy scum being first taken off, the albumen has a better chance to act on those impurities for which it is especially designed, than spending a part of its force in raising the heavy scums.

NEW ORLEANS.

With these instructions, on the morning of December 1, the ninth run was begun with 11 tons of cane, Mr. Remmers directing the details.

### Ninth Run.

Limed to alkalinity in cells; acidified in clarifier with sulphur, and then added about 1¼ lbs. albumen to each clarifier of 350 gallons of juice, heated to 190° Fahr.; shut off steam and neutralised with lime; took off blanket and brushed clean; a very pretty juice was made, though all the albumen failed to dissolve. The process is a slow one and furnishes a large amount of scums and skimmings before cleaning the juice. The following are the results:

| Description. | Total Solids. | Sucrose. | Glucose. | Glucose Ratio. | Purity Co-efficient. | Fibre. |
|---|---|---|---|---|---|---|
| Mill juices | 13·64 | 9·86 | 1·83 | 18·0 | 71·96 | 8·10 |
| Diffusion juices | ... | 7·52 | 1·22 | 16·2 | ... | ... |
| Clarified ,, | ... | 6·68 | 1·13 | 16·9 | ... | ... |
| Syrup | 46·07 | 34·10 | 6·06 | 17·7 | 73·00 | ... |

There were obtained 124 lbs. of chemically pure sugar as firsts, or 71 per cent. of total sugar in the cane. There were 20 lbs. seconds, making a total of 144 lbs., or 82 per cent. of total sugar. The extraction was 88·3 per cent. of the cane.

### Tenth Run.—Nine Tons of Cane used.

Wilcox's process continued. This time no lime was used in the boiling. The raw diffusion juice was sulphured to acidity, 1¼ lbs. albumen, well dissolved, added to each clarifier of 350 gallons, heated to 100° Fahr. and limed to neutrality, took off blanket and brushed. A pretty juice, but was sticky and gummy in the pan and centrifugal. Not as good as method used in ninth run. Following are the results:

| Description. | Total Solids. | Sucrose. | Glucose. | Glucose Ratio. | Purity. Co-efficient. | Fibre. |
|---|---|---|---|---|---|---|
| Mill juices | 13·31 | 18·18 | 1·61 | 16·01 | 76·37 | 9·27 |
| Diffusion juices | ... | 6·00 | 1·11 | 16·09 | ... | ... |
| Clarified ,, | ... | 7·27 | 1·18 | 16·23 | ... | ... |
| Syrup | 49·30 | 36·20 | 6·06 | 16·70 | 73·04 | ... |

117 lbs. chemically pure sugar per ton of cane were obtained as firsts, or 71 per cent. on total sugar present in juice; and 16 lbs. seconds; total, 133 lbs. per ton, or nearly 80 per cent. on total sugar.

### Eleventh Run.—Twelve Tons of Cane used.

On account of failure to meet expectations in run 10, a

return was made to liming in the cell. The alkaline juice was treated in the clarifier to acidity with sulphur and acid phosphate of calcium. The albumen solution added and limed to neutrality. This time a free sugar was made. The following are the results:

| Description. | Total Solids. | Sucrose. | Glucose. | Glucose Ratio. | Purity Co-efficient. | Fibre. |
|---|---|---|---|---|---|---|
| Mill juices | 12·73 | 9·06 | 1·65 | 17·0 | 75·4 | 9·00 |
| Diffusion juices | ... | 6·63 | 1·01 | 15·2 | ... | ... |
| Clarified ,, | ... | 6·53 | 0·98 | 15·0 | ... | ... |
| Syrup | 48·07 | 36·50 | 5·55 | 15·2 | 74·9 | ... |

There were extracted 126 lbs. of chemically pure first sugars per ton out of a total of 171 lbs. in the syrup, or 73 per cent. of sugar present; amount of seconds obtained, 15 lbs.; total, per ton of cane, 141 lbs., or 82 per cent. of sugar present.

Lime, sulphur and acid phosphate of calcium were used with indifferent results in

### Run No. 12.—Eleven Tons of Cane used.

Lime to alkalinity in cells. In clarifier rendered distinctly acid, with sulphur and acid phosphate. Limed again to neutrality and cleaned. Slow work and very indifferent results. The following are the results:

| Description. | Total Solids. | Sucrose. | Glucose. | Glucose Ratio. | Purity Co-efficient. | Fibre. |
|---|---|---|---|---|---|---|
| Mill juices | 13·03 | 9·41 | 1·56 | 16·6 | 72·15 | 9·00 |
| Diffusion juices | ... | 6·28 | 0·93 | 14·7 | ... | ... |
| Clarified ,, | ... | 6·38 | 0·86 | 13·4 | ... | ... |
| Syrup | 47·70 | 34·30 | 5·12 | 14·9 | ... | ... |

There were recovered in first sugars, 126 lbs. chemically pure sugar per ton of cane, out of a total of 164 lbs. in the syrup, or 16 per cent. of total present. The sugar was, however, very indifferent. There were also 14 lbs. seconds, making a total of 140 lbs. or 85 per cent. of total sugars present. This gave the largest yield of sugar during the season, but the sugar was very indifferent and hard to dry—polarising very low.

Sulphate of alumina was used as a reagent in

### Run No. 15.—Eighteen Tons of Cane were used in the Trial.

The sulphate of alumina was kindly furnished by Mr. A. R. Shattuck, of the well-known firm of Shattuck & Hoffmann, who in person witnessed the progress of the experiment until convinced of its inefficacy. This substance was used in many ways. By adding 1¼ lbs. to a clarifier, and neutralising with lime, or reversing, and liming in cells to alkalinity, and then 1¼ lbs. of sulphate of alumina in clarifier. Then both lime and sulphate were increased and reversed, until excessive quantities of each were used. Every attempt to utilise it gave disastrous results. Juice could not be settled; made a poor syrup, which would not *settle*, and occasioned inversion. It was cooked to grain in the pan, and an attempt made to centrifugal it, with disastrous results. It was dumped into cars, and put in the hot room, and after remaining there nine months, on September 9, ineffectual attempts were made by Mr. E. A. Newman, an experienced sugar maker, to dry it in the centrifugal. It would not purge by any methods known to us. As the United States Government required the sugar house to be emptied of sugar and molasses before beginning another campaign, it was put in molasses barrels, and consigned to a commission merchant to do what he could with it.

Besides the above a partial experiment was made with superphosphate of alumina with very unsatisfactory results.

### A Review of Clarifying Agents used.

A clarifying agent to meet public demands, must perform excellent work, and admit of a reasonable amount of expedition in that work. It, too, must be inexpensive. The present low prices of sugars prohibit expenditure of 1 c. in its manufacture that is not absolutely necessary. Lime and sulphur are the great reagents now extensively used in this State. They are both inexpensive, and when properly used make excellent sugars without much loss. Until something equally as inexpensive, and permitting in its use of as rapid work can be found to supplant them, they will doubtless remain, even though the reagents may have superior merits. The first cost and the delay occasioned by its use are inseparable objections to any new reagent, possessing decided merit. Any delay in the march of sugar making means a large expenditure for additional setting and juice tanks or a curtailing of the daily output. Neither of these can at present be done, unless it is unequivocally shown that the reagent is of permanent merit. Unfortunately none of the reagents used can be so classified, and therefore none can be unhesitatingly recommended for general use.

When simply unwashed sugars are made, lime seems to be the only agent needed, especially if the juices are worked as rapidly as they are made, but when white and high-grade yellows are desired, some bleaching agent is needed, which is at present supplied by the use of various kinds of acids or acid salts. Sulphur as at present used not only bleaches but aids in defecation. It acts also as a disinfectant and antiseptic. When properly made, sulphurous acid (for such is the name of the gas of burning sulphur) is the least harmful of the mineral acids, but the following precautions are necessary in its use: See that no sulphuric acid is also formed at the same time, which, if formed, should be speedily removed by well washing the gas with a stream of pure water. Juice, after being sulphured, should not be heated until it is neutralised with lime. Used in this way its injurious effects are reduced to a minimum. Sulphured juices seem always to carry a goodly amount of sulphites and sulphates of lime into the molasses, with exactly what effect on the crystallisation of sugar is as yet undetermined. In the place of sulphur may be used bisulphite of lime, with same chemical results and with the advantage of having the amount used entirely under control. Wilcox's process with albumen showed no special merit, with the decided objection of time required to perform the different operations. The entire sugar house was delayed by its use; it is, therefore, not to be recommended. It made a pretty sugar and a goodly quantity of it, but so did several other methods used, far less difficult to operate, and perhaps less costly.

For diffusion juice coming hot from the battery which takes sulphur with difficulty, the acid phosphate of calcium seems specially adapted. By liming to excess in the cells and neutralising the juices at once in the clarifier with acid phosphate of calcium, excellent results are obtained. In mill houses where sulphuring precedes the lime, the application of acid phosphate is not so easy nor so rapid. It is therefore of doubtful utility in these houses, especially at its present price. With weak diffusion juices it took 3 quarts of 20° of Baume density for 350 gallons. It would require at least 1 gallon for every 300 gallons to 400 gallons of mill juices. A barrel of 50 gallons of this substance, I am told, cost 16 dol., or about 32 c. a gallon. A mill working 100,000 gallons a day would require 300 gallons to 400 gallons or 6 barrels to 8 barrels, or 96 dol. to 128 dol. per day for this special reagent. At these figures, it will be hard to convince our planters that it should supersede our present practices or be a valuable addition to the already existing methods.

The use of alum, sulphate of alumina, and super-phosphate of alumina are from our experience to be strongly condemned, as not only injurious to the juice, but strongly resistant to every effort of rapid settling. They make bright pretty juices when settled, but a large addition must be made to the settling tanks or filter presses of our sugar houses before they can be universally used. Our results are so disastrous as to condemn them in positive terms.

*Fancher and Clarke's Patent.*

Early in the sugar campaign, the station received from a friend in Queensland a letter, enclosing a circular giving "Fancher and Clarke's patented process for the conversion of molasses into sugar." The process consists in reducing the molasses with water and treating it in clarifier with boracic acid and powdered sulphur, thoroughly boiling, then skimming off carefully the scums, sending the latter through filter presses, and the filtered liquor returns to the molasses. This molasses is then mixed with the cane juice. By this process it is claimed that no molasses is made and only sugar is obtained. What becomes of the molasses the patentee sayeth not. To test the question three experiments were made on a small scale.

No. 1. 25 lbs. of molasses, diluted with 19 lbs. of water, and 100 grams of boracic acid, and 50 grams of sulphur added, boiled and skimmed; analysed sample before and after. See analyses.

No. 2. Same, with 100 boracic acid and 100 sulphur.
No. 3. Same, with 150 boracic acid and 100 sulphur.

### ANALYSES.

| Description. | Total Solids. | Sucrose Single. | Sucrose Double. | Glucose. | Glucose Ratio. |
|---|---|---|---|---|---|
| Original molasses | 40·8 | 20·5 | 22·40 | 10·26 | 45·80 |
| No. 1 after treatment | 45·6 | 24·6 | 25·90 | 11·42 | 48·10 |
| ,, 2 ,, | 55·9 | 29·7 | 31·70 | 14·28 | 45·00 |
| ,, 3 ,, | 53·4 | 26·8 | 28·30 | 14·10 | 49·82 |

These three samples were cooked to masse cuite, and 7 lbs. sugar obtained after nine months in hot room.

After a prolonged boiling little or no effect was produced whatever upon the glucose and solids not sugar, the molasses elements, and therefore it was useless to go further with the investigation.

The juice of our canes contains melassigenic elements, which, if not removed, will certainly form molasses. Could some substance be found which would unite with all the solids not sucrose, and precipitate them so that they could be removed, sugar-making would be greatly simplified. But, unfortunately, such a discovery has not yet been made, and to return the molasses to the juice or syrup is simply to temporarily obscure it. It is bound ultimately to reappear, and may in its transit injure the juice syrup.

### Destruction of Glucose.

In the work on the diffusion battery our attention was attracted to the decrease in the glucose ratio of the diffusion juice over the mill juice whenever an excess of lime was used in the battery. It has also been noted that in many sugar houses where the so-called neutral but really alkaline juices had been treated, a similar reduction of glucose occurred. Investigations on a small scale showed that either dextrose or lævulose alone or together (as invert sugar, called glucose, in cane juices), when treated with an alkali or alkaline earth was destroyed. Accordingly a number of small experiments in the sugar house were made by treating molasses with an excessive quantity of lime—boiling and brushing. Professors Ross, Wipprecht, and Hutchinson followed us with careful chemical analyses. Second molasses was taken and treated with 1 per cent., 2 per cent., 4 per cent., 6 per cent., and 10 per cent. of lime with following results:—

| Description. | Total Solids. | Sucrose Single. | Sucrose Double. | Glucose. |
|---|---|---|---|---|
| Original molasses | 40·8 | 20·5 | 22·4 | 10·26 |
| Same, with 1 per cent. lime | 43·8 | 23·0 | 23·3 | 8·88 |
| ,, ,, 2 ,, ,, | 45·0 | 25·2 | .. | 7·40 |
| ,, ,, 4 ,, ,, | 43·1 | 23·8 | 23·8 | 4·82 |
| ,, ,, 6 ,, ,, | 46·0 | 22·8 | .. | 2·00 |
| ,, ,, 10 ,, ,, | 49·4 | 23·2 | .. | 1·23 |

Here the glucose had almost disappeared, and repeated analyses showed but a slight difference in the double and single polarisations. The sugar was also determined by inversion and with Fehling's solution and found to corroborate polariscopic tests. The last experiment above was taken into the small vacuum pan to see if our chemical results would be established in the sugar house. Here great difficulties were encountered. Do what we would we could not get the stuff to cook. It was finally withdrawn and acid phosphate of calcium added to precipitate the lime used. An immense precipitate was obtained which contained 18 per cent. sucrose and 1·3 per cent. glucose besides much phosphate of calcium. The filtered liquid, however, after a slight dilution showed only 1·28 per cent. glucose. This liquid was again used in the pan with the hopes it would grain. Failing in this we cooked to string and put in the hot room where it grained very slowly and indifferently.

Encouraged by this small experiment, two gallons each of a second molasses, holding nearly equal quantities of glucose and sucrose, were experimented upon, using the large vacuum pan for work. The glucose was readily destroyed, the lime precipitated with acid phosphate of calcium and filtered, and the filtered liquor sent to the pan to grain. All efforts at graining were abortive—so it was cooked into string, and put in the hot room. On September 12, nine months after, it was centrifugaled, with the following results: 889 lbs. molasses and 135 lbs. sugar, or nearly 1 lb. sugar from a gallon of the original molasses. The sugar is of a good grain, but very dark, and poplarised low.

A sample of masse cuite was taken at the time of discharge and analysed, and found to contain 12 per cent. of glucose, when only a trace had been discovered in the beginning. On trial the masse cuite was found to be quite acid, and glucose had been produced during the boiling under the influence of the acid.

The next day another trial was made with same amount acid phosphate of calcium added to only neutrality. This was sent to vacuum pan, and an entire day consumed in trying to reduce it to masse cuite, without effect. On Christmas Eve at 11 P.M. it was turned out of the pan with only a density of 38 degrees Baume cold, after 15 hours cooking. Analyses showed it to contain a considerable amount of lime, which caused it to roll in waves in the pan, instead of the usual ebullition. Any overlimed juice offers obstacles to rapid cooking and should be avoided. During Christmas holidays our investigations were transferred to the laboratory, where a thorough chemical investigation was made, with following results:

Whenever a solution of glucose, or dextrose, or lævulose is treated with an excess of lime, a darkening of the solution takes place with the conversion of these substances into acids which gradually neutralised the lime until finally, if enough lime be present, the entire glucose is destroyed and there remains in the black solution, soluble salts of lime. These acids have been named glucinic and saccharic, and they form with lime soluble salts. When the lime is precipitated from these solutions, the acids are left in a free state ready to destroy the sucrose whenever heat is applied. Could some way be found to precipitate these acids after precipitating the lime, valuable results could be obtained from this process, but unfortunately the only precipitant of these acids (oxides of mercury) are poisons and can not be used in the arts. In a laboratory experiment, after thoroughly removing the lime with acid phosphate, ammonia was added to neutralise the acids, and the molasses boiled to masse cuite and analysed as follows: Total solids, 87 per cent.; water, 13 per cent.; sucrose, 49 per cent.; lime, 1·46 per cent.; glucose, 4·21 per cent., and solids not sugar, 24 per cent. This failed to granulate. During the process of cooking with lime a large loss of albuminoids took place, which action was plainly discernable by the escape of free ammonia. In the laboratory experiments the albuminoids were reduced from 2·90 per cent. to 0·81 per cent. These experiments are given to the public only to explain chemical and physical phenomena frequently occurring in the sugar house and with no result as yet of their practical use.

### *Experiments in Centrifugaling.*

The following experiments were made to determine the influence of wash water on the centrifugal: The masse cuite had a composition of sucrose, 73·1 per cent.; glucose, 7·69 per cent.; moisture, 9·15 per cent.; solids not sugar, 10·04 per cent.

It was taken hot from the pan and put into a car, and from this weights were taken. This work continued until the masse cuite got so hard that it had to be handled with a spade. Nine different experiments were made, three without any water, and the rest with water varying from 2¼ per cent. to 25 per cent. It was contemplated at the beginning of the experiment to use saturated (white) sugar solutions in different quantities, as with pure water; but before getting to them another influencing factor becomes visible, not counted on in the outset. As we proceeded the masse cuite cooled and became harder, and gave relatively greater yields, until finally, by experiment No. 6, it was revealed that the cold masse cuite, washed with 5 per cent. of water, gave 7·8 per cent. and 5 per cent. more than the unwashed in the beginning of the experiment. It was now apparent that an increase of crystals was taking place with the cooling, and any further experiments with a sugar solution as a wash could not be compared with those made while hot. Accordingly only three more were made, two with same quantity of water, and one without water.

The following are the experiments:

| Number. | Amount Used, masse cuite. | How Treated. | Sugar. | Analyses. | C. P. Sugar. |
|---|---|---|---|---|---|
| | Lbs. | | Lbs. | | |
| 1 | 100 | Without water | 57·01 | 94·0 | 53·76 |
| 2 | 100 | ,, ,, | 60·00 | 90·5 | 54·30 |
| 3 | 100 | With 12½ lbs. water | 40·00 | 97·2 | 38·88 |
| 4 | 100 | ,, 25 ,, ,, | 35·00 | 98·5 | 34·47 |
| 5 | 100 | ,, 2½ ,, ,, | 60·62 | 94·8 | 57·46 |
| 6 | 100 | ,, 5 ,, ,, | 65·00 | 95·2 | 61·88 |
| 7 | 100 | ,, 7½ ,, ,, | 45·60 | 93·8 | 42·76 |
| 8 | 100 | Mixed with 7½ lbs. water before centrifugaling | 55·34 | 95·2 | 52·68 |
| 9 | 100 | Without water | 70·20 | 90·0 | 63·18 |

The centrifugal was taken to pieces and cleaned after each experiment, and in experiments three and four, after the masse cuite was dried and before adding the water, the basket was cleaned, and the subsequent washings caught, weighed and analysed with following results:

No. 3 gave 30·6 lbs. of washings containing 48·2 per cent. sucrose, and 4·48 per cent. glucose.

No. 4 gave 56·2 lbs. of washings containing 48·8 per cent. sucrose, and 4 per cent. glucose; 12½ lbs. water then washed out of the centrifugal, 14·74 lbs. sugar, and 1·37 lbs. glucose, and 25 lbs. water removed 27·42 lbs. sugar and 2·24 lbs. glucose.

From these experiments these conclusions can be drawn:

1. That masse cuite in cooling gives a greater yield in the centrifugal, and suggests the propriety, adopted by many planters, of dropping their masse cuite into waggons and keeping for several hours in the hot room.

2. That mixing the water with masse cuite, before centrifugaling, gives larger yields than using the same amount in the centrifugal.

3. That for every lb. of water used in the centrifugal, more than 1 lb. of sugar is dissolved.

The ash and albuminoids of the mill juices were determined several times during the season, and are here given.

|  | Ash. | Albuminoids. |
|---|---|---|
| Field Experiment 13, Plat III. .. | .. | ·332 |
| ,, ,, 14, ,, ,, .. | ·563 | ·285 |
| ,, ,, 15, ,, ,, .. | ·480 | ·285 |
| ,, ,, 16, ,, ,, .. | ·572 | ·285 |
| ,, ,, 3, ,, IV. .. | .. | ·335 |
| ,, ,, 5, ,, ,, .. | .. | ·396 |
| ,, ,, 7, ,, ,, .. | .. | ·446 |
| ,, ,, 8, ,, ,, .. | .. | ·305 |
| ,, ,, 17, ,, V. .. | ·51 | ·400 |
| ,, ,, 18, ,, ,, .. | ·53 | ·359 |
| ,, ,, 19, ,, ,, .. | ·50 | ·392 |

Experiment 13 above was manured with potash only.

Experiment 14 above was manured with potash and nitrogen.

Experiment 15 above was manured with potash, phosphoric acid and nitrogen.

Experiment 16 above was unmanured.

Experiment 3 above was manured with potash, phosphoric acid and nitrogen.

Experiment 5 above was manured with phosphoric acid only.

Experiment 7 above was manured with phosphoric acid, potash and nitrogen.

Experiment 8 was unmanured.

Experiment 17 above was manured with nitrogen only.

Experiment 18 above was manured with nitrogen and potash.

Experiment 19 above was manured with nitrogen, potash and phosphoric acid.

The object in analysing above was to determine, if possible, the effects of the different ingredients of the fertilisers upon the ash and albuminoids of the juice. An inspection will show that little or no influence was produced by the different fertilisers upon these constituents of the juice.

The final molasses of different runs have been subjected to the following analyses with a view of additional light on the same subject:

## UNITED STATES.

**Analyses of Molasses from Experiment Station Sugar House, 1890.**

| Fertilisers Used in the Field. | Number of Run. | Density by Brix. | Ash. | CaO in Molasses. | CaO in Ash. | P2O5 in Molasses. | P2O5 in Ash. | K2O in Molasses. | K2O in Ash. | Nitrogen in Molasses. | Albuminoids. | Process of Clarification in Sugar House. |
|---|---|---|---|---|---|---|---|---|---|---|---|---|
| Kainite group | 1 | 80·4 | 5·18 | 0·42 | 8·11 | 0·16 | 3·08 | 2·13 | 41·12 | 0·78 | 4·87 | Lime |
| Sulphate potash group | 2 | 73·7 | 3·97 | 0·31 | 7·80 | 0·21 | 5·29 | 1·46 | 36·77 | 0·66 | 4·13 | ,, |
| Muriate potash ,, | 3 | 76·9 | 4·71 | 0·86 | 18·25 | 0·03 | 0·64 | 1·83 | 37·86 | 0·67 | 4·19 | Lime and bisulphite. |
| Soluble phosphate ,, | 5 | 68·0 | 2·71 | 0·26 | 9·59 | 0·06 | 2·21 | 1·00 | 36·90 | 0·59 | 3·69 | ,, ,, acid phosphate. |
| Insoluble phosphate ,, | 6 | 75·7 | 3·17 | 0·49 | 15·45 | 0·18 | 5·67 | 1·27 | 40·00 | 0·69 | 4·39 | ,, ,, sulphur. |
| Organic nitrogen ,, | 8 | 66·4 | 2·93 | 0·54 | 18·43 | 0·12 | 4·08 | 1·32 | 45·05 | 0·75 | 4·69 | ,, ,, |
| Mineral nitrogen ,, | 9 | 74·7 | 3·27 | 0·16 | 4·90 | 0·20 | 6·11 | 1·58 | 48·31 | 8·81 | 5·06 | Wilcox albumen. |

Attention is called to the excessive amounts of lime present in Nos. 3, 6, and 8, where lime and bisulphite, lime and acid phosphate, and lime and sulphur were respectively used in the clarification; also to the increased nitrogen in the Wilcox process.

### Bleaching Molasses.

On January 29, 1891, a firm in Boston wrote to the Department of Agriculture in Washington, complaining bitterly of the practice prevailing in New Orleans of bleaching molasses with chemicals. This letter was sent me by Dr. H. W. Wiley, with the request that I would find out all I could about the matter, particularly their methods of treating and bleaching molasses. Upon the receipt of this letter we started an investigation, and soon found that the R. R. Chemical Company, of New York, were selling compounds for bleaching molasses under the name of "Sulphine" and "Boxyde." Samples of these were obtained and examined, and the following report of Professor B. B. Ross will show how thoroughly the work was performed. These substances are recommended to be used as follows: 3 lbs. sulphine, 3 ozs. boxyde, to 50 gallons of molasses.

### Professor Ross' Report.

Samples of the two clarifying agents now largely used in brightening dark molasses, and sold under the name of "sulphine" and "boxyde" respectively, have been recently subjected to a careful analysis in this laboratory, and, in addition, quite a number of practical tests have been made to determine their utility as decolourising agents. The sample marked "boxyde" was found on examination to consist of nearly chemically pure zinc, or "zinc dust," and in making clarification tests the pure zinc dust of the laboratory gave results identical with those obtained by the use of the "boxyde." The sample marked "sulphine" on analysis proved to be a solution of commercial bisulphite of soda, with a small quantity of sulphuric acid.

### ANALYSES of Sulphine.

|  | Per Cent. |
|---|---|
| Sulphurous acid | 21·25 |
| Sulphuric „ | 0·93 |
| Chlorine | 0·15 |
| Soda | 10·43 |
| Sodium bisulphite | 34·53 |

Quite a number of tests with molasses were made with the use of the "sulphine" alone, but in no instance was the clarification as good as where zinc was used in addition. In several tests, finely pulverised iron filings were used as a substitute for the "boxyde," but the results obtained by it were lacking in uniformity. Two or three clarifications with the use of "sulphine" and iron were extremely good, but the length of time consumed in securing a clear liquid was very considerable, and on some subsequent tests made with other samples of molasses, the brightening effects were not nearly so apparent. It was found by quite a number of experiments that sodium bisulphate and zinc dust gave a clarification fully as good as that secured by the bisulphite and zinc, and that the sediment settled with equal rapidity.

Sodium sulphate, with a very small quantity of very dilute sulphuric acid (not enough to correspond to the acidity of the bisulphate used in the test above-mentioned) together with zinc dust, gave a very clear solution, fully equal in brightness to the bisulphate test. With sodium sulphite substituted for the sulphate, and with the addition of sulphuric acid and zinc dust as before, the degree of brightness secured was greater than that obtained by any other method, and this brightening also took place more rapidly. Dilute sulphuric acid and zinc, when used in the absence of the salts just named, gave in some experiments a very fair clarification, and in others only a moderate brightening was produced.

The samples brightened by the use of the "sulphine" gave quite a considerable reaction for sulphuric acid when tested, showing that, as might be presumed, the bleaching was accomplished by reduction, the sulphurous acid taking up oxygen from the colouring matters of the syrup and being converted into sulphuric acid.

The function of the zinc is also essentially that of a reducing agent, being especially active in the presence of free acids or of salts having an acid reaction, and in its use, in conjunction with "sulphine," appears merely to reinforce the reducing influence of the latter substance. The samples of molasses, brightened by these agents, when diluted with water and exposed to the air, commenced darkening from the surface downward, confirming, by the restoration of colour by the oxygen of the air, the presumption that the bleaching was due exclusively to reduction. Other reducing agents, including several metallic sulphides were used in the place of zinc dust in conjunction with the "sulphine," but no satisfactory results followed the use of any of these substitutes. The superior reducing properties of zinc dust have long been utilised in the laboratory in the removal of oxygen from the most thoroughly oxidised substances, and it will be difficult to find a solid substance more active in producing these effects than zinc.

With this report before them, the planters can, if they wish, bleach their own goods. I see no reason why they should not reap the profit now going to the middle men.

Annex C.—REPORT OF THE STATE EXPERIMENT STATION AT BATON ROUGE, 1890.

In pursuance with the lines already mapped out in former bulletins this station has devoted its time, first, to a study of the principal farm products of this neighbourhood—the chief ones of which are cotton and corn; second, to determining the adaptability and value of new crops to this section; and third, to the relative merits of different breeds of live stock for this locality.

Under the first head the experiments have been of three kinds: 1st. An investigation of the merits of the different varieties of seed. The next subject of investigation was the manurial requirements of these crops on this soil, embracing the subjects of both kind and quantity that is best applied. Then the physiological questions of distance, &c., are of no small consequence, and these also received their share of attention.

### Corn.

In this report the experiments in corn will be first treated of, and these will be introduced by the study of the

### Varieties.

On March 17, the land being thoroughly prepared, 12 varieties of corn were planted. The beds (5 feet apart) were opened with a bull-tongue. In the furrow thus opened were dropped at regular intervals of 2 feet three grains of the variety being planted—there being three rows devoted to each variety. The grain was then carefully covered with a hoe. A seasonable rain brought the crop up very prettily, but unfortunately these rains continued for some time. As soon as the weather permitted this corn (then about 12 inches high) was carefully thinned to one stalk to the hill. The grass, however, had grown rapidly during the rains, and despite all care in removing it the stand was more or less injured. After the corn matured, each variety was carefully gathered and weighed, and the percentages of shuck, cob, and grain determined.

Below is a table giving the results:—

## UNITED STATES.

### Varieties of Corn.

| Name. | Yield per acre. Corn in the shuck. | Yield per acre. Grain. | Per cent. Shuck. | Per cent. Cob. | Per cent. Grain. |
|---|---|---|---|---|---|
|  | Lbs. | Bushels. |  |  |  |
| White St. Charles | 2,622 | 36·8 | 8·1 | 13·1 | 78·8 |
| *Golden Beauty | 965 | .. | .. | .. | .. |
| Blount's Prolific | 3,397 | 45·6 | 9·9 | 16·6 | 74·5 |
| Champion White Pearl | 2,302 | 31·2 | 8·2 | 15·4 | 76·4 |
| Mosby's | 4,172 | 58·9 | 6·6 | 14·2 | 79·2 |
| Young's Hybrid | 3,648 | 46·0 | 14·1 | 14·9 | 70·8 |
| Hickory King | 2,280 | 31·6 | 10·3 | 12·0 | 77·7 |
| McQuade | 3,967 | 53·4 | 10·5 | 14·1 | 75·4 |
| Golden Dent Gourd Seed | 3,522 | 46·9 | 11·6 | 13·8 | 74·6 |
| Improved Leoming | 2,736 | 35·0 | 11·0 | 17·2 | 71·8 |
| *Large White Flint | 989 | .. | .. | .. | .. |
| Brazilian Flower | 1,696 | 23·5 | 5·8 | 15·9 | 78·3 |

\* So badly weevil eaten when gathered that the percentages could not be determined.

By an examination of this table it will be seen that Mosby, McQuade, Golden Dent, Young's Hybrid, and Blount's Prolific lead the list in the order named. During 3 years' test the Mosby, Blount's Prolific, and McQuade have been among the first, thus showing themselves to be good. The Golden Dent and Young's Hybrid are new corns to us, but both bear high recommendations for favour. Especially is this the case with the former, as it is at least 2 weeks earlier than any of its rivals. Another corn whose earliness recommends it, though not among the largest yielders, is the Improved Leoming. The low yields of Golden Beauty and Large White Flint are partially accounted for by the fact that, though gathered as early as possible, they were almost totally destroyed by weevils—hence no determination could be made of the relations between shuck, cob, and grain.

While examining the results, it is well for those at a distance to remember that they can only be taken for these conditions of climate and soil. All plants are sensitive to a change in these conditions, and none more so than corn.

### Manurial Experiments in Corn.

Plats 9, 10, and 11 were devoted to the question of the best kinds and quantities of fertiliser for corn. The question "Does this soil need potash, phosphorous acid, or nitrogen to grow corn, and if so, in what form and quantity are they needed?" was put to each plat. All the experiments were planted March 6,

## NEW ORLEANS.

with Red Cob Gourd Seed corn. On March 27, the stand being very poor, this was ploughed up and replanted with a nondescript corn, the only seed we then had. Even then a poor stand was obtained. The following table gives the fertilisation and yield per acre:—

### Corn.—Plat 9.—Potash.

| Number of Experiment. | How Fertilised. | Yield per acre. Shuck corn. | Grain. |
|---|---|---|---|
| | | Lbs. | Bushels. |
| 1 | Meal phosphate, *168 lbs. kainite | 2,968 | 39·7 |
| 2 | ,, 336 lbs. kainite | 3,808 | 50·9 |
| 3 | ,, | 3,684 | 49·3 |
| 4 | ,, 42 lbs. muriate potash | 3,864 | 51·7 |
| 5 | ,, 84 ,, ,, | 3,804 | 50·9 |
| 6 | ,, | 3,684 | 49·3 |
| 7 | Nothing | 2,968 | 39·7 |
| 8 | Meal phosphate, 42 lbs. sulphate potash | 3,852 | 51·1 |
| 9 | ,, 84 ,, ,, | 3,524 | 47·1 |
| 10 | ,, | 3,920 | 52·4 |
| 11 | 280 lbs. acid phosphate, 196 lbs. cotton seed meal, 49 lbs. nitrate potash | 3,684 | 49·3 |
| 12 | 280 lbs. acid phosphate, 84 lbs. cotton seed meal, 98 lbs. nitrate potash | 3,864 | 51·7 |

\* Meal phosphate—280 lbs. cotton seed meal.
280 lbs. acid phosphate.

### Corn.—Plat 10.—Phosphoric Acid.

| Number of Experiment. | How Fertilised. | Yield per Acre. Shuck Corn. | Grain. |
|---|---|---|---|
| | | Lbs. | Bushels. |
| 1 | Basal mixture,* 280 lbs. dissolved bone | 3,080 | 41·1 |
| 2 | ,, 560 ,, ,, | 3,472 | 46·5 |
| 3 | ,, | 3,080 | 41·1 |
| 4 | ,, 280 lbs. acid phosphate | 3,864 | 51·7 |
| 5 | ,, 560 ,, ,, | 3,808 | 51·0 |
| 6 | ,, | 3,640 | 48·7 |
| 7 | Nothing | 2,912 | 39·0 |
| 8 | Basal mixture, 280 lbs. bone meal | 3,864 | 51·7 |
| 9 | ,, 560 ,, ,, | 3,752 | 50·2 |
| 10 | ,, | 3,528 | 47·2 |
| 11 | ,, 140 lbs. gypsum | 3,292 | 44·0 |
| 12 | ,, 280 ,, ,, | 3,080 | 41·1 |

\* Basal mixture—280 lbs. cotton-seed meal.
347·2 lbs. kainite.

## UNITED STATES.

### Corn.—Plat 11.—Nitrogen.

| Number of Experiment. | How Fertilised. | Yield Per Acre. Shuck Corn. Lbs. | Grain. Bushels. |
|---|---|---|---|
| 1 | Mixed minerals,* 79·8 lbs. nitrate soda | 2,912 | 39·0 |
| 2 | ,,                159·6 ,,     ,, | 3,696 | 49·5 |
| 3 | ,,                 53·2 ,, sulphate ammonia | 3,304 | 44·2 |
| 4 | ,,                106·4 ,,     ,, | 3,808 | 51·0 |
| 5 | ,,                112   ,, dried blood | 3,192 | 42·7 |
| 6 | ,,                224   ,,     ,, | 3,304 | 44·2 |
| 7 | ,,                140   ,, fish scrap | 2,688 | 36·0 |
| 8 | ,,                280   ,,     ,, | 3,416 | 45·6 |
| 9 | ,,                168   ,, cotton-seed meal | 2,800 | 37·5 |
| 10 | ,,               336   ,,     ,, | 3,360 | 45·0 |
| 11 | ,,               504   ,, cotton-seed | 2,800 | 37·5 |
| 12 | ,,             1,008   ,,     ,, | 1,232 | 22·0 |

\* Mixed minerals—280 lbs. acid phosphate.
347·2 lbs. kainite.

From such slight variations in yield it is impossible to draw any conclusions, and hence the questions of form and quantity of fertiliser will have to remain for renewed study. But a careful comparison of the three plats will prove instructive, and results in more than a suspicion that we have found the answer as to the kind of plant food most needed. It will be found that in each plat wherever the fertiliser contains phosphoric acid there is an increase in yield. Did this only occur in a few instances, we would be wary of stating it as a fact, but when it is so universally the case we think we are safe in announcing that the most important element of plant-food on these bluff soils for corn is phosphoric acid. Nor are these results the sole evidence on which this statement is based. It will be remembered by those who have studied the bulletins of this station that, though injured by drought, last year's experiments hinted to us that this was the case. The beneficial effects of the phosphoric acid was very plain upon the growing corn, both last season and this. It is particularly to be regretted that there was so poor a stand this year as the benefits of phosphoric acid would in all probability have been much plainer.

*Physiological Experiments with Corn.*

Plat No. 15 was set aside for this purpose. It is perfectly level, and having been in cotton the year before and been broken up in the fall was in splendid order. It was broken in March 21, with a two-horse sulky plough and harrowed till thoroughly pulverised and level. It was then checked off 3 feet by 4 feet with bull-tongue.

From three to four grains of McQuade's corn were dropped by hand at the intersection of the check, the whole covered with a smoothing harrow and water drains opened all round the edge of the plat. When the corn was about 6 inches high this plat was first divided into two equal parts longitudinally. Each of these parts were in their turn divided equally by an imaginary line running across the plat. The following diagram will illustrate it better.

PLAT 5.
225 Feet.

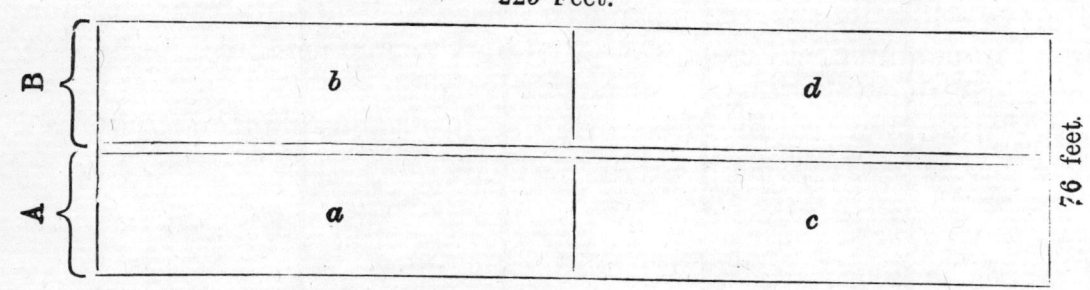

```
     ┌─────────────────────┬─────────────────────┐
B {   │          b          │          d          │
     ├─────────────────────┼─────────────────────┤  76 feet.
A {   │          a          │          c          │
     └─────────────────────┴─────────────────────┘
```

A and B are the first divisions of the plat, a, b, c, and d, subdivisions.

a and b were then thinned by hand to one stalk to hill, c and d to two stalks.

Then a mixture of equal parts of cotton seed meal and acid phosphate was applied to A at the rate of 200 lbs. per acre.

This was dropped by hand at the foot of the corn, and a smoothing harrow run both ways. Three weeks later the harrow was again run through the crop. This was all the cultivation it received.

The questions for solution were:

1st. Will flat cultivation succeed here? Answered by whole plat.

2nd. With flat cultivation, how thick will corn succeed on this soil unfertilised?

3rd. When moderately fertilised?

The following is the yield per acre (in bushels of shelled corn) of the minor plats a, b, c, and d.

    a. Fertilised,   1 stalk to the hill, 42·4 bushels.
    b. Unfertilised, 1   ,,   ,,   ,,   41·7   ,,
    c. Fertilised,   2 stalks   ,,   ,,   63·0   ,,
    d. Unfertilised, 2   ,,   ,,   ,,   65·4   ,,

This has been a very wet season, so the plat undoubtedly answers the question of flat cultivation in the affirmative, at least for that sized field. Two stalks are none too thick for corn planted 3 feet by 4 feet in a wet season. Fertiliser applied after the corn was up at that rate on good land has done no good. This experiment should be closely studied by every farmer, for it not only economises labour, but avoids the tremendous loss caused by careless handling of the hoe.

## Cotton.

Cotton.

This has only been a moderate season for this staple. During early growth excessive rains interfered very seriously with cultivation. Dry weather, however, succeeding this period of rain enabled the plant to catch up with what it had lost, and at one time it looked as though the phenomenal yields of last year would be repeated. Heavy rains again set in, however, causing a great deal of shedding, and where at all thick rotting a great many half matured bolls of the bottom crop. A greater part of this crop was lost by this cause, and the rest was badly injured. When picking commenced, exceptionally fine weather enabled the saving of nearly every lock.

With much trouble the station secured and planted under, as near like conditions as possible, twenty.

## Varieties of Cotton.

Great care was exercised, both in the cultivation and saving of each—all conditions being kept as near the same as possible. After the cotton was all picked, each variety was carefully ginned on a small 20-saw Gullett gin, and the percentages of lint, seed, and motes carefully calculated.

The following table gives results per acre:—

VARIETIES of Cotton.—Plat O.—Yield per Acre.

| Name of Variety. | Seed Cotton, Lbs. ||||  Per Cent. Lint. | Per Cent. Seed. | Per Cent. Trash. | Lbs. Lint per Acre. |
| | 1st Picking. | 2nd Picking. | 3rd Picking. | Total. | | | | |
|---|---|---|---|---|---|---|---|---|
| Allen's Long Staple | 728 | 504 | 224 | 1,456 | 25·00 | 70·00 | 5·00 | 364·0 |
| Peterkin | 560 | 728 | 392 | 1,680 | 25·00 | 70·00 | 5·00 | 420·0 |
| Dickson's Improved | 420 | 616 | 280 | 1,516 | 28·00 | 69·00 | 3·00 | 335·4 |
| Bolivar-County | 616 | 672 | .. | 1,288 | 29·41 | 69·11 | 1·58 | 378·8 |
| Peerless | 672 | 504 | 28 | 1,204 | 32·50 | 66·00 | 1·50 | 391·3 |
| Petit Gulf | 532 | 560 | 252 | 1,344 | 30·76 | 67·30 | 1·94 | 413·4 |
| Mexican | 476 | 588 | 280 | 1,244 | 27·50 | 69·64 | 2·86 | 331·1 |
| Ellsworth | 378 | 378 | 42 | 798 | .. | .. | .. | .. |
| Fishburn | 252 | 672 | 252 | 1,176 | .. | .. | .. | .. |
| Boyd's | 672 | 448 | 168 | 1,288 | 30·00 | 67·50 | 2·50 | 386·4 |
| W. J. Cook | 448 | 420 | 196 | 1,064 | 25·00 | 71·88 | 3·12 | 266·0 |
| T. J. King | 952 | 420 | 28 | 1,400 | 32·50 | 65·00 | 2·50 | 455·0 |
| Haggerman | 560 | 896 | 728 | 2,184 | 29·31 | 68·10 | 2·59 | 640·1 |
| Southern Hope | 504 | 896 | 728 | 2,128 | 27·50 | 70·00 | 2·50 | 581·2 |
| Texas Storm and Drouth Proof | 196 | 588 | 560 | 1,344 | 33·33 | 64·28 | 2·39 | 448·0 |
| Okra | 840 | 728 | 196 | 1,760 | 31·70 | 67·07 | 1·23 | 557·9 |
| Welbon's Pet | 784 | 952 | 364 | 2,100 | 29·00 | 70·00 | 1·00 | 609·0 |
| Hawkins | 140 | 700 | 728 | 1,568 | 32·35 | 65·00 | 2·65 | 507·2 |
| Herlong | 224 | 840 | 672 | 1,736 | 30·95 | 67·15 | 1·90 | 537·2 |
| Little Brannon | 462 | 546 | 616 | 1,624 | 29·31 | 68·10 | 2·59 | 475·9 |

It will be noticed that the percentages are far below those of last year. This was so marked upon the first determination, that, for fear that from some unknown cause the tests were not reliable, the work was done again. This second determination only corroborated the first; hence we are forced to the conclusion that the low percentages are due to the climatic conditions of this season. A comparison, therefore, on this season's work would scarcely be just.

By an inspection of the first three columns of the above table, however, some idea of the merits of the various cottons as regards earliness may be formed. The Bolivar County, Peerless, Ellsworth, and T. J. King had virtually matured all their crop by the time of the second picking. Next came Allen, Peerless, Boyd's and Okra, with 50 per cent. and so on down, while Hawkins does not open the majority of its crop until the last.

*Experiments in Fertilising Cotton.*

Very near the same experiments were made with cotton as with corn, the difference being that in the nitrogen and phosphoric acid plats a greater variety of substances was used.

In plat 12 it was endeavoured to obtain answers to the questions: Does this soil need nitrogen? If so, in what form and quantity is that ingredient best supplied? The following table gives the experiments with their results:

## NEW ORLEANS.

### COTTON.—Plat 12.—Nitrogen.

| Number of Experiment. | How Fertilised. | Yield per Acre. Seed Cotton. Lbs. | Lint. Lbs. |
|---|---|---|---|
| 1 | Mixed minerals,* 79·8 lbs. nitrate soda | 2,346 | 782 |
| 2 | ,,    ,,    159·6 ,,    ,, | 2,534 | 844 |
| 3 | ,,    ,,    53·2 ,, sulphate ammonia | 2,184 | 728 |
| 4 | ,,    ,,    106·4 ,,    ,, | 2,346 | 782 |
| 5 | ,,    ,, | 2,374 | 791 |
| 6 | Nothing | 1,554 | 518 |
| 7 | Mixed minerals, 112 lbs. dried blood | 2,240 | 746 |
| 8 | ,,    ,,    224 ,,    ,, | 2,128 | 709 |
| 9 | ,,    ,,    140 ,, fish scrap | 2,366 | 788 |
| 10 | ,,    ,,    280 ,,    ,, | 2,296 | 798 |
| 11 | ,,    ,, | 2,170 | 723 |
| 12 | Nothing | 1,274 | 424 |
| 13 | Mixed minerals, 168 lbs. cotton-seed meal | 2,030 | 673 |
| 14 | ,,    ,,    336 ,,    ,, | 2,520 | 840 |
| 15 | ,,    ,,    504 ,, cotton-seed | 2,240 | 746 |
| 16 | ,,    ,,    1,008 ,,    ,, | 2,198 | 732 |
| 17 | ,,    ,, | 1,946 | 642 |
| 18 | Nothing | 997 | 332 |

\* Mixed Minerals—280 lbs. acid phosphate.
347·20 lbs. kainite.

A study of this table will show that no positive answers can be drawn from it. The results of experiments 2 and 14, however, would seem to indicate that nitrogen in the forms of nitrate of soda and cotton seed meal in large quantities does yield some benefit. We are the more willing to attribute the increase in experiment No. 2 to the nitrate of soda, since the yield of last year was similar. This experiment leading all the others in both years. With these two exceptions there is very little to be said of the benefits of nitrogen, for it will be seen that "mixed minerals" in which this substance was totally wanting compares very favourably with all its nitrogenous competitors.

Plat No. 13 was devoted to phosphatic fertilisers.

The following table gives results:

### Cotton.—Plat 13.—Phosphoric Acid.

| Number of Experiment. | How Fertilised. | Yield per Acre. Seed Cotton. | Lint. |
|---|---|---|---|
| | | Lbs. | Lbs. |
| 1 | Basal mixture,* 280 lbs. dissolved bone.. .. | 1,610 | 533 |
| 2 | „ 560 „ „ .. .. | 2,184 | 728 |
| 3 | „ 280 „ acid phosphate.. .. | 2,294 | 764 |
| 4 | „ 560 „ „ .. .. | 2,464 | 821 |
| 5 | „ .. .. .. .. .. | 2,198 | 732 |
| 6 | Nothing .. .. .. .. .. .. | 1,120 | 373 |
| 7 | Basal mixture, 280 lbs. reverted dissolved bone | 2,338 | 779 |
| 8 | „ 560 „ „ „ | 2,058 | 686 |
| 9 | „ 280 „ „ acid phosphate | 2,240 | 746 |
| 10 | „ 560 „ „ „ | 2,156 | 715 |
| 11 | „ .. .. .. .. .. | 1,834 | 611 |
| 12 | Nothing .. .. .. .. .. .. | 1,624 | 541 |
| 13 | Basal mixture, 280 lbs. bone meal .. .. | 1,984 | 661 |
| 14 | „ 560 „ „ .. .. | 2,282 | 760 |
| 15 | „ 140 „ gypsum .. .. .. | 2,184 | 728 |
| 16 | „ 280 „ „ .. .. .. | 1,946 | 648 |
| 17 | „ .. .. .. .. .. | 1,862 | 620 |
| 18 | Nothing .. .. .. .. .. .. | 1,667 | 555 |

\* Basal Mixture, 280 lbs. cotton-seed meal, 347·2 lbs. kainite.

Here, too, the yields are so nearly alike that conclusions as to form and quantity would not be reliable. In only one instance (see experiment No. 4) has there been any marked increase over other experiments containing phosphoric acid. This would seem to argue that phosphoric acid in the form of acid phosphate is best. If such were a fact, experiment No. 3, where half the quantity of acid phosphate was used, should give the next largest yield. This, however, is not the case; hence the increased yield of No. 4 is probably more due to some slight difference of conditions, such as a greater fertility of soil, or a better stand, than to any particular benefit of acid phosphate.

An examination of the whole plat, however, will lead to very near the same conclusion (though not so plain) as was arrived at with corn, *i.e.*, that phosphoric acid in some form is greatly needed on this soil. As with corn so here the presence of phosphoric acid always insures an increased yield. This is not only the case in this plat, but also in those of nitrogen and potash.

### Plat 14.—*Potash.*

At first glance at these results, and indeed after a close study, one, who was not acquainted with the circumstances, would pronounce that potash was most decidedly beneficial. This, however, is not necessarily the case. Although experiments Nos. 5, 6, 11 and

12, where potash is absent, are much lower than their neighbours, this falling-off is easily accounted for by the fact that these four were badly attacked by blight early in the season, while the others were comparatively free from it. Might not the presence of potash have acted as a germicide to prevent this disease? This is only a question that arises, but one which we are not prepared to answer. It is probably not so, as from all investigations on the subject, and from our own observations, we are strongly inclined to attribute this disease to excessive moisture rather than to any inherent defect in the soil. These figures, however, are worthy of remembrance in investigations on this subject. Annexed we give the results of these experiments:

COTTON.—Plat 14.—Potash.

| Number of Experiment. | How Fertilised. | Yield per Acre. Seed Cotton. | Lint. |
|---|---|---|---|
| | | Lbs. | Lbs. |
| 1 | Meal phosphate,* 168 lbs. kainite | 1,792 | 597 |
| 2 | ,, 336 ,, ,, | 2,176 | 725 |
| 3 | ,, 42 ,, muriate potash | 2,114 | 704 |
| 4 | ,, 84 ,, ,, | 2,100 | 700 |
| 5 | ,, | 1,484 | 494 |
| 6 | Nothing | 1,288 | 429 |
| 7 | Meal phosphate, 42 lbs. sulphate potash.. | 1,638 | 546 |
| 8 | ,, 84 ,, ,, | 2,254 | 751 |
| 9 | 196 lbs. cotton seed meal, 280 lbs. acid phosphate, 49 lbs. nitrate potash | 2,436 | 812 |
| 10 | 84 lbs. cotton seed meal, 280 lbs. acid phosphate, 98 lbs. nitrate potash | 2,534 | 844 |
| 11 | Meal phosphate | 1,456 | 485 |
| 12 | Nothing | 1,274 | 424 |

\* Meal phosphate.—280 lbs. cotton seed meal.
280 lbs. acid phosphate.

*Forage Crops.*

It is too often the custom, when corn is a little past the milk, to go through the fields and strip the leaves from the stalk and save them as fodder. This is a pernicious practice, for not only is the expense greater than the stuff is worth, but by so doing the yield of grain is materially lessened. There are a great many plants that make far better forage than these dried corn leaves, and that can be raised and saved at much less cost.

With a view of determining those of this class (forage crops) best suited to this locality the following were planted:—

Yellow Millo Maize—A large, tall, thick foliage plant, readily eaten by stock, both green and after curing. Requires from six to eight hours sun to cure. Yielded 19·38 tons of dry forage per acre. The stand was very poor.

Pearl Millet—Familiarly known as cat-tail, horse and Egyptian millet. Furnishes a large amount of green food, but does not make good fodder. Can be cut several times in a year.

Soja Bean—A short woody plant, bearing a tremendous amount of short, flat, poorly filled pods. The beans are small and round and very hard. Has never proved of much value here.

Conch Pea—This is of the same class as the "clay pea." It has a much smaller vine and is a great vine producer. It is said that one quart of these peas when planted will produce enough vines to cover an acre of ground. The vines are easily cured into an excellent hay.

Hungarian grass—Planted May 16, cut June 30; yielded 2,644 lbs. per acre of an excellent hay. One to two hours' sun is plenty for the purpose of curing. German Millet—Planted May 16; cut July 4; yielded 3,746 lbs. of good hay per acre. Golden Millet—Planted May 16; cut July 4; giving a yield of 3,282 lbs. per acre.

Particular attention is called to these plants. In this climate where rain is such a bane to the hay makers' existence, a plant that cures so rapidly is particularly valuable. None of these required more than four hours' sun, and the product was a good yield of very excellent hay, as the following analyses show:—

| Description. | Moisture. | Fat. | Crude Protein. | Crude Fibre. | Carbo-hydrates. | Ash. |
| --- | --- | --- | --- | --- | --- | --- |
| German millet | 6·70 | 2·45 | 7·87 | 30·85 | 43·53 | 8·60 |
| Golden ,, | 6·52 | 3·75 | 7·50 | 31·95 | 41·53 | 8·75 |
| Hungarian grass | 10·22 | 2·92 | 8·75 | 25·90 | 40·51 | 11·70 |

Besides the above there were planted patches of white, blue, and yellow lupins, and silver hulled, early Japanese and common buckwheat. The lupins were a total failure from incipiency. The buckwheats grew well and to the eye promised fine yields. When cut, however, there was not a grain of fruit—the copious rains having caused a good growth of plant, but prevented the formation of fruit.

*Grasses.*

Besides the above, plats of one-fourth acre were, on February 10, planted with the following grasses and clovers:—Kentucky blue, "poa pratensis"; rescue, "bromus shaderi"; red top, "agrostis vulgaris"; orchard, "dactylis glomerata"; tall meadow oat, "arrhenatherum avenaceum"; of grasses and of clovers, crimson, "trifolium incarnatum"; alsike, "T. hybridum"; red,

"T. pratense"; and burr, "medicago maculata." Owing to the long period of dry weather succeeding their planting these were a total failure. A patch of perennial rye, "lolium perenne," planted two weeks later, was more fortunate. This formed a beautiful bed until finally choked out by native "crab" grass.

Early this fall this native grass was closely cut and removed in hopes that, it being a perennial, its roots would have survived the summer and put out again. So far, however, not a blade has appeared, and it is more than probable that it is completely killed. These grasses were all replanted this fall with better fortune, and are all now up and growing nicely. The results will be given later in a bulletin on grasses and hay.

There were also planted small plats of a large number of other grasses, all of which met with the same fate as the larger ones, i.e. failed to germinate. They were, therefore, replanted this fall, and are now up and growing nicely. The following is a list of them:—

Alfalfa, "medicago sativa"; red clover, "T. pratense"; alsike clover, "T. hybridum"; Bokhara clover, "melilotus alba"; burr clover, "medicago maculata"; crimson clover, "T. incarnatum"; esparsette, "hedysarum onobichis"; Timothy, "phleum pratense"; Kentucky blue, "poa pratensis"; red top, "agrostis vulgaris"; vetch, "vicia sativa"; crested dog tail, "cynosurus cristatus"; tall oat, "arrhenatherum avenaceum"; orchard, "dactylis glomarata"; meadow fescue, "festuca pratensis"; rough stalked meadow, "poa nemoralis"; meadow soft, "holcus lanatus;" meadow fox tail, "alopecurus pratensis"; hard fescue, "festuca duriuscula"; sheeps fescue. "festuca ovina"; Italian rye, "lolium perenne"; rescue, "bromus shaderi"; Texas blue grass, "poa arachnifera"; Para grass, "panicum borbonode."

Of these the two last have been grown on the station for the last three years. They seem to be the only grasses yet tried that are able to survive our warm summers and native grasses. The Texas blue grass has recommended itself, particularly as it makes an excellent winter pasture. The Para grass is rather too course to be of much value, besides it is a summer grass, and we already have a number of natives its superior.

The following oats and wheats are also now growing nicely:—

Welcome oats, black Russian oats, golden cross wheat, Everitt's high grade wheat, Fulcaster wheat, hybrid Mediterranean wheat, German amber wheat, Martin's amber wheat, fultz wheat, early red clawson wheat.

*Fruit, &c.*

It was expected and hoped that we would be able in this bulletin to give a good report from the fine orchard. A very unexpected and unseasonable frost on March 1, after the trees were in full bloom, blasted all such hopes. We were more fortunate than many, however, for only two trees were killed.

## UNITED STATES.

Though not killed, they were all severely injured, and it required most of the growing season to enable them to recuperate. The same was the case with the smaller fruits, strawberries, raspberries and blackberries.

The grapes had also started growth when caught by the frost. Though the injury to them was not as great as to the other fruits, yet when combined with the excessive rains of the late spring the two were sufficient to make this crop a failure also. Indeed, some of the less hardy varieties have completely succumbed.

### Sugar Cane.

**Sugar cane.** The following are the analyses of 25 varieties of sugar cane grown on the station this year:—

ANALYSES of Varieties of Cane Grown on State Experiment Station, Baton Rouge, La., 1890.

| Variety. | Total Solids. | Sucrose. | Glucose. | Solids not Sugar. |
|---|---|---|---|---|
| Purple | 15·0 | 12·1 | 2·65 | 0·25 |
| Striped Mexican | 16·0 | 12·4 | 2·00 | 1·60 |
| Rose Bamboo | 12·8 | 9·9 | 2·77 | 0·13 |
| Hanuala | 12·4 | 7·4 | 2·94 | 2·06 |
| Ohia | 13·1 | 8·1 | 4·07 | 0·93 |
| Papaa | 12·6 | 7·3 | 4·24 | 1·06 |
| Otaheite | 14·4 | 8·7 | 4·24 | 1·46 |
| Kokea | 13·5 | 9·5 | 3·41 | 0·59 |
| Lahaina | 13·3 | 8·7 | 3·65 | 0·95 |
| Akiolo | 13·8 | 7·8 | 5·04 | 0·96 |
| Ainakea | 12·4 | 7·4 | 4·66 | 0·34 |
| Crystallina | 16·5 | 12·9 | 3·21 | 0·39 |
| Yellow | 14·1 | 9·3 | 3·12 | 1·68 |
| Kanio | 9·9 | 3·0 | 5·70 | 1·20 |
| Cavengerie | 11·0 | 6·0 | 4·07 | 0·93 |
| Loucier (No. 1) | 14·0 | 8·7 | 4·68 | 0·62 |
| Green | 14·0 | 9·0 | 3·03 | 1·97 |
| Bourbon | 14·5 | 11·3 | 2·04 | 1·16 |
| Black Java | 15·5 | 12·9 | 1·73 | 0·87 |
| Portier | 13·4 | 9·1 | 2·69 | 1·61 |
| Blanca d' Otaheite | 13·5 | 8·5 | 4·08 | 0·92 |
| Loucier (No. 2) | 12·5 | 7·6 | 3·92 | 0·98 |
| Japanese | 15·1 | 9·0 | 3·29 | 2·81 |

These analyses are quite low, but this is easily accounted for by the fact that these are all foreign varieties and are now undergoing a process of acclimation. After this process is completed some of these may prove very valuable as sugar producers.

### Live Stock.

**Live stock.** The live stock of the station consists of a herd of Holstein cattle, composed of a male, Horace Southland, four years old, and three females, *i.e.*, a full-grown cow, "Sophia D," a two-year old heifer, "Ada," and a nine months' old calf, "Bessie."

A herd of Jersey's, namely: One male, Prince of Baton Rouge, and "Princess of Beechwood," three years old, "Loucretia S" (this animal has just been sold to Mr. Henry McCall of Donaldsonville, La.), 21 months old, and a ten days old heifer calf.

The object of these cattle is to test their adaptability to this soil and climate. They have both done well. A sick animal has not been known amongst them.

"Sophia D," the Holstein cow, has given with her last calf, dropped October 15, six gallons of milk per day, from which was obtained $1\frac{1}{4}$ lbs. of butter. "Princess of Beechwood" has just dropped her third calf, and so far no tests have been made with her. With her last calf she gave three gallons per day, this also yielding $1\frac{1}{4}$ lbs. of butter.

The Holstein heifer "Ada" gave birth to her first calf at the unusually (for this large breed) early age of 17 months. Owing to her youth no tests have been made with her. She gives promise of being a deep, long milker.

These are all the animals at the pail. The station also has a three months old calf, the son of "Sophia D." This was not mentioned in the above list, as it has already been sold. Perhaps a word as to the method of raising these calves would not be amiss.

It is generally the custom to allow the calf to run with its mother, *i.e.*, to draw the milk from its mother's udder. This is, to say the least, poor economy, and should never be tolerated where the animals are kept for the money to be made from their milk.

In well regulated dairies a few hours after birth the calf is removed from its mother and never sees her to know her again. It should be given its mother's milk for the first week or so; a few days of patience is all that is required to teach it to eat. This is done by the feeder allowing it to suck the two fingers, they being immersed in milk. After a few lessons the calf will forget the fingers and drink the milk from the pan. All trouble is then over. For the first month it should have pure milk. This can then be gradually changed to skim milk, with a little bran stirred in. Gradually increase the bran, and if the animal has a tender green pasture by the time it is four months old, the milk can be entirely stopped. Thus it is seen there is a great saving of milk, besides there is a tremendous saving in worry. The roping of the calf and pulling him away, and the repetition of this operation two or three times during the process of milking to make the cow "let down" her milk are familiar scenes to all. Then, how often when we find no milk at the table are we met with the answer that "the cow and calf got together." All of this is avoided by removing the calf. Nor does the calf suffer, but, on the contrary, when properly fed, seems to thrive better.

Those who try this method once never return to the other. A word of warning, however, is perhaps necessary. When this method is practised, be careful to milk the cow dry. Unless this is done there is great risk of spoiling the bag. In the event the bag does not spoil there is a loss, for Dame Nature is economical and only supplies what is needed. Unless all the milk is removed, by just so much as is left will the future supply be diminished. For this reason a cow should always be milked at least twice a day.

The bulls are both fine specimens of their breed. They are allowed to serve other cattle for the moderate charge of 5 dol.

As to which breed is the best is a question we are not prepared to answer. Both have their admirers. This is a question that the embryo breeder will have to determine for himself, as it is largely influenced by proximity to market, scarcity or abundance of food, &c.

The Holsteins are large cattle, requiring an abundance of food, but easily fattened, and giving in return an abundance of a moderately rich milk.

The Jerseys are, on the contrary, small, requiring actually a smaller (but relatively larger) amount of food, very difficult to fatten, and giving in return a medium quantity of very rich milk.

If near a market and there is an abundance of feed, then the Holsteins would probably be the best. If, on the other hand, the products of the dairy have to be shipped before finding a market, or if feed be scarce, then wisdom would point to the Jerseys as the proper animal.

### Poultry.

**Poultry.**

The poultry yards were so severely and repeatedly depleted by thieves in the early spring and summer that no data as to the relative merits of the different breeds could be kept. The yards are well stocked now, however, and this spring a close study will be made of them.

The following is a list of breeds on hand:—White Crested Polish, Brown Leghorns, Light Brahmas, Langshans, Black Minorcas, White Plymouth Rocks, Barred Plymouth Rocks, White Minorcas, Partridge Cochins, Buff Cochins, White Wyondott.

### Building and Improvements.

**Building and improvements.**

The building has been of a rather limited amount this year, as nearly all the requisite buildings had been erected in previous years. A small labourer's cabin was erected in May, as much for the protection of the poultry as for the convenience of the labourer. Besides this there was added to the farm residence a back gallery and kitchen, two very much needed improvements, and which make it as comfortable a house as could be wished. Some little additions to the stables to accommodate the increasing number of cattle and a little fencing complete the list.

### Tiling.

The greatest improvement of the year has been in the form of drainage. The average inhabitant of the bottom lands will, no doubt, be surprised that thorough drainage is as necessary to these hill lands as it is to his. To put it a little differently, these hill lands suffer as greatly from excess of moisture as do the bottoms. Convinced of the great benefits of drainage on this soil, the station has put in about five acres of tiling, not only for the purpose of improving that soil, but also to illustrate to the farmers of this section the value of this kind of drainage. The station has not only sought to illustrate the benefits of tile drainage, but is also trying to determine the best depth and distance for placing the tile.

Plats 9, 10, 11, 12, 13, and 14 are devoted to these questions. In plat 9 the 3-inch tiles are placed at an average depth of 3 feet, and are 40 feet apart. In plat 10 the same distance is preserved, but the drains are one-half foot deeper. Again, in plat 11 the distance is the same, but the depth is 4 feet. In plats 12, 13, and 14 this depth is preserved, but the distance varies, being 20 feet in 12, 30 feet in 13, and again 40 feet in 14. These are very important questions in tile drainage, as upon them depend, in a large degree, the cost. Of course, no report can yet be made on this work, as it has not been done long enough to show any very great benefit. Yet the benefits are already perceptible.

Now as to the cost of tile drainage. The 3-inch tile can be bought f.o.b. in New Orleans for 17 dol. per 1,000. The freight per car load lots (18,000 lbs.) to this point is 24 dol., making the drains cost at Baton Rouge 20 dol. per 1,000, or 2 c. a-piece. Mr. Adolph Theil, who did this work, will put down the tile at a charge of 5 dol. 30 c. per string of 210 feet. Now, assuming 40 feet apart to be sufficient, we have the following cost per acre:—

|  | Dol. | c. |
|---|---|---|
| 1,050 tiles at 2 c. | 21 | 00 |
| 5 strings of 210 feet, at 5 dol. 30 c. | 26 | 50 |
| Total | 47 | 50 |

Of course, to this must be added the cost of delivering to the field, and also some little allowance for breakage.

## UNITED STATES.

### Agricultural Report for Mobile for the Year 1891.

#### ABSTRACT of Contents.

|  | PAGE |
|---|---|
| Agricultural advantages of Alabama | 96 |
| Fruit and vegetable culture | 96 |
| Soil and climate | 96 |
| Annex A.—Map of Alabama | 96 |

Mr. Vice-Consul Barnewall reports as follows:—

The promised reports from the Agricultural Department of Alabama for unknown reasons have never been received, in default I inclose some few items culled from the leading papers of the times, mostly from J. P. Still's agricultural articles in the "Mobile Register."

**General agricultural prosperity.** The whole south seems to be on an eve of prosperity never before known in its history: trades are flourishing, industries are developing, and this section is fast assuming commercial proportions on an equality with the east and west.

**Annex A.** The inclosed map of Alabama will give more accurate idea of the resources of the State than the most elaborate description could.

Taken as a whole, no State presents such agricultural advantages. The farmer can find exactly what he wants within its boundaries as well as many things that could not be found further north, should he be a corn and wheat man no better corn and wheat county is known to the world than that of the Tennessee Valley. **Climate and soil.** Hogs, the main stay of the corn grower, are in perfection here, for the mildness of the winter climate necessitating lighter feeding renders this product more profitable than it could be at any point north of the Ohio River.

Then if the taste of the farmer inclines him to grape, wine, or fruit production he can come lower down to the mountain regions and suit himself to perfection. At Culhoun and other points large vineyards yielding wine that is equal to the best are in full blast, while in the high table-lands are flourishing orchards of **Fruit culture.** apples, peaches, pears, plums. This region, though called mountainous, is simply a region of high lands broken here and there by rich valleys, whose productiveness is unequalled: corn, cotton, wheat, rye, oats, barley, sorghum, potatoes, tobacco, rice, and peas flourish in this belt. Those belts already mentioned and others to be named extend entirely across the State from east to west.

**Pine country.** Below the mountain belt sets in a belt of pine country with light soil and gravelly subsoil on the uplands, and very deep and rich soils in the valleys; this is a fair fruit belt and a good cotton, corn, and stock belt.

**"Black belt" for cereals.** Below this comes the black prairies or black belt, the finest corn and cotton belt known to the world—the geological formation is cretaceous, it is literally a chalk foundation, strictly it is an immense marl outcrop—and the yield is tremendous. There is more cotton raised in this belt, as it extends across the Southern

States, than is raised in all the rest of the world together. Clover, millet, corn, grasses, peas of all varieties for forage and ensilage thrive to perfection, rendering it a grand region for the production of stock.

Below the black prairie belt comes a high belt of red land, this has been called peculiarly the fruit region; below this red belt are the lower prairies, a region extremely rich in lime, phosphoric acid, and potash, it is not hilly, it is not prairie, for it is well and heavily timbered, immense deposits of rich marls make up one of its peculiarities, among which are green sand marls identical with the celebrated green sand marls of New Jersey. Hence this region is rich in potash and suited to the raising of the finest tobacco as well as cotton, corn, vegetables, and fruit.

Below the lower prairies sets in the long leaf pine coast belt of Alabama; this soil is light, but responds so well to fertilisers that it is the great truck farming region of America. This interest is still in its infancy, yet Mobile ships 1,000,000 dol. worth of products annually. Commencing at Mobile and extending to the Gulf is an area possessing every characteristic of the cultivation of Sea Island cotton, the most profitable cotton grown.

The climate of the Gulf coast is sub-tropical. The land lies high, as a rule. The formation is what geologists call the orange sand drift; it is not sandy but a clay loam, well watered by cold springs of the purest water.

The attractions and advantages of Alabama are being recognised almost daily, this is shown by the increase of population, as the rates of expansion is greater than at any time in her history. The most rapid increase is in the mining district, although the improvement has been everywhere.

## PENSACOLA.

### Report on Agriculture for the Year 1891.

#### ABSTRACT of Contents.

| | Page |
|---|---|
| Extent of agriculture at Pensacola | 97 |
| Market gardens and gardeners | 98 |
| Fruit culture | 98 |
| Caution as to seeds for planting | 99 |
| Family vegetable gardens | 99 |
| Hints about planting lawns or parks | 100 |
| Grasses | 100 |
| Animals for food | 102 |
| Poultry, eggs, and milk | 103 |

Mr. Vice-Consul Howe reports as follows:—

Agriculture

As remarked before in my reports on agricultural matters at this post, Pensacola is not to any extent an agricultural portion of Florida, the timber industry being almost exclusively followed

98                        UNITED STATES.

Vegetables.

here. However, there are many farms and market gardens at and in the villages around Pensacola which are well managed by thrifty and intelligent agriculturists (among these farmers there are some coloured persons, smaller farmers), which yield paying returns, and these vegetable products—in their ordinary variety for these parts—are abundant to supply the wants of this community (some families have their own kitchen gardens) for everyday table purposes, according to the season for each description.

Interesting to British agriculturist.

In compiling these agricultural reports, which ought to contain particulars that would likely be of utility or interest to British agriculturists generally, I especially endeavour to interest and benefit the agriculturists of those places in the British dominion where the climates are mostly like that of Florida.

Fruits.

The fruits of Florida, in their season, among which are, notably (I will write about the orange below), peaches, pears, plums, figs, grapes, strawberries, &c., are mostly in good supply here in their seasons—in the spring and summer of each year—being largely these fruits, the produce of the same farms and gardens from which the vegetable supplies are reaped.

Moderate cost.

Community supplied at their doors.

All of the products above referred to are, as a rule, to be obtained at moderate cost, in keeping with the periodical yield of the several crops, which is generally good, and peddled about in carts from door to door, as these fruits and vegetables generally are, the wants of the community in this respect are daily and conveniently supplied.

Oranges.

The growth of the orange cannot be positively counted upon at Pensacola the same as most of the other fruits that are cultivated here, affected as it is in the winter months by cold weather, hence the regular gardeners and others here and in the villages around do not plant large groves of orange trees, as is done in other portions of Florida. Some orange trees are cultivated at Pensacola and its surroundings, and the yield is sometimes very good for domestic uses, very few lots of oranges being in the market of this home growth. The supplies of oranges at Pensacola are mostly from other places in Florida, and are always in plenty while the crop is in—from autumn to spring.

Supply at Pensacola.

Large crop.

The orange crop of Florida is very large this year. I see by a publication on the subject that it is estimated at 4,500,000 boxes. It may be of interest to give the following remarks about the successful orange growers, taken from a late number of the New Orleans "Times Democrat":—

"Our neighbours of Florida have raised some 4,500,000 boxes of oranges this year, and will make a handsome profit on the crop.

Good profit.

"Our neighbours of Florida are to be congratulated on a success due to their enterprise and perseverance. The orange crop is a slow one; it takes some years for the tree to grow to maturity and bear fruit, and it requires a great deal of patience to wait, but the Floridians had the proper spirit and won. When the great freeze came a few years ago, destroyed their crops, and injured their trees, it looked as though the industry had received a serious and almost fatal blow, but the orange growers never abandoned hope, and stuck to their groves with the result we now see." *Freezing weather bad for oranges*

The boxes of oranges average 175 each in quantity, and the average wholesale price is 1 dol. 25 c. to 1 dol. 50 c. per box. *Average price per box.*

If our people of the British West Indies would only, in a systematic and business-like way, take hold of the quantities of waste and fertile land in those islands, what a fine business they could build up, what an industry could be added to the present (some drooping) industries of those places, by the extensive cultivation there of oranges. Those climates, soils, and other surroundings are the very best for the growth of the orange, as evidenced by the (limited) quantities of this fruit there now grown. No frosts there to destroy crops, and by no means do any of the obstacles arise there that have to be contended with in Florida, therefore, the orange industry, if regularly gone into in those islands, ought to be, I think, very successful. Shipments would always be made to the near markets of the United States, where this best of all fruits, the orange, would never be in over supply. *Orange culture in British West Indies. Climate and soil good. Could be made very successful. Shipments to United States.*

It may appear to be superfluous to call the attention of agricultural people to the particularity that should be observed in the selection of seeds for planting, but, in many publications on agricultural matters, I observe that advice in this respect is frequently given. Advice like this, at least, is good for non-agriculturists, or amateurs in gardening. "Vegetables of good quality cannot be grown without first sowing reliable seeds. It is exceedingly annoying after ploughing, sowing, and cultivating your garden for an entire season to find that, instead of having spent your time and money profitably, you have lost heavily in obtaining a spurious article. *Gardening, selection of seeds.*

"Seeds, like people, have their peculiarities and different natures, and to know the nature of the various varieties is one of the principles of successful gardening. Some sorts will withstand great moisture, while others will perish. Some are liable to attack of insects and are completely eaten up, while others can withstand such assaults. *Seeds for successful gardening.*

"Sima beans, okra, cucumber, squashes, melons, pumpkins, corn, and wrinkled peas, have very delicate germs, and if a succession of cold wet weather succeed their planting, they will invariably perish in the ground; on the contrary, peas, radish, lettuce, turnip, onion, beet, snap beans, carrot, salsify, and spinach, will withstand quite a spell of such weather; therefore, many failures result from the inexperience of the planter in either selecting an improper time for sowing or in covering small delicate seeds too deep, but when failure arises with a person who is familiar with the sowing of seeds, the reason is invariably because they are worthless from either bad harvesting or too old to grow; the latter is really the principal cause. Good seeds, unlike good wine, are not improved by being aged." *Vegetables. Hints about cultivating.*

**Vegetable gardens.**

A vegetable, or kitchen garden, is an important appendage to a country villa. The lawn is certainly very beautiful with its velvety carpet and graceful trees, and is, without doubt, the most attractive object for any rural home; but the garden from which you draw your daily supply of vegetables is a source of great economy, and the amount thus saved would be a snug fund in a single season.

**Bread-stuffs.**

I am not aware that bread-stuffs are grown in this part of Florida to any extent. I know, however, that a certain species of corn receives much attention, and is used more particularly at table, served up round and tender, and taking its place amongst the vegetables proper. The pods of corn are plucked from the stalk when the corn is young and juicy. The pods are boiled and the corn eaten right from the pods with butter. The pods are also stripped, and the corn used in soups. This is particularly an article of kitchen-garden culture. The planting of this corn commences here in the spring; it is planted in hills, about three feet apart, a shovelful of manure, or a handful of good phosphate should be in each, 5 grains or 6 grains to a hill is sufficient; when up thin them out, allowing those of the strongest plants to remain; thorough cultivation is necessary to secure a good crop. When a succession is required for the table, plant every two weeks until the middle of summer.

**Corn.**

**Species of corn. New England, &c.**

Some of the several species of this corn are:—

"New England eight-rowed early sugar. Unequalled for an early sort; the ears are of large size, has but eight rows, and of delicious quality.

**Egyptian sugar.**

"Egyptian sugar. This is one of the best of the large varieties, of vigorous habit, ears large, having from 12 rows to 15 rows, kernels of good size, and very productive; it is very sweet and tender, and of delicious flavour; invaluable for canning.

**Black Mexican.**

"Black Mexican. A very peculiar looking variety, from its bluish-black grains, but is quite early, and of delicious quality."

**Grass for ornamental use.**

Referring to the cultivation of grass for ornamental use, "When a lawn or park is properly planted the next most important feature is the grass which covers it, for no matter how beautifully a lawn is situated and planted, if it lacks this one requisite it ceases to be attractive, and is like unto a beautiful mansion furnished with rag carpet. To accomplish this pay great attention to the preparation of the soil; in a larger extent of grounds it should be ploughed, sub-soiled, and cross-ploughed, in contracted spaces dug and trenched, the surface properly graded and finely prepared, taking care to collect every weed or root of a weed that can be found. Sow the seed in the month of February, March, or April, with a slight broad casting of oats; and August, September, or October, with a small proportion of rye. What kind of seed to sow is the next question, as all that is called lawn grass seed is by no means the same. To be ignorant of the growth and nature of the various varieties of grass is for the purpose above given, leads into errors that prove ruinous to the lawn, and cause great loss and disappointment.

"After preparing the ground as directed, sow the seed at the rate of 3 bushels to 4 bushels to the acre; cover in with a light seed harrow or thin branches tied together, to serve the purpose of harrowing, and give the whole a light roll with a field or lawn roller. Mow early and mow frequently is the secret of your after success, which gives strength and stability to the sward. During the warm summer months permit the mown grass to remain on the lawn, as it will greatly strengthen the roots, and prevent the young grass from being burnt out. And, as a top dressing or manuring, never use stable manure, as it always contains seeds of weeds, but apply fine bone dust at the rate of 300 cwts. or 400 cwts. per acre, or 200 cwts. of Peruvian guano.

"The lawn mowers in preference to the scythe, as it is not only a source of economy, but a lawn kept shorn with a machine is always more beautiful than one mown with a scythe, as the sod becomes more compact, the surface more even, and the grass more luxuriant."

*Lawn mowers*

I give, as follows, some of the varieties of grass seeds used here for hay and permanent pasture, &c.

For stock feeding the Johnson grass is particularly alluded to in an agricultural publication as follows:—

"Johnson grass ('Sorghum Halapense'). The Johnson grass has become one of the most popular varieties of grasses in the southern States, and is destined to become still more so when better known, it appears to be especially adapted for all tropical climates, as the roots penetrate the soil to a great depth; it is perennial, a rapid grower, very nutritious, being eagerly devoured by all kinds of stock; comes early in the spring, grows until the frost cuts it down in the fall, stands the drought better than any grass, having long cane-like roots, which penetrate the soil for moisture, superior, both as a grazing and hay grass; has abundance of roots which decay, thereby enriching the ground rather than exhausting it as Timothy does; belonging to the Sorghum family, it contains

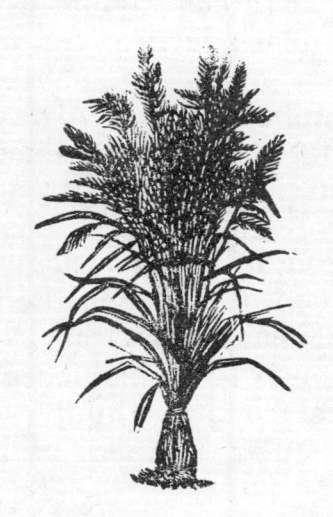

*Johnson grass*

JOHNSON GRASS.

much saccharine matter, which is an important factor in the food of stock. It will grow on any land where corn will grow; on lands that will produce a bale of cotton to the acre, 4 tons to 6 tons of hay can be cut per annum, cutting three or four times. Heavy fertilising would produce greater results. The best results follow sowing the seed in August and September, enabling the seed to get a good root by fall, and forming a better turf the following season. Sow broad coast, with clean seed, at a rate of 1 bushel to the acre, or seed in the chaff at the rate of 2 bushels to the acre, and cover with a light brush, or sow just before a heavy rain. Three good crops the following year will be the result if the season is favourable. Sowing in the spring does well, but the crop would not be as heavy the first year.

*Texas blue grass.* "Texas Blue Grass ('Poa arachonifera'). This variety is destined to become as popular in the south as the Kentucky blue grass is in the north; it is regarded as the best and the earliest spring grass known for that section of the country; the reason of its great success south is on account of the great depth to which its roots penetrate the ground, which supplies the plant with moisture, and enables it to withstand the longest drought. It will not wilt even in the warmest and dryest season. Its greatest period of growth is from the first fall rains in September until the last of May. Its height of growth ranges from $2\frac{1}{2}$ feet to 4 feet; it is a perennial plant, and when once established will last indefinitely. It can be grown from both seed sets, the latter should be planted from early fall until the last of April.

*English perennial rye grass.* "English Perennial Rye Grass ('Lolium Perenne'). A very nutritious and valuable grass for meadows and permanent pastures.

*Red top grass.* "Red Top Grass ('Agrostis vulgaris'). Valuable as a mixture in either pasture or lawn grasses, succeeds well in almost any soil.

*Italian rye grass.* "Italian Rye Grass ('Lolium Italicum'). A valuable European variety, thriving in any soil, and yielding early and abundant crops.

*Sheep's fescue.* "Sheep's Fescue ('Festuca ovina'). Excellent for sheep pastures; is short and dense in growth, making it valuable for grass plots."

*Fresh meat supply.* Animals for food appear to be always in good supply at Pensacola. The chief fresh meat consumed here is beef. Cattle for beef and sheep and hogs for mutton and pork are in fair supply at and in the villages around Pensacola and its vicinity. Texas cattle are also brought here for slaughter.

As a rule it is not considered that the meats here are of best quality. Hogs are not slaughtered at Pensacola except in the winter months. Venison is to be had here in the winter months, secured by the butchers from the hunters in the country places around, who make a regular business of hunting and supplying the deer.

The butchers here, as shown by a regular publication over their signatures, have lately formed a combination, and apparently increased their rates for meats, classifying them as to prices. Amongst the prices for families, hotels, and boarding houses, stevedores, &c., meats for ships are quoted at 12½ c. (6¼d.) per lb. The association of butchers have also advertised that ships will only be supplied in future with meats, vegetables, &c., through a sole agent appointed by them. The trade with the shipping at Pensacola in butchers' meat forms an immense amount per annum expended with the butchers. I have observed that all vessels in the harbour are always kept well supplied with fresh meat and vegetables (the butchers are also greengrocers for the shipping and families). I think this should be so; let the seamen have all of these things in plenty while their vessels are in port.

Sheep raising. While writing this report, I see it announced in the papers here that some new-comers from the Western States have arrived in Pensacola, bringing with them a large number of sheep, with the intention of going regularly into sheep-raising. It is said that they have settled on extensive well-suited lands a few miles from Pensacola. I do not think that the grasses of this soil are calculated for the growth and size of sheep, and quality of their mutton. On this point I may remark that the grasses of the British West India Islands are about the best in the world for sheep-raising.

Poultry and eggs. Poultry and eggs are always in good supply at Pensacola, and are a source of large revenue to those engaged in supplying these things.

Milk. The dairies here supply good milk, which is always in abundance for the wants of the community. The price of milk is not very low—another combination—it having been lately raised from 40 c. to 50 c. (2s. 1d.) per gallon.

(1233)

LONDON:
Printed for Her Majesty's Stationery Office,
By HARRISON AND SONS,
Printers in Ordinary to Her Majesty.
(75  3 | 92—H & S  1233)

# FOREIGN OFFICE.
## 1892.
## ANNUAL SERIES.

### No. 989.

### DIPLOMATIC AND CONSULAR REPORTS ON TRADE AND FINANCE.

# UNITED STATES.

### REPORT FOR THE YEAR 1891
ON THE
### TRADE &c. OF THE CONSULAR DISTRICT OF GALVESTON.

REFERENCE TO PREVIOUS REPORT, Annual Series No. 823.

*Presented to both Houses of Parliament by Command of Her Majesty, MARCH, 1892.*

LONDON:
PRINTED FOR HER MAJESTY'S STATIONERY OFFICE,
BY HARRISON AND SONS, ST. MARTIN'S LANE,
PRINTERS IN ORDINARY TO HER MAJESTY.

And to be purchased, either directly or through any Bookseller, from
EYRE & SPOTTISWOODE, EAST HARDING STREET, FLEET STREET, E.C., and
32, ABINGDON STREET, WESTMINSTER, S.W.; or
JOHN MENZIES & Co., 12, HANOVER STREET, EDINBURGH, and
90, WEST NILE STREET, GLASGOW; or
HODGES, FIGGIS, & Co., 104, GRAFTON STREET, DUBLIN.

1892.

[C. 6550—51.] *Price Three Halfpence.*

## New Series of Reports.

Reports of the Annual Series have been issued from Her Majesty's Diplomatic and Consular Officers at the following places, and may be obtained from the sources indicated on the title-page:—

| No. | | Price. | No. | | Price. |
|---|---|---|---|---|---|
| 869. | Suakin | ½d. | 929. | Constantinople | ½d. |
| 870. | Berlin | 1d. | 930. | Erzeroum | 1½d. |
| 871. | Batoum | 1½d. | 931. | Gothenburg | 2d. |
| 872. | Rosario | ½d. | 932. | Tunis | 1d. |
| 873. | Buenos Ayres | ½d. | 933. | New York | 1d. |
| 874. | Mogador | 1d. | 934. | Nagasaki | 1d. |
| 875. | Tainan | 6½d. | 935. | Hakodate | 1½d. |
| 876. | Pakhoi | 1d. | 936. | Sofia | 3d. |
| 877. | Odessa | 2½d. | 937. | Frankfort | 2d. |
| 878. | Trebizond | 1½d. | 938. | Bangkok | 9d. |
| 879. | Mollendo | ½d. | 939. | Berne | 1½d. |
| 880. | Kiukiang | 1d. | 940. | The Hague | 1½d. |
| 881. | Antananarivo | 1d. | 941. | Christiania | 1d. |
| 882. | Stettin | 2½d. | 942. | Christiania | ½d. |
| 883. | Fiume | 1½d. | 943. | Brunei | 1½d. |
| 884. | Batavia | 1d. | 944. | Alexandria | 1½d. |
| 885. | Samoa | ½d. | 945. | Therapia | ½d. |
| 886. | Cherbourg | 1d. | 946. | Bushire | 1½d. |
| 887. | Cagliari | 1d. | 947. | Tokio | 2d. |
| 888. | Hankow | 1½d. | 948. | Stockholm | 2d. |
| 889. | Vienna | 1½d. | 949. | Palermo | 2½d. |
| 890. | Amoy | 1d. | 950. | St. Petersburg | 2½d. |
| 891. | Adrianople | ½d. | 951. | Quito | ½d. |
| 892. | Chicago | 2½d. | 952. | Rio de Janeiro | 2d. |
| 893. | Brest | 1d. | 953. | Naples | 2d. |
| 894. | Smyrna | 1d. | 954. | Amsterdam | 1d. |
| 895. | Cadiz | 1d. | 955. | Tangier | 2d. |
| 896. | Aleppo | 1d. | 956. | Paramaribo | 1d. |
| 897. | Foochow | 1d. | 957. | Teneriffe | 1d. |
| 898. | Kiungchow | 1d. | 958. | Athens | 2d. |
| 899. | The Hague | 1½d. | 959. | Odessa | 1d. |
| 900. | Nice | 1½d. | 960. | Copenhagen | 9d. |
| 901. | Nantes | 1½d. | 961. | Tokio | 1d. |
| 902. | Port-au-Prince | 1½d. | 962. | Salonica | 1¼d. |
| 903. | Bengazi | 1d. | 963. | Stettin | 3½d. |
| 904. | Tahiti | ½d. | 964. | Philadelphia | 2d. |
| 905. | Chinkiang | 1d. | 965. | Mexico | 2d. |
| 906. | San Francisco | 3d. | 966. | Malaga | 2½d. |
| 907. | Brindisi | 2d. | 967. | Berne | 1d. |
| 908. | Beyrout | 1d. | 968. | Puerto-Rico | ½d. |
| 909. | Noumea | ½d. | 969. | Buda-Pesth | 1d. |
| 910. | San Francisco | 1d. | 970. | Bogotá | 1d. |
| 911. | New York | 1½d. | 971. | Panama | 1½d. |
| 912. | Caracas | 1½d. | 972. | Munich | 2d. |
| 913. | Greytown | ½d. | 973. | Copenhagen | 4d. |
| 914. | Corunna | 2d. | 974. | Guatemala | 1d. |
| 915. | Christiania | 5½d. | 975. | Munich | 2d. |
| 916. | Callao | 1d. | 976. | Meshed | 1½d. |
| 917. | Macao | 1d. | 977. | Para | ½d. |
| 918. | Söul | 1d. | 978. | Florence | 1d. |
| 919. | Dunkirk | 1d. | 979. | The Hague | 1½d. |
| 920. | Tamsui | 1d. | 980. | Patras | 1d. |
| 921. | Bussorah | ½d. | 981. | Paris | 1½d. |
| 922. | Yokohama | 3½d. | 982. | Zanzibar | 2½d. |
| 923. | Bilbao | 1½d. | 983. | Buenos Ayres | ½d. |
| 924. | Barcelona | 2½d. | 984. | Copenhagen | 1d. |
| 925. | Netherlands-India | 1d. | 985. | Stuttgart | 1d. |
| 926. | Chefoo | 1d. | 986. | New Orleans | 1½d. |
| 927. | Buenos Ayres | ½d. | 987. | New Orleans | 10d. |
| 928. | Santo Domingo | ½d. | 988. | Suakin | ½d. |

# No. 989.

*Reference to previous Report, Annual Series No. 823.*

## UNITED STATES.

### GALVESTON.

*Captain Boyle to the Marquis of Salisbury.*

My Lord,  Galveston, February 2, 1892.

I HAVE the honour to enclose a Report on the Trade and Commerce of my Consular District for the past year, 1891.

I have, &c.
(Signed)  JAMES BOYLE.

---

*Report on the Trade and Commerce of Texas for the Year 1891.*

ABSTRACT of Contents.

|  | PAGE. |
|---|---|
| **Texas—** | |
| Alien land law.. | 1 |
| Population, manufactories | 2 |
| Emigration ; climate.. | 3 |
| Steamship communication ; exports ; agriculture.. | 4 |
| Fruit culture ; real estate ; loan companies | 5 |
| Rights of aliens ; crime | 6 |
| Railways ; town of Velasco | 7 |
| Harbour ; general remarks | 8 |
| Finances ; taxation ; education ; history | 9 |
| **New Mexico—** | |
| Land ; population ; finances ; education | 10 |
| Public works ; schools ; climate ; irrigation ; agriculture | 11 |
| Cattle, sheep, mines, &c. | 12 |
| Timber ; railways | 13 |
| Tables | 14–19 |

The Alien Land Law,* which has at last been proclaimed by the Supreme Court of this State as unconstitutional, has caused more discussion than anything else during the past year, and it is, perhaps, the most important matter that has taken place in Texas during 1891. The Law itself was passed at the last regular Session, and was in operation only a short time, but during

*Alien Land Law Act.*

---

\* The text of this Law is contained in Parliamentary Paper No. 25, Commercial, 1891 (C. 6512, price 1*d*.).—ED.

(1231)

that time it was almost universally denounced. Opinions differ as to whether this Law was good or bad, but the general opinion all through the State is that the Law as it passed is bad, as tending to drive foreign capital from the State. Texas is a young State and wants capital in all ways to develop its rich resources and lands, and where it comes from may not matter much as long as it does come. If such an Act as this is ever to be excused, it is certainly not excusable in a new country like Texas, where land is so plentiful, and where what is most needed for its development is capital.

This Law may be amended in the next State Legislature, and possibly may be annulled, but whatever action is taken, it is quite certain that the failure of the Alien Ownership Law in Texas (for even its advocates admit its failure) will prevent any similar legislation by Congress or the States, as seemed extremely probable a year ago. The idea was to prevent the acquisition of large tracts of land by foreign syndicates and their being held unimproved for a length of time, as has been already done in Texas, but in the attempt to do this they included and prevented each and every foreigner from even owning a homestead. This appears to be the literal meaning of the Law as it originally stood.

*Population.* From the last official count of the population of the State of Texas it was computed as follows:—In 1880, it was 1,591,749; in 1890, it was 2,235,523, showing an increase of 643,774, or 40·44 per cent., and it must be at least, I think, 2,500,000 in 1891.

The population of Galveston in 1880 was 22,248; in 1890 it was 29,084, an increase of 30·73 per cent.; but I think this estimate of 1890 is far below the proper figures. At the present time it must be between 35,000 and 40,000.

The census returns last taken here during the summer of 1890 show that only 16 of the 244 counties in the State indicate a decrease in population. Texas has 14 cities, with a population of from 10,000 to 50,000 inhabitants.

*Manufactories.* Galveston, as a great port and commercial centre, is attracting a great deal of attention, almost more so than any other city in the United States. There is here, and in full work, a cotton factory with all the newest machinery, employing about 600 hands. The chief articles that it produces are sheetings, shirtings, and drillings, all in different qualities and widths, weighing from 2·50 yards to 5·30 yards per pound.

A rope and twine factory, producing annually about 4,680,000 lbs. of rope, and 300,000 lbs. of twine.

A jute and bagging factory, of 300 hands, which turns out about 500,000 yards of bagging, and a large quantity of twine. The demand at present is more than the mill can meet.

A lace curtain factory is also about to be built about seven miles from the city. The corner stone has been laid, and machinery is shortly expected from Nottingham, England, and also skilled labour.

There are also other mills in the city of Galveston, and other manufactories are springing up in many other cities of this State, and there is employment in all these factories, I think, for many hands, and at good wages.

There are in this city large cotton-seed oil mills. Their capital stock is 300,000 dol. They crush about 120 tons of seed per day, converting it into 4,560 gallons, or 90 barrels of oil. They also produce 40 tons of cake during the same period. A good deal of the product finds a market in Mexico and in California, where it is used to make a so-called olive oil.

Another enterprise is the American branch of William Cooper and Nephews, proprietors of Cooper's Sheep Dipping Powders, who have made the town of Galveston their headquarters.

Emigrants. The emigration into the United States averages about 600,000 per annum, of which Texas gets her full share, while the emigration from the other States of the Union to Texas is becoming greater each year. There appears to be work in the State of Texas for any number, but the class of emigrant that is chiefly wanted is the labouring class, skilled or otherwise, and the mechanic. More often than not young men arrive from England who have been clerks in offices there, and who, knowing absolutely nothing of farming, &c., in any way, think that it is a profitable source of wages and of business, and that all they have to do is to go up into the country and obtain a situation at once on some farm. This is much to be deplored, for never was there a greater delusion, and it is only within the last month that two of these cases have come personally before me. It would be advisable for all who emigrate here to think well over the matter, and if they make up their minds to come, to possess some little money of their own so that they could look round and see for themselves before finally settling what to do and where to go to. There is a very great demand and opening for female servants. At present it is impossible almost to get any at all, and what there are are inferior. Wages for common female servants are very high, and vary from 12 dol. to 30 dol. per month. Housemaids, 12 dol. to 18 dol.; cooks, from 12 dol. to 30 dol.

The expenses of living are very high indeed, and it is a notorious fact that in Galveston they exceed those of any other place in the south by 25 per cent. to 50 per cent., and it is the same in proportion all through the State of Texas.

Climate The climate of Texas is most variable, but not unhealthy on the whole. Sudden changes of 20 to 30 degrees in a few hours often happen, and one has to be very careful how one is clothed. Cases of malarious fever are not frequent about Galveston, but in the interior of the State they are more so, and people who come to it for the first time are generally the first to suffer, as they go on as if they were at home. Frost is unusual in the south, but in some winters it is severe, and in the month of January, 1892, there were from 8 to 10 degrees.

(1231)

## UNITED STATES.

**Steamship communication.**

The export grain trade by steamships will, I think, become most important from the port of Galveston. It has increased very much during 1891, and already three new grain elevators are about to be put up on the wharves for handling grain. One is being built now to cost 250,000 dol., and of a capacity of 1,000,000 bushels. There is a weekly service of steamers bringing tropical fruits from Blue Fields, Central America, and which is shipped through Galveston to St. Louis, Chicago, &c. It is also intended to ship flour by steamers to the West Indies, but up to the present only two sailing vessels have been chartered for this export. The Governments of the West India Islands have offered special inducements for the importation of breadstuffs. There is also a weekly service of excellent steamships, fitted luxuriously for passengers, from Galveston to New York, a voyage which takes about five days.

**Foreign exports, see annex.**

The exports for 1891-92, up to date, of cotton, oil-cake, flour, wheat, and miscellaneous goods to foreign countries have been the largest in the history of this port. The increase is not due entirely to the phenomenal cotton crops, but to the fact that there has been an extension and growth of this State's export trade in every way. The exporting of wheat and flour this year is a feature of the business that was in embryo last season, and scarcely counted at all in the final result.

**Agriculture**

The cotton crop of 1891 and 1892 indeed is the largest in Texas which has ever been known. It is estimated at about 2,200,000 bales, and the increase is calculated to be 10 per cent. over the official report of last year. In fact already the cry is that there is too much cotton, and that prices have not been so low since the French Revolution of 1848, and farmers are evidently seeing that growing cotton at present prices does not pay, and cannot pay.

The bare or insufficient profit accruing to the grower under the present system had led to the formation of companies for the purpose of erecting cotton mills, water power being abundant in certain portions of this State; and as cotton can be manufactured where it is grown cheaper than in New England, calculating cost of freight on the raw produce, and of the manufactured article when brought back here, Texas is likely, with its increasing immigration, before many years, to be a formidable rival to New England manufactories; and to prevent this, the capitalists who are interested in New England mills may likewise advocate a reduction of tariffs, so as to prevent the southern trade from leaving them.

It is an undoubted fact, that though there is plenty of money in banks lying idle, traders from up country, who have come to obtain their usual supplies of groceries and dry goods in Galveston, or loans from the banks, on the security of the next cotton crop, have in many cases been refused any credit at all, and that if they wanted supplies for farmers they have been informed that on account of the low price of cotton they must pay in cash.

The question is, What are the farmers to grow? If they grow corn to feed hogs and cattle they cannot get advances from the merchants who want to sell it to them, and it does seem an anomaly that beeves should be sent from Texas to St. Louis and Chicago, and come back to Texas in the form of dressed beef, to be consumed by the very farmers who raised, bred, and fed the original cattle.

There is no doubt but that the cultivation of cotton will be increased each year in Texas, as fresh land will be broken up by incoming settlers, and the whole present crop of the United States might be very easily grown within this one area; and it seems more and more probable that owing to the superiority of Texas cotton its cultivation may increase, and the crops of the older States decrease year by year until they assume insignificant proportions, while the Great Empire State of the South secures the monopoly of this great staple.

The extremely low price of cattle and cotton, the two staple farming products in Texas, has engendered a good deal of discontent amongst the agricultural population, who do not see why they should sell the products of their toil on a free trade basis, while they have to pay on a protective tariff of between 40 per cent. and 50 per cent. on all their agricultural implements, and on the clothing for themselves and family. Hence we see political combinations, such as Farmers' Alliances, &c., demanding redress from Congress through their representatives in Washington; and as farmers control the political machinery of the State, their demands are not likely to be altogether unheeded by the federal authorities. Consequently a radical reduction of the tariff, and more extended foreign commerce of the State and country, may result sooner than is generally expected.

Most of the land all through the State of Texas is admirably suited for maize and oats; and the crop-growing season is so long that two crops may very often be grown in the same year, whilst the prairie land in many parts is found to be excellent and well adapted for fruit growing, such as pears, apples, strawberries, &c. The county of Galveston is a great centre for this industry, and the experience of those engaged in fruit growing is that in the cultivation of small fruits, such as I have mentioned, as well as of grapes and vegetables, the productiveness and money value can hardly be over estimated. *Fruit, &c.*

Vegetables as fine as any in England, Australia, or New Zealand are to be seen daily, and are all of excellent quality. An industry that gives promise of success in the State is olive growing, but the great drawback at present to this industry is the harm done by an insect called "black-scale."

Texas owns her entire public domain, differing from the other States in the Union, the public domain of which is owned by the United States.

*Public domain land and real estate.*

Most land titles originated with the State, but when Texas gained her independence from Mexico, she recognised the Mexican grants, which had been made by the State of Coahuila,

*Aliens and loan companies.*

and nearly all the titled land was granted subsequently to the Revolution, which resulted in the formation of the Republic of Texas. Land is owned in fee simple by the citizens of the State, and holdings run all the way from the small town and city lot to holdings of from 250,000 acres to 300,000 acres. Most of the land titles originated with the State, as I have said, and are short, simple, and to the point. There are a few corporations in the State owning large tracts of land, whose business is the raising of stock. These corporations are for the most part British.

There is no doubt that the outside public are having their attention attracted to this State in all ways, and this has had the effect of a very marked advance in the value of land and real estate both in the country and in all the principal cities. Waste lands are now known to be capable of producing fruit and vegetables (this refers both to lands near the seashore and also further inland), which a few years ago were considered as perfectly useless.

*Rights of aliens and corporations.*

Aliens have the same right to hold real and personal property in Texas, which citizens of Texas enjoy in the country of which such aliens may be citizens.*

Alien corporations are authorised to do business in the State under the Act of July 6, 1889, upon filing their Memorandum of Association with the Secretary of State of Texas, and paying a fee in proportion to the amount of their capital stock, which fee in no case is to exceed 200 dol. Permits are granted by the Secretary of State of Texas to do business for any period not longer than 10 years.

British loan companies have invested in mortgages in Texas from 30,000,000 dol. to 40,000,000 dol. They operate under the Act of July 6, 1889. Their business has uniformly been successful, and their yearly dividends average from 8 per cent. to 15 per cent.

These companies own some real estates on which they have found it necessary to foreclose their mortgages, owing to default in payment of principal or interest; but the amount so owned by them is insignificant, and many of them hold no real estate.

*Crime.*

It is doubtless a fact, and one that cannot be denied, I think, that there is a great deal of crime committed in the State of Texas; but when one considers the vast size and extent of this State, the size of which is 274,000 square miles—almost as large as Great Britain and France joined together—and that a great deal of this vast tract of country is very thinly populated, one may wonder that there is not still more lawlessness. The vicinity of Texas to the borders of Mexico facilitates the escape of many of the miscreants and law breakers of the two countries.

Great efforts are being made to put an end to this state of things, and to show the perpetrators of crime that the law is to be obeyed, and that it will be enforced and carried out with the utmost vigour and severity.

* See Article 9 of Law of January 13, 1891, referred to in footnote on page 1.—ED.

Speaking personally of the town of Galveston, I have never seen one more orderly, or better conducted.

A Railway Commission was appointed by the last Legislature, in order to settle the basis if possible of railway rates. It is no doubt correct in principle, and is meant to be fair and just, but up to the present it has neither satisfied railway companies, nor in many instances merchants.

*Railway Commission.*

*Railways and financial status.*

It may be that, whereas it was probably only designed to adjust existing discrepancies in freights, it has made freight rates of its own, which though doubtless correct in theory, do not prove universally satisfactory in practice, and until some mutual adjustment takes place it is likely to retard the building of new railroads.

The railroad companies say that they cannot meet their current expenses, much less pay a dividend on the rates made by the Commission, and they have in some cases appealed to the Courts against the same.

There are between 8,000 and 9,000 miles of main lines in the State of Texas, besides branches, extensions, and connections of about 300 miles.

The San Antonio and Aransas Pass Railway from San Antonio to Waco is just completed, and a railway is about to be made from Colombia in the south to Velasco on the Sea. There are also other lines projected.

Taking the distinctively Texas lines, they appear to be doing poorly, when the through lines are doing well. By the Texas lines I mean the Texas and Pacific, San Antonio and Aransas Pass, International and Great Northern Railroads. I may point out that the Aransas Pass road on over 1,000,000 dol. gross earnings made only 112,909 dol. net, and the International and Great Northern on nearly 2,750,000 dol. gross earnings has but 85,146 dol. net.

The Texas and New Orleans showed a decrease of 208,176 dol., and the Louisiana Western 130,229 dol., while the increase on the Galveston, Harrisburg, and San Antonio, and the New York, Texas, and Mexican are respectively only 176,670 dol. and 10,351 dol. I have taken these few statistics from the "Financial Chronicle," New York, which paper is well known and most reliable in all its statements regarding railways and their workings.

The town of Velasco has been extensively advertised for the past year, with a view, probably, of disposing of large sections of land round its neighbourhood, which have been purchased by a syndicate of northern capitalists. That they have developed from 16 feet to 17 feet of water in the harbour there is unquestioned, but under the New Railway Commission of Texas it is difficult to see what advantage it would possess as a port for the export of cotton, &c., over Galveston, as the rates are regulated according to mileage. The parties interested in Velasco will very probably procure the loading of a few steamers there, so as to make it apparent to the world in general that it is capable of doing some export business.

*Town of Velasco.*

Velasco is about 40 miles or 45 miles by sea from Galveston. The nearest railway to it is at Colombia, which is 40 miles above Velasco on the Brazos River, but a railway is about to be laid from Colombia to Velasco.

**Galveston harbour works.**

Acting-Consul Heyworth, in his commercial report for 1890, commences by referring to the grant for harbour works at Galveston, which, no doubt, is of the utmost importance to this port.

Through the courtesy and kindness of Major Allen, who is in command here of the corps of engineers, United States Army, and who is also in charge of the works now proceeding in harbour, I am able to give a few statistics of this most important work.

The work was commenced in 1887 in construction of the south jetty. The plan consists of two jetties of rip-rap, protected by heavy blocks against the action of waves; the jetties were to be built to an elevation of 5 feet above mean low tide, and to be 7,000 feet apart at their sea ends.

The total length of jetty work, when completed, will be about 62,000 feet, or nearly 12 miles. The estimated cost of this work is 7,000,000 dol., of this amount the sum of 800,000 dol. was expended on the work up to August 30, 1890. Congress, by Act of September 19, 1890, appropriated 500,000 dol. for continuing the work, and by Act of March 3, 1891, 600,000 dol. more was appropriated.

The Act of September 19, 1890, authorises the Secretary of War to make contracts for material and labour necessary to carry out the plan of 1886, the material and labour to be paid for as appropriations may from time to time be made according to law. The appropriations of September 19, 1890, and of March 3, 1891, are expected to carry the south jetty to the crest of the outer bar. There are now 19,000 linear feet of south jetty completed, and about 3,200 feet partly built.

The total of jetty, complete and incomplete, is 22,600 feet.

Upon the expenditure of the 1,100,000 dol. just mentioned, there will remain to be appropriated, in order to finish the work, 5,100,000 dol.

The contract under which the work is progressing provides that the contractors shall earn not less than 1,000,000 dol. a year. The money now available for the work should be earned by August 1, 1892.

If Congress continues to furnish money as required, the jetties should be completed within about 6 years.

**General remarks.**

There is strong feeling, I think, among all parties that a combination bridge should be built, by this I mean a road for waggons, carts, &c., and a railway bridge to connect Galveston with the mainland. At present there is only a railway one. It is being strongly advocated. It is estimated approximately that to build a combination bridge, such as I describe, with double track for railway, would cost 1,000,000 dol., and to maintain this bridge would not cost less than 25,000 dol. per annum. If this is correct, bonds would be issued, and tolls would have to be paid by the railroad companies. I believe that a proposition or petition has been filed with the Bridge Committee for action by the County Commissioners.

The entire indebtedness of the State of Texas is said to be 4.237,730 dol., of which she holds in her school and other funds 3,017,100 dol., making her sole debt to others but 1,220,630 dol. *Indebtedness of State.*

The official assessed valuation of real and personal property of Texas, other than that owned by the State and churches, was:— *Assessed valuation.*

|      | Dollars. |
|------|----------|
| 1880.. | 311,470,736 |
| 1890.. | 786,111,883 |
| 1891.. | 844,000,000 (estimated) |

The rate of taxation per 1,000 dol. is about 3 dol. 25 c. *Rate of taxation.*

| Description. |  | Quantity. |
|---|---|---|
| Sugar crop of 1891 | Lbs. | 19,000,000 |
| ,, average yield per acre | ,, | 2,600 |
| Wheat, 1891 | Bushels | 8,000,000 |
| Corn, 1891 | ,, | 71,000,000 |
| Oats, 1891 | ,, | 15,000,900 |
| Head of cattle, 1891 |  | 8,000,000 |
| Horses and mules, 1891 |  | 1,500,000 |
| Hogs, 1891 |  | 1,500,000 |
| Cotton in bales, 1891 |  | 2,200,000* |

*Some statistics.*

\* One fourth crop of United States.

The schools, both public and private, and education generally, in all its branches, are advancing year by year, and are attaining a very high standard. Texas in all her cities has excellent schools. The Government gives a grant to every school, white or coloured, and this grant is regulated by the size of the community, which is called the capitation grant. *Education.*

Acting-Consul Heyworth in his report for 1890 went very fully into facts from the reports of the Secretary of the Texas State Bureau of Immigration, regarding the status of schools, school funds, and the number attending these institutions, and I have been unable to gather anything further regarding them. In Galveston city the two most prominent schools are The Bell High School and Rosenberg School, both of them admirable institutions in all ways and magnificent buildings.

*Th History of Texas is Short but Eventful.*

1. Claimed and controlled by Spain by right of discovery. *Texas history.*
2. Ceded by Spain to France pursuant to Treaty of 1800.
3. Transferred by France to the United States by the Treaty of April, 1806.

4. Exchanged for Florida and receded to Spain by the United States under the treaty of February, 1809.

5. Severed from Spain and made part of Mexico by Revolution prior to 1824.

6. Erected into the Republic of Texas by the Revolution of 1835-36.

7. Annexed to the United States by the consent of the people of Texas, and became a State of the Union, retaining her entire public domain, in February, 1846.

8. Adopted her ordinance of secession and became one of the Confederate States of America in 1861.

9. Restored to the Union, after the fall of the Confederacy, in 1865, and is now the largest State in the Union, making great progress and development.

## New Mexico.

**Land titles and small holdings.** In an irrigated country, which New Mexico is for the most part, the cultivated land lies between the acesnia, or irrigating ditch, and the river. This is cut up into small farms. When it was first settled, the original occupants usually owned a plot of from 50 varas to 300 varas wide (vara is a short yard, 33 inches), running from river to the foot-hills. As generations succeeded, these tracts were divided among heirs until strips of land became very narrow. The land is of great fertility. The Land Court Bill provides that anyone owning a small holding, upon making his residence known as a fact, may enter such legal sub-division, not exceeding 160 acres, as shall include his said possession. The smallest legal sub-division known to Land Office Law is 40 acres.

**Population.** There is a gradual and healthy growth all over the territory. The number of votes cast in the election of November, 1890, was between 180,000 and 185,000, and it is calculated to increase about 1,000 each year.

**Finances.** The last financial total of assessed valuation in the State was about 45,199,847 dol. 91 c.

The territorial indebtedness of the State was about 866,433 dol. 3 c., at close of the forty-first fiscal year, March 3, 1891. The territorial expenses were 178,679 dol. 3 c.

The financial condition of New Mexico is remarkably sound.

The assessed valuation of 1891 will considerably exceed above valuation, but I have not been able to ascertain exact amount.

**Education.** In no respect is New Mexico making such progress as in public education. There are 533 schools in this State. In east Las Vegas, a beautiful stone schoolhouse has just been erected, and five other districts in San Miguel county have voted bonds for a similar purpose. Other schools are opened in the counties of Albuquerque, Raton, Denning, Roswell, and San Juan.

**Public buildings.** Under head of public buildings three territorial educational institutions are referred to. They are the University of Albuquerque, the Agricultural College at Las Cruces, and the School of Mines at Socorro. There is also a school for the deaf and dumb at Santa Fé, and an orphan's home and industrial school as well.

**Schools.** These are mostly sustained by religious denominations or societies. There are a number of schools and academies, and they are all doing good work towards the general education of the south of the State and territory.

The most successful private school, which is not denominational, is said to be the Goss Military Institute for boys at Roswell. It is a boarding school and has already 45 students in attendance, with a prospect of a rapid increase.

**Climate.** So far as its delightful character is concerned there is no climate equal to New Mexico in America, and perhaps in the world. The percentage of deaths from pulmonary diseases is lower here than in any other point almost in the United States. For those in good health, nothing can be more delightful than the summer climate of Santa Fé, Las Vegas, and the hot springs. The rainfall varies about 1 inch to 2 inches per month. Temperature from 45 degrees to 85 degrees all the year. Of course, there are cold spells and frost at certain times.

**Irrigation.** Irrigation is of great and increasing importance in the State, and there are many companies formed for this purpose. The system appears to be by canals and laterals, and the best known systems are the Springer and the Vermejo. Acting-Consul Heyworth in his commercial report for 1890 of Texas and New Mexico stated what has been achieved in civil and hydraulic engineering in this area; but in course of time, as the State is opened up, this system of irrigation will no doubt open up the fertile lands which only want water to make them almost the finest grazing and agricultural pastures in the world.

**Agriculture and horticulture.** The advance of both these important branches is very marked. The acreage of every staple product is increased, and in some parts it is reported to have increased fully 20 per cent. The increase in the hay crop is specially marked. Alfalfa is a great success and frequently reaches from 7 tons to 12 tons per acre, and gives from 3 crops to 5 crops per annum. Many farmers have from 100 tons to 200 tons of it. Timothy and other grasses are being extensively cultivated, and in Sans Miguel county there are now fully 5,000 acres of timothy, where three years ago there was none.

From 25 per cent. to 30 per cent. is the usual return for wheat sown:—

|  | Bushels per Acre. |
|---|---|
| Wheat | 40 to 50 |
| Maize | 60   80 |
| Oats | 50   60 |
| Barley | 40   60 |

Nowhere do grapes, peaches, apricots, pears, quinces, apples, arrive at such perfection as they do in New Mexico. Orchards are springing up everywhere, and a careful estimate calculates the number of fruit trees planted in 1891 about 200,000. The greatly increased product of fruit of all kinds makes a canning factory a necessity, and no doubt very shortly these factories will spring up. The valleys about Roswell seem to be chosen as the choicest lands for cultivation of fruit.

**Cattle.** The estimated number in 1890 was about 1,129,088, but owing to considerable losses in some localities during the winter months this number will, I think, have decreased instead of increased.

The prices for each are as follows, approximately:—

|  | Dollars. |
|---|---|
| Yearlings | 6 to 10 |
| Two year olds | 8   14 |
| Three year olds | 12   20 |
| Stock cattle | 8   16 |

**Sheep.** The industry of sheep farming is in a very prosperous state. Prices have been good, and yields about 20 per cent. on the capital invested. There is no such disease known as "dry rot," as the climate is so dry. Prices of sheep in herds differ in different counties in New Mexico. The increase in sheep from 1890 is about 50 per cent. in the eastern part of the State, but it is impossible to get and obtain accurate accounts and statements from the other counties.

The total amount of the wool crop is estimated at 16,000,000 lbs. There is plenty of good grass and water in all the districts for sheep. Prices have been good, and the average price is: yearling wethers, 1 dol. 25 c.; older wethers, 2 dol. 50 c.

**Mines and mining.** Mining throughout the whole State has increased in amount and profit during the past year. In every section of the State there is an enlarged development. The total mineral product for 1890 was 3,000,000 dol. almost exactly. It is estimated from the last official reports that the output for 1891 will be fully as much if not more. Mining in New Mexico is in its elementary stages, but there is known to be iron, coal, fire-clay, alumina, serpentine, marbles (black and white), kaolin, salt, sulphate of lime, and silicate of magnesia. The mining population is most orderly. Now that the Alien Land Law Act has been decided as unconstitutional, there is no doubt the further development of the mining industry will be extraordinary, and this would be increased by an adoption of a system of commercial reciprocity with the Republic of Mexico, inasmuch as it would doubtlessly lead to the establishment of numerous manufactories in the State. Much attention is being paid to both zinc and copper ore, and it is more than probable that within a year smelting furnaces will rise up. Precious stones, such as beautiful turquoises, topazes, garnets, rubies, carbuncles, &c., are found in San Juan valley and in the Burro mountains.

Bullion shipments from January 1, 1891, to October, 1891, were as follows: gold, 131,055 dol.; silver, 9,876 dol.

Valuable timber is found all over the State, especially the finest pine, and sawmills are already working in Tres Piedras. There are also seven mills in Colfax county. In the regions north-west of Las Vegas and in San Miguel and Mora counties there is a vast amount of timber, and mills are also in full working order there and are doing a large and increasing trade. *Timber.*

Railways are being built and laid rapidly all over the State. The parent company, if one may so express it, is the South-West Coal and Iron Company, with a capital of 1,000,000 dol., and bonded indebtedness of 200,000 dol. The total railroad mileage in New Mexico is between 1,400 miles and 1,500 miles. As railways increase and spread, it will of course be of the greatest help to farmers, miners, and others, and their products will then easily be carried to the different markets in the United States. *Railways.*

The Governor, in his report, says: "Another year has passed, and I am able to report that in every branch of production we are having a wonderful increase and development. For years we have suffered under the incubus of unsettled land titles, but at last the long hoped for relief has come. The Land Court is already established. This will give stability to titles and confidence to investors, it will bring to us both men and money. The late Legislature passed an Act for the incorporation of community grants, which will settle vexed questions with regard to them. The Legislature was most progressive. It provided for improvements of roads, suppression of trusts, impartial selection of juries, protection of the cattle interest, reduction of liquor selling, and most important of all, the establishment of an efficient system of public schools and education." *Future development of State.*

## 14          UNITED STATES.

STATEMENT of Vessels Engaged in the Foreign Trade in the District of Galveston, Texas, during the Year ending December 31, 1891.

ENTERED.

| Nationality. | Ballast. Number of Vessels. | Ballast. Tons. | Cargo. Number of Vessels. | Cargo. Tons. | Total. Number of Vessels. | Total. Tons. |
|---|---|---|---|---|---|---|
| American | 8 | 890 | 13 | 4,596 | 21 | 5,486 |
| British | 121 | 153,140 | 37 | 51,203 | 158 | 204,343 |
| German | 2 | 490 | 1 | 461 | 3 | 951 |
| Mexican | 1 | 108 | ... | ... | 1 | 108 |
| Norwegian | 7 | 3,399 | 24 | 7,632 | 31 | 11,031 |
| Spanish | 8 | 10,627 | ... | ... | 8 | 10,627 |
| Swedish | 1 | 356 | ... | ... | 1 | 356 |
| Total | 148 | 169,010 | 75 | 63,892 | 223 | 232,902 |
| ,, for the year preceding | 149 | 112,514 | 72 | 57,795 | 221 | 170,309 |

CLEARED.

| Nationality. | Ballast. Number of Vessels. | Ballast. Tons. | Cargo. Number of Vessels. | Cargo. Tons. | Total. Number of Vessels. | Total. Tons. |
|---|---|---|---|---|---|---|
| American | 11 | 4,163 | 24 | 7,992 | 35 | 12,155 |
| British | ... | ... | 163 | 220,265 | 163 | 220,265 |
| German | ... | ... | 4 | 1,217 | 4 | 1,217 |
| Mexican | ... | ... | 1 | 108 | 1 | 108 |
| Norwegian | 1 | 269 | 30 | 10,546 | 31 | 10,815 |
| Spanish | ... | ... | 10 | 10,543 | 10 | 10,543 |
| Swedish | ... | ... | ... | ... | ... | ... |
| Total | 12 | 4,432 | 232 | 250,671 | 244 | 255,103 |
| ,, for the year preceding | 3 | 333 | 219 | 183,358 | 222 | 183,691 |

STATEMENT of Imports at the Port of Galveston, Texas, for the Year ending December 31, 1891.

GALVESTON.

| Commodities. | Germany. | Great Britain. | France. | Netherlands. | Nicaragua. | Colombia. | Mexico. | Cuba. | Turkey. | Japan. | Spain. | Italy. | Brazil. | Total for 1891. | Total for 1890. |
|---|---|---|---|---|---|---|---|---|---|---|---|---|---|---|---|
| | Dollars. | Dollars. | Dollars. | Dollars. | Dollars. | Dollars. | Dollars. | Dollars. | Dollars. | Dollars. | Dollars. | Dollars. | Dollars. | Dollars. | Dollars. |
| Free of duty— | | | | | | | | | | | | | | | |
| Coffee | ... | ... | ... | ... | 113,565 | 7,517 | 39,073 | ... | ... | ... | ... | ... | 329,385 | 368,458 | ... |
| Fruits and nuts | ... | ... | ... | ... | ... | ... | 291 | ... | ... | ... | ... | ... | ... | 121,473 | ... |
| Fustic, dye-wood | ... | ... | ... | ... | ... | ... | 2,692 | ... | ... | ... | ... | ... | ... | 2,692 | ... |
| Gold dust | ... | ... | ... | ... | 10,270 | 2,603 | ... | ... | ... | ... | ... | ... | ... | 12,873 | ... |
| Rubber, crude | ... | ... | ... | ... | 39,476 | ... | ... | ... | ... | ... | ... | ... | ... | 39,476 | ... |
| Sugar, below 16 d.s. | ... | 640 | ... | ... | ... | ... | ... | ... | ... | ... | ... | ... | ... | 640 | ... |
| Coin, Mexican | ... | ... | ... | ... | ... | ... | 1,570 | ... | ... | ... | ... | ... | ... | 1,570 | ... |
| Works of art, and al' other free goods, including household effects | 468 | 9,919 | 145 | ... | 25 | ... | 242 | ... | ... | ... | ... | ... | ... | 10,799 | ... |
| Subject to duty— | | | | | | | | | | | | | | | |
| Books and printed matter | 3,284 | 1,210 | 90 | ... | ... | ... | ... | ... | ... | ... | ... | ... | ... | 1,300 | ... |
| Cement in barrels | ... | 86,230 | ... | 34,989 | ... | ... | ... | ... | ... | ... | ... | ... | ... | 124,503 | ... |
| Chemicals, viz.— | | | | | | | | | | | | | | | |
| Soda, ash | ... | 2,923 | ... | ... | ... | ... | ... | ... | ... | ... | ... | ... | ... | 2,923 | ... |
| " caustic | ... | 2,037 | ... | ... | ... | ... | ... | ... | ... | ... | ... | ... | ... | 2,037 | ... |
| Sheep, dip | ... | 56,459 | ... | ... | ... | ... | ... | ... | ... | ... | ... | ... | ... | 56,459 | ... |
| Coal, bituminous | ... | 20,184 | ... | ... | ... | ... | ... | ... | ... | ... | ... | ... | ... | 20,184 | ... |
| Cotton, manufactures of | 208 | 2,665 | ... | ... | ... | ... | ... | ... | 399 | ... | ... | ... | ... | 3,272 | ... |
| Earth and stoneware— | | | | | | | | | | | | | | | |
| Slates, roofing | ... | 1,148 | ... | ... | ... | ... | ... | ... | ... | ... | ... | ... | ... | 1,148 | ... |
| Bricks, fire | ... | 1,173 | ... | ... | ... | ... | ... | ... | ... | ... | ... | ... | ... | 1,173 | ... |
| Tiles, all kinds | ... | 99 | ... | ... | ... | ... | ... | ... | ... | ... | ... | ... | ... | 99 | ... |
| Crockery ware | 785 | 9,033 | ... | ... | ... | ... | ... | ... | ... | ... | ... | ... | ... | 9,818 | ... |

## UNITED STATES.

STATEMENT of Imports at the Port of Galveston, Texas, for the Year ending December 31, 1891—continued.

| Commodities. | Germany. | Great Britain. | France. | Netherlands. | Nicaragua. | Colombia. | Mexico. | Cuba. | Turkey. | Japan. | Spain. | Italy. | Brazil. | Total for 1891. | Total for 1890. |
|---|---|---|---|---|---|---|---|---|---|---|---|---|---|---|---|
| | Dollars. | Dollars. | Dollars. | Dollars. | Dollars. | Dollars. | Dollars. | Dollars. | Dollars. | Dollars. | Dollars. | Dollars. | Dollars. | Dollars. | Dollars. |
| Fish, in oil | ... | ... | 6,882 | ... | ... | ... | ... | ... | ... | ... | ... | ... | ... | 6,882 | ... |
| Fruits and vegetables | ... | 5,383 | 6,938 | ... | ... | ... | ... | ... | ... | ... | ... | ... | ... | 12,321 | ... |
| Glass, window | ... | ... | ... | 4,181 | ... | ... | ... | ... | ... | ... | ... | ... | ... | 4,881 | ... |
| Iron, manufactures of | ... | 8,857 | 110 | ... | ... | ... | 240 | ... | ... | 437 | ... | ... | ... | 9,639 | ... |
| „ in pigs | ... | 1,351 | ... | ... | ... | ... | ... | ... | ... | ... | ... | ... | ... | 1,351 | ... |
| Ale and porter | ... | 13,803 | ... | ... | ... | ... | ... | ... | ... | ... | ... | ... | ... | 13,803 | ... |
| Mineral water, natural | ... | ... | ... | 2,631 | ... | ... | ... | ... | ... | ... | ... | ... | ... | 2,631 | ... |
| Musical instruments | 1,530 | ... | ... | ... | ... | ... | ... | ... | ... | ... | ... | ... | ... | 1,530 | ... |
| Oil, tar or lead | ... | 43,091 | ... | ... | ... | ... | ... | ... | ... | ... | ... | ... | ... | 43,091 | ... |
| Salt in bags | ... | 32,391 | ... | ... | ... | ... | ... | ... | ... | ... | ... | ... | ... | 32,391 | ... |
| Shells, polished | 148 | ... | ... | ... | ... | ... | ... | ... | ... | ... | ... | ... | ... | 148 | ... |
| Whiskey, American re-imported | 29,958 | ... | ... | ... | ... | ... | ... | ... | ... | ... | ... | ... | ... | 29,858 | ... |
| Sugar, beet, over 16 d.s. | 40,071 | ... | ... | ... | ... | ... | ... | ... | ... | ... | ... | ... | ... | 40,071 | ... |
| Wine, all kinds | 1,086 | ... | 1,916 | ... | ... | ... | ... | ... | ... | ... | 99 | 75 | ... | 3,176 | ... |
| Spirits in bottles | ... | 212 | 26 | ... | ... | ... | ... | ... | ... | ... | ... | ... | ... | 238 | ... |
| Tin and terne plates | ... | 86,726 | ... | ... | ... | ... | ... | ... | ... | ... | ... | ... | ... | 86,726 | ... |
| Tobacco leaf, and manufactures of | ... | ... | ... | ... | ... | ... | 222 | 1,452 | ... | ... | ... | ... | ... | 1,674 | ... |
| Miscellaneous | ... | 8,949 | 1,916 | 347 | 67 | ... | 207 | ... | ... | ... | ... | ... | 57 | 11,543 | ... |
| Total for 1891 | 77,438 | 394,083 | 18,023 | 42,148 | 163,403 | 10,120 | 44,637 | 1,452 | 399 | 437 | 99 | 75 | 329,442 | 1,082,151 | ... |
| „ 1890 | 35,160 | 340,435 | 7,635 | 11,736 | 13,170 | ... | 50,735 | 557 | 10,409 | 4,734 | 625 | 502 | ... | China. 284 | 475,982 |

## GALVESTON.

STATEMENT of Exports of Commodities of Domestic Growth and Manufacture from the Port of Galveston, Texas, for the Year ending December 31, 1891.

| Destination. | Cotton. Quantity. | Cotton. Value. | Oil Cake. Quantity. | Oil Cake. Value. | Wheat. Quantity. | Wheat. Value. | Flour. Quantity. | Flour. Value. | Corn. Quantity | Corn. Value. |
|---|---|---|---|---|---|---|---|---|---|---|
| | Bales. | Dollars. | Tons. | Dollars. | Bushels. | Dollars. | Barrels. | Dollars. | Bushels. | Dollars. |
| Great Britain | 668,353 | 29,747,951 | 21,105 | 470,302 | 202,500 | 203,408 | 9,390 | 39,280 | 8,000 | 4,160 |
| France | 45,240 | 1,815,871 | 212 | 4,750 | 327,015 | 323,760 | 800 | 3,350 | .. | .. |
| Germany | 44,269 | 1,939,791 | 16,670 | 415,791 | 57,880 | 60,890 | .. | .. | .. | .. |
| Russia | 9,755 | 407,366 | .. | .. | .. | .. | .. | .. | .. | .. |
| Denmark | .. | .. | 4,072 | 93,656 | .. | .. | .. | .. | .. | .. |
| Netherlands | .. | .. | 1,137 | 24,042 | .. | .. | .. | .. | .. | .. |
| Italy | 1,329 | 58,649 | .. | .. | .. | .. | .. | .. | .. | .. |
| Cuba | .. | .. | .. | .. | .. | .. | 1,305 | 6,383 | 3,000 | 1,722 |
| Mexico | 5,874 | 247,864 | .. | .. | .. | .. | .. | .. | .. | .. |
| Nicaragua | .. | .. | .. | .. | .. | .. | 434 | 2,307 | 1,741 | 1,369 |
| Total for 1891 | 774,828 | 34,217,492 | 43,196 | 1,008,541 | 587,395 | 588,058 | 11,929 | 51,320 | 12,741 | 7,251 |
| " 1890 | 499,189 | 26,303,400 | 53,484 | 1,202,779 | .. | .. | 19,481 | 80,511 | 35,246 | 11,989 |

STATEMENT of Exports of Commodities of Domestic Growth and Manufacture from the Port of Galveston, Texas, for the Year ending December 31, 1891—continued.

| Destination. | Cotton-seed Oil. | Lumber, &c. | Bottled Beer. | Sugar. | Manufacture of Iron, &c. | Boots and Shoes, Wearing Apparel. | Sundries. | Total. |
|---|---|---|---|---|---|---|---|---|
| | Dollars. | Dollars. | Dollars. | Dollars. | Dollars. | Dollars. | Dollars. | Dollars. |
| Great Britain | .. | .. | .. | .. | .. | .. | 1,238 | 30,466,339 |
| France | .. | .. | .. | .. | .. | .. | 2,140 | 2,149,871 |
| Germany | .. | .. | .. | .. | .. | .. | 910 | 2,417,382 |
| Russia | .. | .. | .. | .. | .. | .. | .. | 407,366 |
| Denmark | .. | .. | .. | .. | .. | .. | .. | 93,656 |
| Netherlands | .. | .. | .. | .. | .. | .. | .. | 24,042 |
| Italy | .. | .. | .. | .. | .. | .. | .. | 58,649 |
| Cuba | .. | .. | .. | .. | .. | .. | .. | 8,105 |
| Mexico | 2,250 | 15,878 | 5,472 | .. | 380 | .. | 34,868 | 306,712 |
| Nicaragua | .. | 1,015 | 1,295 | 2,208 | 2,364 | 7,653 | 14,127 | 32,338 |
| Total for 1891 | 2,250 | 16,893 | 6,767 | 2,208 | 2,744 | 7,653 | 53,283 | 35,964,460 |
| ,, 1890 | .. | 200,600 | 14,623 | .. | .. | .. | 39,587 | 27,853,489 |

## GALVESTON.

GENERAL Statement of Value of Merchandise Entered at the Port of Galveston, Texas, from Foreign Countries and Exported in Transit to the United States of Mexico, from January 1, 1891, to December 31, 1891.

| From | January. | February. | March. | April. | May. | June. | July. | August. | September. | October. | November. | December. | Total, 1891. | Total, 1890. |
|---|---|---|---|---|---|---|---|---|---|---|---|---|---|---|
| | Dollars. | Dollars. | Dollars. | Dollars. | Dollars. | Dollars. | Dollars. | Dollars. | Dollars. | Dollars. | Dollars. | Dollars. | Dollars. | Dollars. |
| Belgium | 1,478 | 23,001 | 2,729 | ... | ... | ... | ... | ... | ... | ... | ... | 1,761 | 27,491 | 145,327 |
| France | ... | ... | 4,213 | 3,468 | 226 | 14,407 | 21 | ... | ... | 6,627 | 1,836 | 435 | 32,711 | 84,363 |
| Germany | 8,037 | 2,010 | 4,899 | ... | ... | 10,163 | ... | ... | ... | 932 | 5,536 | 4,815 | 36,392 | 165,890 |
| Great Britain | 30,360 | 47,969 | 13,780 | ... | 73 | 31,515 | ... | 33,304 | 38,236 | 9,715 | 37,179 | 30,250 | 272,381 | 368,618 |
| Mexico | 1,178 | 609 | 511 | ... | ... | ... | ... | ... | ... | ... | ... | ... | 2,298 | 2,455 |
| Total, 1891 | 41,053 | 73,589 | 26,132 | 3,468 | 299 | 56,085 | 21 | 33,304 | 38,236 | 17,274 | 44,551 | 37,261 | 371,273 | ... |
| Total, 1890 | 61,454 | 72,536 | 110,689 | 29,795 | 139,721 | 969 | 70,165 | 48,818 | 35,188 | 28,958 | 90,711 | 77,599 | ... | 766,653 |

| Transported, viâ the following Frontier Ports. | January. | February. | March. | April. | May. | June. | July. | August. | September. | October. | November. | December. | Grand Total for each Frontier Port. |
|---|---|---|---|---|---|---|---|---|---|---|---|---|---|
| | Dollars. | Dollars. | Dollars. | Dollars. | Dollars. | Dollars. | Dollars. | Dollars. | Dollars. | Dollars. | Dollars. | Dollars. | Dollars. |
| Brownsville, Texas | 620 | ... | 1,340 | ... | ... | 4,909 | ... | 467 | ... | ... | ... | ... | 7,336 |
| Eagle Pass, Texas | 3,919 | 8,351 | 6,914 | ... | ... | 5,421 | 21 | 1,829 | 14,124 | 7,686 | 8,414 | 2,351 | 59,030 |
| El Paso, Texas | 1,970 | 97 | 195 | ... | 73 | 4,754 | ... | 3,580 | 3,612 | 1,399 | 830 | 1,078 | 17,588 |
| Laredo, Texas | 32,241 | 60,495 | 16,830 | 3,468 | 226 | 41,001 | ... | 27,428 | 20,500 | 6,187 | 11,883 | 33,832 | 254,091 |
| Nogales, North Texas | 2,303 | 4,646 | 853 | ... | ... | ... | ... | ... | ... | 2,002 | 23,424 | ... | 33,228 |
| Total for each month | 41,053 | 73,589 | 26,132 | 3,468 | 299 | 56,085 | 21 | 33,304 | 38,236 | 17,274 | 44,551 | 37,261 | 371,273 |

(1231)

LONDON :
Printed for Her Majesty's Stationery Office,
By HARRISON AND SONS,
Printers in Ordinary to Her Majesty.
(75   3 | 92—H & S   1231)

# FOREIGN OFFICE.
## 1892.
## ANNUAL SERIES.

### No. 994.

### DIPLOMATIC AND CONSULAR REPORTS ON TRADE AND FINANCE.

# UNITED STATES.

### REPORT FOR THE YEAR 1891
### ON THE
### TRADE OF PENSACOLA.

REFERENCE TO PREVIOUS REPORT, Annual Series No. 833 (page 10).

*Presented to both Houses of Parliament by Command of Her Majesty,*
*MARCH, 1892.*

LONDON:
**PRINTED FOR HER MAJESTY'S STATIONERY OFFICE,**
BY HARRISON AND SONS, ST. MARTIN'S LANE,
PRINTERS IN ORDINARY TO HER MAJESTY.

And to be purchased, either directly or through any Bookseller, from
EYRE & SPOTTISWOODE, East Harding Street, Fleet Street, E.C., and
32, Abingdon Street, Westminster, S.W.; or
JOHN MENZIES & Co., 12, Hanover Street, Edinburgh, and
90, West Nile Street, Glasgow; or
HODGES, FIGGIS, & Co., 104, Grafton Street, Dublin.

1892.

[C. 6550—56.] *Price One Penny.*

# New Series of Reports.

Reports of the Annual Series have been issued from Her Majesty's Diplomatic and Consular Officers at the following places, and may be obtained from the sources indicated on the title-page:—

| No. | | Price. | No. | | Price. |
|---|---|---|---|---|---|
| 872. | Rosario | ½d. | 933. | New York | 1d. |
| 873. | Buenos Ayres | ½d. | 934. | Nagasaki | 1d. |
| 874. | Mogador | 1d. | 935. | Hakodate | 1½d. |
| 875. | Tainan | 6½d. | 936. | Sofia | 3d. |
| 876. | Pakhoi | 1d. | 937. | Frankfort | 2d. |
| 877. | Odessa | 2½d. | 938. | Bangkok | 9d. |
| 878. | Trebizond | 1½d. | 939. | Berne | 1½d. |
| 879. | Mollendo | ½d. | 940. | The Hague | 1½d. |
| 880. | Kiukiang | 1d. | 941. | Christiania | 1d. |
| 881. | Antananarivo | 1d. | 942. | Christiania | ½d. |
| 882. | Stettin | 2½d. | 943. | Brunei | 1½d. |
| 883. | Fiume | 1½d. | 944. | Alexandria | 1½d. |
| 884. | Batavia | 1d. | 945. | Therapia | ½d. |
| 885. | Samoa | ½d. | 946. | Bushire | 1½d. |
| 886. | Cherbourg | 1d. | 947. | Tokio | 2½d. |
| 887. | Cagliari | 1d. | 948. | Stockholm | 2d. |
| 888. | Hankow | 1½d. | 949. | Palermo | 2½d. |
| 889. | Vienna | 1½d. | 950. | St. Petersburg | 2½d. |
| 890. | Amoy | 1d. | 951. | Quito | ½d. |
| 891. | Adrianople | ½d. | 952. | Rio de Janeiro | 2d. |
| 892. | Chicago | 2½d. | 953. | Naples | 2d. |
| 893. | Brest | 1d. | 954. | Amsterdam | 1d. |
| 894. | Smyrna | 1d. | 955. | Tangier | 2d. |
| 895. | Cadiz | 1d. | 956. | Paramaribo | 1d. |
| 896. | Aleppo | 1d. | 957. | Teneriffe | 1d. |
| 897. | Foochow | 1d. | 958. | Athens | 2d. |
| 898. | Kiungchow | 1d. | 959. | Odessa | 1d. |
| 899. | The Hague | 1½d. | 960. | Copenhagen | 9d. |
| 900. | Nice | 1½d. | 961. | Tokio | 1d. |
| 901. | Nantes | 1½d. | 962. | Salonica | 1½d. |
| 902. | Port-au-Prince | 1½d. | 963. | Stettin | 3½d. |
| 903. | Bengazi | 1d. | 964. | Philadelphia | 2d. |
| 904. | Tahiti | ½d. | 965. | Mexico | 2d. |
| 905. | Chinkiang | 1d. | 966. | Malaga | 2½d. |
| 906. | San Francisco | 3d. | 967. | Berne | 1d. |
| 907. | Brindisi | 2d. | 968. | Puerto Rico | ½d. |
| 908. | Beyrout | 1d. | 969. | Buda-Pesth | 1d. |
| 909. | Noumea | ½d. | 970. | Bogotá | 1d. |
| 910. | San Francisco | 1d. | 971. | Panama | 1½d. |
| 911. | New York | 1½d. | 972. | Munich | 2d. |
| 912. | Caracas | 1½d. | 973. | Copenhagen | 4d. |
| 913. | Greytown | ½d. | 974. | Guatemala | 1d. |
| 914. | Corunna | 2d. | 975. | Munich | 2d. |
| 915. | Christiania | 5½d. | 976. | Meshed | 1½d. |
| 916. | Callao | 1d. | 977. | Para | ½d. |
| 917. | Macao | 1d. | 978. | Florence | 1d. |
| 918. | Söul | 1d. | 979. | The Hague | 1½d. |
| 919. | Dunkirk | 1d. | 980. | Patras | 1d. |
| 920. | Tamsui | 1d. | 981. | Paris | 1½d. |
| 921. | Bussorah | ½d. | 982. | Zanzibar | 2½d. |
| 922. | Yokohama | 3½d. | 983. | Buenos Ayres | ½d. |
| 923. | Bilbao | 1½d | 984. | Copenhagen | 1d. |
| 924. | Barcelona | 2½d. | 985. | Stuttgart | 1d. |
| 925. | Netherlands-India | 1d. | 986. | New Orleans | 1½d. |
| 926. | Chefoo | 1d. | 987. | New Orleans | 10d. |
| 927. | Buenos Ayres | ½d. | 988. | Suakin | ½d. |
| 928. | Santo Domingo | ½d. | 989. | Galveston | 1½d. |
| 929. | Constantinople | ½d. | 990. | Berlin | 1d. |
| 930. | Erzeroum | 1½d. | 991. | Zanzibar | 1½d. |
| 931. | Gothenburg | 2d. | 992. | Guayaquil | 1d. |
| 932. | Tunis | 1d. | 993. | Tonga | 1d. |

# No. 994.

*Reference to previous Report, Annual Series No. 833 (page 10).*

## UNITED STATES.

### NEW ORLEANS.

*Consul de Fonblanque to the Marquis of Salisbury.*

My Lord,                  *New Orleans, February* 10, 1892.
    I HAVE the honour to enclose herewith Trade Report from Vice-Consul Howe, of Pensacola, for the year 1891.
              I have, &c.
           (Signed)      A. de G. de FONBLANQUE.

*Report on the Trade of Pensacola for the Year* 1891.

ABSTRACT of Contents.

| | PAGE |
|---|---|
| Timber trade | 1, 8 |
| Imports | 2 |
| Shipping and navigation | 2 |
| Fertilisers; machinery; coal; railways | 3 |
| Fish; sanitary; labour question | 4 |
| Imports and exports | 5 |
| Shipping | 6 |
| Pine-wood shipments | 8, 9 |

Timber trade.

    The tables annexed to this report will show that the trade of Pensacola for the year 1891 was fairly good in comparison with the average yearly business of this port. It will also be seen that the bulk of the exports of pitch-pine wood—the staple export commodity of this place and its surroundings—was, as usual, to ports and places in the United Kingdom. Believing that it will be of interest, I give in this report a table showing the ports and places in the United Kingdom to which shipments of pitch-pine

(1245)

were made during the year from Pensacola and the quantities and description shipped.

The trade of Pensacola is very much supported by some of the commercial houses of the United Kingdom, both in the way of shipments of pitch-pine wood direct to ports there and by some of these shipments being controlled by British houses and sent hence to other countries; therefore, those in the wood trade in the United Kingdom are always glad, I think, to know of the continued prosperity of this great wood exporting port. I also annex a table showing the exports of pitch-pine hence to ports and places abroad, other than in the United Kingdom. My idea in giving this other table is to give an insight into the trade abroad generally with Pensacola in pitch-pine.

My opinion, based upon past supplies and guided by what I have seen and heard of during my many years of service at this post, is that the present yearly average trade of Pensacola may be counted upon for many decades of years yet; and that the demand for pitch-pine wood nearly all over the principal parts of the world will hardly ever decline while the supply lasts, though substitutes for this wood, as iron and steel, in ship-building are now taking its place to some extent.

*Imports.* The imports at Pensacola in the year 1891 from foreign ports were, as usual, about nominal. The chief articles of consumption at Pensacola are brought here from the larger markets of the United States, north and west, and amount to several millions of dollars yearly. Amongst these imports there is a large proportion in cloth fabrics and cutlery, &c., of British goods, even with the late large increase in cost of some of these things by reason of the new tariff of duties.

*Shipping.* The shipping tables in this report will show that British sailing vessels are falling-off very much. In this connection it may be again remarked that of the sailing vessels entered here now, particularly those under the flags of Norway and Sweden, over one-half were, I believe, formerly under the British flag, and traded regularly to Pensacola years ago. I think that as these old vessels get older, when it will be impossible to run them longer, and they are not replaced by purchase of other British sailing vessels (as cannot well be done, for the reason that few, if any, of the old class of sailing vessels are now being built in the United Kingdom, and not many more old sailing vessels there to sell), that British steam tonnage will yearly increase in the carrying trade. The proportion of tonnage of British vessels which loaded at Pensacola with pitch-pine wood during the year, in comparison with the tonnage of other flags, amounted to nearly one-fourth. The net tonnage of British steam and sailing vessels loading cargoes of pitch-pine amounted to 87,016 tons. The steamers (64,656 tons) took an average of about $1\frac{3}{4}$ tons of cargo per net register of ton. The sailing vessels (22,360 tons) took an average of about $1\frac{1}{2}$ tons of cargo per net register of ton. Taking the tonnage of the other foreign vessels which loaded pitch-pine wood at Pensacola during the year, allowing for their carrying capacity about the same ratio as the British vessels, I find that British vessels loaded nearly one-third of the cargoes in weight, although they were only about one-fourth in tonnage of the other vessels.

*Fertilisers.* In my last yearly report I mentioned that a factory was being built at Pensacola for the purpose of preparing fertilisers on a large scale for general use and shipment hence, and that the chief proprietors in this establishment were of Ireland. The factory has been finished and occupies a large area of ground with its main and other buildings. *Machinery.* The machinery for the works was brought there from the United Kingdom at a large cost. This factory is a short distance from the town, near to the railroad, and is in immediate connection, by railway, to the wharves of Pensacola, and from the works to all parts of the United States. This new enterprising industry, it is considered, will be a great acquisition to Pensacola. In the first place the outlay of money in the lands and buildings of the factory has been very large, and, following this, is permanent labour for a large number of persons. This enterprise will, I think, be also beneficial to all persons interested in it, in the way of capital invested. The proprietors will no doubt receive a good return on their investments, and the agricultural people in this and the adjoining States will be supplied with fertilising compounds, and, no doubt, with much better facilities than hitherto, when all such fertilising articles had to be imported, coming viâ this and other seaport towns. These works are styled the "Gaulding Fertiliser Company," having its headquarters in Dublin I believe.

*Marine railway.* The marine railway here, which I have hitherto written about in these reports, is now finished, and in good working order, I am told, for taking on vessels for repairs. A short time since the company were able to give a reply to an inquiry from Galveston to the effect that it was prepared to take up for repairs a British steamer which was damaged and a vessel of about 2,000 tons gross.

*Coal.* Referring to the export of coal from Pensacola, which is brought to the wharves here by railroad from the mines in Alabama, these shipments go to Mexico, Cuba, and Central America. A British steamer of 1,109 tons net, on time charter, was loaded here frequently during the year with some of this coal for Colon. Her cargo each time was about 2,100 tons. The coal company engaged in this export business do some, or most, of their shipping in barges. These barges are decked and have a crew on board, but are helpless as regards making their own way. Powerful steam tugs are used to tow these barges, one at a time usually, to their destination. One of the steam vessels used for this purpose is under the British flag. This vessel was built at Glasgow, and has been engaged here in this business for several years past, towing some of these barges of coal to places in Cuba and Mexico.

To ports in Central America the cargoes are loaded on steamers and sailing vessels.

(1245)

From time to time some of the barges, with their entire cargoes of coal, are lost at sea from stress of weather during the voyage. They sprung a leak and had to be cast off by the steam vessels towing them, and abandoned, after their crews were rescued. Three of these barges, loaded with coal, have been lost within the last few months of the year from foundering, or having been abandoned in a leaky state, I am told.

There is insurance on the coal loaded on these barges, but not on the barges, as I am informed, the company taking the risk on the latter in these shipments. Some of these wooden barges are the hulls of sailing vessels which had suffered casualty, and were condemned and sold, and refitted for the coal-carrying business as described. Some of them are mainly of iron—hulls of old condemned steamers.

**Fish.** Fish is in abundance and cheap at Pensacola, and is hawked about the streets immediately after being caught by the fishermen who are engaged in this retail fish trade. Some of the kinds of fish caught in these waters are very fine. In the bay of Pensacola, and in the several inland streams around here, almost every description of salt-water fish abound, and in the season 50 c. (2s. 1d.) will purchase a dozen Spanish mackerel. The "snapper-banks" off the harbour of Pensacola are famous for the fine fish, the "snapper" being in abundance there. This fish "can be caught often two at a time on one line, weighing from 5 lbs. to 60 lbs., as rapidly as the line is thrown in. The limit to the quantity that may be caught is commensurate with the physical endurance of the catcher." At least, so says the pamphlet, "Facts about Florida." It is claimed, however, that no one can know the flavour of fresh fish until he has eaten a "pompano" at Pensacola. This fish is scarce, and rather higher in price; it is caught and can only be obtained in certain months of the year, about autumn and spring, mostly in the latter season. A good deal of fish is shipped from Pensacola to markets far and near in the United States. This wholesale business in fish is carried on by dealers in the business, who have fishing fleets of small vessels regularly employed. These shipments go forward packed in ice in express railroad cars. The vessels engaged in these catchings are supplied with cisterns, and a large portion of the fish caught is brought to land alive. Ice is used on these vessels for packing the fish that cannot be saved alive.

**Sanitary.** Pensacola was free from epidemics of any kind during the year 1891, and the town has been fairly healthy, and as regards the general condition of the 12,000 inhabitants here, I think it has been ordinarily good. I have before stated in these reports that, as a rule, the mass of the people of this place appear to be free from want always, and their routine of life, so far as I can observe, presents cheerfulness and contentment. Strikes, or like **Labour question.** obstacles to trade, seldom or never occur here. I may still then, with much pleasure, repeat my remarks in former reports in favour of the apparent continued prosperity of this community, and of the continued activity of the business of this great timber-exporting port.

## NEW ORLEANS.

Now follow the tables connected with this report :—

Annex A.—RETURN of Principal Articles of Export from Pensacola during the Years 1890-91.

| Articles. | | 1891. | | 1890. | |
|---|---|---|---|---|---|
| | | Quantity. | Value. | Quantity. | Value. |
| | | | £ s. d. | | £ s. d. |
| Pitch-pine lumber | Super. ft. | 113,569,000 | 283,890 0 0 | 129,329,000 | 323,322 10 0 |
| Sawn pitch-pine timber | Cubic ft. | 11,179,576 | 279,419 8 0 | 12,528,440 | 313,211 0 0 |
| Hewn " " | " " | 539,930 | 12,373 7 11 | 1,387,878 | 31,805 10 9 |
| Cotton | Bales | ... | ... | 21,713 | 229,506 11 3 |
| Coal | Tons | 48,191 | 32,627 11 4 | 31,738 | 18,780 18 9 |
| Cedar | Cubic ft. | 2,400 | 175 0 0 | 5,000 | 364 11 8 |
| Other articles | ... | ... | 25,000 0 0 | ... | 1,854 19 2 |
| Total | ... | ... | 611,055 7 3 | ... | 918,846 1 7 |

The following, as regards the above table of exports, is descriptive of the quantities, values, weights, and measures, the conversion of money into sterling being at the rate of 4 dol. 80 c. per 1*l*. Lumber at average of 12 dol. (2*l*. 10*s*.) per 1,000 superficial feet, board measure; sawn timber at an average of 12 c. (6*d*.) per cubic foot, basis 40 feet average; hewn timber at average of 11 c. (5½*d*.) per cubic foot, basis 100 feet average; cotton at average of 10 c. (5*d*.) per lb., in bales of 507 lbs. average weight each bale; coal at 3 dol. 25 c. (13*s*. 6½*d*.) per ton; cedar at 35 c. (1*s*. 5½*d*.) per cubic foot.

Annex B.—RETURN of Principal Articles of Import to Pensacola, during the Years 1890-91.

| Articles. | | | | Value. | |
|---|---|---|---|---|---|
| | | | | 1891. | 1890. |
| | | | | £ s. d. | £ s. d. |
| Chief articles | .. | .. | .. | .. | .. |
| Other " | .. | .. | .. | 12,302 0 0 | 11,521 5 0 |

NOTE.—As explained elsewhere in this report, the chief articles of import to Pensacola, which consist of breadstuffs, grocery articles, and such other necessaries of life as are in daily demand, are brought here by railroad from the large western and northern markets of the United States. Also articles of clothing, hardware, &c., come from the same markets, and these goods altogether amount to about 3,000,000 dol. per year. Salt, superphosphates, and some other articles are brought here from the United Kingdom and other countries abroad, and the value thereof is shown

## UNITED STATES.

above. In the items of other articles of import for the year 1891 there was a large item, 2,552*l*. 1*s*. 8*d*., for iron ore brought in a British steamer from Huelva, Spain.

Annex C.—TABLE showing the Total Value of all Articles Exported from Pensacola and Imported to Pensacola from and to Foreign Countries during the Years 1890–91.

|  | Exports. |  | Imports. |  |
|---|---|---|---|---|
| Country. | 1891. | 1890. | 1891. | 1890. |
|  | £ s. d. | £ s. d. | £ s. d. | £ s. d. |
| United Kingdom | 235,412 10 6 | 514,387 13 7 | 6,052 0 0 | 6,004 5 0 |
| South Africa | 4,316 11 8 | ... | ... | ... |
| British West Indies | 662 10 0 | ... | ... | ... |
| France | 94,397 7 4 | 44,761 6 5 | ... | ... |
| Italy | 43,421 2 8 | 68,623 9 3 | ... | ... |
| Brazil | 35,356 7 0 | 26,967 10 0 | ... | ... |
| Netherlands | 33,540 8 9 | 58,795 11 8 | ... | ... |
| Spain and colonies | 25,139 15 3 | 43,808 7 2 | 2,750 0 0 | ... |
| Belgium | 20,581 8 5 | 17,015 15 0 | ... | ... |
| Argentine Republic | 17,830 0 0 | 39,200 15 0 | ... | ... |
| Germany | 14,132 13 0 | 17,919 14 6 | 3,500 0 0 | 5,517 0 0 |
| Portugal | 5,928 2 6 | 7,874 0 0 | ... | ... |
| Mexico | 4,983 7 11 | 2,774 6 5 | ... | ... |
| United States of Colombia | 4,579 15 10 | ... | ... | ... |
| Costa Rica | 3,749 13 9 | ... | ... | ... |
| Uruguay | 3,402 0 0 | 19,582 10 0 | ... | ... |
| Nicaragua | 2,903 6 8 | 3,515 8 4 | ... | ... |
| Austria | 650 12 10 | 1,981 0 3 | ... | ... |
| Norway | ... | 1,247 9 10 | ... | ... |
| Other countries | 594 10 0 | 1,740 15 0 | ... | . |
| Total, foreign countries | 551,582 4 1 | 870,195 12 5 | 12,302 0 0 | 11,521 5 0 |
| „ ports in the United States | 59,473 3 2 | 48,650 9 2 | ... | .. |
| Total | 611,055 7 3 | 918,846 1 7 | 12,302 0 0 | 11,521 5 0 |

Annex D.—RETURN of all Shipping at the Port of Pensacola in the Year 1891.

ENTERED.

|  | Sailing. |  | Steam. |  | Total. |  |
|---|---|---|---|---|---|---|
| Nationality. | Number of Vessels. | Tons. | Number of Vessels. | Tons. | Number of Vessels. | Tons. |
| British | 47 | 23,024 | 47 | 64,656 | 94 | 87,680 |
| American | 139 | 69,642 | 1 | 464 | 140 | 70,106 |
| Swedish and Norwegian | 139 | 115,635 | 17 | 8,942 | 156 | 124,566 |
| Italian | 68 | 46,314 | ... | ... | 68 | 46,374 |
| Russian | 33 | 21,655 | ... | ... | 33 | 21,655 |
| Spanish | 2 | 2,305 | 9 | 14,742 | 11 | 17,047 |
| German | 13 | 12,376 | ... | ... | 13 | 12,376 |
| Netherlands | 8 | 7,078 | ... | ... | 8 | 7,078 |
| Austrian | 10 | 6,706 | ... | ... | 10 | 6,706 |
| French | 8 | 5,018 | ... | ... | 8 | 5,018 |
| Total | 467 | 309,753 | 74 | 88,804 | 541 | 398,617 |
| „ for the year preceding | 534 | 366,954 | 58 | 74,256 | 592 | 441,210 |

## NEW ORLEANS.

#### Cleared.

| Nationality. | Sailing. Number of Vessels. | Sailing. Tons. | Steam. Number of Vessels. | Steam. Tons. | Total. Number of Vessels. | Total. Tons. |
|---|---|---|---|---|---|---|
| British | 48 | 24,309 | 47 | 64,656 | 95 | 88,965 |
| American | 136 | 72,382 | 1 | 464 | 137 | 72,846 |
| Swedish and Norwegian | 138 | 115,042 | 17 | 8,942 | 155 | 123,984 |
| Italian | 69 | 47,060 | ... | ... | 69 | 47,060 |
| Russian | 30 | 19,289 | ... | ... | 30 | 19,289 |
| Spanish | 2 | 2,305 | 9 | 14,742 | 11 | 17,047 |
| German | 11 | 11,063 | ... | ... | 11 | 11,063 |
| Netherlands | 8 | 6,289 | ... | ... | 8 | 6,289 |
| Austrian | 10 | 6,574 | ... | ... | 10 | 6,574 |
| French | 8 | 4,819 | ... | ... | 8 | 4,819 |
| Total | 460 | 309,132 | 74 | 88,804 | 534 | 397,936 |
| ,, for the year preceding | 528 | 369,598 | 58 | 74,256 | 586 | 443,854 |

## UNITED STATES.

Annex E.—TABLE showing the Quantities, Assortment, and Value of Pitch-pine Wood shipped from Pensacola to Ports and Places in the United Kingdom and British Colonies during the Year 1891.*

| Ports and Places. | Sawn Timber. | Hewn Timber. | Deals, Lumber, &c. | Value. |
|---|---|---|---|---|
| | Cubic Feet. | Cubic Feet. | Super. Feet. | £ s. d. |
| Liverpool | 1,553,886 | 8,160 | 4,991,000 | .. |
| London | 707,267 | .. | 2,178,000 | .. |
| Greenock | 897,166 | .. | 1,705,000 | .. |
| The Tyne | 273,416 | .. | 145,000 | .. |
| Newcastle | 64,000 | .. | 41,000 | .. |
| Leith | 99,582 | .. | 122,000 | .. |
| West Hartlepool | 366,000 | .. | 890,000 | .. |
| Queenstown | 370,519 | .. | 138,000 | .. |
| Newhaven | 73,000 | .. | 262,000 | .. |
| Bristol | 202,250 | 10,877 | 88,000 | .. |
| Barrow | 335,324 | | 170,000 | .. |
| Cardiff | 334,666 | 23,152 | 212,000 | .. |
| Middlesbrough | 116,800 | .. | 64,000 | .. |
| Sharpness | 300,683 | .. | 137,000 | .. |
| Hull | 284,840 | .. | 207,000 | .. |
| Falmouth | 75,750 | 15,983 | 54,000 | .. |
| Fleetwood | 218,250 | .. | 62,000 | .. |
| Aberdeen | 53,333 | 2,788 | 72,000 | .. |
| Grimsby | 197,047 | .. | 397,000 | .. |
| Sutton Bridge | 36,833 | .. | 751,000 | .. |
| Dublin | 55,333 | .. | 17,000 | .. |
| The Downs | 66,000 | .. | 22,000 | .. |
| Ayr | 29,166 | 2,138 | 58,000 | .. |
| Dundee | 73,166 | 15,423 | 312,000 | .. |
| Newport | 123,833 | .. | 77,000 | .. |
| King's Lynn | 73,066 | 7,606 | 33,000 | .. |
| Glasgow | 69,916 | .. | 62,000 | .. |
| Swansea | 78,749 | 6,613 | 60,000 | .. |
| Waterford | .. | 1,750 | 573,000 | .. |
| Whitehaven | 36,000 | .. | 20,000 | .. |
| Grangemouth | 168,749 | 11,236 | 90,000 | .. |
| Garstow Dock | 48,916 | .. | 25,000 | .. |
| Southampton | 8,250 | 2,215 | 321,000 | .. |
| Port Glasgow | 118,000 | .. | 75,000 | .. |
| Cape Town | 10,250 | .. | 70,000 | .. |
| Montrose | 28,586 | .. | 200,000 | .. |
| Mithel Dock | 23,416 | 7,561 | 52,000 | .. |
| Sunderland | 62,075 | .. | 19,000 | .. |
| Granton | 46,500 | .. | 8,000 | .. |
| Belize | .. | .. | 265,000 | .. |
| Places in South Africa | 38,000 | 4,166 | 775,000 | .. |
| Total | 7,680,583 | 119,668 | 15,820,000 | 234,306 19 4 |

\* See table Annex A for value of each description of the above assortment of pitch-pine wood, which, if figured up, would show the total value as given above.

## NEW ORLEANS.

Annex F.—TABLE showing the Quantities, Assortment, and Value of Pitch-pine Wood shipped from Pensacolo to Ports and Places in Countries abroad, other than the United Kingdom, during the Year 1891.

| Ports and Places. | Sawn Timber. | Hewn Timber. | Deals, Lumber, &c. | Value. |
|---|---|---|---|---|
|  | Cubic Feet. | Cubic Feet. | Super. Feet. | £ s. d. |
| France— |  |  |  |  |
| Fécamp | 142,249 | .. | 247,000 | .. |
| Calais | 40,916 | 1,652 | 1,113,000 | .. |
| Bordeaux | 100,315 | 24,510 | 3,146,000 | .. |
| St. Servan | .. | .. | 209,000 | .. |
| Havre | 447,869 | .. | 326,000 | .. |
| Cherbourg | 4,260 | 1,485 | 528,000 | .. |
| Honfleur | 141,719 | .. | 2,549,000 | .. |
| Dieppe | 73,586 | .. | 787,000 | .. |
| Marseilles | 80,919 | 16,235 | 2,611,000 | .. |
| Dunkirk | 50,083 | 33,788 | 790,000 | .. |
| Brest | 75,000 | .. | 95,000 | .. |
| Rouen | 82,504 | .. | 701,000 | .. |
| St. Nazaire | 217,832 | 55,828 | 1,041,000 | .. |
| Caen | 39,416 | 2,076 | 907,000 | .. |
| Boulogne | 1,833 | .. | 361,000 | .. |
| Rochefort | 4,416 | 44,790 | 442,000 | .. |
| St. Malo | .. | .. | 118,000 | .. |
| Italy— |  |  |  |  |
| Genoa | 460,675 | 108,455 | 4,944,000 | .. |
| Naples | 90,500 | 3,236 | 713,000 | .. |
| Palermo | .. | .. | 1,047,000 | .. |
| Salerno | 25,586 | 9,507 | 177,000 | .. |
| Spezia | 2,750 | .. | 486,000 | .. |
| Cagliari | 36,000 | 4,840 | 813,000 | .. |
| Civita Vecchia | 1,500 | 1,072 | 151,000 | .. |
| Leghorn | 47,916 | 5,264 | 92,000 | .. |
| Brazil— |  |  |  |  |
| Rio de Janeiro | .. | .. | 11,653,000 | .. |
| Santos | .. | .. | 1,954,000 | .. |
| Netherlands— |  |  |  |  |
| Harlingen | 21,250 | 7,832 | 20,000 | .. |
| Rotterdam | 6,666 | .. | 633,000 | .. |
| Amsterdam | 151,416 | .. | 2,487,000 | .. |
| Terneuzen | 6,000 | 3,011 | 1,053,000 | .. |
| Dordrecht | 144,089 | .. | 2,409,000 | .. |
| Delfezyl | 191,880 | 2,172 | 64,000 | .. |
| Zaandam | 133,189 | .. | 141,000 | .. |
| Spain— |  |  |  |  |
| Bilbao | 80,333 | .. | 1,531,000 | .. |
| Havana | .. | .. | 3,493,000 | .. |
| Denia | .. | .. | 306,000 | .. |
| Cienfuegos | .. | .. | 1,814,000 | .. |
| Caibarien | .. | .. | 707,000 | .. |
| Cardenas | .. | .. | 66,000 | .. |
| Seville | 27,916 | 859 | 26,000 | .. |
| Valencia | .. | .. | 432,000 | .. |
| Barcelona | .. | .. | 405,000 | .. |
| Guantino | .. | .. | 207,000 | .. |
| Belgium— |  |  |  |  |
| Ghent | .. | .. | 1,168,000 | .. |
| Antwerp | 20,982 | 31,588 | 6,823,000 | .. |

## UNITED STATES.

Annex F.—TABLE showing the Quantities, Assortment, and Value of Pitch-pine Wood shipped from Pensacola to Ports and Places in Countries abroad, other than the United Kingdom, during the Year 1891—continued.

| Ports and Places. | Sawn Timber. | Hewn Timber. | Deals, Lumber, &c. | Value. |
|---|---|---|---|---|
| | Cubic Feet. | Cubic Feet. | Super. Feet. | £ s. d. |
| Argentine Republic— | | | | |
| Buenos Ayres | .. | .. | 5,465,000 | .. |
| Rosario | .. | .. | 333,000 | .. |
| Ensenada | .. | .. | 730,000 | .. |
| La Plata | .. | .. | 605,000 | .. |
| Germany— | | | | |
| Geestemunde | 65,416 | .. | 770,000 | .. |
| Brake | .. | .. | 1,391,000 | .. |
| Hamburg | 92,291 | .. | 609,000 | .. |
| Bremen | .. | .. | 549,000 | .. |
| Lubeck | 6,500 | .. | 692,000 | .. |
| Portugal— | | | | |
| Lisbon | 175,000 | 25,277 | 51,000 | .. |
| Oporto | .. | 34,584 | 23,000 | .. |
| Uruguay— | | | | |
| Monte Video | .. | .. | 1,361,000 | .. |
| Mexico— | | | | |
| Tampier | .. | .. | 917,000 | .. |
| Progresso | .. | .. | 59,000 | .. |
| Austria— | | | | |
| Fiume | 2,288 | 14,333 | 106,000 | .. |
| Ports in Central America | .. | .. | 400,383 | .. |
| Total | 3,321,493 | 447,120 | 76,278,000 | 283,978 17 0 |

LONDON:
Printed for Her Majesty's Stationery Office,
By HARRISON AND SONS,
Printers in Ordinary to Her Majesty.
(75  3 | 92—H & S  1245)

# FOREIGN OFFICE.
## 1892.
## ANNUAL SERIES.

### N⁰ 1001.
### DIPLOMATIC AND CONSULAR REPORTS ON TRADE AND FINANCE.

# UNITED STATES.

### REPORT FOR THE YEAR 1891
#### ON THE
### TRADE OF BALTIMORE AND DISTRICT.

REFERENCE TO PREVIOUS REPORT, Annual Series No. 835.

*Presented to both Houses of Parliament by Command of Her Majesty,*
*MARCH, 1892.*

LONDON:
PRINTED FOR HER MAJESTY'S STATIONERY OFFICE,
BY HARRISON AND SONS, ST. MARTIN'S LANE,
PRINTERS IN ORDINARY TO HER MAJESTY.

And to be purchased, either directly or through any Bookseller, from
EYRE & SPOTTISWOODE, EAST HARDING STREET, FLEET STREET, E.C., and
32, ABINGDON STREET, WESTMINSTER, S.W.; or
JOHN MENZIES & Co., 12, HANOVER STREET, EDINBURGH, and
90, WEST NILE STREET, GLASGOW; or
HODGES, FIGGIS, & Co., 104, GRAFTON STREET, DUBLIN.

1892.
*Price Three Halfpence.*

[C. 6550—63.]

# New Series of Reports.

Reports of the Annual Series have been issued from Her Majesty's Diplomatic and Consular Officers at the following places, and may be obtained from the sources indicated on the title-page:—

| No. | | Price. | No. | | Price. |
|---|---|---|---|---|---|
| 879. | Mollendo | ½d. | 940. | The Hague | 1½d. |
| 880. | Kiukiang | 1d. | 941. | Christiania | 1d. |
| 881. | Antananarivo | 1d. | 942. | Christiania | ½d. |
| 882. | Stettin | 2½d. | 943. | Brunei | 1½d. |
| 883. | Fiume | 1½d. | 944. | Alexandria | 1½d. |
| 884. | Batavia | 1d. | 945. | Therapia | ½d. |
| 885. | Samoa | ½d. | 946. | Bushire | 1½d. |
| 886. | Cherbourg | 1d. | 947. | Tokio | 2½d. |
| 887. | Cagliari | 1d | 948. | Stockholm | 2d. |
| 888. | Hankow | 1½d. | 949. | Palermo | 2½d. |
| 889. | Vienna | 1½d. | 950. | St. Petersburg | 2½d. |
| 890. | Amoy | 1d. | 951. | Quito | ½d. |
| 891. | Adrianople | ½d. | 952. | Rio de Janeiro | 2d. |
| 892. | Chicago | 2½d. | 953. | Naples | 2d. |
| 893. | Brest | 1d. | 954. | Amsterdam | 1d. |
| 894. | Smyrna | 1d. | 955. | Tangiers | 2d. |
| 895. | Cadiz | 1d. | 956. | Paramaribo | 1d. |
| 896. | Aleppo | 1d. | 957. | Teneriffe | 1d. |
| 897. | Foochow | 1d. | 958. | Athens | 2d. |
| 898. | Kiungchow | 1d. | 959. | Odessa | 1d. |
| 899. | The Hague | 1½d. | 960. | Copenhagen | 9d. |
| 900. | Nice | 1½d. | 961. | Tokio | 1d. |
| 901. | Nantes | 1½d. | 962. | Salonica | 1½d. |
| 902. | Port-au-Prince | 1½d. | 963. | Stettin | 3½d. |
| 903. | Bengazi | 1d. | 964. | Philadelphia | 2d. |
| 904. | Tahiti | ½d. | 965. | Mexico | 2d. |
| 905. | Chinkiang | 1d. | 966. | Malaga | 2½d. |
| 906. | San Francisco | 3d. | 967. | Berne | 1d. |
| 907. | Brindisi | 2d. | 968. | Puerto-Rico | ½d. |
| 908. | Beyrout | 1d. | 969. | Buda-Pesth | 1d. |
| 909. | Noumea | ½d. | 970. | Bogotá | 1d. |
| 910. | San Francisco | 1d. | 971. | Panama | 1½d. |
| 911. | New York | 1½d. | 972. | Munich | 2d. |
| 912. | Caracas | 1½d. | 973. | Copenhagen | 4d. |
| 913. | Greytown | ½d. | 974. | Guatemala | 1d. |
| 914. | Corunna | 2d. | 975. | Munich | 2d. |
| 915. | Christiania | 5½d. | 976. | Meshed | 1½d. |
| 916. | Callao | 1d. | 977. | Para | ½d. |
| 917. | Macao | 1d. | 978. | Florence | 1d. |
| 918. | Söul | 1d. | 979. | The Hague | 1½d. |
| 919. | Dunkirk | 1d. | 980. | Patras | 1d. |
| 920. | Tamsui | 1d. | 981. | Paris | 1½d. |
| 921. | Bussorah | ½d. | 982. | Zanzibar | 2½d. |
| 922. | Yokohama | 3½d. | 983. | Buenos Ayres | ½d. |
| 923. | Bilbao | 1½d. | 984. | Copenhagen | 1d. |
| 924. | Barcelona | 2½d. | 985. | Stuttgart | 1d. |
| 925. | Netherlands India | 1d. | 986. | New Orleans | 1½d. |
| 926. | Chefoo | 1d. | 987. | New Orleans | 10d. |
| 927. | Buenos Ayres | ½d. | 988. | Suakin | ½d. |
| 928. | Santo Domingo | ½d. | 989. | Galveston | 1½d. |
| 929. | Constantinople | ½d. | 990. | Berlin | 1d. |
| 930. | Erzeroum | 1½d. | 991. | Zanzibar | 1½d. |
| 931. | Gothenburg | 2d. | 992. | Guayaquil | 1d. |
| 932. | Tunis | 1d. | 993. | Tonga | 1d. |
| 933. | New York | 1d. | 994. | New Orleans | 1d. |
| 934. | Nagasaki | 1d. | 995. | Mozambique | 1½d. |
| 935. | Hakodate | 1½d. | 996. | Galatz | 1½d. |
| 936. | Sofia | 3d. | 997. | Nantes | 1½d. |
| 937. | Frankfort | 2d. | 998. | Algiers | 1d. |
| 938. | Bangkok | 9d. | 999. | Havre | 2½d. |
| 939. | Berne | 1½d. | 1000. | Buenos Ayres | 6d. |

# No. 1001.

*Reference to previous Report, Annual Series No. 835*

## UNITED STATES.

### BALTIMORE.

*Consul Segrave to the Marquis of Salisbury.*

My Lord,         Baltimore, February 20, 1892.

I HAVE the honour to transmit herewith to your Lordship Reports on the Trade and Commerce of Baltimore, Norfolk, and Richmond, for the year 1891.

           I have, &c.
        (Signed)   E. SEGRAVE.

---

*Report on the Trade and Commerce of Baltimore for the Year 1891.*

### ABSTRACT of Contents.

| | PAGE |
|---|---|
| Recent legislation and its effects on trade | 2 |
| Commercial situation | 3 |
| Port: works in connection with | 3 |
| Chinese exclusion demonstrated | 3 |
| Immigration | 4 |
| Taxation | 4 |
| Trial by jury | 5 |
| Oysters | 5 |
| Railway: underground works | 5 |
| Commercial position: advantages of | 6 |
| Trade: details of | 6 |
| Freights | 8 |
| Immigration: table of | 9 |
| Tables | 10–13 |
| Trade of Richmond | 13 |
| Trade of Norfolk | 15 |

(1256)

## UNITED STATES.

**Effects of recent legislation on trade.**

Notwithstanding the confident statements of the most eminent commentators, the time has not, as yet, arrived to form any conclusive opinion as to the effect of the McKinley Tariff Bill on the foreign commerce of Baltimore.

We have been told, indeed, and on the best authority, that "the Bill was a genuine American measure, passed by an American Legislature in the best interests solely of the American people, high and low; that there was not a clause, sentence, or word of the Bill that was not dictated by American patriotism, and that it would rejoice the heart of every American and gladden and brighten his home."

The people in this country are accustomed to hyperbole, they like it, and, no doubt, set a truer value upon it than any outsider could be expected to do, but, as a significative comment on the universal gladness, comes a doleful note from a "Caucus of Canners" to the effect that in the past year tin plate had cost them 10,000,000 dol. more than in the previous year, and that they had got less for their money.

And, as with tin plate, so in the fullness of time will it be with other commodities.

The Bill has been termed a monopoly Bill in so far as its tendency is to exclude outside goods from competition with home products, for, as a great political economist once said, "Where there is not competition there is monopoly."

It is argued that internal competition will safeguard the consumer, with the evidence recently adduced of the methods of the great producers, and the skill and dexterity with which combinations and trusts are brought into existence, there is neither comfort or security in such a plea.

Now the alleged object of trusts is to promote economy of production by the centralisation of labour; to do this, small dispersed and possibly competing works are bought up and closed, by which means the few, no doubt, gain an increase of wages, but by throwing the many out of employment; and as regards the reduction in prices to the consumer, that has, no doubt, in many cases been effected, but by no means in all cases.

But the trust controls the market, and what remedy has the public if one of these combinations were to decree a 25 per cent. rise in prices, say in illuminating oil for example? The only resource of the consumer, deprived of any competition or the possibility of creating it, would be to burn less oil or go to bed with the sun.

The long and short of this Bill is that the consumer has to pay for it, and as a sop to his susceptibility a promise of increased wages is held out to him.

So far, with the solitary exception of tin plate, it does not appear that the Bill has had much effect on the foreign trade of Baltimore, and even tin plate is beginning to come in in increased quantities.

In chemicals, earthenware, wines, paints, oil cloth, salt, pickles, sugar, and rice, the import has seriously increased, whilst in metals and ores, clays, toys, and coffee there has been a sensible decrease, that in tin plate alone having fallen from a value of 1,250,000*l.* in the first six months of the year to about 120,000*l.* in the second six months.

On the whole, the commercial situation of Baltimore during 1891 offers legitimate grounds for congratulation. *Commercial situation.*

Foreign exports have increased from 14,800,000*l.* in 1890 to 16,330,000*l.* in 1891, and foreign imports from 2,993,000*l.* to 3,737,000*l.*, or an aggregate increase in foreign trade of 2,250,000*l.* sterling.

Bank clearances show a slight fall on those of the previous year, but the condition of the money market in the early months of 1891 accounts for this decrease, and the returns for the last six months, which show a sensible increase over the corresponding period of 1890, offer sufficient evidence of the activity and soundness of Baltimore business.

Reference has been made in former reports to the great advantages possessed by Baltimore as a shipping port for foreign trade, and which render it, for that purpose, second to none on the Atlantic seaboard. *Port—works in connection with.*

That these advantages are daily becoming more apparent to shipowners and others interested is evident from the increased volume of its foreign trade, and the facilities which it affords through its magnificent system of railways in communication with the west, as well as local appliances for the speedy despatch of shipping show how amply it deserves its reputation. On more than one occasion a vessel has entered, loaded, and cleared for a European port within 24 hours.

The system of elevators has been enlarged and rendered as perfect as science and money can make them, and have now an aggregate storage capacity of 6,000,000 bushels of grain, and labour is plentiful and fairly cheap from an American point of view.

In addition, the work of deepening and widening the channel of approach has been vigorously prosecuted, 500,000 dol. having been spent on this work during the past year.

The contract provides for the widening of the channel to 600 feet, with a depth throughout of 27 feet at low water, and this has now been practically accomplished.

A curious instance occurred during the past year showing the inelasticity of American law in the eyes of those appointed to administer it. *Chinese exclusion.*

An English steamer entered this port manned by a crew of Hong-Kong (British Colonial) subjects.

The most perfunctory examination would have disclosed that fact, as well as that they had been legally shipped before the proper officer in the colony, and that all the provisions of English law had been duly complied with. Further, that they had been for months, if not over a year, in the ship, and that, on an average, at least three months' wages were due to them.

Nevertheless, the local officer lost no time in warning the

master that if his hands were found on shore they would be promptly arrested, under the existing law, on the ground of Chinese nationality.

The matter was referred to the Federal Government, and in process of time orders came permitting these seamen to land, provided always that they did not desert their ship and remain in Maryland.

The ship had lain at Baltimore for 12 days, but the embargo on her crew was not taken off till three days after her departure.

*Immigration—Maryland and Virginia a field for.*

It is a subject of wonder and regret that the numerous well-to-do English and Scottish immigrants who annually arrive in the United States, instead of proceeding to the west, do not turn their attention to the far more favourable field for immigration offered by Maryland and Virginia.

In place of the torrid heats of summer and the Arctic rigours of a winter in Dakota and adjoining States they have here an equable climate, rarely colder than in England, and although in summer it is occasionally under the influence of a "hot wave," warmer than the average English husbandman is accustomed to, there are few days when work in the open air may not be carried on.

Land is plentiful, either to purchase or to lease, some good, a great deal bad, as in most countries, and generally fetching prices according to quality.

The soil varies so as to admit of almost every variety of culture, from market gardening in the neighbourhood of towns to cattle breeding and fruit culture.

Markets are plentiful and good, and the facilities of transport leave nothing to be desired.

Labour (coloured) is also obtainable; it is by no means ideally perfect, but still it is available, and would no doubt prove acceptable to the British immigrant just arrived in a new country.

Of course the foregoing remarks are intended to be directed to the immigrant who may be possessed of some small capital.

*Taxation.*

An influential portion of the commercial community is much exercised with regard to the system of taxation now in force in this State, and a movement is on foot towards legislation for its alteration.

As the law is at present in force, real and personal property are assumed to comprise everything that should be amenable to taxation.

It is stated that there is no difference of public opinion as to the defective nature of the present system, nor the manner of enforcing it, with the result that the present tendency is towards the establishment of an income tax.

Another question is raised as to the propriety of taxing mortgages and ground rents. On this subject it is alleged that at each succeeding session of the legislature an attempt is made to revive the question of a tax on mortgages, a scheme which is declared to be opposed to the interests of the lender, the borrower, and the community at large by taxing the same thing twice over.

As to ground rents, in spite of their fitness as an investment, they have recently been subject to legislative restrictions. But as the validity of those in existence cannot be called in question, it is now proposed to embarrass such holdings by compelling the landlord to pay the tax which the tenant has covenanted to pay. If the tenant has contracted under lease to pay the taxes, and the law decrees that he must pay the landlord's as well, how can the burden which he has voluntarily assumed be lessened by interfering with the existing contract?

It is urged that if the value of the rental be impaired as an investment, the landlord will be compelled to sell, and the tenant will then purchase the freehold of his holding. Apart from the unrighteous principle involved, there is no evidence of any desire on his part to do so.

And it would be safe to say that if the entire ground rents of Baltimore were offered for sale at a fair market value, a very small proportion would be purchased by tenants. They are borrowers, but other people who are investors would certainly buy them up.

Trial by jury in this State under the modern dispensation does not appear to meet with unqualified approval.

*Trial by jury.*

The able and accomplished President of the Board of Trade in his annual address speaks of it as "once the boasted bulwark of human rights, now conspicuous in its degeneracy, which might be regarded as a jest if the solemnity of the subject did not forbid it."

He says further, "Avoided and evaded by persons of ability and position, and resisted in consequence of the conscriptive and merciless character of the summons, the jury-box is often filled from the ranks of indolence and incapacity. The most momentous interests in life are entrusted to the caprices of incompetency, and are frequently at the mercy of social, religious, and political prejudices."

With the commencement of the winter, the inevitable oyster question invariably crops up, and public opinion is worked upon with a view to putting pressure on the legislature to give some protection to this great industry.

*Oysters.*

The control of the State oyster beds, whether by purchase, lease, or royalty, is declared to be absolutely indispensable, if the people are not prepared to see the utter extinction of the oyster.

Twenty-five years back the business of the oyster canner was in its infancy.

At the present moment there are 85 firms engaged in this business, with a capital of some 6,000,000 dol., unless the legislature bestirs itself, this trade with the oyster appears to be doomed to extinction.

There has always been a missing link in the otherwise perfect railway communications at Baltimore. This is now in process of being forged by the construction of what is termed the "Belt Railway," a short underground line running under the heart of the city. By means of this line considerably greater facilities

*Railways, underground.*

(1256)

will be given to the commercial and travelling public. Through its means one French line will obtain a direct road from north to south, another line access to tidal waters, whilst a third which serves a populous suburb will obtain a terminus in the centre of the city for its daily increasing customers.

The length of tunnel is about 2,900 yards. It will be lighted by electricity, and maintained absolutely free from smoke through a system of hot-air currents, fans, and flues, and by the use of cable traction.

The cost of this great engineering work will be about 1,000,000*l.*, and it is expected that trains will be running through it in the course of another 12 months.

**Commercial position.**
Up to three or four years back Baltimore had practically stood still, possibly even retrograded. She had developed some trades but had lost others. She had established a large grain business, but had lost the most important sugar trade on the Atlantic seaboard.

If the balance could have been struck, comparing her position with that of 15 years earlier, it would probably have been shown that this city had barely if actually held its own.

With the establishment, however, of the great Pennsylvania steelworks in the immediate vicinity of the city, a new departure was taken, and it shortly became evident that Baltimore was admirably adapted to become the centre of great manufacturing industry. It possesses advantages to be found in few, if any, other cities in this country. It has vast resources in timber, coal, and iron within reasonable distance, and abundant and cheap transport, as well by water as by rail; and further, its climate gives it great advantages over cities further north.

Complaints, however, are made of the failure this year of the railway companies to meet the vastly increased demand for transport of grain. It is alleged that in consequence of the two great railroads, which serve this city from the west, not having been adequately equipped with rolling stock, Baltimore has lost a quarter of the grain trade which should of a right have been hers, and which was diverted in other directions. It is asserted that corn which was sent from the west for December delivery at Baltimore has not as yet (in the middle of February) reached this port.

**Trade— details of. Grain trade.**
The returns for the past year show that Baltimore still maintains its proud pre-eminence as the largest exporter of grain in the country after New York.

The short crops in many continental countries, together with the bountiful harvest in this country, has greatly stimulated the commercial movement at Baltimore, and will continue to show its active influence for many months in the present year.

The annexed Table B gives details of the export.

The reduction in the shipment of corn (maize) is owing to the short crop in 1890, but it will be more than made up in the next four months, as more than the entire of last year's shipments are even now contracted for, and vessels are already taken up for its export.

The stock in the city's elevators on the last day of the year was as under:—

|  | Bushels. |
|---|---|
| Wheat | 1,602,000 |
| Corn (maize) | 998,000 |
| Oats | 153,000 |
| Rye | 102,000 |

The year has been a very profitable one for the canned goods industry, and there has been a very large increase in the business. Crops of all kinds were prolific, and the packer reaped the benefit by an increased output.

*Canned goods.*

The stock of preserved peaches was the largest ever known in this State, and amounted to 1,500,000 cases, as against 500 cases in 1890.

The trade has been reported as more active than at any time since 1888, and prices were fairly remunerative.

Oysters canned were 25 per cent. to 50 per cent. in excess of 1890, in spite of the depletion of the beds, and this active trade will, no doubt, have contributed to the impending catastrophe.

The very large cotton harvest gathered in the past year, and the prospect of another large yield, caused a certain stagnation in the market. The price declined 1½ c. per lb. during the year, making it lower than at any time since 1874.

*Cotton.*

The crop last season was 8,600,000 bales. The receipts for the year were 306,307 bales, the export 190,827 bales. Local mills took 70,000 bales, and 88,000 bales were shipped coastwise.

The receipts of tobacco were less than the average in quantity, but were made up in quality, and the market was more active than in any previous year.

*Tobacco.*

France contracted for the usual quantity, about 10,000 hogsheads. The remainder was promptly absorbed by other European markets, leaving no accumulation of stock at any time in dealers' hands.

Prices were firm during the season, and slightly above the average of 1890, which must have been very satisfactory to producers. Stocks in warehouses are reduced to the lowest figure on record, viz., 5,899 hogsheads.

There was considerable diminution in the export of live cattle during the year, amounting to over 22,000 head.

*Cattle.*

Violent fluctuations in prices have been the marked feature in the coffee market during 1891. The political situation in Brazil, from whence Baltimore takes all its coffee, may in a great measure be held accountable for this. An active speculation has marked dealings, and business has been very brisk at this place.

*Coffee.*

The price opened in January at 16 dol. 20 c., and was quoted in December at 12 dol. 30 c.

The decrease in import at this port is said to be owing to

merchants here sending their stock to New York to take advantage of a better market and of the higher prices prevailing there.

**Customs.** The total receipts of customs during 1891 from all sources amounted to 3,267,034 dol., being an increase of 161,234 dol. over those of 1890. This is possibly in the main attributable to the rush during the first six months of the year to get in goods before the McKinley Tariff Bill came finally into operation.

**Freights.** Transatlantic rates opened at the commencement of the year in a very depressed condition. There was but a small surplus of grain for export, and many steamers were thrown on the market for other cargoes, thus reducing rates.

During the first half of the year as low as 10s. a ton to the United Kingdom, and 11s. to the Continent, was accepted, but as the season advanced rates rapidly hardened, under the influence of the undoubted surplus of the grain crop which became apparent, until 4s. 6d. a quarter to 4s. 9d. a quarter for grain was to be obtained, and for general cargo as high as 22s. 6d. a quarter.

These rates subsequently slightly declined, and at the close of the year stood at 4s. 3d. a quarter, and 19s. to 20s. respectively, with fair demand, for tonnage.

A matter deserving of serious consideration by those interested is how far, as the effects of the McKinley Tariff Bill develop, will its provisions influence rates of freight.

Month by month the proportion of vessels arriving in ballast becomes greater, and it is quite within the limits of possibility, if not of probability, that a time may come when the British shipowner, influenced whether by more remunerative employment for his vessels elsewhere, or for any other reason, may not care to incur the costs and risks of a transatlantic voyage for a single freight only.

Should fate decree that such an eventuality should concur with a superabundant harvest such as the United States is this year blessed with, the situation of the Western farmer would be piteous in the extreme.

Over-burdened with unremunerative wealth, he would have no resource but to bury or burn his grain, or to harden his heart and consent to double freight being paid for its transport across the sea. It is hardly necessary to point out that the latter alternative would not tend to its prompt sale unless in direful extremity; and thus the British farmer might finally prevail over his American competitor.

I leave it to more competent critics to speculate on what effects, moral, political, and financial, such a combination of by no means impossible circumstances might have in this country.

It must, however, by no means be lost sight of that, at the present moment, the solution of a great financial problem is actually in the hands of a few score of British shipowners, entirely independent of any legislative enactments which might be passed in this country, and who might possibly be influenced, from one cause or another, to absolutely renounce American trade.

## BALTIMORE.

**Immigration.** During the past year 49,638 immigrants disembarked at this port, an increase of 19,198 over those of the previous year, and the largest number on record.

|  | Number. |
|---|---|
| Men | 26,499 |
| Women | 23,139 |

The following nationalities were represented:—

|  |  | Number. |
|---|---|---|
| England | 385 |  |
| Ireland | 140 |  |
| Scotland | 5 |  |
| Colonies | 1 |  |
|  |  | 531 |
| Argentine |  | 1 |
| Austro-Hungary |  | 1,806 |
| Belgium |  | 2,938 |
| Denmark |  | 394 |
| France |  | 2 |
| Germany |  | 31,111 |
| Italy |  | 8 |
| Netherlands |  | 28 |
| Portugal |  | 2 |
| Roumania |  | 13 |
| Russia and Poland |  | 8,480 |
| Spain |  | 1 |
| Sweden and Norway |  | 255 |
| Switzerland |  | 24 |
| Turkey |  | 12 |
| United States |  | 1,175 |

Subjoined are transmitted:—

Annex A.—Return of all shipping at the Port of Baltimore in the year 1891.

Annex B.—Return of the principal articles of export from Baltimore in 1891.

Annex C.—Principal articles of import into Baltimore in 1891.

Annex D.—Table showing the total value of all articles exported from, or imported into, Baltimore to and from foreign countries in 1891.

Annex A.—RETURN of all Shipping at Baltimore in the Year 1891.

ENTERED.

| Nationality. | Sailing. Number of Vessels. | Sailing. Tons. | Steam. Number of Vessels. | Steam. Tons. | Total. Number of Vessels. | Total. Tons. |
|---|---|---|---|---|---|---|
| British* | 26 | 8,511 | 570 | 856,890 | 596 | 864,301 |
| American, foreign only | 175 | 61,421 | 6 | 1,305 | 181 | 62,726 |
| German† | ... | ... | 93 | 314,645 | 93 | 314,645 |
| Italian | 14 | 9,855 | ... | ... | 14 | 9,855 |
| Swedish and Norwegian | 4 | 2,282 | 12 | 6,983 | 16 | 9,265 |
| Netherlands | ... | ... | 13 | 26,330 | 13 | 26,330 |
| Spanish | ... | ... | 6 | 13,504 | 6 | 13,504 |
| All others | 3 | 856 | 1 | 1,542 | 4 | 2,398 |
| Total | 222 | 82,925 | 701 | 1,221,199 | 923 | 1,304,124 |
| ,, for the year preceding | 183 | 66,018 | 730 | 1,064,681 | 913 | 1,130,699 |

\* British decrease, vessels, 31; increase, tonnage, 6,449.
† German tonnage is evidently gross tonnage.

CLEARED.

| Nationality. | Sailing. Number of Vessels. | Sailing. Tons. | Steam. Number of Vessels. | Steam. Tons. | Total. Number of Vessels. | Total. Tons. |
|---|---|---|---|---|---|---|
| British* | 26 | 8,511 | 563 | 833,202 | 589 | 841,713 |
| American, foreign only | 167 | 54,315 | ... | ... | 167 | 54,315 |
| German† | ... | ... | 90 | 294,643 | 90 | 294,643 |
| Italian | 14 | 9,855 | ... | ... | 14 | 9,855 |
| Swedish and Norwegian | 3 | 1,886 | 14 | 7,653 | 17 | 9,539 |
| Netherlands | ... | ... | 13 | 26,333 | 13 | 26,333 |
| Spanish | ... | ... | 6 | 13,504 | 6 | 13,504 |
| All others | 4 | 930 | 1 | 1,542 | 5 | 2,472 |
| Total | 214 | 75,497 | 687 | 1,176,877 | 901 | 1,252,374 |
| ,, for the year preceding | 175 | 53,435 | 715 | 1,107,407 | 890 | 1,160,842 |

\* British decrease, vessels, 25; decrease, tonnage, 51,398.
† German tonnage is evidently gross tonnage.

## BALTIMORE.

### Annex B.—RETURN of the Principal Articles of Export from Baltimore during the Years 1891–90.

| Articles. | | 1891. Quantity. | 1891. Value.* | 1890. Quantity. | 1890. Value.* |
|---|---|---|---|---|---|
| | | | Dollars. | | Dollars. |
| Grain and bread stuffs— | | | | | |
| Wheat | Quarters | 1,951,912 | ... | 641,496 | ... |
| Flour | Tons | 303,735 | ... | 330,243 | ... |
| Corn, maize | Cwts. | 175,370 | ... | 592,569 | ... |
| ,,  meal | Tons | 2,276 | ... | 725 | ... |
| Rye | Bushels | 754,826 | ... | 28,890 | ... |
| Provisions— | | | | | |
| Cattle, live | Head | 65,399 | ... | 88,172 | ... |
| Beef, various | Tons | 20,648 | ... | 28,458 | ... |
| Pork, hams, and bacon | ,, | 13,285 | ... | 9,523 | ... |
| Canned goods | Cases | 65,856 | ... | ... | ... |
| Lard, tallow, and grease | Tons | 41,941 | ... | 55,530 | ... |
| Oils— | | | | | |
| Illuminating | Barrels | 270,000 | ... | 387,000 | ... |
| Vegetable and animal | ,, | 170,450 | ... | 173,853 | ... |
| Oilcake | Tons | 27,798 | ... | 27,926 | ... |
| Minerals— | | | | | |
| Copper, various | ,, | 17,317 | ... | 25,925 | ... |
| Silver | ,, | 570 | ... | 1,616 | ... |
| Zinc | ,, | 1,277 | ... | 318 | ... |
| Coals | ,, | 115,290 | ... | 61,491 | ... |
| Timber— | | | | | |
| Lumber | Met. feet | 31,318 | ... | 29,126 | ... |
| Logs | Number | 6,193 | ... | 41,856 | ... |
| Staves | Thousands | 1,735 | ... | 2,423 | ... |
| Various— | | | | | |
| Apples, various | Tons | 3,578 | ... | 2,086 | ... |
| Bark | Bags | 29,389 | ... | 46,300 | ... |
| ,,  extract | Barrels | 16,329 | ... | 10,837 | ... |
| Cotton | Bales | 190,827 | ... | 146,573 | ... |
| Resin | Barrels | 111,414 | ... | 116,181 | ... |
| Seeds, clover and grass | Tons | 6,879 | ... | 6,409 | ... |
| Sugar and glucose | ,, | 1,205 | ... | 3,612 | ... |
| Starch | ,, | 1,927 | ... | 1,721 | ... |
| Tobacco | Hogsheads | 55,808 | ... | 53,924 | ... |
| Wax | Tons | 1,419 | ... | 1,173 | ... |
| Whisky | Barrels | 7,136 | ... | 2,516 | ... |
| Total | ... | ... | 79,365,959 | ... | 71,780,959 |
| Equivalent in sterling £ | ... | ... | 18,193,199 | ... | 14,800,185 |

\* 4 dol. 85 c. = 1*l*.

## Annex C.—Return of the Principal Articles of Import into Baltimore during the Years 1891–90.

| Articles. | | 1891. Quantity. | 1891. Value.* | 1890. Quantity. | 1890. Value.* |
|---|---|---|---|---|---|
| | | | Dollars. | | Dollars. |
| Metals and minerals— | | | | | |
|   Iron ore | Tons | 418,833 | ... | 515,382 | ... |
|   „ manganese | „ | 12,780 | ... | 9,192 | ... |
|   „ speigle | „ | 3,150 | ... | 7,432 | ... |
|   Purple ore | „ | 19,351 | ... | 37,161 | ... |
|   „ various | „ | 1,240 | ... | 21,966 | ... |
|   Steel, various | „ | 1,560 | ... | 5,127 | ... |
|   Tin plate | Boxes | 976,647 | ... | 1,199,408 | .. |
| Chemicals and fertilisers— | | | | | |
|   Salt, manure | Bags | 62,166 | ... | 75,785 | ... |
|   „ cake | Casks | 6,982 | ... | 3,982 | ... |
|   Soda, ash | „ | 39,929 | ... | 24,028 | ... |
|   „ caustic | „ | 2,120 | ... | 1,464 | ... |
|   Sulphur | Tons | 14,995 | ... | 15,964 | ... |
|   Bleaching powder | Tierces | 5,102 | ... | 3,183 | ... |
|   Fertilisers, other | Bags | 152,366 | ... | ... | ... |
| Clay, various— | | | | | |
|   Cement | Barrels | 125,607 | ... | 83,839 | ... |
|   Clays | Tons | 25,043 | ... | 14,345 | ... |
|   Earthenware | Crates | 24,099 | ... | 19,305 | ... |
| Toys | Cases | 10,433 | ... | 15,912 | ... |
| Fish, salt | Barrels | 30,287 | ... | 23,978 | ... |
| Beer | „ | 3,067 | ... | 3,233 | ... |
| Mineral waters | Cases | 6,611 | ... | 10,640 | ... |
| Whisky | Barrels | 14,081 | ... | 16,671 | ... |
| Wines and liqueurs | Cases | 7,237 | ... | 1,890 | ... |
| Tar, gas, and coal | Casks | 17,083 | ... | .. | ... |
| Hides | Bales | 19,203 | ... | 16,703 | ... |
| Oilcloth | „ | 18,295 | ... | 4,671 | ... |
| Paints | Tubs | 8,542 | ... | 4,712 | ... |
| Sugar | Bags | 201,452 | ... | ... | ... |
| Fruits— | | | | | |
|   Bananas | Bunches | 590,624 | ... | 614,161 | ... |
|   Cocoa nuts | Thousands | 1,425 | ... | 1,942 | ... |
|   Pineapples | Dozens | 375,277 | ... | 335,153 | ... |
|   Lemons and oranges | Cases | 44,956 | ... | 9,272 | ... |
|   Fruit, dried | Packages | 22,212 | ... | ... | ... |
| Coffee | Bags | 172,727 | ... | 190,195 | ... |
| Rice | „ | 58,490 | ... | 39,882 | ... |
| Pepper and spices | „ | 3,876 | ... | 4,843 | ... |
| Pickles | Cases | 6,383 | ... | 3,742 | ... |
| Salt | Tons | 17,749 | ... | 13,687 | ... |
| Total | ... | ... | 18,193,199 | ... | 14,519,041 |
| Equivalent in sterling | £ | .. | 3,638,639 | ... | 3,182,551 |

\* 4 dol. 85 c. = 1*l*.

## BALTIMORE.

Annex D.—TABLE showing the Total Value of all Articles Exported from or Imported into Baltimore during the Years 1890–91.

| Country. | Exports. 1891. | Exports. 1890. | Imports. 1891. | Imports. 1890. |
|---|---|---|---|---|
| | £ | £ | £ | £ |
| Great Britain | 10,500,000 | 9,000,000 | 1,850,000 | 1,750,000 |
| Germany | 2,500,000 | 1,850,000 | 275,000 | 200,000 |
| Netherlands | 1,750,000 | 1,170,000 | 150,000 | 125,000 |
| Brazil | 600,000 | 650,000 | 400,000 | 350,000 |
| France | 950,000 | 750,000 | 100,000 | .. |
| Belgium | 1,000,000 | 620,000 | 50,000 | .. |
| Italy | .. | .. | 125,000 | .. |
| Spain and Cuba | 100,000 | .. | 350,000 | 250,000 |
| Denmark | 250,000 | 85,000 | .. | .. |
| Other countries | 540,000 | 100,000 | 300,000 | 150,000 |
| Total | 18,190,000 | 14,225,000 | 3,600,000 | 2,825,000 |

## RICHMOND.

Mr. Vice-Consul Handcock reports as follows:—

*General trade.* The trade of Richmond has, during the past year, been most prosperous, continuing almost everywhere to show promising signs of development.

The commencement of the year was gloomy in the extreme, most of the markets being depressed, owing to excessive speculation and over-investment in the so-called "land booms." The crisis, too, that occurred in London had effect here, in that the prevailing distrust made money tight and loans unobtainable. The outlook for 1891 was, therefore, anything but hopeful, capital being diverted from the usual useful channels was locked up in more or less wild speculations in real estate, which in the end in many instances proved mere "bubbles."

Things began to mend early in the year, as the rage for land speculation died out, and high hopes for the future characterised the closing of 1891, which were increased somewhat by the report that a settlement of the State Debt had been agreed upon in England. This settlement, which had been so long postponed and had caused so much heart-burning to the bondholders, is now before the State Legislature, and many people are sanguine enough to predict that Virginia will benefit greatly when the interest on its debt is paid.

It is easy to believe how deferred payment of the State Debt may have made foreign investors shy, and how increased credit will attract increased capital from abroad.

*Tobacco.* Tobacco, the staple industry of Richmond, has prospered and increased during the year; only one failure is reported, and that for a small sum—an unimportant firm.

It seems that more attention is being paid of late towards the extension of the manufacture of cigarettes, owing to the ever-increasing demand for the same; nevertheless, the out-turn of cheroots and cigars shows no diminution.

Several of the large firms have with advantage to themselves enlarged their capacity for the manufacture of plug-tobacco. Owing principally to the fast-increasing demand for bright tobacco used in cigarettes, &c., in July last the attempt was successfully inaugurated of selling bright tobacco loose on the warehouse floor direct from the planters of Virginia and North Carolina, instead of, as has hitherto been the custom, in hogsheads and tierces. This system has so well succeeded that no less than five large warehouses are now employed in this business.

A large trade is carried on in Richmond in Western (Burley) tobacco, viz., tobacco from the Western States of Kentucky and Missouri. This tobacco, though not of the same fine quality as Virginian leaf, has the advantage of being cheaper and being procurable at all times.

The tobacco crop for 1891, both as regards dark shipping and bright tobacco, is reported below the estimate; excessive rain during the maturing of the leaf seems to have weakened the crop.

England, Germany, and Austria are reported as buying the best tobacco in open market, while France, Spain, and Italy buy the worst. The "Regie" system which obtains in these latter countries is the cause of this; the agencies through whom the leaf is purchased contract to do so at fixed rates, and are considerably tied down as to the prices they pay in the markets.

Richmond now manufactures many of the articles connected with the making up of tobacco, such as liquorice, oils, gums, &c. The manufacture of decorated tin boxes was floated as a new industry during the past year, with a capital of 100,000 dol., and promises well.

*Shipping.* The port of Richmond includes West Point, at the head of the York River, 38 miles from Richmond, the terminus of the Richmond and Danville Railway system, and the port proper of Richmond, 127 miles from the sea on the James River. As the draft of water in the channel of the river is only 16 feet, the size of ships coming up here is very limited. At the wharf at West Point there is a depth of 23 feet of water.

A scheme for deepening the channel of the James River to $25\frac{1}{2}$ feet is being carried out by very slow degrees, the grants of money made for the purpose by the State being very inadequate.

## BALTIMORE.

### Statistics of the Port of Richmond, Va., for 1891.

Arrivals from Foreign Countries.

| Nationality. | Entered. Number of Vessels. | Tons. | Cleared. Number of Vessels. | Tons. |
|---|---|---|---|---|
| British steamers | 29 | 49,218 | 29 | 49,218 |
| „ sailing | 4 | 1,026 | 4 | 1,026 |
| Foreign steamers | 10 | 16,888 | 10 | 16,888 |
| „ sailing | 7 | 1,574 | 7 | 1,574 |
| American steamers | .. | .. | .. | .. |
| „ sailing | 1 | 421 | 1 | 525 |
| Total | 51 | 69,127 | 51 | 69,231 |

### Imports, Port of Richmond, Va., for 1891.

|  | Dollars. |
|---|---|
| Garden, flower, and farm seeds | 6,880 |
| Sugar bonded from New York | 59,243 |
| Liqueurs and wines | 2,074 |
| Chinaware | 1,883 |
| Miscellaneous | 12,690 |
| Total | 82,770 |

## NORFOLK.

Mr. Vice-Consul Myers reports as follows:—

The port of Norfolk, Virginia, for the last year has had a fairly good trade, and, compared with other ports in this country, has progressed considerably.

Norfolk is fast becoming the most important seaport of the Southern States, being the terminus of the Norfolk and Western Railroad which, with its connections, extends to the Mississippi Valley in the south-west, and to the grain-producing sections of the great north-west, and taps the famous Pocahontas coalfields in south-west Virginia. Its future as a coaling port for steamers from all South Atlantic and Gulf ports is assured. Shipmasters are partial to Pocahontas coal, not only on account of its price, but on account of its steaming qualities.

The Atlantic trade being no longer carried by sailing vessels, steamers are monopolising the freightage; therefore, a first-class coaling port on the Atlantic seaboard will, a little later on, be the centre of the steamer business.

It is probable that the World's Columbian Exposition, to be held at Chicago in 1893, will further bring the port of Norfolk and her advantages to the attention of the commercial nations, Hampton Roads having been designated by the Congress of the United States as the place of rendezvous for the navies of the

## UNITED STATES.

world; and as vigorous efforts are being made to get through connections with Chicago and the West in time for business when the Exposition opens, Norfolk, being much nearer Chicago than New York, will likely have many transatlantic visitors on their way to the World's Fair.

The railway facilities are inadequate at present for the great amount of freight bound to this port from the interior, and improvements in this direction are progressing rapidly.

It will be noted from the following tables that the shipping has largely increased in the past year.

The shipping of grain has become quite a large business. Coal shipments have increased beyond all expectations. Considering the market, cotton has been better than usual. The manufacture of cotton goods is an industry of recent introduction here, but is on the increase, with two mills already in operation and paying well, and two others in process of construction.

The continued financial depression, so prevalent all over the country, has been felt very little in Norfolk. There are now ten banks here, but there being demand for more banking capital, a new National Bank has been organised, and will shortly open its doors.

Many fine new buildings have been put up within the last year. House building is brisk, with occupants for all houses as soon as they are finished.

Strangers and visitors remark on the cleanliness and general healthfulness of Norfolk. A great deal is due to the climate, which is temperate and equable, and generally free from the extremes common elsewhere in the United States.

The principal articles of trade are cotton, grain, oysters, lumber and vegetables.

The growth, sale, and distribution of market vegetables (known here as "trucking") is an extensive industry, and the trade in this respect is worth several million dollars annually to Norfolk.

The lumber business is a very heavy one, there being in the vicinity about 60 mills engaged in its manufacture.

TABLE showing the Movement of Shipping at this Port (not including the Coasting Trade in American Vessels), representing the Entries and Clearances to and from Foreign Ports only.

ENTERED.

| Nationality. | Sailing. Number of Vessels. | Sailing. Tons. | Steam. Number of Vessels. | Steam. Tons. | Total. Number of Vessels. | Total. Tons. |
|---|---|---|---|---|---|---|
| British | 4 | 3,105 | 490 | 673,082 | 494 | 676,187 |
| American | 20 | 8,267 | 3 | 3,506 | 23 | 11,773 |
| Spanish | ... | ... | 62 | 96,905 | 62 | 96,905 |
| Norwegian | ... | ... | 11 | 6,594 | 11 | 6,594 |
| Italian | 5 | 2,575 | 1 | 1,324 | 6 | 3,899 |
| German | ... | ... | 3 | 3,961 | 3 | 3,961 |
| Swedish | ... | ... | 1 | 680 | 1 | 680 |
| Austrian | 1 | 574 | ... | ... | 1 | 574 |
| Total | 30 | 14,521 | 571 | 786,052 | 601 | 800,573 |

## BALTIMORE.

### Cleared.

| Nationality. | Steam. Number of Vessels. | Tons. | Sailing. Number of Vessels. | Tons. | Total. Number of Vessels. | Tons. |
|---|---|---|---|---|---|---|
| British | 6 | 3,668 | 478 | 665,643 | 484 | 669,311 |
| American | 24 | 9,897 | 3 | 633 | 27 | 10,530 |
| Spanish | ... | ... | 59 | 92,323 | 59 | 92,323 |
| Norwegian | ... | ... | 12 | 6,976 | 12 | 6,976 |
| Italian | 4 | 2,496 | 1 | 1,324 | 5 | 3,820 |
| German | ... | ... | 4 | 5,182 | 4 | 5,182 |
| Swedish | ... | ... | 1 | 680 | 1 | 680 |
| Austrian | 1 | 574 | ... | ... | 1 | 574 |
| Total | 35 | 16,635 | 558 | 772,761 | 593 | 789,396 |

TABLE showing the Principal Articles of Export and Import at this Port during the past year, value calculated at 5 dol. to the 1l.

### Exports.

| Articles. | | Quantity. | Value. |
|---|---|---|---|
| | | | £ |
| Cotton | Bales | 262,285 | .. |
| Coal | Tons | 153,214 | .. |
| Lumber | .. | .. | 20,204 |
| Logs | .. | .. | 46,286 |
| Staves | .. | .. | 29,464 |
| Shingles | Tons | 225,000 | .. |
| Wheat | Bushels | 1,492,024 | .. |
| Corn | ,, | 83,617 | .. |
| Rye | ,, | 63,787 | .. |
| Oats | ,, | 210,720 | .. |
| Flour | Sacks | 195 | .. |
| ,, | Barrels | 100,246 | .. |
| Tobacco | Lbs | 942,193 | .. |
| ,,  manufactured | ,, | 11,322 | .. |
| ,,  ,, | Tierces | 7 | .. |
| Cotton seed | Sacks | 5 | .. |
| Cotton seed meal | ,, | 7,837 | .. |
| Fence | Bales | 225 | .. |
| Bark | Bags | 2,933 | .. |
| Boat oars | Number | 2,327 | .. |
| Lard | Lbs. | 206,120 | .. |
| Turpentine | Cases | 50 | .. |
| Zinc ore | Barrels | 2 | .. |
| Peanuts | Bags | 50 | .. |
| Hay | Bales | 620 | .. |
| ,, | Tons | 37 | .. |
| Posphate rock | ,, | 1,650 | .. |
| Dried apples | Lbs. | 50,525 | .. |
| Apples | .. | .. | .. |
| Bones | Bags | 164 | .. |
| Engine | .. | 1 | .. |
| *Total value | .. | .. | 3,039,079 |

# UNITED STATES.

## Imports.

| Articles. | | Quantity. | Value. |
|---|---|---:|---:|
| | | | £ |
| Salt | Lbs. | 4,038,720 | .. |
| Wine | Octaves | 11 | .. |
| ,, | Gallons | 193 | .. |
| Dried figs | Lbs. | 50 | .. |
| Sperm oil | Casks | 72 | .. |
| Manure salt | Lbs. | 1,334,802 | .. |
| Kainit | ,, | 5,857,625 | .. |
| Tar, creosote acid | Barrels | 3,979 | .. |
| Grain sacks | | 23,045 | .. |
| Olive oil | Gallons | 20 | .. |
| Hair pins | Gross | 100 | .. |
| ,, | Boxes | 6 | .. |
| Razors | Dozen | 99 | .. |
| Pocket knives | ,, | 108 | .. |
| Cheese | Lbs. | 220 | .. |
| Bituminous coal | Tons | 75 | .. |
| Jewellery | Boxes | 1 | .. |
| Dry goods | Cases | 6 | .. |
| Total value | .. | .. | 10,500 |

LONDON:
Printed for Her Majesty's Stationery Office,
By HARRISON AND SONS,
Printers in Ordinary to Her Majesty.
(75  3 | 92—H & S  1256)

# FOREIGN OFFICE.
## 1892.
## ANNUAL SERIES.

### Nº. 1015.
### DIPLOMATIC AND CONSULAR REPORTS ON TRADE AND FINANCE.

# UNITED STATES.

### REPORT FOR THE YEAR 1891
ON THE
## TRADE OF BOSTON (MASS.).

REFERENCE TO PREVIOUS REPORT, Annual Series No. 843.

*Presented to both Houses of Parliament by Command of Her Majesty,*
*APRIL, 1892.*

LONDON:
PRINTED FOR HER MAJESTY'S STATIONERY OFFICE,
BY HARRISON AND SONS, ST. MARTIN'S LANE,
PRINTERS IN ORDINARY TO HER MAJESTY.

And to be purchased, either directly or through any Bookseller, from
EYRE & SPOTTISWOODE, East Harding Street, Fleet Street, E.C., and
32, Abingdon Street, Westminster, S.W.; or
JOHN MENZIES & Co., 12, Hanover Street, Edinburgh, and
90, West Nile Street, Glasgow; or
HODGES, FIGGIS, & Co., 104, Grafton Street, Dublin.

1892.

[C. 6550—77.] *Price One Penny.*

# New Series of Reports.

Reports of the Annual Series have been issued from Her Majesty's Diplomatic and Consular Officers at the following places, and may be obtained from the sources indicated on the title-page:—

| No. | | Price. | No. | | Price. |
|---|---|---|---|---|---|
| 893. | Brest | 1d. | 954. | Amsterdam | 1d. |
| 894. | Smyrna | 1d. | 955. | Tangier | 2d. |
| 895. | Cadiz | 1d. | 956. | Paramaribo | 1d. |
| 896. | Aleppo | 1d. | 957. | Teneriffe | 1d. |
| 897. | Foochow | 1d. | 958. | Athens | 2d. |
| 898. | Kiungchow | 1d. | 959. | Odessa | 1d. |
| 899. | The Hague | 1½d. | 960. | Copenhagen | 9d. |
| 900. | Nice | 1½d. | 961. | Tokio | 1d. |
| 901. | Nantes | 1½d. | 962. | Salonica | 1½d. |
| 902. | Port-au-Prince | 1½d. | 963. | Stettin | 3½d. |
| 903. | Bengazi | 1d. | 964. | Philadelphia | 2d. |
| 904. | Tahiti | ½d. | 965. | Mexico | 2d. |
| 905. | Chinkiang | 1d. | 966. | Malaga | 2½d. |
| 906. | San Francisco | 3d. | 967. | Berne | 1d. |
| 907. | Brindisi | 2d. | 968. | Puerto Rico | ½d. |
| 908. | Beyrout | 1d. | 969. | Buda-Pesth | 1d. |
| 909. | Noumea | ½d. | 970. | Bogotá | 1d. |
| 910. | San Francisco | 1d. | 971. | Panama | 1½d. |
| 911. | New York | 1½d. | 972. | Munich | 2d. |
| 912. | Caracas | 1½d. | 973. | Copenhagen | 4d. |
| 913. | Greytown | ½d. | 974. | Guatemala | 1d. |
| 914. | Corunna | 2d. | 975. | Munich | 2d. |
| 915. | Christiania | 5½d. | 976. | Meshed | 1½d. |
| 916. | Callao | 1d. | 977. | Para | ½d. |
| 917. | Macao | 1d. | 978. | Florence | 1d. |
| 918. | Sôul | 1d. | 979. | The Hague | 1½d. |
| 919. | Dunkirk | 1d. | 980. | Patras | 1d. |
| 920. | Tamsui | 1d. | 981. | Paris | 1½d. |
| 921. | Bussorah | ½d. | 982. | Zanzibar | 2½d. |
| 922. | Yokohama | 3½d. | 983. | Buenos Ayres | ½d. |
| 923. | Bilbao | 1½d. | 984. | Copenhagen | 1d. |
| 924. | Barcelona | 2½d. | 985. | Stuttgart | 1d. |
| 925. | Netherlands-India | 1d. | 986. | New Orleans | 1½d. |
| 926. | Chefoo | 1d. | 987. | New Orleans | 10d. |
| 927. | Buenos Ayres | ½d. | 988. | Suakin | ½d. |
| 928. | Santo Domingo | ½d. | 989. | Galveston | 1½d. |
| 929. | Constantinople | ½d. | 990. | Berlin | 1d. |
| 930. | Erzeroum | 1½d. | 991. | Zanzibar | 1½d. |
| 931. | Gothenburg | 2d. | 992. | Guayaquil | 1d. |
| 932. | Tunis | 1d. | 993. | Tonga | 1d. |
| 933. | New York | 1d. | 994. | New Orleans | 1d. |
| 934. | Nagasaki | 1d. | 995. | Mozambique | 1½d. |
| 935. | Hakodate | 1½d. | 996. | Galatz | 1½d. |
| 936. | Sofia | 3d. | 997. | Nantes | 1½d. |
| 937. | Frankfort | 2d. | 998. | Algiers | 1d. |
| 938. | Bangkok | 9d. | 999. | Havre | 2½d. |
| 939. | Berne | 1½d. | 1000. | Buenos Ayres | 6d. |
| 940. | The Hague | 1½d. | 1001. | Baltimore | 1½d. |
| 941. | Christiania | 1d. | 1002. | Taganrog | 1d. |
| 942. | Christiania | ½d. | 1003. | Riga | 2d. |
| 943. | Brunei | 1½d. | 1004. | Bordeaux | 2½d. |
| 944. | Alexandria | 1½d. | 1005. | The Hague | 1½d. |
| 945. | Therapia | ½d. | 1006. | Paraguay | 1½d. |
| 946. | Bushire | 1½d. | 1007. | Constantinople | 1½d. |
| 947. | Tokio | 2½d. | 1008. | Rome | 1d. |
| 948. | Stockholm | 2d. | 1009. | Mozambique | 1d. |
| 949. | Palermo | 2½d. | 1010. | Wênchow | 1d. |
| 950. | St. Petersburg | 2½d. | 1011. | Mogador | 2½d. |
| 951. | Quito | ½d. | 1012. | Amoy | 1d. |
| 952. | Rio de Janeiro | 2d. | 1013. | Kiúkiang | 1d. |
| 953. | Naples | 2d. | 1014. | Stettin | 1½d. |

# No. 1015.

*Reference to previous Report, Annual Series No. 843.*

## UNITED STATES.
### BOSTON.

*Consul Henderson to the Marquis of Salisbury.*

My Lord, Boston, March 15, 1892.

I HAVE the honour to enclose a Report on the Trade and Commerce of Boston and the Boston Consular District for the year 1891.

I have, &c.
(Signed) C. A. HENDERSON.

---

*Report on the Trade and Commerce of Boston for the Year* 1891.

ABSTRACT of Contents.

| | Page |
|---|---|
| Condition of trade | 1 |
| Foreign exports and imports at Boston | 3 |
| Foreign maritime trade at Boston | 3 |
| Rates of exchange | 4 |
| Mercantile failures in district | 4 |
| Population and immigration | 4 |
| Statistics of manufactures in Massachusetts | 4 |
| Annexes A, B, C: Shipping, exports, and imports | 7–9 |

The financial stringency which marked the latter part of the year 1890, and the occurrence of some heavy and unexpected failures later on, continued to have a depressing effect on the general business of this Consular district throughout the year, and, by restricting credit and diminishing consumption, caused an almost unexampled fall in prices on a large majority of marketable commodities. [General condition of trade.]

In all other respects the year was an uneventful one for trade; for whilst the volume and profits were uniformly small, it was not affected by rash speculation, sudden fluctuations or important strikes.

NOTE.—Sterling amounts in this report are given at 5 dol. to the 1*l*.

(1265)

## UNITED STATES.

**Cotton and cotton goods.** The cotton crop of 1891 was the largest on record, but of inferior quality, and prices, after some slight fluctuations, fell before the end of the year to the lowest point known for 40 years.

Cotton goods were in active demand, and the New England mills were kept constantly at work, but prices were forced down simultaneously with the decline in the cost of the raw material.

**Wool and woollens.** There were no sudden fluctuations in the wool market, but a steady downward tendency during the year, closing prices, with the exception of coarse grades, being from 1*d.* to 2*d.* lower than at the end of 1890, whilst stocks held by dealers and manufacturers were comparatively heavy.

Notwithstanding the low cost of wool, woollen manufacturers did not, on the whole, do a prosperous business, for while certain goods, such as dress-stuffs and cassimeres, sold fairly well, flannels and blanketings, owing to exceptionally mild weather, were in small demand.

**Hides and leather.** The year opened with a good market for both foreign and domestic hides, but it slackened later on, and prices were exceedingly low at its close.

This was attributable to the gradual decline in leather, which ultimately fell to less than cost, and resulted in the shutting down of a large number of tanneries in this section of the country.

**Boots and shoes.** The depression in the leather market was itself to be traced to the short demand for boots and shoes, which fell from 3,585,000 cases in 1890 to 3,465,000 cases in 1891, and this in the face of an average yearly increase of about 100,000 cases for several previous years, as a natural consequence of the growth of the population.

**Iron and steel.** A dull market at the beginning of the year, and a prolonged strike in the coke districts led to the blowing out of many furnaces in all parts of the United States where they existed, and to a large decrease in production, but a better demand later on, though unaccompanied by any material advance in prices, caused work to be resumed in some of them. The present high duty on imported ore, however, and the great distance and heavy freight from those places in the country where it is most abundantly produced, has driven the manufacturers of iron and steel out of the New England States, where, especially in Massachusetts, it was formerly extensively carried on, and this industry is now all but extinct here.

**Lumber trade.** Building operations have been very general and extensive to meet the wants of an increasing population, and the lumber trade has been brisk, but dealers complain of low prices and small profits.

**Flour and grain.** The flour and grain market was very buoyant during the year, and notwithstanding the exceptionally abundant crop prices were fairly well maintained, owing to the brisk demand for foreign markets.

**Fish trade.** The fish trade was more prosperous in 1891 than for several years past, although sales were checked to a certain extent by the prices demanded, which were high as compared with the reduced cost of other articles of food.

Mackerel brought to market was of small size, but of good quality, and that received from Ireland was more carefully packed and more readily saleable than in previous years. The preserved mackerel received was—

|  | 1891. | 1890. |
|---|---|---|
|  | Barrels. | Barrels. |
| From New England fleet | 47,814 | 19,000 |
| Canada | 44,659 | 54,543 |
| British Isles | 4,583 | 16,953 |
| France | 865 | 811 |
| Norway and Sweden | 607 | 2,492 |
| Total | 98,528 | 93,799 |

The market supply of cod fish was 110,127 quintals, and that of other ground fish was 507,813 quintals.

**Foreign exports and imports.** Foreign commerce at the port of Boston shows a considerable advance on the previous year both in exports and imports, the former amounting to 16,351,931*l*., or a gain of over 1,900,000*l*., and the latter to 14,160,924*l*., or a gain of nearly 950,000*l*.

The increase in exports was principally represented by domestic goods, the value of foreign goods re-exported (amounting to 83,562*l*.) being only about 14,000*l*. more than in 1890. Of the value of goods imported 6,631,737*l*. represented free goods, and 7,529,187*l*. those which were dutiable, against 3,605,000*l*. and 9,608,000*l*. respectively in 1890.

**Foreign maritime trade.** The custom-house return of vessels in the foreign trade arriving at Boston from all, except United States, ports, shows 1,806 British vessels of 1,233,099 tons, 342 Americans of 157,965 tons, and 194, of 162,536 tons, of other nationalities, or a total of 2,342 vessels and 1,553,600 tons, compared with the previous year; British tonnage is thus shown to have increased by 76,177 tons, American to have decreased by 10,377 tons, and that under other foreign flags to have increased by 53,003 tons.

According to the Consulate records, the total arrivals at Boston of British vessels from all, including United States, ports, were 1,848 vessels of 1,237,702 tons, namely, 640 steamers of 1,080,770 tons, and 1,208 sailing vessels of 156,932 tons, being an increase over the previous year of 49,999 tons in steamers and 17,971 tons in sailing vessels, or a total increase of 69,970 tons.

**Ocean freights—Inwards.** Inward freights at Boston from the United Kingdom did not vary materially from the previous year, rates as a rule being based on time contracts.

**Outwards.** Outward freights to the United Kingdom declined steadily from the beginning to about the middle of the year, when they improved and continued to rise, closing in December higher in most cases than they had been in any previous month.

(1265)

Freights on live cattle were 3*l*. 7*s*. 6*d*. per head in January, 1*l*. 2*s*. 10*d*. per head in April, and 3*l*. per head in December. Grain was 2¾*d*. per bushel in January, 1*d*. per bushel in June, and 5½*d*. per bushel in December; and in these last-named months, respectively, flour was 12*s*., 6*s*., and 18*s*. per 100 lbs.; provisions were 1*l*. 4*s*., 4*s*., and 1*l*. 10*s*. per ton; cotton was $\frac{11}{64}d.$, $\frac{1}{32}d.$, and $\frac{7}{32}d.$ per lb.; leather was 2*l*., 17*s*. 6*d*., and 2*l*. 5*s*. per ton; whilst apples were 2*s*. per barrel from January to September, 2*s*. 3*d*. per barrel in October, and 3*s*. per barrel in November and December.

**Sterling exchange.** Exchange took a start in January, when bankers' sight bills went up from 4 dol. 83½ c. per 1*l*. in the previous month, to 4 dol. 87¾ c.; was 4 dol. 88¼ c. in April; 4 dol. 88¾ c. in June; 4 dol. 87½ c. in August; was down to 4 dol. 83¾ c. in September; and rose to 4 dol. 85 c. by the end of December.

**Mercantile failures.** Whilst the number of firms in business in this Consular district was 80,228, or an increase of 1,508 on the previous year, the number of failures was 892, against 886, and their liabilities only amounted to 3,025,703*l*., showing a decrease of 1,432,369*l*.

**Population and immigration.** The population of the four States comprised in this Consular district is given as follows in the United States census for 1890:— Massachusetts, 2,238,943; Vermont, 332,422; New Hampshire, 376,530; Maine, 661,086; being an increase, as compared with the year 1880, of 25·57 per cent., 0·04 per cent., 8·51 per cent., and 1·87 per cent. respectively.

The number of immigrants (exclusive of those who arrived overland from British North America and Mexico) who landed at ports in this district during the year ended June 30, 1891, was 32,199. Of these 21,035 were British, viz., 7,370 English, 1,855 Scotch, 11,746 Irish, 3 Maltese, 7 Indian, 53 British West Indian, and 1 New Zealander.

**Statistics of Massachusetts manufactures.** The 21st annual report, published in 1891 for 1890, of the Massachusetts Bureau of Statistics of Labour contains the result of an inquiry in regard to the question of net profits in the manufacturing industries of the State, of which the following is an abstract:—

Manufacturing establishments, as shown in the State census for 1885, numbered in that year 23,431, and were managed by 22,482 private firms and 949 corporations. Of these establishments, in 1890, 13,418 did not report as to net profits, whilst 10,013, representing 75·45 per cent. of the total capital invested in, and 70 per cent. of the value of products of, all the establishments, did report as to net profits. Of these 10,013, 9,251 made net profits, and 762 did not make net profits.

The capital invested in 1890 by 23,431 establishments was 100,118,875*l*., viz.:—

|  | £ |
|---|---|
| By 9,251, showing net profits | 61,358,385 |
| 762 „ no „ | 14,183,976 |
| 13,418 not reporting net profits | 24,576,514 |

The invested capital is thus classified:—

## BOSTON.

|  |  | £ |
|---|---|---|
| Value of land, buildings, and fixtures | | 23,777,329 |
| „ machinery, implements, and tools | | 23,050,866 |
| Cash capital | | 34,688,189 |
| Credit „ | | 18,602,491 |

The selling price of products of the 23,431 establishments was 134,926,854*l*., viz.:—

|  |  | £ |
|---|---|---|
| Of 9,251 establishments | | 82,903,287 |
| 762 „ | | 10,483,324 |
| 13,418 „ | | 41,540,243 |

The average percentage of cost of items in relation to the total cost of production and to selling price respectively in the 10,013 establishments which reported as to the net profits was:—

| Items. | Percentage of Cost. | Percentage of Selling Price. |
|---|---|---|
| Stock used | 67·67 | 58·91 |
| Salaries | 1·98 | 1·73 |
| Wages | 25·66 | 22·35 |
| Rent | 0·85 | 0·73 |
| Taxes | 0·64 | 0·56 |
| Insurance | 0·33 | 0·33 |
| Freights | 1·46 | 1·27 |
| New equipment | 0·28 | 0·24 |
| Repairs | 0·93 | 0·81 |
| Other expenses | 0·15 | 0·13 |
| Total | 100·00 | 87·05 |
| Gross profit | | 12·95 |
| Total | | 100·00 |

The average distribution of gross profit was:—

|  | Per cent. |
|---|---|
| Interest on cash and credit capital | 2·15 |
| Depreciation account | 1·90 |
| Selling expenses and bad debts | 5·00 |
| Net profit | 3·90 |
| Gross profit as above | 12·95 |

The number of persons employed, and average yearly earnings of all (including men, women, and children) in 213,431 establishments was:—

|  | Number. | Average Earnings. |
|---|---|---|
|  |  | £ s. d. |
| Employed by private firms | 257,656 | 72 9 0 |
| „ corporations | 162,310 | 66 13 0 |

Or an average for all of 70*l*. 4*s*. 1*d*.

## UNITED STATES.

In conclusion, the report contains the statement that, whereas the average yearly earnings of employés were 70*l.* 4*s.* 1*d.*, whilst the average net profits of partners of private firms, as nearly as can be computed from the available data, were 68*l.* 4*s.* 10*d*, and those of stockholders in corporations 67*l.* 18*s.* 10*d.*, the result of an equal sub-division of the combined earnings of employés and the net profits of partners and stockholders, would be the yearly receipt in each case of an average of 69*l.* 17*s.* 10*d*, or an average loss to employés of 6*s.* 3*d.* per year, and a gain to partners of 1*l.* 13*s.*, and to stockholders of 1*l.* 19*s.*

In conjunction with the above report the same bureau has published the annual statistics of manufactures in Massachusetts for the year 1890, of which the following is an abstract:—

From the returns in the United States census for 1890 it appears that manufacturing establishments in Massachusetts had increased from 23,431 in 1885 to nearly 25,000 in 1890.

The number of these establishments from which returns were received in 1890 was 5,380, and of these the number available for comparison with one or more previous years was 4,297.

Of the above 4,297 establishments 3,733 show an increase in product, 544 a decrease, and 20 no change, as compared with the year 1888; whilst 3,008 show an increase, 1,189 a decrease, and 100 no change since 1889.

3,696 establishments, classified as high grade, medium grade, and low grade, offer the means of comparison as to the relative value of their products in 1885 and 1890, and show a large increase, as may be deduced from the following table:—

| Grade. | Establishment. | Value of Products. | |
|---|---|---|---|
| | | 1885. | 1890. |
| | Number. | £ | £ |
| High | 686 | 63,343,792 | 78,163,460 |
| Medium | 968 | 15,852,523 | 21,373,727 |
| Low | 2,042 | 6,838,681 | 10,332,123 |
| Total | 3,696 | 86,034,996 | 109,869,310 |

3,041 establishments made returns in 1890 corresponding to those made by them in 1889, and the following figures show the comparative result for these establishments:—

| Heads of Returns. | 1889. Amount. | 1889. Number. | 1890. Amount. | 1890. Number. |
|---|---|---|---|---|
| | £ s. d. | | £ s. d. | |
| Capital invested | 74,077,883 0 0 | ... | 78,240,054 0 0 | ... |
| Value of stock used | 60,623,990 0 0 | ... | 64,983,988 0 0 | ... |
| „ goods made | 104,610,346 0 0 | ... | 109,178,140 0 0 | ... |
| Amount of wages paid | 22,357,999 0 0 | ... | 23,428,997 0 0 | ... |
| Persons employed | ... | 263,083 | ... | 270,195 |
| Average number of days' work | ... | 289·56 | ... | 289·51 |
| Average yearly earnings of employés | 85 7 4 | ... | 86 14 3 | ... |

From a collation of all returns in the year 1885 (when the State census was taken), in conjunction with those received subsequently, it is assumed by the bureau that, embracing as they do the leading establishments in the most important industries, and the principal portion of the total product value of manufactures, this product value can be fairly estimated for the year 1890 at the sum of 174,000,000*l*.

Annex A.—RETURN of Shipping in the Foreign Trade at the Ports in the Boston Consular District in the Fiscal Year ended June 30, 1891.

ENTERED.

| Nationality. | Sailing. Number of Vessels. | Sailing. Tons. | Steam. Number of Vessels. | Steam. Tons. | Total. Number of Vessels. | Total. Tons. |
|---|---|---|---|---|---|---|
| British and other foreign | 3,197 | 396,715 | 987 | 1,205,404 | 4,184 | 1,602,119 |
| American | 606 | 168,140 | 282 | 282,495 | 888 | 450,635 |
| Total | 3,803 | 564,855 | 1,269 | 1,487,899 | 5,072 | 2,052,754 |
| „ for the year preceding | 3,898 | 528,211 | 1,177 | 1,395,334 | 5,075 | 1,923,545 |

CLEARED.

| Nationality. | Sailing. Number of Vessels. | Sailing. Tons. | Steam. Number of Vessels. | Steam. Tons. | Total. Number of Vessels. | Total. Tons. |
|---|---|---|---|---|---|---|
| British and other foreign | 3,160 | 367,879 | 817 | 961,484 | 3,977 | 1,332,363 |
| American | 1,090 | 253,527 | 273 | 272,962 | 1,363 | 526,489 |
| Total | 4,250 | 621,406 | 1,090 | 1,237,446 | 5,340 | 1,858,852 |
| „ for the year preceding | 4,396 | 688,577 | 1,035 | 1,165,732 | 5,431 | 1,854,309 |

Annex B.—RETURN of Principal Articles of Export from and Imports to Ports in the Boston Consular District during the Fiscal Years ended June 30, 1891-90.

EXPORTS.

| Articles. | Value. 1891. | Value. 1890. |
|---|---|---|
| | £ | £ |
| Dairy and meat products | 6,462,522 | 5,824,578 |
| Horned cattle | 1,879,359 | 1,800,474 |
| Corn, flour, and other bread-stuffs | 2,056,091 | 2,274,418 |
| Raw cotton | 2,463,655 | 1,558,497 |
| Cotton manufactures | 211,922 | 228,542 |
| Tobacco in leaf and manufactured | 219,941 | 305,855 |
| Iron, steel, and manufactures of | 375,229 | 331,569 |
| Sugar and molasses | 102,787 | 22,638 |
| All other domestic merchandise | 3,013,582 | 2,894,782 |
| Foreign merchandise re-exported | 86,149 | 235,397 |
| Coin and bullion | 251,989 | .. |
| Total | 17,087,226 | 15,476,750 |

IMPORTS.

| Articles. | Value. 1891. | Value. 1890. |
|---|---|---|
| | £ | £ |
| Sugar and molasses | 2,694,017 | 1,944,511 |
| Wool | 1,819,498 | 1,499,487 |
| Woollen goods | 436,987 | 711,165 |
| Hides, goat and fur skins, and furs | 1,076,457 | 772,561 |
| Iron, steel, and manufactures of | 1,142,406 | 945,971 |
| Chemicals, drugs and dyes | 1,024,795 | 917,625 |
| Flax, hemp, and jute, and manufactures of | 1,369,834 | 1,499,992 |
| Cotton manufactures | 286,965 | 302,579 |
| Fish | 363,805 | 407,300 |
| Coin and bullion | 6,547 | 9,863 |
| All other goods (including returned domestic exports valued at 94,764l.) | 5,800,778 | 5,559,517 |
| Total | 16,022,089 | 14,570,571 |

## BOSTON.

Annex C.—TABLE showing the Value of all Articles Exported from and Imported to Ports in the Boston Consular District during the Fiscal Years ended June 30, 1891–90.

| Country. | Exports. 1891. | Exports. 1890. | Imports. 1891. | Imports. 1890. |
|---|---|---|---|---|
| | £ | £ | £ | £ |
| United Kingdom and colonies | 15,960,875 | 14,375,393 | 9,758,789 | 9,034,082 |
| Germany | 238,852 | 34,261 | 857,963 | 733,056 |
| France and colonies | 195,170 | 152,773 | 487,429 | 582,432 |
| Austria-Hungary | .. | .. | 81,395 | 47,420 |
| Spain and colonies | 29,938 | 57,159 | 2,257,796 | 1,986,802 |
| Netherlands and colonies | 34,276 | 38,605 | 280,468 | 266,750 |
| Belgium | 309,537 | 282,608 | 300,589 | 285,547 |
| Sweden and Norway | .. | 2,200 | 185,208 | 162,079 |
| Italy | 15,916 | 6,121 | 315,468 | 262,367 |
| Russia | .. | .. | 101,329 | 100,537 |
| Turkey | 16,568 | 3,982 | 144,050 | 137,655 |
| Argentine Republic | 28,427 | 149,547 | 639,054 | 545,033 |
| Uruguay | 13,776 | 60,675 | 94,888 | 69,129 |
| Brazil | 2,156 | 1,716 | 73,104 | 32,127 |
| Chile | 56,715 | 94,100 | 60,439 | 64,494 |
| Mexico | .. | .. | 138,682 | 84,654 |
| Hayti | 19,868 | 19,555 | 65,329 | 55,919 |
| All other countries | 165,152 | 198,055 | 180,159 | 120,478 |
| Total | 17,087,226 | 15,476,750 | 16,022,089 | 14,570,571 |

LONDON:
Printed for Her Majesty's Stationery Office,
By HARRISON AND SONS,
Printers in Ordinary to Her Majesty.
(75  4 | 92—H & S  1265)

# FOREIGN OFFICE.
## 1892.
## ANNUAL SERIES.

### No. 1072.

### DIPLOMATIC AND CONSULAR REPORTS ON TRADE AND FINANCE.

# UNITED STATES.

### REPORT FOR THE YEAR 1891
#### ON THE
### TRADE OF CHARLESTON AND DISTRICT.

REFERENCE TO PREVIOUS REPORT, Annual Series No. 845.

*Presented to both Houses of Parliament by Command of Her Majesty,*
*JUNE, 1892.*

---

LONDON:
PRINTED FOR HER MAJESTY'S STATIONERY OFFICE,
BY HARRISON AND SONS, ST. MARTIN'S LANE,
PRINTERS IN ORDINARY TO HER MAJESTY.

And to be purchased, either directly or through any Bookseller, from
EYRE & SPOTTISWOODE, EAST HARDING STREET, FLEET STREET, E.C., and
32, ABINGDON STREET, WESTMINSTER, S.W.; or
JOHN MENZIES & Co., 12, HANOVER STREET, EDINBURGH, and
90, WEST NILE STREET, GLASGOW; or
HODGES, FIGGIS, & Co., 104, GRAFTON STREET, DUBLIN.

1892.

[C. 6550—134.] *Price Twopence Halfpenny.*

# New Series of Reports.

Reports of the Annual Series have been issued from Her Majesty's Diplomatic and Consular Officers at the following places, and may be obtained from the sources indicated on the title-page:—

| No. |  | Price. | No. |  | Price. |
|---|---|---|---|---|---|
| 954. | Amsterdam | 1d. | 1013. | Kiukiang | 1d. |
| 955. | Tangier | 2d. | 1014. | Stettin | 1½d. |
| 956. | Paramaribo | 1d. | 1015. | Boston | 1d. |
| 957. | Teneriffe | 1d. | 1016. | Callao | 1d. |
| 958. | Athens | 2d. | 1017. | Aleppo | 1d. |
| 959. | Odessa | 1d. | 1018. | Santos | 2½d. |
| 960. | Copenhagen | 9d. | 1019. | Piræus | 1d. |
| 961. | Tokio | 1d. | 1020. | Mogador | 1d. |
| 962. | Salonica | 1½d. | 1021. | Adrianople | ½d. |
| 963. | Stettin | 3½d. | 1022. | Tripoli | 1d. |
| 964. | Philadelphia | 2d. | 1023. | Jerusalem | 1d. |
| 965. | Mexico | 2d. | 1024. | Odessa | 6d. |
| 966. | Malaga | 2½d. | 1025. | Genoa | 1½d. |
| 967. | Berne | 1d. | 1026. | Kiungchow | 1d. |
| 968. | Puerto Rico | ½d. | 1027. | Batoum | 4½d. |
| 969. | Buda-Pesth | 1d. | 1028. | Buenos Ayres | 1d. |
| 970. | Bogotá | 1d. | 1029. | Batavia | 1d. |
| 971. | Panama | 1½d. | 1030. | Santo Domingo | ½d. |
| 972. | Munich | 2d. | 1031. | San José | 1d. |
| 973. | Copenhagen | 4d. | 1032. | Manila | 1½d. |
| 974. | Guatemala | 1d. | 1033. | Marseilles | 1d. |
| 975. | Munich | 2d. | 1034. | Swatow | 1d. |
| 976. | Meshed | 1½d. | 1035. | Paris | 1d. |
| 977. | Para | ½d. | 1036. | Ichang | 5d. |
| 978. | Florence | 1d. | 1037. | Pakhoi | 1d. |
| 979. | The Hague | 1½d. | 1038. | Foochow | 1d. |
| 980. | Patras | 1d. | 1039. | Brest | 1d. |
| 981. | Paris | 1½d. | 1040. | Madeira | ½d. |
| 982. | Zanzibar | 2½d. | 1041. | Antwerp | 1½d. |
| 983. | Buenos Ayres | ½d. | 1042. | Taganrog | 2½d. |
| 984. | Copenhagen | 1d. | 1043. | Algiers | 2½d. |
| 985. | Stuttgart | 1d. | 1044. | Hankow | 1½d. |
| 986. | New Orleans | 1½d. | 1045. | Nantes | 1½d. |
| 987. | New Orleans | 10d. | 1046. | Belgrade | 2d. |
| 988. | Suakin | ½d. | 1047. | Fiume | 1d. |
| 989. | Galveston | 1½d. | 1048. | Wuhu | 1d. |
| 990. | Berlin | 1d. | 1049. | Cagliari | 1d. |
| 991. | Zanzibar | 1½d. | 1050. | Erzeroum | 1d. |
| 992. | Guayaquil | 1d. | 1051. | Syra | 1d. |
| 993. | Tonga | 1d. | 1052. | Cherbourg | 1d. |
| 994. | New Orleans | 1d. | 1053. | Lima | 1d. |
| 995. | Mozambique | 1½d. | 1054. | Bilbao | 1½d. |
| 996. | Galatz | 1½d. | 1055. | Cadiz | 2d. |
| 997. | Nantes | 1½d. | 1056. | Corunna | 2½d. |
| 998. | Algiers | 1d. | 1057. | Saigon | 1d. |
| 999. | Havre | 2½d. | 1058. | Port-au-Prince | 1d. |
| 1000. | Buenos Ayres | 6d. | 1059. | Trebizond | 1d. |
| 1001. | Baltimore | 1½d. | 1060. | Barcelona | 1½d. |
| 1002. | Taganrog | 1d. | 1061. | Tainan | 1d. |
| 1003. | Riga | 2d. | 1062. | Smyrna | 1½d. |
| 1004. | Bordeaux | 2½d. | 1063. | Old Calabar | ½d. |
| 1005. | The Hague | 1½d. | 1064. | Samoa | ½d. |
| 1006. | Paraguay | 1½d. | 1065. | Tahiti | 1d. |
| 1007. | Constantinople | 1½d. | 1066. | Chefoo | 6d. |
| 1008. | Rome | 1d. | 1067. | Gothenburg | 2d. |
| 1009. | Mozambique | 1d. | 1068. | Buenos Ayres | 1½d. |
| 1010. | Wenchow | 1d. | 1069. | Loanda | 1½d. |
| 1011. | Mogador | 2½d. | 1070. | Guatemala | 1d. |
| 1012. | Amoy | 1d. | 1071. | Zanzibar | 1d. |

## No. 1072.

*Reference to previous Report, Annual Series No. 845.*

# UNITED STATES.

## CHARLESTON.

*Consul St. John to the Marquis of Salisbury.*

My Lord,              *Charleston, May* 23, 1892.

I HAVE the honour to transmit herewith Annual Reports on the Trade and Commerce of Charleston, Savannah, and Brunswick.

I have, &c.
(Signed)     C. ST. JOHN.

---

*Report on the Trade and Commerce of Charleston for* 1891.

### ABSTRACT of Contents.

| | PAGE |
|---|---|
| General remarks | 1 |
| Fires on cotton ships | 6 |
| Cotton trade | 8 |
| Phosphates and fertilisers | 11 |
| Rice | 19 |
| Naval stores | 21 |
| Lumber | 25 |
| Shipping | 27 |
| Miscellaneous, sanitary, &c. | 28 |
| Reports from Vice-Consul at Savannah | 29 |
| ,, ,, ,, Brunswick | 33 |

### General Remarks.

According to official figures, the total trade and commerce of Charleston for the commercial year ending September 1, 1891, amounted, in round numbers, to 98,000,000 dol. (20,000,000*l.*).

This sum shows a net increase in favour of the present year of 18,000,000 dol. (3,600,000*l.*), as compared with 80,000,000 dol. (16,000,000*l.*) for the year before.

A reference to last year's report will show that, at the time it was sent in, the indications gave reason to expect that an

(1320)

unusually large business would be probably done during the season now under review. These expectations have, on the whole, been fairly realised, although there has been a small decrease in the value of the trade done in rice, resin, turpentine, and lumber.

In cotton, however, notwithstanding the low prices which prevailed for that staple, there was an increase over the previous year of 9,000,000 dol. (1,800,000*l.*), while crude phosphate rock increased 275,000 dol. (55,000*l.*); cotton goods, 480,000 dol. (96,000*l.*); fruits and vegetables, 930,000 dol. (180,000*l.*); manufactured products, 2,000,000 dol. (400,000*l.*); and the wholesale and retail trade, 5,000,000 dol. (1,000,000*l.*).

Five years ago the annual trade of Charleston amounted to but 66,000,000 dol. (13,200,000*l.*), when, it will be remembered, millions of dollars' worth of property were destroyed by the severe earthquake shock which took place on the night of August 31, 1886, laying in total, or partial, ruin many of the best buildings of the city.

During the five years that have elapsed since that time, however, by intelligent effort and the exercise of the conservative business methods, characteristic of this place, nearly all traces have been removed of the havoc caused by the earthquake, and a gain is recorded in the trade and commerce of the port, for the above-named five years, of 31,000,000 dol. (6,200,000*l.*).

With a banking capital of nearly 1,500,000 dol. (300,000*l.*), Charleston is doing a safe and steadily increasing business of about 100,000,000 dol. (20,000,000*l.*) per year, although at the close of 1891 nearly all branches of trade were more or less depressed or unfavourably affected by the extremely low prices of cotton. These prices have naturally resulted from the enormous crop of 8,600,000 bales produced in the United States during the past season, with the probability of another crop as large, or even larger, for the current year of 1891-92.

Indeed, the prices now offered for cotton in some of the interior markets of this Consular district are the lowest known for the past 30 years, and farmers, merchants, and business men generally at this port and throughout the entire State suffer from the stagnation or general congestion prevailing in cotton, inasmuch as this business is interwoven, or related to, nearly all other branches of trade in this section, and whatever affects cotton therefore affects everything.

There is, however, a very general belief that the excessive production of last year, with the consequent decline in values, will, to a certain extent, beget its own remedy, as there is almost sure to be a marked curtailment in the amount of cotton grown next season (1892-93), as many producers are, at present prices, quite unable to pay for cash advances and fertilisers furnished them last year, and, with these claims unpaid, low prices prevailing and a large stock of surplus cotton on hand, both in this country and in Europe, it is likely that money and fertilisers will be advanced less liberally by merchants and manufacturers for the coming season than has heretofore been the case.

A curious contrast is presented at the close of 1891 between the condition of the cotton-growing Southern States of the American Union and the grain-growing States of the West. In both sections crops of cotton and grain respectively were produced in prodigal abundance. But the unusually large grain crop of the West was met by an unusually large demand for wheat and corn from Europe, owing to famine and other causes keeping up the prices of these cereals to a good paying figure, while, on the contrary, the Southern States, having produced the largest cotton crop ever made in this country, were without a corresponding increased European demand, and have consequently suffered widespread distress from the collapse of prices.

The western farmer has grown prosperous from the superabundance of his crops, while the southern planter is impoverished from the same cause.

The disastrous decline in cotton prices has, among other things, emphasised very strongly, to many minds, the importance of placing Charleston hereafter in a position to handle and export the grain of the west.

Up to the present time Charleston has never been a grain exporting port, nor is it likely that grain ships can profitably load cargoes here for Europe until the completion of the jetty system of works now being prosecuted by the United States Government for deepening the water on the bar.

If, however, a sufficient depth of water can be secured at the entrance to this harbour, there seems to be no apparent reason why Charleston should not become a place of considerable importance as a grain-exporting point. At the present time the railway terminal facilities are excellent—better than they have ever been before—the tracks and docks completed last year having been considerably improved and extended since then by the East Shore Terminal Company.

During the past season this company has built tracks from the custom-house to the Cotton Exchange, built or repaired 10 or 12 more wharves, and propose further improvements for next year, so that with the ample water accommodation afforded by Charleston's superb harbour of 15 square miles, lying in front of the city, and with two broad rivers on either side of it, nothing seems lacking in climatic conditions or otherwise to accomplish the desired result but a sufficient depth of water on Charleston bar; such a depth as would enable a grain-loaded ship to go to sea drawing, say, 23 feet or 24 feet of water.

Attention to the question of making this place a grain port is now being entertained by parties in the west, and business men here, being fully alive to the possibilities which lie in this direction, are making strong efforts to urge upon Congress the necessity of an early completion of the jettys.

It is well known that rival ports, particularly Port Royal and Savannah, are likely to compete strongly with Charleston for the grain trade of the west; but though Port Royal has now sufficient water for grain vessels, she has not as yet the necessary railway

(1320)

connections with the western systems, while Savannah must always be more or less handicapped by her narrow river and her 18 miles distance from the ocean. Still it may be well to remember that the enterprising citizens of that town (Savannah) have 26 feet of water on their bar at the present time, compared with 18 feet at Charleston; and, moreover, that they have managed to increase the depth of water in the river about 4 feet more than it was 10 or 12 years ago. Now, a steamer can load to 22 feet at the Savannah docks and proceed to sea without lighterage, whereas in 1880 17 feet to 18 feet was the maximum limit for city loading.

But, nevertheless, in spite of these advantages, the narrow river and still narrower channel is against Savannah, rendering vessels frequenting that port liable to a class of casualties from which they are comparatively exempt in Charleston harbour, such as collisions, groundings, &c., which often result from slight errors of judgment, faulty steering, &c., while working down the narrow, crooked river channel from Savannah to the sea.

Although there has been a good deal of substantial work done upon the Charleston jettys during the year 1891, as is shown by the published reports of Captain Abbott, the United States engineer in charge, there is as yet no decided deepening to be recorded of the water on the bar, nor, indeed, as pointed out by that officer, is this to be expected until the accomplishment of a good deal more necessary work, the successful prosecution of which is dependent upon the appropriations that may be made by Congress for this purpose.

But, to some extent, British shipowners have overcome the disadvantages of the present low water on the bar by building and sending out a class of flat bottomed, light draft vessels this year, able to take in full cotton cargoes at the Charleston docks, and only drawing 16 feet or 17 feet. These vessels, after crossing the bar with ease and safety, obtained the necessary stability in a sea way by immersing the ships 1 foot or 2 feet more with the aid of the water ballast tanks.

The result has been that British ships have, as a general rule, experienced very little delay this season in getting to sea promptly after taking in their cargoes, whereas last year, and in previous years, there was a good deal of loss of time and money by waiting for spring tides and favourable winds; weeks sometimes being wasted in this way after ships were loaded and ready to sail.

This is all the more apparent as a larger number of British steamers came to this port in 1891 than ever before in any one year, several of them being of exceptionally large size and capacity.

A reference to the shipping return, published elsewhere, will show that 96 vessels flying the British flag, mostly steamers, aggregating 114,767 tons, came to Charleston during 1891, as compared with 87 arrivals for 1890, and 63 for the year before;

and yet the records show but one serious casualty (by fire) to any of these vessels while at this port.

The minor mishaps being confined to two or three cases in which vessels have touched bottom crossing the bar, together with one slight collision at Ashley River bridge by a British steamer imprudently attempting to pass through the narrow draw in tow of tugs, but without steam up in her own boilers.

The damages in none of the above-mentioned cases being more than trifling.

In reviewing the trade of Charleston for 1891, several features present themselves to which it may be well to call attention. In the first place the cotton and shipping business, which was unusually good at the opening of the year, continued very much later into the season than has generally been the case in previous years.

As a rule the bulk of this trade is over by or soon after the new year holidays, but cotton and shipping kept brisk this year up to April and May, and something was doing even on through the summer until the opening of the autumn trade. During the summer months a number of British steamers arrived with cargoes of pyrites, kainit, and sulphur; this, together with the exportation of phosphate rock, gave employment to these vessels during June, July, and August, a season when the British flag on merchant steamers has heretofore been rather a rare sight at this port.

During the year 14 British steamers arrived loaded with kainit, 7 with cargoes of iron pyrites, and 5 with sulphur, and it may be mentioned that pyrites as an article of importation is something new in the history of Charleston. Several of the phosphate-manufacturing establishments in this neighbourhood have recently equipped themselves with the necessary appliances for making sulphuric acid from pyrites instead of sulphur. This acid, which is largely used in the manufacture of fertilisers and treatment of crude phosphate rock, it has been found, can be made from sulphur pyrites at a cost from 40 per cent. to 60 per cent. cheaper than from sulphur. Hence, it is probable that pyrites, as an article of importation, if it does not largely displace sulphur, will, hereafter figure as a permanent and prominent feature in the imports at this place.

During the year 1890 the cotton season was fairly under way by August 20, but the cotton receipts and shipping business for 1891 were not well started until September 20, when the staple commenced to come in with a rush that continued until about the middle of December, when the bulk of the trade was practically over for the season.

During the two months from September 20 to December 20, 1891, a good deal of inconvenience was caused by the inability of the railways, with the means at their disposal, to convey so much cotton promptly to the ships' sides. For several weeks something in the nature of a block prevailed on the railways, and numbers of vessels were put on demurrage from this cause. Indeed, when the season had fully commenced in September, the railways, ship-brokers, and draymen were kept exceedingly busy handling the inflowing fleecy staple, and by the middle of November the port had never had larger receipts of cotton, the increase over last year was very marked in this respect; cotton came to Charleston this season from points that had never sent a bale here before, and no port on the Atlantic coast could show anything like a proportionate increase in receipts.

Charleston received this year one bale to every two sent to Savannah; whereas for the previous year, the receipts at Charleston and Savannah respectively were as three bales to one in favour of Savannah.

Although the railways were taxed to their utmost capacity for a short time during the autumn, the situation was considerably relieved as soon as the East Shore Terminal Company extended its lines and built in side tracks to accommodate the traffic.

Better arrangements, however, are promised for the future, and it is believed that a recurrence of trouble from inadequate traffic accommodation is not likely to happen another year.

*Fires on cotton ships.* A very gratifying feature of the year's business has been the infrequency of cotton fires on foreign vessels at Charleston during 1891. The British steamer "Yesso," loaded with 5,125 bales, took fire about the beginning of the year, the loss to ship and cargo being quite a serious one to the underwriters, but this was the only cotton fire at this port where considerable damage was sustained; the cause of this fire, as usual in such cases, being unknown.

Several instances of slight fires, or incipient blazes, among cotton on British vessels were reported by the masters, but the damage was trifling.

The record for the year, therefore, compares very favourably with previous seasons, notwithstanding the large amount of tonnage in port and the unusually heavy receipts and exports of cotton.

Several years ago so many fires occurred here on cotton ships that Charleston was almost a black list port in the eyes of underwriters and insurers, but the record for 1891 shows a marked improvement in this respect for that year.

The United States Government have recently issued circular instructions to the custom-house officials here calling attention to the necessity of enforcing strictly the regulations with reference to the loading and stowing of cotton with a view to the prevention of fires on shipboard. The local police laws bearing on this are also quite strict and appear to be fairly well carried out.

Although no serious cotton ship fires occurred immediately at Charleston in 1891 with the exception already mentioned, there was, however, one case of fire developed after leaving this port in the hold of the British steamship "Wastwater" loaded here last autumn, the cotton in her hold being on fire when she arrived at Liverpool. But whether or not this was the result of causes originating at Charleston or after leaving this port is not known. The damage done in this case was considerable.

Some apprehension was felt towards the close of the year that the large quantities of cotton on hand, together with the low prices for the staple and general depression of the market, would offer a strong temptation to evil-disposed persons to defraud insurance companies by burning up cotton expensive to store and hold, and unprofitable to sell at prevailing prices. But these fears were not realised up to the end of the year.

Whether the good record in regard to cotton fires will continue through the winter and spring remains to be seen. Charleston has certainly had rather a bad name of late years in this respect which, it is hoped, the future will now redeem.

The following statement will show the amount of the general trade of Charleston for the fiscal year ending August 31, 1891, together with its money value as compared with the previous season.

| Articles. | | Quantity. | |
|---|---|---|---|
| | | 1890-91. | 1889-90. |
| Cotton, upland | Bales | 544,330 | 342,572 |
| ,, Sea Island | Bags | 13,414 | 7,256 |
| Rice | Barrels | 87,657 | 97,240 |
| Turpentine | Caks | 35,414 | 50,548 |
| Resin | Barrels | 175,871 | 219,773 |
| Phosphate rock, crude | Tons | 392,743 | 349,762 |
| ,, ,, ground | ,, | 2,000 | 1,250 |
| Fertilisers | ,, | 287,975 | 261,650 |
| Lumber and cross-ties | Feet | 61,226,827 | 73,397,400 |
| Cotton goods | Bales | 72,253 | 63,467 |

| Articles. | Value. | |
|---|---|---|
| | 1890-91. | 1889-90. |
| | Dollars. | Dollars. |
| Cotton, uplands | 24,494,850 | 15,415,740 |
| ,, Sea Islands | 1,073,120 | 719,230 |
| Rice | 1,314,855 | 1,458,600 |
| Turpentine | 708,280 | 1,010,960 |
| Resin | 286,678 | 384,602 |
| Phosphate rock, crude | 4,275,000 | 4,000,000 |
| ,, ,, ground | 23,400 | 10,000 |
| Fertilisers | 5,869,525 | 5,494,650 |
| Cotton goods, domestics, &c. | 3,973,915 | 3,490,685 |
| Lumber and cross-ties | 673,595 | 807,371 |
| Fruits and vegetables | 2,410,000 | 1,480,000 |
| Manufactures (exclusive of fertilisers) | 11,611,500 | 9,527,879 |
| Wholesale and retail trade | 41,840,000 | 36,820,000 |
| Total | 98,554,718 | 80,619,717 |

## UNITED STATES.

### Cotton.

**Cotton.**

The net receipts of cotton at this port for the commercial year ending August 31, 1891, were 557,744 bales, against 349,824 bales received in 1890 and 416,490 bales for the year before.

So far as any reliable information can be obtained on the subject the receipts this year have only been exceeded twice before; the two exceptions were during the years 1880–81, when 628,187 bales were received, and in 1882–83 568,217 bales.

The increase in last year's business, as compared with that of the two previous seasons, was foreshadowed in the annual trade report sent in for 1890; the indications at that time all pointing to an unusually heavy cotton trade for the season now under review.

The gratifying results of this year's business at Charleston have not been due solely to the fact that the United States produced a cotton crop last year of 8,624,156 bales, the largest ever made in this country, but also to the change in the administration of the most important feeder to this port, the South Carolina Railway Company, and the opening up of the East and West Shore Companies' terminal lines along the city water fronts.

Although these enterprises have not yet been fully developed, their effect on the business of the port has already been felt to a remarkable degree by the reduction in the expense of shipments of cotton from interior points to the ships' holds. The lighterage and drayage charges also, which have hitherto been a serious burden to commerce, are now, to a great extent, abolished, and Charleston is enabled to compete on more equal terms than at any period since the American Civil War with the rival ports of Savannah, Norfolk, and Wilmington in carrying the crops of the west and south-west to foreign and domestic ports.

The official figures show that Charleston's cotton receipts last year were about 40 per cent. greater than the year before, a proportionate increase much in excess of any of the other cotton ports. This record has been made with terminal facilities but partly completed, and with no appreciable increase in the water on the bar.

It is generally believed that with the full development of the harbour improvements and railway systems and the perfecting of the terminal arrangements the results to the business of this port, hereafter, will be of a permanent and most gratifying character.

**Exports.**

The total amount of the cotton exported from this port during the year ending August 31, 1891, was as follows:—

|  | Bales. |
|---|---|
| To Liverpool, uplands | 143,942 |
| „ Sea Islands | 5,634 |
| Havre, uplands | 16,330 |
| Continental ports, uplands | 248,842 |
| „ „ Sea Islands | 127 |
| New York, uplands | 126,489 |
| „ Sea Islands | 7,265 |
| Total | 548,629 |

With reference to the condition of the growing cotton crop at the end of August, 1891, reports received from all sections of the cotton belt showed it to be very favourable; although, as a rule, the season was about two weeks later than last year.

The stands, however, were good and the plants were generally healthy and free from grass, and it was noted there was a considerable improvement shown in the cultivation.

The outlook at that time indicated that the crop for the coming year of 1892 would probably equal the 8,600,000 bales made the last year, and might possibly exceed it, some authorities placing their estimates for the next crop as approximating 9,000,000 bales. This prospect, therefore, together with a stock of 1,200,000 bales of American cotton on hand in Europe and the United States to be consumed, and the new crop coming in, made the question of future prices become a very important one.

The situation of affairs was made more serious by the failure of the grain crops in many parts of Europe and Asia, the general dulness of trade in the European manufacturing centres, the scarcity of money and the speculative advances in the prices of bread-stuffs, all of which had a more or less unfavourable effect upon the cotton market.

At this time the cry began to be heard that prices had reached a point which made it unprofitable to raise cotton, and that any further decline would result in a positive loss to the grower.

Utopian remedies of various kinds were suggested for the evil conditions of things, but the fact soon became plainly apparent that the planters had produced more cotton than the world wanted to buy, and that an article is dear at any price when not needed.

Too much cotton had been grown and too few of the necessaries of life. The inevitable result was that with the continued further decline in prices a general collapse of the cotton trade occurred and by the end of the year, bankruptcy and ruin staring many planters in the face.

The prices quoted for cotton in this market on September 1, 1890, were $10\frac{1}{2}$ c. per lb. for middling uplands and 25 c. for medium fine Carolina Sea Islands. One year later, on September 1, 1891, the same grades were quoted at 8 c. for middlings and 19 c. for Sea Islands; and at the close of the year 1891 middlings brought $6\frac{1}{2}$ c. to 7 c. per lb., and for medium fine Sea Islands the quotations were 16 c. to 17 c., according to the colour and condition of the staple.

These quotations show that the loss sustained by the cotton

producers of this country, in consequence of the decline in prices for the 16 months above indicated, has amounted to upwards of 50,000,000 dol. (10,000,000*l.*), estimating the year's crop at 8,600,000 bales, and the weight per bale at, say, 500 lbs. The loss of a sum so large, although it has been widely distributed throughout 12 or 13 different States, easily explains the prevailing distress among the planters and the general depression of business at the end of 1891.

Particularly is this the case when it is recollected that cotton is the principal, and in many sections the sole, money crop of the Southern States of the American Union.

*Sea Island cotton.* At the opening of the cotton year in September, 1890, the weather was very favourable for Sea Islands, and the crop promised to be a very large one as compared with the previous year; but after this time, with each successive harvest month, came such weather as had scarcely been experienced by the present generation. The rainfall was very heavy and injured the quality of the fibre, although atmospheric conditions otherwise were favourable to the formation of the pod. The result, at the end of the season, showed that the crop made was about 50 per cent. greater than the previous year, but of deteriorated quality.

Prices opened in September at 24 c. per lb. for medium fine Carolina Sea Island cotton, and $22\frac{1}{2}$ c. for fine Floridas. From this time until February, under increasing estimates in the yield, the decline was constant, and medium fine Carolinas touched 18 c. and Floridas 17 c.

In March, the stock of bright cotton having been almost exhausted, Carolinas commenced to advance, and by April were quoted at 20 c., while Floridas were $17\frac{1}{2}$ c. During the summer months some sales were made on easier terms, but spinners became unwilling to buy more of the inferior quality, of which the remaining stock was principally composed.

The indications at the close of the season of 1891 were fairly good for the next year's crop, but even the most sanguine do not anticipate a crop nearly as large as that made last year.

The receipts and exports of Sea Islands at Charleston during the year ending August 31, 1891, as compared with the previous year, were as follows:—

RECEIPTS.

| | Quantity. | |
|---|---|---|
| | 1890–91. | 1889–90. |
| | Bales. | Bales. |
| Receipts of Sea Islands | 13,241 | 7,170 |
| Georgia and Floridas | 173 | 86 |
| Old stock | 67 | 3 |
| Total | 13,481 | 7,259 |

### Exports.

| | Quantity | |
|---|---|---|
| | 1890-91. | 1889-90. |
| | Bales. | Bales. |
| Exports of Islands | 12,744 | 7,108 |
| Georgia and Floridas.. | 173 | 36 |
| Stock, Islands.. | 564 | 67 |
| Total | 13,481 | 7,211 |

STATEMENT of Comparative Exports of Sea Island Cotton from the Port of Charleston for the Year ending August 31, 1891.

| | Quantity. | |
|---|---|---|
| | 1890-91. | 1889-90. |
| | Bales. | Bales. |
| Liverpool | 7,324 | 4,673 |
| Havre .. | 679 | 411 |
| Continental ports | 117 | .. |
| New York | 4,787 | 2,108 |
| Total | 12,907 | 7,192 |

In addition to the figures given in the foregoing statements, which were for the commercial year ending August 31, 1891, it may be added that from September 1, 1891, to December 31, 1891, the total receipts of cotton at this port were 410,473 bales; and that the exports during the same time were 333,208 bales. Of the cotton exported during these four months 137,473 bales went to Liverpool, 5,550 bales to Havre, 110,055 bales to continental ports and 84,176 bales to New York.

This period, which forms the first-third of the cotton year for 1891-92, will also be included and fully reported on in the next annual trade return from this office.

At the close of the year a recapitulation of the cotton business for the autumn months shows that its most characteristic features have been great and unusual depression of prices, a short but very active season, lasting practically only about 12 weeks, say from September 20 to December 20, and lastly a closing year with the trade in a complete state of prostration, little or nothing doing in the carrying trade, warehouses filled to overflowing with cotton for which there is no demand at remunerative prices, and gloomy prospects for any considerable rise in values.

*Phosphates and fertilisers.*

Up to about four years ago Charleston was a yearly importer

of fertilisers and manufactured manures from foreign countries, but this business has now practically ceased, owing to the enlargement, which has taken place in the last few years, of the establishments for making fertilisers situated at, or near, this port. All of the phosphate companies, however, continue to import such articles required by them in the manufacture of fertilisers as kainit, muriate of potash, nitrate of soda, sulphur and pyrites.

But little of these imports now come from Great Britain or British colonies. Most of the kainit, muriate, and nitrate being brought from Hamburg, sulphur from Italy, and pyrites from Spain and Portugal.

The many advantages possessed by Charleston as a centre for the manufacture of commercial fertilisers having phosphate rock as a basis have not been overlooked by capitalists, who have shown by their investments during the past 10 years how fully they have appreciated them.

The situation of this place secures to the manufacturer excellent railway connections, good water transportation facilities and close proximity to the raw material; advantages not enjoyed in an equal degree by any of the other south Atlantic ports on this coast. This is emphasised in a practical way by the rapidly increasing value of eligible sites with water fronts near Charleston, and the increased demand for these locations.

During the past year five new fertiliser companies have been organised in this State, and their product is now added to the total output for the year. The names of these new companies are the Chicora, Royal, Imperial, Piedmont, and Georgia Chemical; the first two, the Chicora and Royal, have immense fertiliser factories, and both have been fortunate enough to secure very favourable sites for their works.

The comparative progress in the fertiliser business here is shown by the fact that in 1880 there were 190,760 tons of crude phosphate rock mined, and 80,000 tons of fertilisers manufactured, while in 1891 the number of tons of rock mined were 572,949, and fertilisers made, 287,975 tons.

Notwithstanding the increased competition, the profits of the business have, so far, paid a handsome rate of interest on the investments made, and Charleston capitalists, during the past year, have added to these investments more than a 1,000,000 dol. Mills which were running in 1890, with a capacity of 20,000 tons to 30,000 tons per annum, were enlarged in 1891, and new mills were built with capacities of 50,000 tons to 75,000 tons yearly, one mill even claiming a capacity of 100,000 tons.

The last four mills built are model establishments, combining all the latest improvements in mill construction, acid chambers, wharves, store rooms, &c.

A number of mills are equipped this year with the necessary appliances for making sulphuric acid from pyrites instead of brimstone; it having been found that at present prices acid can be made from pyrites at a saving of 50 per cent. to 60 per cent.

After the close of the shipping season in the spring of 1891 the companies were all busy during the summer months, in putting their machinery in first class condition, making general repairs and adding improvements to their works. At the opening of the new season on September 1, the mills were all ready and prepared for turning out the largest product known in the history of Charleston; but the disastrous decline in the cotton market, however, towards the close of the year 1891, naturally had a very unfavourable effect upon the fertiliser business.

Up to the new year the sales were reported as being 50 per cent. to 60 per cent. behind last year, collections were difficult to make, and the prospects for the coming season of 1892 were, on the whole, very depressing for the trade. The impression in some quarters was quite general that many cotton planters would be obliged next season to make a crop without the use of phosphate fertilisers, or else abandon cotton growing altogether, and substitute some other crop in its place.

The season of 1890-91 was perhaps the most satisfactory one ever enjoyed by the phosphate rock trade here. Prices were remunerative throughout the year ending August 31, 1891, and the demand was good, affording satisfactory returns for shipments and home deliveries. The land miners had an exceptionally good opportunity for a profitable output this season, owing to the litigation between the State Government and the Coosaw Mining Company, which reduced the yield from river mining for the season about 80,000 tons.

Upon the whole, however, the year was one of great activity with advanced prices, and a marked absence of those fluctuations which have attended the trade for some time past.

The question of increased royalty by the State was a matter provoking a good deal of discussion, and some friction was brought into play by the State's new method of taxing the land mining companies owning their own phosphate grounds. But these enterprises, being profitable ones, the question of taxation was generally settled without any great difficulty.

The principal obstacle, checking the steady output of phosphate rock, was the scarcity of labour. The negro, who is the best and most reliable labourer for phosphate mining in this climate, has had other fields opened to him, where he could exchange his labour for money with more profit to himself.

The new fertiliser companies and the increased railway construction throughout the State have absorbed many hands, thus sensibly decreasing the supply of labour for the phosphate mines. Several of the companies, endeavoured, with more or less success, to supply the deficiency of negro labour by Italians, brought here under contract from New York; and two companies, the Horse Shoe and Bolton Mines, at the close of the year were using land dredges as a substitute for the negro.

The following is a complete list of the fertiliser manufacturing companies in this State on August 31, 1891:—Ashley Company, Atlantic Phosphate, Ashepoo, Berkley, Edisto, Etiwan, Stono, Wappoo Mills, Wando, Wilcox, Gibbes, and Co., Pacific Guano

## UNITED STATES.

Co., Meadville Mines, Chicora, Imperial, Royal, Piedmont, Georgia Chemical Works, Greenville Fertiliser Co., Baldwin Fertiliser Co., Port Royal Fertiliser Co., Columbia Fertiliser Co., Globe Fertiliser Co.

Of the foregoing list, the following companies are new, having been organised within the past 15 months, namely, the Chicora, Imperial, Royal, Piedmont, and Georgia Chemical. The latter manufactory has been taken into the phosphate fields on the Edisto River at Pon Pon, the first instance of the kind where this has been done.

In addition to the above-mentioned companies there are nearly as many more cotton seed oil mills in this State, combining with their oil business the manufacture of commercial fertilisers having phosphate rock as a basis. This branch of the business has steadily increased, the mills have prospered and their wants have created an additional demand for crude rock.

**Shipments of fertilisers.** The shipments of manufactured fertilisers from the ports of Charleston, Savannah, and Port Royal during the past three years have been as follows:—

| Ports. | Quantity. | | |
|---|---|---|---|
| | 1889. | 1890. | 1891. |
| | Tons. | Tons. | Tons. |
| Charleston | 172,050 | 261,650 | 287,975 |
| Savannah | 85,550 | 75,000 | 112,000 |
| Port Royal | 55,000 | 50,000 | .. |

**Sales of fertilisers.** The total sales of manufactured fertilisers for the past three years were:—

| Ports. | Quantity. | | |
|---|---|---|---|
| | 1889. | 1890. | 1891. |
| | Tons. | Tons. | Tons. |
| Charleston | 172,550 | 261,650 | 287,975 |
| Savannah | 85,550 | 75,000 | 112,000 |
| Port Royal | 55,000 | 50,000 | 48,400 |

**Imports of chemicals.** The following chemicals, &c., used in the manufacture of phosphate fertilisers were imported at the port of Charleston during the past two years:—

## CHARLESTON.

| Articles. | 1889-90. | |
|---|---|---|
| | Quantity. | Value. |
| | Tons. | Dollars. |
| Kainit | 13,619 | 93,376 |
| Brimstone | 19,302 | 324,938 |
| Nitrate soda | 3,284 | 104,273 |
| Muriate potash | 2,730 | 90,058 |
| Total | 38,935 | 612,645 |

| Articles. | 1890-91. | |
|---|---|---|
| | Quantity. | Value. |
| | Tons. | Dollars. |
| Kainit | 21,676 | 139,499 |
| Brimstone | 25,556 | 541,969 |
| Nitrate soda | 2,014 | 52,747 |
| Muriate potash | 3,232 | 113,841 |
| Pyrites | 5,500 | 31,020 |
| Fertilisers | 548 | 5,480 |
| Total | 58,526 | 884,556 |

The total amount of business done at Charleston in crude phosphate rock during the year 1890-91 was 572,949 tons, valued at 4,275,000 dol. (855,000*l*.).

*Crude phosphate rock.*

This does not include the fertiliser business proper, which consisted, as already stated, of 287,987 tons, valued at 5,869,525 dol. (1,173,900*l*.).

South Carolina crude phosphate rock continues to maintain its leading position in the markets of the world as a standard article, reliable and uniform both in quality and analysis, and containing so little deleterious matter that it is generally regarded as chemically perfect. The superior quality of the Carolina rock has been most clearly shown by its ability to hold its own for the last two years, notwithstanding the increasing competition of the Florida companies.

During this time many millions of dollars have been invested in Florida enterprises. Several large, well situated, and well equipped companies are now mining rock in that State, and many smaller companies are preparing to go into the business.

Still the output of Florida rock up to the present time has by no means been commensurate with the capital now invested there in mining operations. The best expert opinions on the subject regard the output, thus far, of Florida rock as not more than 25 per cent. of what it should be under existing circumstances.

Nevertheless, the Carolina miners recognise the fact that

(1320)

Florida contains some excellent phosphate deposits, and it is very evident that, after the business there has passed through the speculative fever period, these deposits will be successfully mined, used and exported. But the Florida miners cannot hope to attain success except by complying with those inevitable conditions and natural laws which environ and control the business elsewhere. They must learn, as the Carolina miners did before them, that successful phosphate mining requires time, labour, patience, knowledge, and money. It must also be remembered that after the rock is mined it is a bulky article, and ample facilities must be provided for moving it to market, and that the more cheaply this is done the greater must be the profit.

When all of these conditions are made favourable, as they doubtless will be in course of time, Florida will most likely come to the front, and possibly be a serious competitor with the Carolina mining industries.

Once Florida has learned the necessary lessons in order to make her a successful miner of phosphate rock, it is perhaps only natural to suppose that she will become a manufacturer of fertilisers, when she will compete with the Carolina manufacturers as well as the miners. But the fertiliser business is a growing industry in a growing country, and although temporarily depressed at the end of 1891, it may be only fair to assume that when Florida's phosphate industries are fully developed, and the time has come for her to make fertilisers as well as mine rock, that the increased supply of manufactured fertilisers brought into the market will be met by an increased demand.

For the present, however, the Charleston manufacturers use about 200,000 tons of crude rock a year, but they have not, so far, been able to use Florida low grade rock, as it cannot compete with the Carolina article; neither could they use the Florida 80 per cent. to 85 per cent. high grade rock, as it is too high priced and variable, both as to colour and quality.

The high grade Florida rock, together with the 23,000 tons of apatite yearly shipped from Canada, had to be sent abroad to markets where there is only a limited demand for rock with high testing qualities.

The Canadian apatite, however, is only a small factor, as the annual output for the past five years has only averaged about 23,000 tons.

**Carolina phosphate lands.**

Sales of phosphate lands have been few during the year. One large tract and a few smaller ones changed hands since last report. Parties holding well situated and valuable lands have, as a rule, been unwilling to sell, and sales of lands in this State have been difficult to make.

**Mining companies.**

The following is a list of the land and river phosphate mining companies in this State, with the annual capacity of each :—

## CHARLESTON.

|  | Tons Capacity. |
|---|---|
| William Gregg | 10,000 |
| Charleston and Mining Manufacturing Company | 100,000 |
| C. C. Pinckney junr. | 30,000 |
| Charles H. Drayton | 15,000 |
| Rose Mining Company | 20,000 |
| William L. Bradley | 30,000 |
| St. Andrew's Mines | 20,000 |
| Bolton | 20,000 |
| Wando Phosphate | 15,000 |
| F. C. Fishburne | 20,000 |
| C. O. Campbell | 15,000 |
| E. J. Hanahan | 20,000 |
| E. B. Fishburne | 20,000 |
| Horseshoe Mines | 20,000 |
| Meadville | 25,000 |
| Mount Holly Company | 15,000 |
| Palmetto | 10,000 |
| Shier Mines | 5,000 |
| Beaufort Phosphate Company | 25,000 |
| Coosaw Company | 100,000 |
| Carolina Company | 50,000 |
| Farmers' Company | 30,000 |
| W. Y. Fripp Company | 5,000 |
| Oak Point Mines | 40,000 |
| Sea Island Chemical Company | 50,000 |
| Williams' Island Company | 20,000 |
| E. C. William | 5,000 |
| Archdale Company | 15,000 |
| Eureka Mine | 15,000 |
| Dotterer Mine | 15,000 |
| Pacific Guano Company | 10,000 |

Prices. The quotations for land and river rock alongside of the vessels at Charleston, at the end of the business year, were as follows:—

|  |  | Value. ||
|---|---|---|---|
|  |  | Land Rock. | River Rock. |
|  |  | Dol.  c. | Dol.  c. |
| Crude | Ton | 7  00 | 7  25 |
| Hot air | Dried | 8  00 | 8  25 |
| Ground rock | Sacks | 9  50 | 9  75 |

Shipments. The shipments of ground and crude rock from Charleston during the past year have been:—To domestic ports of the United States and to the west, by railway, 252,305 tons, against 291,046 tons for the year before; and the shipments to foreign ports during the same period were 5,438 tons of rock for 1891, and 5,876 tons for 1890.

Recapitulation. The following comparative statement shows the total amount of phosphate rock consumed and exported from the two ports of Charleston and Beaufort, South Carolina, during the past two years, together with the total value in dollars:—

## UNITED STATES.

### Exports from Charleston.

| To— | Quantity. | |
| --- | --- | --- |
| | 1890-91. | 1889-90. |
| | Tons. | Tons. |
| Foreign countries | 5,438 | 48,716 |
| Coastwise | 181,641 | 135,298 |
| Interior | 70,664 | 65,748 |
| Consumed | 135,000 | 100,000 |
| Total | 392,743 | 349,762 |

### Exports from Beaufort.

| To— | Quantity. | |
| --- | --- | --- |
| | 1890-91. | 1889-90. |
| | Tons. | Tons. |
| Foreign countries | 121,360 | 171,106 |
| Coastwise | 33,846 | 41,890 |
| Interior | 9,000 | 8,000 |
| Consumed | 16,000 | 16,000 |
| Total | 180,206 | 236,996 |

| From— | Total Value. | |
| --- | --- | --- |
| | 1890-91. | 1889-90. |
| | Dollars. | Dollars. |
| Charleston and Beaufort | 4,275,000 | 4,000,000 |

Total phosphate and fertiliser business for the year.

The following brief statement will show the total amount and value of the phosphate rock and fertiliser business done at Charleston during the year:—

| | Quantity. | Value. |
| --- | --- | --- |
| | Tons. | Dollars. |
| Phosphate rock | 572,949 | 4,275,000 |
| Fertilisers | 287,975 | 5,869,525 |
| Total | 860,924 | 10,144,525 |

## Rice.

At the beginning of September, 1890, the prospects were very favourable for a fine rice harvest, but were soon destroyed by the heavy rains which commenced early in the month, and continued, with scarcely an intermission, throughout the whole of September, seriously impeding the cutting and gathering of the rice, preventing the planters from properly curing the grain, and causing it in some instances to heat and sprout in the cocks.

This necessitated the bestowal of much extra labour on the crop, besides greatly increasing the cost of getting it stored away in the barns. Much of the rice land on the Cooper River had not been planted at all this season, and the yield from that portion under culture was generally of poor quality and short in quantity. It therefore became evident early in the season that there would be a considerable falling-off in the receipts at the Charleston mills as compared with the year before.

The total receipts of rice at this port, from September 1, 1890, to September 1, 1891, were only 681,369 bushels, against 799,144 bushels received at the city mills last year, showing a shortage for the present season of 117,775 bushels. But this deficiency was partly counterbalanced by the fact that the rice lands in South Carolina, on rivers situated north of the Cooper, had yielded better crops than during 1890, this increased yield reducing the entire shortage in the crop for the whole State of South Carolina to 35,225 bushels as compared with the previous year.

There was also a reduction in the crop of Georgia rice this year of 60,000 bushels, resulting from very much the same causes that made the Carolina crop short; but the rice reports from the State of North Carolina, and also from Louisiana, show increased yields for the present year. The total rice crop produced in the United States during the season of 1891 was 5,036,332 bushels, while the estimated crop for 1890 was placed at 4,669,616 bushels. These figures show that, notwithstanding the deficiency in Carolina rice, there was an increase in the total crop produced this season throughout the country of 366,716 bushels.

The first shipment of new rice this year reached Charleston August 20, 1890, was pounded at the West Point Mill, and sold the day following at $6\frac{1}{2}$ c. per pound. This was soon followed by other shipments, but a few days later the weather became so unfavourable that shipments from the country entirely ceased for several weeks. Some of the rice on the way to market about this time became too damp for milling, and to be handled and dried before it could be cleaned.

The market, therefore, was not fairly opened until towards the end of September. In October there was a moderately good demand for rice, the prices then quoted being $4\frac{3}{4}$ c. to 5 c. per pound for fair, $5\frac{1}{8}$ c. to $5\frac{1}{2}$ c. per pound for good, and 6 c. to $6\frac{1}{4}$ c per pound for prime. During November there was less demand, and prices fell off $\frac{1}{4}$ c. to $\frac{1}{2}$ c. The decline was unchecked in

## UNITED STATES.

December, the money troubles in Europe at this time causing uneasiness and distrust in this country, and producing complications and curtailment of transactions, to some extent, notwithstanding the apparent shortage in the Atlantic coast crop.

Prices continued to drop until about the middle of January, 1891, when a reaction took place, lost ground was recovered during the following months, and most of the rice offered for sale was freely taken at prices that ruled at the beginning of the season.

During the spring months large quantities of foreign rice were brought into this market, and about 80,000 bushels of uncleaned rice from Japan was milled in Charleston in addition to the domestic crop.

*Rice crop.*

Up to the year 1884 Carolina rice was packed in tierces averaging 600 lbs. net weight each, but for the past six seasons it has been packed in barrels containing about 300 lbs. The following figures, including the references to the Louisiana crop, are therefore given in barrels of the above-mentioned average weight.

The total crop of South Carolina rice for the season of 1890–91 was as follows:—

|   |   | Barrels. |
|---|---|---|
| Milled at Charleston | .. .. .. .. .. | 61,507 |
| „ Georgetown | .. .. .. .. .. | 34,237 |
| Total for South Carolina | .. .. .. | 95,744 |

The total amount of the crop for Georgia milled at Savannah during the same year was 46,506 barrels, while the North Carolina crop milled at Wilmington, Washington, and Newbern was 25,456 barrels, making the crop produced on the Atlantic coast during the year ending August 31, 1891, amount to 167,706 barrels, which, added to the Louisiana crop of 296,363 barrels, would make the total crop of the United States for the year 464,069 barrels.

*Rice exports and home consumption.*

The following table shows the exports, shipments by railway, and home consumption of rice at Charleston for the past two years:—

### SHIPMENTS.

| To— | 1890–91. | 1889–90. |
|---|---|---|
|   | Barrels. | Barrels. |
| New York | 33,187 | 41,543 |
| Foreign ports | .. | 150 |
| Interior, by rail | 33,270 | 38,547 |
| City consumption | 20,000 | 17,000 |
| Total | 86,457 | 97,240 |

## CHARLESTON.

### RICE RECEIPTS.

| Place. | Quantity. | |
|---|---|---|
| | 1890-91. | 1889-90. |
| Receipts at Charleston | Barrels. 87,657 | Barrels. 97,240 |
| Deduct shipments and city consumption | 86,457 | 97,240 |
| Stock remaining on hand August 31, 1891 | 1,200 | .. |

The foregoing figures are for the commercial year ending August 31, 1891, but in addition to this it may be stated that from September 1, 1891, to December 31, the total receipts of rice at Charleston amounted to 24,394 barrels against 33,260 barrels received during the corresponding period in 1890; and the total exports during the last four months of the year 1891 were 16,754 barrels, against 26,462 barrels for the same time the year before, leaving a stock on hand and shipboard on the last day of 1891 of 4,862 barrels.

Of the above stated 16,754 barrels exported, 9,029 barrels were shipped to New York, and 7,725 barrels went by rail to interior points of the United States, there being no shipments of rice to foreign countries during this time.

### *Naval Stores.*

The receipts of turpentine and resin at this port during the 12 months ending August 31, 1891, were less than for the previous year. The decrease is attributable in part to the reduced territory now shipping naval stores to Charleston, in consequence of the gradual exhaustion and clearing away of the yellow pine forests in this section, and also to the fact that considerable quantities of naval stores from Georgetown, formerly going to northern ports viâ Charleston, are now shipped direct by steamers plying between Wilmington, Georgetown, and New York.

The turpentine, resin, and tar products of the pine tree, however, sent to Charleston this year were disposed of at fairly remunerative prices, the factors expressing themselves as moderately satisfied with the volume of business done this season, and anticipating larger receipts and profitable prices for next year.

The Charleston resin and turpentine sheds are situated in close proximity to the tracts of the East Shore Railway Company, and are convenient to the docks at which vessels loading naval stores for foreign ports are generally moored. Resin and turpentine

(1320)

shipped to the north can be taken now, without breaking bulk, to the wharves of the New York steamship line and loaded directly into the ships.

For many years Wilmington, North Carolina, was the principal naval stores' market in America, but as the Carolina forests have been gradually worked out, the turpentine hands, year by year, pushed forward into the virgin forests of south-west Georgia, Florida, and Alabama, so that at the present day Savannah is one of the first naval stores' ports in the world, and prices elsewhere are controlled by that market.

But notwithstanding the movement of the turpentine distillers and resin producers, which, like the star of empire on the American continent, steadily takes its westward course, it is likely that Charleston will be able, for many years yet, to do a fair share of the naval stores' business, owing to that ingenious device of modern times known in this country as the "long haul," to railway extensions keeping pace with the growth of trade, to improved terminal facilities and to better water accommodation for handling the business which are now furnished by this port.

The following comparative statement shows the receipts and exports of naval stores at Charleston for the year ending August 31, 1891, and also for the year before.

TABLE showing Receipts, Exports, and Stock on Hand of Naval Stores at Charleston.

|  | 1890–91. | | 1889–90. | |
| --- | --- | --- | --- | --- |
|  | Spirits. | Resin. | Spirits. | Resin. |
|  | Casks. | Barrels. | Casks. | Barrels. |
| Stock on hand .. .. | 3,710 | 19,774 | 2,394 | 17,886 |
| Receipts .. .. | 35,414 | 163,816 | 50,548 | 219,773 |
| Total .. .. | 39,124 | 183,590 | 52,942 | 237,659 |

## CHARLESTON.

*Exports.*

TABLE showing Exports of Naval Stores to Foreign Ports during the Past Two Years.

FOREIGN.

| Ports. | 1890-91. Spirits. | 1890-91. Resin. | 1889-90. Spirits. | 1889-90. Resin. |
|---|---|---|---|---|
|  | Casks. | Barrels. | Casks. | arrels. |
| Rotterdam | 3,888 | 15,573 | 4,812 | 12,873 |
| Hamburg | 5,098 | 13,836 | 1,872 | 27,965 |
| Bristol | 3,027 | 3,268 | 4,553 | 4,200 |
| Goole | .. | .. | .. | 2,639 |
| Cardiff | .. | .. | .. | 2,726 |
| Trieste | 100 | 23,079 | 100 | 22,877 |
| Glasgow | 1,343 | 3,093 | 1,750 | 4,020 |
| Genoa | 2,132 | 13,126 | 846 | 10,809 |
| London | 2,864 | 6,301 | 9,299 | 8,498 |
| Garston Dock | .. | .. | 150 | 5,082 |
| Liverpool | .. | 11,353 | .. | 3,158 |
| Naples | 60 | 2,775 | .. | 2,352 |
| Hull | .. | 2,445 | 200 | 3,700 |
| Granton | .. | .. | .. | 3,613 |
| Marseilles | .. | .. | .. | 2,375 |
| Harburg | .. | 12,943 | .. | 9,478 |
| Riga | .. | 2,225 | .. | 2,759 |
| Barcelona | .. | 298 | .. | 300 |
| Venice | .. | .. | .. | 2,770 |
| Stettin | .. | 4,442 | .. | 5,033 |
| Nordkopping | .. | .. | .. | 600 |
| Sor's Hel's | .. | .. | .. | 2,156 |
| Newcastle | .. | 5,223 | .. | 3,200 |
| Gottenburg | .. | 299 | .. | 1,000 |
| Bremen | .. | 8,750 | .. | .. |
| Antwerp | .. | 2,842 | .. | .. |
| Bremerhaven | .. | 2,734 | .. | .. |
| Aberdeen | .. | 500 | .. | .. |
| Total foreign | 18,512 | 135,105 | 19,585 | 144,183 |

TABLE showing Comparative Coastwise Exports of Naval Stores for the Past Two Years.

COASTWISE.

| | 1890-91. Spirits. | 1890-91. Resin. | 1889-90. Spirits. | 1889-90. Resin. |
|---|---|---|---|---|
|  | Casks. | Barrels. | Casks. | Barrels. |
| New York | 14,507 | 37,308 | 22,475 | 67,229 |
| Interior, rail | 2,823 | 2,156 | 3,175 | 6,453 |
| Total | 17,330 | 39,464 | 25,650 | 73,682 |

## UNITED STATES.

### RECAPITULATION.

|  | 1890-91. | | 1889-90. | |
|---|---|---|---|---|
|  | Spirits. | Resin. | Spirits. | Resin. |
|  | Casks. | Barrels. | Casks. | Barrels. |
| Stock on hand and the receipts for year | 39,124 | 183,590 | 52,942 | 237,639 |
| Total exports of foreign and domestic | 35,842 | 174,579 | 49,232 | 217,865 |
| Stock on hand September 1 | 3,282 | 9,011 | 3,710 | 19,774 |

*Prices.*

The prices quoted for the leading grades of resin and spirits of turpentine on September 1, 1890, were:—for rosin, grade C., 1 dol. 15 c. per barrel; grade F., 1 dol. 25 c. per barrel; grade G., 1 dol. 35 c. per barrel; grade H., 1 dol. 55 c. per barrel; grade I., 1 dol. 75 c. per barrel; grade K., 1 dol. 95 c. per barrel; grade M., 2 dol. 5 c. per barrel; and grade N., 2 dol. 50 c.; for spirits of turpentine, 36 c. per gallon.

In October grade C. resin declined to 1 dol. 12 c., and other grades in proportion, but prices rose again in November to 1 dol. 25 c. for grade C., 1 dol. 35 c. for grade F., and 1 dol. 45 c. for grade G. resin. There were various fluctuations throughout the rest of the season, and the highest price during the year for low grades resins was in May, 1891, when grade C. was quoted at 1 dol. 40 c., grade F. 1 dol. 50 c., and grade G. 1 dol. 65 c. Later on prices declined again, and closed August 31, 1891, at 1 dol. 15 c. for grade C., 1 dol. 20 c. for grade F., and 1 dol. 25 c. for grade G.

The highest price quoted for spirits of turpentine during the year was $38\frac{1}{2}$ c. in November, 1890. The closing price in August, 1891, being 34 c. per gallon.

*Supplementary.*

From September 1, 1891, until December 31, 1891, the naval stores' market showed but little activity, and there was a gradual decline in the prices of turpentine. Early in September spirits were sold at 34 c. to 35 c. per gallon, but by the middle of December the quotations were 30 c.; a slight advance then took place, and at the end of the year it closed at 31 c.

Resin was sold during the first part of September at 1 dol. 25 c. per barrel for grade C., 1 dol. 90 c. for grade I., and 2 dol. 90 c. for window glass, and 3 dol. 10 c. for water white; but by October 1 there was a recession of values to 1 dol. 60 c. for the lowest grades and 2 dol. 85 c. and 3 dol. respectively for window glass and water white. From this time the market improved, and after various fluctuations it closed December 31, 1891, at the following quotations: for grade C. resin 1 dol. 25 c., water white 3 dol. 75 c., and window glass 3 dol. 35 c. per barrel.

The receipts of naval stores at Charleston from September 1, 1891, to December 31, 1891, were 50,127 barrels of resin and

9,334 casks of spirits of turpentine, and the exports during the same period were 47,765 barrels of resin and 9,070 casks of turpentine. Of the amounts exported 6,631 barrels of resin and 5,133 casks of turpentine went to New York or interior points by rail, 1,350 casks and 20,613 barrels were shipped to Great Britain, and most of the rest was sent to places in the north of Europe.

## Lumber.

The encouraging outlook early in the season for the lumber business was not fully realised, and as the year advanced orders decreased, the demand slacked off, and prices declined towards the end of the year to a point so low that the terms offered were hardly sufficient to compensate either manufacturers or shippers. [Lumber.]

The stringency of the financial market and the caution arising from the doubtful supply of money may probably account for this, because improvements and enterprises which would have been undertaken under more favourable conditions have been restricted, resulting in a decreased demand for lumber.

The market was well stocked during the year with the best grades of timber for the use of the city mills, while the excellent facilities now enjoyed by Charleston for handling lumber by rail to the terminal points, and the accessible means for river transportation, renders this one of the most desirable markets for the business, and make it possible to execute orders on the best terms and at the shortest notice.

There has been some inquiry for distant future delivery, and the indications were that business would improve towards the end of the winter and the opening up of the spring trade. Prospective improvements to be made together with expected railway connections with the western river front, corresponding to the present eastern terminal arrangements, would appear calculated to make a trade commensurate with the advantages offered.

The comparative exports of lumber, timber, and cross-ties from the port of Charleston from September 1, 1890, to August 31, 1891, as well as for the same period in 1889-90, will be found in the following table:— [Exports.]

| Exported to. | Quantity. | |
|---|---|---|
| | 1890-91. | 1889-90. |
| | Feet. | Feet. |
| New York | 27,941,951 | 30,638,452 |
| Boston | 251,000 | .. |
| Philadelphia | 6,021,000 | 23,611,652 |
| Baltimore | 2,760,900 | 1,118,000 |
| Other American ports | 8,582,371 | 8,319,609 |
| Total coastwise | 45,557,222 | 63,687,713 |
| West Indies | 5,129,195 | 4,268,437 |
| South America | 540,410 | .. |
| Nova Scotia | .. | 430,000 |
| Other foreign ports | .. | 11,250 |
| Total foreign | 5,669,605 | 4,709,687 |
| „ coastwise | 45,557,222 | 63,687,713 |
| Grand total | 51,226,827 | 68,397,400 |

## Shipping.

Shipping.

The total number of vessels arriving at this port during the year 1891, exclusive of vessels under 100 tons register and river steamers, were as follows:—

| Nationality. | Number of Vessels. | Tonnage. |
|---|---|---|
| American | 763 | 785,962 |
| British | 96 | 114,767 |
| Italian | 30 | 12,840 |
| Norwegian | 24 | 13,736 |
| Spanish | 16 | 7,044 |
| German | 14 | 5,662 |
| Swedish | 3 | 1,065 |
| Danish | 3 | 917 |
| Austrian | 2 | 1,340 |
| Total | 951 | 943,333 |

The proportion of the year's shipping trade done by British vessels is shown, fully detailed, in the following shipping return for 1891.

## CHARLESTON.

### Return of British Shipping at the Port of Charleston in the Year 1891.

*Direct Trade in British Vessels from and to Great Britain and British Colonies.*

| | Entered. | | | | | | | Cleared. | | | | | | |
|---|---|---|---|---|---|---|---|---|---|---|---|---|---|---|
| **Total Number of Vessels.** | | | **Total Tonnage.** | | | Total Number of Crews. | Total Value of Cargoes. | **Total Number of Vessels.** | | | **Total Tonnage.** | | | Total Number of Crews. | Total Value of Cargoes. |
| With Cargoes. | In Ballast. | Total. | With Cargoes. | In Ballast. | Total. | | | With Cargoes. | In Ballast. | Total. | With Cargoes. | In Ballast. | Total. | | |
| 4 | 18 | 22 | 2,357 | 21,068 | 23,425 | 444 | £ 4,830 | 39 | ... | 39 | 50,817 | ... | 50,817 | 858 | £ 1,740,000 |

*Indirect or Carrying Trade in British Vessels from and to other Countries.*

#### Entered.

| Countries whence Arrived. | Number of Vessels. | | | Tonnage. | | | Number of Crews. | Value of Cargoes. |
|---|---|---|---|---|---|---|---|---|
| | With Cargoes. | In Ballast. | Total. | With Cargoes. | In Ballast. | Total. | | |
| Belgium | ... | 3 | 3 | ... | 5,184 | 5,184 | 77 | £ ... |
| Brazil | ... | 1 | 1 | ... | 1,415 | 1,415 | 23 | ... |
| Denmark | ... | 1 | 1 | ... | 356 | 356 | 10 | ... |
| France | ... | 2 | 2 | ... | 2,725 | 2,725 | 47 | ... |
| Germany | 15 | ... | 15 | 20,097 | ... | 20,097 | 319 | 64,800 |
| Holland | ... | 1 | 1 | ... | 482 | 482 | 11 | ... |
| Hayti | ... | 1 | 1 | ... | 182 | 182 | 7 | ... |
| Mexico | ... | 1 | 1 | ... | 1,240 | 1,240 | 24 | ... |
| Italy | 3 | ... | 3 | 4,074 | ... | 4,074 | 72 | 22,600 |
| Portugal | 1 | 4 | 5 | 1,067 | 5,506 | 6,573 | 110 | 1,800 |
| Spain | 7 | 3 | 10 | 7,345 | 3,743 | 11,088 | 203 | 40,846 |
| Uruguay | ... | 1 | 1 | ... | 959 | 959 | 13 | ... |
| United States | ... | 30 | 30 | ... | 36,967 | 36,967 | 693 | ... |
| Total | 26 | 48 | 74 | 32,583 | 58,759 | 91,342 | 1,609 | 130,046 |

#### Cleared.

| Countries to which Departed. | Number of Vessels. | | | Tonnage. | | | Number of Crews. | Value of Cargoes. |
|---|---|---|---|---|---|---|---|---|
| | With Cargoes. | In Ballast. | Total. | With Cargoes. | In Ballast. | Total. | | |
| Germany | 25 | ... | 25 | 33,021 | ... | 33,021 | 552 | £ 1,302,000 |
| Russia | 4 | ... | 4 | 4,234 | ... | 4,234 | 87 | 183,000 |
| Spain | 5 | 1 | 6 | 6,363 | 1,096 | 7,459 | 140 | 191,467 |
| Sweden | 4 | ... | 4 | 3,395 | ... | 3,395 | 60 | 62,000 |
| United States | ... | 13 | 13 | ... | 12,397 | 12,397 | 232 | ... |
| Total | 38 | 14 | 52 | 47,013 | 13,498 | 60,506 | 1,071 | 1,738,467 |

## 28  UNITED STATES.

### Miscellaneous.

EXTRACT of Report furnished by Charleston Health Officer, H. B. Holbrook, M.D.

**Miscellaneous.** There has been no epidemic in this city during the past year of 1891, except a visitation of "La Grippe," which also visited the entire country; 15 white and 21 coloured deaths occurred. The epidemic was most general.

A few deaths have occurred from diphtheria; whites two, coloured one. No scarlet fever deaths, and very few deaths from typhoid fever; in fact there has been fewer deaths from typhoid fever in 1891 than for 20 years past. This is most encouraging, and might well be regarded as a good test of cleanliness and good water.

There were 234 deaths from diarrhœal diseases—far above the average. Consumption claims 41 whites and 203 coloured victims.

**Quarantine.** The quarantine station of Charleston Harbour at Fort Johnson continues to give the greatest satisfaction. It is furnished with all modern scientific appliances; the Holt system, embracing steam heating at 230 degrees, bichloride of mercury spray and sulphur fumigation 18 per cent., furnishes a complete system of disinfection.

**Disinfection.** This very important work is most satisfactorily done by a rigid custom of furnishing a full supply of disinfectants to every house, reported as having a case of contagious or infectious disease, a fumigation with sulphur dioxide gas being used.

During the summer months deodorising solutions are placed in all public places requiring it, and a supply of disinfectants is furnished to any and all who ask for it. Sixty-two houses were fumigated and disinfected, 6,892 persons were supplied with chloride of lime, and 38,700 gallons of copperas solution was distributed.

### MORTUARY Statistics for 1891.

|  | Number. |
|---|---|
| Male, white | 296 |
| Female ,, | 257 |
| Total white | 553 |
| Male, coloured | 641 |
| Female ,, | 730 |
| Total coloured | 1,371 |

**Population and deaths.** Estimated population, whites 28,870, coloured 36,295; total 65,165.

Proportion of deaths, whites 1 in 52, coloured 1 in 26; total proportion 1 in 33.

Mean, 66·5 degrees; the average annual temperature of Charleston for 20 years is 66 degrees, and for the months of January, 49·9 degrees; February, 53·7 degrees; March, 56·7 degrees; April, 64·2 degrees; May, 72·7 degrees; June, 78·8 degrees; July, 82·3 degrees; August, 79·8 degrees; September, 75·4 degrees; October, 67·7 degrees; November, 58·9 degrees; December, 51·9 degrees. Highest temperature, 95 degrees, on July 4; lowest, 27 degrees, on February 27 and December 1. *Air temperature.*

Number of days in which temperature was above 90 degrees, 21 days in May, June, July, and August; there were 120 cloudless days.

Prevailing direction, north-east, highest velocity, 36 miles north-west, November 18. The last frost occurred April 6, and the first frost October 21. *Winds.*

## SAVANNAH.

Mr. Vice-Consul Robertson reports as follows:—

The trade and commerce of Savannah during the year 1891 was not, in all respects, as satisfactory as that of the previous year, for the reason that a tight money market upset and depressed trade to a very considerable extent, and the low price and inferior quality of much of the cotton were not without hurtful influence.

The actual volume of the city's business—as will be shown later on—however, was much greater than that of any previous year.

One of the features of this increase was, that it was not in cotton alone. The increase in cotton valuation was very small, on account of low prices. Had the prices equalled those of last year, the increased value of the trade of the port would have been remarkable.

Savannah has long been recognised as the leading naval stores' market of the world, and there is not much doubt that she will continue to be for many years to come. It will be many years before the pine forests are exhausted, and, in the meantime, the proportion of naval stores handled at Savannah will steadily grow larger.

Savannah's business and manufacturing enterprises are growing with rapid strides. The volume of her wholesale and retail business during the past year (1891) was greater than ever before in her history, and the prospects for a steady annual increase are particularly bright. *Business generally.*

The following is a comparative estimate of the valuation of Savannah's trade for the years 1890–91.

UNITED STATES.

TABLE showing Comparative Estimate of Savannah's Trade during the Years 1891-90.

|  | 1891. | | 1890. | |
| --- | --- | --- | --- | --- |
|  | Currency. | Sterling. | Currency. | Sterling. |
|  | Dollars. | £ | Dollars. | £ |
| Cotton | 52,000,000 | 10,400,000 | 51,500,000 | 10,300,000 |
| Naval stores | 6,300,000 | 1,260,000 | 6,000,000 | 1,200,000 |
| Lumber | 4,500,000 | 900,000 | 3,300,000 | 660,000 |
| Fertilisers | 3,000,000 | 600,000 | 2,750,000 | 550,000 |
| Groceries | 25,000,000 | 5,000,000 | 22,750,009 | 4,550,000 |
| Liquor and tobacco | 4,250,000 | 850,000 | 4,000,000 | 800,000 |
| Provisions | 5,000,000 | 1,000,000 | 4,750,000 | 950,000 |
| Dry goods | 4,500,000 | 900,000 | 4,200,000 | 840,000 |
| Clothing | 1,000,000 | 200,000 | unobtainable | |
| Boots, shoes and hats | 2,000,002 | 400,000 | 1,000,000 | 200,000 |
| Hardware | 1,500,000 | 300,000 | 1,300,000 | 260,000 |
| Furniture | 1,000,000 | 200,000 | 500,000 | 100,000 |
| Jewellery | 750,000 | 150,000 | 500,000 | 100,000 |
| Drugs, oils, and paint | 1,250,000 | 250,000 | 1,000,000 | 200,000 |
| Manufactures | 7,500,000 | 1,500,000 | 3,250,000 | 650,000 |
| Retail trade | 26,000,000 | 5,200,000 | 22,000,000 | 4,400,000 |
| Miscellaneous | 8,000,000 | 1,600,000 | 5,000,000 | 1,000,000 |
| Total | 153,550,000 | 30,710,000 | 133,800,000 | 26,760,000 |

The year under review was remarkable for the exceeding stringency of money.

*Real estate.* But for the difficulty in obtaining money, the transactions in real estate would have been immense. Naturally the effect of tight money was to reduce the volume of business in this line. The disposition to invest was very marked, and only restrained by the difficulty experienced in negotiating loans.

Notwithstanding this fact the price of real estate kept up, and the demand—on an easier money market—has again become active.

*Financial.* Although the banking capital of Savannah has been increased by nearly 1,000,000 dol. (200,000*l.*) during the year the great need of more money is still apparent, and fully 2,000,000 dol. (400,000*l.*) more capital could be easily used here advantageously for the actual requirements of strictly legitimate trade.

*Railroads.* Savannah has the best transportation facilities of any city on the south Atlantic coast.

It is the coast terminus of two of the largest railroad systems of the south, the Central Railroad and the Plant System.

These two great systems combined make Savannah the seaport terminus of 3,700 miles of road.

In addition to this vast mileage two new railroads are being rapidly built into Savannah, and it is hoped will be in active operation by the end of the present year.

*Harbour improvements.* The improvements heretofore executed in the harbour of

Savannah, and the expectations of further improvements yet to be made, have been the inducements to develop the railway systems before-mentioned. The sections of country made tributary to Savannah by those railways are among the richest in the United States, and to enable the port to furnish an outlet to the rapidly growing commerce offered to it from the interior deep water is more than ever needed.

To this end the people of Savannah have devoted both time and money during the year with very great success, and with the support granted by nearly all the southern and western States it is highly probable that an appropriation sufficiently large to carry on the work of improvement will be granted at an early date.

Crops. The increase in the receipts of cotton at this port during 1891 was larger than that of any previous year. The total receipts amounting to 1,140,000 bales, an increase of 183,091 bales over 1890, which was the greatest in the history of the port.

Naval stores. The year's business in this department of trade was the most prosperous in the history of the port. The receipts in turpentine alone was 11,000 casks over the receipts of 1890.

Lumber. While the lumber trade generally has held its own during the year, the business was not a prosperous one for the merchants. The financial and other troubles in South America shut off exports of lumber in that direction, and consequently prices in the home markets were knocked down by the extraordinary volume of the offerings.

Investments. I would again draw the attention of investors to the advantages offered by Savannah for the profitable investment of capital. Savannah at the present time is very similar to New York 20 years ago. Who would have dreamed at that time that real estate in that city would have enhanced in value so tremendously as it has done.

The same can be said of the whole south, 20 years ago the southern States were in ruins, and the people beggared; now look at the magnificent showing she makes in the trade returns of the country. If such rapid increase has been made in the past 20 years, what may not be expected in the future.

This is particularly the case with Savannah; from her natural position as a port, and with the continued increase in her railway connections with the west, I think Savannah in the near future will become the New York of the southern States.

Imports and exports generally. Imports. The imports and exports for the year have been generally satisfactory.

The annexed Tables A and B show an improvement in the valuation of imports over 1890.

Fertilisers. There was a considerable increase in the importation of fertilisers over the year 1890.

Cotton ties. No cotton ties were imported through this port during the year. All shipments arrived viâ New York.

Other articles. All other articles of importation with the exception of salt show an increase over the past year.

Exports. By reference to the annexed returns it will be seen that

(1320)

|                | Cotton. |
|---|---|
nearly all articles under this heading have increased during the year under review.

The exportation of cotton during the year was the heaviest in the history of the port.

While the quantity of cotton shipped was much more than during 1890 and all previous years, the valuation was less owing to the low prices which reigned during the greater part of the season, consequent on an enormous crop, and the heavy stocks carried by the spinners from the crop of 1890.

*Cotton seed.* The exportation of cotton seed continues to increase.

*Lumber and timber.* The quantity of lumber shipped from Savannah was larger than during 1890; but owing to the principal markets being closed to all business the prices realised were far below the average.

*Spirits of turpentine.* The exportation of this article of commerce was larger than any previous year. Over 8,000,000 gallons were shipped during the year.

*Resin.* A large increase is also shown in the exportation of resin.

*All other articles.* A large increase is noticeable under this heading, and accounted for by the shipment at this port of several cargoes of phosphate from the Florida mines.

Annex A.—RETURN of Principal Articles of Export from Savannah during the Years 1891–90.

| Articles. | | 1891. | | 1890. | |
|---|---|---|---|---|---|
| | | Quantity. | Value. | Quantity. | Value. |
| | | | £ | | £ |
| Cotton | Lbs. | 272,427,878 | 4,857,807 | 260,767,535 | 5,464,428 |
| „ seed | „ | 3,006,634 | 5,839 | 2,026,718 | 4,162 |
| Lumber and timber | Feet | 39,019,181 | 50,565 | 32,006,065 | 59,396 |
| Spirits of turpentine | Gallons | 8,168,562 | 584,077 | 5,907,924 | 439,154 |
| Resin | Barrels | 811,917 | 271,637 | 659,320 | 212,847 |
| Other articles | ... | ... | 122,829 | ... | 9,460 |
| Total | ... | ... | 5,892,754 | ... | 6,189,447 |

RETURN of Principal Articles of Import to Savannah during the Years 1891–90.

| Articles. | | 1891. | | 1890. | |
|---|---|---|---|---|---|
| | | Quantity. | Value. | Quantity. | Value. |
| | | | £ | | £ |
| Fertilisers | Tons | 16,711 | 26,108 | 8,053 | 17,296 |
| Cotton ties | Bundles | ... | ... | 32,509 | 6,465 |
| Salt | Lbs. | 5,551,474 | 1,341 | 11,228,736 | 2,825 |
| Molasses | Gallons | 132,575 | 3,940 | 44,625 | 1,433 |
| Brimstone | Tons | 3,745 | 15,386 | 4,960 | 14,993 |
| Fruit and nuts | ... | ... | 17,241 | ... | 10,008 |
| Other articles | ... | ... | 30,463 | ... | 28,143 |
| Total | ... | ... | 94,479 | ... | 81,163 |

## CHARLESTON.

**Annex B.**—TABLE showing the Total Value of all Articles Exported from Savannah and Imported to Savannah from and to Foreign Countries during the Years 1891-90.

| Country. | Exports. 1891. | Exports. 1890. | Imports. 1891. | Imports. 1890. |
|---|---|---|---|---|
|  | £ | £ | £ | £ |
| Britain | 2,293,175 | 1,677,076 | 15,623 | 23,844 |
| Germany | 1,380,010 | 1,732,823 | 33,340 | 23,207 |
| Spain | 663,083 | 722,217 | 8,045 | 34 |
| Russia | 269,161 | 614,625 | .. | .. |
| Netherlands | 194,665 | 231,547 | .. | 50 |
| Belgium | 94,131 | 102,756 | 4,866 | 2,260 |
| Brazil | 12,280 | 4,248 | 226 | 243 |
| Italy | 415,085 | 478,695 | 15,616 | 15,001 |
| France | 323,624 | 297,195 | 268 | 173 |
| Other countries | 247,540 | 328,265 | 16,495 | 16,351 |
| Total | 5,892,754 | 6,189,447 | 94,479 | 81,163 |

**Annex C.**—RETURN of all Shipping at the Port of Savannah in the Year 1891.

ENTERED.

| Nationality. | Sailing. Number of Vessels. | Sailing. Tons. | Steam. Number of Vessels. | Steam. Tons. | Total. Number of Vessels. | Total. Tons. |
|---|---|---|---|---|---|---|
| American | 71 | 42,478 | 392 | 341,951 | 463 | 384,429 |
| British | 28 | 16,719 | 94 | 121,613 | 122 | 138,332 |
| Norwegian | 136 | 80,630 | 15 | 8,236 | 151 | 88,866 |
| German | 12 | 7,912 | 3 | 4,877 | 15 | 12,789 |
| All others | 71 | 39,306 | 3 | 5,570 | 74 | 44,876 |
| Total | 318 | 187,045 | 507 | 482,247 | 825 | 669,292 |

CLEARED.

| Nationality. | Sailing. Number of Vessels. | Sailing. Tons. | Steam. Number of Vessels. | Steam. Tons. | Total. Number of Vessels. | Total. Tons. |
|---|---|---|---|---|---|---|
| American | 64 | 39,909 | 386 | 331,147 | 450 | 371,056 |
| British | 29 | 17,241 | 98 | 128,362 | 127 | 145,603 |
| Norwegian | 120 | 71,344 | 14 | 5,779 | 134 | 77,123 |
| German | 13 | 10,369 | 2 | 3,113 | 15 | 13,482 |
| All others | 72 | 40,221 | 4 | 6,076 | 76 | 46,297 |
| Total | 298 | 179,084 | 504 | 474,477 | 802 | 653,561 |

## BRUNSWICK.

Mr. Vice-Consul Torras reports as follows:—
During the year 1891 the cotton trade of the port of Bruns-

wick has been very satisfactory; but the export of yellow pine lumber and timber has fallen off considerably, and the prices of the principal products of this portion of Georgia, such as yellow pine timber and lumber, resin, spirits of turpentine, and cotton, have been remarkably low as compared with previous years. The rates of freight during the same period of time were the lowest that have prevailed for many years past.

The Board of Health of this city has lately passed an ordinance allowing all vessels from the Bahama Islands laden with fruit to discharge their cargoes at the city docks at any time during the year. Heretofore it was forbidden to import any fruit from the said islands from May 1 to November 1 of each year.

Most of the fruits, vegetables, and meats consumed here are imported from other counties and States, largely from New York. This is probably due, to some extent, to the scarcity of good farmers, who could reap good benefits from the soil of this county and city if properly worked.

The climate is one of the finest in the southern States, vegetables of many varieties growing here at all seasons.

During the month of August of 1891 the Board of Trade of this city, in order to encourage commerce, recommended to the City Council the deepening of the outer, or St. Simon's, bar by blasting with dynamite, and for that purpose the said City Council appropriated the necessary funds to carry on the work. The process by which the bar was deepened consisted in burying dynamite cartridges some 2 feet beneath the sand at the bottom of the outer bar, which cartridges were discharged by an electric battery, to which they were attached, at the moment when the ebb tide should be at its greatest force. It is claimed that by the process just mentioned some $2\frac{1}{2}$ feet of dirt in depth, by near 1,000 feet in length and 500 feet in width, has been removed from the bottom of the bar. The whole process occupied 45 days, and cost exactly 6,500 dol. It has been reported by the local authorities that the actual depth of the St. Simon's bar is over 20 feet at mean high tide.

The annexed returns show the amount of articles exported to other countries during the year 1891.

RETURN of Foreign Exports from Brunswick, Ga, for the Year 1891.

CHARLESTON.

| Ports. | Cotton. Quantity. Bales.* | Cotton. Value. Dollars. | Cotton. Quantity. Bales.† | Cotton. Value. Dollars. | Resin. Quantity. Lbs. | Resin. Value. Dollars. | Turpentine. Quantity. Gallons. | Turpentine. Value. Dollars. | Lumber. Quantity. Feet. | Lumber. Value. Dollars. | Timber. Quantity. Feet. | Timber. Value. Dollars. | All other Articles. Quantity. | All other Articles. Value. Dollars. | Total Value. Dollars. |
|---|---|---|---|---|---|---|---|---|---|---|---|---|---|---|---|
| Aberdovey, Wales (England) | ... | ... | ... | ... | ... | ... | ... | ... | 332,090 | 3,420 | 14,493 | 150 | ... | ... | 3,570 |
| Amsterdam (Holland) | ... | ... | ... | ... | 3,207,395 | 15,880 | ... | ... | ... | ... | ... | ... | ... | ... | 15,880 |
| Antwerp (Belgium) | ... | ... | ... | ... | 54,525 | 265 | 117,154 | 41,590 | ... | ... | ... | ... | ... | ... | 41,855 |
| Bahia (Brazil) | ... | ... | ... | ... | 38,210 | 285 | ... | ... | 262,798 | 3,302 | ... | ... | ... | ... | 3,587 |
| Barcelona (Spain) | ... | ... | ... | ... | 2,257,715 | 11,700 | ... | ... | 778,156 | 9,727 | ... | ... | ... | ... | 21,427 |
| Barbadoes, W. I. (England) | ... | ... | ... | ... | ... | ... | ... | ... | 403,099 | 4,925 | ... | ... | ... | ... | 4,925 |
| Bremen (Germany) | 8,907 | 233,370 | ... | ... | ... | ... | ... | ... | ... | ... | ... | ... | ... | ... | 233,370 |
| Brest (France) | ... | ... | ... | ... | ... | ... | ... | ... | 12,000 | 150 | 330,000 | 4,000 | ... | ... | 4,150 |
| Bridgetown, W... (England) | ... | ... | ... | ... | ... | ... | ... | ... | 296,013 | 4,144 | 72,121 | 1,010 | ... | ... | 5,154 |
| Birkenhead (England) | ... | ... | ... | ... | 526,595 | 5,268 | ... | ... | 12,436 | 124 | 387,840 | 3,878 | ... | ... | 4,002 |
| Bristol (England) | ... | ... | ... | ... | ... | ... | 219,117 | 77,165 | ... | ... | ... | ... | ... | ... | 82,433 |
| Buenos Ayres (Argentine Republic) | ... | ... | ... | ... | ... | ... | ... | ... | 573,006 | 7,162 | 58,507 | 732 | ... | ... | 7,894 |
| Cardenas, Cuba (Spain) | ... | ... | ... | ... | ... | ... | ... | ... | 264,000 | 3,200 | ... | ... | ... | ... | 3,200 |
| Cardiff, Wales (England) | ... | ... | ... | ... | ... | ... | 186,819 | 61,500 | 27,912 | 279 | 714,454 | 7,145 | ... | ... | 7,424 |
| Cork (Ireland) | ... | ... | ... | ... | 284,090 | 1,000 | ... | ... | 12,015 | 144 | 502,424 | 5,527 | ... | ... | 68,171 |
| Chatham (England) | ... | ... | ... | ... | ... | ... | ... | ... | 18,059 | 235 | 389,149 | 3,891 | ... | ... | 4,126 |
| Delfynze (Holland) | ... | ... | ... | ... | ... | ... | ... | ... | 9,701 | 97 | 489,725 | 4,897 | ... | ... | 4,994 |
| Dordrecht (Holland) | ... | ... | ... | ... | ... | ... | ... | ... | 10,432 | 104 | 471,312 | 4,713 | ... | ... | 4,817 |
| Dublin (Ireland) | ... | ... | ... | ... | ... | ... | ... | ... | 13,030 | 130 | 515,327 | 5,153 | ... | ... | 5,283 |
| Dunkirk (Scotland) | 4,849 | 164,564 | ... | ... | ... | ... | ... | ... | 18,514 | 185 | 403,258 | 4,033 | ... | ... | 168,782 |
| Elenthera, B. W. I. (England) | ... | ... | ... | ... | ... | ... | ... | ... | 34,000 | 561 | ... | ... | ... | ... | 561 |
| Erith (England) | ... | ... | ... | ... | ... | ... | ... | ... | 182,114 | 6,863 | 216,712 | 1,941 | ... | ... | 8,804 |
| Fécamp (France) | ... | ... | ... | ... | ... | ... | ... | ... | 280,000 | 4,200 | 36,000 | 540 | ... | ... | 4,740 |
| Fleetwood (England) | ... | ... | ... | ... | ... | ... | 12,811 | 6,190 | 16,938 | 169 | 488,508 | 4,885 | ... | ... | 5,054 |
| Garston Dock (England) | ... | ... | ... | ... | 5,300,700 | 42,505 | ... | ... | ... | ... | ... | ... | ... | ... | 48,695 |
| Geestemunde (Germany) | ... | ... | ... | ... | 4,878,105 | 35,530 | 166,139 | 55,695 | 20,634 | 200 | 503,319 | 5,033 | ... | ... | 5,233 |
| Glasgow (Scotland) | ... | ... | ... | ... | ... | ... | ... | ... | 5,995 | 60 | 467,098 | 4,671 | ... | ... | 91,225 |
| Gibraltar, Bri.Poss. (England) | ... | ... | ... | ... | 3,719,470 | 32,840 | ... | ... | ... | ... | ... | ... | ... | ... | 32,840 |
| Goole (England) | ... | ... | ... | ... | ... | ... | ... | ... | 43,820 | 463 | 1,178,302 | 16,883 | ... | ... | 17,346 |
| Grangemouth (Scotland) | ... | ... | ... | ... | ... | ... | ... | ... | 55,705 | 907 | 644,512 | 6,434 | ... | ... | 7,341 |
| Great Yarmouth (England) | ... | ... | ... | ... | ... | ... | ... | ... | ... | ... | 406,119 | 5,000 | ... | ... | 5,000 |
| Greenock (Scotland) | ... | ... | ... | ... | 2,109,210 | 13,970 | ... | ... | ... | ... | ... | ... | ... | ... | 13,970 |
| Gutiejewsky (Russia) | ... | ... | ... | ... | ... | ... | 128,267 | ... | 10,063 | 131 | 522,067 | 6,786 | ... | ... | 6,917 |
| Halifax, N.S. (England) | ... | ... | ... | ... | 2,339,500 | 10,875 | 128,267 | 45,560 | ... | ... | ... | ... | ... | ... | 56,435 |
| Hamburg (Germany) | ... | ... | ... | ... | ... | ... | ... | ... | ... | ... | ... | ... | ... | ... | |

## UNITED STATES.

### Return of Foreign Exports from Brunswick, Ga, for the Year 1891—continued.

| Ports. | Cotton. Quantity. Bales.* | Cotton. Value. Dollars. | Resin. Quantity. Lbs. | Resin. Value. Dollars. | Turpentine. Quantity. Gallons. | Turpentine. Value. Dollars. | Lumber. Quantity. Feet. | Lumber. Value. Dollars. | Timber. Quantity. Feet. | Timber. Value. Dollars. | All other Articles. Quantity. | All other Articles. Value. Dollars. | Total Value. Dollars. |
|---|---|---|---|---|---|---|---|---|---|---|---|---|---|
| Harbour Island, B. W. I. (England) | ... | ... | ... | ... | ... | ... | ... | 500 | ... | ... | ... | ... | 500 |
| Havana, Cuba (Spain) | ... | ... | 9,044,840 | 46,260 | ... | ... | 30,000 | ... | 21,365 | 256 | ... | ... | 4,171 |
| Harburg (Germany) | ... | ... | 113,655 | 690 | 133,430 | 42,360 | 326,257 | 3,915 | ... | ... | ... | ... | 46,260 |
| Hull (England) | ... | ... | ... | ... | ... | ... | ... | ... | ... | ... | ... | ... | 43,050 |
| Ilha do Poyo, Cape Verde I. (Portugal) | ... | ... | ... | ... | ... | ... | 87,270 | 1,045 | ... | ... | ... | ... | 1,045 |
| Java (Spain) | ... | ... | ... | ... | ... | ... | 141,441 | 1,844 | ... | ... | ... | ... | 1,844 |
| Kingston, Jamaica (England) | ... | ... | ... | 28 | ... | ... | 259,561 | 3,228 | 31,041 | 439 | ... | ... | 3,667 |
| Las Palmas, Canary I. (Spain) | ... | ... | 4,910 | ... | 516 | 194 | 388,664 | 4,843 | ... | ... | ... | ... | 5,065 |
| London (England) | ... | ... | 517,985 | 3,600 | ... | ... | 20,070 | 200 | 680,121 | 6,800 | ... | ... | 10,600 |
| Liverpool " | 97,527 | 4,050,971 | 817,180 | 6,740 | 79,554 | 26,250 | 616,447 | 8,559 | 1,449,715 | 14,497 | 38,812‡ | 32,160 | 4,207,383 |
| "   " | ... | ... | ... | ... | ... | ... | ... | ... | ... | ... | 2,380§ | 33,600 | 33,600 |
| Menai Bridge (England) | ... | ... | ... | ... | ... | ... | 9,120 | 115 | 383,019 | 3,846 | ... | ... | 3,961 |
| Matanzas, Cuba (Spain) | ... | ... | ... | ... | ... | ... | 770,154 | 9,400 | ... | ... | ... | ... | 9,400 |
| Monte Video (Uruguay Republic) | ... | ... | ... | ... | ... | ... | 216,432 | 2,705 | ... | ... | ... | ... | 2,705 |
| Mayaguez, Porto Rico (Spain) | ... | ... | ... | ... | ... | ... | 231,312 | 3,300 | ... | ... | ... | ... | 3,300 |
| Mistley (England) | ... | ... | ... | ... | ... | ... | 22,200 | 175 | 384,882 | 3,879 | ... | ... | 4,054 |
| Nassau, B. W. I. (England) | ... | ... | ... | ... | ... | ... | 164,761 | 1,986 | 35,000 | 528 | ... | ... | 2,514 |
| Newry (Ireland) | ... | ... | ... | ... | ... | ... | 7,475 | 67 | 402,022 | 4,210 | ... | ... | 4,277 |
| Newcastle-on-Tyne (England) | ... | ... | 1,382,505 | 7,250 | ... | ... | 38,966 | 389 | 1,304,833 | 13,049 | ... | ... | 20,688 |
| Palamos (Spain) | ... | ... | 25,045 | 143 | ... | ... | 201,040 | 2,536 | ... | ... | ... | ... | 2,679 |
| Parbore, N. S. (England) | ... | ... | ... | ... | ... | ... | 28,944 | 283 | 98,552 | 1,183 | ... | ... | 1,183 |
| Portsmouth (England) | ... | ... | 1,931,920 | 13,715 | ... | ... | ... | ... | 1,045,577 | 10,455 | ... | ... | 10,738 |
| Putiloff Harbour (Russia) | ... | ... | ... | ... | ... | ... | 64,884 | 798 | ... | ... | ... | ... | 13,715 |
| Queenstown (Ireland) | ... | ... | 19,129,750 | 92,129 | 891,776 | 327,725 | 6,149,756 | 77,663 | 1,880,507 | 19,799 | ... | ... | 20,597 |
| Rotterdam (Holland) | ... | ... | ... | ... | ... | ... | ... | ... | 789,365 | 10,552 | ... | ... | 419,854 |
| Rio de Janeiro (Brazil) | ... | ... | ... | ... | ... | ... | 40,257 | 811 | 286,637 | 7,784 | 614,315∥ | 10,962 | 88,215 |
| Santiago de Cuba, Cuba (Spain) | ... | ... | ... | ... | ... | ... | 1,269,258 | 17,346 | 97,969 | 1,322 | ... | ... | 19,557 |
| Santos (Brazil) | ... | ... | ... | ... | ... | ... | ... | ... | ... | ... | ... | ... | 18,668 |
| Santo Antonio, Cape Verde I. (Portugal) | ... | ... | 5,395 | 31 | ... | ... | 189,180 | 1,194 | ... | ... | ... | ... | 1,225 |
| St. Thomas, W. I. (England) | ... | ... | ... | ... | ... | ... | 72,244 | 1,270 | 23,906 | 359 | ... | ... | 1,629 |
| St. John's (New Brunswick) | ... | ... | ... | ... | ... | ... | 104,433 | 1,512 | 413,650 | 6,103 | ... | ... | 7,615 |

## CHARLESTON.

### RETURN of Foreign Exports from Brunswick, Ga, for the Year 1891—continued.

| Ports. | Cotton. Quantity. | Cotton. Value. | Cotton. Quantity. | Cotton. Value. | Resin. Quantity. | Resin. Value. | Turpentine. Quantity. | Turpentine. Value. | Lumber. Quantity. | Lumber. Value. | Timber. Quantity. | Timber. Value. | All other Articles. Quantity. | All other Articles. Value. | Total Value. |
|---|---|---|---|---|---|---|---|---|---|---|---|---|---|---|---|
|  | Bales.* | Dollars. | Bales.† | Dollars. | Lbs. | Dollars. | Gallons. | Dollars. | Feet. | Dollars. | Feet. | Dollars. | | Dollars. | Dollars. |
| St. John's, Porto Rico (Spain) | ... | ... | ... | ... | ... | ... | ... | ... | 300,006 | 3,329 | ... | ... | ... | ... | 3,329 |
| St. Pierre, Martinique (France) | ... | ... | ... | ... | ... | ... | ... | ... | 301,482 | 4,524 | ... | ... | ... | ... | 4,524 |
| Stettin (German) | ... | ... | ... | ... | 2,113,335 | 12,205 | ... | ... | ... | ... | ... | ... | ... | ... | 12,205 |
| Tralee (Ireland) | ... | ... | ... | ... | ... | ... | ... | ... | ... | ... | 389,110 | 3,928 | ... | ... | 3,928 |
| Valencia (Spain) | ... | ... | ... | ... | ... | ... | ... | ... | 1,009,441 | 15,886 | 445,715 | 5,635 | ... | ... | 21,521 |
| Venice (Italy) | ... | ... | ... | ... | 3,256,245 | 15,995 | ... | ... | ... | ... | ... | ... | ... | ... | 15,995 |
| Waterford (Ireland) | ... | ... | ... | ... | ... | ... | ... | ... | ... | ... | 362,108 | 3,739 | ... | ... | 3,739 |
| West Hartlepool (England) | ... | ... | ... | ... | ... | ... | ... | ... | 49,979 | 650 | 560,490 | 6,726 | ... | ... | 7,376 |
| Total | 111,283 | 4,448,905 | 1,171 | 68,206 | 63,058,280 | 368,904 | 1,935,583 | 684,229 | 16,804,564 | 220,955 | 19,896,831 | 222,391 | ... | 76,722 | 6,090,312 |

* Upland bales.  † Sea Island bales.  ‡ Say cotton seed.  § Tons, phosphate.  ∥ Feet, Palmetto packages.

### RECAPITULATION.

| Ports. | Cotton. Quantity. | Cotton. Value. | Cotton. Quantity. | Cotton. Value. | Resin. Quantity. | Resin. Value. | Turpentine. Quantity. | Turpentine. Value. | Lumber. Quantity. | Lumber. Value. | Timber. Quantity. | Timber. Value. | All other Articles. Quantity. | All other Articles. Value. | Total Value. |
|---|---|---|---|---|---|---|---|---|---|---|---|---|---|---|---|
|  | Bales.* | Dollars. | Bales.† | Dollars. | Lbs. | Dollars. | Gallons. | Dollars. | Feet. | Dollars. | Feet. | Dollars. | | Dollars. | Dollars. |
| British ports | 102,376 | 4,215,535 | 1,117 | 68,206 | 17,540,285 | 135,423 | 797,870 | 269,160 | 2,982,319 | 42,576 | 6,838,229 | 181,640 | ... | 65,760 | 4,978,300 |
| Germany | 8,907 | 233,370 | ... | ... | 13,497,675 | 69,340 | 128,267 | 45,560 | 20,634 | 200 | 503,319 | 5,033 | ... | ... | 353,503 |
| Holland | ... | ... | ... | ... | 22,337,145 | 108,009 | 891,776 | 327,725 | 9,701 | 97 | 489,725 | 4,897 | ... | ... | 440,728 |
| Belgium | ... | ... | ... | ... | 54,525 | 265 | 117,154 | 41,590 | ... | ... | ... | ... | ... | ... | 41,855 |
| Brazil | ... | ... | ... | ... | 38,210 | 285 | ... | ... | 7,681,812 | 98,311 | 887,334 | 11,874 | ... | ... | 110,470 |
| Spain | ... | ... | ... | ... | 2,287,670 | 11,871 | 516 | 194 | 4,450,728 | 58,791 | 753,717 | 13,675 | ... | 10,962 | 95,493 |
| France | ... | ... | ... | ... | ... | ... | ... | ... | 593,482 | 8,874 | 366,000 | 4,540 | ... | ... | 13,414 |
| Argentine Republic | ... | ... | ... | ... | 4,041,130 | 27,685 | ... | ... | 573,006 | 7,162 | 58,507 | 732 | ... | ... | 7,894 |
| Russia | ... | ... | ... | ... | 5,395 | 31 | ... | ... | ... | ... | ... | ... | ... | ... | 27,685 |
| Portugal | ... | ... | ... | ... | ... | ... | ... | ... | 276,450 | 2,239 | ... | ... | ... | ... | 2,270 |
| Uruguay Republic | ... | ... | ... | ... | ... | ... | ... | ... | 216,432 | 2,705 | ... | ... | ... | ... | 2,705 |
| Italy | ... | ... | ... | ... | 3,256,245 | 15,995 | ... | ... | ... | ... | ... | ... | ... | ... | 15,959 |
| Total | 111,283 | 4,448,905 | 1,117 | 68,206 | 63,058,280 | 368,904 | 1,935,583 | 684,229 | 16,804,564 | 220,955 | 19,896,831 | 222,391 | ... | 76,722 | 6,090,312 |

* Upland bales.  † Sea Island bales.

LONDON:
Printed for Her Majesty's Stationery Office,
By HARRISON AND SONS,
Printers in Ordinary to Her Majesty.
(75  6 | 92—H & S  1320)

# FOREIGN OFFICE.
## 1892.
### ANNUAL SERIES.

### No. 1078.

### DIPLOMATIC AND CONSULAR REPORTS ON TRADE AND FINANCE.

# UNITED STATES.

### REPORT FOR THE YEAR 1891

ON THE

### TRADE OF THE CONSULAR DISTRICT OF PHILADELPHIA.

REFERENCE TO PREVIOUS REPORT, Annual Series No. 964.

*Issued during the Recess and Presented to both Houses of Parliament by Command of Her Majesty.*

LONDON:
**PRINTED FOR HER MAJESTY'S STATIONERY OFFICE,**
BY HARRISON AND SONS, ST. MARTIN'S LANE,
PRINTERS IN ORDINARY TO HER MAJESTY.

And to be purchased, either directly or through any Bookseller, from
EYRE & SPOTTISWOODE, EAST HARDING STREET, FLEET STREET, E.C., and 32, ABINGDON STREET, WESTMINSTER, S.W.; or
JOHN MENZIES & Co., 12, HANOVER STREET, EDINBURGH, and 90, WEST NILE STREET, GLASGOW; or
HODGES, FIGGIS, & Co., 104, GRAFTON STREET, DUBLIN.

1892.

[C. 6812–3.]   *Price Twopence Halfpenny.*

## New Series of Reports.

Reports of the Annual Series have been issued from Her Majesty's Diplomatic and Consular Officers at the following places, and may be obtained from the sources indicated on the title-page:—

| No. | | Price. |
|---|---|---|
| 958. | Athens | 2d. |
| 959. | Odessa | 1d. |
| 960. | Copenhagen | 9d. |
| 961. | Tokio | 1d. |
| 962. | Salonica | 1½d. |
| 963. | Stettin | 3½d. |
| 964. | Philadelphia | 2d. |
| 965. | Mexico | 2d. |
| 966. | Malaga | 2½d. |
| 967. | Berne | 1d. |
| 968. | Puerto Rico | ½d. |
| 969. | Buda-Pesth | 1d. |
| 970. | Bogotá | 1d. |
| 971. | Panama | 1½d. |
| 972. | Munich | 2d. |
| 973. | Copenhagen | 4d. |
| 974. | Guatemala | 1d. |
| 975. | Munich | 2d. |
| 976. | Meshed | 1½d. |
| 977. | Para | ½d. |
| 978. | Florence | 1d. |
| 979. | The Hague | 1½d. |
| 980. | Patras | 1d. |
| 981. | Paris | 1½d. |
| 982. | Zanzibar | 2½d. |
| 983. | Buenos Ayres | ½d. |
| 984. | Copenhagen | 1d. |
| 985. | Stuttgart | 1d. |
| 986. | New Orleans | 1½d. |
| 987. | New Orleans | 10d. |
| 988. | Suakin | ½d. |
| 989. | Galveston | 1½d. |
| 990. | Berlin | 1d. |
| 991. | Zanzibar | 1½d. |
| 992. | Guayaquil | 1d. |
| 993. | Tonga | 1d. |
| 994. | New Orleans | 1d. |
| 995. | Mozambique | 1½d. |
| 996. | Galatz | 1½d. |
| 997. | Nantes | 1½d. |
| 998. | Algiers | 1d. |
| 999. | Havre | 2½d. |
| 1000. | Buenos Ayres | 6d. |
| 1001. | Baltimore | 1½d. |
| 1002. | Taganrog | 1d. |
| 1003. | Riga | 2d. |
| 1004. | Bordeaux | 2½d. |
| 1005. | The Hague | 1½d. |
| 1006. | Paraguay | 1½d. |
| 1007. | Constantinople | 1½d. |
| 1008. | Rome | 1d. |
| 1009. | Mozambique | 1d. |
| 1010. | Wênchow | 1d. |
| 1011. | Mogador | 2½d. |
| 1012. | Amoy | 1d. |
| 1013. | Kiukiang | 1d. |
| 1014. | Stettin | 1½d. |
| 1015. | Boston | 1d. |
| 1016. | Callao | 1d. |
| 1017. | Aleppo | 1d. |
| 1018. | Santos | 2½d. |
| 1019. | Piræus | 1d. |
| 1020. | Mogador | 1d. |
| 1021. | Adrianople | ½d. |
| 1022. | Tripoli | 1d. |
| 1023. | Jerusalem | 1d. |
| 1024. | Odessa | 6d. |
| 1025. | Genoa | 1½d. |
| 1026. | Kiungchow | 1d. |
| 1027. | Batoum | 4½d. |
| 1028. | Buenos Ayres | 1d. |
| 1029. | Batavia | 1d. |
| 1030. | Santo Domingo | ½d. |
| 1031. | San José | 1d. |
| 1032. | Manila | 1½d. |
| 1033. | Marseilles | 1d. |
| 1034. | Swatow | 1d. |
| 1035. | Paris | 1d. |
| 1036. | Ichang | 5d. |
| 1037. | Pakhoi | 1d. |
| 1038. | Foochow | 1d. |
| 1039. | Brest | 1d. |
| 1040. | Madeira | ½d. |
| 1041. | Antwerp | 1½d. |
| 1042. | Taganrog | 2½d. |
| 1043. | Algiers | 2½d. |
| 1044. | Hankow | 1½d. |
| 1045. | Nantes | 1½d. |
| 1046. | Belgrade | 2d. |
| 1047. | Fiume | 1d. |
| 1048. | Wuhu | 1d. |
| 1049. | Cagliari | 1d. |
| 1050. | Erzeroum | 1d. |
| 1051. | Syra | 1d. |
| 1052. | Cherbourg | 1d. |
| 1053. | Lima | 1d. |
| 1054. | Bilbao | 1½d. |
| 1055. | Cadiz | 2d. |
| 1056. | Corunna | 2½d. |
| 1057. | Saigon | 1d. |
| 1058. | Port-au-Prince | 1d. |
| 1059. | Trebizond | 1d. |
| 1060. | Barcelona | 1½d. |
| 1061. | Tainan | 1d. |
| 1062. | Smyrna | 1½d. |
| 1063. | Old Calabar | ½d. |
| 1064. | Samoa | ½d. |
| 1065. | Tahiti | 1d. |
| 1066. | Chefoo | 6d. |
| 1067. | Gothenburg | 2d. |
| 1068. | Buenos Ayres | 1½d. |
| 1069. | Loanda | 1½d. |
| 1070. | Guatemala | 1d. |
| 1071. | Zanzibar | 1d. |
| 1072. | Charleston | 2½d. |
| 1073. | Nice | 1d. |
| 1074. | Caracas | 1d. |
| 1075. | Lisbon | 2d. |
| 1076. | Calais | 2d. |
| 1077. | Rio Grande do Sul | 5½d. |

# No. 1078.

*Reference to previous Report, Annual Series No. 964.*

## UNITED STATES.

## PHILADELPHIA.

*Consul Clipperton to the Marquis of Salisbury.*

My Lord,         *Philadelphia, May* 24, 1892.
 I BEG leave to enclose a Report on the Trade, Commerce, and Manufactures of this Consular District during the year 1891.
    I have, &c.
    (Signed)    ROBT. CHAS. CLIPPERTON.

---

*Report on the Trade and Commerce of Philadelphia for* 1891.

### ABSTRACT of Contents.

| | PAGE |
|---|---|
| Introduction | 2 |
| General business outlook | 2 |
| Free coinage of silver | 2 |
| Labour | 3 |
| Shipping and navigation; fast ocean steamships; transfer of foreign built ships | 5–7 |
| Fish culture | 8 |
| Trade and commerce | 8 |
| Imports and exports | 11 |
| Immigration | 13 |
| Deaths; suicides; destitution; stowaways; naturalisation laws | 16, 17 |
| Cattle and cattle diseases; trichinosis | 17 |
| Iron and steel; natural gas | 18, 19 |
| Anthracite and bituminous coals | 20 |
| Gas testing in mines; dynamite | 21–23 |
| Petroleum | 23 |
| Tin-plate | 27 |
| Railroads; free passes illegal | 27, 28 |
| Trusts | 28 |
| City of Philadelphia | 29 |
| Vital statistics; sanitary | 30 |
| Finances of Philadelphia | 31 |
| Failures | 32 |
| Liquor licenses | 34 |

(1342)

## UNITED STATES.

**Introduction.**

The States composing this Consular district experienced, in 1891, a continued prosperity, equalling if not exceeding that of 1890. The productive interests have been largely increased, and a lively competition among manufacturers has caused the prices of the middle and lower grades of textiles to very materially fall in prices. The coal trade has been unprecedented, both in production and sales. Railway traffic, passenger and freight, has more than held its own. Farmers, especially the cereal growers, have reaped large harvests. The iron and steel industry has been active in all of the iron-producing districts. On the whole, the year 1891 has closed with general prosperity to production and labour throughout the country, especially so to the chief centres of trade and commerce.

**General business outlook.**

The advance of foreign exchange, &c., the decline of silver and cotton, have caused disturbance from time to time in the financial markets. On the other hand, since the end of the year, business in most mercantile circles is much more encouraging. The bank clearances are heavier, and a number of important centres report a renewed activity. An increased trade on the stock exchanges and stiffened prices have aided to stimulate the general channels of trade. Gold exportations have ceased, and there is even talk of the possibility of gold imports. It is said that much of the gold exported last year was shipped when rates of exchange made the movement unprofitable, a premium being paid in Europe for the precious metal. Silver has declined to $90\frac{1}{2}$ c. ($3s.\ 9\frac{1}{4}d.$), the lowest price on record, and Congress has rejected what is known as the "Silver Bill," the public sentiment having grown against the measure; and the law still in force compelling the Government to purchase large quantities of silver and issuing notes against it, seems to be growing in popularity.

Cotton has declined in price since the end of the year, the Southern States having had an enormous crop, and as the planters are obliged to market the product, the supply in the manufacturing districts necessarily became greater than the demand. Cheap raw cotton means cheaper cotton goods, and the public at large will necessarily be benefited, provided there is not a falling off in the rate of wages.

It is believed that trade as a whole is gradually enlarging and that the year 1892 will turn out prosperous for the country at large. The State of Pennsylvania will, perhaps, not reap much addition, as the western business is largely met by western distributing centres, while the southern States, chiefly supplied by the eastern manufacturing districts, are usually dull.

**Free coinage of silver.**

This project now being actively pushed forward by many members of Congress at Washington, is met with opposition from various commercial circles throughout the eastern sections of the country. A special committee from the Philadelphia Board of Trade was sent to Washington and argued against the adoption of the Free Coinage Bill then under consideration by the House Committee on coinage, weights and measures. The measure is alleged to be one of inevitable danger and is likely to lead to

## PHILADELPHIA.

financial disaster, should free and unlimited coinage of the silver of the whole world be adopted upon the artificial standard contemplated. The question is still before Congress.

The precious metals production of the United States, west of the Missouri River, in 1891, amounted to 6,337,023*l*. in gold; silver, 12,122,801*l*.; and copper at 2,652,333*l*.

*Precious metals.*

In the production of gold, California keeps the lead with 2,091,098*l*. for 1891, and Colorado with 929,464*l*., but in the aggregate, the latter named State exceeds in total production, having turned out 5,640,609*l*.; Montana's total of 5,602,200*l*. is the next largest quantity of silver bullion expressed, figuring for 3,402,400*l*. with ores and base bullion forwarded by freight, 1,631,800*l*.; Utah comes in third with a total of 2,681,699*l*.; California with 2,443,047*l*. fourth; and Idaho with 2,319,000*l*. fifth. Segregated, the gross yield for 1891 is approximately as follows:—Gold, 6,305,199*l*., 27·04 per cent. of the total; silver, 12,122,801*l*., or 51·26 per cent. of the total; copper, 2,652,333*l*., or 11·22 per cent.; and lead 2,477,156*l*., or 10·48 per cent.

Taking all the reports at hand, the total mineral production of the United States is given, from reliable sources, as follows:—

| Articles. | | Quantity. |
| --- | --- | --- |
| | | 1890. | 1891. |
| Gold | Ounces | 1,588,880 | 1,620,000 |
| Silver | ,, | 54,500,000 | 58,000,000 |
| Pig-iron | Tons (2,000 lbs.) | 10,307,028 | 8,976,000 |
| Steel rails | ,, (2,240 lbs.) | 2,095,996 | 1,090,900 |
| Copper | Lbs. | 264,020,000 | 292,620,000 |
| Lead | Tons (2,000 lbs.) | 181,494 | 205,488 |
| Zinc | ,, | 66,342 | 76,500 |
| Nickel | Lbs. | 200,332 | 144,841 |
| Quicksilver | Flasks | 22,926 | 21,022 |
| Aluminium | Lbs. | 94,881 | 163,820 |
| Tin | ,, | .. | 123,366 |
| Antimony ore | Tons (2,240 lbs.) | .. | 700 |
| Anthracite coal | ,, | 38,006,483 | 42,839,799 |
| Bituminous coal | ,, | 93,000,000 | 98,000,000 |
| Phosphate rock | ,, (2,000 lbs.) | 637,000 | 659,731 |
| Salt | Barrels (280 lbs.) | 9,727,697 | 10,229,691 |
| Bromine | Lbs. | 310,000 | 415,000 |
| Pyrites | Tons (2,000 lbs.) | 109,431 | 122,438 |
| Sulphur | ,, | .. | 1,200 |

The anti-Chinese feeling is very strong in most of the labour unions of the country, and the expiration of the Chinese Exclusion Act is stirring up a great deal of activity among those who entertain the feeling, with the result that resolutions in favour of the continuance of the exclusion are being passed almost everywhere. In the western States the workers are most active, but they do not lack sympathisers in the east, where union after union and assembly after assembly have expressed their antagonism to Chinese immigration.

*Labour.*

(1342)

## UNITED STATES.

This question, like that relating to the Huns, Italians, and other foreign elements of labour not in general favour with the working men's organisations in this country, is one of the most troublesome to those who champion unionism, socialism, and other systems of protection and industrial reforms. They claim that the Chinese and others who do not assimilate with local workers, and do not accept or adopt the manners, customs, and responsibilities of the country, ought to be debarred from landing. The average working man cares little for the diplomatic or international aspect of the question. He looks at the matter as a practical man who has to earn a living for himself and his family, and who, sustaining the duties of citizenship, objects to work, that he should have, going to others who are not citizens, who do not speak the language or accept the customs of the country, and who, if report be true, send or carry away the money they make to be spent and enjoyed abroad.

The general master workman of the Knights of Labour proposes an alliance, "offensive and defensive," of employers and employed, interested in protecting their home industries. Mr. Powderly takes the carpet industry as a test case. He urges that the manufacturers should agree with the employed upon a price list for carpets, and scale of wages such as will be equitable, and based upon the exact conditions which prevail at each point of operations. The parties to play fair with each other and have no strikes on either side, and that the first one to cut prices, turn out inferior work, or attempt to impose on another, will be shut out from the trade. It is alleged that this can be done very easily, and the standard of wages and the quality of the manufactured article kept where they ought to be.

Another person, connected with the Machinery Moulders' Union, argues for the efficacy and influence of trade unions, and refutes the objections of those who would be glad to have them broken up. The opponents to unions allege that they foster strikes, create trouble among workmen, &c. This argument is again refuted by the Amalgamated Society of Engineers, who have an income of 124,000*l*., out of which they expended in disputes, including assistance given to other trades, 889*l*., or a good sum less than 1 per cent. out of their income.

In the State of Ohio a journeyman ironworker expresses his views as to giving financial assistance to working men:—"The men have become tired of subscribing for those unable to follow their daily labour, for the reason that whenever it did occur that one usually careful and economical was not in a position to take care of himself for a little while, he is not in need of anything, but he is always called upon to help those who have had the same opportunity he had to prepare for a rainy day." The system of paying sick, disability, and death benefits will continue, but there is likely to be a severe contraction in the subscriptions for members out of employment, and for prolonged support of those on strikes.

In the eastern States a great number of union printers are

## PHILADELPHIA.

out of employment. This applies particularly to the cities of Philadelphia and New York. One of the typographical unions has decided that no member shall work over five days a week, the object is to give unemployed men places. As a temporary movement, under peculiar stress, such a step may be admirable, but as a permanent arrangement it does not appear to be an effective way to correct the condition of the printers' market being overstocked.

The shipping at the port of Philadelphia for the year 1891 is recorded as follows:— *Shipping and navigation.*

The entrances of British ships, sail and steam, were—

|  | 1890. | 1891. |
|---|---|---|
|  | Tons | Tons. |
| Steam | 833,630 | 886,691 |
| Sail | 99,031 | 103,102 |
| Total | 932,661 | 989,793 |

The returns furnished by the United States custom-house, for 1891, for the shipping of all nations at this port are as follows (the figures of the British shipping are taken from the Consular registers):—

### ENTRANCES, SAIL.

| Nationality. | With Cargo. Number of Vessels. | With Cargo. Tons. | In Ballast. Number of Vessels. | In Ballast. Tons. | Total. Number of Vessels. | Total. Tons. |
|---|---|---|---|---|---|---|
| Austrian | 3 | 1,925 | 1 | 1,418 | 4 | 3,343 |
| Brazilian | 1 | 338 | ... | ... | 1 | 338 |
| British | 151 | 83,667 | 15 | 19,435 | 166 | 103,102 |
| Danish | 1 | 268 | ... | ... | 1 | 268 |
| French | 1 | 1,075 | 4 | 3,382 | 5 | 4,457 |
| German | 15 | 9,954 | 2 | 2,711 | 17 | 12,665 |
| Italian | 48 | 31,281 | 4 | 2,629 | 52 | 33,910 |
| Norwegian | 35 | 22,106 | 10 | 7,547 | 45 | 29,653 |
| Portuguese | 10 | 3,699 | ... | ... | 10 | 3,699 |
| Spanish | 3 | 972 | ... | ... | 3 | 972 |
| Swedish | 6 | 2,191 | ... | ... | 6 | 2,191 |
| Total | 274 | 157,476 | 36 | 37,122 | 310 | 194,598 |

(1342)

# UNITED STATES.

### ENTRANCES, STEAM.

| Nationality. | With Cargo. Number of Vessels. | Tons. | In Ballast. Number of Vessels. | Tons. | Total. Number of Vessels. | Tons. |
|---|---|---|---|---|---|---|
| Belgian | 16 | 39,616 | ... | ... | 16 | 39,616 |
| British | 455 | 676,493 | 140 | 210,198 | 595 | 886,691 |
| Danish | ... | ... | 5 | 8,210 | 5 | 8,210 |
| Dutch | ... | ... | 6 | 11,207 | 6 | 11,207 |
| French | 2 | 2,997 | 7 | 7,763 | 9 | 10,760 |
| German | 10 | 16,911 | 34 | 68,000 | 44 | 84,911 |
| Norwegian | 75 | 36,900 | 1 | 427 | 76 | 37,327 |
| Spanish | 7 | 11,124 | ... | ... | 7 | 11,124 |
| Total | 565 | 784,041 | 193 | 305,805 | 758 | 1,089,846 |
| ,, foreign sail and steam | ... | ... | ... | ... | 1,068 | 1,284,414 |

### CLEARANCES, SAIL.

| Nationality. | With Cargo. Number of Vessels. | Tons. | In Ballast. Number of Vessels. | Tons. | Total. Number of Vessels. | Tons. |
|---|---|---|---|---|---|---|
| Austrian | 6 | 4,887 | ... | ... | 6 | 4,887 |
| British | 127 | 77,949 | 16 | 8,214 | 143 | 86,163 |
| Danish | 1 | 581 | ... | ... | 1 | 581 |
| French | 6 | 5,686 | ... | ... | 6 | 5,686 |
| German | 17 | 12,586 | ... | ... | 17 | 12,586 |
| Italian | 58 | 38,063 | ... | ... | 58 | 38,063 |
| Norwegian | 42 | 28,254 | 1 | 234 | 43 | 28,488 |
| Portuguese | 11 | 4,215 | ... | ... | 11 | 4,215 |
| Russian | 1 | 1,137 | ... | ... | 1 | 1,137 |
| Spanish | 3 | 972 | ... | ... | 3 | 972 |
| Swedish | 4 | 1,491 | ... | ... | 4 | 1,491 |
| Total | 276 | 175,821 | 17 | 8,448 | 293 | 184,269 |

### CLEARANCES, STEAM.

| Nationality. | With Cargo. Number of Vessels. | Tons. | In Ballast. Number of Vessels. | Tons. | Total. Number of Vessels. | Tons. |
|---|---|---|---|---|---|---|
| Belgian | 16 | 39,616 | ... | ... | 16 | 39,616 |
| British | 305 | 437,952 | 32 | 31,668 | 337 | 519,620 |
| Danish | 5 | 8,210 | ... | ... | 5 | 8,210 |
| Dutch | 6 | 11,207 | ... | ... | 6 | 11,207 |
| French | 7 | 7,763 | ... | ... | 7 | 7,763 |
| German | 38 | 75,438 | 1 | 1,771 | 39 | 77,209 |
| Italian | 1 | 1,818 | ... | ... | 1 | 1,818 |
| Norwegian | 20 | 10,968 | 45 | 20,689 | 65 | 31,657 |
| Mexican | 1 | 160 | ... | ... | 1 | 160 |
| Spanish | 2 | 1,730 | ... | ... | 2 | 1,730 |
| Total | 401 | 644,862 | 78 | 54,128 | 479 | 698,990 |
| ,, foreign sail and steam | ... | ... | ... | ... | 772 | 883,259 |

## COASTWISE* Entrances and Clearances from the Port of Philadelphia for the Year 1891.

| Description. | Steamers. | Ships. | Barques. | Brigs. | Schooners. | Total. |
|---|---|---|---|---|---|---|
| Coastwise arrivals | 1,474 | 16 | 44 | 8 | 2,706 | 4,248 |
| ,, clearances | 1,684 | 11 | 88 | 27 | 2,742 | 4,552 |

\* No flag but American is allowed in this trade.

## PHILADELPHIA.

ARRIVALS at the Delaware Breakwater for Orders, &c., 1891.

|  | For Orders. | For Harbour. | In Distress. | Total. |
|---|---|---|---|---|
|  | Number. | Number. | Number. | Number. |
| Steamers | 135 | 39 | 2 | 176 |
| Ships | 9 | 11 | .. | 20 |
| Barques | 143 | 67 | .. | 210 |
| Brigs | 58 | 20 | .. | 78 |
| Schooners | 145 | 1,952 | 6 | 2,103 |
| Total | 490 | 2,089 | 8 | 2,587 |

### ARRIVALS, 1891.

| Description. | Steamers. | Ships. | Barques. | Brigs. | Schooners. | Total. |
|---|---|---|---|---|---|---|
| American vessels entered from foreign ports | 41 | 14 | 83 | 39 | 189 | 366 |
| Foreign vessels entered from foreign ports | 727 | 22 | 220 | 44 | 25 | 1,038 |
| Coastwise entrances | 1,474 | 16 | 44 | 8 | 2,706 | 4,248 |
| Total | 2,242 | 52 | 347 | 91 | 2,920 | 5,652 |

### CLEARANCES, 1891.

| Description. | Steamers. | Ships. | Barques. | Brigs. | Schooners. | Total. |
|---|---|---|---|---|---|---|
| American vessels cleared for foreign ports | 43 | 10 | 57 | 23 | 210 | 343 |
| Foreign vessels cleared for foreign ports | 522 | 26 | 211 | 32 | 24 | 815 |
| Coastwise clearances | 1,684 | 11 | 88 | 27 | 2,742 | 4,552 |
| Total | 2,249 | 47 | 356 | 82 | 2,976 | 5,710 |

The advance in the speed of ocean steamships is briefly shown by the following data :— *Fast ocean steamships.*

| Year. | Steamships. | From— | Time. |
|---|---|---|---|
|  |  |  | Days hrs. min. |
| 1819 | "Savannah" | New York to Liverpool | 22 0 0 |
| 1851 | "Persia" | Liverpool to New York | 9 20 0 |
| 1869 | "City of Brussels" | New York to Queenstown | 7 18 2 |
| 1882 | "Alaska" | Liverpool to New York | 6 22 10 |
| 1889 | "City of Paris" | ,, ,, | 5 23 7 |
| 1891 | "Teutonic" | ,, ,, | 5 16 31 |

The proposed transfer of two British first class steamers of the Inman Line by special Act of Congress is likely to become an accomplished fact. The Act will contain a clause that steamships registered under the provisions of the Act may be taken by the United States as cruisers or transports. The registration of such *Transfer of foreign-built ships to the American flag.*

ships as the "City of Paris" and the "City of New York" will insure the addition of at least four cruisers to the United States navy, and their maintenance without expense to the Government, until the emergency arises for their use in connection with the naval forces. As commerce destroyers steamships of this class would prove as effective as the armed cruisers of the navy. Under this Act it would appear that two ships equal to the "City of Paris" and the "City of New York" must be built in the United States, would have to measure 8,000 tons, and excel the two ships named in speed. If the two ships be granted American register, they will be entitled to the postal allowance for carrying the mails. The ships will be required to be officered by Americans, and to take as apprentices one American-born boy under 21 years of age for each 1,000 tons gross register, " who shall be educated in the duties of seamanship, rank as petty officers, and receive such pay for their services as may be reasonable."

*Fish culture.* The Pennsylvania Fish Commission have done valuable work during the past few years. Six years ago the commission had 300,000 trout fry for free distribution, and it was only with the greatest trouble that they were disposed of. The success following so increased as to make it difficult to supply the demand. This year the demand cannot be fully met as the applications call for over 4,500,000, and there are only a little over 3,000,000 on hand.

Two years ago 100,000 salmon fry were placed in the upper part of the Delaware River where the water was considered most favourable to their growth. As a result of this planting, quite a number of salmon measuring 12 inches to 20 inches were caught last summer. Large numbers were seen making their way down to the sea. The commission are so encouraged that they are hatching 300,000 Penobscot River salmon eggs at its hatcheries. Lake trout are being hatched for distribution in suitable waters.

White fish fry are being hatched at Erie to the extent of 12,000,000 eggs. White perch is considered of important commercial value on the lakes, and 40,000,000 fry of this were deposited in Lake Erie last year, and large quantities will be placed in the lakes in 1892. Rock and strawberry bass abound in the Delaware and Schuylkill Rivers after the successful planting of four years ago.

Pike-perch, or Susquehanna salmon, known sometimes as wall-eyed pike, have exceeded all expectations. Black bass is becoming abundant in the rivers named. Pike-perch are frequently caught weighing 9 pounds and 10 pounds. All the brands of fish hereinmentioned are most valuable, and are the result of the Fish Commission's labours. The laws against fishing out of season and with prohibited materials are rigidly enforced. Pennsylvania will have an extended fish exhibit at the Columbian Exhibition at Chicago.

*Trade and commerce.* The trade in cereals during 1891 was dull till the latter part of the year when the demand for grain and flour in Europe increased the shipments from all seaports. In the beginning of this year (1892) the shipments from this port increased rapidly.

## PHILADELPHIA.

The receipts of cereals, provisions, &c., at Philadelphia during 1891 were as follows:—

| Articles. | | Quantity. |
|---|---|---|
| Flour | Barrels | 2,451,113 |
| Wheat | Bushels | 6,893,166 |
| Corn | ,, | 5,622,000 |
| Oats | ,, | 4,895,500 |
| Barley | ,, | 974,400 |
| Wool | Bales | 147,959 |
| Cotton | ,, | 911,045 |
| Lard | Tierces | 15,699 |
| ,, | Packages | 60,715 |
| Pork | Barrels | 5,820 |
| Butter | Tubs | 238,412 |
| ,, | Boxes | 87,693 |
| Cheese | ,, | 218,600 |
| Eggs | Barrels | 36,373 |
| ,, | Crates | 521,417 |
| Tobacco, leaf | Packages | 51,276 |
| ,, manufactured | ,, | 87,749 |
| Whiskey | Barrels | 43,539 |

For February, 1892, the shipments continued to keep up to an unusual standard as compared with those of the same month of the previous year.

The following is a statement of the total shipments of all cereals from Philadelphia to Europe during the year 1891:—

| Month. | Wheat. | Corn. | Oats. | Flour. |
|---|---|---|---|---|
| | Bushels. | Bushels. | Bushels. | Barrels. |
| January | 29,913 | 60,598 | .. | 105,671 |
| February | 43,417 | 217,800 | .. | 46,682 |
| March | 58,079 | 309,577 | .. | 85,699 |
| April | 51,725 | 27,107 | .. | 107,899 |
| May | 87,973 | 198,917 | .. | 91,608 |
| June | 172,062 | 244,911 | .. | 65,426 |
| July | 314,417 | 131,424 | .. | 86,397 |
| August | 2,450,589 | 3,695 | .. | 92,405 |
| September | 1,394,843 | 171,076 | .. | 101,424 |
| October | 1,059,812 | 148,382 | .. | 88,712 |
| November | 626,544 | 161,883 | .. | 109,865 |
| December | 525,787 | 1,083,765 | 312,211 | 174,554 |
| Total | 6,815,161 | 2,759,135 | 312,211 | 1,156,342 |

## 10 UNITED STATES.

## Philadelphia Grain Elevators.

**Philadelphia grain elevators.**

GIRARD POINT STORAGE COMPANY (Pennsylvania Railroad System).

| Elevator. | Location. | Storage Capacity. | Receiving Capacity (10 hours). | Delivering Capacity (10 hours). |
|---|---|---|---|---|
| | | Bushels. | Cars. | Bushels. |
| A .. .. | Girard Point .. | 800,000 | 150 | 150,000 |
| B .. .. | ,, ,, .. | 1,000,000 | 300 | 250,000 |
| C .. .. | Washington St. | 400,000 | 100 | 130,000 |

\* Pennsylvania Railroad Company's grain depot; capacity, 300,000 bushels.

PHILADELPHIA GRAIN ELEVATOR COMPANY (Philadelphia and Reading Railroad System).

| Elevator. | Location. | Storage Capacity | Receiving Capacity (10 hours). | Delivering Capacity (10 hours). |
|---|---|---|---|---|
| | | Bushels. | Cars. | Bushels. |
| Pt. Richmond.. | Pt. Richmond | 1,000,000 | 300 | 300,000 |
| Twentieth St. .. | Twentieth St. | 400,000 | 100 | 100,000 |

TRADESMEN'S GRAIN ELEVATOR AND STORAGE COMPANY (Baltimore and Ohio Railroad System).

| Elevator. | Location. | Storage Capacity. | Receiving Capacity (10 hours). | Delivering Capacity (10 hours). |
|---|---|---|---|---|
| | | Bushels. | Cars. | Bushels. |
| 23d St. .. | 23d & Race sts. | 125,000 | .. | .. |

### FLOATING ELEVATORS.

| Elevator. | Proprietors. | Capacity per Hour. |
|---|---|---|
| | | Bushels. |
| Columbia .. | Girard Point Storage Company .. | 4,000 |
| St. Nicholas .. | ,, ,, ,, .. | 2,500 |
| Empire .. | Philadelphia Floating Elevator Association .. .. .. .. .. | 6,000 |
| Republic.. | Philadelphia Floating Elevator Association .. .. .. .. .. | 2,500 |

The following is a comparative statement of the imports into the United States for the years 1881 and 1891, giving the names of the countries whence they were shipped:—

## PHILADELPHIA.

Imports.

| Countries. | Value. 1881. | Value. 1891. |
|---|---|---|
|  | Dollars. | Dollars. |
| Argentine Republic | 6,214,575 | 5,976,554 |
| Austria-Hungary | 1,415,611 | 11,595,310 |
| Belgium | 12,603,435 | 10,915,672 |
| Brazil | 52,782,536 | 83,230,295 |
| Central American States | 3,159,786 | 9,799,713 |
| Chile | 1,435,970 | 3,448,290 |
| China | 24,020,707 | 19,321,850 |
| Colombia | 5,991,890 | 4,765,354 |
| Denmark | 762,879 | 652,562 |
| France | 69,806,375 | 76,688,995 |
| French Possessions | 2,928,750 | 795,899 |
| Germany | 52,989,181 | 97,316,383 |
| Great Britain and Ireland | 174,493,738 | 194,723,262 |
| Canada and British North America | 38,041,947 | 39,434,535 |
| All other British Possessions | 30,975,498 | 54,093,884 |
| Greece | 550,638 | 1,378,333 |
| Hayti and San Domingo | 5,643,050 | 4,853,814 |
| Hawaian Islands | 5,533,000 | 13,895,597 |
| Italy | 11,643,987 | 21,678,208 |
| Japan | 14,217,600 | 19,309,198 |
| Liberia | 131,082 | 13,512 |
| Mexico | 8,317,802 | 27,295,992 |
| Netherlands | 5,802,306 | 12,422,174 |
| Dutch Possessions | 10,246,706 | 7,627,533 |
| Peru | 760,556 | 386,518 |
| Portugal | 987,629 | 1,651,025 |
| Russia | 2,887,153 | 4,833,345 |
| Spain | 5,933,995 | 6,033,481 |
| Cuba | 63,033,404 | 61,714,395 |
| Puerto Rico | 3,860,199 | 3,164,110 |
| All other Spanish Possessions | 9,318,966 | 5,206,746 |
| Sweden and Norway | 947,896 | 3,723,201 |
| Switzerland |  | 14,118,805 |
| Turkey | 1,582,307 | 6,260,835 |
| Uruguay | 4,164,663 | 2,356,739 |
| Venezuela | 6,601,817 | 12,078,541 |
| All other Countries and Ports | 2,756,479 | 2,125,837 |
| Total | 642,664,628 | 844,916,196 |

The totals in sterling at 5 dol. the 1*l.* are as follows:—In 1881, 128,532,926*l.*; in 1891, 168,983,239*l.*

Exports.

Of the exports, 191,467,941*l.*, of domestic production 143,565,471*l.*, or more than two-thirds, were composed of cotton, breadstuffs, provisions, and mineral oils, leaving only 47,902,470*l.* for all other exports. The striking feature of the great increase in the exports for the year is that breadstuffs were sent out to the value of 18,200,000*l.*, and cotton 4,560,000*l.*; while there was a decrease in the value of exports of provisions, cattle, and oil, the staple articles of production. The entire increase of exports of 1891 over the previous year, 22,269,020*l.*, was made up by the abnormal foreign demand for breadstuffs. It is not flattering that the increase in the export trade of the United States in 1891 was due almost entirely to a bread famine in certain parts of Europe, and not to a steadily expanding market for a constantly increasing number of American products.

The imports at Philadelphia during the year 1891, tabulated in brief, were as follows:—

| Countries. | Free. | Dutiable. | American. | Foreign. | Total. |
|---|---|---|---|---|---|
| | Dollars. | Dollars. | Dollars. | Dollars. | Dollars. |
| Argentine Republic | 61,048 | ... | ... | 61,048 | 61,048 |
| Austria | 502,732 | 426,143 | 14,677 | 914,198 | 928,875 |
| Belgium | 107,977 | 292,263 | 556 | 399,684 | 400,240 |
| Brazil | 1,810,659 | 505,087 | 266,835 | 2,048,911 | 2,315,746 |
| Honduras | 14,000 | ... | ... | 14,000 | 14,000 |
| Nicaragua | 192,852 | ... | 25,339 | 167,513 | 192,852 |
| Chile | 111,587 | 50 | 29,844 | 81,793 | 111,637 |
| China | 36,338 | 57,545 | ... | 93,883 | 93,883 |
| Denmark | 752 | 3,669 | ... | 4,421 | 4,421 |
| Danish West Indies | 16,175 | ... | ... | 16,175 | 16,175 |
| Greenland | 76,350 | ... | 393 | 75,957 | 76,350 |
| France | 155,476 | 1,692,424 | 196,624 | 1,651,276 | 1,847,900 |
| French West Indies | 5,530 | ... | ... | 5,530 | 5,530 |
| „ Guiana | 5,850 | ... | ... | 5,850 | 5,850 |
| „ Possessions in Africa | 247,726 | 147,464 | 27,028 | 368,162 | 395,190 |
| Germany | 4,982,556 | 3,340,616 | 17,816 | 8,305,356 | 8,323,172 |
| England | 2,503,371 | 11,158,599 | 2,098,257 | 11,563,713 | 13,661,970 |
| Scotland | 55,684 | 1,004,027 | 37,774 | 1,021,937 | 1,059,711 |
| Ireland | 1,302 | 276,428 | 46,686 | 231,044 | 277,730 |
| Nova Scotia | 15,926 | 34,140 | 12,635 | 37,431 | 50,066 |
| Ontario | 75,289 | 22,072 | ... | 97,361 | 97,361 |
| Newfoundland | ... | 1,414 | ... | 1,414 | 1,414 |
| British West Indies | 2,199,660 | 15,401 | 702,463 | 1,512,598 | 2,215,061 |
| „ Guiana | 2,262,796 | 544,956 | 1,024,693 | 1,783,059 | 2,807,752 |
| „ Honduras | 5,358 | ... | ... | 5,358 | 5,358 |
| „ East Indies | 866,624 | 124,589 | 6,466 | 984,747 | 991,213 |
| Hong-Kong | 24,180 | 2,833 | ... | 27,013 | 27,013 |
| British Possessions in Africa | 104,730 | 2,858 | ... | 107,588 | 107,588 |
| Australasia | 1,053 | 356,472 | ... | 357,525 | 357,525 |
| British Possessions, all other | 1,502 | ... | ... | 1,502 | 1,502 |
| Greece | 109 | 31,241 | ... | 31,350 | 31,350 |
| Hayti | 136,373 | 32,995 | 65,436 | 103,932 | 169,368 |
| Italy | 382,507 | 808,173 | 13,588 | 1,177,092 | 1,190,680 |
| Japan | 504 | 2,744 | ... | 3,248 | 3,248 |
| Mexico | 4,995 | 2,628 | ... | 7,623 | 7,623 |
| Netherlands | 104,227 | 52,098 | 1,135 | 155,190 | 156,325 |
| Dutch East Indies | 1,903,312 | 419,474 | ... | 2,322,786 | 2,322,786 |
| Peru | 1,535 | ... | ... | 1,535 | 1,535 |
| Portugal | 122,376 | 26,277 | 8,331 | 140,322 | 148,653 |
| Madeira Islands | ... | 1,284 | 615 | 669 | 1,284 |
| Russia on the Baltic Sea | 153,015 | 312,018 | ... | 465,033 | 465,033 |
| „ Black „ | 829 | 38,433 | ... | 39,262 | 39,262 |
| San Domingo | 14,651 | ... | 14,651 | ... | 14,651 |
| Spain | 173,532 | 425,857 | 23,620 | 575,769 | 599,389 |
| Cuba | 14,465,046 | 3,260,927 | 8,512,920 | 9,213,053 | 17,725,973 |
| Puerto Rico | 552,742 | 23,586 | 115,698 | 460,630 | 576,328 |
| Philippine Islands | 944,425 | ... | 92,475 | 851,950 | 944,425 |
| Sweden and Norway | 1,007 | 122,351 | ... | 123,358 | 123,358 |
| Switzerland | 24,740 | 408,942 | 5,789 | 427,893 | 433,682 |
| Turkey in Europe | 142,970 | 172,727 | 61,975 | 253,722 | 315,697 |
| „ Asia | 275,355 | 124,999 | 22,974 | 377,407 | 400,354 |
| „ Africa | 68,476 | 8,399 | 17,243 | 59,632 | 76,875 |
| United States of Colombia | 131,556 | 19 | 11,511 | 120,064 | 131,575 |
| Uruguay | 46,319 | ... | ... | 46,319 | 46,319 |
| Arabia | 5,435 | 23,723 | ... | 29,158 | 29,158 |
| Morocco | 29,150 | 5 | ... | 29,155 | 29,155 |
| Total | 36,130,269 | 26,807,050 | 13,476,020 | 48,962,199 | 62,438,219 |

The fact is prominent that of the goods imported as per the foregoing table, only 2,695,204*l.* were in American vessels, while the rest, 9,792,240*l.*, were brought in foreign bottoms.

The exports from Philadelphia were 8,569,103*l.*, and the countries to which they were sent are stated to be:—

|  |  | Dollars. |
|---|---|---|
| Austria | .. | 150,287 |
| Belgium | .. | 2,752,166 |
| Brazil | .. | 1,596,228 |
| Nicaragua | .. | 20,080 |
| Chile | .. | 29,976 |
| Colombo | .. | 79,466 |
| Denmark | .. | 361,114 |
| Danish West Indies | .. | 80,660 |
| France | .. | 4,546,276 |
| French West Indies | .. | 66,708 |
| French Possessions in Africa | .. | 24,863 |
| Germany | .. | 2,302,592 |
| Greece | .. | 161,427 |
| Italy | .. | 1,275,554 |
| Japan | .. | 1,054,834 |
| Mexico | .. | 7,913 |
| Netherlands | .. | 1,039,586 |
| Dutch Guiana | .. | 775 |
| Portugal | .. | 340,878 |
| Spain | .. | 617,802 |
| Cuba | .. | 1,037,989 |
| Puerto Rico | .. | 23,067 |
| Sweden and Norway | .. | 98,467 |
| England | .. | 20,021,635 |
| Scotland | .. | 3,450,362 |
| Ireland | .. | 1,092,369 |
| Nova Scotia | .. | 31,680 |
| Quebec | .. | 6,224 |
| Newfoundland | .. | 15,422 |
| British West Indies | .. | 32,600 |
| British India | .. | 138,136 |
| Australasia | .. | 288,323 |
| Venezuela | .. | 10,265 |
| Total | .. | 42,845,724 |

The total in sterling at 5 dol. to the 1*l.* equals 8,569,145*l.*

The item refined petroleum stands first on the list in value, being 1,615,855*l.*; wheat follows with 1,472,336*l.*; wheat flour, 1,140,324*l.*; crude petroleum, 542,809*l.*; tobacco leaf, 378,620*l.*; corn, 350,974*l.*; locomotives, 293,326*l.*; bacon, 293,291*l.*; cattle, 316,976*l.*; and cotton, 259,186*l.*

England took the heaviest amount of these exports to the value of 4,004,327*l.*; next follows France, 909,255*l.*; Scotland, 630,072*l.*; Belgium, 550,433*l.*; Germany, 460,518*l.*; Italy, 255,111*l.*; Brazil, 301,246*l.*; Japan, 210,967*l.*; Ireland, 218,474*l.*; Netherlands, 207,917*l.*; and Cuba, 207,598*l.*

Public attention has been called to the nature of the immi- *Immigration.* grants arriving from many European countries, notably Russia, Poland, Hungary, Italy. The numbers annually coming in at all the chief ports of entry are increasing, especially among the low and depraved classes. The aliens who arrive can and do become citizens within 5 years; while native-born citizens cannot avail themselves of the franchise until they are 21 years of age. Politicians encourage this wholesale naturalisation, as the political strength of party leaders is increased by the additional votes.

The statistics of immigration at all the ports show that nearly 600,000 landed during the year 1891, which is the largest figure since the memorable year 1882. The immigration from those countries sending the most desirable people, viz., Great Britain, Germany, the Netherlands, and the Scandinavian nations, was somewhat increased, but the hosts of undesirable people came chiefly from Russia.

The following table exhibits the sex, nativity, health, &c., of all persons coming into the port of Philadelphia during the year ending June 30 1891.

The total arrivals were 28,257, of whom 25,798 were immigrants, and 2,459 were citizens of the United States and non-immigrants. Of the 25,798 the sexes were:—

|  | Number. | Per Cent. |
|---|---|---|
| Males | 15,770 | 61·13 |
| Females | 10,028 | 38·87 |
| Total | 25,798 | 100·00 |

The ages were:—

|  | Number. | Per Cent. |
|---|---|---|
| Under 15 years | 5,137 | 21·83 |
| 15 years and under 40 years | 16,897 | 67·97 |
| 40 years and over | 2,538 | 10·20 |
| Not stated | 1,226 | .. |
| Total | 25,798 | .. |

The nativity of the immigrants is officially reported as follows:—

| Country. | Number. | Per Cent. |
|---|---|---|
| Ireland | 5,137 | 19·91 |
| England | 3,702 | 14·35 |
| Wales | 50 | 0·19 |
| Scotland | 790 | 3·06 |
| Germany | 5,396 | 20·92 |
| France | 70 | 0·27 |
| Russia | 1,763 | 6·83 |
| Poland | 2,348 | 9·10 |
| Switzerland | 138 | 0·54 |
| Sweden | 2,225 | 8·63 |
| Norway | 925 | 3·59 |
| Belgium | 246 | 0·95 |
| Holland | 15 | 0·06 |
| Italy | 44 | 0·17 |
| Spain | 5 | 0·02 |
| Denmark | 451 | 1·75 |
| Hungary | 552 | 2·14 |
| Austria | 547 | 2·12 |
| Turkey | 65 | 0·25 |
| Greece | 103 | 0·40 |
| Austria-Hungary | 132 | 0·54 |
| Finland | 10 | 0·04 |
| Armenia | 27 | 0·11 |
| Australia | 1 | .. |
| All other countries | 1,056 | 4·09 |
| Total | 25,798 | 100·00 |

Among these 25,798 immigrants the health statistics are as follows :—

|  | Physical. | Mental. |
|---|---|---|
|  | Number. | Number. |
| Good | 25,778 | 25,792 |
| Impaired | 20 | 6 |

(1342)

## 16 UNITED STATES.

Their occupations are reported as follows:—

| Occupation | Number |
|---|---|
| Architect | 1 |
| Brewers | 29 |
| Butchers | 88 |
| Barbers | 21 |
| Bakers | 77 |
| Blacksmiths | 68 |
| Bartenders | 5 |
| Bricklayers | 24 |
| Carpenters | 123 |
| Cabinetmakers | 50 |
| Cooks | 23 |
| Coopers | 24 |
| Farmers | 1,005 |
| Gardeners | 46 |
| Hatters | 7 |
| Labourers | 8,136 |
| Locksmiths | 15 |
| Masons | 57 |
| Miners | 220 |
| Machinists | 20 |
| Millers | 36 |
| Musicians | 5 |
| Painters | 80 |
| Peddlers | 59 |
| Plasterers | 5 |
| Porter | 1 |
| Printers | 21 |
| Saddlers | 14 |
| Shoemakers | 198 |
| Spinners | 20 |
| Tailors | 279 |
| Tinsmiths | 10 |
| Tanners | 7 |
| Wagonsmiths | 8 |
| Weavers | 163 |
| Waiters | 17 |
| All other occupations | 3,955 |
| No occupation, including women and children | 10,605 |
| Not stated | 258 |
| Total | 25,798 |

The destination of these people has been chiefly the States of Pennsylvania and New York, the former receiving 13,198 and the latter 4,309. Illinois and West Virginia come next with 2,680 and 1,824 respectively. The remainder scattered in all directions over the country, northerly and westerly.

*Deaths.* During the year 20 deaths occurred on shipboard. With few exceptions they were infants or children, who were buried at sea.

*Suicides.* There were two suicides of male immigrants.

*Destitution.* There were 1,117 worthy immigrants who needed assistance; temporary relief being afforded them. Of the nationality of this number the Russians predominated—301; Poles, 197; Irish, 177; Germans, 149; Swedes, 103; and other flags running from 54 British to one Belgian.

*Stowaways.* There were 62 stowaways discovered during the year and 11 workaways; 16 were sent back to their countries, and the remainder, after careful examination, were permitted to land. The masters of all vessels are required to securely retain on shipboard and take all stowaways and workaways who are refused a landing by the Commissioners away from the country. The penalty for neglect, purposely or otherwise, is a fine of 60*l*. for each person allowed by the master to land; and there are several suits now pending against British vessels in the United States courts for this offence.

A Bill has been favourably reported in Congress restricting the present facilities for the naturalisation of aliens. The Bill provides that "no foreigner who has been convicted of a felony or other infamous crime or misdemeanour involving moral turpitude, or who is an Anarchist or polygamist or immigrant to the United States in violation of any of our laws, or who cannot read the Constitution of the United States, shall be naturalised." {Naturalisation laws.}

Five years continual residence in the United States, and one within the State in which application is made, are established as pre-requisites to naturalisation.

It is generally conceded that some radical changes in the existing laws are needed. Among these changes are the abolition of the "declaration of intention" to become a citizen, and a requirement that naturalisation proceedings shall take the form of a court trial, in which five years' residence, ability to read the Constitution, and absence of certain moral disqualifications to citizenship must be proved.

The immigration at the principal ports of the United States for the year 1891 amounted to 590,666, against 491,026 for 1890. This included 123,401 from Germany, 73,177 from Russia, 70,711 from Austria-Hungary, 68,481 from Italy, 55,888 from Ireland, 52,350 from England and Wales, 52,262 from Sweden and Norway, 31,285 from Poland, 12,484 from Scotland, 10,466 from Denmark, 6,928 from Switzerland, 6,527 from France, and 5,364 from the Netherlands.

The trade in cattle at this port has grown largely. The shipments of live animals hence for England have been at the rate of several steamers per week, averaging 375 head for each ship. An attendant is required as an extra hand, known as a "cattle man," for each 25 head. These men are signed on the ship's articles of agreement as supernumeraries, and their engagement duly attested on board by an official sent from the Consulate. This trade has become a feature of the port, and the laws of the United States require a rigid system of cleanliness, fitting quarters, and ample attendance. {Cattle and cattle diseases.}

Tuberculosis still prevails in certain districts, and under the laws the afflicted animals are killed by order of the State Veterinary Surgeon, the State paying 6*l*. per head.

Notwithstanding the precautionary measures taken in all sections of the country, this dread disease continues from time to time to show itself, especially in the Western States of this Consular district where there are immense herds of swine being driven in and across the States of Ohio, Indiana, and Michigan to market. {Trichinosis in swine.}

(1342)

## UNITED STATES.

In Pennsylvania there were a few cases of poisoning by trichinosis, it being clearly shown in each case that they were the result of eating raw or partially cooked pork, either in the shape of hams or sausages. One noted case recently occurred in one of the upper counties, where a family of five persons were suddenly stricken, and it is said two small children fatally.

No figures of the casualties can be given at present, as the official reports of the various States have not yet been published. No live swine are exported from Philadelphia to Europe.

**Iron and steel.**

The manufacture of cast-iron pipe in the United States, as reported by the Department of the Interior, has been large, 36 establishments having reported the manufacture as a leading speciality of their business. The total capital invested in these works was in 1890 2,860,187*l*. The number of hands employed, including officers and clerks, numbered 7,788, to whom 758,882*l*. in wages was paid. The total cost of the materials consumed was 1,896,678*l*., and the value of the products was 3,033,737*l*. The principal material consumed by the pipe foundries was pig-iron, the quantity used amounting to 591,258 net tons, costing 1,552,082*l*., while cast-iron pipe formed the principal product, the output being 513,030 tons (of 2,000 lbs.), valued at 2,511,263*l*. The greatest growth of the pipe industry in the United States has been chiefly in the south and west.

The wages averaged as follows:—

| Rates per Week. | Males above 16 Years. | Children. |
|---|---|---|
| | Number. | Number. |
| Under 5 dol. | 215 | 22 |
| 5 dol. and over, but under 6 dol. | 121 | 9 |
| 6 ,, ,, 7 ,, | 654 | 2 |
| 7 ,, ,, 8 ,, | 1,321 | .. |
| 8 ,, ,, 9 ,, | 1,358 | .. |
| 9 ,, ,, 10 ,, | 1,023 | .. |
| 10 ,, ,, 12 ,, | 896 | .. |
| 12 ,, ,, 15 ,, | 940 | .. |
| 15 ,, ,, 20 ,, | 689 | .. |
| 20 ,, ,, 25 ,, | 157 | .. |
| 25 dol. and over | 118 | .. |

The cast-iron pipe foundries were in operation during an average of 10 months each. The average term of employment was 11 months.

In 1890 there was great activity in the iron and steel industries, as well as in most other industries, but the production of pig-iron and of some other leading products declined. In 1890 there was more activity in projecting and erecting new iron and steel works than during last year. During 1891 financial reverses were encountered, and a number of enterprises were abandoned in toto. This statement is especially true of many southern enterprises. In 1891, however, considerable activity was shown in the building of new rolling mills and steel works. Since the close of the year much depression in the trade has been experienced, the production having exceeded the demand, and some failures have occurred. The tariff will most effectually exclude all importations of iron from the United Kingdom, and as the chief blast furnaces of the country, as well as the rolling mills and steel works, Bessemer included, will curtail their output, it is not likely that any serious adversity will occur to any branch of the iron and steel industries of the country on which the McKinley tariff places the duty.

The Bessemer steel industry has grown to such proportions as to be probably the first in the world, and during the past two years enlarged development has taken place. Six new standard plants have been established, some for steel castings, others for steel rails, steel nail plates, and billets. The open hearth steel works have made great progress. In 1890 and 1891 17 new open hearth steel plants were started in the country, while only three were abandoned, and they of not large capacity. The crucible steel works, basic steel, cut-nail machines, wire-nail works, and the forgeries and bloomeries have met with varying success. The latter, however, declined during the past year.

The use of natural gas as fuel in the rolling mills and steel works of the United States largely increased from year to year, but of late there has been a falling-off in the use of this material for iron and steel works. The entire number now using this product in whole or in part is 74, showing a reduction of 30 works in two years. The development of the natural gas region in the central part of Indiana has been marked during the past two years, and it has occasioned the establishment of several new iron and steel industries; but in all the other natural gas sections of the country the use of natural gas as fuel in iron and steel works has declined owing to the shrinkage in its supply. In most of the works which have been compelled to abandon, or to partly abandon the use of natural gas, a return has been made to the use of bituminous coal; but some of these works have also introduced the use of gas made from coal, or of petroleum.

*Natural gas.*

The iron and steel works in the whole country in 1891 were as follows:—

Bituminous, 267; anthracite and coke, 164; and charcoal, 138; total, 569. Annual capacity of completed blast furnaces, 16,296,703 net tons; annual capacity of the bituminous furnaces, 11,309,700 net tons; annual capacity of completed rolling mills, 11,831,294 net tons; annual capacity in ingots, 6,500,000 net tons. In Pennsylvania the number of furnaces was, for anthracite, 124; bituminous, 80; charcoal, 15; total, 219. The annual capacity of completed furnaces was, anthracite, 2,742,848 net tons; bituminous, 3,858,200 net tons; charcoal, 61,700 net tons; total, 6,662,748 net tons. In Ohio there are no anthracite, and only 60 bituminous, with 12 of charcoal, making a total of 72; the capacity being 2,123,500 net tons for bituminous, and 53,000 net tons for charcoal, being a total of

(1342)

2,176,500 net tons. Indiana and Michigan, the two remaining States of this Consular district, have but small development in this industry, showing but 25 plants, with a capacity of 466,000 net tons.

Of rolling mills and steel works Pennsylvania heads the list with 211 rolling mills and steel works; iron and steel rolling mills, 192, and cut-nail machines, 1,555. The steel plants of all kinds number 98.

*Anthracite coal.*

The anthracite coal trade during the year 1891 was more active than in any previous year in the history of mining. The output was larger than that of all previous years. Since the Philadelphia and Reading Railroad effected what is called the "deal," in which the coal mining and the coal-carrying companies were affected, it has been difficult to obtain concise and analytical statistical tables as to the tonnage of the different railways. The combination of the coal-carrying railways, viz., the Lehigh Valley Railroad, the New Jersey Central Railroad, and the Delaware, Lackawanna, and Western Railroad, and the expected absorption of the Delaware and Hudson Railroad, has virtually placed the control of the anthracite coal trade in the power of the Philadelphia and Reading Railroad Company.

The total production of anthracite coal for 1891 was as follows:—

|  | Tons. |
|---|---|
| Reading Railroad Company | 8,601,121 |
| Lehigh Valley | 7,220,497 |
| New Jersey Central | 5,857,988 |
| Delaware, Lackawanna, and Western | 6,198,048 |
| Delaware and Hudson | 3,939,917 |
| Pennsylvania Railroad | 1,692,419 |
| Erie | 1,204,271 |
| Ontario and Western | 695,770 |
| D.S. and S. Railroad (one month) | 43,882 |
| Total | 40,448,336 |

It would be of little use to quote the market prices of anthracite coal here for the information of the British public, as the variations, though not great, are frequent. For the years 1890–91 the average prices were 15s. for Schuylkill and for Lehigh 18s. per ton.

*Bituminous coal.*

The bituminous, or soft coal, output in the United States now aggregates 100,000,000 tons annually. The demand throughout the country has kept up with the supply, and at least 15 per cent. increase annually of the supply has been experienced, some of the districts having shown a growth far beyond the percentage mentioned. The output of the States of Pennsylvania, Virginia, West Virginia, and Maryland continued to operate under "a pool" or association. They made the prices at the various loading points, and agreed to abide thereby. The Pennsylvania districts largely increased their mining during the year. An effort was made to strengthen the market by an advance in the rate of tolls and transportation on the railway lines, but the low-water freights offset this where coal was sold and delivered.

The importations of coal amounted to 1,362,387 tons, being an excess of 523,825 tons over the imports of 1890. The importations were 863,555 tons of anthracite, and 1,613,565 tons bituminous.

The production in the Pennsylvania bituminous districts was 36,000,000 tons, being an increase of 2,000,000 tons on the production of 1890. This State heads the list of the coal-producing States of the Union in both bituminous and anthracite. The coals mined here are used in gas making iron smelting, forging, blacksmithing, and steam raising in all the industrial sections of the middle and eastern States, and on nearly all ocean steamers.

The people employed in the Pennsylvania districts numbered as high as 7,000, and their average earnings are based upon the average price of coal at the mines, which was during the year 10s. per ton.

The casualties that occur at the mines, especially in the bituminous districts, continue as a matter of course, although it may be said that the number of fatal casualties has not increased with the growing output of all the mines. For the year 1890 the fatal accidents from all sources, explosive, caving-in, and miscellaneous, figured 524, and the number of non-fatal accidents was 1,388. There were 275 widows and 813 orphans left by these casualties. The official figures for 1891 have not yet been issued, but the foregoing is a fair average for some years past, and it is believed that the figures for the last year will not exceed, but, it is predicted, are likely to be less than those quoted above.

There is a general interest taken by all persons connected with mining towards any endeavour or project to reduce the list of mining casualties, and it is the present belief that the mechanical device hereinafter referred to is apparently up to the present date the most practical.

I referred in despatches to the Foreign Office dated May 22, 1889, and July 12, 1890, to Thomas Shaw's mine signal system, and his inspector's instrument and gas tester, with which it becomes possible to determine the character of ventilation both as to fire-damp and choke-damp in mines; and I then gave a full description of the nature and operation of both instrument and system. *Gas testing in mines.*

The value of this instrument by which tests can be made in 1 minute or 2 minutes is being realised in the mining districts, and is gradually receiving the attention and adoption that its merits deserve.

The system has been in use during the past three years in the Morrell Mines, situated in the Fifth Bituminous District of Pennsylvania, and is represented by the inspector of that district as giving entire satisfaction there; he also calls attention to the fact " that on one day a change of five-tenths of 1 per cent. to 16 per cent. occurred in a space of 5 minutes."

Similar endorsement is given after nearly three years' opera-

(1342)

tions by the general manager of the Fulton Ironworks at Johnstown in the State of Pennsylvania, who writes:—

"As to the accuracy of this system there can be no question of doubt, and its value in fiery mines is equally evident," and "its determinations are exceedingly quick and accurate, enabling the superintendent of coal mines to determine beyond doubt the condition of the air in his mine, and, of course, to correct it promptly."

I referred to it originally, as it was said that its scientific basis was entirely new, and its superiority over the miner's lamp, with which, under the most favourable circumstances, it is difficult to observe the presence of less than 4 per cent. of gas in the atmosphere, which is 66 per cent. towards the igniting line, whereas Shaw's system gives a positive alarm when 1 per cent. is present and is sensitive to the one-thousandth part of fire-damp, besides which the condition of the air in the mine can be ascertained previous to the entrance of men into the mine.

The "inspector's instrument" has been made the official standard of test in Pennsylvania and Ohio. In the former State the Legislature has made appropriations for providing all the districts with this instrument.

Professor George Lawson, Ph.D., LL.D., Fellow of the Institute of Chemistry of Great Britain and Ireland, and ex-President of the Royal Society of Canada, lately wrote from the University of Dalhousie College, Halifax, N.S., after witnessing trials of the "gas tester":—

"I may say freely that I was quite unprepared for the admirable results obtained by experiments of the Shaw machine. The exactitude with which it determined, in repeated and always confirmatory trials, the fractional percentages of combustible gas present, down to the minimum capable of forming an explosive mixture of air, reached far beyond any possible approach to precision which I ever expected to live to see, and bore unmistakable testimony at once to the accuracy of the principles upon which the machine is founded, and the nicety of manufacture of the article used."

It has also a practical utility for oil refineries, steamships, city sewers, auditoriums—in fact, all places where polluted atmosphere is dangerous.

The Government of the United States are now examining into its utility on board vessels for giving particulars as to the condition of the air in coalbunkers, paint-rooms, and holds, with the object of minimising the liability to spontaneous combustion.

The operation of the instrument is so simple that persons of ordinary common sense can learn, after one or two hours of instruction, how to detect the presence of half of 1 per cent. of gas in the air.

The freedom with which explosives can be obtained in this country has caused a marked attention in public sentiment, and a Bill has been introduced in Congress requiring a permit system by which the manufacture, sale, and storage of high explosives

## PHILADELPHIA.

may be regulated.  The recent reports of explosions and destruction of property in Paris have awakened a public feeling that some stringent measures are necessary to curtail the bold and aggressive element that is spreading, apparently without reference to the form of Government.  Many of these agitators, or Anarchists, will doubtless seek asylum in America, where there are already a limited number, and it is proposed to prohibit, so far as possible, the landing of such persons.  The alleged negligence of the authorities has already enabled this criminal element to obtain a slight footing in some of the large cities. *Dynamite.*

The petroleum trade of Philadelphia is gradually returning to the port, whence a majority of the trade should be shipped, as the greater part of the production is in Pennsylvania.  There have been two pipe lines laid from the oil fields of Virginia, and a new refinery has been established at a point below the city, known as Marcus Point.  It has since been alleged, however, that this new enterprise has already been swallowed by the Standard Company, which is virtually the gigantic "oil trust," having an absolute monopoly of the refining and shipments of the product. It is predicted that Philadelphia will be the centre of the oil trade not only of America but of all the world.  It will be observed by the following tables that Philadelphia's percentage of the trade rose from 27·3 in the months prior to the pipe line to 35·75 in the 10 months following it. *Petroleum.*

### Prior to Opening of New Pipe Line (January 1 to February 27, 1891).

| States. | Quantity. | Per Cent. | Quantity. | Per Cent. | Quantity. | Per Cent. | Total. | Per Cent. |
|---|---|---|---|---|---|---|---|---|
| | Barrels.* | | Barrels.† | | Cases. | | Barrels.‡ | |
| Philadelphia | 326,098 | 35·1 | 23,404 | 10·3 | 390,507 | 19·1 | 427,046 | 27·3 |
| New York | 554,795 | 59·8 | 203,899 | 89·7 | 1,655,533 | 80·9 | 1,089,700 | 69·6 |
| Baltimore | 47,282 | 5·1 | .. | .. | .. | .. | 47,282 | 3·1 |
| Total | 928,175 | 100·0 | 227,303 | 100·0 | 2,046,040 | 100·0 | 1,564,586 | 100·0 |

### Subsequent to Opening of New Pipe Line (February 27 to December 31, 1891).

| States. | Quantity. | Per Cent. | Quantity. | Per Cent. | Quantity. | Per Cent. | Total. | Per Cent. |
|---|---|---|---|---|---|---|---|---|
| | Barrels.* | | Barrels.† | | Cases. | | Barrels.‡ | |
| Philadelphia | 2,488,355 | 47·07 | 417,384 | 19·90 | 3,034,574 | 24·86 | 3,512,654 | 35·75 |
| New York | 2,699,603 | 51·07 | 1,648,346 | 78·58 | 9,174,124 | 75·14 | 6,182,767 | 62·92 |
| Baltimore | 98,890 | 1·86 | 31,850 | 1·52 | .. | .. | 130,740 | 1·33 |
| Total | 5,286,848 | 100·00 | 2,097,570 | 100·00 | 12,208,698 | 100·00 | 9,326,161 | 100·00 |

\* In bulk.     † In round.     ‡ In 50-gallon barrels.

## PHILADELPHIA.

The "bulk" trade here at the present time is close to that of New York, which heretofore enjoyed nearly a monopoly of it. The relative figures now stand 47.07 to 51.07. In the shipments by barrels and cases, however, New York has decidedly the lead, its barrel exports being four times as great as Philadelphia and its "case" trade three times as great. These branches of the export trade are of greater importance to a city than the bulk trade, as they necessitate the employment of a greater number of men for coopering and making cases, and in handling of them. Philadelphia shows a small increase in these two branches, and it will grow.

## UNITED STATES.

The following table shows the growth of Philadelphia's oil exports during the past six years, the total for 1891 being over 1,000,000 barrels greater than in 1886, and 712,816 barrels greater than in 1887, the year of greatest exports up to 1891. In estimating the amount, 50 gallons of bulk oil are taken as making a barrel, and five cases a barrel:—

| States. | 1886. Barrels. | 1886. Per cent. | 1887. Barrels. | 1887. Per cent. | 1888. Barrels. | 1888. Per cent. | 1889. Barrels. | 1889. Per cent. | 1890. Barrels. | 1890. Per cent. | 1891.* Barrels. | 1891.* Per cent. |
|---|---|---|---|---|---|---|---|---|---|---|---|---|
| Philadelphia | 2,933,245 | 28·8 | 3,227,442 | 30·3 | 2,657,743 | 26·5 | 3,168,745 | 26·50 | 3,185,924 | 25·82 | 3,940,258 | 34·59 |
| New York | 7,012,621 | 69·0 | 7,235,031 | 67·8 | 7,206,724 | 72·1 | 8,607,281 | 72·03 | 8,871,059 | 71·92 | 7,272,467 | 63·85 |
| Baltimore | 224,783 | 2·2 | 208,031 | 1·9 | 144,039 | 1·4 | 173,210 | 1·47 | 278,643 | 2·26 | 178,022 | 1·56 |
| Total | 10,170,649 | .. | 10,670,504 | .. | 10,008,506 | .. | 11,949,236 | .. | 12,335,626 | .. | 11,390,747 | .. |

\* From January 1st to December 31st.

The Marcus Hook traffic in bulk and barrel oil has increased 8·77, and it is predicted that most of the export trade will be from that point, which is within the customs jurisdiction of Philadelphia. The refinery works there are progressing rapidly to completion, and when they are completed the shipments to and from the piers will be greatly increased.

The average price of petroleum has been 57 c. per barrel. The yield of some of these petroleum wells is surprising. For instance, one well has put out 575,000 barrels, being a net product of 322,400 dol., at 60 c. per barrel, deducting for transit charges and waste.

Tin-plate. It is claimed by the tin-plate men that by the heavy duties on tin-plate the time is not far distant when the development of the supposed tin mines and the manufacture of tin-plate will cause the 6,000,000*l*. per annum shipped to Wales for tin to be saved to the country. The fact is that it is not money that is sent to Wales but wheat, flour, petroleum, cotton, beef and pork that are sent from this country. It is difficult to understand how, should tin be produced in this country to any extent, the agriculturist and all tin consumers would be benefited to the extent of 8,000,000*l*. per annum. The commercial fact is that by a free exchange of this country's home products for Welsh tin-plate the American consumers would get an equivalent. This law came into effect on July 1, 1891, and is to continue for six years. In case the manufacture should be less than one-third of the quantity of imported tin-plate consumed in the country in any one of the six years of trial, then, after 1897, tin-plate is to go on the free list. The yearly average imports of tin-plates and terne-plates amount to 678,000,000 lbs. Taking 300 working days in the year, gives a daily consumption in the United States of 2,600,000 lbs. per day of eight hours. The American output has been less than four hours' consumption, and at the present time it does not seem to equal 1 per cent. of the imports and consumption. Of 19 establishments, only four make steel sheets, which they subsequently coat with tin or lead. Four out of the 19 make ordinary bright tin-plate, such as is used for canning and domestic purposes, and the other 15 make roofing plate.

Railroads. The extension, improvements, and traffic of the railways in this Consular district continue to increase. The city of Philadelphia has now terminal facilities and enlarged stations that have been wanting for many years. The Philadelphia and Reading Railroad have placed the coal-producing and carrying interests of the State and city on a firm footing. The road has been for several years past in a state of bankruptcy, but now it is believed that the president of the road has placed it on a safe basis, as he has embraced in his plans one of the most extensive financial enterprises ever undertaken in this country. He has taken under his control the Lehigh Valley Railroad, the Port Reading Railroad, and the Central Railroad of New Jersey; and this scheme also includes control of the Lehigh and Susquehanna Railroad, all the chief coal-carriers of the country. Under these leases will be paid a guaranteed dividend of 7 per cent., and in a short time this guarantee will gradually increase till it reaches 10 per cent. per annum. The Reading are also constructing a splendid terminal in this city with an elevated outlet, and will have also magnificent terminals on New York harbour. Millions of pounds will be expended in the contemplated improvements, and there would appear to be no doubt that these gigantic enterprises will greatly promote the commercial interests of Philadelphia and the State of Pennsylvania, hence all the commercial exchanges have congratulated President McLeod for the bold step he has taken.

City councils have passed an ordinance authorising the running of tramways in the streets by electricity on overhead wires, called the trolley system. The claim is made that the construction of these roads will be detrimental to the city's interests and dangerous to life as well as a serious obstacle to the efficient workings of the fire department. Almost universal opposition is made by the citizens and business interests.

*Free passes illegal.*

The Interstate Commerce Commission, under an Act of Congress, has decided that the law excludes the right to give "passes" for railway travel, from State to State, to "gentlemen eminent in public service, higher officials of the States, prominent officers of the United States, members of Legislative Railroad Committees, or persons whose goodwill is important to the Corporation." As to newspaper passes, in exchange for advertising, and others issued for direct and valuable consideration, decision is reserved.

*Trusts.*

The "trusts" or combination of trades, for the purpose of controlling the channels of trade, continue to grow. The enormous sugar refineries have all combined, and sugar has already made an advance in price. Trusts have also been formed in the rubber trade and in numerous other branches of business. A strong protest has been made against the sugar trust, and a Bill will doubtless be introduced in Congress to take the duty off imported sugar in order that the consumers may not be entirely at the mercy of the combination.

An account of these trusts was given in full in the last report from this Consulate, and it is deemed unnecessary to go over the ground again as there have been no new developments, but only an increase in the numbers.

*The sugar trust.*

The all-powerful American sugar trust has been strenuously opposed for years by three great refineries of this city, viz., Spreckle's, E. C. Knight's, and the Franklin's; but there is a prediction that the trust will soon absorb these three great refineries. The trust known as the American Sugar Refining Company had a capital of 10,000,000*l*., which has within the past two months been increased to 15,000,000*l*. This addition to its financial power has caused the Company to redouble its efforts to bring within its control all outstanding refineries. There were, it is understood, 3,000 individual holders of the trust stock before the increase in capitalisation. The certificates paid 7 per cent.

interest on preferred, and 8 per cent. on the common stock. A profit of ⅜ c. per pound on sugar means 3,000,000l. a year to the sugar trust.

The refineries located in Philadelphia are undoubtedly the greatest in the country. The fresh water facilities of the Delaware River are unexcelled by those of any other city in America, and the railway tracks run into the refineries here, which they do not do at New York or Boston. Fresh water is one of the most valuable of all commodities connected with the manufacture of sugar. The Philadelphia refineries turn out an average of 13,000 barrels of sugar daily. The Franklin refinery makes nearly 6,000 barrels, the Spreckle's 5,000, and the Knight's about 2,000. Before the tariff was taken off sugar there were 1,450,000 tons of raw sugar boiled up in the United States. In 1891 the increase was remarkable, 1,800,000 tons being used by refineries, and for 1892, if the year's fruit crop is as good as it is expected it will be, there will be consumed at the refineries 2,000,000 tons of raw sugar. Four years ago the price of refined sugar was 9 c. a pound, now it is 4 c. a pound. The population uses about 70 pounds of refined sugar per capita, and the increase each year is supposed to keep pace with population, about 5 per cent.

Since writing the above, the three Philadelphia refineries referred to accepted the terms and were incorporated in the American Sugar Refining Company, which increased its capital to 75,000,000 dol.

The city of Philadelphia has within the past few years made rapid strides in the way of improvements, increased trade, industries, and commercial facilities, as well as becoming one of the chief financial centres of the country. The future of the port and city is assured so far as continuous public improvements and enlarged railway facilities are especially concerned. The city is at the junction of the Rivers Delaware and Schuylkill; its population is 1,046,964, to which may be added about 200,000 living adjacent; the area being 129·4 square miles; there is a frontage of 18 miles on the Delaware River, all navigable with wharfage running for 5 miles, and the channel in many sections runs in a depth of 35 to 40 feet at low water. The Schuylkill River flows through the city for 16 miles, and there are 4 miles of dockage and wharfage along its banks. Point Breeze and Girard Point are the two principal shipping points for the exportation of cereals and petroleum. There are 1,151 miles of open streets and alleys, and these figures are continuously increasing; the lighting, gas, and electricity, and the drainage are good, and the water supply ample, additional reservoirs being constructed from time to time, the consumption being 138,199,248 gallons, equal to 132 gallons per capita, while in the year 1888 it was 100 gallons, and 71 gallons in 1880. The maximum pumpage in one day was 170,600,577 gallons. The police force consists of 2,000 men with patrol waggons, mounted officers, police surgeons, and station-house matrons. The fire department is a very efficient department of the city government, consisting

*The city of Philadelphia.*

of 525 men and 40 steam-engines, 2 chemical and 10 hook and ladder trucks; there are about 900 miles of wire in the fire-alarm system, and about 600 alarm boxes. The population for 1892 is set down at 1,100,000. In 1683 it was 600; in 1783, 42,000; in 1880, 846,980; and in 1890, 1,046,964. The city is adorned by numerous small parks, or "squares," and one, naturally and artificially made beautiful, of 2,800 acres, and improvements costing over 1,200,000*l.* The City Hall, where the municipal departments are located, is the largest structure in the United States. This handsome building is not as yet completed, but up to date the expenditures have reached 3,000,000*l.*, and it is estimated that another 1,000,000*l.* is necessary to finish the structure, which is of white marble with lavish ornamentation. It is now proposed to erect a general exchange to be known as the "Bourse," wherein all commercial and stock exchanges will be located. The structure will be on a large scale and cost some hundreds of thousands of pounds. The building authorities of the different cities of the United States have reported the improvements made during the year 1891, and the progress in growth, particularly of the larger cities, has been surprising. Philadelphia had erected 6,991 new buildings at a cost of 3,533,341*l.*, and Chicago 11,805 at an expenditure of 10,800,360*l.*, and New York 2,827, costing 11,231,326*l.* For the chief cities of the whole country, the figures are 65,348 buildings erected at a cost of 48,556,450*l.* These figures do not include the immense and costly buildings erected by the United States Government authorities, and the moneys expended for the alterations and additions to old buildings, which brings the grand total to 65,000,000*l.*

*Vital statistics.* With reference to contagious diseases, Congress is about to order an investigation into the cases of typhus fever that have recently occurred at one or two ports of entry. The Law of March 3, 1891, is explicit in two particulars. No person is allowed to land if suffering from a loathsome or dangerously contagious disease, and no person is allowed to land who is likely to become a public charge. On either of these grounds the cases herein referred to should have been excluded. Being Russian Hebrews they were taken in charge by a Hebrew charity association and distributed, especially in New York and Brooklyn, in various boarding houses. The deadly typhus fever soon broke out. Some of the immigrants getting away from New York and coming to Philadelphia, several cases occurred here. The contagion has aroused the community to the danger which constantly menaces the ports of landing of immigrants, such as New York, Philadelphia, and Boston, through the admission of such unfortunate people as the Russian Jews. In order to curtail the evil effects of this class of immigration it is proposed to increase the head tax. As it is, it becomes important for the steamship companies to use greater precaution, as all detained immigrants are housed, fed, and cared for at the expense of the company, and the costs will cut heavily into the profits of the lines. The matter does not even rest here. First class passengers are discriminating between those boats which carry Russian and Polish immigrants and those which do not. It is believed, therefore, that the best lines will, in self-defence, refuse hereafter to take any of these very undesirable emigrants.

The general mortality list in Philadelphia has for some time been above the average. For one week the deaths were 537, being 134 more than for the corresponding period of one year ago. Influenza, scarlet fever, and diphtheria have been unusually prevalent.

The deaths for the year 1891 were:—

|  | Number. |
|---|---|
| From specific diseases | 21,793 |
| old age | 805 |
| violence | 649 |
| Total | 23,247 |

The population for the middle of the year 1891 is placed at 1,069,264, based upon the increase from the census of 1880 and that of 1890. The deaths from consumption number 2,624. It is becoming the belief in the medical faculty that this dread disease will eventually succumb to the physician's skill. It is but a few years ago when the loathsome disease small-pox awakened so much horror in the community, while now it is absolutely eradicated from the mortuary statistics. From 2,585 deaths in the year 1872—when that epidemic was started from a single case—to none at all in the year 1890. During last year there were five deaths—four in one family, and one in the near neighbourhood. This outbreak was the result of a child playing near a vessel on which an undiscovered convalescent sailor was employed. Stringent sanitary precautions were at once taken by the Board of Health, and a spread of the disease was promptly and effectually prevented.

The deaths from the epidemic influenza have been on the increase during the past few months, especially among those of advanced years. The increased mortality was chiefly from affections of the respiratory organs. The discovery of a case of leprosy in the most thickly-populated part of the city of Philadelphia has caused a degree of public alarm, and the health authorities have taken immediate steps for the disinfection of the premises where the case was discovered. The fact that the authorities have found that the leper was engaged as a cook in a temperance hostelry, frequented chiefly by actors and actresses, has added a feeling of horror to the disgusting disclosures. The proprietor has been placed under arrest. The appearance of leprosy from time to time among the oriental population of the country justifies the most stringent precautionary measures being taken by the proper authorities.

*Finances of Philadelphia.*—The assessed valuation of property in the city of Philadelphia by the Board of the Revision of Taxes is as follows:—

## UNITED STATES.

|  | £ |
|---|---|
| In the year 1891 | 142,780,568 |
| For the year 1892 | 147,139,354 |
| Being an increase of | 4,358,786 |

The value of property, both real and personal, are much more than these figures indicate; still the intent is to make the assessments as near to actual value as it is possible to do.

The appropriations for the various municipal departments are 3,296,805·40*l*. for 1892, which is an increase of 254,235·15*l*., being about the average yearly increase during the past 10 years.

The defalcation of the City Treasurer and his subsequent confession of guilt and imprisonment depleted the city's finances to the extent of over 100,000*l*.

The total value of buildings and alterations for which permits were issued was 4,017,647·30*l*. The improvements and expenditures of all departments have increased in proportion to the general growth of the population and the expansion of the city.

The increase in the collection of delinquent taxes in 1891 exceeded those of the previous year by 38,997*l*. Counting, however, all expenses, interest and the sum paid into the sinking fund, there was a deficit of 104,529*l*., which was provided for by deducting it from the amount subject to the appropriation for 1892. The funded debt of the year was 11,340,264*l*.

**Failures.** The total failures of business houses throughout the country during the year 1891 numbered 12,394, with liabilities aggregating 38,635,600*l*., while the total actual assets were 20,578,600*l*. In 1890 the failures were 10,673, and the liabilities 34,999,800*l*., and actual assets 18,552,200*l*. Banks, bankers, and brokers suffered severely. In 1890 there were 32 failures of private banks, State, national, and savings banks, with about 3,800,000*l*. liabilities. Last year the total number of bank failures is reported at 53, with approximate liabilities of 7,000,000*l*.

The failures in Philadelphia numbered 404, assets 1,424,145*l*., and the liabilities 2,258,068*l*. In Pennsylvania the failures aggregated liabilities of 600,000*l*., in Ohio 400,000*l*., and Michigan 860,000*l*.

The failures, liabilities, and assets were distributed among the different trades as follows:—

## PHILADELPHIA.

| Trades. | Number. | Liabilities. | Assets. |
|---|---|---|---|
|  |  | £ | £ |
| Bankers and brokers | 4 | 843,174 | 317,940 |
| Carpenters and builders | 20 | 199,990 | 131,060 |
| Carriages, bicycles, &c. | 5 | 11,103 | 6,020 |
| Clothing, manufacturing, wholesale and retail.. | 20 | 19,683 | 8,315 |
| Coal, wood, and ice | 7 | 66,455 | 52,051 |
| Drugs, paints, and dyers | 26 | 33,644 | 15,136 |
| Dry goods and notions.. | 20 | 62,007 | 16,715 |
| Grain, flour, bakers, &c. | 17 | 76,010 | 50,768 |
| Furniture, carpets, &c. | 37 | 52,409 | 36,975 |
| Grocers | 31 | 24,609 | 6,692 |
| Hardware, roofers, &c... | 11 | 95,826 | 32,906 |
| Hats, manufacturing, wholesale and retail | 8 | 17,670 | 11,884 |
| Iron | 10 | 68,692 | 59,296 |
| Ladies and men's furnishing | 11 | 4,854 | 2,031 |
| Leather dealers and manufacturers | 13 | 78,107 | 49,399 |
| Liquor dealers and restaurants | 11 | 57,560 | 18,835 |
| Lumber, &c. | 15 | 108,978 | 102,300 |
| Machinery | 14 | 38,747 | 20,857 |
| Paper, stationers, &c. | 9 | 16,360 | 3,680 |
| Printers and publishers | 10 | 12,340 | 6,330 |
| Produce, commission | 18 | 47,146 | 15,032 |
| Shoes, wholesale and retail | 20 | 26,301 | 12,104 |
| Textile fabrics, manufactures.. | 13 | 200,900 | 399,900 |
| Tobacco and cigars | 8 | 13,891 | 5,733 |
| Jewellers and opticians | 14 | 21,552 | 16,441 |
| Miscellaneous | 32 | 88,426 | 15,648 |

Compared with 1890, when there were 307 failures, with liabilities of 1,376,522*l*., and assets of 738,913*l*., this is an unfavourable showing, but it is explained by the crash of the Keystone and Spring Garden banks. Deducting the liability of these, 843,175*l*., the total liabilities for 1891 are very little greater than those of 1890. Next after the banks the most serious losses were in the textile trade, where the assets, however, were nearly double the liabilities.

The following statement of the business done per week is a fair exhibit of the condition of the banks in Philadelphia, and may be accepted as applicable to the transactions of the year 1891 from week to week.

|  | £ |
|---|---|
| Capital | 4,354,000 |
| Loans | 19,290,400 |
| Reserve | 7,003,600 |
| Bank notes | 42,400 |
| Due from banks | 1,710,400 |
| „ to „ | 4,437,800 |
| Deposits | 16,419,000 |
| Circulation | 667,200 |
| Clearings | 14,061,759 |
| Balances | 2,063,482 |

Greater freedom was used in the granting of licenses for

## UNITED STATES.

**Liquor licenses.**

opening of public houses for the year 1891, and it is generally believed that this will extend for the year 1892, notwithstanding that renewed efforts will be made by the prohibitionists and the Law and Order Society to curtail the issues. The License Court has entire power and control. It can increase or decrease the number as it sees fit.

At the present time an effort will be made to increase the number of licensed houses, the argument used being that an even distribution of public houses will decrease the number of "speak-easies," viz., private unlicensed clubs, illicit places for the sale of spirits, and perambulators who sell drinks from a bottle in secluded alleys.

It is stated that the number of licensed houses will be enlarged by at least 1,000, or, in other words, double the present number of public houses. The Law and Order Society claim that any addition to the licensed houses will not decrease the number of "speak-easies," alleging that as they do a large Sunday trade, when the licensed houses are closed, it will be quite as difficult to discover them and place them under arrest, while an increase in the number of regular taverns will be an increased injury to the morals and sobriety of the community during week-days.

There are at present 1,253 licensed saloons, 1,402 bakeries, 279 public schools, and 682 churches, making, on the basis of 205,444 votes—the largest ever cast in the Commonwealth—a saloon to every 163 voters, a bakery to every 146, a public school to every 736, and a church to every 301.

---

LONDON:
Printed for Her Majesty's Stationery Office,
By HARRISON AND SONS,
Printers in Ordinary to Her Majesty.
(75   7 | 92—H & S   1342)

# FOREIGN OFFICE.
## 1892.
## ANNUAL SERIES.

### No 1080.

### DIPLOMATIC AND CONSULAR REPORTS ON TRADE AND FINANCE.

# UNITED STATES.

REPORT FOR THE YEAR 1891

ON THE

TRADE, &c., OF THE DISTRICT OF THE CONSULATE-GENERAL OF NEW YORK.

REFERENCE TO PREVIOUS REPORT, Annual Series No. 911.

LONDON:
PRINTED FOR HER MAJESTY'S STATIONERY OFFICE,
BY HARRISON AND SONS, ST. MARTIN'S LANE,
PRINTERS IN ORDINARY TO HER MAJESTY.

And to be purchased, either directly or through any Bookseller, from
EYRE & SPOTTISWOODE, EAST HARDING STREET, FLEET STREET, E.C., and
32, ABINGDON STREET, WESTMINSTER, S.W.; or
JOHN MENZIES & Co., 12, HANOVER STREET, EDINBURGH, and
90, WEST NILE STREET, GLASGOW; or
HODGES, FIGGIS, & Co., 104, GRAFTON STREET, DUBLIN.

1892.

*Price Twopence.*

# New Series of Reports.

Reports of the Annual Series have been issued from Her Majesty's Diplomatic and Consular Officers at the following places, and may be obtained from the sources indicated on the title-page:—

| No. | | Page. | No. | | Page. |
|---|---|---|---|---|---|
| 964. | Philadelphia | 2d. | 1022. | Tripoli | 1d. |
| 965. | Mexico | 2d. | 1023. | Jerusalem | 1d. |
| 966. | Malaga | 2½d. | 1024. | Odessa | 6d. |
| 967. | Berne | 1d. | 1025. | Genoa | 1½d. |
| 968. | Puerto Rico | ½d. | 1026. | Kiungchow | 1d. |
| 969. | Buda-Pesth | 1d. | 1027. | Batoum | 4½d. |
| 970. | Bogotá | 1d. | 1028. | Buenos Ayres | 1d. |
| 971. | Panama | 1½d. | 1029. | Batavia | 1d. |
| 972. | Munich | 2d. | 1030. | Santo Domingo | ½d. |
| 973. | Copenhagen | 4d. | 1031. | San José | 1d. |
| 974. | Guatemala | 1d. | 1032. | Manila | 1½d. |
| 975. | Munich | 2d. | 1033. | Marseilles | 1d. |
| 976. | Meshed | 1½d. | 1034. | Swatow | 1d. |
| 977. | Para | ½d. | 1035. | Paris | 1d. |
| 978. | Florence | 1d. | 1036. | Ichang | 5d. |
| 979. | The Hague | 1½d. | 1037. | Pakhoi | 1d. |
| 980. | Patras | 1d. | 1038. | Foochow | 1d. |
| 981. | Paris | 1½d. | 1039. | Brest | 1d. |
| 982. | Zanzibar | 2½d. | 1040. | Madeira | ½d. |
| 983. | Buenos Ayres | ½d. | 1041. | Antwerp | 1½d. |
| 984. | Copenhagen | 1d. | 1042. | Taganrog | 2½d. |
| 985. | Stuttgart | 1d. | 1043. | Algiers | 2½d. |
| 986. | New Orleans | 1½d. | 1044. | Hankow | 1½d. |
| 987. | New Orleans | 10d. | 1045. | Nantes | 1½d. |
| 988. | Suakin | ½d. | 1046. | Belgrade | 2d. |
| 989. | Galveston | 1½d. | 1047. | Fiume | 1d. |
| 990. | Berlin | 1d. | 1048. | Wuhu | 1d. |
| 991. | Zanzibar | 1½d. | 1049. | Cagliari | 1d. |
| 992. | Guayaquil | 1d. | 1050. | Erzeroum | 1d. |
| 993. | Tonga | 1d. | 1051. | Syra | 1d. |
| 994. | New Orleans | 1d. | 1052. | Cherbourg | 1d. |
| 995. | Mozambique | 1½d. | 1053. | Lima | 1d. |
| 996. | Galatz | 1½d. | 1054. | Bilbao | 1½d. |
| 997. | Nantes | 1½d. | 1055. | Cadiz | 2d. |
| 998. | Algiers | 1d. | 1056. | Corunna | 2½d. |
| 999. | Havre | 2½d. | 1057. | Saigon | 1d. |
| 1000. | Buenos Ayres | 6d. | 1058. | Port-au-Prince | 1d. |
| 1001. | Baltimore | 1½d. | 1059. | Trebizond | 1d. |
| 1002. | Taganrog | 1d. | 1060. | Barcelona | 1½d. |
| 1003. | Riga | 2d. | 1061. | Tainan | 1d. |
| 1004. | Bordeaux | 2½d. | 1062. | Smyrna | 1½d. |
| 1005. | The Hague | 1½d. | 1063. | Old Calabar | ½d. |
| 1006. | Paraguay | 1½d. | 1064. | Samoa | ½d. |
| 1007. | Constantinople | 1½d. | 1065. | Tahiti | 1d. |
| 1008. | Rome | 1d. | 1066. | Chefoo | 6d. |
| 1009. | Mozambique | 1d. | 1067. | Gothenburg | 2d. |
| 1010. | Wênchow | 1d. | 1068. | Buenos Ayres | 1½d. |
| 1011. | Mogador | 2½d. | 1069. | Loanda | 1½d. |
| 1012. | Amoy | 1d. | 1070. | Guatemala | 1d. |
| 1013. | Kiukiang | 1d. | 1071. | Zanzibar | 1d. |
| 1014. | Stettin | 1½d. | 1072. | Charleston | 2½d. |
| 1015. | Boston | 1d. | 1073. | Nice | 1d. |
| 1016. | Callao | 1d. | 1074. | Caracas | 1d. |
| 1017. | Aleppo | 1d. | 1075. | Lisbon | 2d. |
| 1018. | Santos | 2½d. | 1076. | Calais | 2d. |
| 1019. | Piræus | 1d. | 1077. | Rio Grande do Sul | 5½d. |
| 1020. | Mogador | 1d. | 1078. | Philadelphia | 2½d. |
| 1021. | Adrianople | ½d. | 1079. | Brindisi | 2d. |

# No. 1080.

*Reference to previous Report, Annual Series No. 911.*

## UNITED STATES.
### NEW YORK.

*Consul-General Booker to the Marquis of Salisbury.*

My Lord,                          *New York, May* 16, 1892.

I HAVE the honour to transmit herewith my Annual Report upon the Trade of New York, with some information in regard to other parts of my Consular District.

I have, &c.
(Signed)     WM. LANE BOOKER

---

*Report on the Trade of New York for* 1891.

ABSTRACT of Contents.

| | PAGE |
|---|---|
| General remarks— | |
|   General review | 2 |
|   Bank returns | 4 |
|   Banking report | 4 |
|   Sterling exchange | 5 |
|   Failures | 5 |
|   State and city finances | 6 |
| Trade and commerce— | |
|   Dry goods | 6 |
|   Exports and imports (vide Annexes B and C) | 16–18 |
|   Grain shipments | 8 |
| Shipping and navigation— | |
|   Ocean freights | 8 |
|   Return of shipping (vide Annex A) | 15 |
|   Return of seamen (vide Annex D) | 25 |
| Public works— | |
|   Canals | 10 |
|   Railroads | 11 |
| Population and industry— | |
|   Census returns | 11 |
|   Vital statistics | 11 |
|   Immigration | 12 |
|   Labour | 14 |
| Annexes— | |
|   Return of shipping (Annex A) | 15 |
|      ,, exports (Annex B) | 16 |
|      ,, imports ,, | 16 |
|      ,, exports and imports (Annex C) | 18 |
|      ,, seamen (Annex D) | 19 |
| Providence, R.I.— | |
|   Vide report for contents | 19 |

## UNITED STATES.

### General Remarks.

General review of trade.

The trade of the port in the first half of 1891 was not satisfactory; it was a period of depression in which mercantile and manufacturing interests suffered; prices were low, and profits correspondingly small. In the latter half there was some improvement, but the reaction was not equal to expectations, under an enormous crop of grain, and remunerative prices for the leading cereals. The large receipts and exports of grain in the autumn, while giving a stimulus to trade, did not materially affect the prices of merchandise. The demand from the interior of the country was confined to immediate requirements, and the benefit to arise from the increased circulation of money from sales of the year's crop had barely set in when the year closed.

The large importation in 1890 of many articles to be affected by the new (McKinley) tariff was one of the leading causes for the generally low prices, and the cautious dealing of interior purchasers; but as an offset to the unsatisfactory condition of trade was the gratifying manner in which collections were made. The New York Cotton Exchange had a most active year. The crop of 1890 turned out to be a 8,655,518 bales, larger than any previous year, and the crop of 1891 was not much less, although the exact figures are not yet obtainable. The rapidity with which the crop was marketed caused the unusual activity, and at the same time forced prices down lower than at any other period in the last 30 years. The total sales of "futures" at the exchange amounted to 26,692,300 bales, against 23,926,500 bales in 1890.

In regard to the crops, the United States Agricultural Department estimates the farm value of wheat, maize, and oats to have been, in 1891, nearly 58,000,000*l*. in value in excess of that of 1890, but there was a loss of fully 12,000,000*l*. in the value of the cotton crop, in consequence of the low prices ruling.

The stock market joined in the general depression of the early months of the year but improved later, and in August there was an active demand for railroad and industrial stocks and bonds with generally rising prices, which became more marked in September, but fell off in October, when there was shown a disposition in some quarters to realise on the advance; but prices were fairly well maintained, notwithstanding the large quantity of stocks and bonds returned from Europe, the transactions, however, being confined chiefly to the regular operators, the outside public looking on.

Gold exports commenced in February, and by July the unusually large sum of 15,000,000*l*. had been shipped, but in September the shipments of grain began to affect the exchanges, and gold between that time and the end of the year had been returned to the extent of 7,000,000*l*.

The clearing-house returns show a considerable falling-off in the volume of trade as compared with 1890. The total clearings at the New York clearing-house in 1891 were 6,952,360,374*l*., and eliminating 1,963,307,424*l*. as representing stock sales, the clearings in trade transactions amounted to 4,989,052,950*l.*, a reduction of 12 per cent. on those of 1890. The total clearings at all the clearing-houses outside of New York city were 4,714,827,890*l.*

The increase in railroad receipts in 1891 shows a marked improvement over 1890, amounting to about 4½ per cent. in gross receipts and 6·80 per cent. in net earnings. The increase in net earnings is due to the general good condition of the roads from large previous outlays on them, and to the maintenance of rates. The great increase in net earnings was in the latter part of the year, when the grain-carrying roads were worked to their utmost capacity at remunerative rates. The North-Western and Pacific Coast Railroads showed the best results, but the improvement was well spread throughout the country. A few railroad companies reduced their dividends in the spring, but in the summer and autumn several increased theirs, and in doing so generally kept well within their earnings. About 4,100 miles of roads were constructed, distributed pretty equally between the different sections of the country. According to leading railroad journals, 33 per cent. of the new tracks laid were in the south-eastern States, 23 per cent. in the north-eastern, 18 per cent. in the south-western, 15 per cent. in the north-western, and 11 per cent. in the Pacific States, distributed among so many lines as to show the work of the year to have been mainly in the construction of short branches or connections.

The value of merchandise imports (excluding specie) was 107,427,135*l.*, or about 7 per cent. less than in 1890; of these imports 51·36 per cent. entered on the free list, against 35·62 per cent. in 1890.

In exports (excluding specie) there was an increase of about 1 per cent. in favour of 1891 over 1890.

The value of all dry goods entered for consumption in 1891 was 18,585,708*l.*, and there was withdrawn from bonded warehouse in the same period 5,714,339*l.*; these amounts, 24,300,047*l.*, fairly represent, as all are dutiable, the amount of dry goods marketed in the year, and show a falling-off from 1890 of 5,333,409*l.* and from 1889 of 3,703,509*l.*

The customs receipts at this port in 1891 were 25,291,004*l.*, against 33,627,085*l.* in 1890.

There were no very serious fluctuations in the money market at any time during the year. In the early part of January call loans were made as high as 8 to 9 per cent., but later, and through February the range was 2 per cent. to 5 per cent., with an average of about 3 per cent., good commercial paper commanding from 5½ per cent. to 6½ per cent. In March call loans ranged from 2 per cent. to 4 per cent, and commercial paper from 5 per cent. to 5½ per cent. In April, till towards the close, call loans were made at 2½ per cent. to 3 per cent., and in the last week, and through May, call loans ranged from 3 per cent. to 7 per cent., with an average of about 4¼ per cent., 5 per cent. to 6 per cent. being the rate for good paper.

(1328)

## UNITED STATES.

In June and July the money market was easy, with call loans ranging from 1 per cent. to 4½ per cent., with no change for commercial paper. In August there was an active demand for money, which could be obtained within a range of from 1½ per cent. to 5 per cent., the average being about 2¼ per cent. Commercial paper brought rather higher rates, averaging about 6 per cent. In the early part of September, call loans ranged from 2½ per cent. to 5 per cent., but towards the close much higher rates were paid; after the first week in October, call loans ranged from 3 per cent. to 6 per cent., with an average of 4 per cent., commercial paper without change. In the early part of November a demand from outside quarters caused the rate for call loans to advance considerably, but it was only of a very temporary character, and the rate fell to 3 per cent. to 4 per cent., and commercial paper was done at 5 per cent. to 5¾ per cent. In December, with an easy money market, call loans ranged from 2 per cent. to 5 per cent., and commercial paper from 4¾ per cent. to 5½ per cent.

In last year's report I referred to the relief given in November, in consequence of numerous failures and great distrust, by the New York clearing-house in authorising the issue of loan certificates, which was taken advantage of by banks to the extent of 3,132,000*l.* At the close of the year this amount was reduced to 2,677,000*l.*, and the reduction continued so rapidly that by the end of January in the year under review the certificates had all been retired except one for 8,000*l.*, which also was soon after cancelled.

The legal tender notes, payable in coin, issued by the Secretary of the Treasury in payment for the monthly purchases of 4,500,000 ounces of silver, under the Act of Congress of 1890, have been a very useful addition to the currency in circulation.

Bank returns. The condition of the associated banks of the city at different periods of the year is shown in the following table:—

AVERAGE Amount of Associated Banks of New York City.

| 1891. | Loans. | Specie. | Legal Tenders. | Deposits. | Circulation. | Surplus over Reserve required against Deposits. |
|---|---|---|---|---|---|---|
| | £ | £ | £ | £ | £ | £ |
| January 3 | 79,449,771 | 16,204,620 | 5,743,770 | 79,646,213 | 741,497 | 1,766,836 |
| March 28 | 84,071,175 | 16,013,740 | 7,121,750 | 85,585,708 | 721,227 | 1,739,062 |
| June 27 | 80,325,642 | 13,976,195 | 10,521,450 | 82,819,416 | 727,860 | 3,792,790 |
| September 26 | 84,010,324 | 12,855,040 | 8,809,672 | 83,356,149 | 1,147,502 | 825,675 |
| December 26 | 88,426,612 | 19,856,855 | 7,604,306 | 93,793,098 | 1,154,568 | 4,012,885 |

Banks The annual report of the Superintendent of the State Banking Department for the fiscal year ending September 30, 1891, has been presented to the Legislature, and from it I extract the following items of interest: 20 new banks were organised during the fiscal year with a capital of 488,200*l.*; one only of these, with a capital of 51,500*l.*, is located in this city. Three banks of this city closed during the year, and one was converted into a national bank. The capital of all the banks was increased during the year by 447,200*l.* Three new trust companies were organised, and one was closed. The capital of the 33 trust companies under the supervision of the State Banking Department is 5,366,300*l.*; only 515,000*l.* belongs to companies outside of New York and Brooklyn.

The savings banks of the city generally paid $3\frac{1}{2}$ per cent. interest, but a few paid $3\frac{3}{4}$ per cent. and 4 per cent.

The following gives the rates of bankers sterling exchange for the year 1891:— *Sterling exchange.*

| Month. | | At 60 Days. | At Sight. |
|---|---|---|---|
| January | highest | 4·86 | 4·89 |
| | lowest | 4·80$\frac{1}{2}$ | 4·85 |
| February | highest | 4·87 | 4·89 |
| | lowest | 4·85$\frac{1}{2}$ | 4·88 |
| March | highest | 4·87 | 4·89 |
| | lowest | 4·86 | 4·88 |
| April | highest | 4·87 | 4·90 |
| | lowest | 4·86 | 4·89 |
| May | highest | 4·86$\frac{1}{2}$ | 4·90 |
| | lowest | 4·84$\frac{1}{2}$ | 4·88$\frac{1}{2}$ |
| June | highest | 4·87$\frac{1}{2}$ | 4·89$\frac{1}{2}$ |
| | lowest | 4·85$\frac{1}{2}$ | 4·88 |
| July | highest | 4·86$\frac{1}{2}$ | 4·88$\frac{1}{2}$ |
| | lowest | 4·84$\frac{1}{2}$ | 4·87 |
| August | highest | 4·85$\frac{1}{2}$ | 4·87$\frac{1}{2}$ |
| | lowest | 4·83 | 4·85 |
| September | highest | 4·83 | 4·86 |
| | lowest | 4·81 | 4·84 |
| October | highest | 4·82 | 4·85 |
| | lowest | 4·80 | 4·84 |
| November | highest | 4·82 | 4·85 |
| | lowest | 4·80$\frac{1}{2}$ | 4·84 |
| December | highest | 4·84 | 4·86 |
| | lowest | 4·81$\frac{1}{2}$ | 4·84$\frac{1}{2}$ |

In the following table, taken from Dun's Commercial Agency's Report, will be found the number of failures in the past two years in New York and Brooklyn cities, and the States of my district. It will be seen that the number of failures in this city and Brooklyn is greater than in 1890, but the liabilities are very much less. There were very few suspensions of firms of prominence in this city. *Failures*

## UNITED STATES.

|  | Number of Failures. | | Amount of Liabilities. | |
|---|---|---|---|---|
|  | 1891. | 1890. | 1891. | 1890. |
|  |  |  | £ | £ |
| New York and Brooklyn cities | 637 | 576 | 5,375,075 | 9,077,410 |
| New York, outside of New York city and Brooklyn | 712 | 748 | 1,627,270 | 1,745,942 |
| Connecticut | 193 | 176 | 560,120 | 298,210 |
| New Jersey | 187 | 154 | 922,786 | 572,653 |
| Rhode Island | 102 | 107 | 317,516 | 831,550 |
| Delaware | 29 | 18 | 89,528 | 44,047 |

*State finances.* The State gross indebtedness at the close of the fiscal year (September 30) was 577,822*l*., against which there is a sinking fund of 394,085*l*., leaving a net debt of 183,737*l*., a reduction during the year of 161,909*l*.

The tax rate for the current year is (1⅜) one and three-eighths mills, the lowest which has been levied by the State since 1855, and on an assessed valuation of property of 778,555,110*l*. will yield 1,070,514*l*.; to be devoted to school purposes 778,555*l*., canals, including canal debt, 291,959*l*.

The direct school tax for the fiscal year produced the sum of 789,186*l*., and the total amount expended from the State treasury was 920,102*l*.

*City finances.* The total funded debt of the city of New York amounted at the close of the year to 30,968,695*l*., against which there is a sinking fund of 10,873,386*l*., leaving a net funded debt of 20,095,310*l*., a reduction of 163,380*l*. on the debt as it stood at the end of 1890.

TABLE showing Valuation and Tax Rates for the past Five Years.

| Year. | Real Estate. | Personal. | City Tax. |
|---|---|---|---|
|  | £ | £ | Per cent. |
| 1891 | 301,635,050 | 66,250,531 | 1·90 |
| 1890 | 288,047,740 | 61,529,806 | 1·97 |
| 1889 | 274,305,127 | 56,085,729 | 1·95 |
| 1888 | 268,380,689 | 51,628,451 | 2·22 |
| 1887 | 258,425,300 | 52,148,655 | 2·16 |

*Trade and Commerce.*

*Dry goods.* During the year 1891 the dry goods trade was carried on under different influences from those of the previous year. As shown in my last report, business had been very active during the last half of 1890, stimulated by the passage of the KcKinley Bill, which had led importers to bring out goods very liberally in anticipation of the increased duties, and of the wants of the country, while in 1891 there was a natural reaction from this activity, and many of those interested were disappointed in the results. The markets were over-supplied with many classes of foreign goods, large quantities of which went but slowly into consumption, and realised proceeds for their owners only late in the year, and then often without profit. These accumulated stocks were a menace to the market during the whole year, and the difficulty of distributing the goods through the regular trade channels resulted in passing an unusual quantity through the auction rooms. During the autumn business returned more nearly to its natural channels, and prices having become established more in accordance with the new and increased cost the results were more satisfactory. American manufacturers, in the meantime, may be said, as a whole, to have been doing fairly well.

Cottons. Spinners and manufacturers of cotton have had to deal, for the most part, with declining prices, but these have been fully and in many cases more than offset by the unprecedented decline of the great staple. The natural effect of low prices on consumption has through the year been in favour of a large distribution of products; but at the same time the constant uncertainty as to the course of prices has made purchasers cautious, while the low prices realised for cotton have diminished the ability of consumers in the cotton-producing States; thus, although the cotton mills have generally declared dividends, many, however, at a considerable reduced rate, a certain depression in feeling has accompanied the year, and there has been an entire absence of speculative activity. The products of the mills, however, have not accumulated, and the feeling for 1892 is one of confidence.

Worsteds and woollens. In worsted and woollen goods an improvement has no doubt taken place since my last. Mills have been fairly well employed, and those making the better classes of goods are said to be well filled with orders. Many manufacturers, however, continue to agitate for the repeal of the duties upon wool, and the feeling appears to be growing among them in favour of such a movement. This would probably spread more rapidly were not the apprehension felt that the freer admission of wool would come later also to mean the freer importation of goods. The demand for foreign goods has not been equal to what it was in the previous year.

There has been but little gain in the volume of business in Burlaps during the year as compared with last, although the enormous crops of grain would indicate a much greater consumption. The business was in the early months of the year more profitable, and prices have more nearly reflected the Dundee values than they did in 1890.

Silks. Little change can be said to have taken place in the silk industry during the past year; no new mills have been erected,

# UNITED STATES.

but the demand for various fabrics has generally been sufficient to keep the existing mills profitably employed. The fabrics most in favour, however, have been of a more or less fancy nature, calling for frequent changes, and the production of black silks has been much smaller than in previous years.

*Grain shipments.*

The following table shows the total grain shipments from this port to Great Britain and the Continent, with the nationality of the vessels engaged in the transport:—

| Country. | Number of Vessels. | Number of Bushels. |
| --- | --- | --- |
| Great Britain | 792 | 48,569,356 |
| Germany | 143 | 5,117,323 |
| Netherlands | 74 | 2,483,692 |
| Belgium | 61 | 3,379,088 |
| France | 34 | 1,711,706 |
| Norway | 29 | 1,667,029 |
| Denmark | 25 | 982,077 |
| Italy | 24 | 1,410,990 |
| Portugal | 16 | 881,797 |
| Spain | 10 | 617,484 |
| Austria | 5 | 129,262 |
| United States | 25 | 1,273,724 |
| Total | 1,238 | 68,223,528 |

The American ships consisted of four steamers, the old passenger ships of the Philadelphia Line. Of the foregoing only 15 were sailing vessels.

There was also included in the return of grain 2,133,366 bushels of flax seed. There was also shipped, and not included in the above return, 260,377 bushels of buck wheat, which has not before been exported in any quantity.

### Shipping and Navigation.

*Ocean freights.*

The shipping business from this Continent was a very limited one during the spring and early summer, and freights at their lowest ebb, in consequence of the small wheat crop and the greatly reduced yield of maize in the preceding year, the latter article advancing to a prohibitive figure, and as a result the regular liners were restricted during the spring months to starvation rates, unable in most cases to secure full cargoes, and frequently compelled to take coal and other similar makeshifts for ballast. As a matter of course, there was no inquiry whatever at that time for steamers for Europe in excess of the regular liners. Cotton freights had, in the meanwhile, been fairly remunerative from the southern ports, and a number of steamers —overwhelmingly under the British flag—found profitable employment thence until towards the close of February, when the freights in the south likewise collapsed. In this period there had been a fair demand for steamers to carry sugar from Cuba to the United States ports north of Hatteras, but the poor business offering from here left little profit to owners. Lumber, timber, and deal freights from the southern ports, and from the Bay of Fundy, declined in sympathy with the low rates prevailing here, and freights on cargoes of petroleum in cases for the East Indies, China, and Japan had likewise to suffer, and fell to a lower level than before reached under the aggressive competition by Russian shipments from Batoum.

Matters remained in this unsatisfactory state until June, when it became evident that the crop of winter wheat was likely to turn out of unusually good quality and large volume, whilst the condition of the other grain crops was very promising—in direct contrast with the general outlook for the European harvests. Freights commenced thenceforward to improve gradually, rising steadily under the stimulating influence of our large crops of spring as well as winter wheat, followed by a very heavy harvest of maize, to the demand for all of which the partial failure of the Russian crops and the prohibition of further exportation thence of cereals in September very largely added. Our export of grain has thus become the largest for years, and freights remained active and advancing until early in December, when they culminated at the figure of 5s. per quarter to Cork f.o. From that time they gradually receded, the decline being largely attributable to the comparative scarcity of supplies at the seaboard, whilst there are still very large stocks distributed throughout the west or held in first hands.

The enormous yield of cotton during the season of 1891-92 gave rise to great expectations as to freights for this commodity, but these expectations have been most signally disappointed. The large crop caused a persistent decline in prices in Europe, under which the staple has sold at abnormally low prices, and freights have had to bear their share of this decline. In addition to low freight rates, the unusually dry weather preceding the picking of the staple rendered it spongy, and consequently more bulky than in average years, so that further loss occurred to the carrier thereby. It appears an anomaly, but it is a fact, nevertheless, that a much smaller yield of cotton would doubtless have much benefited the ocean-carrying trade, as well as many other interests.

The good figures obtainable for grain were naturally to some extent reflected in all the freights from this coast since the activity in grain shipments commenced, and it may be stated in summing up that the second half-year's business somewhat compensated for the very dull state of our carrying trade in the early part of the year.

Sailing vessels continue to lose their grip on markets of the Atlantic coast of the United States, in quite the proportion apparent in most parts of the world. The carrying of petroleum in barrels, by sailing vessels, has practically ceased, all the large European ports being now supplied by tank steamers. Apart some cargoes in barrels for the Baltic and some French ports, Italy and a number of ports in the East Indies, China, and Japan, have been supplied by cargoes of case oil still largely by sailers, although the competition of steamers is rapidly encroaching on the latter business. Smaller vessels have found employment in the naval store trade hence for Europe, and larger ones in the timber and lumber business from southern ports and in carrying deals from the Bay of Fundy, but the rates in general have been little remunerative. The continued stagnation of business in the River Plate has rendered lumber shipments for that country—in average years a source of employment for a large number of vessels—unfortunately inoperative. Shipments of general cargo for the west coast of South America, for the Cape Colonies, and for Australia, have continued by means of sailing vessels, but rates have gradually declined from former satisfactory freights to starvation figures. Owing to the comparative lack of value of our export staples, a change from sail to steamer for these trades has not yet taken place, in spite of continued efforts on part of charterers to bring about this change.

## Public Works.

**Canals.**

The report of the Superintendent of Public Works on the trade and tonnage of the canals shows that 4,563,472 tons (of 2,000 lbs.) passed through the canals in 1891, 682,630 tons less than in 1890, but in the latter year there were sent 467,537 tons of ice which had been gathered on Lake Champlain, an unusual commodity. Of the tonnage transported in 1891 there was carried by the

|  | Tons (of 2,000 lbs). |
|---|---|
| Erie Canal | 3,097,853 |
| Champlain Canal | 1,101,123 |
| Black River „ | 122,116 |
| Oswego „ | 161,426 |
| Cayuga and Seneca Canal | 80,954 |

Of the total amount of freight moved, 3,190,331 tons were carried east, and 1,373,141 tons west.

The tonnage of the canals the past season was composed mainly of the following articles:—

|  | Tons. |
|---|---|
| Product of the forest | 1,206,986 |
| „ agriculture | 1,171,192 |
| Domestic salt | 73,152 |
| Anthracite coal | 789,763 |
| Bituminous „ | 91,739 |
| Iron ore | 215,686 |

The Superintendent ascribes the reduction in tonnage passage through the canals in 1891 to the neglect of the State to make proper provision for the improvement and development of the canals, and to keep pace with the improvements that are constantly being made to the railroads that compete for the carrying trade of the west and north, and to the reduction of railroad rates during the time the canals are open.

During the year 1,491,950 tons (of 2,000 lbs.) were sent westward to Buffalo, Pittsburg, &c., by the railroads from New York, and 4,998,208 tons were received, originating at or west of Buffalo, Pittsburg, &c. In 1890 the westward freight was 1,435,189 tons, and eastward 3,736,995 tons. *Railroads.*

## Population and Industry.

The United States census of 1890 gave New York city a population of 1,515,301, and Brooklyn 804,377. Under the State census of 1891 the population of this city is 1,801,739, and Brooklyn 930,633. The State of New York by the United States census 5,997,853, and by the State census 6,483,632, of whom 720,605 are aliens, and of these about 375,090 are credited to this city. *Census.*

### VITAL Statistics, New York City.

|  | 1891. | 1890. |
|---|---|---|
|  | Number. | Number. |
| Births | 46,804 | 39,250 |
| Marriages | 15,764 | 14,992 |
| Deaths | 43,659 | 40,103 |

*Vital statistics.*

Of the deaths reported 11,241 were under 1 year of age, and 18,224 under 5 years of age.

The causes of death were principally as follows:—

|  | Number. |
|---|---|
| Phthisis | 5,160 |
| Pneumonia | 5,818 |
| Bronchitis | 1,836 |
| Influenza | 854 |
| Croup | 609 |
| Measles | 663 |
| Whooping cough | 352 |
| Diphtheria | 1,361 |
| Scarlet fever | 1,220 |
| Cerebro-spinal meningitis | 189 |
| Diarrhœal diseases | 3,587 |
| Heart disease | 2,284 |
| Typhoid fever | 384 |
| Malarial fevers | 185 |
| Bright's disease | 2,501 |
| Violence | 1,953 |

Death rate 25·97 per 1,000,

## 12 UNITED STATES.

**Immigration.** There were 430,884 immigrants landed at this port in 1891, of whom 153,939 were females, from the following countries:—

| Countries. | 1891. | 1890. |
|---|---|---|
|  | Number. | Number. |
| Great Britain | 28,163 | 29,225 |
| Ireland | 35,951 | 33,604 |
| Germany | 79,496 | 68,058 |
| France | 4,189 | 4,208 |
| Russia | 83,552 | 49,119 |
| Sweden | 32,426 | 24,291 |
| Norway | 10,600 | 9,569 |
| Switzerland | 6,264 | 6,436 |
| Belgium | 2,773 | 2,118 |
| Holland | 4,295 | 3,209 |
| Italy | 65,084 | 58,243 |
| Spain | 124 | 144 |
| Portugal | 1,985 | 863 |
| Denmark | 9,024 | 8,220 |
| Hungary | 25,409 | 23,003 |
| Austria | 27,433 | 30,442 |
| Turkey | 1,020 | 540 |
| Greece | 1,038 | 273 |
| All other countries | 12,058 | 6,945 |
| Total | 430,884 | 358,510 |

Their destinations were as follows:—

## NEW YORK.

| | Number. |
|---|---|
| Alabama | 356 |
| Arizona | 263 |
| Arkansas | 482 |
| Connecticut | 8,390 |
| Colorado | 2,602 |
| California | 6,222 |
| Delaware | 814 |
| District of Columbia | 649 |
| Florida | 489 |
| Georgia | 499 |
| Indiana | 2,063 |
| Indian territory | 412 |
| Illinois | 28,329 |
| Iowa | 4,787 |
| Idaho | 473 |
| Kentucky | 845 |
| Kansas | 2,064 |
| Louisiana | 826 |
| Maine | 749 |
| Maryland | 1,757 |
| Michigan | 9,173 |
| Missouri | 3,833 |
| Minnesota | 8,475 |
| Mississippi | 511 |
| Montana | 1,383 |
| Massachusetts | 12,474 |
| New Hampshire | 705 |
| North Carolina | 667 |
| North Dakota | 681 |
| Nebraska | 3,275 |
| Nevada | 754 |
| New Jersey | 14,454 |
| New Mexico | 503 |
| New York | 232,102 |
| Ohio | 9,420 |
| Oregon | 1,394 |
| Pennsylvania | 48,218 |
| Rhode Island | 2,731 |
| South Carolina | 345 |
| South Dakota | 1,126 |
| Tennessee | 594 |
| Texas | 3,065 |
| Utah | 913 |
| Vermont | 739 |
| Virginia | 582 |
| West Virginia | 521 |
| Wisconsin | 7,507 |
| Washington | 1,214 |
| Wyoming | 454 |
| Total | 430,884 |

1,045 immigrants were returned as coming within the prohibited class; their nationalities are given in the following table:—

|  | Number. |
|---|---|
| Great Britain | 63 |
| Ireland | 71 |
| Germany | 99 |
| France | 13 |
| Russia | 193 |
| Switzerland | 14 |
| Sweden | 13 |
| Norway | 3 |
| Belgium | 3 |
| Holland | 4 |
| Italy | 387 |
| Portugal | 2 |
| Denmark | 6 |
| Hungary | 43 |
| Austria | 03 |
| Turkey | 24 |
| Greece | 4 |
| Total | 1,045 |

The landing-place of immigrants has been moved to Ellis Island in the bay about a mile from the old landing-places, Castle Garden and the Barge Office. The change was made as the island afforded greater facilities for transacting the business connected with the landing of the increasing number of immigrants.

*Labour.* There is nothing of great importance to record in regard to labour in my Consular district; the main feature is the success attending the strikes for a reduction of hours of labour. The annual reports of the various bureaux connected with labour for 1891 are not yet published. From a printed abstract of the report of the board of arbitration and mediation I learn that the number of strikes in the State of New York was in the year 6,258, of which 494 were abandoned. The strikes were mainly in regard to hours of labour and wages; in a few instances the trouble was caused by the opposition of employés to organised labour. A reduction of the hours of labour was obtained by the strikers in 2,083 instances, and in 1,941 the wages were increased. The cases where violence was used, in proportion to the number of strikes, were small, only 257 cases being reported.

The board referred to makes protest against the "sweating system" in New York and other large cities.

# NEW YORK.

Annex A.—RETURN of all Shipping at the Port of New York in the Year 1891.

**ENTERED.**

| Nationality. | Sailing. Number of Vessels. | Sailing. Tons. | Steam. Number of Vessels. | Steam. Tons. | Total. Number of Vessels. | Total. Tons. |
|---|---|---|---|---|---|---|
| British | 1,077 | 481,981 | 1,646 | 3,078,620 | 2,723 | 3,560,601 |
| American | 970 | 467,540 | 345 | 534,486 | 1,315 | 1,002,026 |
| German | 88 | 91,080 | 388 | 1,041,392 | 476 | 1,132,472 |
| French | 5 | 3,348 | 111 | 306,083 | 116 | 309,431 |
| Swedish and Norwegian | 134 | 99,700 | 248 | 144,088 | 382 | 243,788 |
| Belgian | 3 | 5,127 | 74 | 241,536 | 77 | 246,663 |
| Italian | 159 | 103,986 | 25 | 37,227 | 184 | 141,213 |
| Mexican | ... | ... | 1 | 630 | 1 | 630 |
| Dutch | 10 | 12,380 | 117 | 244,179 | 127 | 258,559 |
| Austrian | 15 | 10,875 | ... | ... | 15 | 10,875 |
| Spanish | 11 | 3,201 | 60 | 88,805 | 71 | 92,006 |
| Danish | 7 | 2,710 | 34 | 68,272 | 41 | 70,982 |
| Other European countries | 10 | 6,271 | 22 | 35,332 | 32 | 41,603 |
| South American | 1 | 530 | ... | ... | 1 | 530 |
| Central American | ... | ... | ... | ... | ... | ... |
| Other countries | ... | ... | 1 | 1,500 | 1 | 1,500 |
| Total | 2,490 | 1,288,729 | 3,072 | 5,822,150 | 5,562 | 7,110,879 |
| ,, for the year preceding | 2,864 | 1,390,397 | 2,883 | 5,245,890 | 5,747 | 6,636,287 |

**CLEARED.**

| Nationality. | Sailing. Number of Vessels. | Sailing. Tons. | Steam. Number of Vessels. | Steam. Tons. | Total. Number of Vessels. | Total. Tons. |
|---|---|---|---|---|---|---|
| British | 1,062 | 499,793 | 1,618 | 2,988,821 | 2,680 | 3,488,614 |
| American | 682 | 328,832 | 338 | 523,643 | 1,020 | 852,475 |
| German | 76 | 78,707 | 351 | 942,214 | 427 | 1,020,921 |
| French | 3 | 2,009 | 109 | 300,553 | 112 | 302,562 |
| Swedish and Norwegian | 137 | 102,030 | 257 | 149,372 | 394 | 251,402 |
| Belgian | 1 | 1,709 | 77 | 251,351 | 78 | 253,060 |
| Italian | 141 | 92,215 | 24 | 35,738 | 165 | 127,953 |
| Mexican | ... | ... | ... | ... | ... | ... |
| Dutch | 7 | 8,671 | 113 | 235,853 | 120 | 244,524 |
| Austrian | 11 | 7,974 | ... | ... | 11 | 7,974 |
| Spanish | 8 | 2,330 | 59 | 87,325 | 67 | 89,655 |
| Danish | 7 | 2,710 | 31 | 62,192 | 38 | 64,902 |
| Other European countries | 10 | 6,271 | 19 | 30,517 | 29 | 36,788 |
| South American | 4 | 2,122 | 1 | 314 | 5 | 2,436 |
| Central American | ... | ... | ... | ... | ... | ... |
| Other countries | ... | ... | ... | ... | ... | ... |
| Total | 2,149 | 1,135,373 | 2,997 | 5,607,893 | 5,146 | 6,743,266 |
| ,, for the year preceding | 2,484 | 1,352,288 | 2,653 | 4,745,825 | 5,137 | 6,098,113 |

(1328)

## UNITED STATES.

ANNEX B.—Return of the Principal Articles of Export from New York during the Years 1891-90.

| Articles. | | 1891. Quantity. | 1891. Value. | 1890. Quantity. | 1890. Value. |
|---|---|---|---|---|---|
| | | | £ | | £ |
| Agricultural implements | ... | ... | 578,150 | ... | 589,870 |
| Bacon and ham | Lbs. | 257,775,178 | 4,279,075 | 293,011,373 | 4,815,890 |
| Beef, fresh | ,, | 118,824,638 | 1,925,315 | 114,663,946 | 1,867,745 |
| ,, canned | ,, | 43,406,001 | 689,740 | 51,789,037 | 792,661 |
| ,, salted | ,, | 41,644,780 | 494,930 | ... | ... |
| Butter | ,, | 11,115,505 | 376,090 | 20,623,534 | 557,495 |
| Cattle, live | Number | 128,759 | 2,320,990 | 166,084 | 2,748,255 |
| Cotton, domestic | Packages | 221,804 | 4,752,440 | 185,630 | 2,036,315 |
| ,, raw | Bales | 813,021 | 7,853,725 | 738,963 | 7,810,735 |
| Cheese | Lbs. | 61,299,205 | 1,155,815 | 70,208,270 | 1,271,420 |
| Coffee | ,, | 5,475,793 | 183,575 | ... | ... |
| Flour | Barrels | 4,128,360 | 4,142,875 | 3,694,112 | 3,523,100 |
| Hops | Lbs. | 9,064,996 | 428,720 | 6,152,440 | 352,438 |
| Indian corn | Bushels (56 lbs.) | 13,145,268 | 1,813,790 | 23,885,541 | 2,159,820 |
| Lard | Lbs. | 279,744,291 | 3,964,310 | 335,324,851 | 4,670,606 |
| Oilcake and meal | ,, | 253,215,682 | 658,160 | 241,610,409 | 605,380 |
| Oleomargarine | ,, | 68,485,146 | 1,391,730 | 84,805,836 | 1,660,970 |
| Oats | Bushels | 2,767,993 | 253,835 | ... | ... |
| Petroleum, refined | Gallons | 365,037,924 | 5,204,430 | 399,097,169 | 6,095,170 |
| ,, crude | ,, | 38,700,384 | 508,560 | 48,101,235 | 757,550 |
| ,, lubricating | ,, | 26,779,820 | 865,190 | 27,714,259 | 870,480 |
| Pork, fresh and pickled | Lbs. | 45,539,128 | 572,430 | ... | ... |
| Rye | Bushels | 4,173,825 | 842,350 | ... | ... |
| Sewing machines | ... | ... | 568,780 | ... | 526,650 |
| Sugar | Lbs. | 55,638,725 | 579,220 | 53,406,617 | 710,130 |
| Specie and bullion | ... | ... | 19,987,630 | ... | 8,752,250 |
| Tallow | Lbs. | 43,342,109 | 461,330 | 54,329,996 | 548,850 |
| Wheat | Bushels (60 lbs.) | 45,312,553 | 10,085,270 | 12,607,484 | 2,481,443 |
| Other articles | ... | ... | 22,593,025 | ... | 31,242,537 |
| Total | ... | ... | 99,531,480 | ... | 87,447,760 |

## NEW YORK.

Annex B (continued).—RETURN of Principal Articles of Import from New York during the Years 1891–90.

| Articles. | | 1891 Quantity. | 1891 Value. | 1890 Quantity. | 1890 Value. |
|---|---|---|---|---|---|
| | | | £ | | £ |
| Cocoa | Bags | 112,851 | 522,416 | 112,162 | 446,090 |
| Coffee | ,, | 3,536,512 | 18,872,755 | 3,113,253 | 13,906,165 |
| China, glass, and earthenware | ... | ... | 1,957,230 | ... | 1,966,032 |
| Cotton | Bales | 26,964 | 442,560 | 17,967 | 274,133 |
| Dry goods— | | | | | |
|   Manufactures of cotton | ... | ... | 4,090,896 | ... | 4,981,800 |
|   ,, flax | ... | ... | 3,544,530 | ... | 3,852,485 |
|   ,, silk | ... | ... | 7,974,164 | ... | 9,996,230 |
|   ,, wool | ... | ... | 5,667,243 | ... | 8,620,205 |
|   Miscellaneous | ... | ... | 2,680,636 | ... | 2,634,746 |
| Furs | Packages | 29,110 | 1,564,505 | 23,339 | 1,371,675 |
| Fruits | ... | ... | 3,275,090 | ... | 3,582,588 |
| Hair | Packages | 26,242 | 266,123 | 27,122 | 316,992 |
| Hemp | Bales | 383,329 | 1,640,840 | 372,398 | 1,511,926 |
| Hides, dressed | ... | ... | 679,500 | ... | 696,267 |
|   ,, undressed | ... | ... | 3,986,368 | ... | 4,026,860 |
| Hops | Bales | 5,117 | 162,945 | 10,420 | 183,982 |
| Indiarubber | ... | ... | 3,209,760 | ... | 3,164,378 |
| Jewellery, watches, and precious stones | ... | ... | 2,687,530 | ... | 2,951,468 |
| Jute and jute butts | ... | ... | 570,930 | ... | 605,350 |
| Linseed | ... | ... | 164,666 | ... | 488,130 |
| Molasses | ... | ... | 132,887 | ... | 251,115 |
| Paper stock | ... | ... | 498,055 | ... | 513,034 |
| Metals— | | | | | |
|   Cutlery | ... | ... | 218,020 | ... | 445,897 |
|   Iron, pig | Tons | 6,521 | 19,494 | 11,965 | 53,546 |
|   ,, spiegel | ,, | 30,554 | 146,507 | 84,074 | 479,018 |
|   ,, other | ... | ... | 275,080 | ... | 196,432 |
|   Metal goods | ... | ... | 831,828 | ... | 520,945 |
|   Steel | ... | ... | 363,310 | ... | 493,490 |
|   Tin plates | Boxes | 2,598,530 | 2,402,254 | 2,365,488 | 2,016,750 |
|   ,, slabs | Tons | 16,158 | 1,506,417 | 13,864 | 1,070,790 |
| Soda ash | ... | ... | 369,595 | ... | 351,285 |
|   ,, caustic | ... | ... | 189,950 | ... | 196,233 |
| Spices | ... | ... | 536,570 | ... | 584,056 |
| Stationery and books | ... | ... | 1,161,000 | ... | 1,190,712 |
| Sugar | Tons | ... | 10,077,600 | 704,507 | 8,612,609 |
| Specie and bullion | ... | ... | 7,241,200 | ... | 4,196,220 |
| Tea | Packages | 1,181,937 | 1,953,290 | 1,248,858 | 2,060,855 |
| Tobacco and cigars | ... | ... | 1,523,500 | ... | 3,494,498 |
| Wines, spirits, &c. | ... | ... | 2,084,070 | ... | 2,246,006 |
| Wood | ... | ... | 1,120,280 | ... | 1,024,783 |
| Wool | Lbs. | 53,432,550 | 1,205,495 | 43,205,565 | 1,085,474 |
| Other articles | ... | ... | 16,851,246 | ... | 23,132,690 |
| Total | ... | ... | 114,668,335 | ... | 119,703,940 |

(1328)

Annex C.—TABLE showing the Total Value of all Articles Exported from and Imported to New York to and from Foreign Countries during the Years 1891–90.

| Country. | Exports. 1891. | Exports. 1890. | Imports. 1891. | Imports. 1890. |
|---|---|---|---|---|
| | £ | £ | £ | £ |
| Great Britain and Ireland | 45,158,400 | 42,879,435 | 22,924,735 | 26,406,675 |
| British possessions | 6,595,235 | 6,024,545 | 7,753,445 | 7,895,215 |
| Germany | 10,404,320 | 8,185,285 | 14,720,350 | 18,781,715 |
| France and possessions | 9,219,230 | 4,302,855 | 14,613,660 | 15,529,990 |
| Belgium | 5,596,360 | 3,386,545 | 1,548,860 | 1,470,050 |
| Spain and possessions | 4,069,375 | 4,695,915 | 8,657,890 | 9,038,170 |
| Netherlands and possessions | 4,028,950 | 3,831,735 | 2,345,980 | 4,064,380 |
| United States of Colombia | 590,620 | 574,000 | 1,162,695 | 1,948,160 |
| Central American States | 738,585 | 799,525 | 813,435 | 826,605 |
| Italy | 1,132,445 | 1,177,015 | 3,352,400 | 3,515,935 |
| Brazil | 1,779,850 | 1,604,970 | 18,144,015 | 12,012,715 |
| China | 1,597,030 | 930,510 | 2,625,820 | 2,352,400 |
| Denmark and possessions | 1,012,840 | 716,285 | 112,330 | 190,025 |
| Venezuela | 1,439,055 | 1,549,110 | 2,549,405 | 2,045,475 |
| Portugal and possessions | 861,630 | 766,940 | 305,095 | 255,140 |
| Argentine Republic | 283,460 | 636,645 | 483,030 | 559,255 |
| Mexico | 970,950 | 877,255 | 2,146,315 | 2,027,040 |
| Hayti | 1,170,430 | 1,651,405 | 552,365 | 478,620 |
| Sweden and Norway | 966,235 | 526,515 | 483,530 | 520,805 |
| Japan | 388,955 | 500,900 | 1,526,540 | 1,349,110 |
| Chile | 328,030 | 538,465 | 347,115 | 463,260 |
| San Domingo | 203,045 | 218,015 | 309,990 | 539,580 |
| Uruguay | 178,435 | 245,420 | 250,070 | 382,500 |
| Austria | 152,540 | 87,460 | 1,840,260 | 2,037,450 |
| Russia | 87,420 | 68,140 | 844,055 | 615,580 |
| Peru | 198,155 | 299,155 | 68,515 | 82,975 |
| Switzerland | 9,050 | 5,775 | 2,454,245 | 3,002,675 |
| Other countries | 370,850 | 367,940 | 1,732,190 | 1,312,440 |
| Total | 99,531,480 | 87,447,760 | 114,668,335 | 119,703,940 |

## NEW YORK.

The specie included in the tables was exported to and imported from the following countries during the years 1891–90:—

| Country. | Exports. 1891. | Exports. 1890. | Imports. 1891. | Imports. 1890. |
|---|---|---|---|---|
| | £ | £ | £ | £ |
| Great Britain, &c. | 11,418,330 | 6,394,770 | 2,527,000 | 1,057,770 |
| France | 3,702,210 | 236,320 | 2,437,415 | 469,445 |
| Germany | 3,509,410 | 571,905 | 845,465 | 1,045,030 |
| West Indies | 753,245 | 282,415 | 716,945 | 85,740 |
| Mexico | 11,785 | 2,080 | 243,240 | 190,915 |
| South America | 552,900 | 522,340 | 250,850 | 599,690 |
| Other countries | 39,750 | 742,420 | 220,285 | 747,620 |
| Total | 19,987,630 | 8,752,250 | 7,241,200 | 4,196,220 |

## PROVIDENCE, R.I.

### ABSTRACT of Contents.

|   | PAGE |
|---|---|
| General remarks— | |
|   General review | 19 |
|   Port statistics | 19 |
| Trade and manufactures— | |
|   Cotton and cotton goods | 20 |
|   Wool and woollens | 21 |
|   Jewellery | 21 |
|   Machinery | 22 |
| Public improvements— | |
|   City progress and improvement | 22 |
| Annexes— | |
|   Return of shipping (Annex A) | 23 |
|   „ exports (Annex B) | 23 |
|   „ imports ( „ ) | 23 |
|   „ exports and imports (Annex C) | 24 |

### General Remarks.

Mr. Vice-Consul Stockwell reports as follows:—

*General report on trade.* During the year 1891 no features especially prominent marked the history, commercial or otherwise, of the State of Rhode Island and Providence plantations.

The volume of business was larger than that of the previous year, but the increase came from natural growth rather than from any quickening of the pulse of trade. The bank clearings in 1890 aggregated 55,017,100*l*., and in 1891 57,331,285*l*., showing an increase in the year 1891 of 2,314,185*l*. During the month of October, 1891, the clearings amounted to 6,124,500*l*.

*Port statistics.* The total number of vessels arriving at the port of Providence from foreign countries during the year 1891 was 110, of which

36 were American. Ships from foreign countries brought the following merchandise:—

| Articles. | | Quantity. |
|---|---|---|
| Lumber .. .. .. .. | Feet .. | 4,508,750 |
| Pickets .. .. .. .. | Pieces .. | 22,460 |
| Coal .. .. .. .. | Tons .. | 866 |
| Salt .. .. .. .. .. | Barrels .. | 8,756,568 |
| Fustic .. .. .. .. | Tons .. | 110 |
| Potato starch .. .. .. | Casks .. | 933 |
| Piling .. .. .. .. | Pieces .. | 6,671 |
| Laths .. .. .. .. | " .. | 15,819,000 |
| Shingles .. .. .. .. | .. | 18,012,000 |
| Logwood .. .. .. .. | Tons .. | 4,099 |
| Rubber .. .. .. .. | Lbs. .. | 731,231 |

The duties collected in the year 1891 amounted to 72,100*l.* All receipts 74,645*l.*; tonnage of the port, sailing vessels, 77, tonnage, 9,790·20 tons; steam vessels, 38, tonnage, 21,240·9 tons.

*Trade and Manufactures.*

Cottons.

During the year 1891 205,589 bales of cotton were received in this market, against 169,190 bales in 1890. This may not show an increase in cotton manufacturing. The low price of cotton led manufacturers to buy largely in excess of present requirements, for it was believed that prices would not decline further. The increase in sales was in the finer grades.

The dividends of New England mills averaged about one-third less than in 1890, and the dividends of 1890 were one-fourth less than those of 1889. This tells the story of cotton manufacturing in New England.

Prices of cotton, yearly extremes, in the Providence market since 1880—

| | Cents. | |
|---|---|---|
| 1881 .. .. .. .. .. .. .. | 11 to | $12\frac{3}{4}$ |
| 1882 .. .. .. .. .. .. .. | $10\frac{3}{4}$ | $13\frac{3}{8}$ |
| 1883 .. .. .. .. .. .. .. | $10\frac{1}{2}$ | $11\frac{1}{4}$ |
| 1884 .. .. .. .. .. .. .. | $10\frac{1}{4}$ | $12\frac{5}{8}$ |
| 1885 .. .. .. .. .. .. .. | $9\frac{3}{4}$ | $11\frac{5}{8}$ |
| 1886 .. .. .. .. .. .. .. | $9\frac{3}{8}$ | $10\frac{1}{8}$ |
| 1887 .. .. .. .. .. .. .. | $9\frac{1}{2}$ | $11\frac{1}{2}$ |
| 1888 .. .. .. .. .. .. .. | $10\frac{1}{8}$ | $11\frac{3}{8}$ |
| 1889 .. .. .. .. .. .. .. | $10\frac{3}{8}$ | $11\frac{7}{8}$ |
| 1890 .. .. .. .. .. .. .. | 10 | $12\frac{3}{4}$ |
| 1891 .. .. .. .. .. .. .. | $8\frac{1}{4}$ | $10\frac{1}{4}$ |

The print cloth manufacturers made a little profit during the year. Although the prices ruled low, yet the low price of cotton made profit, what there was, possible. In January, 1891, 64's were quoted at $3\frac{1}{16}$ c., one-quarter off. In November the price was $2\frac{15}{16}$ c., one off, but at the close of the year the price rallied to $3\frac{1}{16}$ c. net, when the stocks on hand were the lowest since 1881. At the close of the year there were only 170,000 pieces of 64's on hand, against 282,000 pieces at the close of 1890. The demand at the end of the year compensated in a measure for the lack of it.

The history of woollen manufacture during the year 1891 was not satisfactory to the sellers. Large importations of woollens and over-production in anticipation of the effect of the McKinley Tariff Bill over-stocked the market.

*Woollen goods and worsteds.*

The worsted trade has been fairly profitable. The demand was good generally, at least better than during the preceding year. There have been large importations of the cheaper grades of worsted, and as foreign manufacturers can buy wool at lower prices, American manufacturers do not attempt to compete with the lower grade of the worsted product. There is also close competition between the western and the eastern manufacturer which tends to lower the price.

As a whole the year has been unsatisfactory to woollen manufacturers. The weather is a factor. In the latitude of Providence (latitude 41° 49' 26") if not throughout lower New England and in some other parts of the country there has been for several years little cold weather, and the demand for clothing woollens has fallen off in consequence.

Of the wool market at this port what is true in one year is usually true in another. There is little change, and the market is controlled by the Boston market. The market has been a little more active in sympathy with other markets than it was last year. There has been an increased sale of foreign wools, chiefly the Australian fleeces. The reason given is that domestic fleeces of some grades contain so much refuse that it is cheaper to buy the Australian wools.

This is one of the great industries of Rhode Island, confined to the City of Providence, being the largest, or next to the largest (Newark) in the country. It is an up and down business, and, while all are employed a part of the year, perhaps half, yet during the other part a large number—the greater number—are idle.

*Jewellery.*

To the workman who spends as fast as he earns the jewellery business is not adapted, for, figuratively speaking, he lives on the fat of the land a part of the year and nearly starves the rest of the year.

Englishmen and Germans (jewellers) who had a sure thing at home should have kept it, small, comparatively, as might have been the income. They learned that 18 dol. to 25 dol. a week (3l. 15s. to 5l.) could be earned here, and they came to find too late that labour, especially to foreigners, was given only a part of the year, and that they must depend upon charity the rest of the year, as shown not by one case but many.

The cause of this intermittent manufacture of jewellery is due to the fact, proclaimed by actual statistics, that this country has a manufacturing capacity to supply 100,000,000 people, while the country has only 65,000,000 people, counting every man, woman, and child to wear jewellery. The importations of jewellery are, and have been, large, but they are falling-off.

The importations of jewellery for the ten months ended October 1, 1891, were valued at 2,258,640*l.*, and in 1890, same period, the value was 2,672,695*l.* But there will be a greater falling-off in the future, probably owing to the effect of the McKinley Tariff Bill.

The exports of jewellery for ten months ended October 1, 1891, were valued at only 119,850*l.*, against 136,370*l.* in 1890. Considering the over-supply and the importations, the flooding of the market, the interruption of manufacture is accounted for.

*Machinery.* The manufacture of tools, machinery, and locomotives was uninterrupted during the year. The product of this market goes to many countries. The Corliss engine is made here, and is accepted throughout the world as the most perfect engine. The engines were sold originally on this plan: the inventor, the Hon. George H. Corliss, offered to sell his engine for the amount saved in fuel, for a given time, by the substitution of his engine, and many were sold on this basis. There are several machine shops here, employing each about 1,000 workmen, and they have not been idle during the year.

*Public improvements.* Two great public improvements—a new system of sewerage and new terminal railway facilities—are nearing completion. The new railway station here will be one of the finest in the country. A new post-office building and a new custom-house are proposed, and a Bill has been introduced into Congress to provide for the purchase of land and the erection of buildings.

The State of Rhode Island proposes to erect a new State House, as the old one has been in use since 1760, or about that time, and has been too small for many years to accommodate the State's business, several offices being in outside buildings. The plans have been made and presented, and the Commission appointed for the purpose has selected one, and will submit to the General Assembly at the present Session. The building is to cost 1,000,000 dol.

During the year electric cars, trolley system, were introduced between the city proper and a suburb. We have now cable cars and electric cars. These improvements have led to many new structures along the route of each line. In this fast age people cannot wait for horses. Rapid transit is the cry and demand, and we have it.

The increase in building was very large during the year, and the lumber market was active. The city was never in a more prosperous condition than at present, and never more desirable in city or suburb as a place of residence.

## Annex A.—Return of all Shipping at the Port of Providence in the Year 1891.

### Entered.

| Nationality. | Sailing. Number of Vessels. | Sailing. Tons. | Steam. Number of Vessels. | Steam. Tons. | Total. Number of Vessels. | Total. Tons. |
|---|---|---|---|---|---|---|
| British | 74 | 7,392 | ... | ... | ... | ... |
| American | 36 | 9,387 | ... | ... | ... | ... |
| Total | 110 | 16,779 | ... | ... | ... | ... |
| ,, for the year preceding | 139 | 18,531 | ... | ... | ... | ... |

### Cleared.

| Nationality. | Sailing. Number of Vessels. | Sailing. Tons. | Steam. Number of Vessels. | Steam. Tons. | Total. Number of Vessels. | Total. Tons. |
|---|---|---|---|---|---|---|
| British | 69 | 6,003 | 1 | 35 | 70 | 6,038 |
| American | 6 | 1,785 | ... | ... | 6 | 1,782 |
| Total | 75 | 7,788 | 1 | 35 | 76 | 7,820 |
| ,, for the year preceding | 107 | 9,140 | ... | ... | ... | ... |

## Annex B.—Return of the Principal Articles of Export from Providence during the Years 1891–90.

| Articles. | | 1891. Quantity. | 1891. Value. | 1890. Quantity. | 1890. Value. |
|---|---|---|---|---|---|
| | | | £ | | £ |
| Vessel | ... | ... | 500 | ... | 413 |
| Lumber | Feet | 22,968 | 45 | ... | ... |
| Fish | Barrels | 27 | 12 | ... | ... |
| Furniture | ... | ... | 8 | ... | ... |
| Provisions | ... | ... | 6 | ... | ... |
| Coal | Tons | ... | ... | 16 | 15 |
| Total | ... | ... | 571 | ... | 428 |

## Return of Principal Articles of Import into Providence during the Years 1891–90.

| Articles. | Value. 1891. | Value. 1890. |
|---|---|---|
| | £ | £ |
| Dry goods | 41,115 | 39,210 |
| Chemicals | 22,759 | 25,707 |
| Metals | 52,919 | 27,195 |
| Rubber | 107,183 | 28,188 |
| Others | 67,409 | 70,572 |
| Total | 291,385 | 190,872 |

(1328)

Annex C.—TABLE showing the Total Value of all Articles Exported from Providence and Imported into Providence from and to all Countries during the Years 1891-90.

| Country. | Exports. 1891. | Exports. 1890. | Imports. 1891. | Imports. 1890. |
|---|---|---|---|---|
| | £ | £ | £ | £ |
| Austria | .. | .. | 3,691 | 4,128 |
| Belgium | .. | .. | 7,200 | 556 |
| Brazil | .. | .. | 107,992 | 28,258 |
| British West Indies | .. | .. | 12,784 | 14,198 |
| Canada | 71 | 428 | 12,637 | 13,239 |
| Cuba | .. | .. | 6,366 | 12,509 |
| Dutch West Indies | .. | .. | 334 | .. |
| England | .. | .. | 70,401 | 71,544 |
| France | .. | .. | 26,831 | 18,907 |
| Germany | .. | .. | 18,675 | 7,443 |
| Greece | .. | .. | 20 | .. |
| Hayti | .. | .. | 6,012 | 310 |
| Ireland | .. | .. | 637 | 207 |
| Italy | .. | .. | 333 | 2,385 |
| Madeira Islands | .. | .. | 2,758 | .. |
| Netherlands | .. | .. | 752 | 428 |
| Newfoundland | 500 | .. | .. | .. |
| Portugal | .. | .. | .. | 247 |
| Scotland | .. | .. | 3,275 | 1,318 |
| Spain | .. | .. | 57 | 372 |
| Sweden | .. | .. | 7,200 | .. |
| Switzerland | .. | .. | 3,430 | 3,803 |
| All others.. | .. | .. | .. | 20 |
| Total | 571 | 428 | 291,385 | 190,872 |

# NEW YORK.

RETURN of the number of Seamen who have been Engaged, Discharged, Left Behind, Reported Dead, or Deserted, or who have been relieved at the British Consulate-General, New York, and showing the total number of British and Foreign sailors who were Engaged, Discharged, &c., from British ships, with the Amount of Wages paid at the Consulate to Seamen on discharge from their Ships and from Hospital or Jail, and also showing the number of new Agreements entered into during the Year 1891.

| | | Seamen. | | | | | | | | Nationality. | | | Wages. | | | Agreements. |
|---|---|---|---|---|---|---|---|---|---|---|---|---|---|---|---|---|
| Engaged. | Discharged. | Left Behind. | | | Dead. | | | Deserted. | Relieved. | British. | Foreign. | Total Number of Seamen. | Paid on Discharge from Vessels. | Paid on Discharge from Hospital or Jail. | Total Wages Paid. | Number Opened. |
| | | In Hospital. | In Jail. | Total. | At Sea. | On Shore. | Total. | | | | | | Dol. c. | Dol. c. | Dol. c. | |
| 12,266 | 9,767 | 194 | 14 | 208 | 59 | 33 | 92 | 2,910 | 221 | 14,324 | 11,140 | 25,464 | 430,601 41 | 5,303 14 | 435,904 55 | 281 |

LONDON :
Printed for Her Majesty's Stationery Office,
By HARRISON AND SONS,
Printers in Ordinary to Her Majesty.
(75   7 | 92—H & S   1344)

# FOREIGN OFFICE.
## 1892.
## ANNUAL SERIES.

### N.º 1081.
### DIPLOMATIC AND CONSULAR REPORTS ON TRADE AND FINANCE.

# UNITED STATES.

### REPORT FOR THE YEAR 1891
#### ON THE
### AGRICULTURE OF THE CONSULAR DISTRICT OF SAN FRANCISCO.

REFERENCE TO PREVIOUS REPORT, Annual Series No. 910.

*Issued during the Recess and Presented to both Houses of Parliament by Command of Her Majesty.*

LONDON:
PRINTED FOR HER MAJESTY'S STATIONERY OFFICE,
BY HARRISON AND SONS, ST. MARTIN'S LANE,
PRINTERS IN ORDINARY TO HER MAJESTY.

And to be purchased, either directly or through any Bookseller, from
EYRE & SPOTTISWOODE, EAST HARDING STREET, FLEET STREET, E.C., and
32, ABINGDON STREET, WESTMINSTER, S.W.; or
JOHN MENZIES & Co., 12, HANOVER STREET, EDINBURGH, and
90, WEST NILE STREET, GLASGOW; or
HODGES, FIGGIS, & Co., 104, GRAFTON STREET, DUBLIN.

1892

[C. 6812–6.]   *Price Three Halfpence.*

# New Series of Reports.

Reports of the Annual Series have been issued from Her Majesty's Diplomatic and Consular Officers at the following places, and may be obtained from the sources indicated on the title-page:—

| No. | | Price. | No. | | Price. |
|---|---|---|---|---|---|
| 959. | Odessa | 1d. | 1020. | Mogador | 1d. |
| 960. | Copenhagen | 9d. | 1021. | Adrianople | ½d. |
| 961. | Tokio | 1d. | 1022. | Tripoli | 1d. |
| 962. | Salonica | 1½d. | 1023. | Jerusalem | 1d. |
| 963. | Stettin | 3½d. | 1024. | Odessa | 6d. |
| 964. | Philadelphia | 2d. | 1025. | Genoa | 1½d. |
| 965. | Mexico | 2d. | 1026. | Kiungchow | 1d. |
| 966. | Malaga | 2½d. | 1027. | Batoum | 4½d. |
| 967. | Berne | 1d. | 1028. | Buenos Ayres | 1d. |
| 968. | Puerto Rico | ½d. | 1029. | Batavia | 1d. |
| 969. | Buda-Pesth | 1d. | 1030. | Santo Domingo | ½d. |
| 970. | Bogotá | 1d. | 1031. | San José | 1d. |
| 971. | Panama | 1½d. | 1032. | Manila | 1½d. |
| 972. | Munich | 2d. | 1033. | Marseilles | 1d. |
| 973. | Copenhagen | 4d. | 1034. | Swatow | 1d. |
| 974. | Guatemala | 1d. | 1035. | Paris | 1d. |
| 975. | Munich | 2d. | 1036. | Ichang | 5d. |
| 976. | Meshed | 1½d. | 1037. | Pakhoi | 1d. |
| 977. | Para | ½d. | 1038. | Foochow | 1d. |
| 978. | Florence | 1d. | 1039. | Brest | 1d. |
| 979. | The Hague | 1½d. | 1040. | Madeira | ½d. |
| 980. | Patras | 1d. | 1041. | Antwerp | 1½d. |
| 981. | Paris | 1½d. | 1042. | Taganrog | 2½d. |
| 982. | Zanzibar | 2½d. | 1043. | Algiers | 2½d. |
| 983. | Buenos Ayres | ½d. | 1044. | Hankow | 1½d. |
| 984. | Copenhagen | 1d. | 1045. | Nantes | 1½d. |
| 985. | Stuttgart | 1d. | 1046. | Belgrade | 2d. |
| 986. | New Orleans | 1½d. | 1047. | Fiume | 1d. |
| 987. | New Orleans | 10d. | 1048. | Wuhu | 1d. |
| 988. | Suakin | ½d. | 1049. | Cagliari | 1d. |
| 989. | Galveston | 1½d. | 1050. | Erzeroum | 1d. |
| 990. | Berlin | 1d. | 1051. | Syra | 1d. |
| 991. | Zanzibar | 1½d. | 1052. | Cherbourg | 1d. |
| 992. | Guayaquil | 1d. | 1053. | Lima | 1d. |
| 993. | Tonga | 1d. | 1054. | Bilbao | 1½d. |
| 994. | New Orleans | 1d. | 1055. | Cadiz | 2d. |
| 995. | Mozambique | 1½d. | 1056. | Corunna | 2½d. |
| 996. | Galatz | 1½d. | 1057. | Saigon | 1d. |
| 997. | Nantes | 1½d. | 1058. | Port-au-Prince | 1d. |
| 998. | Algiers | 1d. | 1059. | Trebizond | 1d. |
| 999. | Havre | 2½d. | 1060. | Barcelona | 1½d. |
| 1000. | Buenos Ayres | 6d. | 1061. | Tainan | 1d. |
| 1001. | Baltimore | 1½d. | 1062. | Smyrna | 1½d. |
| 1002. | Taganrog | 1d. | 1063. | Old Calabar | ½d. |
| 1003. | Riga | 2d. | 1064. | Samoa | ½d. |
| 1004. | Bordeaux | 2½d. | 1065. | Tahiti | 1d. |
| 1005. | The Hague | 1½d. | 1066. | Chefoo | 6d. |
| 1006. | Paraguay | 1½d. | 1067. | Gothenburg | 2d. |
| 1007. | Constantinople | 1½d. | 1068. | Buenos Ayres | 1½d. |
| 1008. | Rome | 1d. | 1069. | Loanda | 1½d. |
| 1009. | Mozambique | 1d. | 1070. | Guatemala | 1d. |
| 1010. | Wênchow | 1d. | 1071. | Zanzibar | 1d. |
| 1011. | Mogador | 2½d. | 1072. | Charleston | 2½d. |
| 1012. | Amoy | 1d. | 1073. | Nice | 1d. |
| 1013. | Kiukiang | 1d. | 1074. | Caracas | 1d. |
| 1014. | Stettin | 1½d. | 1075. | Lisbon | 2d. |
| 1015. | Boston | 1d. | 1076. | Calais | 2d. |
| 1016. | Callao | 1d. | 1077. | Rio Grande do Sul | 5½d. |
| 1017. | Aleppo | 1d. | 1078. | Philadelphia | 2½d. |
| 1018. | Santos | 2½d. | 1079. | Brindisi | 2d. |
| 1019. | Piræus | 1d. | 1080. | New York | 1d. |

# No. 1081.

*Reference to previous Report, Annual Series No. 910.*

## UNITED STATES.

### SAN FRANCISCO

*Consul Donohoe to the Marquis of Salisbury.*

My Lord,   San Francisco, May 11, 1892.

I HAVE the honour to enclose herewith a Report on Agricultural matters from this Consulate, which has been prepared by Mr. Vice-Consul Moore, and Reports from the Vice-Consulates at Portland, Port Townsend, and Los Angeles, for the year 1891.

No Reports will be furnished this year by the Vice-Consuls at Astoria and San Diego.

I have, &c.
(Signed)   DENIS DONOHOE.

---

*Report on Agriculture for San Francisco for 1891.*

### ABSTRACT of Contents.

| | PAGE |
|---|---|
| San Francisco Consulate— | |
| Cereals; fruits; olives; walnuts, &c. | 2 |
| Wine and brandy | 3 |
| Hops; wool; sheep | 6 |
| Cattle; horses; vegetables; advice to settlers | 7 |
| Raisins; fruit diseases | 8 |
| Portland Vice-Consulate— | |
| Cereals | 9–10 |
| Fruit; hops; sheep and wool | 11 |
| Port Townsend Vice-Consulate— | |
| Cereals; vegetables | 12 |
| Hay; hops; fruits; live stock | 13 |
| Swine and swine diseases; prices | 14 |
| Los Angeles Vice-Consulate— | |
| Alfalfa | 14 |
| Vegetables; cereals | 15 |

(1344)

## UNITED STATES.

**Wheat.** Notwithstanding the general complaints of business men as to the dulness of trade in 1891, the year proved a prosperous one generally for the agricultural interest of the State.

The crops of cereals were large, and realised high prices owing to the partial failure of similar crops in Europe. The amount of wheat produced in the State is estimated at 33,000,000 bushels. The average value per cental on board ship was 6s. 8d., or about 1s. 3d. higher than in 1890. The great feature of the wheat business during the year was the unprecedented amount shipped direct to France.

**Barley.** The crop of barley is estimated at 10,000,000 bushels, and prices have been very good.

**Fruits.** The overland exports of fruit by rail viâ the Southern Pacific Railway in 1891 were as follows:—

|   |   | Lbs. |
|---|---|---|
| Green fruit | .. | 109,367,710 |
| Canned „ | .. | 46,334,080 |
| Dried „ | .. | 58,000,240 |
| Raisins .. | .. | 36,657,710 |
| Total | .. | 250,359,740 |

This shows a considerable increase over 1890, when the shipments over the same line reached 234,965,050 lbs.

**Fruit crop.** The crop produced in 1891 was larger than the year preceding, but the prices obtained were very much less. It was especially abundant in peaches and apricots, while in cherries and most of the varieties of berries it was short. Prunes were a fair average, and the system of drying them has so greatly improved that they are likely to prove a serious rival to the French product, which has so long been unapproachable. Our raisin and dried fruit crop generally was greater than ever before. The local market was demoralised, large quantities of green fruit being sold for little or nothing. The shipment of oranges reached 1,200,000 boxes, valued at 2,400,000 dol.

**Olive culture and oil.** The culture of the olive is extending. A portion of the crop is preserved for the table, but the bulk is manufactured into oil, which is of good quality. The trees do not become productive until they are about 8 years old. The product of olive oil for the last 4 years is given as follows:—

|   |   | Gallons. |
|---|---|---|
| 1888 | .. | 590 |
| 1889 | .. | 1,142 |
| 1890 | .. | 5,202 |
| 1891 | .. | 11,011 |

**Walnuts.** English walnuts do well in the southern portion of the State, and about Ventura there are trees whose individual crops have sold as high as 12l. 7s. 11d. The French varieties have been tried, and are said to be larger bearers.

**Raisins.** The estimated pack for 1891 is put down as 2,000,000 boxes, against 1,500,000 boxes for 1890. The bulk of the crop continues to be sent to the Eastern States, where it is gradually supplanting the imported article. Every year sees a large increase of land planted with raisin vines, and it is possible that at no distant period competition will bring down prices to an unremunerative basis, especially as the local consumption is limited and the transportation charges to the Eastern States heavy.

Receipts of wine and brandy in this city for the past 13 years compare as follows:— *Wine and brandy.*

| Year. | Quantity. | |
|---|---|---|
| | Wine. | Brandy. |
| | Gallons. | Gallons. |
| 1891 | 12,810,675 | 701,125 |
| 1890 | 11,171,641 | 590,173 |
| 1889 | 10,452,301 | 497,108 |
| 1888 | 8,871,312 | 237,099 |
| 1887 | 8,502,028 | 246,306 |
| 1886 | 6,155,408 | 180,453 |
| 1885 | 5,895,110 | 157,152 |
| 1884 | 4,818,439 | 112,265 |
| 1883 | 4,858,628 | 131,711 |
| 1882 | 4,430,095 | 133,956 |
| 1881 | 4,935,222 | 150,028 |
| 1880 | 3,588,904 | 133,725 |
| 1879 | 3,364,607 | 94,768 |

There has been a very satisfactory increase in the trade as shown by the fact that the receipts for 1891 have been 15 per cent. to 16 per cent. over those of 1890. It is of course not likely that the trade would continue to increase at this rate. Although receipts have doubled in four years we must not expect that they will increase at the same rate in future years, as the returns to the grower do not appear to be in all cases satisfactory. In wine, however, everything depends upon quality. What we need is to produce better wine and brandies rather than to increase the amount of the vintage. When this is done prices will be much better than they have been, as the world has not any surplus of good wines, and those of the requisite quality will always find a market. Another thing required is more knowledge on the part of the vineyardist. Prices have been low the past three years, and this has created a deep-seated dissatisfaction on the part of the grape-grower. During the year steps were taken to enable the country wine-makers to market their own product; but I have not heard of any results as yet. The complaint is that the middle man as the wine merchant makes the money, and that the vineyardist has to do with little or no profit. Some have talked of rooting up their vines. In a few cases this I believe has been done. All this will, however, right itself in due time. The receipts of wine in this city for the year, added to the exports from the

*Increase in wine trade.*

*Better quality require*

interior, make 15,041,121 gallons for 1891. Adding to this receipts of brandy and shipments from interior points converted into wine, we have a total equal to 20,211,345 gallons arriving in this market or shipped from the interior in the past year. For 1890 these figures represented 16,750,000 gallons. It is evident that the whole of the vintage of 1891 has thus in some method been disposed of. There is, however, a difference of about 4,000,000 gallons between receipts and shipments from this city. For the same time in 1889 wine receipts were 5,295,825 gallons, showing a gain of over 1,250,000 gallons in two years. For the same time in 1889 brandy receipts were 194,644 gallons, showing an increase of nearly double the quantity in two years. This shows that the advice to wine-makers to distil their products into brandy has not been altogether thrown away. Making due allowance for the quantity of wine taken to manufacture brandy, we received during the first 6 months of the year the equivalent of 8,613,957 gallons. If we add to that shipments from the interior, we have held the disposition of 11,269,874 gallons, not to speak of the consumption of the State and coast itself, which almost equals 1,250,000 gallons. We have thus had the disposition of 12,500,000 gallons during the half year. Of the wine and brandy received in this city, the equivalent of 8,323,307 gallons has been shipped by sea and rail.

It would appear from the facts here given that the equivalent of the vintage of 1890 has been pretty effectively disposed of. The yield for 1891 is stated to be as follows:—

|  | Gallons. |
| --- | --- |
| Napa | 4,000,000 |
| Sanoma | 2,500,000 |
| Santa Clara | 2,500,000 |
| Alameda and Contra Costa | 1,750,000 |
| Presno | 3,000,000 |
| Los Angeles and Santa Barbara | 1,500,000 |
| Sacramento | 1,600,000 |
| San Joaquin | 900,000 |
| Santa Cruz | 500,000 |
| Other counties | 1,700,000 |
| Total | 19,950,000 |

The low price of grapes formed a subject of much dissatisfaction during the year, though prospects at present are much better for viticulturists and others than they have been. In May a syndicate with a capital of 120,000*l*. was formed to ship must from this State to England and France, where it was to be made into brandy. A great champagne manufacturing company is also on the boards.

The retiring viticultural officer, C. A. Wetmore, outlined a plan by which wine-growers in the various districts might co-operate to relieve the market. Mr. Wetmore's scheme was for the delivery of grapes to a trustee in each district under contracts, the trustee being authorised to form a company, and distil the grapes. After the sale of the product the distillery, plant, and

## SAN FRANCISCO.

fixtures are to be transferred to the company, and stock issued to those who furnished grapes. 3,099*l*. 3*s*. 6*d*. would probably cover the cost of the plant, and 2,000 tons of grapes would realise as brandy, say, 4,132*l*. 4*s*. 7*d*. Each stockholder would thus have good collateral.

*New regulations.* The new regulations of the Internal Revenue Department during the year favoured the wine makers. One of them provided that a separate room must be assigned in each winery for fortification purposes, and this room must be bonded. All sweet wines will be fortified therein. Pipes will convey the freshly-made wine into vats located in the bonded rooms, and the flow may be stopped by the United States gaugers in charge, who will have keys to the room, and a means of shutting off the wine whenever they so desire. This is the only method under which brandy with the tax unpaid will be allowed to be used in fortifying sweet wines. Another privilege the manufacturers will have under the new regulations will be that of returning the fortified wine to the winery, where it will be allowed to remain until the full process of manufacture has been completed. A regulation providing that the fortification process cannot be used in any winery not situated at a vineyard will be strictly enforced by the revenue officials who are authorised to seize any wine fortified with brandy, with the tax unpaid, in any other establishment. The owner may purchase fresh grapes wherever he chooses. The juice of grapes crushed elsewhere than at the winery cannot be used. Wine makers must report to the Office of Internal Revenue at certain intervals the quantity of grapes they have produced. There will be a special department attached to the office of the revenue collector, where apparatus will be provided for analysing wines to determine their saccharine and alcoholic proportions. The bonded room must be entirely separate from the winery. The entrance will be secured by Government seals, and egress and ingress will be controlled by special officers.

*Foreign demand for wine.* The demand for our wine from abroad has been very large. We shipped a considerable quantity to Germany, whence also comes a demand for our brandy. It is said that there will be an increase of about 1,000,000 gallons, due to vineyards coming into bearing. Our wine is improved in colour and quality due to more care in treatment, one-half sound, one-half defect; defect due to bad fermentation and inferior fruit. Prices were 15 per cent. better. There was greater demand for finer wines. Mission and Malvoisie were used for distillation.

*Prices of grapes.* Prices of grapes have been:—1*l*. 4*s*. 9*d*., 1*l*. 17*s*. 2*d*., and 2*l*. 1*s*. 4*d*. per ton for mission; 2*l*. 1*s*. 4*d*., 2*l*. 9*s*. 7*d*., and 2*l*. 13*s*. 8*d*. per ton for zinfaudel; 2*l*. 1*s*. 4*d*. and 3*l*. 2*s*. per ton for reisling and burgundy; 5*l*. 3*s*. 3*d*. to 7*l*. 4*s*. 7*d*. for sauterne and medoc.

*Foreign shipments.* The demand for the best qualities of wine is increasing. It is going mostly to France and England. Our brandy goes principally to Hamburg and Bremen. The foreign demand for our wines is likely to be checked by the increase of 15 per cent. duty in France. Prices on dry wines are lower on

(1344)

account of large production. In sweet wines prices are higher, because the demand exceeds the supply. California brands are in greater demand. Brandies command better prices, and are in greater demand. Wines at low prices are being distilled into brandy. We quote dry wines, new, at 7$d$. to 8½$d$.; old, 10$d$. to 13½$d$., naked without cooperage; mission wines, 6½$d$. to 7$d$; foreign, 7$d$. to 8½$d$. per gallon; grapes, 2$l$. 9$s$. 7$d$. to 3$l$. 2$s$. per ton; mission, 2$l$. 1$s$. 4$d$. to 2$l$. 9$s$. 7$d$. per ton.

The initial shipment, 5,000 gallons of claret, was made from Cloverdale to Yokohama in the fall. We have been shipping largely to Japan during the latter half of the year. In September we made very heavy shipments of wine to England, as large as we used to make to New York viâ Panama, while shipments of brandy were the largest that ever left this port. A train of 10 cars, loaded with wine, left Napa in October for Marseilles, France, and as each car contained 3,000 gallons, the shipment represents an aggregate of 30,000 gallons. It was all claret, and was the largest single shipment ever made from this country to Europe. It was taken to New York, probably for 6$d$. per gallon, and was probably landed at Marseilles for less than 10$d$. On December 12 the winemakers of Upper Napa Valley decided not to sell wines of the vintage of 1891 at less than 7½$d$. at the depôt, net cash, without commission. There have been heavy shipments to the Hawaiian Islands and Central America during the year. Indeed, on all hands, foreign demand has improved.

*Hops.*

The crop of California hops produced in 1891 is estimated at 35,000 bales, or about 25 per cent. more than was produced in 1890. The quality was fully up to the average, and the prices obtained remunerative to the growers.

*Wool.*

During the winter of 1890-91 the rains were light, and did not come at seasonable times to insure a large crop of grass. In consequence of which the wool-growers had to buy a large quantity of extra feed at high prices. The withdrawal of a great many hundred thousand acres of grazing land from market by the United States Government for Yosemite Park purposes, excluding all stock from that desirable range, has been a great drawback to this industry. Excluded from a longer use of the lands on the west side of the San Joaquin as a free common by the railroad reducing the same to possession, and charging from 16$l$. 10$s$. 7$d$. to 20$l$. 13$s$. 3$d$. per section, has added largely to the expense of sheep husbandry. Instead of closing the year with a profit, the wool-growers generally found themselves at the end of the year in debt. High prices for mutton alone sustained this industry during the past year. But if we are again short of grass, with which we now appear to be threatened, the tendency will be to decrease sheep farming in this State. The result of 1892 will depend much upon this, because we are actually short of range to maintain, even in an average grass year, the reduced number of sheep now in this State.

*Sheep.*

If the sheep at shearing time are poor the wool clip will naturally be inferior, and prices will be less in consequence.

## SAN FRANCISCO.

Prices ought to be higher this year than they were last, but the Eastern market does not yet indicate it. The only thing we can confidently predict is, prices for mutton will rule high. Like everything governed by the law of supply and demand, and as the supply is less than the demand, good prices for mutton are assured. This industry, like anything else, has its ups and downs, and in time, no doubt, we shall soon see full prosperity re-established. The year 1891 has not been very prosperous for the wool growers, and the wool dealers do not appear to have made much money. Prices have ranged lower than they were for the previous year.

The Agricultural Department at Washington has issued its annual report upon the numbers and value of farm animals in the United States. It is a statement in some instances falling below the census reports. The following are some of the figures for California:— *Cattle.*

| Description. | Number. | Value. Currency. | Value. Sterling. |
|---|---|---|---|
|  |  | Dollars. | £ |
| Horses | 415,059 | 26,010,045 | 5,202,009 |
| Mules | 54,574 | 4,077,548 | 805,550 |
| Milch cows | 290,521 | 7,829,541 | 1,565,908 |
| Oxen and other cattle | 602,904 | 10,481,663 | 2,096,333 |
| Sheep | 4,083,531 | 9,884,211 | 1,976,842 |
| Hogs | 512,424 | 2,741,675 | 548,335 |

The report says of California:—"The aggregate number of horses is slightly above that of January 1, 1891. While the quality has been greatly improved during the past 10 years by the introduction of better breeds, prices at present are depressed owing to the supply being greater than the demand. A great deal of work heretofore performed by horses is now done by railways and by machinery, which is, no doubt, another cause of this depression. Mules are about the same as to number as last year, and the demand is somewhat better than for horses, as is also the price. *Improvement in horses.*

"While milch cows remain about the same as one year ago, oxen and other cattle have materially decreased and prices are lower. The number of sheep is also less, but prices have been higher. Hogs have not diminished, and the supply is about equal to the demand."

There was a large crop in 1891, but for want of transportation much of it brought low prices and went to waste. Prices were very unprofitable towards the close of the year. *Potatoes.*

Vegetables are largely grown in the State, and the markets are stocked with a great variety at all seasons of the year. *Vegetables.*

Settlers coming to this State cannot be too careful in selecting a suitable location before purchasing land. Most of the pub- *Advice to settlers.*

lished accounts of the large profits to be made here by those engaged in farming, and which appear in the European papers, come from interested parties, and should be accepted with caution. They estimate the capital required at too low a figure for fruit farming, and which leaves no margin should their crops not succeed in the most satisfactory manner.

My advice to persons intending to engage in farming or fruit raising in this State is to stay here at least one year before deciding where to buy. They might during that time work on a farm and pick up practical knowledge as to the land, climate, marketing facilities, and branch of agriculture they wish to undertake, and are much more likely to succeed than those who purchase without having the benefit of their experience. It must be borne in mind that the climate found in the interior of the State is very warm for several months of the year, and this is especially the case in the portions suitable for raisin and orange culture.

<small>Approximate cost of 20 acres for raisin growing.</small>

The following statement shows the approximate cost of 20 acres of land for raisin growing in the southern portion of the State, together with the amount required until the land becomes productive:—

|  | Dollars. |
|---|---|
| Cost of 20 acres at 60 dol. (12*l*. 7*s*. 11*d*.) per acre | 1,200 |
| „ vines, one year old, 40 dol. (8*l*. 5*s*. 3½*d*.) per acre, including planting | 800 |
| „ attending to vines, second year, at 20 dol. (4*l*. 2*s*. 7½*d*.) per acre | 400 |
| „ „ „ third year, at 15 dol. (3*l*. 2*s*.) per acre | 300 |
| „ water, at 1 dol. (4*s*. 1½*d*.) per acre per annum for three years | 60 |
| Total | 2,760 |
| „ four-roomed house (103*l*. 6*s*. 1*d*.) | 500 |
| „ stable and outhouses (30*l*. 19*s*. 10*d*.) | 150 |
| „ two horses, waggon, and harness (51*l*. 13*s*. 1*d*.) | 250 |
| „ farming implements (20*l*. 13*s*. 3*d*.) | 100 |
| „ living expenses at 25 dol. (5*l*. 3*s*. 4*d*.) per month for three years | 900 |
| Total | 4,660 |

In some colonies the water right is sold with the land, but the companies make a charge for flooding the land. I have not included any charges for servants' wages as many settlers do their own cooking and housework.

Board could probably be obtained in the neighbourhood for 40 dol. (8*l*. 5*s*. 3*d*.) per month, which would save the expense of building a house untill the land became productive. The figures given for planting and attending to the vines are those obtainable at contract price, but an experienced vineyardist or horticulturist could attend to the vines himself and save considerably from the figures given, though if he kept house he would require someone to manage it, as all his time would be occupied on the land. A man to assist could be hired for 35 dol. (7*l*. 4*s*. 7*d*.) a month, and found.

<small>Pests and tree diseases.</small>

There are a large number of insect pests and tree diseases, which horticulturists have to contend with in this State, and great care is being exercised to prevent their number being increased. With this object in view all imported plants are carefully examined, and any found to be infected are destroyed. Beneficial insects, so called because they prey or feed upon those that injure fruit trees, have been imported from Australia and are being colonised here, and their introduction is expected to prove highly successful.

The following figures taken from the census returns show the number of fruit trees in this State and in Florida. The comparison between California and Florida in relation to fruit trees, is interesting. In this State there are 7,861,647 acres devoted to bearing and non-bearing trees. Florida has 16,875,463 acres. California has 2,652,021 bearing trees or plants, while Florida boasts of 25,317,536. California has 4,247,789 non-bearing trees, and Florida has 9,200,764. California has 38,367 acres devoted to oranges, while Florida has 144,769. This State has 1,153,881 orange trees bearing, against Florida's 2,725,272; non-bearing orange trees in California, 2,223,710; Florida has 7,408,543.

*Comparison between California and Florida.*

## PORTLAND.

Mr. Vice-Consul Laidlaw reports as follows:—

The year 1891 was an exceptionally profitable one for farmers in both eastern and western Oregon, as nearly all crops were above an average, and prices of the great staple wheat were higher than for eight years past.

*Crops.*

The report of the United States Agricultural Department, which agrees very closely with reports from observers here, gives the following figures on wheat production in this State and the neighbouring State of Washington (the latter being given in this report for the reason that a large proportion is marketed in this district):—

*Wheat crop.*

| State. | 1891. Acres. | 1891. Bushels. | 1890. Acres. | 1890. Bushels. | 1889. Acres. | 1889. Bushels. |
| --- | --- | --- | --- | --- | --- | --- |
| Oregon | 692,055 | 13,149,000 | 887,250 | 12,865,000 | 845,000 | 13,689,000 |
| Washington | 698,040 | 12,216,000 | 436,275 | 8,071,000 | 415,500 | 6,856,000 |

These figures give an average per acre of 19 bushels for Oregon, and 18 bushels for Washington. Another authority gives the average for Oregon as 22 bushels.

The receipts of wheat and flour were as under during the cereal years ending July 31 each year:—

*Receipts at Portland.*

| Cereal Year. | Willamette Valley. || Eastern Oregon. ||
| --- | --- | --- | --- | --- |
|  | Wheat. | Flour. | Wheat. | Flour. |
|  | Quarters. | Sacks. | Quarters. | Sacks. |
| 1890-91.. | 208,448 | 229,067 | 692,840 | 130,218 |
| 1889-90.. | 283,536 | 195,455 | 320,300 | 91,378 |
| August-December, 1891 | 132,206 | 120,600 | 677,885 | 53,216 |
| „    „    1890 | 124,673 | 101,177 | 378,406 | 41,852 |

Average prices sacked and delivered here were 1 dol. 52 c. per cental, equal to 1*l.* 10*s.* 4*d.* per quarter for Valley, and 1 dol. 45 c. per cental, equal to 1*l.* 9*s.* per quarter for eastern Oregon.

**Oats crop.** The figures of the United States Agricultural Department of the oat crop of 1891 are as follows, viz. :—

| State. | Extent. | Production. |
| --- | --- | --- |
|  | Acres. | Bushels. |
| Oregon .. .. .. | 233,037 | 7,341,000 |
| Washington .. .. | 177,466 | 6,744,000 |

An average per acre of 31 bushels in Oregon and 38 bushels in Washington. Prices during the first four months of the year were very high, but gradually dropped after the new crop came to market. Average price of prime oats during the year was 54 c. (2*s.* 3½*d.*) per cental.

The following is a comparison of receipts here :—

| Cereal Years. | Quantity. | Five Months Ending December 31. | Quantity. |
| --- | --- | --- | --- |
|  | Centals. |  | Centals. |
| 1890-91 .. .. .. | 392,901 | 1891 | 228,857 |
| 1889-90 .. .. .. | 479,654 | 1890 | 223,032 |

**Barley** Farmers in eastern Oregon are apparently giving more attention of late years to the growth of barley. Receipts during the calendar year were 141,831 centals. Throughout the first eight months of the year market prices were very good, but were low during the last four months. Average for the year was about 1 dol. 15 c. (4*s.* 7½*d.*) per cental.

**Flaxseed.** Little attention was given last year to the growth of flaxseed, and receipts fell off from 9,463,969 lbs. in 1890, to 2,591,985 lbs. in 1891.

**Other field crops.** The receipts of potatoes were larger than last year, and at the close of the year prices were low. Hay and other farm products gave good returns to the agriculturist.

**Fruit.** There has been a great improvement in the quality of Oregon fruits during the last few years, and much care and attention has been given to orchards. In view of the fact that millions of fruit trees have been planted of late years, and the good market found for fruits in the middle western States, there is little doubt that this business will grow to an enormous extent. It has been a profitable crop for farmers, and although fruit here does not come in so early as in California, the apples, pears, prunes, and peaches grown in Oregon, and also strawberries, cherries, and other small fruits are superior. The codlin moth, of late years, has caused much trouble in the apple orchards. During the year 196,596 boxes and 383 car loads of green fruit were received here.

**Tinned fruits.** There are four canneries in Portland engaged in canning fruit and vegetables, but the market for these goods was at least 40 per cent. lower than during the previous year.

**Hops.** The hop crop was not so profitable as in 1890, and many vineyards were rendered useless or badly damaged by the hop louse. The Oregon crop was about 16,000 bales of 185 lbs. each. The highest quotation during the year was 31 c. (1s. 3½d.) for choice, while last year as high as 1s. 8d. was paid. The average for the year in this market was about 11¼d. per lb.

**Sheep and cattle.** According to the figures of the Agricultural Department the number of animals in Oregon is—

| Animals. | Number. | Value per Head. |
|---|---|---|
|  |  | Dol. c. |
| Oxen and cattle.. | 797,051 | 16 42 |
| Milch cows | 106,122 | 25 0 |
| Swine | 227,343 | 4 32 |
| Horses | 226,545 | 43 75 |
| Mules | 4,741 | 59 34 |

Based upon the last clip there are about 2,250,000 sheep in the State of an average value of 2 dol. 24 c. per head.

**Wool.** Wool dealers in eastern Oregon offered 9d. per lb. at shearing time in May last, but flockowners generally held for 10d. Afterwards most of the wool sold for 7d. to 8½d. It is stated that sheep are not profitable. When wool is below 7½d. eastern Oregon wools are heavy and shrink in scouring 55 per cent. to 75 per cent. There are now comparatively few sheep in the Willamette Valley, but they are finer grades and their wool brings better prices.

**Sheep.** Sheep on the large ranges are in very good condition, the increase has been unusually large and the year has been very favourable. The ranges are not so crowded as they were two years ago. Many bands of sheep in eastern Oregon will average 10 lbs. to the fleece, others only 5 lbs. or 6 lbs., the general average being 7 lbs. The most profitable grade of sheep on the eastern Oregon ranges is ½ merino or ⅞ merino.

## UNITED STATES.

**Mutton.**

Mutton has been high, and dealers have paid on an average of the year's prices 2d. per lb. live weight delivered on cars.

**Cattle.**

The season has been a favourable one for cattle on the ranges, so far as weather is concerned. The loss of stock has been light, but the prices have been too low for profit, as the range is now short. The average prices paid by dealers for 3-year-old steers to 5-year-old steers on the ranges during the year was about 1½d. per lb. live weight. Eastern Oregon steers will average about 1,250 lbs. live weight.

### Port Townsend.

Mr. Vice-Consul Alexander reports as follows:—

The year 1891 has been memorable as one of the rainiest seasons ever experienced in this State, particularly in Western Washington.

Here heavy rains came in the spring which interrupted the seeding and planting of the ground, to be followed only by many cloudy, dull days, obscuring the sun in the summer, which delayed the growth and maturing of the crops, and when the time for harvesting did arrive, the crops were found to be not only in a very backward stage, but in many instances greatly damaged both in quality and quantity.

**Wheat.**

The staple farm product of Eastern Washington was materially benefited by the late spring rains and the yield was above the average, estimated to be about 20,000,000 bushels; the average yield per acre throughout the State being 21 bushels, prices ranging from 3s. 4d. per bushel to 4s. 2d. per bushel. Now that irrigation is being adopted, and with such satisfactory results, we may safely say that the acreage sown with wheat this coming year will far exceed that of any previous one.

**Oats**

The yield of oats, chiefly grown in Western Washington on the reclaimed swamp lands, is estimated at 9,860,000 bushels this year, having averaged 35 bushels to the acre for the whole State. The season has been somewhat unpropitious, which has interfered detrimentally with the quality, discolouring the grain very much. Prices have remained very firm for good samples.

**Barley, &c**

The average yield of barley for the State has been 31·5 bushels to the acre; rye, 14·3 bushels to the acre; and corn, 90 bushels to the acre.

**Potatoes and other roots, &c.**

The season has been very good for the root crop generally, and in many instances enormous crops are reported, although in some places the yield of potatoes has been very poor and the quality very bad, particularly upon the low-lying lands, where the potatoes seem to have rotted in the ground from getting too much moisture, and again in other parts a good portion of the crop was damaged by a worm which bored into the potato. A great rush was made to get these potatoes on the market as early as possible, which immediately became overstocked, and sent prices so low down that it did not compensate the producer to pay for the picking and handling of the crop and getting it to market, consequently many thousands of bushels were left decaying on and in the ground. Prices ranged from 1*l.* per 2,000 lbs. to 2*l.* per 2,000 lbs. There is no probability of improvement.

Hay this year was considerably damaged by rain, although in many places good crops were obtained of fine quality. The price has been very low, the farmer getting from 1*l.* 16*s.* per 2,000 lbs. to 2*l.* 2*s.* per 2,000 lbs., and the wholesale merchant from 2*l.* 2*s.* per 2,000 lbs. to 3*l.* 10*s.* per 2,000 lbs., according to quality. The retail price was a trifle above these figures. The cessation of work in the logging camps, where a large number of horses and cattle (oxen) are used, and railway building has decreased the demand, which has had a marked influence on the price. *Hay.*

The yield of hops for 1891 has been about 45,000 bales; the decrease from that of last year must be attributed to the ravages of the hop louse, no yard, as far as I can learn, being free from this disease. Spraying with the quassia wash, after the English method, was commenced early and was kept up late, which had added considerably to the cost of production. The quality has been below the average, with prices ranging from 4*d.* per lb. to 10*d.* per lb. The cost of production is now 5*d.* per lb. to 6*d.* per lb. The acreage is being increased. *Hops.*

The fruit season has been good all through, some districts having had better returns than others; the quality has been average. Many acres of ground have been cleared and planted out in orchards, chiefly with prunes; and if all conditions remain favourable, in another six years the supply will be enormous. This will necessitate the building of establishments for the tinning and drying of fruits, and other methods will have to be adopted for preserving these crops; as it is now, very large quantities of fruit of all kinds perish before they can be used or marketed. More care and study will also have to be given to the cultivation of fruit trees to make the business a thorough success, as blight and insects are making their appearance in the several districts, and trees will have to be carefully watched to guard against the spread and ravages of these pests, which will entail more additional expense for spraying. *Fruit.*

All the small fruits, such as strawberries, currants, gooseberries, and raspberries, have done well this year, and where marketable have brought in large profits, the demand being greater than the supply apparently.

The demand for stock of improved breeds still continues among horses, the Shiva and the Norman Parcheron seem to be the general favourites, while in cattle, Jersey and Guernsey bulls are being used a great deal by farmers, to improve the butter qualities of their herds; Herefords and Holstein Friesians and Shorthorns are also used for milking purposes. Small bands of sheep are found about the State, which are chiefly crosses between Cotswolds and merinos and the "down" varieties; but the supply does not equal the demand, more ought to be kept as they are very profitable both for wool and mutton, and seem to *Stock* be free from diseases of all kinds, receiving very little care and attention. All stock has wintered well, and there has been but very little mortality.

The supply of pigs is very small, farmers merely keeping enough for their own use. More ought to be kept, as they are also profitable. They are principally crosses between Berkshire, Poland-China, and a white variety. There is also a red variety found, which rather resembles the Tamworth breed. The only disease which seems to affect pigs is cholera, which about once a year makes it appearance, brought in usually from some other State; but no very serious results follow, as all the animals are at once killed and burnt. There has been no epidemic of infectious or contagious disease among stock this year. Three or four cases of glanders made their appearance among horses in Seattle, but the diseased animals were at once destroyed, their carcases burnt, and the disease has disappeared.

During the year the price live weight per head has been about as follows:—Beef averaging 1½d. to 2d. per lb.; calves, 2½d. to 3½d. per lb.; sheep, 2d. per lb.; pork, 2½d. to 3d. per lb.; and lamb, 8s. to 10s. per head.

At an industrial exhibition held at Jacoma during the year there was shown:—An apple weighing 2 lbs. 4 ozs.; a strawberry 10 inches in circumference; a bunch of grapes weighing 6 lbs.; strawberries fresh from the garden in October; an onion weighing 4 lbs. 1 oz.; a potato weighing 8 lbs. 4 ozs.; a radish weighing 9½ lbs.; a beet weighing 30 lbs.; a pumpkin weighing 93 lbs.; a watermelon weighing 64 lbs.; a cabbage weighing 53 lbs.; a squash weighing 120 lbs.; Timothy grass 7 feet 8 inches high; clover 5 feet high; alfalfa from a yield of 12 tons per acre; corn stalks 14 feet high; a hill of potatoes that yielded 43 lbs., also 67 lbs. of potatoes from 2 lbs. planted; hops from a yield of 9,592 lbs. per acre; a sample of wheat from a yield of 68 bushels per acre; a sample of oats from 125 bushels per acre; a blackberry bush that grew during the year 21 feet; a branch from a prune tree, 33 inches long, with 46 lbs. of prunes on it; a lump of coal weighing 16,800 lbs.; and a deal plank 50 inches wide, 30 inches thick, and 32 feet long, without a knot visible.

## Los Angeles.

Mr. Vice-Consul Mortimer reports as follows:—

With the exception of grain, the principal crops here are semi-tropic fruits, and I have therefore little to say which is likely to be of any value to English farmers. In my annual report on the trade and commerce of this district for the year 1891 I have given some information about orange and lemon culture, and I beg to refer those interested in these subjects to that report.

Alfalfa, better known in Europe as lucerne, is one of the most profitable crops in this district. It is a plant peculiarly well suited to a dry climate, as the roots extend downward some 30 feet and draw up the moisture. It produces four or five crops a year, and one planting will last 10 or 12 years. Each cutting produces from 1 ton to 2 tons per acre, which sells readily here at an average of 1*l*. 10*s*. per ton. Land suitable for alfalfa costs from 20*l*. to 40*l*. per acre. One strong point is, that it does not exhaust the soil like grain; indeed, it is stated that it has an enriching effect by bringing up nutritive elements from below.

In 1890 some farmers here made a large profit on potatoes, and in consequence so many persons planted potatoes in 1891 that the market was glutted. To utilise the product a number of starch factories were started, and used about 20,000 tons; about the same amount was shipped east and north.  *Potatoes.*

Harvesting machines are now in use here which cut, thresh, and sack the grain at one operation. The result of improved appliances for grain farming has been to lessen the number of persons employed on the large ranches, and to increase the large holdings by the absorption of the small ones. In this district this has not been the case, grain farming having given place to small fruit farms, and in consequence Southern California shows a relatively larger increase in population than any other part of the State.  *Grain.*

LONDON:
Printed for Her Majesty's Stationery Office,
By HARRISON AND SONS,
Printers in Ordinary to Her Majesty.
(75   7 | 92—H & S   1328)

# FOREIGN OFFICE.
## 1892.
## ANNUAL SERIES.

### No. 1086.
### DIPLOMATIC AND CONSULAR REPORTS ON TRADE AND FINANCE.

# UNITED STATES.

### REPORT FOR THE YEAR 1891
ON THE
### TRADE OF THE CONSULAR DISTRICT OF SAN FRANCISCO.

REFERENCE TO PREVIOUS REPORT, Annual Series No. 906.

*Issued during the Recess and Presented to both Houses of Parliament by Command of Her Majesty.*

LONDON:
**PRINTED FOR HER MAJESTY'S STATIONERY OFFICE,**
BY HARRISON AND SONS, ST. MARTIN'S LANE,
PRINTERS IN ORDINARY TO HER MAJESTY.

And to be purchased, either directly or through any Bookseller, from
EYRE & SPOTTISWOODE, EAST HARDING STREET, FLEET STREET, E.C., and
32, ABINGDON STREET, WESTMINSTER, S.W.; or
JOHN MENZIES & Co., 12, HANOVER STREET, EDINBURGH, and
90, WEST NILE STREET, GLASGOW; or
HODGES, FIGGIS, & Co., 104, GRAFTON STREET, DUBLIN.

1892.

[C. 6812—11.] *Price Threepence.*

# New Series of Reports.

Reports of the Annual Series have been issued from Her Majesty's Diplomatic and Consular Officers at the following places, and may be obtained from the sources indicated on the title-page:—

| No. | | Price. | No. | | Price. |
|---|---|---|---|---|---|
| 966. | Malaga | 2½d. | 1026. | Kiungchow | 1d. |
| 967. | Berne | 1d. | 1027. | Batoum | 4½d. |
| 968. | Puerto Rico | ½d. | 1028. | Buenos Ayres | 1d. |
| 969. | Buda-Pesth | 1d. | 1029. | Batavia | 1d. |
| 970. | Bogotá | 1d. | 1030. | Santo Domingo | ½d. |
| 971. | Panama | 1½d. | 1031. | San José | 1d. |
| 972. | Munich | 2d. | 1032. | Manila | 1½d. |
| 973. | Copenhagen | 4d. | 1033. | Marseilles | 1d. |
| 974. | Guatemala | 1d. | 1034. | Swatow | 1d. |
| 975. | Munich | 2d. | 1335. | Paris | 1d. |
| 976. | Meshed | 1½d. | 1036. | Ichang | 5d. |
| 977. | Para | ½d. | 1037. | Pakhoi | 1d. |
| 978. | Florence | 1d. | 1038. | Foochow | 1d. |
| 979. | The Hague | 1½d. | 1039. | Brest | 1d. |
| 980. | Patras | 1d. | 1040. | Madeira | ½d. |
| 981. | Paris | 1½d. | 1041. | Antwerp | 1½d. |
| 982. | Zanzibar | 2½d. | 1042. | Taganrog | 2½d. |
| 983. | Buenos Ayres | ½d. | 1043. | Algiers | 2½d. |
| 984. | Copenhagen | 1d. | 1044. | Hankow | 1½d. |
| 985. | Stuttgart | 1d. | 1045. | Nantes | 1½d. |
| 986. | New Orleans | 1½d. | 1046. | Belgrade | 2d. |
| 987. | New Orleans | 10d. | 1047. | Fiume | 1d. |
| 988. | Suakin | ½d. | 1048. | Wuhu | 1d. |
| 989. | Galveston | 1½d. | 1049. | Cagliari | 1d. |
| 990. | Berlin | 1d. | 1050. | Erzeroum | 1d. |
| 991. | Zanzibar | 1½d. | 1051. | Syra | 1d. |
| 992. | Guayaquil | 1d. | 1052. | Cherbourg | 1d. |
| 993. | Tonga | 1d. | 1053. | Lima | 1d. |
| 994. | New Orleans | 1d. | 1054. | Bilbao | 1½d. |
| 995. | Mozambique | 1½d. | 1055. | Cadiz | 2d. |
| 996. | Galatz | 1½d. | 1056. | Corunna | 2½d. |
| 997. | Nantes | 1½d. | 1057. | Saigon | 1d. |
| 998. | Algiers | 1d. | 1058. | Port-au-Prince | 1d. |
| 999. | Havre | 2½d. | 1059. | Trebizond | 1d. |
| 1000. | Buenos Ayres | 6d. | 1060. | Barcelona | 1½d. |
| 1001. | Baltimore | 1½d. | 1061. | Tainan | 1d. |
| 1002. | Taganrog | 1d. | 1062. | Smyrna | 1½d. |
| 1003. | Riga | 2d. | 1063. | Old Calabar | ½d. |
| 1004. | Bordeaux | 2½d. | 1064. | Samoa | ½d. |
| 1005. | The Hague | 1½d. | 1065. | Tahiti | 1d. |
| 1006. | Paraguay | 1½d. | 1066. | Chefoo | 6d. |
| 1007. | Constantinople | 1½d. | 1067. | Gothenburg | 2d. |
| 1008. | Rome | 1d. | 1068. | Buenos Ayres | 1½d. |
| 1009. | Mozambique | 1d. | 1069. | Loanda | 1½d. |
| 1010. | Wênchow | 1d. | 1070. | Guatemala | 1d. |
| 1011. | Mogador | 2½d. | 1071. | Zanzibar | 1d. |
| 1012. | Amoy | 1d. | 1072. | Charleston | 2½d. |
| 1013. | Kiukiang | 1d. | 1073. | Nice | 1d. |
| 1014. | Stettin | 1½d. | 1074. | Caracas | 1d. |
| 1015. | Boston | 1d. | 1075. | Lisbon | 2d. |
| 1016. | Callao | 1d. | 1076. | Calais | 2d. |
| 1017. | Aleppo | 1d. | 1077. | Rio Grande do Sul | 5½d. |
| 1018. | Santos | 2½d. | 1078. | Philadelphia | 2½d. |
| 1019. | Piræus | 1d. | 1079. | Brindisi | 2d. |
| 1020. | Mogador | 1d. | 1080. | New York | 1d. |
| 1021. | Adrianople | ½d. | 1081. | San Francisco | 1d. |
| 1022. | Tripoli | 1d. | 1082. | Frankfort | 4d. |
| 1023. | Jerusalem | 1d. | 1083. | Hiogo | 1½d. |
| 1024. | Odessa | 6d. | 1084. | Tokio | 1½d. |
| 1025. | Genoa | 1½d. | 1085. | Amsterdam | 1d. |

## No. 1086.

*Reference to previous Report, Annual Series No. 906.*

# UNITED STATES.

## SAN FRANCISCO.

*Consul Donohoe to the Marquis of Salisbury.*

My Lord,  San Francisco, May 11, 1892.

I HAVE the honour to enclose herewith Annual Reports on the Trade and Commerce of San Francisco, Portland, Astoria, Port Townsend, Los Angeles, and San Diego, for the year 1891.

I have, &c.
(Signed)  DENIS DONOHOE.

---

*Report on the Trade and Commerce of San Francisco for 1891.*

### ABSTRACT of Contents.

|  | PAGE |
|---|---|
| San Francisco Consulate— |  |
| Shipping; charters; freights; harbour works | 2–3 |
| Imports and exports | 4–5 |
| Cereals; salmon; cement; fruit | 6 |
| Timber; redwood; wine and brandy | 7 |
| Sugar; coal; quicksilver; metals | 8 |
| Population; health statistics | 9 |
| Railways; banks; labour; strikes, &c. | 10 |
| Hints to English settlers; price of land | 11 |
| Portland Vice-Consulate— |  |
| Harvest; shipping | 11 |
| Glass and cement; flour; wheat; wool | 12 |
| Hops; cereals; timber; fisheries; banking | 13 |
| Exchange; freights; shipping; seamen | 14 |
| Crimping; agriculture | 15 |
| Cattle; metals; mining; river navigation | 16 |
| Harbour; lights; pilotage; public works | 17 |
| Railways; population; taxation; waterworks; bonds | 18 |
| Building; labour | 19 |
| Sanitary; shipping returns | 20 |
| Imports and exports | 20–21 |
| Astoria Vice-Consulate— |  |
| Fisheries; lumber | 22–23 |
| Shipping; sailors; weather; casualties | 24 |
| Imports; exports; shipping returns | 25 |
| Port Townsend Vice-Consulate— |  |
| Rains; cereals | 26 |
| Hops; fruit culture | 27 |
| Irrigation; timber; coal; iron; precious metals | 28 |
| Salmon fisheries; railways | 29 |
| Freights; sanitary; general progress | 30 |
| Tables | 31–34 |

(1343)

## UNITED STATES.

### Abstract of Contents—continued.

|  | Page |
|---|---|
| Los Angeles Vice-Consulate— | |
| Introductory; state of business | 34 |
| Cement; fruit; tin cans (duty); vegetables | 36 |
| Raisins; wine | 37 |
| Shipping; harbour improvements | 39 |
| Agriculture; sugar | 40 |
| Ramie culture | 41 |
| Orange culture | 42 |
| Insect pests | 43 |
| Peaches; vine disease; floriculture | 44 |
| Anthrax | 45 |
| Population; tin ore | 45 |
| Borax; oil; railways | 46 |
| Advice to British capitalists | 47 |
| Irrigation bonds | 48 |
| Public library; school | 49 |
| Vagrants; liquor laws | 50 |
| Advice to emigrants | 51 |
| Administration of law; orange land (cost of); meteorological | 52 |
| Land investments; clothing; climate | 53 |
| Shipping returns; exports | 54–56 |
| San Diego Vice-Consulate— | |
| Shipping | 56 |
| Railways; cereals; fruit | 57 |
| Irrigation; cement; tin; failures | 58 |
| Tables | 58–60 |

NOTE.—All values in this report are reduced to sterling at the rate of 5 dol. to the £.

**Increase in exports and imports.**
**Good crops. Increased export of wheat to France. Wine production unproductive to owners of vineyards.**

The foreign trade of this port, both in exports and imports, shows a considerable increase over that of 1890. The fruit and wheat crops were both good, and the prices realised have left little to be desired by the farmers. As will be seen by the tables given in this report, the export of wheat has increased considerably, especially in the quantity sent to France.

The trade in California wines has been very active during the year, though prices received by the cultivators of the vines still remain low, and unless they can manage to ship their wines direct to the consumer, without going through the hands of the middleman, the growth of the grape for wine purposes will cease to be remunerative to the vineyard proprietor.

**Increase in British shipping.**

The number of British vessels entering at this port during the year has been greatly in excess of those entering in 1890, though the clearances show a large falling-off. The reason for this will be shown in the body of this report. There were 63 British vessels in port on December 31, 1891.

### Shipping and Navigation.

**Break in the freight market.**

The table given under Annex A in the report shows a large increase in the number of vessels engaged in the foreign trade of this port. The 276 British vessels, with a tonnage of 473,283 tons, which entered the port in 1891, many of them with charters to load grain for the United Kingdom or Continent of Europe, and others expecting to easily obtain paying rates were grievously disappointed, and more particularly those arriving in the last half of the year 1891. The following explains the trouble as to charters at this port.

The year 1891 will long be memorable to charterers and ship-owners in connection with Pacific coast business. The first half of the year was not notable for many changes, and those who had ships to charter and who had chartered them were hopeful. Everything pointed to a large wheat crop and lots of business. This brought an unusual number of vessels hither or set them on the way. At one time in the autumn there was a good deal exceeding 400,000 tons of tonnage either on the way or loading. *Charters at San Francisco.*

When the real state of affairs became known there was nothing to prevent a disastrous break, and rates for iron vessels to United Kingdom for orders went rapidly down in a few weeks from 2*l*. 10*s*. asked to 1*l*. *Rates during year.*

Here the sending vessels to other destinations, chartering them for lumber, &c., reduced the list of available tonnage heavily, and the break was stayed at the point referred to. But the losses were reckoned at hundreds of thousands of dollars, and one firm failed. At least one more was on the ragged edge, but matters were settled.

In January wheat charters were 1*l*. 15*s*. for wooden vessels and 2*l*. 2*s*. 6*d*. to 2*l*. 3*s*. for iron vessels. There was a large fleet of vessels that came to hand in February. Wood was quoted at 1*l*. 16*s*. 3*d*., iron at 2*l*. to 2*l*. 1*s*. 6*d*. In March wood was held at 1*l*. 17*s*. 6*d*., iron at 2*l*. to 2*l*. 3*s*. The same figures prevailed to the early part of April. Iron, United Kingdom, in the same month went up to 2*l*. 5*s*. In May, on account of the large amount of tonnage on the way, there was a decline, and the rate was 2*l*. 2*s*. 6*d*. for iron. In June wooden vessels were held at 1*l*. 15*s*. and iron at 2*l*. 1*s*. 3*d*. to 2*l*. 3*s*. 9*d*. The amount on the way at the close of the half year went up to close on to 400,000 tons.

Most of the vessels on the way in May and June were chartered to arrive. In July there was quite a demand for vessels to carry supplies to Chile, and asking rates thence went up to 4*l*. and 5*l*. To Europe rates were 2*l*. 5*s*. to 2*l*. 12*s*. 6*d*. asked for United Kingdom. Wood 2*l*. to 2*l*. 5*s*. *Good freights to Chile.*

In September rates were 2*l*. 7*s*. 6*d*. to 2*l*. 2*s*. iron, United Kingdom orders, wood 2*l*. In October they went down to 2*l*. iron. In November the market dropped rapidly, reaching 1*l*. 8*s*. 9*d*. iron, United Kingdom, to 1*l*. 1*s*. wood. In December they dropped to rates previously mentioned, the year closing disastrously. Lumber freights were low during the year. *Lumber rates low.*

Great improvements are at present under way on the harbour front of San Francisco, and a belt line of railway is to be constructed along the water front, which will add considerably to the facilities for disposing of the cargoes of vessels unloading there. *Improvement to water front.*

(1343)

# UNITED STATES.

## Annex A.—RETURN of all Shipping at the Port of San Francisco in the Year 1891.

### ENTERED.

| Nationality. | Sailing. Number of Vessels. | Sailing. Tons. | Steam. Number of Vessels. | Steam. Tons. | Total. Number of Vessels. | Total. Tons. |
|---|---|---|---|---|---|---|
| British | 220 | 371,798 | 56 | 101,485 | 276 | 473,283 |
| American, from foreign countries | 296 | 201,594 | 221 | 378,126 | 517 | 579,720 |
| American, from Atlantic ports of Union | 47 | 84,252 | 1 | 1,892 | 48 | 86,144 |
| Hawaiian | 7 | 3,819 | 31 | 51,952 | 38 | 55,771 |
| German | 26 | 36,373 | 7 | 11,101 | 33 | 47,474 |
| Nicaraguan | 9 | 8,220 | 24 | 24,378 | 33 | 32,598 |
| Norwegian | 9 | 12,087 | 4 | 6,506 | 13 | 18,593 |
| Italian | 9 | 14,124 | ... | ... | 9 | 14,124 |
| Miscellaneous | 4 | 3,045 | 4 | 1,442 | 8 | 4,487 |
| Total | 627 | 735,312 | 348 | 576,882 | 975 | 1,312,194 |
| " for the year preceding | 519 | 605,217 | 299 | 446,730 | 818 | 1,051,947 |

### CLEARED.

| Nationality. | Sailing. Number of Vessels. | Sailing. Tons. | Steam. Number of Vessels. | Steam. Tons. | Total. Number of Vessels. | Total. Tons. |
|---|---|---|---|---|---|---|
| British | 130 | 198,169 | 54 | 97,791 | 184 | 295,960 |
| American, to foreign countries | 274 | 225,717 | 208 | 355,645 | 482 | 581,362 |
| American, from Atlantic ports of Union | 17 | 28,084 | 1 | 1,892 | 18 | 29,976 |
| Nicaraguan | 12 | 13,585 | 25 | 25,877 | 37 | 39,462 |
| Hawaiian | 7 | 3,659 | 27 | 47,897 | 34 | 51,556 |
| German | 19 | 29,102 | 6 | 9,337 | 25 | 38,439 |
| Norwegian | 3 | 2,857 | 4 | 6,506 | 7 | 9,363 |
| Italian | 7 | 11,262 | ... | ... | 7 | 11,262 |
| Miscellaneous | 6 | 2,477 | 3 | 1,170 | 9 | 3,647 |
| Total | 475 | 514,912 | 328 | 546,115 | 803 | 1,061,027 |
| " for the year preceding | 546 | 601,581 | 282 | 452,772 | 828 | 1,054,353 |

NOTE.—The entrances and clearances of American ships do not include the coasting trade, whaling, or fishing voyages.

### Trade and Commerce.

The following table shows at a glance the trade of San Francisco for 1891 and 1890:—

## Annex B.—RETURN of Principal Articles of Export from San Francisco during the Years 1891-90.

| Articles. | | 1891. Quantity. | 1891. Value. | 1890. Quantity. | 1890. Value. |
|---|---|---|---|---|---|
| | | | £ | | £ |
| Wheat and flour | Tons | 932,757 | 6,714,125 | 726,257 | 4,559,809 |
| Wine | Gallons | 5,370,408 | 417,827 | 4,027,848 | 333,906 |
| Tinned salmon | Cases | 442,581 | 393,100 | 526,894 | 476,516 |
| Barley | Centals | 899,541 | 247,998 | 296,665 | 79,740 |
| Tinned fruit and vegetables | Cases | 230,953 | 189,309 | 146,984 | 118,908 |
| Timber | Feet | 19,931,487 | 94,053 | 18,830,535 | 92,176 |
| Brandy | Gallons | 433,399 | 79,079 | 210,776 | 43,042 |
| Quicksilver | Flasks | 4,010 | 34,485 | 6,252 | 62,577 |
| Other articles | ... | ... | 1,597,969 | ... | 2,240,010 |
| Total | ... | ... | 9,767,945 | ... | 8,006,684 |

## SAN FRANCISCO.

RETURN of Principal Articles of Import to San Francisco during the Years 1890-91.

| Articles. | | 1891. | | 1890. | |
|---|---|---|---|---|---|
| | | Quantity. | Value. | Quantity. | Value. |
| | | | £ | | £ |
| Raw silk | Lbs. | 5,067,758 | 3,242,995 | 2,227,517 | 1,740,204 |
| Sugar | Tons | 138,187 | 2,358,650 | 146,673 | 2,705,944 |
| Coffee | Lbs. | 22,223,214 | 775,101 | 20,023,557 | 691,444 |
| Coals | Tons | 1,015,854 | 683,556 | 563,531 | 405,102 |
| Tin-plates | Boxes | 291,484 | 378,929 | 274,750 | 180,281 |
| Tea | Lbs. | 7,339,069 | 232,617 | 6,338,870 | 188,174 |
| Cement | Barrels | 577,982 | 231,193 | 435,759 | 102,917 |
| Rice | Tons | 19,635 | 173,261 | 21,433 | 254,610 |
| Scrap iron | ,, | 26,669 | 69,335 | 20,025 | 51,492 |
| Pig-iron | ,, | 12,383 | 49,532 | 12,768 | 40,093 |
| Bullion and coin | ... | ... | 2,002,291 | ... | 1,969,431 |
| Other articles | ... | ... | 467,736 | ... | 789,133 |
| Total | ... | ... | 10,665,196 | ... | 9,118,825 |

Annex C.—TABLE showing the Total Value of all Articles Exported from San Francisco and Imported to San Francisco from and to Foreign Countries during the Years 1891-90.

| Country. | Exports. | | Imports. | |
|---|---|---|---|---|
| | 1891. | 1890. | 1891. | 1890. |
| | £ | £ | £ | £ |
| Great Britain | 3,491,887 | 3,329,246 | 1,023,976 | 937,064 |
| France | 2,526,129 | 439,094 | 275,160 | 249,319 |
| Hawaiian Islands | 800,107 | 836,817 | 2,328,183 | 2,472,690 |
| China | 634,499 | 622,951 | 1,546,187 | 1,113,923 |
| Central America | 499,114 | 371,541 | 713,490 | 602,503 |
| Belgium | 370,605 | 214,716 | 152,447 | 145,175 |
| Mexico | 326,306 | 294,129 | 171,841 | 160,012 |
| Australia | 324,081 | 217,725 | 303,469 | 239,009 |
| Canada | 168,094 | 183,292 | 438,657 | 314,604 |
| Japan | 147,835 | 143,472 | 2,681,838 | 1,569,594 |
| Chile | 116,609 | .. | 90,765 | .. |
| Pacific Islands | 98,656 | 93,750 | 61,529 | 53,773 |
| Peru | 61,911 | .. | 3,993 | .. |
| Asiatic Russia | 38,290 | .. | 65,793 | .. |
| Ecuador | 31,191 | .. | 17,323 | .. |
| Germany | 28,279 | 39,459 | 273,568 | 231,201 |
| Brazil | 14,187 | .. | .. | .. |
| Spanish Possessions | 6,601 | 11,933 | 145,090 | 273,052 |
| India | 5,882 | 1,418 | 252,736 | 79,989 |
| Dutch East Indies | 3,308 | .. | 82,153 | 297,158 |
| Other countries | 74,374 | 1,207,141 | 42,048 | 379,759 |
| Total | 9,767,945 | 8,006,684 | 10,665,196 | 9,118,825 |

The exports of wheat and flour show a large increase over those of 1890, and the prices realised are largely in excess of those for the same period. *Wheat and flour.*

The farmers held over a considerable quantity of the 1890 *Prices good.*

## UNITED STATES.

**Receipts in San Francisco.** harvest, waiting for better prices in 1891, and in the last quarter of the year sent their wheat to market, when they realised the best price of the year; the high prices were started upon the intelligence received of a deficiency in the French crop.

The total receipts of wheat in this market 17,943,341 centals and of flour 6,048,745 quarter sacks; this reduced to wheat makes 22,480,101 centals for 1891, as compared with 18,869,869 centals in 1890.

**Export of flour.** The export of flour to Great Britain was 366,202 barrels, and to China and Japan 444,558 barrels, with a total export to all countries of 1,223,875 barrels.

**Barley.** The export of barley shows a large increase over that of 1890, and prices were fairly good during the season.

**Salmon pack.** The total pack of salmon on the Pacific coast is given as follows:—

|  | Cases. |
|---|---|
| Alaska | 710,792 |
| Columbia River | 312,197 |
| British Columbia | 385,000 |
| Sacramento River | 25,000 |
| Other small fisheries | 54,227 |
| Total | 1,487,216 |

The Pacific coast salmon pack for 1890 was 1,623,867 cases.

**Cement, great fall in price.** The imports of cement have, as may be seen, been the largest ever known in this port. The cause was not so much a large demand as the extra facilities for shipment by the lowness of freights; a sudden decline from 14s. and 15s. to 5s.

These heavy imports utterly demoralised the market. There have been fearful cuts in the wholesale prices.

We have had almost 150,000 barrels more than in 1890, there has been a very heavy consumption, but nothing to affect this, and the result is exceedingly heavy stocks.

Some cement sold during the year as low as 8s. per barrel.

**Tin-plates.** The stock in hand at the close of the year 1890 was very light, not more than 20,000 cases. Large quantities were received during the early part of 1891, before the new tariff came into effect. **Good prices.** Prices have been high, and in September went up to 28s. per case, and at the close of the year stood at 25s. to 26s.

**Canned fruits.** The following is an estimate of the pack of the season by a leading packer:—

## SAN FRANCISCO.

|  | Cases. |
|---|---|
| Apples | 7,000 |
| Apricots | 200,000 |
| Asparagus | 11,000 |
| Blackberries | 16,500 |
| Cherries, white | 35,000 |
| " black | 25,000 |
| Currants | 5,500 |
| Gooseberries | 11,000 |
| Grapes | 38,500 |
| Nectarines | 5,500 |
| Pears | 140,000 |
| Peas | 27,500 |
| Peaches | 200,000 |
| Plums | 45,000 |
| Quinces | 3,300 |
| Raspberries | 10,000 |
| Strawberries | 15,000 |
| Total | 795,800 |

Miscellaneous—

| Pie fruits | 50,000 |
|---|---|
| Tomatoes | 250,000 |
| Jams and jellies | 25,000 |
| Total | 325,000 |
| Grand " | 1,120,800 |

|  | Cases. |
|---|---|
| Exports by rail | 685,962 |
| " sea | 170,569 |
| Coast consumption | 60,000 |
| Total | 916,531 |

The lumber receipts for 1891 show an increase as compared with 1890, and are given in the following table:— *Timber.*

|  | Feet. |
|---|---|
| Pine | 266,621,368 |
| Redwood | 165,496,295 |
| Maple | 62,000 |
| Laurel | 18,000 |
| Spruce | 26,725 |
| Ash | 119,335 |
| Hardwood | 50,000 |
| Total | 432,393,723 |
| " 1890 | 412,476,066 |

The export demand has been fairly good, and shows an increase for this year. Redwood, which is much used on the Pacific coast for house building and interior decoration, has only to be better known abroad to cause an increased demand for it. *Redwood for house building.*

The receipts of California wine and brandy at San Francisco in 1891 were as follows:— *Wine and brandy.*

|  | Gallons. |
|---|---|
| Wine | 12,810,675 |
| Brandy | 701,125 |

## UNITED STATES.

**With care better wines.**

There has been a fair increase for the year; what is most needed is an improvement in the quality. Prices have been low for the past three years, and there is much dissatisfaction in consequence on the part of the vineyard owners, but with more attention to manufacture, and seeing that only sound grapes are used in the press, better results will be obtained in the quality of the wines.

**Shipments to England and Germany.**

The quantity of California wine and brandy exported to England has been 64,950 gallons of wine, and 58,560 gallons of brandy, whilst to Germany 15,084 gallons of wine and 102,771 gallons of brandy were exported.

**Large shipments to eastern States.**

The California wines are, however, gradually making some headway in the eastern States, and there is a very considerable increase in the quantity sent across this Continent by railroad; they will yet take a better position in the markets of the world than they occupy at present.

**French tariffs stopped exports.**

A very good business would have been done with France if the tariff on wines had not been lately increased.

**Sugar.**

The principal sugar imports at this port come from the Hawaiian Islands, 127,042 tons having been imported from there and 6,695 tons from Java.

**Sugar from beetroot.**

The soil of portions of California has been found favourable for the growth of beetroot, and as the United States Government now pays a bounty of ¾d. to 1d. a pound on all sugar manufactured in this country, a great impetus has been given to the establishment of factories for the making of sugar from beetroot, and machinery for such factories has either been imported from Germany or made in this country.

**Government bounty.**

There are three beet sugar factories in the State, and the product of the three for 1891 amounted to 3,649 tons, upon which amount the factories received a bounty of about 32,700*l*.

**Coal.**

The receipts of coal from foreign ports have been as follows:—

|  | Tons. |
|---|---|
| From British Columbia | 652,657 |
| Great Britain | 200,426 |
| Australia | 321,197 |
| Japan | 20,679 |
| Total | 1,194,959 |

The receipts of foreign coals in 1890 was 686,926 tons. There was a large increase in the receipts of foreign coal in 1891, and consequently a great fall in prices.

**Quicksilver.**

The total production of quicksilver in California in 1891 amounted to 21,022 flasks, as against 22,926 flasks in 1890. The price has fallen since 1890, and the average for the year is only 8*l*. per flask.

**Metal product.**

From the annual statement of Messrs. Wells, Fargo and Co., the product of metals in the States and territories west of the Missouri River, excluding British Columbia and Mexico, for the last two years is given as follows:—

## SAN FRANCISCO.

| Year. | Gold. | Silver. | Copper. | Lead. | Total. |
|---|---|---|---|---|---|
|  | £ | £ | £ | £ | £ |
| 1891 | 6,337,023 | 12,122,801 | 2,652,332 | 2,477,156 | 23,589,312 |
| 1890 | 6,359,072 | 12,586,166 | 4,113,818 | 2,301,914 | 25,360,970 |

The export of silver from San Francisco during the past year to China, Japan, the Straits, &c., has been 1,582,474*l*. *Silver export.*

### Population and Industries.

The United States Census of 1890 makes the population of the city of San Francisco 300,000, of which 282,000 is given as Caucasian and African, and 18,000 as Chinese. The number of Chinese has decreased in consequence of the restrictions upon their coming to the United States and the number that have returned to China. *Population.*

The deaths from all causes during the year are given by the health department for the fiscal year ending June 30, 1891, at 6,650, of which 6,138 were whites and blacks, and 512 Chinese. *Death rate.*

The prevalent diseases, as given by the health officer's report, are six in number as follows :— *Diseases.*

|  | Deaths. |
|---|---|
| Zymotic diseases | 1,083 |
| Constitutional diseases | 1,069 |
| Local diseases | 2,948 |
| Development diseases | 706 |
| Violent diseases | 322 |
| Unascertained causes | 10 |

This makes the total for whites and blacks.

The following paragraph appeared in one of the local papers at the end of the year :—

"Our City's Physical and Moral Health.—The vital, criminal, and other statistics of our city's condition during the past year are not as comforting to contemplate as they might be. An alarming increase was recorded in the mortuary rate, the deaths in the city being 6,875 for 1891, as against 6,148 for 1890, an increase of 727. During the last month of December the deaths numbered exactly 800, arising largely from diseases entirely preventible.

"Until the rain of last week came, our sewers were in a frightfully congested condition, and no doubt had a large share in the increased death rate. These figures, which speak louder than words, ought to arouse public opinion to the necessity of better sanitation, or we may well despair that anything will be done.

"During the year 1891 there were 35 murders committed in San Francisco, but nobody was hanged; and if any homicide's neck is in serious danger, we are unacquainted with the fact. In addition to these successful murders, 88 persons were arrested for assault to murder, 275 for assault with a deadly weapon, 1,625 for disturbing the peace, and 745 for battery. Truly we are a bellicose people. There were no fewer than 98 suicides and 319 insane commitments; 770 suits for divorce were commenced.

"Of the 1,204 male prisoners in San Quintin 425 are under 25 years of age, many of them being as young as 16 years, and of course these do not include the boys in the industrial school and house of correction. The number of places within the city limits at which intoxicants may be bought is put at 4,223.

"The census gives San Francisco a total population of 300,000. These are lamentable figures that ought to make an impression on every good citizen."

*Railway.* The mileage of all the railways in the State of California on July 1, 1891, was 4,290 miles, and the Southern Pacific has increased its mileage during the year by 177 miles. The total number of passengers carried by all the lines was 19,319,271, of which the Southern Pacific carried 16,556,283. The average rate of fare was 3·7 c. a mile.

*Savings banks.* There were in the State of California on July 1, 1891, 45 savings banks, of which 11 have their place of business in San Francisco. The bank commissioner's report states the resources of the 45 banks to be, at the date mentioned above, as 25,243,618*l*., with deposits amounting to 22,832,950*l*.

The San Francisco savings banks allow interest on term deposits—that is, deposits that require 6 months' notice before withdrawal, 5⅖ per cent.

*Business failures.* The Broad-street Mercantile Agency reports 1,702 failures in the Pacific Coast, States, and territories for the year 1891, with assets 861,302*l*., and liabilities 1,641,402*l*., as compared with 992 of the previous year, with assets 774,795*l*., and liabilities 1,448,631*l*. The following causes are assigned for the failures, viz.:—Incompetency, 250; inexperience, 105; inadequate capital, 362; injudicious crediting, 43; complications of indebtedness, 8; personal extravagance, 44; neglect of business and bad habits, 35; excessive competition, 22; unfavourable circumstances, floods, fires, &c., 82; speculation, 24; fraud, 97.

*Labour and employment.* San Francisco can scarcely be called a manufacturing city, though there are certain branches of business, such as extensive ironworks and canneries, that give a great deal of employment.

*Strikes.* Strikes in various trades have been numerous, and in one particular instance, that of the Union Iron Works, largely engaged in building and repairing ships, one of the most serious strikes amongst the moulders employed there lasted for 18 months, and was only brought to a termination by the men giving up the contest.

*Difficulty of obtaining employment.* Many young men come to San Francisco from the United Kingdom who have been brought up to mercantile pursuits, expecting to readily find employment in mercantile houses here, or in wholesale or retail shops, and who are grievously disappointed to find that such employment is most difficult to procure, and that there are plenty of young Americans who understand the ways of the people, and will be taken in preference to the new arrivals from abroad.

# SAN FRANCISCO.

Many of our countrymen who come in this way are glad to take ordinary labourer's work, and even that about a city like San Francisco is difficult to procure by one who has not been brought up to such work.

Another class of young Englishmen come here with some little money to go into farming. To this class I would say put your money in a solvent savings bank, and go out to the country and hire out to a ranch owner and learn thoroughly your business before you attempt to purchase and cultivate land on your own account. One year's experience will enable such a man to become acquainted with the varieties of soil, the crops suited to each, and by not staying too long in one section, he will eventually see in what part of the State he had better make his home. A young man without encumbrance, and steady in his habits, starting with 20*l*. in his pocket and the balance of his capital in the bank, ought to be able to get along for a year, as he will be fed when employed on a farm, and after he knows something of work will receive from 5*l*. to 6*l*. per month for his labour. *[A young man had better hire on wages before purchasing land.]*

Many Englishmen who have not been to California think that land can be bought here for a low price; that is not the case, farms both large and small command good prices, and if under cultivation and with water rights attached, sometimes very high prices. This subject will be fully entered into in the agricultural report from this Consulate. All I can say here to a young fellow coming to California with capital to put into land, is not to believe any statements made by land agents until he has seen for himself and interviewed persons living in the neighbourhood of the land offered to him; and further to place no confidence in the numerous colonisation pamphlets which are brought to his notice, until he has satisfied himself by personal inspection. *[Land dear.]*

A man with a family coming here for farming if he has capital had better leave his family at home and come out alone and see for himself before choosing a site for his future home. If he is disappointed in the country and people he can go back; if not he can purchase his ranch and send for his family; but he must remember that he will require a good deal of money to live upon, if he goes into fruit farming until his land produces a paying crop. *[Family man coming out for farming.]*

# PORTLAND.

Mr. Vice-Consul Laidlaw reports as follows:—

Throughout the year 1891 in nearly all branches of business the trade of this district shows a very great increase. The foreign imports and exports are larger than for many years past.

The wheat harvest over the entire State and also in Eastern Washington was much above an average both in quantity and quality, and prices were higher than for 8 years past. *[Harvest.]*

The proportion of British tonnage employed in the foreign trade was 89 per cent. of the whole or 9 per cent. more than in 1890. *[British tonnage.]*

## UNITED STATES.

**Imports.**

As is always the case, the largest proportion of the import trade was done by sail and rail from San Francisco and the Eastern States. The returns of the custom-house show an increase of 37 per cent. over the imports of 1890, exclusive of transit trade. The increase is principally in coals, rice, salt, cement, tea, bags, sugar, &c., while tin-plates, earthenware, window glass, pig iron, and fire bricks were smaller. 67 per cent. of the window glass and 20 per cent. of the cement came from Belgium. The import trade in most British goods has been very unprofitable to importers, and the losses, particularly in cement, have been very heavy. The market for this article is glutted and it is selling now at 9s. per barrel, which is far below cost. Of the coals 10,455 tons were received from British Columbia, 10,618 tons from Australia, and 1,580 tons from the United Kingdom, 1,013 tons from Atlantic ports by sail, and from coast mines 45,132 tons. The market is well supplied. Fair prices were realised.

**Glass and cement from Belgium.**

**Importers lost heavily on cement. Coal trade.**

**Rapid increase of trade with China.**

The returns show a rapidly increasing trade with China and Japan, three large British steamers making regular voyages bringing cargoes consisting principally of tea and rice, and returning with flour and lumber. A large proportion of their inward cargoes of tea is shipped by rail in bond for other cities of the United States and Canada.

**Exports.**

The value of exports to foreign countries and coastwise was 73 per cent. more than in 1890.

Values of all produce shipped by sea to domestic ports during the last three years are: 1889, 903,400*l*.; 1890, 825,820*l*.; 1891, 1,182,250*l*.

**Flour trade.**

The flour trade with China and Japan is steadily increasing, the direct line of steamers carrying a much larger proportion than that of the Canadian Pacific Railway. Shipments to these markets during the last three years are as follows: 1889, 49,684 sacks; 1890, 6,684 sacks; 1891, 90,106 sacks.

**With China. Total shipments.**

The total shipments foreign and coastwise were 429,498 sacks, valued at 520,870*l*.; average, 1*l*. 4s. 3d. f.o.b. per sack.

**Wheat trade.**

A much larger proportion of the wheat exports of 1891 were shipped viâ San Francisco than was the case the previous year, but little, if any, was sent east by rail.

**Shipments.**

The total shipments foreign and coastwise were 1,089,425 quarters, valued at 1,620,004*l*. The average values during the years were about 1*l*. 11s. f.o.b. per quarter for Oregon Valley wheat, and 1*l*. 9s. 9d. per quarter f.o.b. for Walla Walla.

**Wool trade.**

The table below shows a continual decrease of receipts of wool at this port. Year by year more of the clip is baled at interior points and shipped east by rail, and therefore does not figure in the returns from Portland. The winter was mild, but the clip was undoubtedly smaller than during 1889 and prices were lower. The quality is steadily improving. Prices ranged from 6¾d. per lb. to 9¾d. per lb. for Valley wools, and from 5d. per lb. to 8½d. per lb. for Eastern Oregon.

The following are the receipts and shipments during the past three years:—

|  | Receipts. | | Shipments. | |
| Year. | Valley. | Eastern. | Viâ San Francisco. | By Rail. |
| --- | --- | --- | --- | --- |
|  | Lbs. | Lbs. | Lbs. | Lbs. |
| 1891 | 702,898 | 6,753,834 | 3,673,400 | 3,639,233 |
| 1890 | 829,130 | 6,843,695 | 4,000,789 | 2,404,340 |
| 1889 | 702,790 | 15,305,095 | 8,313,849 | 6,061,473 |

**Hop trade.** The crop of Oregon was a little over 3,800,000 lbs. Receipts here were smaller than last year, being only 1,899,676 lbs. Prices during the first six months of the year ranged from 16 c. to 31 c. according to quality and of new crop; during the last six months from 11 c. to 18 c. The average for the year was about 16 c. (8d.) per lb. for common to 22½ c. (11¼d.) for choice. The hop louse caused considerable damage in some vineyards.

**Barley and oats.** The receipts of barley and oats, being smaller, would apparently show a lighter crop. Prices were high till new crop came to market, when they dropped to a lower range.

**Flaxseed.** Production of flaxseed has fallen off very materially, the receipts being less than half of those of 1890.

**Fruit trade.** There is a continual increase in the fruit trade which has been profitable during the year.

**Timber trade.** The foreign timber trade though small was larger than last year.

Shipments were:—

|  | Quantity. | Value. |
| --- | --- | --- |
|  | Feet. | £ |
| To foreign ports | 6,320,000 | 15,080 |
| „ coastwise ports | 24,557,000 | 49,114 |
| By rail | 33,040,000 | 66,080 |

**Fisheries. Salmon.** The product of the salmon packing factories of the Columbia River was 402,150 cases, and of other bays and rivers in Oregon 37,500 cases. Shipments to England were 82,178 cases, the rest of the pack being shipped to San Francisco or by rail east. Overland shipments were 235,378 cases. This business is not very profitable now. Average market prices were about 5s. 4d. for tall tins and 5s. 11d. for flats per dozen 1 lb. tins f.o.b. here.

**Financial. Banking capital.** The capital employed in banking business in Portland at the close of 1891 was as follows:—

|  | £ |
| --- | --- |
| 8 national banks' capital and surplus | 776,178 |
| 2 British „ „ „ | 1,359,500 |
| 2 private „ „ „ | 258,500 |
| 6 savings „ „ „ | 296,156 |
| Total | 2,690,334 |
| Deposits at end of the year were | 2,368,380 |

## UNITED STATES.

**Clearing house.**

The transactions of the clearing house for the last two years were as follows:—

|  | 1891. | 1890. |
|---|---|---|
|  | £ | £ |
| Exchanges | 20,515,433 | 18,687,845 |
| Balances | 3,949,883 | 3,557,015 |

**Money market. Exchange.**

Throughout the year there has been no financial embarrassment of any consequence, though money has not been largely available for speculative purpose. Exchange has generally low. Bills on London at 60 days' sight fluctuated between 4 dol. 77 c. and 4 dol. 87 c. per 1*l.* for bank, and from 4 dol. 76 c. to 4 dol. 85¼ c. per 1*l.* for mercantile.

**Freights.**

The average rate of freight for grain charters during the year for iron ships was 2*l.* 5*s.* 8*d.*, about 3*s.* 3*d.* higher than in 1889. Only seven wooden ships loaded grain, and the average rate for the year was 1*l.* 19*s.* 9*d.*, about the same as last year. 2*l.* 13*s.* 9*d.* was the highest and 1*l.* 15*s.* the lowest rate paid for iron ships and 2*l.* 7*s.* 6*d.* and 1*l.* 10*s.* respectively for wooden ships. These rates are to a port in the United Kingdom, and most of the charters were drawn up with the option of Havre, Antwerp, or Dunkirk at the same rate as to the United Kingdom.

**Shipping.**

The following table gives the tonnage engagements for sailing vessels during the last two years, exclusive of coasting voyages:—

| Articles. | Quantity. | |
|---|---|---|
|  | 1891. | 1890. |
|  | Tons. | Tons. |
| Grain and flour cargoes | 135,969 | 73,763 |
| Salmon and assorted cargoes | 3,654 | 3,271 |
| Timber cargoes | 6,335 | 2,528 |
| Miscellaneous cargoes | 853 | 1,656 |
| Total | 146,811 | 81,218 |

96 of the above were British ships, registering 125,761 tons. For the first time in the history of the grain trade on this coast, several vessels came out, in ballast, from British and Continental ports.

**British steamers.**

The British steamers "Zambesi," "Batavia," and "Sussex" made regular monthly voyages from Japan, and the "Monghut" and "Taichow" ran regularly between Vancouver, British Columbia, and this port, connecting with the Canadian Pacific Railway Company's China line.

**Sailors.**

seamen's wages varied between 5*l.* and 6*l.* for able bodied seamen.

## SAN FRANCISCO.

The number and changes in crews of British ships entering this port during the past year have been as follows, viz. :—

| Total Number of Crews. | Deserted. | Discharged. | Engaged. | Reported Dead. | Hospital Permits. |
|---|---|---|---|---|---|
| 3,598 | 276 | 85 | 194 | 2 | 29 |

**Crimping.** My experience of 18 years in this port has convinced me that a Consular Convention with the United States, similar in its provisions to that with France, and the restoration of the punishment of imprisonment for desertion abroad, is not only necessary for the proper discipline of British crews in American ports, but would indirectly tend to suppress crimping. In his report for 1890, my colleague at Astoria makes the statement that the crimps infesting that port had changed to Portland, and gives figures to prove that there were more desertions from British vessels here than at his port. The facts are that nearly all the seamen's boarding houses have been and are located at Astoria, that, with one or two exceptions, all the most notorious crimps reside there, and that during the past year there have been assaults made upon crews of British vessels by these crimps that border upon piracy. Difficulties, technical and otherwise, have been thrown in the way of the operations of the State Law of 1889 for the protection of seamen, and the Town Council of Astoria has always refused to appoint an officer to carry out the provisions of the law. It would be strange if there were not more desertions from vessels here than at that port, as in nearly every instance the ships only lie there long enough to enter, clear, and finish up their business, while here they have to discharge and load; nevertheless, the large majority of deserting seamen are seduced from their duty by Astoria crimps, and immediately taken down to that port. Unlike the authorities and people of Astoria, every disposition has been shown here to assist in carrying out the beneficent State Law of 1889, which aims at the suppression of crimping. The Town Council has appointed and paid an officer, as required by the Act, ever since it became law, and the Chamber of Commerce, throughout the past year, has used all possible means to protect seamen, and spent a good deal of money in employing counsel and prosecuting offenders. It has even tried to protect the masters and seamen in Astoria itself. Some good has been accomplished, but the burden of failure is distinctly chargeable to the supineness of the people of Astoria, the press there treating the whole iniquitous business with a want of seriousness. I regret to say there seems little doubt that shipmasters in some instances profit by the bonuses wrung from the owners, and the extortion practised upon seamen to pamper those parasites upon commerce.

**Agriculture. Cereals, &c.** Farmers have generally had a very profitable year, the wheat harvest having been large and prices very satisfactory. Other cereals and farm produce generally brought good prices. There

(1343)

was a good demand for fruit throughout the year, and the yield generally was good.

**Sheep and cattle.** Losses of stock were light, and the stock business has recovered to some extent from the extraordinary heavy losses during the winter of 1889–90. The sheep and cattle on the ranges are in good condition, and good prices were the rule for both mutton and beef.

**Manufactures.** There has been a continued increase in manufacture in this city, and careful inquiry gives the following results for the year:—

|  | £ |
|---|---|
| Capital employed | 3,642,000 |
| Value of product | 6,170,900 |
| Hands employed | 12,383 |

**Iron and steel.** The product of the Oregon Iron and Steel Company's furnaces was about 10,000 tons of charcoal pig-iron, and their cast-iron pipe works run to full capacity of 500 tons per month.

**Smelting.**
**Lead and silver.** The smelting works at Linton only run part of the year, when they were blown out. Capacity of these works is only 150 tons of lead and silver ores per day. As there is a large section of the mining district of Washington and Idaho from which ores can be profitably sent here to be smelted, the prospects are that from a comparatively small beginning this will become a large business. In this branch there seems to be a good opening for British capital and energy.

**Mining.** Owing to the low price of silver many of the mines in the Cœur d'Alène district of Idaho are shut down. Year by year more attention is being given to mining throughout this and the neighbouring States of Washington and Idaho. I have not been able to procure any reliable statistics of the product of mines in this locality. **Precious metals.** Wells, Fargo and Company give the gold shipments of Oregon in 1891 as 200,800*l.*, and of silver 16,800*l.*; also of the neighbouring State of Washington, gold 43,400*l.*, and silver 22,400*l.*

**Improvements of river bars and channels.** During the year some work has been done by the United States engineers in blasting out rocky bars in the upper reaches of the Columbia and Snake Rivers, so as to render them more navigable for light draft steamers.

**Mouth of Columbia.** The navigable water included in the projects of improvement of the lower rivers, adopted by the United States engineers, extends from the iron railway bridge in the city of Portland to the crest of the bar at the mouth of the Columbia River, a distance of 114 miles. Of this distance 12 miles are on the Willamette River, and the rest on the Columbia. There is in this reach an aggregate of 4 miles on the Willamette and 6 miles on the Columbia, which require improvement before the contemplated depth of 25 feet at low water can be obtained. In other portions of these rivers, between Portland and Astoria, the depth in the channel is from 50 feet to 75 feet.

Throughout the year quite an amount of work has been done

by the United States engineers on the several bars, and the great jetty at the mouth of the Columbia is practically completed, and the last survey in June showed a depth of at least 27 feet at low water in a channel half a mile wide, and nowhere less than 25 feet in a width of 1½ miles. Major Handbury, United States engineer in charge, believes that next survey will show a depth of 30 feet at low water in a channel a mile wide. Practically, therefore, the Columbia River bar has ceased to be a danger, as the mean rise of tide is 7 feet, and the channel is straight, deep, and safe.

The last Legislature created the Port of Portland Commission, with powers to issue bonds to the extent of 100,000*l.* and levy an annual special tax on all property in the county, for the purpose of attaining and maintaining a channel of at least 25 feet in depth between Portland and the sea. This Commission is at work on the project as laid down by the United States engineers, which contemplates the placing of contraction dykes at places where the rivers are wide, and therefore shoal. After dredging between these dykes the engineers believe the force of the current will maintain a permanent, deep channel. {Object of Port of Portland Commission.}

At Coos Bay, under direction of Captain T. W. Symons, United States Engineer Corps, work has been continued on a jetty there, which is now fully a mile long. The improvement of the entrance has been very marked, the last survey giving 18 feet of water where there was at one time only 8 feet to 12 feet. This is quite an important harbour. At Yaquina and Coquille similar works are in progress, and steps are also being taken to improve the mouth of the Siuslaw River. {Minor harbours.}

Contracts have been let for lighthouses at Heceta Head, at the mouth of the Siuslaw, and also at the mouth of Umpque River. The Lighthouse Board has also recommended the placing of a lighthouse on North Head, at the mouth of the Columbia. {Aids to navigation. Lights.}

A lightship is nearly completed, which will be moored off the entrance of the Columbia River. The hull will be painted red, with "Columbia River" in black letters on each side, and "No. 50" on each quarter. It will have a fog signal, and will show two fixed white reflector lights, each 30 feet above the sea level, visible in clear weather from the deck of a vessel 15 feet above the sea and 10½ nautical miles off. The proposed geographical position of the light-vessel is—latitude north, 46° 13′ 15″; longitude west, 124° 13′ 15″. Magnetic bearings from the vessel will be approximately—North Head, N.N.E., ¾ E., Cape Disappointment Lighthouse, N.E.; Port Adams Lighthouse, E. by N. {Lightship at mouth of the Columbia.}

The towage and pilotage service was carried on indifferently, though cheaply, during the busiest part of the year, and a good deal of delay to ships was caused thereby. {Towage and pilotage.}

The work on the great canal and locks at the cascades of the Columbia River above Portland proceeds slowly, and unless Congress should become more lavish in appropriations, it will be {Public works.}

(1343)

years before the work is completed so that boats may pass through.

**Bridges.** Last Legislature created a commission to buy or build bridges across the Willamette River at Portland, free to the public, and authorised the issue of 30-year 5 per cent. bonds to the extent of 100,000*l.* for that purpose.

**Railways.** A portage line is being built, by State aid, along the banks of the Cascades Canal, and another portage road is projected between the Dalles and Celiloaround, the dangerous rapids at that point. Other lines are also projected, but hardly any railroad work has been done in this section during the year. The total mileage of railway in Oregon and portions of Washington tributary to this port is 2,065 miles.

**Consolidation of suburbs.** By Act of the Legislature and vote of the people Portland, East Portland, and Albina were consolidated during 1891.

**Population.** The census of 1890 gave the population of the now consolidated city as 69,893, and it is now believed to be over 75,000, some authorities estimating it as high as 82,000.

**Taxation.** The State and county taxes were levied at the rate of 1·90 per cent., city tax at 1 per cent., and district school tax at 60 per cent., or 3½ per cent. in all. Property is valued at about 40 per cent. of its actual value for taxation purposes. The net valuations of all property assessed in this city, after deduction of taxpayers' indebtedness within the State, was 9,104,215*l.*, and in the entire State 25,555,059*l.*

**City finances.** The total revenue of this city, including balances carried over from 1890, was 150,219*l.*, and the expenditures were 137,452*l.* These figures do not include any revenue or expenditure of the Water, City Hall, or Free Bridge Commissions, nor any expenditure for streets or sewers. The cost of these improvements, paid by owners of contiguous property, was—street improvements, 43,409*l.*; street extensions, 6,307*l.*; sewers, 9,063*l.*

**City hall.** The construction of the City Hall building was taken out of the hands of the Council and turned over to a commission appointed by the Legislature. During the year there was a further expenditure made of 8,289*l.*

**Waterworks.** Receipts of the Commission were equal to 47,683*l.*, and disbursements of the operating department were 19,798*l.*, inclusive of 7,000*l.* interest on bonds. Last Legislature gave the Commission power to issue equal to 500,000*l.* in 30-year 5 per cent. bonds for the purpose of bringing in water from a pure stream 33 miles away.

**Bonds a good investment.** The following are the different issues of bonds guaranteed by the city, and which seemingly present a good investment to British capitalists:—

|  | Authorised. | Issued. | Average Premium when Sold. |
|---|---|---|---|
|  | £ | £ | Per Cent. |
| Water bonds .. .. .. | 640,000 | 140,000 | 7·85 |
| City Hall bonds .. .. | 135,000 | 35,000 | 2·50 |
| Bridge bonds .. .. .. | 100,000 | 20,000 | 1·00 |
| City Park bonds .. .. | 50,000 | .. | .. |

The interest of Port of Portland bonds is guaranteed by a county tax, and the authorised issue is equal to 100,000*l*., of which 20,000*l*. have been issued and sold at a premium of $2\frac{1}{16}$ per cent. All of the above are 5 per cent. bonds, redeemable in 30 years. The first issue of 140,000*l*. water bonds are non-taxable, and a favourite investment; the last lot sold in 1890 brought a premium of $10\frac{1}{2}$ per cent.

The year was not an active one in real estate transactions, Real estate. which were below those of 1890. The transfers and sales of real estate recorded in Multnoman county were 10,944,759 dol., equal to 2,188,950*l*. Over half of this property was within the limits of the city.

The building trade has been very active, and in all directions Buildings. dwellings are in course of construction; some of these are very handsome. Many of the business buildings are magnificent piles of brick and stone, which would be a credit to any city.

The following data, compiled by the Chamber of Commerce, gives some idea of what is being done in Portland and suburbs. The buildings referred to have been completed or begun during the past year:—

|  | Value. | Number. |
|---|---|---|
|  | £ |  |
| Buildings costing under .. .. | 200 | 870 |
| ,, ,, .. .. | 500 | 807 |
| ,, ,, .. .. | 1,000 | 258 |
| ,, ,, .. .. | 2,000 | 112 |
| ,, ,, .. .. | 4,000 | 53 |
| ,, ,, .. .. | 6,000 | 12 |
| ,, ,, .. .. | 10,000 | 9 |
| ,, ,, .. .. | 20,000 | 8 |
| ,, ,, .. .. | 30,000 | 2 |
| ,, ,, .. .. | 40,000 | 1 |
| ,, ,, .. .. | 80,000 | 1 |
| ,, ,, .. .. | 100,000 | 1 |
| Total number of buildings .. | .. | 2,134 |
| Total approximate cost .. .. | 1,329,493 | .. |

Skilled labour is generally in demand, but I must repeat Labour. my warning to clerks and men who have no particular business that they are unlikely to procure immediate employment, and

## UNITED STATES.

may fall into distress, unless they are so situated as to be able to afford to wait.

**Health.** On the whole, the city and country are in a prosperous condition, and the general health of this city has been good throughout the year.

NOTE.—All values given in this report are reduced to sterling at the average rate of 5 dol. per 1*l*.

### Annex A.—RETURN of all Shipping at the Port of Portland, Oregon, in the Year 1891.

ENTERED.

| Nationality. | Sailing. Number of Vessels. | Sailing. Tons. | Steam. Number of Vessels. | Steam. Tons. | Total. Number of Vessels. | Total. Tons. |
|---|---|---|---|---|---|---|
| British | 125 | 126,384 | 26 | 29,241 | 151 | 155,625 |
| American, foreign | 2 | 1,117 | 2 | 921 | 4 | 2,038 |
| ,, Atlantic | 6 | 8,057 | ... | ... | 6 | 8,057 |
| ,, coasting | 30 | 10,149 | 294 | 243,152 | 324 | 253,301 |
| German | 5 | 5,119 | 1 | 1,541 | 6 | 6,660 |
| Norwegian | 1 | 1,500 | ... | ... | 1 | 1,500 |
| Dutch | 1 | 1,207 | ... | ... | 1 | 1,207 |
| Total | 170 | 153,533 | 323 | 274,855 | 493 | 428,388 |
| ,, for the year preceding | ... | ... | ... | ... | 396 | 309,911 |

CLEARED.

| Nationality. | Sailing. Number of Vessels. | Sailing. Tons. | Steam. Number of Vessels. | Steam. Tons. | Total. Number of Vessels. | Total. Tons. |
|---|---|---|---|---|---|---|
| British | 88 | 114,827 | 26 | 29,241 | 114 | 144,068 |
| American, foreign | 8 | 11,702 | 3 | 1,278 | 11 | 12,980 |
| ,, coasting | 25 | 6,481 | 282 | 234,516 | 307 | 240,997 |
| German | 5 | 5,119 | 1 | 1,541 | 6 | 6,660 |
| Norwegian | 1 | 1,500 | ... | ... | 1 | 1,500 |
| Dutch | 1 | 1,207 | ... | ... | 1 | 1,207 |
| Total | 128 | 140,836 | 312 | 266,576 | 440 | 407,412 |
| ,, for the year preceding | ... | ... | ... | ... | 361 | 302,036 |

### Annex B.—RETURN of Principal Articles of Export from Portland, Oregon, during the Years 1891-90.

| Articles. | | 1891. Quantity. | 1891. Value. £ | 1890. Quantity. | 1890. Value. £ |
|---|---|---|---|---|---|
| Wheat | Quarters ... | 722,470 | 1,108,303 | 280,418 | 354,296 |
| ,, flour | Sacks ... | 264,686 | 306,754 | 296,910 | 308,493 |
| Timber | 1,000 feet... | 2,966 | 8,120 | 855 | 2,647 |
| Other articles | ... | ... | 14,595 | ... | 16,061 |
| Total | ... | ... | 1,437,772 | ... | 681,497 |

## SAN FRANCISCO.

**RETURN of Principal Articles of Import to Portland, Oregon, during the Years 1891-90.**

|  |  | 1891. Quantity. | 1891. Value. | 1890. Quantity. | 1890. Value. |
|---|---|---|---|---|---|
|  |  |  | £ |  | £ |
| Coals and coke | Tons | 23,923 | 16,024 | 12,655 | 9,635 |
| Tin and terne-plates | Lbs. | 2,871,367 | 19,200 | 3,724,639 | 23,299 |
| Rice | ,, | 6,958,578 | 28,476 | 3,282,516 | 11,804 |
| Earthenware and glass | ... | ... | 14,812 | ... | 17,657 |
| Salt | Lbs. | 10,344,615 | 6,872 | 2,224,871 | 1,701 |
| Cement | Barrels | 96,438 | 29,701 | 58,989 | 14,791 |
| Cigars and tobaccos | Lbs. | ... | 12,182 | 40,939 | 14,482 |
| Wines and liquors | ... | ... | 2,800 | ... | 2,898 |
| Beer, porter, and ale | Gallons | 27,478 | 5,464 | 31,220 | 4,436 |
| Soda and chemicals | Lbs. | 873,351 | 2,279 | 1,964,104 | 2,977 |
| Oils | Gallons | 19,948 | 2,180 | 21,239 | 1,694 |
| Pig and scrap iron | Tons | 1,188 | 3,142 | 1,828 | 4,543 |
| Bar iron and manufactures of iron and steel, and cutlery | ... | ... | 2,488 | ... | 1,754 |
| Firebricks | Number | 260,200 | 468 | 1,427,705 | 1,134 |
| Fireclay | Tons | 195 | 216 | 208 | 308 |
| Tea | Lbs. | 735,209 | 20,119 | 411,005 | 12,475 |
| Hemp | Tons | 498 | 17,805 | 392 | 16,397 |
| Window glass | Lbs. | ... | 6,274 | 3,028,193 | 13,098 |
| Bags and bagging | ... | ... | 18,360 | ... | 12,602 |
| Pickles and sauces | ... | ... | 1,229 | ... | 1,691 |
| Manufactures of silk | ... | ... | 3,608 | ... | 4,815 |
| ,, cotton | ... | ... | 1,858 | ... | 1,123 |
| Lemons | Boxes | ... | 2,080 | 1,641 | 967 |
| Sugar | Lbs. | 581,599 | 4,436 | ... | ... |
| Crude sulphur | Tons | 686 | 3,743 | ... | ... |
| Rice flour | Lbs. | 468,803 | 1,864 | ... | ... |
| Wood-pulp | Tons | 170 | 1,649 | ... | ... |
| All other articles | ... | ... | 30,315 | ... | 16,184 |
| Total | ... | ... | 259,644 | ... | 192,465 |
| Entered for transportation— |  |  |  |  |  |
| To other districts | ... | ... | 150,763 | ... | ... |
| To Canada | ... | ... | 42,712 | ... | ... |
| Grand total | ... | ... | 453,119 | ... | 192,465 |

N.B.—The above returns do not include exports or imports, coastwise or by rail, with the exception of articles transported in bond.

(1343)

22                    UNITED STATES.

Annex C.—TABLE showing the Total Value of all Articles Exported from Portland, Oregon, and Imported to Portland, Oregon, from and to Foreign Countries during the Years 1891–90.

| Country. | Exports. 1891. | Exports. 1890. | Imports. 1891. | Imports. 1890. |
|---|---|---|---|---|
|  | £ | £ | £ | £ |
| Great Britain | 1,053,735 | 569,309 | 101,875 | 77,418 |
| Belgium | 23,615 | 11,300 | 12,511 | 12,233 |
| British Columbia | 37,776 | 26,521 | 15,661 | 7,984 |
| China and Japan | 92,164 | 74,367 | 77,278 | 42,614 |
| ,, ,, in transit | .. | .. | 193,475 | .. |
| Australia | .. | .. | 5,662 | 4,411 |
| Peru and Chile | 1,400 | .. | 476 | .. |
| France | 219,568 | .. | 662 | 210 |
| Cuba | .. | .. | 11,885 | 14,032 |
| Philippine Islands | 440 | .. | .. | 17,621 |
| India | .. | .. | 27,277 | 11,377 |
| Germany | .. | .. | 3,205 | 3,598 |
| Brazil | 8,801 | .. | .. | .. |
| Italy | .. | .. | 2,364 | 967 |
| All other countries | 273 | .. | 788 | .. |
| Total | 1,437,772 | 681,497 | 453,119 | 192,465 |

ASTORIA.

Mr. Vice-Consul Cherry reports as follows:—

General business. Business has been good for the past year in the whole district, and notably in this city.

Direct foreign Imports. Show some falling-off, a larger quantity coming through San Francisco.

Exports. Show a large increase in salmon and wheat.

Imports of tin-plates. The price of B.V. Grades for the year at retail was from 6 dol. 50 c. (1l. 7s.) to 6 dol. 70 c. (1l. 7s. 8d.). These are coke steel tin-plates.

Salt. About the same quantity as last year, but selling very cheaply owing to over-stocking.

Coals. The extra demand has been met by imports from the domestic ports on the Sound.

Exports of salmon. Show three times the quantity by ship as the year before, all going to England around the Horn.

A fair share still goes by steamer from here to San Francisco, and is shipped from there to Europe and Australia.

Wheat exports. Owing to bountiful crops and a sharp demand in Europe a larger quantity than for some years back has been sent out of the country.

Flour There is a great falling-off in this product. The mills up the country are shipping a large quantity of low grade flour to Japan and China by steamers. This is found more profitable, as it reduces the quantity of offal, which is hard to sell at anything like a profit. These steamer shipments affect the shipments to Europe.

Has gone along fairly steadily, the cannery men offering 1 dol. (say 4s.) per fish, which price, after some demur, was accepted by the fishermen. *Industries. Salmon fishing.*

The number of gill nets was greater last season, and the number of fish caught by them was greater in proportion than the catch by the traps, seines, and fish-wheels, especially the latter.

One large buyer and shipper told me that his shipments in 1890–91 were 800 tons (2,000 lbs.) of frozen sturgeon, mostly by rail for the Eastern States. He also stated that in his belief the sturgeon were diminishing in numbers. Other accounts state that the fish have simply changed their feeding grounds in the river. It is a great pity that some action is not taken by the Government to have a special boat put on the river for the double purpose of studying the habits of the food fishes, and the illicit and indiscriminate fishing that now goes on. Little more than a close time is now all that there is done in the matter. A couple of salmon-breeding establishments, which put out only a small quantity of fry, and in the judgment of many they are not located in the right place. *Sturgeon fishing.*

Two schooners were fitted out in this district to join the sealing fleet. Commencing in January off San Diego, in southern California, and gradually working their way north up the coast after the seals. Arriving off this port at the end of February, or early in March, and continuing on to the Aleutian Islands to June. *Sealing.*

The main part of the little fleet is owned in Victoria, British Columbia, but Puget Sound ports and San Francisco add their quota.

The amount of the catch is kept quiet, but it is supposed to be on an average over 100 skins to each schooner.

The prices received for canned salmon, f.o.b. steamer or sailing vessel, at Astoria ranged from 1*l.* to 1*l.* 5*s.* per case of 48 1 lb. tins. *Salmon canning.*

A larger quantity of various sizes and shapes are noticeable in this year's pack, mostly in ½ lb. and 1 lb. "flat" tins.

The total output is less than for 1890, and all of which was of good quality.

Columbia River had 389,000, against 433,000 in 1890. A still smaller quantity was put up on the adjacent coasts north and south, being 10,000 cases for the coast north, and 25,500 cases for the coast south. Alaska, however, has made a very large showing.

There is a great increase to be noted for the past year. The prices of logs have, however, come down. The scheme of log rafts has, however, not yet been put into practice. *Lumbering.*

Is all still increasing in magnitude, and I observe that the *Lumber manufacturing.*

exports to foreign ports are steadily increasing in the lumber ports to the north.

**Box making.** Still keeps up its output, but it is all taken either for local consumption or for California fruits or Alaska salmon.

**Paper pulp making.** All the output of this small factory is forwarded to San Francisco, and it is more observable each year that a paper-making plant would be a remunerative opening for capital.

**Shipping.** The number of vessels was a great increase on the year before, drawn to this river by the sharp demand for food-stuffs in Europe, raising the price of freights materially, so much so that several vessels that left here early in the year for France and the United Kingdom to return to the Columbia River in November and December in ballast. On account of the number of vessels of small tonnage, the average size of the vessels does not show much increase over last year. Ships under the British flag more than hold their former proportion, the great increase being nearly altogether under that flag.

**Sailors.** I have to note that there are fewer attempts at desertion than heretofore, especially noticeable when taken in connection with the number of ships arriving.

A bold attempt at driving out some of the crew of a British ship was made last November. The matter was taken up by the local authorities promptly. Some of the prisoners arrested were indicted to appear before the Grand Jury, which body holds its meeting in February, and at time of writing two crimps and three of their tools are taking their trial before the Circuit Court on the charges of rioting, attempted kidnapping, and larceny of clothing.

**Unusually stormy weather.** The unusually stormy season in November and December was the means of some vessels due at this port losing their charters. I can safely state that in a residence of 17 years at the port I have not seen such another stormy 60 days, especially notable for the fierceness of the gales blowing at that time.

**Disasters in 1891.** I have to note the loss of a fine British ship, the "Strathblane," on the coast to the north of this river. From the inquiry instituted at the time to find out the cause of the disaster, it developed that the master, though doubtful of the correctness of his chronometer, held the vessel on the inshore tack during a thick and dirty night, with a heavy gale blowing, the vessel having a greater drift than was anticipated. Six lives were lost, and the vessel a total loss.

**Health.** Has been uniformly good for the past year.

## SAN FRANCISCO.

### Annex A.—Return of all Shipping at the Port of Astoria during the Year 1891.

#### Entered.

| Nationality. | Sailing. Number of Vessels. | Sailing. Tons. | Steam. Number of Vessels. | Steam. Tons. | Total. Number of Vessels. | Total. Tons. |
|---|---|---|---|---|---|---|
| British | 101 | 133,048 | 25 | 29,132 | 126 | 162,180 |
| American | 64 | 27,833 | 316 | 244,535 | 380 | 272,368 |
| German | 5 | 5,040 | 1 | 1,764 | 6 | 6,804 |
| Dutch | 1 | 1,007 | ... | ... | 1 | 1,007 |
| Norwegian | 1 | 1,528 | ... | ... | 1 | 1,528 |
| Total | 172 | 168,456 | 342 | 275,331 | 514 | 443 887 |
| ,, for the year preceding | ... | ... | ... | ... | 532 | 518,427 |

#### Cleared.

| Nationality. | Sailing. Number of Vessels. | Sailing. Tons. | Steam. Number of Vessels. | Steam. Tons. | Total. Number of Vessels. | Total. Tons. |
|---|---|---|---|---|---|---|
| British | 91 | 114,667 | 25 | 28,456 | 116 | 143,123 |
| American | 77 | 41,445 | 303 | 238,992 | 380 | 280,437 |
| German | 5 | 5,040 | 1 | 1,764 | 6 | 6,804 |
| Dutch | 1 | 1,007 | ... | ... | 1 | 1,007 |
| Norwegian | 1 | 1,528 | ... | ... | 1 | 1,528 |
| Total | 175 | 163,687 | 329 | 269,212 | 504 | 432,899 |
| ,, for the year preceding | ... | ... | ... | ... | 587 | 531,664 |

### Annex B.—Return of Principal Articles of Export from Astoria during the Years 1891-90.

| Articles. | | 1891. Quantity. | 1891. Value. | 1890. Quantity. | 1890. Value. |
|---|---|---|---|---|---|
| | | | £ | | £ |
| Salmon | Hundreds | 84,178 | 85,118 | 27,701 | 32,540 |
| Wheat | Bushels | 718,268 | 141,509 | 578,805 | 92,700 |
| Flour | Barrels | 14,876 | 12,173 | 35,638 | 27,503 |
| Lumber | Feet | 2,951 | 7,600 | 3,981 | 8,600 |
| Sundries | ... | ... | 185 | ... | 215 |
| Total | ... | ... | 246,585 | ... | 161,558 |

### Return of Principal Articles of Import into Astoria during the Years 1891-90.

| Articles. | | 1891. Quantity. | 1891. Value. | 1890. Quantity. | 1890. Value. |
|---|---|---|---|---|---|
| | | | £ | | £ |
| Tin-plates | Boxes | 23,555 | 18,369 | 36,172 | 24,456 |
| Salt | Tons | 101 | 225 | 172 | 354 |
| Coals | ,, | 2,304 | 1,727 | 4,033 | 3,365 |
| Sundries | ... | ... | 1,625 | ... | 150 |
| Total | ... | ... | 21,946 | ... | 28,325 |

Annex C.—TABLE showing the Total Value of all Articles Exported from Astoria and Imported to Astoria from and to Foreign Countries during the Years 1891-90.

| Country. | Exports. 1891. | Exports. 1890. | Imports. 1891. | Imports. 1890. |
|---|---|---|---|---|
| | £ | £ | £ | £ |
| Great Britain | 175,311 | 139,513 | 18,648 | 24,855 |
| British Colonies | 24,731 | 4,352 | 3,290 | 3,170 |
| Other countries | 47,540 | 13,717 | 3 | .. |
| Total | 247,582 | 157,582 | 21,941 | 27,025 |

## PORT TOWNSEND.

Mr. Vice-Consul Alexander reports as follows:—

The anticipations which were indulged in at the close of 1890 for a prosperous year in 1891 can hardly be said to have been realised all over the State of Washington. The farmers and tradesmen in eastern Washington have fared better than those in the western portion. The universal depression in trade has been most severely felt in this new country, where the general tendency is to reach out further than is sometimes prudent, and when expectations are not realised, disastrous results frequently follow: houses are mortgaged, assignments are made, failures occur, and many leave to seek their fortunes in new places. Such would seem to be more particularly the state of affairs in western Washington.

The heavy rains in the early spring, while beautifying the eastern portion of the State, where the soil is of a sandy, dry character, interfered considerably with the ploughing and seeding of the ground in the western portion. The soil there remaining cold and wet from the winter, the crops, consequently backward, were hindered from ripening and maturing by the dull weather continuing all through the summer, and the rains which commenced again in the early autumn delayed still further the harvesting and spoiled a good portion of the crop. These circumstances and the slow demand for what was gathered sent prices for all farm produce so low down that there was hardly any margin for profit left to the farmer after his crops were actually marketed and sold.

*Wheat.* The rains in the early part of the year benefited the land in eastern Washington, where the great wheat belt is, and the crop was very large, estimated at 20,000,000 bushels, being about 5,000,000 bushels over that of 1890; of this amount about 5,500,000 bushels have been shipped foreign from the ports in Puget Sound, chiefly to Great Britain, France, and Belgium for

## SAN FRANCISCO.

the European market. The lowest price paid for wheat for export was about 3s. 4d. per bushel and the highest 4s. 2d.

The export of flour for the year from the Sound ports has shown a great increase over last year; the total for the year amounts to 160,358 barrels, equal to about 125,040l. *Flour.*

The hop crop of 1891 was about 45,000 bales, of which the Northern Pacific Railway shipped east by rail during the last quarter of the year 34,026 bales. The decrease from last year has been due chiefly to damage from the hop louse which made its appearance in some yards last season and spread through most of the districts this year. In yards where care was taken and the vines sprayed frequently, commencing early in the season, the yield was pretty good. The quassia wash used after the English method seems to be very effective, being perfectly harmless to the growing crop, and is generally adopted. The quality has also been very much below the average. Prices ranging from 4d. to 10d. per lb., averaging about 7d. The cost of production is now estimated from 5d. to 6d. per lb., on account of the expense of spraying and washing. *Hops.*

Many acres of ground have been planted out in fruit trees during the year, chiefly with the Italian or Fallenberg prune, which seems to be the most profitable of all other varieties by reason of its productiveness, size, and good drying qualities, and brings the highest price in any market. The French prune comes next. The German and St. Catharine's plum are also grown to some extent. Bartlett pears were very profitable this year, bringing in the market, in competition with California pears, from 5s. to 6s. per 20-lb. box; for profit in selling green or for the canneries (the shops or places where the fruit is boiled and put up in tins for market), the Bartlett, Seckel, and Idaho pears will always be the most extensively grown. *Fruit growing.*

First grade apples have ranged from 3s. to 9s. per bushel box; the crop has been good.

Small fruits are very profitable. Strawberries and blackberries bringing 5d. per lb. for the whole crop, raspberries 7½d. to 1s. per lb., gooseberries and currants from 3d. to 5d. per lb. this year. An orchard properly kept and in bearing condition, either in large or small fruits, ought to yield a profit of 100l. per acre. More attention will have to be paid now to the cultivation of the soil and the care of the trees, pruning, spraying, &c., as scale, caterpillars, and other destructive insects to fruit trees are increasing rapidly in the districts; fruit-dries and other methods of preserving the crops will also have to be used, as a very large percentage of the crop perishes before it can be marketed in a fresh state.

All fruit, apples, cherries, plums, strawberries, carefully selected, of an even size, and nicely packed in boxes, command a ready sale. Some districts have been more favoured than others, but generally it has been a good fruit season, both in quality and quantity.

Probably over 4,000 acres of ground have been planted with

potatoes this year in western Washington alone, chiefly on land leased by Chinese. The rains in the early part of the year rotted the seed in the ground, which had to be planted over again, making the crop late; when the potatoes were gathered there was no market, prices were so low it did not pay to sack and ship them and pay the freight charges, consequently many thousands of bushels were left to decay and waste on the ground, and in many instances the crop was never picked at all. The quality was also in many districts very bad on account of the wet season. Prices ranged from 1*l*. per ton wholesale to 3*l*. per ton retail.

*Irrigation.* The irrigation companies in eastern Washington are progressing rapidly with their ditches for irrigation purposes, the main ditch will be 60 miles in length when completed; 25 miles are already finished. The ditches are estimated to irrigate over 100,000 acres of valuable land, the soil of which is well adapted for farming, and wherever cultivated has produced large crops.

*Timber.* From reports received from a majority of the saw-mills, the total cut in the State for the year 1891 will aggregate 1,375,000,000 feet, valued at 3,300,000*l*. Owing to the long distances from the eastern market and the heavy freight rates, the shipment of timber east by rail is practically prohibited. The Northern Pacific Railway has recently lowered the rates, so that a great increase may be expected in this business. The export trade, which amounted to about 200,000,000 feet, was materially decreased from last year by the foreign financial stringency, and the revolutions and disturbances in Central and South America. The trade is improving a little. Shipments of spars still continue to be made to Europe, principally to England and Norway.

The shipment to eastern States by rail of cedars, shingles for roofing, &c., has increased very greatly over last year, but the high transportation rates are a great drawback to the development of this industry; many new mills have been put in operation during the year.

*Coal.* The output of coal, which is of lignite and bituminous character, of the various mines of the State during the past year has been about 1,300,000 tons, though it would have been very much larger but for the unfortunate labour difficulties in the King County mines during the spring and early summer of this year, which caused cessation of work, and consequently curtailed production. The average price to consumers in western Washington during the year has been from 16*s*. to 1*l*. per ton (of 2,000 lbs.); at the mines the price has been 10*s*. per ton.

*Iron.* The iron ores in this State consist of magnetite, hematite, limonite, and bog ores. These ores are of excellent quality, and the quantity in some districts seems to be inexhaustible. Very little up to the present has been done towards developing these deposits.

*Precious metals.* The mining for precious metals has been attended with so many obstacles that but little progress has been made, in many instances not much more than mere prospecting. The ores from the Silver Creek mining district are galena with iron and sulphurate of copper, carrying gold, silver, and copper, averaging about 9*l*. per ton in value; about 500 tons have already been taken out and wait means of transportation to the smelter. The ores from the Monte Christo mines are of the same character, carrying from 2*l*. to 10*l*. in gold, from 2*l*. to 15*l*. in silver, and from 14 per cent. to 16 per cent. of lead. These mines are dependent for their value upon their transportation facilities, of which there are none at present.

The ores from the Cascade Mining District are galena, and carrying silver, averaging about 14*l*. to the ton.

The character of the ores from the Snoqualmie district are free-milling, with sulphurets, concentrating and smelting ores, the latter being lead and copper, containing gold and silver. Many of the richest and most valuable mines are located in the most inaccessible part of the State.

Fish. The salmon pack in this State for the year 1891 is estimated at 177,033 cases, of which 144,000 cases were Columbia River salmon. Large quantities are smoked and dried, and many are salted down in barrels for domestic use. Halibut are caught in large quantities on the fishing banks from 15 miles to 20 miles west of Cape Flattery, and in the Straits of Fuca and the Archipelago de Haro; the catch is taken to Port Townsend, packed in ice in boxes, and from there sent by steamer to Jacoma, where it is put in the cold storage warehouse and frozen, or else immediately placed in refrigerator railway trucks, or carriages, and shipped to eastern markets, where is an excellent market—these carriages being especially built to keep fish, meat, fruit, or anything perishable in a cold or frozen state; shipments have successfully been made to New York and Boston, Mass. Large quantities of herring and cod are caught, and houses for smoking and curing these and other fish are contemplated being built, but the demand at present seems limited, and hardly warrants a great outlay of expense. Until freight rates to eastern markets are very much reduced, but very few of such industries and enterprises can be managed to bring in very profitable returns; the present rate per truck by rail to Chicago is from 120*l*. to 180*l*. by passenger train, and from 80*l*. to 120*l*. by goods or freight train, according to the capacity of the truck. There is no doubt that the waters along the whole coast from California up to the northern part of Alaska, almost up to the Arctic Ocean, abound with good fish. The "Albatross," the steamship belonging to the United States Fish Commission, each return from her northern cruise in search of new fishing grounds and other scientific explorations, reports the discovery of new fishing banks where fish were caught, principally halibut and cod, and of fine flavour.

Railways The total new mileage constructed in the State during the year was 288·15 miles, with over 100 miles under construction. Surveys have been made for over 1,000 miles in addition to these, and many more are under contemplation. The total railway mileage of the State for the year 1891, constructed and operated, is 2,281 miles. A very important piece of railway work during the year was the completion of the Seattla and Montana Railway to the boundary line between the United States and Canada, thus completing connections with the Canadian Pacific, which enables Canadian Pacific passengers and freight to go by train all the way from Vancouver, British Columbia, to California. The finishing of the Great Northern Railway to a direct outlet in Puget Sound is likely to be made during the coming year, so there will be not less than four transcontinental routes meeting on the waters of Puget Sound, and competing for the growing business of the North-West and the Asiatic trade.

Freights. The opening rates for the grain season of 1891 and 1892 were firm on a basis of 1*l*. 17*s*. 6*d*. for iron ships, going as high as 2*l*. 7*s*. 6*d*. for convenient-sized vessels for September and October loading. The rush of tonnage to avail such rates, combined with the collapse of the European grain market, caused freight rates to go as low as 21*s*. for iron ships, and several vessels engaged at high rates have compromised with the shippers, accepting a lump sum for cancellation, and either took timber charters or proceed elsewhere for cargoes. Timber freights likewise suffered for superabundance of tonnage, and Melbourne rates have gone from 2*l*. 15*s*. in January to 2*l*. for December loading. West-Coast South America rates decreased from 2*l*. 12*s*. 6*d*. in January to 1*l*. 12*s*. 6*d*. in December. Coal freights, owing to the overstocked condition of the California markets, have been nominal, rates averaging 6*s*. per ton.

Silver export. The export of silver from Port Townsend to British Columbia during the year has been 21,779*l*.

Health. The State has been very healthy during the past year, no epidemic of infectious or contagious diseases having occurred, either among the people or animals.

General progress and prosperity. It will not be inappropriate to mention here the spirit of enterprise and progress of the citizens which is apparent in the towns of this new State, and so characteristic of the country. There is hardly a town of any size in the State with a population of more than 3,000 persons, which has not its gas, water, and electric-light works; fire departments, possessing engines (steam), hose-carts, and ladder apparatus, horses carefully trained, and other contrivances in case of fire (Seattle has a fire-boat for the protection of property on the water-front, with pumps which can throw 7,000 gallons of water per minute); electric motor (using steam engines), and two with cable street railways in operation (Seattle has 22 miles of cable and 59 miles of electric railway in operation). Very fine buildings and business houses constructed of brick, stone, and iron, several storeys in height, are to be found in all the large towns, with lifts, called elevators, and all modern conveniences and contrivances. Fine county and city halls, court houses, churches, &c., are conspicuous objects as you approach these towns, particularly from the water, and handsome residences with pretty gardens are met with in the suburbs.

Very great inducements in the way of donations of land for building sites, &c., money, or other valuable considerations are offered as subsidies by many towns to individuals or companies, who will introduce and put in operation any industry, enterprise, or manufacture which will be a benefit to such town from a commercial point of view.

Among some of the manufacturing industries of the State are sash, door, and house-furniture factories, box factories, machine shops, foundries, breweries, brick, tile, and cement works, cigar making, biscuit (called cracker) factories, soap, broom and ice works, with several minor industries. At Jacoma are the Pacific Naphtha Launch Works, the only ones on the Pacific Coast; within two years they have built 20 launches, besides several small boats, some going into British Columbia. Not far also from this town are the works of the Jacoma Smelting and Refining Company for reducing the ores containing the precious metals; the furnace has been in operation two years, and has a capacity of 120 tons per day. During the year 1891 there was turned out 7,139·60 ounces of gold, 451,972·61 ounces of silver, and 4,247,417 lbs. of lead, the value reckoned at about 156,226*l*. During the year ores have been received from Alaska, California, Mexico, and South America, in addition to those from this and neighbouring States. To bring into greater prominence the productions, resources, trades, and manufactures of this State there was held, and kept open for several days during last autumn, at Jacoma, the Western Washington Industrial Exposition, which was visited by people from all sections of the country and British Columbia, and was considered a very creditable exhibition.

I append the several annexes, marked respectively A, B, and C, to show in detail the commerce and trade in this collection district, which I am able to present through the courtesy of Andrew Watson, Esq., collector of customs for this district.

Annex A.—RETURN of all Shipping at the Port of Port Townsend in the Year 1891.

ENTERED.

| Nationality. | Sailing. Number of Vessels. | Sailing. Tons. | Steam. Number of Vessels. | Steam. Tons. | Total. Number of Vessels. | Total. Tons. |
|---|---|---|---|---|---|---|
| British | 68 | 94,652 | 95 | 28,776 | 163 | 123,428 |
| American | 195 | 180,949 | 1,406 | 1,023,608 | 1,601 | 1,204,557 |
| Norwegian and Swedish | 18 | 18,234 | ... | ... | 18 | 18,234 |
| Chilian | 15 | 14,361 | ... | ... | 15 | 14,361 |
| German | 6 | 8,720 | ... | ... | 6 | 8,720 |
| Nicaraguan | 2 | 1,281 | ... | ... | 2 | 1,281 |
| Italian | 1 | 2,095 | ... | ... | 1 | 2,095 |
| Hawaiian Islands | 1 | 779 | ... | ... | 1 | 779 |
| Ecuadorian | 1 | 778 | ... | ... | 1 | 778 |
| Spanish | 1 | 510 | ... | ... | 1 | 510 |
| Total | 308 | 322,359 | 1,501 | 1,052,384 | 1,809 | 1,374,743 |
| ,, for the year preceding | 258 | 239,440 | 1,244 | 958,726 | 1,502 | 1,198,166 |

(1343)

## UNITED STATES.

CLEARED.

| Nationality. | Steam. Number of Vessels. | Steam. Tons. | Sailing. Number of Vessels. | Sailing. Tons. | Total. Number of Vessels. | Total. Tons. |
|---|---|---|---|---|---|---|
| British | 74 | 101,180 | 100 | 24,509 | 174 | 125,689 |
| American | 198 | 189,875 | 1,469 | 1,040,145 | 1,667 | 1,230,020 |
| Norwegian and Swedish | 19 | 19,574 | ... | ... | 19 | 19,574 |
| Chilian | 16 | 15,749 | ... | ... | 16 | 15,749 |
| German | 5 | 5,109 | ... | ... | 5 | 5,109 |
| Nicaraguan | 2 | 1,281 | ... | ... | 2 | 1,281 |
| Hawaiian Islands | 1 | 779 | ... | ... | 1 | 779 |
| Ecuadorian | 1 | 778 | ... | ... | 1 | 778 |
| Spanish | 1 | 510 | ... | ... | 1 | 510 |
| Total | 317 | 334,835 | 1,569 | 1,064,654 | 1,886 | 1,399,489 |
| ,, for the year preceding | 260 | 237,358 | 1,229 | 935,131 | 1,489 | 1,172,489 |

Annex B.—RETURN of Principal Articles of Export from Port Townsend during the Years 1891–90.

| Articles. | | 1891. Quantity. | 1891. Value. £ | 1890. Quantity. | 1890. Value. £ |
|---|---|---|---|---|---|
| Cattle | Head | 977 | 5,434 | 355 | 3,060 |
| Hogs | ,, | 53 | 114 | 872 | 1,272 |
| Horses | ,, | 303 | 6,756 | 153 | 8,848 |
| Sheep | ,, | 32,931 | 15,247 | 20,940 | 9,397 |
| All other animals | ... | ... | 1,012 | ... | 815 |
| Wheat | Bushels | 5,484,001 | 1,040,981 | 2,025,926 | 320,118 |
| Flour | Barrels | 134,805 | 110,448 | 125,089 | 94,617 |
| All other breadstuffs | ... | ... | 4,039 | ... | 4,801 |
| Provisions, meats, &c., fresh, tinned | ... | ... | 21,398 | ... | 22,120 |
| Dairy products | ... | ... | 1,686 | ... | 3,899 |
| Vegetables, fresh, tinned | ... | ... | 1,098 | ... | 820 |
| Fruits, fresh, tinned | ... | ... | 5,294 | ... | 2,361 |
| Hops | ... | ... | 300 | ... | 77 |
| Fish, fresh, salted, tinned | ... | ... | 3,619 | ... | 2,411 |
| Furs, furskins, hides, dressed | ... | ... | 1,371 | ... | 13,313 |
| Liquors, spirits, wines | ... | ... | 3,866 | ... | 2,165 |
| Oils, animal, mineral, vegetable | ... | ... | 10,975 | ... | 9,105 |
| Tobacco, cigars | ... | ... | 2,430 | ... | 1,546 |
| Agricultural implements, &c. | ... | ... | 793 | ... | 421 |
| Iron, and manufactures of | ... | ... | 31,770 | ... | 22,260 |
| Indiarubber, and manufactures of | ... | ... | 1,995 | ... | ... |
| Leather, and manufactures of | ... | ... | 3,510 | ... | ... |
| Paper, and manufactures of, books, stationery | ... | ... | 4,055 | ... | 3,549 |
| Cotton, and manufactures of, cloth | ... | ... | 3,143 | ... | ... |
| Wool, and manufactures of, carpets, &c. | ... | ... | 1,397 | ... | 736 |
| Wood, and manufactures of, boards, deals, &c. | ... | ... | 217,884 | ... | 258,714 |
| Wood, sawn, hewn, logs | ... | ... | 7,700 | ... | 721 |
| ,, doors, mouldings, house furniture, &c. | ... | ... | 3,836 | ... | 6,007 |
| All other articles, unmanufactured and manufactured | ... | ... | 24,139 | ... | 48,513 |
| Total | ... | ... | 1,536,290 | ... | 841,766 |

## SAN FRANCISCO.

### RETURN of Principal Articles of Import to Port Townsend during the Years 1891–90.

| Articles. | | 1891. Quantity. | 1891. Value. | 1890. Quantity. | 1890. Value. |
|---|---|---|---|---|---|
| | | | £ | | £ |
| **Free—** | | | | | |
| Tea | Lbs. | 241,378 | 7,352 | 229,750 | 6,742 |
| Furs, skins, hides (raw) | ... | ... | 10,581 | ... | 8,059 |
| Household effects | ... | ... | 10,346 | ... | ... |
| Ores | ... | ... | 1,524 | ... | ... |
| Other articles | ... | ... | 13,481 | ... | 1,553 |
| Total | ... | ... | 43,284 | ... | 16,354 |
| **Dutiable—** | | | | | |
| Cement | Lbs. | 23,262,720 | 19,910 | 70,813 | 18,587 |
| Coal | Tons | 18,756 | 14,457 | 3,174 | 3,635 |
| Firebrick | ... | ... | 513 | ... | 1,150 |
| Iron, and manufactures of | ... | ... | 7,470 | ... | ... |
| Earthenware, china, porcelain | ... | ... | 4,418 | ... | ... |
| Cotton and woollen manufactures | ... | ... | 548 | ... | ... |
| Flax, and manufactures of | ... | ... | 211 | ... | ... |
| Rice, granulated | Lbs. | 2,892,173 | 9,595 | 3,067,901 | 10,160 |
| Provisions, meats, vegetables, &c. | ... | ... | 772 | ... | ... |
| Hay and agricultural produce | ... | ... | 987 | ... | ... |
| Furs, dressed | ... | ... | 1,082 | ... | 129 |
| Fish, all kinds | ... | ... | 406 | ... | 361 |
| Liquors, spirits, wine | ... | ... | 1,584 | ... | 2,366 |
| Cattle | Head | 12 | 70 | 48 | 361 |
| Horses and other animals | ... | ... | 76 | ... | ... |
| Other articles | ... | ... | 13,186 | ... | 20,732 |
| Total | ... | ... | 74,517 | ... | 57,481 |
| Free | ... | ... | 43,284 | ... | 16,354 |
| Dutiable | ... | ... | 74,517 | ... | 57,481 |
| Grand total | ... | ... | 117,801 | ... | 73,835 |

NOTE.—The goods and merchandise shipped through in bond to other places in the United States and Canada probably amount to 200,000*l*., but it is very difficult to obtain correct figures of these shipments. The 1*l*. sterling has been reckoned at 4·8665 dol., the custom-house standard at this port.

(1343)

## UNITED STATES.

Annex C.—TABLE showing the Total Value of all Articles Exported from Port Townsend and Imported to Port Townsend from and to Foreign Countries during the Years 1891–90.

|  | Exports. |  | Imports. |  |
| Country. | 1891. | 1890. | 1891. | 1890. |
| --- | --- | --- | --- | --- |
|  | £ | £ | £ | £ |
| Great Britain | 487,096 | 381,646 | 31,741 | 28,894 |
| British Columbia, Canada | 168,928 | 169,398 | 57,184 | 28,493 |
| Australia | 104,376 | 110,623 | .. | 1,391 |
| France | 501,386 | 15,865 | .. | 51 |
| Belgium | 148,608 | 2,633 | .. | .. |
| Hawaiian Islands | 44,954 | 49,405 | 682 | 10 |
| Chile | 22,961 | 52,403 | 783 | 823 |
| China | 18,256 | 13,324 | 12,432 | 7,091 |
| Peru | 16,994 | 26,113 | .. | .. |
| Mexico | 15,758 | 7,584 | .. | .. |
| French Possessions, Australia | 5,492 | 2,131 | .. | .. |
| Brazil | 1,481 | .. | .. | .. |
| Japan | .. | .. | 11,946 | 7,170 |
| Germany | .. | 1,662 | 2,733 | 26 |
| Other countries | .. | 8,978 | 300 | 37 |
| Total | 1,536,290 | 841,765 | 117,801 | 73,986 |

## LOS ANGELES.

Mr. Vice-Consul Mortimer reports as follows:—

*Introductory remarks.* For the last three years I have chronicled an annually-increasing depression in business and financial disasters, resulting chiefly from the "boom" of 1887. In my report for 1890 I stated that I thought the period of depression was nearly at an end; that real property was for sale below its value; and that it was a good time to purchase. The events of the last year have justified the opinion I then expressed, and it is now evident that there is a renewed demand for farm property at good prices, and that in many branches of trade business is in a much better condition. Apart from the fact that the land here is very productive, and raises very valuable crops, this district offers greater inducements to settlers with limited capital than the central and northern counties, in that the small area of the fruit farms admits of companionship and proximity to churches and schools, advantages which are out of the question on the large grain farms in the central portion of the State; and also because the climate in the vicinity of Los Angeles is much more desirable, being warmer in winter and very much cooler in summer than in the central counties. These social and climatic advantages, with other causes, account for the rapidity with which this district is recovering from the wreck made by the "boom."

The best evidence that the reaction is now at an end is found in the increased activity shown in the development of the country. For example, the total number of acres planted in orange trees in San Bernardino county, from the introduction of the industry to the end of 1890, was 13,070 acres. During the year 1891 this acreage was increased to 19,673 acres, the increase, 6,603 acres, being more than 50 per cent. of the total acreage planted in all the years prior to 1891. The other counties in this district show similar results in other branches of horticulture and agriculture. The following comparative statements show that business generally is improving. The Los Angeles clearing-house reports clearings as follows:—

|      | £         |
|------|-----------|
| 1890 | 6,200,000 |
| 1891 | 7,825,000 |

The clearings for the first half of 1891 amounted to 3,622,000*l*., and for the second half to 4,203,000*l*.

The assessed value of all property in the counties of Los Angeles and Santa Barbara after equalisation was as follows:—

|               | Year. | Value.      |
|---------------|-------|-------------|
|               |       | £           |
| Los Angeles   | 1890  | 13,895,000  |
| ”             | 1891  | 16,523,500  |
| Santa Barbara | 1890  | 2,943,000   |
| ”             | 1891  | 3,274,000   |

I have not received returns from the assessors of the other counties in this district. It is stated in the press, however, that there has been an increase in 1891 in the value of taxable property in all the counties of Southern California.

The value of real property sold and conveyed in the city and county of Los Angeles during the year 1891, as shown by recorded deeds, averaged 300,000*l*. per month, the total for the year being 3,600,000*l*. This is a little less than the total for 1890. As, however, the transactions of 1890 included the completion of transactions arising out of the "boom" of 1887, I believe I may say that there was some increase in new transactions in real estate in 1891. In so far as British interests are concerned, the most important matters in this report will be found under the following headings:—"Raisins," "Wine," "Ramie," "Advice to British capitalists," "Tin," "Irrigation bonds," "Advice to emigrants."

*Trade and Commerce.*

The imports are shown in Annex B.

Portland cement.
Portland cement invoiced in London at 1*l.* 4*s.* to 1*l.* 6*s.* per ton sells here for 3*l.* 5*s.* to 3*l.* 10*s.* per ton. The duty is 6*s.* 5*d.* per ton. Messrs. Whittier, Fuller, and Co., the only firm here importing direct from England, write me: "Cement is sold very close, and sales are usually made net cash."

Exports.
The chief exports are oranges and other fruits, wines and brandies, and grain.

Oranges.
The orange crop for 1891 of the counties in this district amounted to 4,437 car loads (44,370 tons), an increase of 1,611 car loads on the product of 1890. This large increase is due chiefly to the extermination of "white scale," a pest which three years ago threatened to destroy the orange groves in this district, and which has been exterminated by the vedolia cardinalis, a parasite imported from Australia. The orange crop for 1892, now being marketed, will be a very light one, owing to heavy losses from windstorms and frost. The loss this year from windstorms is unprecedented. The loss from frost occurs at long intervals, the last serious loss having taken place eight years ago. Oranges are now being shipped to the eastern States in car-load lots at 3*s.* 8*d.* per cwt. This is the lowest rate heretofore made, and is due to the competition between the transcontinental railways. Further particulars of the orange industry are given elsewhere in this report.

Canned fruits.
The manager of the Southern California Packing Company estimates the pack of fruit in this district in 1891 at 3,500,000 cans of $2\frac{1}{2}$ lbs. each, of which his company packed 2,000,000 cans. He adds: "The business is not more overdone here than elsewhere. . . . . The prospects for the coming season are good for fruit, but poor for a large profit, unless the eastern crop should be cut short." A market is found in this country for the canned fruits of this district. A small quantity of dried and evaporated fruits was shipped to London during the year. Should these fruits suit the English market a very large business may be built up.

Refund of tariff on imported tin.
Owing apparently to an oversight on the part of the framers of the new United States customs tariff, canned goods packed in imported tin can be sold in foreign countries at a lower price than in this country, 99 per cent. of the tariff on imported tin being refunded to the packers on export of goods packed in such tin.

Vegetables.
Vegetables from this district are now being shipped to Chicago and other eastern cities, and I am advised that the business is proving profitable. The charges for carriage, formerly 1*l.* 8*s.* per cwt., have recently been reduced by the Atchison, Topika, and Santa Fé Railway to 4*s.* 2*d.*, at which figure the growers here can make a large profit. The agent for Wells, Fargo and Co.'s Express Company writes me as follows:— "The plan to be followed as soon as the farmers produce vegetables in sufficient quantities is to ship in refrigerator car lots to such important points as Kansas City, Denver, Omaha, and Chicago, and then distribute through the express companies to small surrounding towns. This will make the cost of transportation nominal, and

more people can afford to buy. Strawberries are shipped successfully each year during the months of November, December, January, and February, as far east as New York."

The product of raisins is increasing in this district, not so rapidly, however, as in the central counties. Mr. West, a member of the State Board of Viticultural Commissioners, is of opinion that the producers must look to this country only for their market, and that when the vineyards now planted are in bearing the market will be overstocked. In reply to some queries from me he writes me as follows:—" It is true that California raisins are driving the foreign product out of the American market, which is only natural because we are now producing about as many raisins in California as are consumed in this country, and there is consequently no market left for foreign goods. Last year, when prices were very high, the profits per acre from good vineyards were not unfrequently 40$l$. to 60$l$. per acre, or on average vineyards, say, 12$l$. to 20$l$. per acre. This season the price has fallen to 1½$d$. to 2$d$. per lb., and the profits will probably range from 5$l$. to 10$l$. per acre on average vineyards in full bearing. In my opinion, the present demoralised condition of the raisin business is due to the fact that the crop is becoming rather unwieldy. There is a profit to the grower at 1½$d$. per lb. in sacks at a shipping point in California. Whether this price can now be obtained or not I do not know, but am informed by one of the largest commission houses that the market is getting into better condition. I do not believe California can ever market raisins in Europe, because our labour costs us too much. While I think many of the stories of the vast profits of the various horticultural and viticultural products of California are overdrawn, I believe that 40 acres of good land, well and economically cultivated by the owner and devoted to various products, will in all cases yield a comfortable living, for the special reason that nearly everything required to maintain a family can be produced on the land."

A London financial paper of January 16, 1892, contained an article on the raisin industry in California, from which I make the following extracts:—" Packers stand ready to buy the raisins in the sweet box . . . the raisins have a ready cash value, and the business has thus been a tempting one for farmers of every grade. . . . There seems no reason why young Englishmen should not choose this pleasant and promising career." In so far as these sentences convey the impression that there is a ready sale for raisins, that there is no danger of over-production, and that the business is a species of pastime, such impression is distinctly erroneous.

The low price realised in the eastern States for the wines produced here is largely due to the manufacture and sale there of bogus wine. I am indebted to Mr. Charles A. Wetmore, Proprietor of the Cresta Blanca Vineyards, and for many years the Chief Executive Officer of the Viticultural Commission, for an interesting account of the adulteration of California wines and cognate subjects. Mr. Wetmore thinks that the removal of the

(1343)

tax on brandy used in fortifying sweet wines has not been in operation long enough to test its effect on the wine trade. He says, "Imitation sweet wines must necessarily be to some extent displaced so long as the price of grapes in California remains low. Higher prices hereafter must prevail for grapes, which will raise the price of musts, and again enable falsifications to be practised profitably. The London firms who have been placing California wines in England do not seem to think that our common sherries or sweet wines can be marketed there. . . . The quantity of wines shipped to England is gradually but steadily increasing, and London merchants are finding out what we have, and can continue to produce, which will gain favour in England. We can with our best and middle grade clarets, burgundies, white wines (sauternes and hocks), and brandies establish permanent trade relations. What is needed, however, to perfect this business is a system of close connections between agencies here more or less controlled in the interest of London houses, so that supplies may be acquired from young vintages, properly stored here, and sufficiently developed to determine their true character and adaptability before shipment. Such agencies here could prepare wines in the interest of the London houses, reserve sufficient to meet probable demand, and dispose of all surplusage in this country. In this way uniform products could be secured, and skill in overcoming difficulties of transportation be acquired. British capital is needed here to develop this trade. Consignments from growers are generally failures, and sporadic purchases ensure no uniformity in qualities. So far British capital has not sought those sections of our vineyards which produce what the London market really wants, but has entered into competition with British interests in Spain and Portugal. The products of the vineyards of southern California will find henceforth all the outlet they need in the United States at more remunerative prices than in England, while the higher grades of clarets, burgundies, and sauternes of central western California will find connoisseurs to appreciate them in England, even more profitably than in our own country. Except in the case of certain vineyard brands established and locally known, brandy from the south and interior will be the exception, and we shall gain steadily in favour as our distillers improve their output. The sweet wines and brandies of southern California are more appreciated in the eastern States than dry wines from the same section. Low prices have prevailed, however, during the last five years, very discouraging to the growers. Decrease in production, increase of markets, and increased demand, are restoring confidence, and we believe that after this spring a rapid advance in values will take place. Such advance cannot again be checked, except by a large increase in acreage of wine grapes, which under any circumstances could not be immediately inaugurated, nor could the effects of new plantings be felt for a number of years. It is probable that the increase in the value of grapes will continue for at least 10 years. Experimental lots of wines have been shipped to France, but any material advance in our values will cause this to cease, our heavy-bodied dry red wines have been in demand in France, but our ability to meet this demand has only been an evidence of the distress of our growers."

The Chief Executive Officer of the Viticultural Commission writes me as follows:—"The new tariff adopted by the French Government has stopped shipments of wine from California to that country.... Our champagnes are gaining in favour in England. During 1891 500 cases of Haraszethys Eclipse Champagne have been sold in London, and orders have been received for more."

*Shipping and Navigation.*

Wilmington (San Pedro), about 21 miles south of this city, is the principal port for this district. 180,000*l.* has been expended by the Government in improving the inner harbour and the entrance thereto, and vessels drawing 20 feet can now enter the inner harbour at high water and come alongside the wharves. In my Report for 1890 I stated that an inspection of the coast-line of this district from Point Duma to San Juan Capistrano (see map accompanying my Report for 1889) had then recently been made by three officers of the Corps of Engineers, under instructions from the Government to select the most suitable place for a deep-water harbour. Colonel Benyaurd, the Chairman of the Board, writes me as to the decision arrived at, and in reply to other queries (the nature of which are indicated by his replies) as follows:—"The River and Harbour Act of September 19, 1890, provided for the appointment of a Board of Engineer Officers to examine the coast between Point Duma and San Juan Capistrano, with a view of determining the best location for a deep-water harbour within those limits. The choice was necessarily limited to Santa Monica Bay and San Pedro Bay. The Board selected the latter bay, as affording more advantages for a deep-water harbour than were possessed by the former. To secure this harbour the construction of a breakwater is necessary. The estimated cost of the structure is from 825,251*l.* to 918,899*l.*, depending upon the character of the material used in the construction. The Board was not required to make any recommendation or express any opinion as to the requirements of that section of the coast commercially, but simply to select the site and present a project, with estimate of cost of securing a deep-water harbour.

Harbour improvements.

"This outer or deep-water harbour is intended for the accommodation of the large vessels coming to that section of the coast. The draught of some of these ships is 26 feet to 27 feet. In the present condition of San Pedro Bay it is thought that the maximum depth that we will be able to maintain at the entrance to the inner harbour is about 16 feet at mean low tide, or about 20 feet at ordinary high tide. If the construction of the outer breakwater be undertaken it is possible that we can obtain a greater depth at the inner harbour. The amount expended upon the improvement has not been exclusively for the benefit of the coasting trade, but for that class of vessels that could enter the harbour. It is well known that many of the deep-draught foreign vessels could reach the wharves after lightering a part of the freight outside. The amount expended upon the improvement during the year ending December 31, 1891, was 20,720*l*. The amount at present available is 2,183*l*."

It is evident from the foregoing letter that until the breakwater is constructed foreign-going vessels must continue to lighten a portion of their cargo before obtaining the protection afforded by the inner harbour.

A deep water harbour should be constructed here, as this district possesses the following advantages over San Francisco for the overland transportation of Asiatic and Australian commerce: First, the railroad here from the eastern States is 500 miles less than to San Francisco, and is equivalent to 800 miles, owing to the comparatively easy grades, and freedom from snow blockades on this southern route. Second, Los Angeles has two competing transcontinental railways, and will shortly have a third, and San Francisco has practically but one. In view of these facts, I think it probable that Congress will within a few years make an appropriation for the construction of the breakwater recommended by the Board. A large part of the domestic trade of this district is done at Redondo, a port a few miles west of San Pedro and about 18 miles from Los Angeles. The British ship "Kirkcudbrightshire" recently landed a cargo of Portland cement and glass there direct from Antwerp. The president of the Redondo Beach Company, the owners of the wharf, writes me that substantial mooring have been placed near the wharf, sufficient to guarantee vessels against damage by storms. Since writing the foregoing I see in the press that a Bill changing the name of this customs collection district from Wilmington to Los Angeles has been passed by Congress. This Bill makes Los Angeles a port of entry and delivery, San Pedro a sub-port of entry and delivery, and the ports of delivery in this collection district, namely, Santa Barbara, Hueneme, and Ventura, have been increased by the addition of Santa Monica and Redondo.

## Agriculture.

Beet sugar.

In my report for 1890 I commented at some length on the sugar beet industry, now extensively carried on at Mr. Gird's ranch, 35 miles east of this city. Mr. Gird has kindly supplied me with information on the subject, which I summarise as follows: The factory on his ranch has a capacity of 350 tons of beets per day, is the largest in the United States, and in 1891 produced 1,026 tons of refined sugar. As the total product of refined sugar in the United States in 1891 was under 4,500 tons, it appears that the Chino factory in its first year produced nearly one-fourth of the total product. In the recent changes in the United States customs tariff, sugar, under No. 16, Dutch standard, was conditionally placed on the free list, and a bounty of $\frac{3}{4}d.$ to $1d.$ per lb. was offered for all sugar produced in the United States. In answer to a query from me whether this bounty enured to the benefit of the consumer, Mr. Gird replies, "Yes; sugar is $5\frac{1}{2}$ farthings lower now than before the tariff was changed, and even with the bounty of $1d.$ per lb. paid to the manufacturer, sugar remains practically at $1\frac{1}{2}$ farthings per lb. lower than it otherwise would have been." Prior to the granting of a bounty the sugar beet industry had not proved profitable in the United States, except in California. Owing to the mildness of this climate operations can be carried on here for several months longer than in the eastern States, and the expensive plant required in the manufacture is idle for a comparatively short time. Mr. Gird thinks that the length of the planting season counterbalances the high price paid here for labour. I have recommended English farmers settling here to rent land near this factory and engage in beet culture while acquiring knowledge and experience of the country. Mr. Gird writes me that 2,700 acres were planted in beets last year, and says, "The tenants have in some cases done extremely well, and the average have made a reasonable profit; there were some failures, as would naturally be expected in the first season of a new industry to which nearly all were strangers." Quite a number of beet sugar factories on the co-operative plan are projected in this district, and several will, I think, be constructed. A recent United States Government report states that there are nearly 1,500 square miles of land in Los Angeles county suitable for beet cultivation, and as the amount of sugar consumed annually in the United States amounts to nearly 2,000,000 tons, the business may grow to large proportions here.

A good deal of interest has been manifested here in the past year in the culture of ramie. The attempts to introduce it in the southern States have not been very successful, owing partly to the moistures of the climate, and chiefly because the machinery necessary to prepare it for market had not then been invented. It has been demonstrated that the dryness of this climate will admit of the preparation of ramie for market at a lower cost than elsewhere, and it is stated that a decorticating machine has been invented which will prepare the fibre at a sufficiently low cost to admit of its being grown profitably. If this is the case the invention is a most important one for this district, as ramie will grow well on alkali lands, and there are here many thousands of acres so impregnated with alkali as to be of little value for other purposes. At the last session of the Legislature of this State a large appropriation was made to provide for free distribution of ramie roots. Mr. W. H. Murray has been appointed State Superintendent of Ramie Culture, and I am indebted to him for a pamphlet containing the following information : 100 lbs. of crude ramie can be run through the decorticating machine per hour at a

*Ramie culture.*

cost of about ½d. per lb. A trial of the machine was made recently at Bakersfield in the district, when 270 lbs. of dry stalks, the product of one quarter of an acre thinly planted, was converted into marketable fibre in 1½ hours. Specimens of the fibre have been sent by Mr. Murray to all parts of Europe, and have elicited great praise. Messrs. Ide and Christie, fibre brokers, of 72, Mark Lane, London, write him as follows: "We could sell 50 tons of your ramie fibre at 16l. per ton, free London, 2½ per cent. discount." On the other hand, Mr. Wm. C. Stubbs, of Louisiana, in an interview had with him by a newspaper reporter, expressed himself as follows: "No machine yet tried has been able to work over an acre a day, and until they can get one that will go through the ramie from 10 acres to 15 acres a day it will not be profitable to raise ramie. I expect such a machine will be invented some day, and when it is the inventor can collect a prize of 20,000l., offered by the British Government for the benefit of its Indian possessions." I mention the matter as it will interest people in India. If ramie can be profitably cultivated here, owing to improved machinery, it can be more profitably cultivated there.

Oranges. Riverside is the best known orange-growing district in Southern California, and land there suitable for this industry is selling at higher prices than have yet been paid elsewhere. Captain Pym (formerly of Her Majesty's Service), who has an orange grove there, has kindly written me the following particulars of the industry:—

"The number of acres of bearing orange orchards at Riverside is approximately 4,500; counting the young trees the acreage is exactly 7,647, and this does not include 1,300 acres recently planted at Arlington Heights. The average net annual returns of bearing orange trees is 60l. per acre. Ten acres in full bearing sold here recently for 3,600l., and a few days ago a Scotchman paid 4,000l. for 15 acres, on which there was a small house; part of this land was in vines, and of the oranges only a portion were in full bearing."

Mr. MacNeil, a Canadian capitalist, who is planting an orange grove of nearly 500 acres, writes me, in reply to some queries I propounded to him (the nature of which is shown in his replies), as follows:—

"Florida is reported to have shipped 2,500,000 boxes of oranges (about 84,000 tons) in season of 1889-90, and nearly 3,000,000 boxes (100,000 tons) this season. In 1870 there were imported into the United States from foreign countries 300,000 boxes, and notwithstanding the products of Florida and California there were imported in season 1889-90 4,000,000 boxes. I do not think California has any serious cause to fear competition from Mexican oranges. The Mexican crop does not come in direct competition with that of California, as it ripens earlier. Oranges grown in Mexico by reason of climatic influences are insipidly sweet, and could not maintain a place in our markets against the standard varieties of southern California. In flavour they are inferior to the Florida oranges, and when the California oranges come in competition with the Florida they sell for a much higher price than the latter.

"On the 2nd inst. (February, 1892) I noticed the quotations of Chicago dealers were as follows:—Florida bright fine, 5s. to 8s. per box; California common, 12s. to 13s. per box. It is difficult to obtain even approximately the average price of California oranges for 1891. The prices I obtained were the ruling prices for good fruit; in 1891 I got 8s. per box on the tree, that is, the picking, assorting, and boxes were paid for by the purchaser. I can get the same price this season. I believe the price may be as low as 5s. per box in 10 years' time, but did I know it would be as low as 3s. per box, I would continue in the business. First class orange or lemon land, with water, can be purchased at from 40l. to 80l. per acre, according to location. . . . A person who pays these prices will have a great advantage when his fruit comes in competition with that of the one who pays 120l. per acre. I regard the action of the transcontinental railroad companies in temporarily reducing the rates of freight charges from 5s. to 3s. 8d. per 1 cwt. as a blunder, and it might have been a serious one. A temporary cut of freight rates on any class of products or merchandise is always a source of danger, if not of disaster, as too many shippers, with indiscriminate judgment and haste in shipping, overstock markets. The error is more serious when the products shipped are of a perishable nature. I do not think the time is many years distant when we will have a 3s. rate on oranges as far east as Chicago."

Great care is exercised to prevent the importation of fruit trees infested with injurious insect pests. A vessel arrived here from Tahiti with a cargo of orange trees consigned to nurserymen in this vicinity. The quarantine officer of the State Board of Horticulture found purple and green scale, and other pests on the trees, and as it was found impossible to kill all the pests by fumigation, the whole cargo was finally destroyed by order of the superior Court here. Three years ago the destruction of the orange orchards from the ravages of the "white scale" appeared to be only a matter of time; fortunately, as I have stated in previous reports, the "white scale" was exterminated by the "vidolia cardinalis," a parasite imported from Australia. The complete success which attended this experiment induced the Legislature of this State to make an appropriation to be used by the State Board of Horticulture in a search for parasites, which would destroy the "red scale" and other pests. The Board has sent Prof. Koebele to Australia in quest of parasites, and in reply to an inquiry from me the Secretary of the Board writes me as follows:—"Mr. Koebele has met with good success in his search for parasites to destroy insect pests. The orchus chalybeus preys on the red scale, and in the district where it was discovered it is known to have diminished the scale to such an extent that it is no longer a pest. The introduction of this insect means a great deal for this State, as the red scale

*Insect pests.*

has done considerable damage to citrus trees in some localities. He has also introduced a moth that preys on the black scale on the olive. This will also be a great benefit, as in some sections the black scale has done the olive considerable injury. Apart from these, he has introduced other insects which keep other pests in check. Mr. Koebele is now in New Zealand, and will remain there as long as we can keep him abroad."

**Peaches.**

The "yellows" has devastated the peach orchards in the eastern States, entirely destroying a very large percentage of the trees; the lessened and continually lessening production of peaches in all the eastern States where they are grown makes the present an exceptionally good time to grow peaches here. Trees imported from the Eastern States are strictly quarantined, and it is hoped that the disease will not appear in this State.

**Vine disease.**

I have commented in my last three reports on a peculiar disease which attacked the vineyards in this district and destroyed about 20,000 acres of bearing vines. The Viticultural Commission closed the inquiry into this disease about a year ago, as it was found that it was disappearing. Professor Dowlen, the expert employed by the Commission, writes me as follows:—

"So far as I have heard, the vine disease seems to be slowly disappearing in this district, though I am told that it has appeared further north, but this I do not know for certain. So far as my information goes, the mission variety seems to be in better condition than any other; this, however, may be a local peculiarity."

The chief executive viticultural officer writes me on the same subject as follows:—

"I have lately made a trip through the southern counties for the purpose of determining the extent of damage done by the vine disease, and found that at least 20,000 acres were destroyed in Los Angeles and orange counties during the past five years. San Bernardino has not lost many vines by the disease up to the present time, but the disease is there, especially among the mission vines. In Orange county several new vineyards were planted last year, and made a good growth. If they continue to do well another year many acres will be planted in that county. The vine disease has disappeared in that county, because all the vines have been killed. The soil may now have changed so that vines will live in it. The new plantings of last year will soon settle that question. The number of acres of vines in bearing is as follows:—Los Angeles county, 6,000 acres; San Bernardino county, 3,615 acres; Santa Barbara county, 400 acres; Orange county, 136 acres."

It appears from the foregoing that in the past five years the vine disease has destroyed two-thirds of the bearing vineyards in this district.

**Flower farming**

In my last report I stated that I had been informed that flower farming for perfumery purposes would shortly be commenced here by Mr. Solon Palmer, perfume manufacturer of New York. In reply to an enquiry Mr. Palmer writes me as follows: "No definite arrangements have been made to carry out the scheme, as I have about concluded that the enterprise could not be made to pay on account of the high price of labour." The jasmine, tuberose, violet, rose, and other flowers used in the manufacture of perfumes grow here to great perfection, and although the processes of enfleurage and maceration require skilled labour, there is so much that could be done by boys and girls, that I am a little surprised to learn that the business cannot be carried on here profitably.

The death of a cow from anthrax was reported in the press here, and in reply to an enquiry from me Dr. Blackinton, veterinary-surgeon, writes me as follows: "The case to which you refer was undoubtedly anthrax, as I made a post-mortem examination, and could not be mistaken in my diagnosis. This subject was brought in from the wet lands, south-west of the city, a few days before her death, and fortunately did not communicate the disease to the other cattle she was with. Last spring I held a post-mortem on a cow from a herd in a cañon near Eagle Rock, and saw symptoms of anthrax. About 30 died in this lot, and the rest, I understand, are doing well. It is generally understood among veterinary surgeons and stockmen here that cattle on certain wet lands and cañons are very liable to anthrax, but all other localities in the State are remarkably free from this scourge." Anthrax.

### Population and Industries.

The population of Los Angeles county, as shown by the official census, has increased as follows:— Population.

|  | Number. |
|---|---|
| 1880 | 33,381 |
| 1890 | 101,454 |
| 1892 (estimated) | 116,000 |

The total number of children between the ages of 5 and 17, who attended the public schools in the city and county of Los Angeles was as follows:—

|  | Number. |
|---|---|
| 1890 | 23,394 |
| 1891 | 23,646 |

In my report for 1890 I stated that an English company, the San Jacinto Estate, Limited, had purchased 45,000 acres of land near this city containing very valuable deposits of tin ore. As this is the only tin mine in operation in the United States I give the following particulars, kindly supplied to me by Mr. Stephens, the general representative of the company. There are about 30 tin lodes on the company's estate extending over a district of 5 square miles. Of these 30 lodes six are now being worked, and produce an average of 15 tons (2,000 lbs. to the ton) of tin metal Tin.

per month, which sells readily at about 80*l*. per ton, the price fluctuating somewhat according to the state of the market. The largest out-put possible with the machinery now in operation is 50 tons per month, but the company will increase the plant according to circumstances. About 120 men are employed at the mines. The work is chiefly let by contract, and the men earn on an average 12*s*. per day. The price of coals delivered at the mines is 1*l*. 3*s*. to 1*l*. 19*s*. per ton, according to quality. The percentage of tin in the ore is about 5 per cent., Cornwall ores give about 2 per cent. The only labour-saving machine not in use in the Cornwall mines is the American vanner. "Buddles take the place of these machines in the Cornwall mines." The company has invested about 80,000*l*. in the development of the mines. In a recent magazine article on these mines the following figures were given as the world's yearly supply of tin:—

|  | Tons. |
|---|---|
| Malay Peninsula and Island | 28,000 |
| England | 9,000 |
| Australia | 6,500 |
| Other countries | 12,500 |
| Total | 56,000 |

If these figures are approximately correct it will be seen that the present relative importance of the San Jacinto mines is quite small.

*Borax.* — I stated in my last report that large quantities of borax were produced in this district; that it was selling at 28*l*. per ton (2,000 lbs.) at point of shipment; that I was informed that the cost of manufacture did not exceed 7*l*. per ton; that the borax fields were in few hands; and that the price was kept up by limiting the output. The secretary of the San Bernardino Borax Mining Company writes me that the average price in 1891 at point of shipment was 26*l*. per ton, and that the average cost of production was 16*l*. per ton. He adds, "The selling price of 26*l*. per ton is competitive price, there being five different companies producing borates and borax in California and Nevada, all selling to different buyers, dealers, and consumers. The product of the Nevada fields has greatly fallen-off by partial exhaustion, while the Death Valley fields lie idle under present prices."

*Oil.* — New oil fields have been discovered in this district in the past year; the product is increasing, and its use for fuel is solving the great want of the district, cheap fuel for manufacturing purposes. I have no accurate statistics of the output of the year.

## *Public Works.*

*Railway construction.* — Railway construction has been active in this district in the past year, and if all the railways which have been built on paper had been actually constructed, the additions to existing lines would have been phenomenal. The Los Angeles Terminal Railway has completed its line to San Pedro, and the general manager writes me as follows: "Our company is contemplating constructing a branch road to Ventura county, but the matter is still indefinite, and no decision will be reached for some little time to come." He adds, "We expect to make quite extensive improvements at San Pedro in the way of constructing wharves and putting up buildings." The railway connecting Los Angeles with Salt Lake City, Utah, to which I have referred in previous reports, has not yet been completed. Expensive work has, however, been done by the Terminal Railway here and by other railways in Utah, which will not be remunerative until the line be completed. I am reliably informed that the road will soon be finished.

*Railway to Salt Lake City, Utah.*

The general manager of the Southern Pacific Company writes me that contracts will soon be let for the completion of the coast line from San Francisco to Los Angeles by way of Santa Barbara, and that "it is expected that the line will be completed in about $2\frac{1}{2}$ years, possibly in 2 years." He adds that his company is about to construct a large wharf at Santa Monica (16 miles west of Los Angeles, see map accompanying my report for 1889). The vice-president of the Atchison, Topeka, and Santa Fé Railway writes me that his company "does not contemplate making any extension of its lines in Southern California in the near future."

Los Angeles in proportion to its size is better supplied with tramways than any city in this country. There are upwards of 20 miles of cable roads, about the same mileage of horse car lines, and nearly 40 miles of electric railways. The president of the electric railway writes me as follows: "We have in operation a total mileage of track operated by electricity of 37 miles. For the present we do not intend to construct any more than to complete our East Los Angeles line, which will take about 5 miles of track, and to re-construct our depôt line, making about $3\frac{1}{2}$ miles more."

*Street railways.*

## General Remarks.

In my report for 1890 I pointed out that investments of English capital in this district have proved unremunerative owing to heavy promotion money in London, mismanagement by English managers unfamiliar with this country, and other causes, and in consequence I advised English capitalists not to invest in Southern California companies. This advice, which applies with equal force to every part of the world where companies have been wrecked by mismanagement, or robbed by promoters, formed the subject of an associated press despatch to the newspapers in the United States, and was used to "boom" other places on the Pacific Coast (where the investor would probably not fare as well as he would here), at the expense of Los Angeles. I have stated

*Advice to British capitalists.*

(1343)

in former reports, and am still of opinion, that this district offers many openings for the profitable investment of capital either by companies or individuals, and although I made a similar statement in my report for 1890, the unfavourable portion of my report was alone commented on in the press despatch to which I refer. Assuming that I am correct in saying that this district offers good opportunities for investment, it follows that companies operating here can better stand the frauds and mismanagement of which I have complained. If investors cannot dispense with the service of unscrupulous promoters, and cannot secure good managers, I still think they are unwise to invest here, or anywhere else. I mention the matter because I learn with regret that the press notices of my observations prevented the sale in New York and Chicago of the bonds of two companies owned and controlled by American capital. This was a result I did not anticipate or desire, and which I regretted, more especially as the bonds in question are, I believe, good securities.

Irrigation bonds.

The rainfall here is insufficient for the successful cultivation of citrous fruits, and must be supplemented by irrigation. The cost of storing water in the mountains and piping it to the place of use is so considerable that co-operation is necessary to accomplish it, and to facilitate co-operative schemes of irrigation the Legislature of this State has passed Acts to provide for the organisation and government of "irrigation districts." These Acts provide for the formation of irrigation districts on a two-thirds vote of the qualified voters, and authorise the issuance and sale of bonds to carry out the necessary works. The best land for orange and lemon culture is on the mountain slopes, where the land in its natural state is worth only 2$l$. to 3$l$. per acre, and with water is worth from 20$l$. to 40$l$. per acre. At the instance of the president of the State Association of Irrigation Districts, 12 representative bankers of San Francisco have agreed to accept the opinion of Mr. William Hammond Hall, C.E., on the business questions involved in each district. Mr. Hall has reported favourably on two of the districts in this vicinity, the Alessandro district and Perris district, of which the former is issuing bonds to the amount of 153,000$l$., and the latter to the amount of 120,000$l$. I take the following particulars from Mr. Hall's report on Alessandro. The bonds are a first lien on 25,500 acres, being all the lands embraced in the district. The assessed value of these lands prior to the formation of the district was 500,000$l$., which Mr. Hall thinks was 100,000$l$. below the real value at that time. Having regard to the improvements now being made, and the valuable improvements in the shape of orange and lemon groves to be planted, Mr. Hall thinks that in 20 years' time these lands will be worth 2,640,000$l$. If these valuations are approximately correct the lands pledged should be very good security for 153,000$l$., and the bonds a good investment for persons satisfied with 6 per cent. interest. The supreme court of this State has passed judgment upon the constitutionality of the Acts under which these bonds are issued. There are already upwards of 30 districts issuing bonds for about 100,000*l.* each. Many of these bonds can be purchased at a considerable discount, as investors here can get more than 6 per cent. for their money, and there is in consequence little demand for them. The bankers in this city have not yet selected a local engineer to report on the irrigation districts in Southern California, and I cannot therefore specify any district as being a good investment except the ones favourably reported on by Mr. Hall.

This city possesses the best public library on the Pacific coast. It contains upwards of 25,000 volumes, and is entirely free to all residents of the city, who can borrow books for home use without charge. I make the following extracts from the annual report of the directors and librarian for 1891. The income of the library is derived from an annual tax levy on all taxable property in the city, not to exceed 1*s.* on each 100*l.* of all real and personal property. The income last year was 5,000*l*. The library contains all the standard English and American novels. An accurate record is kept of the books taken out for home use, and it shows the following results for the year 1891:— {Public library.}

|  | Volumes. |
|---|---|
| Fiction and periodicals | 87,217 |
| All other books | 29,046 |

Statistics have been compiled showing the authors whose books are most in demand, and the following list is in the order of their popularity:—Miss Alcott, E. P. Roe, W. T. Adams, Captain King, G. A. Henty, W. Besant, Charles Dickens, Sir Walter Scott, and F. Stockton. The number of registered borrowers, that is, persons who take books for home use, is 5,758. This is about one-twelfth of the total population of the city.

At the last session of the Legislature of this State a sum of 80,000*l.* was appropriated for the construction and maintenance of a reform school for juvenile offenders. This school was established at Whittier, about 8 miles east of Los Angeles, was opened on July 1, 1891, and will accommodate about 300 children. The experiment is a most interesting one, owing to the fact that the treatment of the inmates is essentially different from that adopted in similar institutions. The children are treated with great kindness, are taught some trade or occupation, have plenty of time for recreation, and in the evening are allowed to play games, sing, and otherwise amuse themselves. The Act establishing the school provides that children of both sexes between the ages of 10 and 16 years who commit misdemeanours, or are vagrants or incorrigible and vicious, may be committed to the school for terms of 1 year to 5 years. In reply to an inquiry from me the superintendent has kindly written me at some length, and I make the following extracts from his letter:—"There are no persons employed as guards, {Whittier Reform School.}

(1343)

no walls, no barred and bolted windows and doors, and no officer or employé is permitted to carry firearms or other weapons. It is our aim to have nothing about the school that is typical of a prison. In regard to punishment, no officer is permitted to strike a child, and there are fixed rules of chastisement. The punishment, when necessary, is determined after studying the boy to be punished. One boy is learning to be an electrician and engineer, and is deeply in love with his work. His punishment for a certain offence might be to put him at work for a week with pick and shovel. Another boy is a great eater, and his punishment might be a limited diet, while a few kindly words to a boy of a different temperament might have the desired effect. The school is organised on a military plan, the boys being divided into four companies. The officers of these companies are chosen from the boys. The boys already show great proficiency in drill, and consider it a privilege, not a duty. These military companies have gone by invitation to fairs at Los Angeles and other cities, and given exhibition drills. At such times their behaviour would have done credit to any school in America. It is our intention next 4th of July to have the four companies participate in the military procession that always takes place on that day in Los Angeles." The establishment of this school is chiefly due to the efforts of Dr. Lindley, the present superintendent, who tells me that it is proving most successful in the reformation of young criminals. In his management of the school he appears to be acting on the principle that if you treat a boy as he ought to be treated if he were what he ought to be, such treatment will tend to make him what he ought to be.

*Treatment of vagrants.* In previous reports I have commented on the fact that persons convicted of vagrancy and similar minor offences are sentenced to work in chains on the public streets. The press here is opposing this form of punishment, and a local paper in its issue of December 18 last says: "The punishment meted out to these persons is the most degrading imaginable, and in its refined cruelty is fit to be inflicted only on the vilest criminals. . . . . . A heavy logging chain 6 feet in length to which is attached an iron ball as large as a man's head" effectually prevents the escape of prisoners.

*Prohibition.* Notwithstanding the fact that this is a wine-producing country there are several municipalities in the district where the sale of liquor is prohibited by law. The City Council of Pomona, a city of a few thousand inhabitants, about 30 miles east of Los Angeles, recently passed a most stringent anti-liquor ordinance. Under this law various fines ranging from 30*l*. and upwards and short terms of imprisonment may be inflicted for the following offences: selling or giving away malt or spirituous liquors; visiting or entering any place where liquors are sold; transporting, carrying, or hauling any liquors or vessels of any kind designed for holding intoxicants. Five days in jail or 20*l*. fine may be inflicted on any person " found with liquor or vessels for holding liquor on his or her person." Permission is given any policeman to enter places and make search at any time for any liquor or vessels for holding the same. There is also a heavy penalty provided for persons who know where liquor is sold and do not inform the police.

The classes most wanted here are capitalists, and those whose capital consists in their ability to do a good day's work. Those described in Europe as "the lower classes" have many opportunities here to improve their condition in life, they can educate their children without expense, and if able and willing to work hard can make a comfortable living. It is worthy of remark that the conditions of life here, as in all new countries, tend to make men self reliant, and such socialistic legislation as providing free education for all, has not here the bad effects complained of in older countries.

Complaint has been made to me that a London firm of emigration agents is sending young English lads here to be taught farming and is charging a fee of 50*l.*, for which the pupils receive but little value. As a rule the employment obtained for these lads is not any better than that which they could obtain without the aid of the introduction afforded by the agent of the firm in question, and in all cases they would be 50*l.* better off if to use a coloquialism they came "on their own hook." The qualities which will ensure success here are conspicuously absent in young men who will pay 50*l.* for the kind of employment which they suppose they are to obtain here. In one case, reported to me a few days ago by the person to whose house one of the pupils was sent, the "pupil" was led to believe in London that the rough work on the farm he was to be sent to would be done by Chinamen. After 10 day's experience this pupil resigned and left this State.

I gather from conversation with many young Englishmen who have settled here that there is an impression in England that fruit farming is a species of pastime. This is wholly erroneous, fruit farming as practised here is much more arduous than any other agricultural work; young Englishmen who think of settling here should thoroughly understand that they will have to work hard if they want to succeed. Englishmen who come to California to settle usually engage in agricultural operations of some description. They like the out-door life and freedom from restraint. Many of these persons are not fitted for agricultural pursuits and would do better in mining. The mining laws of this country are extremely liberal, and there are many valuable mines undeveloped and many as yet undiscovered in this district. A valuable mining country will shortly be opened by a railway soon to be constructed between Los Angeles and Salt Lake City. Having regard to these facts, I think I may say that there is an opening here for competent mining engineers. A short course of study at the School of Mines in Jermyn Street, London, with a little practical experience here, would qualify an intelligent man to prospect for and locate mines.

*(margin: Advice to emigrants.)*

The law.

Some Englishmen who have settled here have sustained some loss owing to ignorance of the law on points of which the following are examples: a debtor here may own a house and grounds or a farm of the value of 1,000*l*., which cannot be sold for any debt if he files with the county recorder a declaration of homestead. Necessary household furniture and certain earnings of a debtor are also among the long list of property exempt from execution. People can, in fact, be in comfortable circumstances, and yet need not pay their debts unless disposed to do so.

The successful party in a suit or action cannot, with a few exceptions, recover the fees he has paid his attorney, and, in consequence, there is practically no use suing to recover small debts. These, and similar peculiarities in the law, work no hardships on people who know the law on these points when lending money or notes or giving credit. The intention of the Legislature was to prevent people being reduced to poverty, and so becoming a charge on the community, and owing to these laws (or other causes) there are practically no paupers here.

The following will illustrate the necessity of non-resident mortgagees being represented here by an agent. If A borrows money from B on mortgage and subsequently records a declaration of homestead and dies, B must file a claim on A's estate within the time limited for filing claims by creditors, otherwise his claim under his mortgage is barred, and he cannot foreclose or recover his money. As mortgages are frequently made for three or five years with interest payable annually it will be seen that under the foregoing state of the law a non-resident mortgagee might lose his principal and interest before default was made on the first payment of interest.

Price of orange land.

Many British subjects come annually to this district to engage in orange-growing, and pay from 100*l*. per acre to 120*l*. per acre for the naked land and water for irrigation. Although I do not think that the best land here is worth more than 60*l*. per acre, I am not prepared to say that persons paying more are imposed upon. I am quite sure, however, that new comers would be much more successful if they rented land for a year or two, and engaged in general farming before purchasing on their own account.

Observatory.

Owing to the clearness of the atmosphere, the absence of clouds, and other climatic conditions, the mountain peaks in this vicinity offer exceptional advantages for astronomical observations. Some time ago Mr. Spence, an Irish gentleman who is president of a bank here, made a donation of 10,000*l*. to be applied to the establishment of the largest telescope yet made on a peak of the Sierra Madre Mountains overlooking Los Angeles. In reply to an enquiry Mr. Spence writes me that the first lens for this telescope was cast by M. Mantous, of Paris, and was one of the most perfect ever made; the second lens was recently shivered in the melting furnace necessitating a delay of two years in the completion of the primary glasses. He adds: "Allow me to thank you for your interest in the desire of the Southern

Californians to get nearer to the works of God which are shown in the planets and stars, and in your communication to the home Government you will, doubtless, reflect the idea that one of the leading thoughts of the Christian nations is to know more and more of the Great Creator."

The bulk of the English capital in this district is invested in the counties of Los Angeles and San Bernardino; some investments have recently been made in Kern County, chiefly purchases from the Kern County Land Company, referred to in my last report. The manager of this company writes me that in the past year his company has "located" about '35 English families, "in all about 160 persons. The majority of these belong to the middle class, and are uniformly successful and make the best of citizens. The Earl of Gosford and Lord Clifton have each purchased large tracts of land from us, and are now improving them. Their purchases amount to about 15,000*l*., and those of the 35 colonists to about 20,000*l*. Other English capitalists will soon operate nurseries and canning companies here." The great drawback to settlement in Kern County is the intense heat in summer. Although it is 150 miles north of Los Angeles, the heat there is intense, when in Los Angeles it is quite cool. This is owing to the fact that Kern County is separated from the cool ocean breezes by the coast range of mountains. The county offers great inducements to settlers who can afford to spend the summer months in some cooler place. I mention the matter, because I have recently received a number of letters from people in England who think of settling here, and who state that their object in going to the north of Los Angeles is to escape the heat here.

*Kern county investments.*

The folly of purchasing lands in California without seeing them was recently illustrated here. A swindler purchased a large tract of land in the mountains of Santa Barbara County for 2*s*. per acre, and sold to non-residents, principally in the Eastern States, at 15*l*. per acre to 20*l*. per acre, representing it to be good fruit land. The matter was fully ventilated in the local press. I am not aware that any British subjects were caught in this particular swindle. I mention the matter, however, as it was stated in the "Los Angeles Times," of November 4, 1891, that a similar swindle on a large scale was practised on some Scotch people in adjoining county.

*Land swindle.*

Clothing is expensive here, and wears out in a much shorter time than English goods. A suit of clothes costing 4*l*. 10*s*. in London can be delivered here for a little less than 8*l*., and will last as long again as an 8*l*. suit made here. It is possible that a London firm might profitably establish an agency here.

*Clothing.*

Emigration to this district is largely influenced by the desire or necessity of escaping from the intense cold and changeable weather in the Eastern States. The division of the year into dry and wet seasons, corresponding to the summer and winter of the Eastern States, conveys the erroneous impression that the winter here is disagreeably wet, as, however, the average rainfall is only

*Climate.*

17 inches, of which the greater part falls at night, there are not more than 10 to 15 rainy days in the year. The extreme heat on the Mojave Desert causes the air there to rise, and the cold air from the ocean comes in to fill the vacuum thus created. Los Angeles is, in consequence, provided with a cool breeze every day in summer, which blows with unvarying regularity, and owing to the configuration of the mountains this district is quite cool when the heat in the central counties, 200 miles to 400 miles north, is almost unbearable. In a recent report of the State Board of Health, Dr. Orme, of this city, in commenting on consumption, points out that if the bacillus theory be true, the great danger to the general public lies in the myriads of these microbes, which are daily deposited in every thoroughfare in the sputa of the suffering multitudes. Dr. Orme thinks that " the Sierra Madre Mountains in this district, at varying elevations, furnish, whether in summer or winter, the best possible climatic conditions for all patients whose cases are in any degree amenable to climatic relief." And he points out that there are on an average 316 days of sunshine every year. The reports of the State Board of Health will interest physicians who think of sending consumptive patients here. A portion of the desert, about 100 miles east of this city and 50 miles west of Yuma, is more than 100 feet below the level of the sea. In June last an overflow of the Colorado River filled a portion of this desert, an area 30 miles by 80 miles, to a depth of 6 feet. The temperature in this basin frequently reaches 130 degrees in the shade, and the water rapidly evaporated. It was supposed at first that the water came from the Gulf of California, had this been the case the lake would have been permanent, and might have affected climatic conditions here; as it was the temperature in the city during the summer was 5 degrees above the normal temperature; the increase was attributed to the proximity of this large body of hot water. I am indebted to Major Osborne, United States Collector of Customs at San Pedro, for the statistics in Annexes A, B, and C. In this report dollars have been converted into sterling at the rate of 5 dol. per 1*l*.

Annex A.—RETURN of all Shipping at the Port of Wilmington during the Years 1891.

ENTERED.

| Nationality. | Sailing. | | Steam. | | Total. | |
| --- | --- | --- | --- | --- | --- | --- |
| | Number of Vessels. | Tons. | Number of Vessels. | Tons. | Number of Vessels. | Tons. |
| British | 3 | 4,037 | ... | ... | 3 | 4,037 |
| American | 34 | 55,363 | ... | ... | 34 | 55,363 |
| Other countries | 4 | 2,830 | ... | ... | 4 | 2,830 |
| Total | 41 | 63,230 | ... | ... | 41 | 63,230 |
| ,, for the year preceding | 33 | 44,367 | ... | ... | 33 | 44,367 |

## SAN FRANCISCO.

This return does not include 546 sailing and steam coasting vessels, aggregate tonnage 349,066. The coasters for 1890 numbered 468, tonnage 290,733.

The following coating vessels arrived at the port of Redondo, steam, 219; sail, 36; total, 255. Tonnage not stated.

CLEARED.

| Nationality. | Sailing. Number of Vessels. | Sailing. Tons. | Steam. Number of Vessels. | Steam. Tons. | Total. Number of Vessels. | Total. Tons. |
|---|---|---|---|---|---|---|
| British | 3 | 4,037 | ... | ... | 3 | 4,037 |
| American | 33 | 53,354 | ... | ... | 33 | 53,354 |
| Other countries | 3 | 2,814 | ... | ... | 3 | 2,814 |
| Total | 39 | 60,205 | ... | ... | 39 | 60,205 |
| ,, for the year preceding | 29 | 43,229 | ... | ... | 29 | 43,229 |

Annex B.—RETURN of the Principal Articles of Export from Wilmington during the Years 1890-91.

| Articles. | | 1890. Quantity. | 1890. Value. | 1891. Quantity. | 1891. Value. |
|---|---|---|---|---|---|
| | | | £ | | £ |
| Wheat | Tons | ... | ... | 1,580 | 8,000 |
| Canned meats | ... | ... | ... | ... | ... |
| Other articles | Tons | 12 | 44 | ... | ... |
| Total | ... | 12 | 54 | 1,580 | 8,000 |

The following is a summary of imports in coasting vessels:—

| Articles. | | Quantity. |
|---|---|---|
| Lumber | Feet | 53,643,060 |
| Railway ties | Number | 342,525 |
| Other articles | Tons | 14,358 |

And at the port of Redondo—

| Articles. | | Quantity. | Estimated Value. |
|---|---|---|---|
| | | | £ |
| Lumber | Feet | 20,689,464 | } 1,100,000 |
| Other articles | Tons | 29,179 | |

(1343)

## UNITED STATES.

RETURN of the Principal Articles of Import to Wilmington during the Years 1890–91.

| Articles. | | 1890. Quantity. | 1890. Value. | 1891. Quantity. | 1891. Value. |
|---|---|---|---|---|---|
| Coal | Tons. | 65,548 | £ 52,800 | 88,151 | £ 68,000 |
| Cement | Barrels | ... | ... | 12,224 | 3,266 |
| Glass | Cases | ... | ... | 4,923 | 2,600 |
| Other articles | ... | ... | 230 | ... | ... |
| Total | ... | ... | 53,030 | ... | 73,866 |

Annex C.—TABLE showing the Total Value of all Articles Exported from Wilmington and Imported to Wilmington from and to Foreign Countries during the Years 1890–91.

| Country. | Exports. 1890. | Exports. 1891. | Imports. 1890. | Imports. 1891. |
|---|---|---|---|---|
| | £ | £ | £ | £ |
| Great Britain and British Possessions | 44 | 8,000 | 53,030 | 74,030 |
| Other countries | .. | .. | 249 | 1,560 |
| Total | 44 | 8,000 | 53,279 | 75,590 |

### SAN DIEGO.

Mr. Vice-Consul Allen reports as follows:—

*General business.* There has been a considerable increase in the exports and imports during 1891, as shown by the custom-house returns (see Annex C), but in spite of this the complaints of merchants about "dull times" are very general.

*Shipping.* Annex A shows a large increase in the total amount of shipping during 1891. The increase in British steam vessels is due to the registration under British colonies of two such coasting steamers plying between San Diego and Lower California. They were given provisional British certificates, the intention having been to take them to Victoria, B.C., to register. It was found, however, that, owing to the heavy duties exacted, this course was not feasible, the traffic not being sufficiently remunerative to bear the charge, and they have now been placed under the Nicaraguan flag.

*Colonisation Company of Mexico.* These steamers belong to an English company that for some years past has been endeavouring to colonise a tract of land in Lower California, but from all indications with very little prospect of success.

*Naval station.* The seizure of the Chilian steamer "Itata" at San Diego and subsequent events brought the great advantages of this port to the notice of the Admiral-Commanding the U.S. Pacific Squadron. He was so impressed with the fine harbour and the healthiness of the station that he has recommended that all ships fitted at Mare Island, San Francisco, shall rendezvous at San Diego for drill.

The military authorities have also given much attention to San Diego of late, and harbour defences and other Government works will probably be soon put in hand. Among these is a jetty designed to increase the scour of the tide and so deepen the harbour channel. The depth of water on bar is now 23 feet at low water spring tides. *Harbour defences.*

The steamers of the Pacific Mail Company that run between San Francisco and Panama are now under contract with the Government to call here both on the down and up trips, and if the contract is faithfully carried out great benefit must result to San Diego. *Mail steamers to call at San Diego.*

Hitherto the steamers have avoided San Diego, receiving a subsidy from the transcontinental railroad companies to abstain from competition in freights from New York, and to keep San Diego from sharing in the trade with the coasts of Mexico and Central America. The company is still making great efforts to avoid the terms of the contract. As, however, there is a great saving of time in the delivery of mails landed and shipped here, it is probable that the Post-office Department will insist on the steamship company fulfilling the contract or forfeiting the Government subsidy.

In spite of having rail communication, San Diego is still very little known, as it lies off the main line of travel. Not until a competing railway is built affording direct communication with the East viâ Yuma, and independent of the hostile influence of competing towns, will San Diego enjoy any great measure of prosperity. *Railway communication with San Diego.*

But with direct rail communication viâ Yuma, and with the opening of the Nicaragua Canal, I think there can be little doubt than San Diego will rapidly rise to the position of the most important town in the State, after San Francisco, as it will then be the port of entry for the whole of Southern California, New Mexico, and Arizona. *Nicaragua Canal.*

The Australian mails for Europe must eventually pass through San Diego, as there is a gain of nearly four days by this route. *Australian mails.*

And with a railway to Yuma, only 170 miles distant, San Diego would be the Pacific terminus of the shorter transcontinental line, open all the year round. *Pacific terminus.*

A large increase has again been put in barley and wheat, but owing to the rains having been somewhat late, I do not expect to see such a large output of grain this year as we had last. *Grain*

Many lemon orchards are now planting, especially in the immediate neighbourhood of this city. Large profits are expected from this industry, as the conditions of soil and climate in this region have proved peculiarly favourable to lemon culture. *Lemon culture.*

## UNITED STATES.

**Irrigation districts.**

During the past year the new law regarding the formation of irrigation districts has been largely taken advantage of by landowners, and the value of land is rising in consequence. "Irrigation Bonds" bring 6 per cent. interest, and are, I think, a sound investment.

**Water dams.**

Private companies are also at work, building dams and storing water for sale. One of the finest of these dams is that of the Hewer Company in the northern part of this county. From their reservoir the company will supply water to a large tract of land in the San Jacinto Valley, one of the finest and most beautiful valleys in Southern California.

**New summer resort for consumptives.**

Strawberry Valley, situated in the mountains near San Jacinto, at an elevation of about 6,000 feet, is becoming a favourite summer resort. During the hottest periods in the summer the temperature is cool and pleasant, and many consumptives have derived benefit from a sojourn there.

**Jamul Portland cement.**

The manufacture of Jamul Portland cement, mentioned in my last report, has proved a failure, the company not having been able to compete with the imported Portland cement.

**Temescel tin mines.**

These mines, also mentioned by me last year, have attracted considerable attention of late, but I have not been able to obtain information regarding them that I consider thoroughly trustworthy. Some experts assert that the ore is in pockets of no very great extent, and that it is of a very refractory nature. According to other accounts, the mines are the most valuable tin mines known.

**Opera house.**

Among buildings erected during 1891 is a very handsome opera-house, capable of seating 1,400 people.

**Bank failure.**

The breaking of a bank a few months ago has caused some distress; but as it has led to the transfer of much good property from small to large capitalists, I think it may be to the ultimate advantage of the town.

I am indebted to Mr. A. Higgins, Deputy Collector of Customs, for the information given in the subjoined annexes.

Annex A.—RETURN of all Shipping at the Port of San Diego, California, during the Year 1891.

ENTERED.

| Nationality. | Sailing. Number of Vessels. | Sailing. Tons. | Steam. Number of Vessels. | Steam. Tons. | Total. Number of Vessels. | Total. Tons. |
|---|---|---|---|---|---|---|
| British | 13 | 16,184 | 49 | 26,266 | 62 | 42,450 |
| American | 166 | 40,747 | 193 | 133,613 | 359 | 174,360 |
| Other countries | 17 | 12,838 | 2 | 2,402 | 19 | 15,240 |
| Total | 196 | 69,769 | 244 | 162,281 | 440 | 232,050 |
| ,, for the year preceding | 70 | 38,983 | 142 | 36,837 | 212 | 75,822 |

NOTE.—Dollars have been reduced to sterling in the following tables at the rate of 4·8665 dol. to the 1*l*.

## SAN FRANCISCO.

**CLEARED.**

| Nationality. | Sailing. Number of Vessels. | Sailing. Tons. | Steam. Number of Vessels. | Steam. Tons. | Total. Number of Vessels. | Total. Tons. |
|---|---|---|---|---|---|---|
| British | 14 | 17,384 | 47 | 25,823 | 61 | 43,207 |
| American | 164 | 40,747 | 192 | 132,647 | 356 | 173,394 |
| Other countries | 16 | 11,610 | 2 | 2,402 | 18 | 14,012 |
| Total | 194 | 69,741 | 241 | 160,872 | 435 | 230,613 |
| ,, for the year preceding | 44 | 25,788 | 144 | 38,811 | 188 | 64,599 |

Annex B.—RETURN of the Principal Articles of Export from San Diego, California, during the Years 1890–91.

| Articles. | | 1890. Quantity. | 1890. Value. | 1891. Quantity. | 1891. Value. |
|---|---|---|---|---|---|
| | | | £ | | £ |
| Wheat | Tons | ... | 11,569 | 6,897 | 51,841 |
| Agricultural implements | ... | ... | 1,182 | ... | 742 |
| Fruit and nuts | ... | ... | 1,370 | ... | 1,024 |
| Manufactures of iron and steel | ... | ... | 5,981 | ... | 13,785 |
| Wine | Gallons | ... | ... | 1,675 | 215 |
| Powder and explosives | ... | ... | 874 | ... | ... |
| Lumber | ... | ... | 3,184 | ... | ... |
| Lime and cement | ... | ... | 702 | ... | ... |
| Coals | ... | ... | 1,373 | ... | ... |
| Other articles | ... | ... | 36,686 | ... | 45,921 |
| Total | ... | ... | 62,921 | ... | 113,528 |

RETURN of Principal Articles of Import to San Diego, California, during the Years 1890–91.

| Articles. | | 1890. Quantity. | 1890. Value. | 1891. Quantity. | 1891. Value. |
|---|---|---|---|---|---|
| | | | £ | | £ |
| Coals | Tons | 46,226 | 30,788 | 73,265 | 49,587 |
| Pig iron | ,, | 458 | 1,603 | ... | ... |
| Cement | Barrels | 60,557 | 15,595 | 50,362 | 9,516 |
| Other articles | .. | ... | 52,707 | ... | 58,122 |
| Total | ... | ... | 100,693 | ... | 117,225 |

(1343)

Annex C.—TABLE showing the Total Value of all Articles Exported from San Diego and Imported to San Diego from and to Foreign Countries during the Years 1890-91.

| Country. | Exports. 1890. | Exports. 1891. | Imports. 1890. | Imports. 1891. |
|---|---|---|---|---|
| | £ | £ | £ | £ |
| Great Britain and British Possessions | 11,569 | 51,857 | 53,092 | 64,052 |
| Mexico | 47,948 | 39,745 | 45,010 | 41,167 |
| Not classified | 3,404 | 21,926 | 2,591 | 12,006 |
| Total | 62,921 | 113,528 | 100,693 | 117,225 |

LONDON:
Printed for Her Majesty's Stationery Office,
By HARRISON AND SONS,
Printers in Ordinary to Her Majesty.
(75 7|92—H & S 1343)

411

# FOREIGN OFFICE.
## 1892.
## ANNUAL SERIES.

### No. 1103.

### DIPLOMATIC AND CONSULAR REPORTS ON TRADE AND FINANCE.

# UNITED STATES.

### REPORT FOR THE YEAR 1891
#### ON THE
### TRADE OF THE CONSULAR DISTRICT OF CHICAGO.

REFERENCE TO PREVIOUS REPORT, Annual Series No. 892.

*Issued during the Recess and Presented to both Houses of Parliament by Command of Her Majesty.*

LONDON:
PRINTED FOR HER MAJESTY'S STATIONERY OFFICE,
BY HARRISON AND SONS, ST. MARTIN'S LANE,
PRINTERS IN ORDINARY TO HER MAJESTY.

And to be purchased, either directly or through any Bookseller, from
EYRE & SPOTTISWOODE, East Harding Street, Fleet Street, E.C., and
32, Abingdon Street, Westminster, S.W.; or
JOHN MENZIES & Co., 12, Hanover Street, Edinburgh, and
90, West Nile Street, Glasgow; or
HODGES, FIGGIS, & Co., 104, Grafton Street, Dublin.

1892.

[C. 6812—28.] *Price Threepence.*

## New Series of Reports.

Reports of the Annual Series have been issued from Her Majesty's Diplomatic and Consular Officers at the following places, and may be obtained from the sources indicated on the title-page:—

| No. | | Price. | No. | | Price. |
|---|---|---|---|---|---|
| 985. | Stuttgart | 1d. | 1044. | Hankow | 1½d. |
| 986. | New Orleans | 1½d. | 1045. | Nantes | 1½d. |
| 987. | New Orleans | 10d. | 1046. | Belgrade | 2d. |
| 988. | Suakin | ½d. | 1047. | Fiume | 1d. |
| 989. | Galveston | 1½d. | 1048. | Wuhu | 1d. |
| 990. | Berlin | 1d. | 1049. | Cagliari | 1d. |
| 991. | Zanzibar | 1½d. | 1050. | Erzeroum | 1d. |
| 992. | Guayaquil | 1d. | 1051. | Syra | 1d. |
| 993. | Tonga | 1d. | 1052. | Cherbourg | 1d. |
| 994. | New Orleans | 1d. | 1053. | Lima | 1d. |
| 995. | Mozambique | 1½d. | 1054. | Bilbao | 1½d. |
| 996. | Galatz | 1½d. | 1055. | Cadiz | 2d. |
| 997. | Nantes | 1½d. | 1056. | Corunna | 2½d. |
| 998. | Algiers | 1d. | 1057. | Saigon | 1d. |
| 999. | Havre | 2½d. | 1058. | Port-au-Prince | 1d. |
| 1000. | Buenos Ayres | 6d. | 1059. | Trebizond | 1d. |
| 1001. | Baltimore | 1½d. | 1060. | Barcelona | 1½d. |
| 1002. | Taganrog | 1d. | 1061. | Tainan | 1d. |
| 1003. | Riga | 2d. | 1062. | Smyrna | 1½d. |
| 1004. | Bordeaux | 2½d. | 1063. | Old Calabar | ½d. |
| 1005. | The Hague | 1½d. | 1064. | Samoa | ½d. |
| 1006. | Paraguay | 1½d. | 1065. | Tahiti | 1d. |
| 1007. | Constantinople | 1½d. | 1066. | Chefoo | 6d. |
| 1008. | Rome | 1d. | 1067. | Gothenburg | 2d. |
| 1009. | Mozambique | 1d. | 1068. | Buenos Ayres | 1½d. |
| 1010. | Wênchow | 1d | 1069. | Loanda | 1½d. |
| 1011. | Mogador | 2½d | 1070. | Guatemala | 1d. |
| 1012. | Amoy | 1d. | 1071. | Zanzibar | 1d. |
| 1013. | Kiukiang | 1d | 1072. | Charleston | 2½d. |
| 1014. | Stettin | 1½d | 1073. | Nice | 1d. |
| 1015. | Boston | 1d. | 1074. | Caracas | 1d. |
| 1016. | Callao | 1d. | 1075. | Lisbon | 2d. |
| 1017. | Aleppo | 1d. | 1076. | Calais | 2d. |
| 1018. | Santos | 2½d. | 1077. | Rio Grande do Sul | 5½d. |
| 1019. | Piræus | 1d. | 1078. | Philadelphia | 2½d. |
| 1020. | Mogador | 1d. | 1079. | Brindisi | 2d. |
| 1021. | Adrianople | ½d | 1080. | New York | 2d. |
| 1022. | Tripoli | 1d | 1081. | San Francisco | 1½d. |
| 1023. | Jerusalem | 1d. | 1082. | Frankfort | 4d. |
| 1024. | Odessa | 6d. | 1083. | Hiogo | 1½d. |
| 1025. | Genoa | 1½d. | 1084. | Tokio | 1½d. |
| 1026. | Kiungchow | 1d. | 1085. | Amsterdam | 1d. |
| 1027. | Batoum | 4½d. | 1086. | San Francisco | 3d. |
| 1028. | Buenos Ayres | 1d. | 1087. | Bankok | ½d. |
| 1029. | Batavia | 1d. | 1088. | Sŏul | 1½d. |
| 1030. | Santo Domingo | ½d. | 1089. | Chiengmai | 1d. |
| 1031. | San José | 1d. | 1090. | Copenhagen | ½d |
| 1032. | Manila | 1½d | 1091. | New Caledonia | ½d. |
| 1033. | Marseilles | 1d. | 1092. | Bushire | 2d. |
| 1034. | Swatow | 1d. | 1093. | Tamsui | 1d. |
| 1035. | Paris | 1d. | 1094. | Dunkirk | 1d |
| 1036. | Ichang | 5d. | 1095. | Port Said | 1d. |
| 1037. | Pakhoi | 1d. | 1096. | Guatemala | ½d. |
| 1038. | Foochow | 1d. | 1097. | Chunking | 9d. |
| 1039. | Brest | 1d. | 1098. | Nagasaki | 1d. |
| 1040. | Madeira | ½d. | 1099. | Constantinople | 2d. |
| 1041. | Antwerp | 1½d. | 1100. | Buenos Ayres | ½d. |
| 1042. | Taganrog | 2½d. | 1101. | Shanghai | 2d. |
| 1043. | Algiers | 2½d. | 1102. | Turkey | ½d. |

## No. 1103.

*Reference to previous Report, Annual Series No. 892.*

## UNITED STATES.

### CHICAGO.

*Consul Hayes Sadler to the Marquis of Salisbury.*

My Lord,          *Chicago, June* 27, 1892.

I HAVE the honour to transmit herewith a Report on the Trade and Commerce of Chicago, during the year 1891, together with the Annual Reports of the British Vice-Consuls at St. Louis, St. Paul, Denver, and Kansas City.

        I have, &c.
      (Signed)    J. HAYES SADLER.

---

*Report on the Trade and Commerce of Chicago for the Year* 1891.

### ABSTRACT of Contents.

| | Page |
|---|---|
| General remarks; commercial activity | 1 |
| The city of Chicago | 3 |
| Its produce trade | 4 |
| Wholesale trade | 8 |
| Manufactures | 9 |
| Real estate and building | 13, 14 |
| Shipping | 16 |
| Imports and exports | 17 |
| Miscellaneous | 19 |
| Notes on the West | 22 |
| Report from St. Louis | 26 |
| ,, St. Paul | 36 |
| ,, Denver | 45 |
| ,, Kansas City | 49 |

### General Remarks.

Another report of prosperity. Whatever dulness may have prevailed, whatever depression in trade or deficiency in crops may have been experienced in other parts of the world, no troubles

(1372)

elsewhere have checked for a serious moment the progress of Chicago or hindered the development of this part of the United States. The record for 1891 shows continued increase in trade and commerce, and the bulk of business done has exceeded that of any previous period. The past season was distinguished by an extraordinarily abundant harvest, the largest return of cereals ever produced in this region, and this, while directly bringing prosperity to agricultural and country districts, has indirectly and beneficially affected this and other cities, promising further activity in the present year. The prominence given to Chicago by the coming exhibition has also been a marked feature of the year, and in view of the event greater activity has prevailed in many branches of industry, especially in the building trade, which has been reflected in the general business. The prospect has already attracted an unusually large number of persons from all parts; there has been no lack, rather an over-supply, of hands to carry out all the plans proposed; everything is now more on the rush than ever, and the business portion of the city presents a scene of marvellous activity.

The first six months of the year presented no extraordinary features; there was comparative dulness in sympathy with the financial depression which prevailed elsewhere, resulting from the disaster in Argentine affairs, and partly on account of the poor crops of 1890; there was a certain drain caused by the withdrawal of money by sale of securities; the harvest, though promising well, had neither been gathered nor had demonstrated its wonderful abundance; a large quantity of dutiable goods had been imported towards the close of the previous year in anticipation of the McKinley Act, which had to be worked off before fresh orders were given, and the business was comparatively quiet. Perhaps, however, owing to the preparations for the World's Columbia Exposition, the general commercial depression was less felt at Chicago during those earlier months than anywhere else.

It was during the last six months of the year that the great buoyancy was developed; and, when the crops began to be in motion, and the building of the World's Fair was commenced, the trade exceeded any previous record of this city; indeed, without wishing to paint in too bright colours, it may be a question whether any city has ever in a given period shown for its size such commercial activity as Chicago has shown during the latter half of 1891. Orders came fast from country districts; farmers were able to make larger purchases, which the poor harvest of 1890 had caused them to postpone, and agricultural implements were in great demand. Grain was largely bought to supply deficiency in foreign countries. All vessels on the great lakes were soon chartered, and the capacity of the railroads was severely tried, and could scarcely meet requirements. It is also claimed that the various reciprocity arrangements with other countries has already tended to augment the business of the city, and that merchants have extended their exports of cereals and packed goods to other republics on the continent, the West Indies, and those countries with which treaties have been made.

## The City of Chicago.

Yet this city is not 60 years old. Sixty years ago the whole of this part of the State of Illinois was a wild prairie, inhabited solely by the Indian and the buffalo, visited by only an occasional pioneer.

In 1830 the population of Chicago consisted of 70 persons, in 1832 it had increased to 200, and in 1833 to 350. In the latter year it was incorporated as a town, and it was at this time that the first building was used for packing beef and pork for the mercantile and lake trade. At that time there was a bar across the mouth of the river, and the small craft of those days were forced to anchor outside and discharge their cargoes into lighters. In 1837 Chicago was incorporated as a city; it comprised but a very small part of its present site, and a census then taken showed 4,170 inhabitants. In 1850 the population was 29,963, 10 years later 112,172, in 1870 298,977, in 1880 503,185, and in 1890 1,208,669, an increase of 705,484 in 10 years; the city is still increasing, and now contains about 1,300,000 inhabitants. And yet progress was interrupted 21 years ago by a fire which reduced to ruin 2,100 acres in the heart of the city, levelled 17,450 buildings, destroyed one-third of the entire property of the city, and rendered 95,500 persons homeless, while some 200 lost their lives. When the census was taken in 1890 the population was composed of 292,463 Americans, 384,958 Germans, 215,534 Irish, 54,209 Bohemians, 52,756 Poles, 45,867 Swedes, 44,615 Norwegians, 33,785 English, 12,963 French, 6,989 Canadians, about 10,000 Russians, the same number of Danes and Italians, and the remainder was made up of other nationalities. The population of the whole State of Illinois, which in 1810 was 12,282 and in 1880 3,077,871, was 3,826,351 in 1890; but, as during the last decade Chicago increased by 705,484, it results that the number of inhabitants outside that city decreased by 42,996. There is a constant tendency all over the country to flock to the towns, which seem to be benefited thereby, and to shift from the agricultural districts, where improvements in labour-saving machinery enable a smaller number of hands to do the same work.

Chicago now extends along the line of Halsted Street, a distance of 21½ miles, and from east to west at the broadest point 10½ miles; it covers an area of 115,328 acres, or 180·2 square miles, and is almost entirely surrounded by magnificent boulevards, stretching for about 35 miles, and expanding here and there into extensive parks. In 1890 there were 127,871 dwellings and 220,320 families, or an average of 1·72 families to each dwelling. In 1890 buildings to the number of 7,590 were erected, with total frontage of 34 miles, costing 6,500,000*l*., and last year 11,805 buildings were constructed, covering a frontage of 53½ miles, at a cost of 11,134,600*l.*, to which may be added a percentage of probably 20 per cent. for completion beyond the estimates. There were during the year 5,391 passenger elevators or lifts inspected. The river frontage extends 41 miles, and the lake frontage 21 miles. There are 2,332 miles of streets, and counting the boulevards 3,164 miles; 775 miles of streets are paved, of which 481 miles are paved with wood and 23⅓ miles with stone. The park and boulevard system covers 2,597 acres. Nearly 100 miles of fresh sewers were laid last year, with pipes varying from 9 inches to 9 feet in diameter. The bonded debt of the city is about 3,800,000*l.* Education has kept pace with the general advance; there are 218 schools, seating 125,000 pupils, and costing 1,130,000*l.*, 86 per cent. of which is raised by taxation and the balance derived from school property; three years ago the appropriation did not amount to half that sum. A visit, however, is almost necessary to realise the activity and progress of this city.

### *Trade and Manufactures.*

The total trade of Chicago in 1891 is estimated at 300,825,000*l.*, against 284,500,000*l.* in the preceding year, or a little less than one-third of the total bank clearings. This includes the produce, wholesale and manufacturing trades, only such transactions in produce as have been followed by delivery from producer to consumer, and is calculated on the first selling value of all goods arrived, except the precious metals, with the additional value they may have acquired by local manufacture. The great increase of 17½ per cent. made in the volume of trade in 1890 has been maintained, and a further increase of about 5·7 per cent. has been made. The steady advance in business done will be seen by comparing the total trade for a number of years, taken from the best authority on the subject. In 1850 the total trade was, in round numbers, 4,000,000*l.*; in 1860, 20,000,000*l.*; in 1870, 77,000,000*l.*; in 1880, 186,000,000*l.*; in 1885, 198,000,000*l.*; in 1890, 284,000,000*l.*; and in 1891, 300,000,000*l.*

### *Receipts and Shipments.*

The receipts and shipments of the principal articles of produce, according to the Board of Trade, were as follows, compared with 1890:—

## CHICAGO.

| Articles. | | 1891. | | 1890. |
|---|---|---|---|---|
| | | Received. | Shipped. | Received. |
| Flour | Barrels | 4,516,617 | 4,048,129 | 5,358,058 |
| Wheat | Bushels | 42,931,258 | 38,990,169 | 14,248,770 |
| Corn | ,, | 72,770,304 | 66,758,300 | 91,387,754 |
| Oats | ,, | 74,402,413 | 68,771,614 | 75,150,249 |
| Rye | ,, | 9,164,198 | 7,572,991 | 3,520,508 |
| Barley | ,, | 12,228,480 | 7,858,108 | 19,401,489 |
| Grass seeds | Lbs. | 68,166,230 | 55,152,971 | 72,086,100 |
| Flax seed | Bushels | 11,120,138 | 9,990,798 | 6,642,905 |
| Cured meats | Lbs. | 206,898,958 | 751,684,862 | 300,198,241 |
| Canned meats | Cases | 41,744 | 1,253,480 | 36,324 |
| Dressed beef | Lbs. | 105,061,775 | 877,295,883 | 109,704,834 |
| Lard | ,, | 74,021,945 | 362,109,099 | 147,475,267 |
| Cheese | ,, | 63,922,939 | 50,204,235 | 67,338,590 |
| Butter | ,, | 127,765,048 | 140,737,620 | 140,548,850 |
| Live hogs | Number | 8,600,805 | 2,962,514 | 7,663,828 |
| Cattle | ,, | 3,250,359 | 1,066,264 | 3,484,280 |
| Sheep | ,, | 2,153,537 | 688,205 | 2,182,667 |
| Calves | ,, | 205,383 | 48,331 | 175,025 |
| Horses | ,, | 94,396 | 87,273 | 101,566 |
| Hides | Lbs. | 110,891,894 | 198,571,824 | 103,743,421 |
| Wool | ,, | 35,049,664 | 57,189,677 | 22,281,570 |
| Lumber | Met. feet | 2,045,418 | 865,949 | 1,941,392 |
| Pork | Barrels | 13,970 | 278,553 | 77,985 |

The total produce trade of 1891 is estimated at 102,474,000*l.*, against 93,340,000*l.* in 1890. The principal feature was the large increase in the receipts and shipments of wheat. Rye also arrived in larger quantities, while there was a falling-off in corn and barley. There was also a large decrease in the receipts of cured meat and lard. Prices were not subject to many fluctuations, and average prices were much the same as in the preceding year.

The receipts of wheat, 42,931,258 bushels, exceeded those of 1890 by 28,682,488 bushels, and the shipments were 27,000,000 bushels in excess of that year. In the movement of wheat Chicago was only outstripped by Minneapolis, which city received 57,500,000 bushels. As soon as the poverty of the crop in Europe was foreseen, buyers flocked in, and wheat rose to 4*s.* 9*d.*; but the demand was met in an unexpected manner from the north-west, and as the wealth of the harvest in this country became known there was no fear of any shortness occurring, and prices declined. As the crops in other countries proved deficient, orders were largely sent, and hundreds of thousands of bushels came by rail nearly the whole length of the continent to supply the demand, and were sold at a profit, but as the yield in these parts proved to be of exceptional abundance speculative purchases were dropped. The export continued to an unprecedented extent during the last six months, and the resources of railways could scarcely keep pace with requirements. The average price of No. 2 wheat was nearly 4*s.* per bushel. Flour was in great demand,

Cereals: Wheat.

(1372)

and the export from the mills in the north-west was very large. Patent flour seems also to have been in favour, as well as bran, in the foreign markets, and large quantities were exported. Of the great wheat-growing States in this district, the Dakotas produced 82,000,000 bushels, against 40,500,000 bushels in 1890; Kansas produced nearly 55,000,000 bushels; Minnesota, 55,333,333; and Illinois, 35,000,000 bushels.

*Corn.* — Corn ranged at higher prices than in 1890, averaging 2s. 4½d. per bushel in this market; there was a falling-off in receipts, as the new crop does not begin to move till towards the end of the year, and the yield of the preceding year was small. Corn and all cereals were affected by demand on account of the failure of crops in Europe. The enormous quantity of 351,000,000 bushels of corn were grown in the State of Iowa, against 232,000,000 bushels in 1890; Illinois came next, with 234,000,000 bushels; and Missouri, with 203,000,000 bushels. Next to Illinois, with 111,000,000 bushels, Iowa produced the largest quantity of oats, the yield being 102,000,000 bushels.

*Oats.* — The price steadily rose till in April it reached 2s. 4d. per bushel, when it receded, and at the close of the year stood at rather under 1s. 4d. per bushel.

*Live stock.* — The receipts of live stock exceeded those of any previous period, and the prediction that this trade is destined to be diverted to other localities has, at all events, not yet been realised. The number of cattle, calves, hogs, sheep, and horses received last year was 14,304,480, the largest number ever received in one year, and the estimated value was 49,368,600*l*.

The receipts of hogs amounted to 8,600,805, or 1,000,000 more than in 1890, and 1,500,000 more than in any other year. They were in a healthy condition, and it is said there was one-third less disease in the States from which they were supplied to this market than in any of the last five years. Iowa, which produces the largest quantity of corn, has also the greatest number of hogs, 7,105,320. The next greatest number are found in Illinois, which has 4,894,815 hogs, followed by Missouri, with 4,632,264 hogs, and Kansas with 3,175,767 hogs.

There was a slight falling-off in the arrivals of cattle compared with 1890, the numbers being 3,250,359 in 1891, and 3,484,280 in the previous year. The shipments numbered 1,066,264, against 1,260,309 in 1890. All the districts from which the market was supplied were remarkably free from disease, and cattle were healthy, though there was an apparent indication that economy had been in some cases exercised in the matter of feeding for market, the price of hay and corn having been high.

The movement of sheep was about the same as the year before. There were 2,153,537 received and 688,205 shipped, leaving the number of 1,465,332 used for city consumption, and for packing in a variety of forms.

The trade in horses was active, and prices for good animals high. About 87,000 were shipped out of a total of 94,396 received. There was a large demand for fine horses, and most of the supply was promptly taken for Eastern markets. This demand accounts for the large proportion of superior animals bred on the farms and ranches.

The great increase in the last 10 years in the movement of cattle, sheep, and horses will be seen in the following table of receipts at the stock yards, cattle and sheep being much more extensively used in the provision business, and the city having become quite a market for horses, which are chiefly raised in Illinois, Iowa, Texas, and Missouri:—

| Year. | Cattle and Calves. | Hogs. | Sheep. | Horses. | Aggregate Value. |
|---|---|---|---|---|---|
|  | Number. | Number. | Number. | Number. | £ |
| 1880 | 1,382,477 | 7,059,355 | 335,810 | 10,398 | 30,527,346 |
| 1882 | 1,607,495 | 5,817,504 | 620,887 | 13,856 | 40,550,561 |
| 1884 | 1,870,050 | 5,351,967 | 801,630 | 18,602 | 38,636,635 |
| 1886 | 2,015,100 | 6,718,761 | 1,008,790 | 27,599 | 34,379,743 |
| 1888 | 2,707,629 | 4,921,712 | 1,515,014 | 55,333 | 37,567,585 |
| 1890 | 3,659,305 | 7,663,828 | 2,182,667 | 101,566 | 47,699,998 |
| 1891 | 3,455,742 | 8,600,805 | 2,153,537 | 94,396 | 49,368,600 |

Provisions. The provision trade was active throughout the year, and there was a large demand for pork and lard; the removal of the restrictions, imposed 10 years ago by Germany and France, had the effect of increased purchases, but prices towards the close of the year were not maintained. The average price of mess pork was 2*l*. 2*s*. 1*d*., of lard 1*l*. 5*s*. 9*d*., and of short ribs 1*l*. 4*s*. 4*d*.

Dairy products. With regard to dairy produce it is said that the quality of butter was better on the whole, and the average price ranged for all kinds about 9*d*., against 7*d*. in 1890. A good business was done in cheese, but foreign demand exhausted the stock, and the product of the autumn was short, causing the price to rise to 6*d*. per lb. towards the close of the year.

Though the crop of hay was good in the west, prices were unusually high, averaging 2*l*. 9*s*. 6*d*. per ton, choice quality fetching as high as 3*l*. and 3*l*. 10*s*.

The receipts of poultry amounted to 28,000,000 lbs., chicken selling at from 4½*d*. per lb. to 6*d*. per lb., and turkeys from 4*d*. per lb. to 7½*d*. per lb. Eggs to the number of 1,508,417 cases of 30 dozen were received, valued at about 9*d*. per dozen.

Fruit. Chicago is one of the largest fruit markets in the world. The crop of 1891 was as abundant in character as that of cereals, and though prices were consequently low the value of receipts exceeded that of the preceding year, when the fruit crop was short and prices high. About 600,000 barrels of apples were delivered in this city; 1,800,000 baskets of peaches, 500,000 cases of strawberries, 200,000 cases of raspberries, and 150,000 cases of blackberries, 5,000,000 lbs. of grapes, and 3,000 car loads of bananas, valued at 60*l*. each, were received, besides large quantities of other fruits.

### Wholesale Trade.

Merchants have no reason to complain of the trade of 1891, the business done showing a fair advance over the preceding year, the excellent harvest having enabled increased purchases to be made. In many articles the value has not been greater, though a greater volume has been handled, especially in the wholesale grocery trade, in some articles of which the prices realised were far lower than in 1890. Prosperity, however, ruled throughout. The great activity in the building trade caused an unusual demand for all material consumed in construction. In structural iron and in brick and tile an advance of 10 per cent. is reported, but a smaller quantity of the finer tiles are imported than formerly. In the dry goods business is noticed a large increase in demand for goods of American production, and a corresponding reduction in the sale of foreign goods of superior quality, resulting from the higher tariff. The larger houses may import as much as before the new tariff, but the smaller retailers are said not to have found it profitable to import as many articles of foreign manufacture, the disposal of such goods at the higher figure which duties necessitate being less easy; and some goods, such as underclothing carpets, and other articles of home production and inferior make, are supplanting the imported article of finer quality. A very large quantity of goods were, however, imported in anticipation of the tariff, and no positive opinion can yet be formed of the effect of the tariff. In jewellery there has been an estimated increase of 20 per cent. In lumber the demand is greater than the supply. Pig iron has been very stationary in price, from 3*l.* 3*s.* 11*d.* to 3*l.* 4*s.* 11*d.* for No. 1, and 3*l.* to 3*l.* 1*s.* for No. 2 coke iron, while charcoal varied from 3*l.* 16*s.* 3*d.* at the commencement of the year to 3*l.* 9*s.* 1*d.* in December. It is said that 6,000,000 tons were produced in the last six months. For railroad purposes the demand was light. The increase in value of the wholesale trade is calculated altogether at about 6½ per cent.

The following table shows the estimated value of the business done in the principal articles of the wholesale trade; the figures are not official though derived from good authority, and are given for the last three years, so that they may be compared with the official return of imports for the same period, which seems to lead to the best conclusion procurable regarding the effect of the McKinley Act:—

## CHICAGO.

| Articles. | Value. 1889. | 1890. | 1891. |
|---|---|---|---|
|  | £ | £ | £ |
| Dry goods and carpets.. | 18,062,000 | 19,326,000 | 20,292,000 |
| Groceries | 11,134,000 | 11,691,000 | 11,691,000 |
| Lumber.. | 7,423,000 | 7,601,000 | 8,041,000 |
| Manufactured iron | 3,202,000 | 3,202,000 | 3,504,000 |
| Clothing.. | 4,433,000 | 4,433,000 | 4,742,000 |
| Boots and shoes | 4,742,000 | 5,340,000 | 5,670,000 |
| Drugs and chemicals.. | 1,402,000 | 1,464,000 | 1,567,000 |
| Crockery and glassware | 1,051,000 | 1,132,000 | 1,237,000 |
| Hats and caps.. | 1,237,000 | 1,443,000 | 1,650,000 |
| Millinery | 1,340,000 | 1,443,000 | 1,443,000 |
| Tobacco and cigars | 2,778,000 | 2,237,000 | 2,371,000 |
| Fresh and salt fish and oysters | 1,060,000 | 1,126,000 | 1,134,000 |
| Oils | 825,000 | 825,000 | 928,000 |
| Dried fruits | 722,000 | 887,000 | 887,000 |
| Building materials | 765,000 | 919,000 | 928,000 |
| Furs | 309,000 | 309,000 | 361,000 |
| Carriages | 338,000 | 382,000 | 413,000 |
| Pianos, all musical instruments | 1,366,000 | 1,485,000 | 1,608,000 |
| Music books, sheet music | 107,000 | 119,000 | 129,000 |
| Books, stationery, wall paper.. | 4,268,000 | 4,536,000 | 4,536,000 |
| Paper | 6,804,000 | 5,258,000 | 5,773,000 |
| Paper stock | 1,134,000 | 1,031,000 | 1,093,000 |
| Pig-iron.. | 3,340,000 | 4,131,000 | 4,227,000 |
| Coal | 4,792,000 | 5,170,000 | 5,361,000 |
| Hardware, cutlery | .. | 3,608,000 | 3,984,000 |
| Wooden, willow ware.. | 592,000 | 652,000 | 722,000 |
| Liquors.. | 2,371,000 | 2,845,000 | 3,093,000 |
| Jewellery, watches, diamonds.. | 3,505,000 | 4,206,000 | 5,155,000 |
| Leather and findings.. | 495,000 | 520,000 | 567,000 |
| Pig-lead and copper | 775,000 | 1,168,000 | 1,237,000 |
| Iron ore.. | 410,000 | 825,000 | 928,000 |
| Miscellaneous.. | 1,177,000 | 1,058,000 | 1,359,000 |
| Total.. | 91,959,000 | 100,372,000 | 106,631,000 |

### *Manufactures.*

Manufactures were somewhat depressed at the commencement of the year, owing to being overstocked; an increase of capital, too, has been requisite to meet increased expenditure in salaries and the larger staff of travellers which competition yearly renders necessary. The large increase in production in 1890, which amounted to 19½ per cent. over that of 1889, has, however, been maintained, and a further increase of 5½ per cent. is estimated. Chicago is yearly becoming more independent of foreign imports, and yearly extends the market for its manufactures. There were 57 new manufacturing firms established last year, bringing the total number of establishments in the city up to 3,307, and an increase in capital employed calculated at 4,200,000*l*. The wages paid in manufacturing industries increased from 19,837,000*l*. to 21,588,000*l*., and the estimated value of product from 110,928,000*l*. to 116,910,000*l*. The amount of capital employed was 43,361,000*l*.

compared with 39,175,000*l.* in 1890, and the number of workmen was 180,870 against 177,000. Though somewhat inactive during the first six months from overstock and monetary depression, all industries recovered in the latter half of the year, except that of steel.

**Packing.** The packing business is the most important of all the industries, and including the manufacture of butterine and other products amounted to the value of 27,600,000*l.*, against 28,304,000*l.* in the preceding year. There was a slight falling-off in the number of cattle absorbed in the packing and canning business, but the number of hogs was larger. The product of hog packing was valued at 12,371,000*l.* and of beef packing and canning at 11,340,000*l.*, while lard, lard oil, and stearine produced a value of 2,588,000*l.* A considerable increase took place in the manufacture of butterine, of which 33,000,000 lbs. were made. There was one additional firm added during 1891 to the number, which is now 76, and the aggregate capital employed increased from 3,500,000*l.* to 3,750,000*l.*

**Iron and steel.** In the iron and steel industry there was a diminution of five in the number of establishments, which is now 316, including 6 rolling mills, 60 foundries, 32 boiler works, 5 car wheel works, 9 stove and range works, and a number of miscellaneous industries. The aggregate capital employed was increased by about 730,000*l.*, and amounts to 9,073,000*l.*, and 30,185 hands are employed. The rolling mills turned out a value of 5,340,000*l.* and the foundries 2,268,000*l.* The total product of the year is valued at 14,577,000*l.*, or about 281,000*l.* more than the product of 1890. About 4,400 fewer hands were employed, and steel is in a depressed condition.

**Brass, copper, &c.** Next in importance are the brass, copper, and other metal industries, which turned out a value of 9,390,000*l.*, or about 180,000*l.* less than in 1890, though there are 12 new establishments, and the aggregate capital of the 153 existing firms increased from 1,703,000*l.* in 1890 to 2,324,000*l.* in 1891. In these, as in the iron and steel industries, there seems to have been a general depression in the first six months of last year till the abundance of the harvest became known, when trade for the most part recovered, except in those industries connected with the building trade, which were active throughout the year. The four smelting and refining works turned out a value of 4,866,000*l.*, the jewellery manufactories 500,000*l.*, and the tin, stamped and metal ware, 1,541,000*l.* The effect of the McKinley Act has been to raise the cost of material to the canner, and consequently the cost of cans, but a large surplus stock was imported in view of the higher rate, and the duty does not seem to have been felt in any appreciable degree, and no rise has as yet taken place in packed goods.

**Iron and wood.** In the iron and wood industries there was also a falling-off of about 185,000*l.* in value of product, which amounted to 8,495,000*l.*, though the capital employed increased from 2,825,000*l.* to 3,696,000*l.*, and the number of workers by 1,500.

The manufacture of agricultural implements produced about 3,333,333*l*. sterling, and the car and bridge builders turned out a value of 3,567,000*l*. The capital employed in these industries mounts up to 3,696,000*l*., or 871,000*l*. more than in 1890.

In the manufactures of wood twelve new establishments were added to the 470 existing in 1890, and the capital employed increased from 3,814,000*l*. to 3,995,000*l*.; the value of the product was only 10,000*l*. more than in the preceding year, and is said to have amounted to 9,495,000*l*. The furniture establishments produced a value of 4,330,000*l*., and the planing mills about 2,060,000*l*. Fifteen years ago no reed organs were made in this city, and ten years ago only 50 pianos. At the present time more organs are manufactured here than in all the cities of the country, and 9,000 are now annually made, besides a large number of other musical instruments, counting together a value of 1,443,000*l*. {Wood.}

The brickyards of Chicago turned out 640,000,000 bricks; the price averaged low, but there was a good demand. Scarcely any tile or terra cotta is now imported, the domestic product of somewhat inferior quality being preferred, as the cost is less. The same may be said of stained glass, the manufacture of which last year produced a value of 186,000*l*. The capital employed in the various industries under this head is now 1,486,000*l*., against against 1,171,000 in 1890; but the estimated value of the product of 1891 was 386,000*l*. less than in 1890, and amounted to 2,211,000*l*. {Brick, stone, &c.}

In all the above industries, though much more capital is invested, the returns have been generally less than in 1890, prices having been depressed greatly owing to more competition.

Competition reduced profits in the brewing industry, and at one time beer was sold as low as 16*s*. 5*d*. a barrel. As many as 14 new breweries were started last year, greatly in view of increased consumption at the time of the Exhibition. The total produce was valued at 2,720,000*l*. The 84 distilleries and rectifiers produced a value of 3,243,000*l*. {Breweries.}

The McKinley Act has revolutionised the tobacco and cigar trade. The import of cigars is greatly reduced, the price increased, and good cigars are difficult to procure. The product of the industry in this city was greatly in excess of that of 1890. There are now 980 establishments for the manufacture of cigars and cigarettes, which produced last year 176,000,000 cigars, and more than 3,000,000 cigarettes, besides manufactures of tobacco and snuff. {Tobacco.}

There was an increase of more than 20 per cent. in chemical productions, and 30 per cent. in the cost of labour in the manufacture. Competition reduced the value of oil mill products by nearly 50 per cent.; the soap industry brought in 1,650,000*l*., one firm alone out of the eight firms producing 80,000,000 lbs. {Chemicals.}

The 87 firms in the leather business increased their capital by 20 per cent., and the product was about the same as in 1890, or 5,000,000*l*. {Leather.}

## UNITED STATES.

**Textiles.**

Textile industries, including clothing of all sorts, show an enormous increase in the value of production, being stated to have turned out to the amount of 10,825,000*l*., against 7,902,000*l*. in 1890. This is partly the result of larger purchases owing to the bountiful harvest, and partly to the higher duties on foreign goods. The McKinley tariff has raised prices all round. Fewer articles of foreign manufacture were imported, and the cost of such goods is greatly higher. Some of the large houses import as much, or nearly so, as before the tariff came in force; but some of the smaller retailers are said to have given up importing any foreign goods, the cost being such as to make them unmarketable or not easily disposed of, and find the inferior article of domestic manufacture has a readier sale. The consequence has been an increased demand for goods of home manufacture, and a consequent rise in prices, the consumer being now forced to give more for an inferior article. New factories are reported as being organised in different parts of this district to meet the demand, but have not yet entered into competition to cause a levelling of prices, and existing establishments have in the meantime secured large profits. The number of firms engaged in this branch of manufacture at Chicago was 141, or 24 less than in 1890, but the capital employed advanced from 3,448,000*l*. to 4,696,000*l*., and the aggregate wages paid from 1,794,000*l*. to 2,192,000*l*., business getting more in the hands of large houses. The value of men's and boys' clothing made was 6,125,000, and of cloaks and suitings 2,270,000*l*.

**Printing, publishing.**

It is estimated that more than 15,000,000 volumes were printed at Chicago in 1891. The city has a large circulation, and is perhaps the most important in the country as a subscription book centre, as well as in the publication of maps, encyclopædias, &c. Printing, publishing, and newspapers produced an estimated value of 4,535,000*l*., and the total output of the different industries is said to have been 5,752,000*l*., or an increase of 1,442,000*l*. during the year.

**Other industries.**

The industries in aliments produced nearly 7,000,000*l*., of which the coffee and spices mills gave a value of 2,267,000*l*. There are many other smaller manufactures, amongst which the bicycle factories turned out a product of 433,000*l*. Bicycles now form a small item of import; some houses which formerly imported from England now cease to do so, and the demand is almost wholly confined to local manufacture, which is considered quite equal in every way.

Space will not allow of entering further into the industries of Chicago, which has for some time been gradually becoming a great manufacturing city. The following will, however, show at a glance the rapid development which has taken place in the last three years in the different manufacturing industries, as classified by the best authority on the subject:—

| Articles. | 1888. | | 1891. | |
|---|---|---|---|---|
| | Capital. | Product. | Capital. | Product. |
| | £ | £ | £ | £ |
| Meat, provisions | 2,886,000 | 22,268,000 | 3,711,000 | 27,000,000 |
| Iron and steel | 4,953,000 | 11,328,000 | 9,073,000 | 14,577,000 |
| Brass, copper, &c. | 978,000 | 5,805,000 | 2,324,000 | 9,390,000 |
| Iron and wood | 2,378,000 | 6,784,000 | 3,696,000 | 8,495,000 |
| Manufactures of wood | 1,993,000 | 6,974,000 | 3,995,000 | 9,495,000 |
| Brick, stone, &c. | 660,000 | 2,055,000 | 1,486,000 | 2,211,000 |
| Breweries, distilleries, and tobacco | 1,990,000 | 6,237,000 | 4,825,000 | 9,397,000 |
| Chemicals | 1,515,000 | 3,948,000 | 2,757,000 | 5,877,000 |
| Leather | 1,804,000 | 1,691,000 | 2,557,000 | 4,917,000 |
| Textiles | 2,247,000 | 5,964,000 | 4,696,000 | 10,825,000 |
| Printing | 1,361,000 | 3,490,000 | 1,460,000 | 5,752,000 |
| Aliments | 966,000 | 5,876,000 | 2,196,000 | 6,878,000 |
| Miscellaneous | 326,000 | 1,471,000 | 610,000 | 1,896,000 |
| Total | 24,057,000 | 83,891,000 | 43,386,000 | 116,910,000 |

## Real Estate and Building.

*Real estate.* — It could scarcely be expected that the immense rise in the value of real estate in and around the city, mentioned in the annual report for 1890, would continue in the same degree; prices, however, have been well maintained all round, property in the vicinity of the Exhibition has still further increased in value, and there is a disinclination to part with land anywhere except at a considerable advance. Transfers in real estate, which give a fair indication of the market, amounted in 1891 to 36,701,000*l*.; four or five years ago they scarcely reached half that amount, and have only been exceeded in 1890, when they amounted to 46,700,000*l*. In point of large transactions, last year was never surpassed; there were fewer speculative purchases with the view of selling at enhanced price, and investment purchasers were proportionately greater. Rapid transportation service has an immediate effect on property in the suburban districts, and those sections, where rapid means of reaching the business quarter of the city are provided, increase proportionately in value. The new south side elevated railroad is now completed to 39th Street, which is reached from Congress Street in 15 minutes, and before the exhibition is open will be carried as far as the World's Fair grounds, where people will be transported in 31 minutes. Along this line a great increase has taken place in the value of real estate; one vacant block has lately been sold at 4,000*l*. more than it was worth a year ago, and another at a rise of 60*l*. a front foot, or 60 per cent. on former value. For property in the immediate neighbourhood of the Exhibition, the rise in value, which was last year equivalent to 300 per cent. or 400 per cent., has been maintained and higher prices given; quite a new town has sprung up, and many hotels and apartments-houses, are projected, and in some instances commenced. Rentable property in any desirable situation in the city is extremely rare, and may be said almost not to exist; apartment and office rents, though in no case have they decreased, have not very materially increased during the year, as so many new buildings have been constructed; it is difficult to foresee what may be the result next year when the exhibition is open; there are scarcely any unrented houses in any good situation, and the city is increasing at the rate of about 100,000 a year. Leases for 99 years are now not uncommon. Hotel prices are on the rise, and have increased considerably during the year. A single bedroom at one of the principal hotels costs now about 16s. a day, or if on the American principle, 1l. or 1l. 5s. a day, while a sitting room or really good accommodation entails much greater daily expense. What they will charge next year is yet a problem.

Building.  Building was carried on last year to an unprecedented extent, and as has already been stated 11,805 buildings were erected, with a total frontage of 53½ miles. A number of large hotels have been constructed for the accommodation of visitors next year, and the ever increasing population; some capable of receiving many hundred people are already open and absorbing the increased number of people who are constantly arriving, and some in course of completion. Many large business blocks in the heart of the city, containing from 400 sets to 800 sets of officers, have been opened, and are being gradually tenanted; others are being constructed or planned, buildings which formerly were considered fine and solid constructions for business purposes being pulled down to be replaced by loftier erections, so that the maximum amount of rent may be obtained on the minimum space of ground, and some of the largest stores in the world have been opened during the last year. Already, the effect of this concentration of business in a limited space, little more than half a mile square, has begun to be felt, and the masses of people and vehicles of all sorts, with the cable lines forming an almost continuous train of cars, which crowd the principal streets from morning till 7 o'clock in the evening, have become a matter of consideration with a view to some means of relieving the pressure. Almost all the public buildings, theatres, hotels, railway stations, private offices, and large stores are concentrated in or quite close to this limited space, and are not distributed, as in most other cities, over a wider area. Everything here, too, seems in a hurry, and it is not easy to thread a way through the crowded streets. With the sole exception of New York, the value of a site in this portion of the city is perhaps greater than in any part of the world; 40,000l. has lately been given for a corner lot, 20 feet by 40 feet, or 50l. per square foot.

There are other reasons, such as danger in case of fire, which have led to much controversy on the subject of these tall buildings, so many of which have lately been erected from 12 stories to 20 stories high, one of them reaching an elevation of 275 feet, and insurance companies have formulated a fresh schedule, augmenting the rate on such buildings as may be used for mercantile purposes. The city authorities have also stopped granting permits for buildings of unlimited height, pending an ordinance on the subject.

To illustrate the marvellous rapidity with which these tall buildings are constructed, the Ashland block may be mentioned, a construction of steel, stone, and terra cotta at the corner of Randolph and Clark Streets, close to the City Hall, 17 stories in height on an area of 140 feet by 80 feet. It was built in midwinter, and work was continued by day and night by relays of men, strong arc electric lights being used by night; artificial heat was furnished by 100 small salamander stoves, to enable the builders and masons to work at that season of the year, and protection from the cold winds was given by several hundred yards of thick canvas. The skeleton of steel for each floor is first erected, each column, girder, and rafter being lifted and placed in position by steam power, and as these are riveted with red-hot rivets, and as the stories rise, they are filled in with square blocks of terra cotta and brick. On December 6, last year, six floors were completed and the steel skeleton for the three next stories was for the most part placed. On December 19, ten floors were completed, and the steel shell for three more stories was mostly in position. Thus the entire construction of four floors of a building 140 feet by 80 feet, divided into numerous rooms was solidly built in 13 days, or one floor in $3\frac{1}{4}$ days. About 60 iron and steel workers, 100 brick masons, and 35 terra cotta setters were continually at work. The enormous quantity of iron and steel used in this new mode of construction, which was only first tried six years ago, has created quite a new industry, and the employés have already their organization under the term architectural iron workers. Steel has now almost entirely taken the place of iron, of which the first few of these tall buildings were constructed. The foundations are tiers of steel rails, embedded in concrete, the beams stretching 10 feet or 12 feet under the street; this plan was found necessary, on account of the nature of the soil, so as to bear the great imposed weight. These beams are made at the Illinois steel works, or come from Pennsylvania. This new method of building is said to be lighter and stronger than the old system, and to be absolutely fire-proof; the greatest variation in the plumb line from base to top of these tall buildings has been found not to exceed half-an-inch.

Houses removed.

Fifteen hundred permits to remove buildings were granted last year at an average charge of about 12s. each; frame buildings are no longer allowed to be built within certain city limits, and it has for some time been a common practice, when new residences are erected or the land sold, to bodily remove the old wooden or brick house to some distance away from the district where improvements are made. This is done by raising the house by means of screw levers on to a platform of baulks under which rollers are placed, and by chains and windlass worked by horse-power, the house is slowly moved along the centre of the streets until it reaches the spot where it is destined to remain on a new foundation. Out of the houses moved last year, 140 were of brick and the rest of wood; two of them were four stories high, and 33 of three stories. It is not uncommon for the families to remain in these houses, as usual, during the process of removal. Sometimes houses are removed on barges, and taken up the river to be replaced in a more remote situation.

*Shipping.*

A return of all shipping at the port of Chicago is given below, including those coasting vessels which arrive and clear from the small adjacent ports of South Chicago and Michigan City, which are in the customs district of this city. There are 384 vessels owned in the district, with a total tonnage of 65,280 tons. Six were built during the year, with an aggregate tonnage of 4,046 tons, two being propellers of 1,992 tons each. Another steel steamship, the fourth built by the Chicago Shipbuilding Company, for the Minnesota iron-ore trade, has since been launched; it will carry 4,000 tons in less than 15 feet of water. New York is the only port in the United States which approaches Chicago in the number of vessels annually entered and cleared; according to the report of the supervising special agent, June 30, 1891, the total number at New York was 16,014, at the nine principal seaports of the country 41,273, and at Chicago 20,227. The total number at the principal ports of the great lakes was 96,024, Milwaukee having exceeded Chicago and numbering 20,994 vessels entered and cleared. On these lakes more than 9,000,000 tons of ore were transported and sent to feed the foundries. Five years ago there were only six steel vessels on the lakes, with total tonnage of 6,459 tons; there are now 89, with a tonnage of 127,624 tons. In 1859 the cost of transporting a bushel of wheat from Chicago to Buffalo was 8$d$.; during a part of last year it was $\frac{1}{2}d$., though it rose later in the season to $1\frac{1}{2}d$. and 2$d$. The average rate of freight for wheat from Chicago to New York by lake and canal was $3\frac{1}{2}d$., by lake and rail $4\frac{1}{2}d$., and by all rail $7\frac{1}{2}d$.; for corn the rate was rather less.

RETURN of all Shipping at the Port of Chicago in the Year 1891.

| Nationality. | Entered. Number of Vessels. | Entered. Tons. | Cleared. Number of Vessels. | Cleared. Tons. | Total. Number of Vessels. | Total. Tons. |
|---|---|---|---|---|---|---|
| Coasting trade | 10,076 | 5,451,632 | 10,109 | 5,363,321 | 20,185 | 10,814,953 |
| Foreign trade, British | 84 | 51,015 | 89 | 53,319 | 173 | 104,334 |
| Foreign trade, American | 64 | 22,205 | 196 | 90,060 | 260 | 112,265 |
| Total, 1891 | 10,224 | 5,524,852 | 10,394 | 5,506,700 | 20,618 | 11,031,552 |
| ,, 1890 | 10,507 | 5,136,253 | 10,547 | 5,150,615 | 21,054 | 10,286,868 |
| ,, 1889 | 9,802 | 4,521,886 | 10,023 | 4,629,184 | 19,825 | 9,151,070 |

# CHICAGO.

Chicago is a customs port of entry, but large quantities of goods for consumption here pay duty at the seaboard ports. The duties collected on imported merchandise at Chicago during the last five years were as follows:—

|  | £ |
|---|---|
| 1887 | 978,244 |
| 1888 | 1,026,266 |
| 1889 | 1,040,984 |
| 1890 | 1,069,582 |
| 1891 | 1,233,730 |

Customs.

The merchandise entered for export, with benefit of drawback, at the port of Chicago during the year 1891 was as follows:—

| Articles. | Packages. | Quantity. |
|---|---|---|
|  | Number. | Lbs. |
| Canned meat | 892,676 | 54,877,719 |
| Salted ,, | 127,446 | 21,224,440 |
| Bales binder twine | 16,075 | 1,128,468 |

| Articles Entitled to Drawback. | Quantity. | Amount of Drawback. |
|---|---|---|
|  | Lbs. | £ |
| Tin-plate | 8,735,992 | 18,542 |
| Salt | 4,808,473 | 929 |
| Hemp | 1,128,468 | 1,586 |
| Total | .. | 21,057 |

*Imports and Exports.*

The following statement shows the value of imported merchandise entered for consumption at the port of Chicago for the last three years:—

# UNITED STATES.

| Articles. | Value. | | |
|---|---|---|---|
| | 1889. | 1890. | 1891. |
| | £ | £ | £ |
| Free goods | 496,257 | 702,121 | 672,482 |
| Ale, beer, and porter | 8,312 | 10,377 | 9,747 |
| Art materials | 13,369 | 15,248 | 9,650 |
| Books, printed | 9,220 | 10,624 | 8,192 |
| Brushes | 4,322 | 5,600 | 7,187 |
| Chemicals | 6,681 | 3,871 | 5,772 |
| China and glassware | 106,836 | 115,710 | 161,765 |
| Caustic soda | 13,280 | 18,888 | 11,998 |
| Cigars and tobacco manufactures | 112,309 | 136,744 | 61,842 |
| Cutlery | 6,181 | 4,907 | 4,880 |
| Diamonds and precious stones | 66,103 | 74,486 | 25,853 |
| Dressed furs | 26,621 | 32,240 | 49,405 |
| Dried fruits and nuts | 70,003 | 113,050 | 66,050 |
| Drug sundries | 9,625 | 9,006 | 8,836 |
| Dry goods | 933,980 | 991,231 | 832,262 |
| Fish, all kinds | 40,117 | 31,371 | 48,501 |
| Gums | 9,506 | 8,940 | 4,414 |
| Iron, manufactures, and wire | 22,656 | 37,961 | 78,605 |
| Jewellery | 3,915 | 3,160 | 11,361 |
| Leaf tobacco | 41,273 | 34,326 | 42,298 |
| Leather manufactures | 61,285 | 52,115 | 50,320 |
| Looking-glass plates | 2,000 | 3,455 | 11,950 |
| Metal manufactures | 32,422 | 45,222 | 57,530 |
| Millinery goods | 17,346 | 18,284 | 18,801 |
| Musical instruments | 39,704 | 43,216 | 43,890 |
| Needles | 2,445 | 2,328 | 272 |
| Paintings and statuary | 12,066 | 15,069 | 11,619 |
| Paper manufactures | 4,266 | 4,504 | 12,589 |
| Paper-hangings | 924 | 459 | 1,082 |
| Pickles and sauces | 3,250 | 2,968 | 5,264 |
| Plate window-glass | 16,534 | 12,214 | 8,509 |
| Smokers' articles | 1,818 | 2,616 | 5,559 |
| Steel bars, bloom, &c. | 310 | 183 | 896 |
| Stone and marble | 2,458 | 7,681 | 8,618 |
| Tin-plates | 296,925 | 336,599 | 328,094 |
| Toys and fancy articles | 25,532 | 24,796 | 15,802 |
| Varnish | 757 | 866 | 1,055 |
| Wines and liquors | 67,381 | 76,178 | 88,567 |
| Wood manufactures | 13,203 | 19,104 | 38,956 |
| Total, including a few other articles | 2,785,018 | 3,174,617 | 3,116,653 |

It will be seen that the imports in 1891, though 57,964*l.* less than in 1890, exceeded in value those of 1889 by 331,635*l.* The increase in value of free goods, however, compared with 1889, amounted to 176,225*l.*, so that the value of dutiable goods imported in 1891 increased only by 165,410*l.* in the two years; and, not counting free goods, the imports of dutiable goods in 1891 were only 38,325*l.* less in value than those of 1890, and amounted to 2,434,171*l.* The amount of duties levied increased by 169,652*l.* from 1889 to 1891, so that the result of this comparison would be that since 1889 free goods, dutiable goods, and customs duties have each increased by about 170,000*l*. The condition in 1890 was abnormal, on account of the quantity of goods imported in anticipation of the McKinley tariff, and probably some of this extra stock was not worked off till the early months of 1891.

Again, comparing the imports of 1891 with those of 1889, and it must not be forgotten that the trade of the city has greatly increased, as shown in tables already given, it will be seen that the commodities which appear to be most affected by the tariff, and of which the import has decreased, are art materials, cigars, cutlery, diamonds and precious stones, drug sundries, dry goods, guns, leather goods, needles, plate window glass, and toys and fancy articles. Caustic soda and dried fruits have also been imported in smaller quantities, as well as paintings and statuary. The trade in cigars has been revolutionised, and a great impetus given to home manufacture. In dry goods, on account of diminution in the imports and the greater cost of the foreign product, articles of domestic manufacture have been in much demand. Diamonds and precious stones have decreased almost two-thirds in value. Guns have been greatly affected, and needles have almost disappeared as an import.

On the other hand, china and glassware, dressed furs, iron manufactures, jewellery, looking-glass plates, metal manufacture, paper, smokers' articles, wines, and wood manufactures have largely increased in import, while the value of some other articles imported has increased, and amongst them that of tin-plate. As yet the output of the tin-plate manufactories which have started here scarcely supplies 1 per cent. of the ever-increasing consumption of the country; and though it is said larger quantities will be turned out shortly, when new machinery is in order, seems probable that many years will elapse before the industry, if it succeeds, will do much more than absorb the natural increase in demand. The factory at St. Louis, which turns out about 350 boxes a-day, is the only one producing a marketable quantity in this district at the present time.

The exports by lake to Canada, consisting almost entirely of flour, wheat, corn, and rye, were more than double those of the preceding year, and amounted in value to 808,000*l*. The exports of domestic produce to Europe on through bills of lading was also large, but no record of the value is obtainable; they consisted chiefly of flour, wheat, corn, clover, and other seeds (11,500,000 lbs.), fresh beef, lard, cheese (6,500,000 lbs.), and oil-cake (17,250,000 lbs.).

### *Miscellaneous.*

Finance. Notwithstanding a certain want of confidence and drain of gold to Europe in the early part of the year, money has been plentiful, and a large number of new enterprises were started, and increased securities issued. The increase in the banking business was remarkable; the number of State banks in Chicago increased from 17 to 23, and the capital from 1,763,000*l*. to 2,562,000*l*., the deposits and loans were also much larger. The national banks in the city increased their capital during the year from 3,320,000*l*. to 4,380,000*l*., while the deposits rose from 19,479,000*l*. to 24,287,000*l*., and the loans and discounts from 14,926,000*l*. to 18,411,000*l*., the surplus and profits amounting to 2,562,000*l*., or 413,000*l*. more than in the preceding year. The total clearing of the associated banks were 918,944,000*l*., an increase of 381,000,000*l*. in the the last five years. To the financial difficulties arising out of the collapse in Argentine affairs is attributed the fact that no corporation of importance was last year formed after the method of English syndicates. One new company, with principal offices in London and Chicago, has since been organised by an amalgamation of seven existing packing firms, covering 20 acres of the stock yards, and having branches in other cities. In 1889 and 1890 nearly 10,000,000*l*. were invested by English capitalists in the stock yards, packing companies, and breweries of this city, and other securities based on Chicago property were largely floated; the business, however, which is purchased at a value far beyond the original capital invested, is often handicapped in the competition which large profits inevitably induce.

Labour. The question of labour in this district has been so recently treated in a special report that there is little to add on the subject, though it may be repeated that the market here is overcrowded in most branches of employment. The influx of immigrants continues; many come from parts of the world where labour is extremely cheap, and, accustomed to less luxury, these men can live on little, and will consequently take employment at low remuneration. Last year 250,000 immigrants came to this country from Austria, Italy, and Russia; but few could read or write or knew the language. The majority, of course, flock to the cities, and a large proportion were sent or found their way to Chicago. Wages of skilled labour have been forced or kept up where trade organisations have been able to exercise their power, but outside of connection with unions the wages paid scarcely enable those who come from countries where labour is reasonably remunerated to meet expenses, even if they can pay for the greater cost of living. As long as they are able-bodied they, no doubt, eventually get employment; but if they fall sick or are maimed, their lot is hard, and the existing resources of hospitals and relief are severely tried. At present the demand for labour is more than supplied, except in agricultural districts (where from 3*l*. 14*s*. to 4*l*. 11*s*. is given, with board, for those who know their work), or for domestic service, which is out of favour.

Health. The total number of deaths in the city of Chicago in 1891 was 27,754, and the rate was 22·20 per 1,000. Of these deaths 1,997 were entered as resulting from typhoid fever, against 1,008 in 1890, but the Commissioner of Health states that many resulted from other causes, and that the doctor's certificates are misleading. Some few cases were investigated, and only 2 out of 15, it is said, proved to have been typhoid fever. This fever, however, if not an epidemic, has been prevalent during the last year, and has been attributed to impurity in the water, and to accumulated dirt from the want of properly cleansing the streets. These had been looked upon by some as dangerous sources of disease, but the purity of the air no doubt carries off much which might cause worse results in another climate. Great attention has lately been paid to the water and sewerage questions, and extensive works are in hand for their improvement. As regards the water supply, Chicago has the advantage of its position on the largest body of fresh water in the world, from which an unlimited supply of pure water can be obtained. At present the main supply is derived by means of a tunnel from a crib two miles out in the lake; there are 25 pumping engines of different size and power, with capacity of 314,000,000 gallons a day, the actual amount of water furnished in 1891 having been 63,522,000 gallons, against 56,338,000 gallons in 1890. The quality of the water has not been wholly satisfactory, or what it should be, especially when spring floods cause the river to flow into the lake. The whole sewerage of the city falls into this river, and is pumped at the rate of 40,000 gallons a minute into a canal, thence finding its way to the Illinois river, but a certain portion reaches the lake. The new tunnel, however, is nearly completed, and in a few months time the water supply of the city will be derived from four miles out in the lake, where it is said to be absolutely pure. The drainage question is one which has long been discussed; the Board appointed for the purpose have now contracted for the excavation of a new canal by means of which the waters of the Chicago River will be conducted into the Illinois River, the carrying power to be 600,000 gallons per minute, so that in a few years' time it is expected that no city sewerage will reach the lake, as the power will be sufficient to cause the flow in the other direction.

Public works.

As so much has been written on the World's Columbian Exposition, and as all particulars have been published in the Journal of the Society of Arts in London, where any information can be obtained, it is not proposed to enter on the subject in this report. The question is one, however, which is very closely allied with trade and commerce, and this great Exhibition may, not improbably, have a powerful influence, not only on the trade of this city and country, but also a greater influence on the channels of trade all over the world than any similar event has ever had. It will furnish a great field for advertisement, and afford the best opportunity for people from all parts to compare the manufactures and commodities of different nations, an opportunity never perhaps equalled.

The Exhibition.

What the effect of the McKinley Act may ultimately be if it continue in force is impossible to foretell; what has been the effect as yet, it has been endeavoured to show as far as possible in this report by comparison with two years ago, but the tariff has not been yet sufficiently long in force to give definite results; opinions are easy to procure, but facts are difficult. Before long the country will probably decide whether it is to

The McKinley Act.

(1372)

continue in force, and no doubt uncertainty on this point has delayed the development of some enterprises, which have been proposed, and might, had the tariff question been a certainty, have gone ahead more quickly. But whether it continue, or a less protective policy be pursued, the race for trade will still be run, and those who push the most forward have the best chance of success.

Nothing has yet stayed the progress which is being made towards carrying the vast enterprise of the Exhibition. The works were commenced in the late summer last year. Many buildings are now completed, and there is no doubt that all will be ready for the inauguration on October 20, or for the opening on May 1 next year. The more the works advance, and the overwhelming applications for space come in, the more easily can it be appreciated that this will be the most important exhibition which has ever taken place.

### Notes on the West.

Abundant crops, development of manufacturing and mining industries, large increase in the population of cities and towns, and a fair advance in the value of agricultural land have been general, and indicate a condition of prosperity for the past year over the whole district, the influence of which has been felt in every branch of business.

**Iowa.** In no previous year has the State of Iowa been favoured with so bounteous a harvest; the grain firms paid out 400,000*l.* more than in the preceding season, and farmers, who for many years have complained that cereals did not bring a fair return on capital invested—indeed, that loss was sustained in the cultivation of land after deducting the prevailing local interest on such capital—have last year had little ground for dissatisfaction. The total value of the agricultural product of the State in 1891 was 92,783,011*l.*, including live stock and timber. The crop of corn was 335,000,000 bushels; wheat, 33,000,000; oats, 116,000,000; potatoes, 25,500,000 bushels; hay, 5,820,000 tons, which, with 169,000,000 lbs. of butter, together reached a value of about 47,000,000*l.*; while 3,959,000 cattle, 5,921,000 hogs, and more than 1,000,000 horses produced a value in the year of about 32,000,000*l.* This State now contains 8,440 miles of railway track, employing 27,580 men, and stands fifth among the States of the union in railway mileage. The number of passengers carried in 1891 was 6,669,659, and of tons of freight nearly 20,000,000, while the total earnings on Iowa business were 8,887,093*l.*, or an increase of 367,890*l.*, and the operating expenses amounted to 5,905,009*l.* There were 178 persons killed in this State and 773 injured, chiefly employés.

During the last two years, savings and State banks have increased 40 per cent. in number and in amount of deposits. Mining has assumed a prominent position, and nearly 10,000 men are constantly employed. This is a prohibition State, and the system seems scarcely to have worked satisfactorily: in the Governor's opinion the experiment has proved a failure, it has converted into crimes acts which the vast majority of the people consider innocent, has interfered with personal rights, and enforcement of the law, which is openly violated, has failed; he considers that it has proved an obstacle to material progress and recommends reconsideration of the law.

Business in the cities has been active in harmony with agricultural prosperity. At Des Moines great advance has been made in industries, 32 new establishments have been added to the list, the business transacted has increased, and in no instance, it is said, has business fallen off in the old houses; the increase in the production of factories in 1891 was more than 500,000*l.*, and the total production amounted to 2,921,568*l.*; the jobbing business increased by about 1,000,000*l.*, and the total business was 7,081,569*l.* The bank clearings were 8,407,812*l.*, an increase of 23·3 per cent. in the year. The savings banks increased in number from 50 to 83, and State banks from 80 to 122, with aggregate capital of 2,273,402*l.* Improvements and public works are actively carried on, and 691 new buildings were constructed in the year. Des Moines is only an example of the manner in which the western cities increase yearly in importance and their business develops as the country fills up: the advance at Sioux City in the same State has been far more rapid.

The State of Wisconsin has also experienced a season of great prosperity and progress. The city of Milwaukee has advanced in no less proportion than Chicago, its population has nearly doubled in the last 10 years, and is now in round numbers 236,000; in 1840 the population was 1,712. A large number of new buildings were erected in 1891, and nearly 2,000,000*l.* expended in their construction. The number of manufacturing establishments increased from 3,027 to 3,258, and the aggregate capital now employed exceeds 16,000,000*l.* sterling. The value of all the productive industries of the city amounted to 26,669,667*l.*, an increase of production in the year of 4,759,667*l.*, chiefly in beer, machinery, iron, and steel, malt and wood working, which are the principal manufacturing industries of the city, and each of which increased by about 200,000*l.* The number of employés in all industries is 55,890, and the amount of wages paid nearly 5,000,000*l.* Improvements have been made in the machinery buildings of the Bay View rolling mills of the Illinois Steel Company, and the mills were run to their full capacity during the year. The Milwaukee cement industry is taking large proportions and gaining ground in the markets of the north-west. The worsted mills are stated to have more than doubled their output during the year, greatly owing to the McKinley tariff; and a new company has been organised, called the Milwaukee Worsted Cloth Company, with a capital of 16,500*l.* The breweries expended about 500,000*l.* in improvements to their plant and in construction of other buildings; the Pabst Brewing Company

*Wisconsin.*
*Milwaukee.*

alone erected 40 buildings at a cost of more than 200,000*l*., and the Schlitz Brewing Company buildings costing nearly 150,000*l*. The output of the Milwaukee breweries in 1891 was 2,051,290 barrels (an increase of 194,224 barrels), which sold at an average price of 1*l*. 6*s*. 10*d*. per barrel, making an aggregate value of about 2,770,000*l*. This is double the quantity brewed eight years ago. The largest tin ware manufacturing firm in the city has been incorporated as a company, with a capital of 123,700.

The total arrival of vessels at the port of Milwaukee was 5,853, with aggregate tonnage of 3,542,421 tons, an increase of 476 vessels and 532,225 tons; the clearances were 5,535, with total tonnage of 3,482,084. Vessels to the value of about 200,000*l*. were added to the customs district during the year. Besides schooners and other small craft, 12 steamers were built at Milwaukee in 1891, one of which was 2,082 tons. The imports increased from 179,948*l*. to 266,099*l*., and the duties on goods from 67,703*l*. to 75,502*l*.

*Nebraska.* — Perhaps, in no State of the Union has greater material progress been made during the last 20 years than in Nebraska. Ten years ago there were only eight States with a smaller population; there are now 18 with a less number of inhabitants. In 1870 the population was only 122,000; in 1880, 450,500, and according to the census report the State was credited in 1890 with a population of 1,056,793, which is still rapidly increasing. The year following the one in which she was admitted as a State, the assessed valuation was 6,721,649*l*.; in 1891 the State had an actual value of real and personal property assessed at 326,837,175*l*., or an increase since 1880 of 196,940,268*l*. There are still in the State some 13,000,000 acres of unimproved land, a great part of which is said to be arable. All grains appear to flourish, and it is essentially an agricultural district, though there are some important factories, which are yearly developing at a rapid rate. 50 creameries, employing 400 men and 350 teams, have an estimated capacity of 50,000 lbs. of butter a day; the dairy produce of the State ranks high, and many prizes have been awarded in national competitions. The country is now dotted over with flour mills, worked either by the numerous streams or by steam, with a daily capacity of 40,000 barrels. A large number of cattle are raised on the ranches. Seven years ago not an animal was killed in the State except for consumption. The *City of Omaha.* — city of Omaha has now the third largest live stock market and packing business in the country. In 1890 the shipments were 1,107,592 cattle, 1,189,206 hogs, 399,755 sheep, and 21,023 horses, mostly raised in the State. In 1891, 606,699 cattle, 1,673,314 hogs, 156,186 sheep, and 26,603 horses and mules were received at Omaha. This city according to the census of 1890 has a population of 140,452, an increase of 360 per cent. compared with 1880, when the population was 30,518. It covers an area of nearly 25 square miles, and has an estimated actual valuation of 46,400,000*l*. It has 103 miles of electric and other car line, and has become a distributing point of considerable importance, being a centre of 13 railroads. A number of new manufacturing enterprises have been established; the number of firms in June, 1891, was 168 with invested capital of 1,631,959*l*. The bank clearings were 53,038,184*l*., an increase of more than 21 per cent. over those of the previous year.

The manufacture of sugar is taking a prominent place among the industries of Nebraska, the soil being stated to be well adapted for the cultivation of beet. Two large factories were started about four years ago, representing an outlay of 400,000*l*., and having a capacity of 40,000 lbs. per day each. Though final conclusions cannot be based on one or even two seasons' trial, the result of work as yet has been considered favourable with regard to tonnage, yield, and cost of production, Nebraska-grown beets having been found sufficiently rich in sugar to warrant success to the industry. The beet being grown on new soil and by inexperienced cultivators, some caution was found necessary in arriving at any conclusion, and improvements in methods are counted upon. Sub-stations have been established in different districts convenient to the railway lines and the average results in 1890 obtained at these sub-stations were as follows: net weight after cleaning and topping, 17·1 ounces; percentage of sucrose, 13·96; and purity, 78. The year was a trying one for beet cultivators; the highest temperature was 112° Farhr., and the lowest 34° below zero; the rainfall in 1890 was 12·71 inches against a normal fall of 17·10 inches, and the temperature, expressed in heat units, in the whole State from April to October was 13,600, compared with a normal heat of 12,990 and 12,730 in Europe.

*Beet sugar making.*

The experiments covered an area of 75,000 square miles, and beets suitable for sugar-making purposes were produced in all parts of the State, 500 farmers sending specimens for analysis. The best variety in the north was found to be the Klein Wauzlebener; in the centre of the State, the Valmorin; and in the south, the Desprez. Insect enemies are among the difficulties to be contended with, and a thorough investigation made has been published, giving a description and the habits of those insects which are found to be the most destructive to the sugar beet, together with suggestions for the best methods of combating their ravages. The factory at Lincoln last autumn was working about 300 tons of beet per day, and turning out 50,000 lbs. of white granulated sugar, besides other products. It is said 6,000,000 lbs. were last year produced at the two factories. A bounty of ½*d*. is given per lb. of sugar produced.

Though in the report of the State Board of Agriculture it is stated that the problem is solved, and confidence is expressed that more money, ready for the purpose, will be put in the enterprise this year, it is acknowledged that efforts have not yet accomplished all that was desired, and that still there are questions of a more or less vexed character, whether the farmer can produce paying beets and in quantity to supply the demand of refineries, and whether both can be made sufficiently remunerative to secure maximum work and results.

Beet requires thorough cultivation, and costs about 2*l*. 10*s*. an acre to raise, while corn costs half that sum, the average yield of which is 40 bushels. If, as is stated, a farmer cultivating beet can expect nearly 20 tons of product per acre, and 14*s*. 5*d*. per ton, there is a large margin in his favour even if it cost him 10*l*. to raise and haul to the factory.

*Sorghum sugar in Kansas.* — The output of the sorghum sugar factories in the State of Kansas last year is said to be 3,000,000 lbs. The chemist of the Department of Medicine Lodge announces a very satisfactory run with the new machinery under the alcohol process. It is reported that 156 lbs. were produced from the cane, while the molasses was estimated to produce 50 lbs. per ton more, and that there was scarcely any loss of alcohol. This, with the 1*d*. per lb. bounty, is thought to be very satisfactory.

*Tin in the Black Hills.* — So many conflicting opinions are circulated regarding the tin deposits in the Black Hills of South Dakota that the true position is difficult to ascertain, and the Harney Peak mines have been very silent for some time. No doubt appears to be held as to the existence of the ore or of its richness, but time is required as well as money and patience to develop a tin mine, and the present difficulty is to solve the question of separating the mica with which the ore is intermixed. The problem is not whether there is tin in Dakota, but whether it exists in paying quantities and can be reduced at a profit. As yet the question is in an experimental stage, and no marketable tin in any quantity is produced; such pigs as have been turned out are said to have cost their weight in gold. Faith can scarcely be placed in the numerous reports circulated; some say that the tin is of unsurpassed quality and quantity, but expensive machinery is required to crush the ore, and some depth must be reached to secure the best quality, and 50 feet per month is as much as can be done; some reports have been spread that, granting there is tin in the Black Hills, it will not pay to work, and that half the men have been discharged. On the other hand, the last accounts seem to be more encouraging, and it is said that in one or two mines a 600-feet level has been reached, good bodies of ore found, and that the new mills would be erected as soon as side tracks were completed. It is rumoured that a rich ledge of tin has been discovered in Wyoming.

## ST. LOUIS.

Mr. Vice-Consul Western Bascombe reports as follows:—

In presenting this report of the trade, finance, and commerce of St. Louis for the year 1891, I have endeavoured, in addition to the statistics of the business transacted at the Exchanges, to give such other information and data in reference to the city's activity and business growth as could be obtained, trusting it may be found of interest.

*Tonnage.* — While the tonnage of freight handled by the various railroads

## CHICAGO.

and steamboats centering in the city shows a slight diminution in the amount of 85,706 tons, in an aggregate of 16,420,027 tons, yet it is conceded that many lines of trade have largely exceeded the business of 1890, both in quantity and profit.

Banks. The financial stability of the city is shown by the Clearing-house statement of an increase of 1·88 per cent., the total clearings being 569,799,787*l*. in 1891, and 559,286,605*l*. in 1890.

The total capital of the 23 banks was, December 31, 1891, 3,210,000*l*.; undivided profits, 1,422,215*l*.

Trust companies. The total capital of the four Trust Companies was 1,300,000*l*., giving a grand total of banking capital of 5,932,215*l*. The stiff rate of discount of 7 per cent. and 8 per cent. has ruled throughout the year, owing to the unusual heavy demand caused by the stringency in the money markets of the country during the latter months of 1890, accompanied by a consequent heavy outflow of gold and the withdrawal of European capital from American investment.

With the export of crops to Europe in 1891 began the inflow of money, and compelled European gold to return to this country in exchange for American grain, cotton, and other articles of export.

Groceries. During the first six months of the year 1891 the business was rather of an unsatisfactory character, owing to a steadily declining market; the last six months trade was very active, and a sufficient profit is claimed to make the result for the year satisfactory, and an increase in the volume of business of 12 per cent. over that of 1890.

Sugar. Owing to the duty being taken off of low grade sugar a great impetus was given the business, the receipts exceeding those of 1890 by 611 hogsheads, 194,826 barrels, and 226,217 bags, and the profit, taking in consideration the reduced cost, has averaged fully up to that of the preceding year.

Coffee. This is the largest interior coffee market in the United States, being a leading distributing point for Rio and Santos coffees. The receipts for 1891 were 253,154 bags, and shipments 232,997 bags, an increase of 30,000 bags over 1890.

Boots and shoes. A conservative view of the year's business shows a gain of 17 per cent. over last year's manufacture of boots and shoes, while in the jobbing trade the output is nearly a half greater.

A decade ago St. Louis manufactured boots and shoes to the value of only 120,000*l*.; for the year 1890 and the past year 1891, 7,600,000*l*. The jobbing trade has not been less active. The receipts for 1891 being 577,630 cases, consisting chiefly of leather goods in 36 and 72 pair cases, at an average valuation of 7*l*. per case; these amount to the sum of over 4,000,000*l*., an increase over last year of 40 per cent.

Boston is the shoe distributing centre of this country. In 1890 St. Louis received 244,000 cases from Boston, while Chicago and New York received more by 60,000 cases. The year 1891 St. Louis passed her two superiors, and now fills first place with 310,489 cases to her credit. Chicago comes second with 288,001 cases, and New York with 284,544 cases. At this rate of progress it will not take long for this city to become the leading market for boots and shoes in this country.

*Furniture.* — Within the last decade this industry has increased 100 per cent. in this city. The business is fully 4,000,000*l*. for 1891. There were 57 furniture factories, employing 4,000 men, and an increased product of 10 per cent. over 1890. An extensive new business is being built up with Mexico and Central American States even as far south as Costa Rica.

*Dry goods.* — The dry goods trade of St. Louis for 1891 does not indicate any marked increase in the volume of business. The total volume of business for 1891 is reported as slightly in excess of 7,000,000*l*.

*Hardware.* — The business done by St. Louis shows a steady increase in 1891; the total value reaches an aggregate of 3,200,000*l*.

*Hats and caps.* — The sales are reported at 800,000*l*., showing an improvement for the last half of the year, which promises a greater increase in volume for 1892.

*Saddlery and harness.* — The record of the saddlery and harness trade of St. Louis for 1891 was on a par with that of 1889 and 1890, viz., total sales aggregating 3,000,000*l*., although the two leading manufacturers have erected new factories looking to an increased output.

*Wood and willow ware.* — While there are no published statistics of this business for 1891, it is reported as being very satisfactory, showing an increase over 1890. It is now a widely established fact that about one-half of the entire business done in this line in the United States is from one mammoth St. Louis establishment.

*Clothing.* — Sales have shown a regular annual increase, as well as the output of the manufactories, which now aggregate 1,200,000*l*.

*Electrical supplies.* — In consequence of the lighting of the city by electricity, the manufacture of electrical supplies has been greatly augmented, until it now aggregates 1,000,000*l*.

*Bakeries.* — The four leading bakeries of St. Louis are now members of the American Biscuit and Manufacturing Company, which embraces the largest bakers of the country within its organisation; the St. Louis establishments have done a satisfactory and increased business the past year, but the results have not been published.

*Wagons and carriages.* — The manufacture of these articles is reported as showing a gain of 10 per cent., the volume being over 800,000*l*.

*Breweries.* — The brewing interests of St. Louis show a slight falling-off in the manufacture of 46,071 barrels, or 2,356,642 gallons.

The capital invested is 4,000,000*l*., and the product is shipped to every State in the Union, Old Mexico, Australia, and Europe. Shipments to foreign countries for 1891 were 314,199 gallons.

*Grain.* — The volume of the grain business of St. Louis for 1891 shows a decrease as compared with 1890 of about 10,000,000 bushels. This decrease was entirely in corn, the receipts of other cereals except barley being in excess of the previous year, making good to within 10,000,000 bushels the loss on corn, which was nearly 24,000,000 bushels.

## CHICAGO.

| Articles. | Receipts. | |
|---|---|---|
| | 1891. | 1890. |
| | Bushels. | Bushels. |
| Wheat | 25,523,183 | 11,730,774 |
| Corn | 21,530,940 | 45,003,681 |
| Oats | 12,432,215 | 12,299,955 |
| Rye | 1,149,490 | 501,054 |
| Barley | 2,108,546 | 2,794,880 |
| Total | 62,744,374 | 72,260,344 |

Including flour reduced to wheat, the receipts would be as follows:—

| Articles. | Receipts. | |
|---|---|---|
| | 1891. | 1890. |
| | Bushels. | Bushels. |
| Flour and wheat | 68,835,754 | 77,795,232 |

The wheat crop of 1890 was a short crop, but the crop of 1891 was the largest ever grown, amounting to 611,788,000 bushels. The quality was not equal to the crop of 1890, but was fairly good. There was a steady foreign demand, which bid fair to largely increase the export, but the last four months of the year the low stage of water in the river curtailed shipments, and consequently the receipts. The destination of these exports was to England 2,621,849 bushels; to France, 6,733,947 bushels; to Germany, 108,079 bushels; to Belgium and Holland, 550,476 bushels. In addition to the shipments by river a considerable quantity was exported viâ Atlantic seaboard, of which 728,500 was on through bills of lading.

*Grain export.*

The receipts of corn show a large falling-off, being but 21,530,940 bushels, against 45,003,681 bushels for 1890. This is accounted for partly by the fact that the crop of 1890, which was marketed in 1891, was less in quantity and of inferior quality to that of 1889, and a less export demand viâ New Orleans.

*Corn.*

The shipments viâ New Orleans, mostly to England, were nearly 2,000,000 bushels, and about half that quantity was exported direct viâ Atlantic ports.

The crop of 1891 was the largest, with the exception of 1889, amounting to 2,060,154,000 bushels, with a yield of 27 bushels per acre. Missouri ranks third among the corn-producing States of the United States.

The oat crop of 1891 was about an average one, the estimate

*Oats.*

being 738,394,900 bushels. The receipts at this point were 12,431,213 bushels; shipments, 7,772,838 bushels, of which the larger part went to the Southern States.

**Rye.** There was a considerable increase in the receipt of rye, the quantity being 1,149,410 bushels, against 504,054 bushels in 1890. The shipments were 1,089,403 bushels, of which 45,600 bushels went to New Orleans.

**Barley.** The receipts of barley were 2,108,546 bushels, a slight falling-off from 1890 of about 686,254 bushels. Of the above amount 38,932 bushels was received from Canada.

**Cotton.** The cotton crop of the United States for 1890-91 was 8,655,518 bales, the largest ever grown, and an increase over the previous year of nearly 19 per cent.

The gross receipts for St. Louis were 706,469 bales, against 538,910 bales the previous season, an increase of over 31 per cent.

There was a steady decline in values the whole cotton year; middling cotton opened at $10\frac{1}{2}$ c. in September, and closed at $7\frac{13}{16}$ c. in August following.

**Provisions.** The business of the past year in pork products was satisfactory, being slightly in excess of the previous year. The increase in the volume of trade is shown by the following statement:—

|  | Quantity. | |
| --- | --- | --- |
|  | 1891. | 1890. |
|  | Lbs. | Lbs. |
| Receipts .. .. .. | 292,760,263 | 270,820,143 |

**Cattle.** The cattle business of the past year shows an increase in receipts of all kinds of 179,662 head.

St. Louis was the only one of the four great cattle markets which made a gain.

**Hogs.** The receipts of hogs were 1,380,569 head, an increase of 40,000 head over 1890. The demand was good and never fully supplied; the same may be said of sheep, the supply not being equal to the demand of butchers and shippers.

**Horses and mules.** There was a decrease in the receipts of horses and mules, accounted for partially by the change in the motive power of several street car lines to electricity and cable.

**Tobacco.** St. Louis still holds first place as a tobacco manufacturing city in the world. For the fiscal year ending June 30, 1890, the quantity manufactured was 46,709,897 lbs., and for the fiscal year ending June 30, 1891, 52,214,862 lbs., or $21\frac{1}{2}$ per cent. of the entire production of the United States. There are some 15 manufactories of chewing and smoking tobacco, with a combined capital of 1,000,000*l*. and an output of about 3,000,000*l*.

## CHICAGO.

The amount manufactured in 1891 was 50,384,439 lbs. The falling-off in tax paid is accounted for by the fact that the tax per lb. was reduced to 6 c. for the year 1891.

The manufacture of cigars shows an increase of nearly 37 per cent., reaching 53,000,000, as against 39,000,000 the previous year.

Bagging. The manufacture of jute bagging has increased the past year, aggregating a total of 15,000,000 yards. The demand was active throughout the season. Prices ranged from 6 c. to 6½ c. for 2-lb. bagging. The stock on hand at close of the year was 50,000 yards.

Iron ties. The existing tariff is so high that importation is quite stopped. They are now entirely supplied of domestic manufacture. Prices have ruled lower than the previous year, selling from 1 dol. 15 c. to 1 dol. 30 c. per bundle during the season.

Lumber. The receipts of lumber in 1891 were 108,306,011 feet; about 700,000 feet less than in 1890.

High wines and whisky. The receipts of high wines and whiskies for 1891 were 100,040 barrels, against 86,713 barrels in 1890. The shipments of whiskey were 117,210 barrels, against 101,885 barrels in 1890.

Leather. The receipts of hides the past year were 6,500,000 lbs. more than the previous year, and the shipments show an increase of 1,000,000 lbs. over 1890.

The receipts of leather for 1891 were 93,043 rolls, against 83,464 rolls in 1890; while the volume of business increased the prices were not satisfactory.

STATEMENT showing Bank Clearing-House Business of 1891 compared with 1890.

| Month. | Clearings 1890. | Clearings 1891. | Balances 1890. | Balances 1891. |
|---|---|---|---|---|
| | £ | £ | £ | £ |
| January | 18,943,028 | 19,524,149 | 3,516,198 | 2,460,951 |
| February | 16,634,768 | 16,403,608 | 3,445,117 | 1,775,223 |
| March | 17,447,358 | 17,929,729 | 3,123,289 | 1,854,768 |
| April | 18,691,107 | 17,899,916 | 3,203,859 | 1,999,644 |
| May | 20,185,128 | 18,121,168 | 3,799,983 | 1,997,294 |
| June | 18,450,127 | 17,424,063 | 3,050,653 | 2,239,409 |
| July | 18,588,180 | 19,137,733 | 2,449,666 | 2,225,767 |
| August | 17,648,401 | 19,500,840 | 1,961,726 | 2,517,006 |
| September | 18,706,585 | 19,482,320 | 2,302,984 | 2,055,244 |
| October | 19,942,928 | 20,886,748 | 2,091,926 | 2,103,332 |
| November | 18,906,806 | 19,561,692 | 1,862,684 | 2,049,199 |
| December | 19,556,223 | 22,047,944 | 1,940,932 | 2,681,342 |
| Aggregate | 223,714,642 | 227,919,910 | 32,756,019 | 25,959,179 |

|  | 1891. ||
|--|----------|----------|
|  | Increase. | Decrease. |
|  | Per cent. | £ |
| Clearings.. | 1·88 | .. |
| Balances.. | .. | 6,797,840 |

TABLE showing Internal Revenue Collections of St. Louis, United States, during the Years 1891–90.

| Designation. | 1891. | | | 1890. | | |
|---|---:|---:|---:|---:|---:|---:|
|  | £ | s. | d. | £ | s. | d. |
| Lists, chiefly banks | 2,812 | 6 | 6 | 969 | 8 | 0 |
| Spirit stamps.. | 381,851 | 0 | 0 | 320,022 | 8 | 0 |
| Tobacco  „ | 604,624 | 1 | 5 | 839,242 | 17 | 0 |
| Cigar    „ | 31,964 | 19 | 5 | 30,824 | 8 | 0 |
| Snuff    „ | 380 | 0 | 7 | 509 | 10 | 0 |
| Beer     „ | 334,914 | 14 | 8 | 343,193 | 17 | 0 |
| Special tax | 32,860 | 19 | 0 | 30,890 | 19 | 0 |
| Oleomargerine* stamps | .. | | | 43 | 2 | 0 |
| Total | 1,389,438 | 1 | 7 | 1,565,696 | 9 | 0 |
| Decrease | 176,258 | 0 | 0 | .. | | |

\* No oleo factories here; the collections were made on illicit goods seized at this port and released under compromise.

## CHICAGO.

CONDENSED Classification of Commodities Imported into St. Louis during the Year 1891, showing Foreign Values and Duties Paid.

| Articles. | Value. | Duty. |
|---|---|---|
| | £ s. d. | £ s. d. |
| Ale and beer | 5,847 16 0 | 2,268 3 2 |
| Anvils | 4,774 16 0 | 1,711 7 5 |
| Art works | 1,122 0 0 | 173 0 5 |
| Books and printed matter | 992 11 0 | 272 3 5 |
| Bricks and tiles | 53 8 0 | 24 0 7 |
| Barley (38,232 bushels) | 4,808 16 0 | 2,293 6 6 |
| Brushes | 3,972 0 0 | 1,588 16 0 |
| Carpets | 724 8 0 | 468 1 8 |
| Cement | 11,972 12 0 | 2,460 8 8 |
| Chemicals and drugs | 26,952 4 0 | 6,308 12 0 |
| China and earthenware | 33,516 0 0 | 19,521 4 0 |
| Corks, and manufactures of | 10,943 16 0 | 2,846 5 3 |
| Cutlery | 7,340 0 0 | 6,072 18 5 |
| Diamonds and precious stones | 8,997 16 0 | 899 15 7 |
| Fancy goods | 6,331 0 0 | 2,783 1 2 |
| Fish | 2,766 12 0 | 781 1 8 |
| Free goods | 66,926 4 0 | .. |
| Glassware | 14,652 8 0 | 10,754 5 4 |
| Guns, firearms, &c. | 14,376 8 0 | 5,674 0 5 |
| Hops | 6,089 8 0 | 2,066 7 5 |
| Jewellers' merchandise | 5,797 6 10 | 1,487 9 0 |
| Manufactures of cotton | 50,418 16 0 | 28,610 11 10 |
| ,, linen | 24,413 16 0 | 10,527 16 0 |
| ,, iron | 3,468 16 0 | 1,071 16 3 |
| ,, leather | 1,774 4 0 | 399 1 3 |
| ,, metals | 42,629 4 0 | 19,168 15 10 |
| ,, paper | 2,719 4 0 | 779 18 7 |
| ,, silk | 6,184 8 0 | 3,292 15 10 |
| ,, wood | 3,473 16 0 | 1,304 18 3 |
| ,, wool | 6,155 4 0 | 4,973 10 7 |
| Musical instruments | 774 12 0 | 289 11 10 |
| Nuts and fruits | 1,503 8 0 | 405 12 6 |
| Paints and colours | 2,581 12 0 | 664 8 2 |
| Rice, granulated | 33,493 12 0 | 5,051 19 10 |
| Seeds | 2,460 16 0 | 515 10 4 |
| Steel bars | 2,104 0 0 | 674 5 0 |
| ,, wire | 24,529 12 0 | 11,478 18 4 |
| Tin plate | 59,835 12 0 | 17,574 0 0 |
| Tobacco, cigars, and cigarettes | 21,163 12 0 | 25,275 15 10 |
| Varnishes | 258 4 0 | 90 7 7 |
| Wines | 23,987 4 0 | 12,935 16 10 |
| Window glass | 40,349 12 0 | 10,877 3 7 |
| Woollen dress goods | 12,252 16 0 | 10,695 1 9 |
| Spirituous liquors | 10,366 12 0 | 10,534 17 10 |
| Sugar, maple and other | 1,259 12 0 | 177 8 10 |
| ,, free after April 1, 1891 | 132,059 0 0 | .. |
| Miscellaneous merchandise | 7,970 1 0 | 3,161 9 2 |
| Total, 1891 | 757,144 14 0 | 250,991 0 0 |
| ,, 1890 | 754,445 18 0 | 271,802 19 0 |
| Increase in value | 2,698 16 0 | .. |
| Decrease in duties | .. | 20,811 19 0 |

(1372)

## UNITED STATES.

RETURN of Merchandise brought into St. Louis in Bond from the following Ports of Entry during the Year 1891, showing Foreign Values and Duties.

| Ports. | Value. | | | Duty. | | |
|---|---:|---:|---:|---:|---:|---:|
| | £ | s. | d. | £ | s. | d. |
| Baltimore | 90,286 | 8 | 0 | 23,511 | 16 | 0 |
| Boston | 3,561 | 8 | 0 | 520 | 8 | 0 |
| Detroit | 11,064 | 0 | 0 | 3,706 | 8 | 0 |
| New Orleans | 129,456 | 4 | 0 | 47,152 | 0 | 0 |
| New York | 378,478 | 10 | 0 | 129,749 | 7 | 0 |
| Philadelphia | 95,714 | 8 | 0 | 31,184 | 8 | 0 |
| Port Huron | 9,955 | 12 | 0 | 3,988 | 4 | 0 |
| Portland, Maine | 38,390 | 0 | 0 | 11,117 | 2 | 0 |
| Portland, Oregon | 54 | 4 | 0 | .. | | |
| San Francisco | 184 | 0 | 0 | 61 | 6 | 0 |
| Total | 757,144 | 14 | 0 | 250,991 | 0 | 0 |

| | £ | s. |
|---|---:|---:|
| In warehouse December 31, 1891 | 20,066 | 16 |

RETURN of Foreign Shipments of Flour from St. Louis viâ Atlantic Seaports during the Years 1890–91.

| Destination. | Quantity. | |
|---|---:|---:|
| | 1891. | 1890. |
| | Barrels. | Barrels. |
| Europe | 327,043 | 271,484 |
| South America | 238 | 1,224 |
| Newfoundland | 1,775 | 26,438 |
| Canada | 12,490 | 15,872 |
| Cuba | 2,958 | 510 |
| Seaboard for export | .. | 3,158 |
| Total | 344,506 | 318,668 |

Nearly all the above were shipped in sacks of various weights, and is reduced to barrels for convenience of calculation, and shows an increase of 25,838 barrels.

The business of the rivers in tons shows a continued decrease, being 160,523 tons less than 1890—

| | Quantity. | |
|---|---:|---:|
| | 1890. | 1891. |
| | Tons. | Tons. |
| Received by steamers and barges | 530,790 | 450,050 |
| " rafts | 132,940 | 142,090 |
| Shipped by steamers and barges | 601,862 | 512,930 |
| Total | 1,265,593 | 1,105,070 |

## CHICAGO.

**AVERAGE** Rates of Freight on Grain in Cents. per Bushel by Barges and Steamers to Liverpool viâ New Orleans in the Years 1891-90.

| Month. | St. Louis to New Orleans. 1891. | St. Louis to New Orleans. 1890. | New Orleans to Liverpool. 1891. | New Orleans to Liverpool. 1890. | St. Louis to Liverpool. 1891. | St. Louis to Liverpool. 1891. |
|---|---|---|---|---|---|---|
|  | Cents. | Cents. | Cents. | Cents. | Cents. | Cents. |
| January | 7½ | 7½ | 8½ | 13 | 16 | 20 |
| February | 7½ | 7½ | 8 | 14 | 15½ | 21½ |
| March | 6½ | 7 | 7½ | 12½ | 14 | 19½ |
| April | 6 | 5½ | 6½ | 11½ | 12½ | 17 |
| May | 5½ | 5½ | 6 | 7 | 11½ | 12½ |
| June | 5½ | 5½ | 5½ | 6 | 11 | 11½ |
| July | 6 | 6 | 6 | 6½ | 12 | 12½ |
| August | 6½ | 6½ | 8½ | 5½ | 15 | 12 |
| September | 7½ | 7 | 9½ | 4½ | 17 | 11½ |
| October | 8 | 7 | 11 | 4 | 19 | 14 |
| November | 8 | 7 | 12 | 2½ | 20 | 9½ |
| December | 8 | 7 | 12 | 6 | 20 | 13 |

**Wool.** The receipts of wool for 1891 were 21,975,954 lbs., against 20,240,503 lbs. in 1890, and shipments 21,464,052 lbs. The stock on hand on the first of this year 1892 was 7,130,000 lbs., since which a number of heavy transactions have taken place to reduce it.

My district embraces the whole State of Missouri, except the county of Jackson.

**Population of district.** The State shows a population at the last census in 1891 of 2,979,184, and the district 2,818,674.

**Valuation.** The total valuation of real and personal property was 163,095,916*l*. for 1891, and Railroad, Bridge, and Telegraph Companies, 12,450,439*l*., making a total of 175,546,355*l*.

**Surplus commodities.** The surplus commodities marketed are shown by the last report of the Labour Commissioner to have been as follows:—

| Description. |  | Quantity. |  | Value. Dol. c. | Total Value. Dollars. |
|---|---|---|---|---|---|
| Cattle | Head | 685,585 | Per head | 40 00 | 27,423,400 |
| Hogs | ,, | 1,965,614 | ,, | 8 00 | 15,724,912 |
| Horses and mules | ,, | 70,664 | ,, | 100 00 | 7,066,400 |
| Sheep | ,, | 224,246 | ,, | 3 75 | 840,922 |
| Wheat | Bushels | 8,819,608 | Per bushel | 0 80 | 7,055,686 |
| Corn | ,, | 6,898,620 | ,, | 0 25 | 1,724,655 |
| Oats | ,, | 5,375,400 | ,, | 0 25 | 1,343,850 |
| Ties | ... | 4,224,918 | ... | 0 30 | 1,267,476 |
| Poultry | Coops | 54,684 | 80 lbs. per coop | 0 10 | 437,472 |
| Coal | Tons | 2,169,382 | Per ton | 1 40 | 3,037,134 |
| Flax seed | Bushels | 972,500 | Per bushel | 1 34 | 1,303,150 |
| Lead | Tons | 60,210 | Per ton | 45 00 | 2,709,450 |
| Zinc | ,, | 37,098 | ,, | 24 00 | 1,754,352 |
| Hay | ,, | 124,182 | ,, | 5 00 | 620,910 |
| Fruit | Barrels | 862,740 | Per barrel | 1 50 | 1,293,110 |
| Timothy and clover | Bushels | 160,500 | Per bushel | 3 00 | 481,500 |
| Iron | Tons | 326,232 | Per ton | 2 45 | 799,268 |
| Lumber | Feet | 328,363,000 | Per 1,000 | 10 00 | 3,283,630 |
| Flour | Barrels | 1,752,600 | Per barrel | 4 50 | 7,836,760 |
| Lime | ,, | 1,618,912 | ,, | 0 50 | 809,450 |
| Cooperage | Cars | 2,253 | ... | ... | 675,900 |
| Miscellaneous | ,, | 72,828 | Per car | 250 00 | 18,207,000 |
| St. Louis press brick | ,, | 10,601 | ,, | 98 57 | 1,044,943 |
| Kansas City press brick | ,, | 1,778 | ,, | 91 06 | 161,908 |
| Total | ... | ... | ... | ... | 106,803,183 |

(1372)

## UNITED STATES.

**COMPARATIVE** Business in Leading Articles at St. Louis during the Years 1890-91.

| Articles. | | Quantity. | |
|---|---|---|---|
| | | 1890. | 1891. |
| Flour, amount manufactured | Barrels | 1,872,005 | 1,148,190 |
| ,, handled | ,, | 4,313,567 | 4,932,464 |
| Wheat, total receipts | Bushels | 11,730,774 | 25,523,183 |
| Corn ,, | ,, | 45,003,681 | 21,530,940 |
| Oats ,, | ,, | 12,229,955 | 12,432,215 |
| Rye ,, | ,, | 501,054 | 1,149,490 |
| Barley ,, | ,, | 2,794,880 | 2,108,546 |
| All grain received, including flour reduced to wheat | ,, | 77,795.232 | 68,835,754 |
| Cotton, receipts | Bales | 587,187 | 765,784 |
| Bagging, manufactured | Yards | 12,000,000 | 15,000,000 |
| Hay, receipts | Tons | 116,346 | 141,398 |
| Tobacco ,, | Hogsheads | 38,082 | 41,042 |
| Lead ,, in pigs of 80 lb. | Pigs | 1,756,850 | 1,739,977 |
| Hog product, total shipments | Lbs. | 379,346,147 | 358,595,516 |
| Cattle, receipts | Head | 630,014 | 779,499 |
| Sheep ,, | ,, | 358,496 | 402,989 |
| Hogs ,, | ,, | 1,359,789 | 1,380,569 |
| Horses and mules, receipts | ,, | 82,071 | 55,975 |
| Lumber and logs ,, | Feet | 681,810,588 | 865,398,011 |
| Shingles, receipts | Pieces | 64,173,150 | 73,980,750 |
| Lath ,, | ,, | 16,336,650 | 20,231,050 |
| Wool, total receipts | Lbs. | 20,540,503 | 21,975,954 |
| Hides ,, | ,, | 28,245,828 | 34,744,949 |
| Sugar, received | ,, | 140,281,225 | 253,960,132 |
| Molasses, shipped | Gallons | 2,467,060 | 2,657,990 |
| Coffee, received | Bags | 222,765 | 253,154 |
| Rice ,, | Packages | 115,970 | 87,192 |
| Coal, receipts | Bushels | 69,477,225 | 72,078,225 |
| Nails ,, | Kegs | 471,352 | 440,679 |
| Potatoes ,, | Bushels | 1,476,913 | 1,832,137 |
| Salt ,, | Barrels | 326,189 | 381,671 |
| ,, ,, | Sacks | 33,848 | 42,478 |
| ,, ,, (in bulk) | Bushels | 168,030 | 388,440 |
| Butter | Lbs. | 13,661,924 | 13,791,258 |
| Freight of all kinds received and shipped | Tons | 16,505,733 | 16,420,027 |

### ST. PAUL.

Mr. Vice-Consul Morphy reports as follows:—

In submitting my annual report I wish to say a few words concerning the State of Minnesota, of which the city of St. Paul is the capital.

*State of Minnesota.*

*Its boundaries.*

The State of Minnesota lies between the State of Wisconsin on the east, and the States of North Dakota and South Dakota on the west, stretching from the State of Iowa on the south to the British possessions on the north. It extends through 5½ degrees of latitude, the 49th parallel being its boundary from the Red River of the north-eastward to the Lake of the Woods, from which the line of demarkation between the State and the British possessions follows the course of Rainy Lake River and the chain of lakes to the eastward, almost to the western point of Lake Superior. Its western boundary is regular, its eastern boundary irregular. Its average breadth is about 250 miles and its length 381 miles. Its area, according to the Government surveys, is 83,513 square miles, or 53,459,840 acres. More than 3,000,000 acres of this is water surface. Only 42,477,682 acres of its surface have been surveyed. The most of the unsurveyed portion lies in the northern and north-eastern counties, which are largely timber and mineral lands. Its area exceeds that of all the New-England States together, and is nearly as great as that of Ohio and Pennsylvania combined. The general elevation of the State above sea-level is high. While there are no mountains within its boundaries, the surface is pleasantly varied, and there are sufficient elevations of a considerable height to redeem it from monotony and to give ample drainage. The highest point is about 2,200 feet above sea-level. Within the State three river systems have their source. The most important is the Mississippi, sometimes called the "Father of Waters," rising in the group of small lakes north of the centre of the State and flowing southward, receiving in its course the waters of the Minnesota and its numerous tributaries. A narrow watershed divides this from the streams that flow into the Red River of the north on its western boundary, while to the north-east other waters join the St. Louis and reach Lake Superior. The position of the State is practically at the head of the waters of the continent. *Area. River system.*

The territory east of the Mississippi River has a light and sandy soil, while everywhere west of it is found the heavy black loam of the prairie. The only unfertile section of the State is found in the rocky region about the head of Lake Superior, and this section contains immense mineral resources. *Soil.*

The climate is peculiar. Its dryness mitigates the severity of both summer and winter temperatures. The extreme long days of this northern latitude having a forcing effect upon vegetation. *Climate.*

The earliest census was taken in June, 1849, and gave the then territory of Minnesota a population of 4,513. Just before its admission as a State the population had grown to 150,037. In 1860 the Federal census credited it with 172,023. The Federal census of 1880 gave it 780,773, and that of 1890, 1,300,017. *Population.*

The city of St. Paul is the capital of the State of Minnesota, the county town of the county of Ramsey, and is situated on the Mississippi River 2,150 miles from its mouth, at the natural head of navigation, 360 miles north-west of Chicago, and 150 miles from the head of Lake Superior and water navigation from the Atlantic Ocean. *St. Paul.*

St. Paul is the commercial city of the great north-west and is rapidly becoming a manufacturing centre of importance. Each year witnesses many new additions to the number of her establishments and the enlargement of existing factories to meet the *The commercial city for the great north-west.*

(1372)

## UNITED STATES.

**Area.**

increasing demand for goods made expressly for this section of the United States.

When the town of St. Paul was incorporated in 1849 it contained 90 acres. In 1854 the city was incorporated with 2,561 acres. Additions have from time to time been made, and the city of St. Paul has now within its corporate limits 35,482 acres, or a little over 55 square miles. The distance between the eastern and western boundaries of the city is 10 miles, and between the northern and southern boundaries a little over 5 miles.

**Population.**

The population of the city began with the year 1838 and numbered three souls. By the following tabulated statement the growth of the city from 1838 to 1890, by the Federal and State authorities, also the number of names in the directory for the last decade, are given for comparison:—

|       | Population. |
|-------|-------------|
| 1838  | 3           |
| 1847  | 50          |
| 1849  | 400         |
| 1850* | 850         |
| 1855* | 4,400       |
| 1860* | 10,600      |
| 1865* | 13,100      |
| 1870* | 20,300      |
| 1875* | 33,178      |
| 1880* | 41,498      |
| 1885* | 111,397     |
| 1890* | 133,156     |

\* Census reports.

| Year. | Number of Names in Directory. |
|-------|-------------------------------|
| 1880  | 18,317                        |
| 1881  | 23,386                        |
| 1882  | 30,334                        |
| 1883  | 35,351                        |
| 1884  | 39,729                        |
| 1885  | 43,960                        |
| 1886  | 49,358                        |
| 1887  | 62,231                        |
| 1888  | 70,234                        |
| 1889  | 74,304                        |
| 1890  | 78,271                        |
| 1891  | 84,403                        |

**Post office income.**

The post office was established in 1846. There have been 11 postmasters. This office is a political one, the appointment being controlled by the Senate. The gross yearly income of the post office from 1887 to 1891 is as follows:—

|       | Dollars. | c. |
|-------|----------|----|
| 1887  | 272,181  | 87 |
| 1888  | 297,327  | 37 |
| 1889  | 300,997  | 33 |
| 1890  | 315,902  | 83 |
| 1891  | 340,150  | 15 |

**Wholesale trade.** St. Paul is by far the most important wholesale centre in the north-west. Its prominence as such has grown steadily with the development of the railway system. In the early days of the settlement of this State the little town standing at the head of navigation on the Mississippi River had a natural advantage for selling goods to the frontier trading posts and farming settlements. That advantage gave St. Paul its first start. When railways were built, the importance the city had already required made it the focus of activity for the new transportation system. To-day St. Paul is the commanding trade centre of the north-west for two reasons. First, because she is the chief railway centre, and, second, because of her proximity to the head of Lake Superior, which gives her the great advantage of cheap water communication with the east. In fact, the waterway of the great lakes is the key to the commercial position of St. Paul. The lake and river routes are regulators of freight rates by rail, which enables the St. Paul merchant to compete with Chicago on equal terms. The following table shows the amount of the wholesale business done in St. Paul for the years 1887–91:—

| | Dollars. |
|---|---|
| 1887 | 101,025,600 |
| 1888 | 106,076,880 |
| 1889 | 109,126,829 |
| 1890 | 122,223,048 |
| 1891 | 131,289,385 |

**Manufacturing industries.** Hitherto very little attention has been given to manufactures. About a year ago, however, a movement to encourage manufacturing enterprises in St. Paul originated in the Chamber of Commerce. Then a company was formed, composed of some of the leading business men, to accumulate capital and make loans to new and old concerns and to subscribe stock. Then the Business Men's Union was formed, which has a capital directly available for the substantial encouragement of new manufacturing enterprises. These organisations, together with the Commercial Club, form a chain of co-operating public-spirited bodies working in harmony to a common end. The following table shows the amount of manufacturing business done in St. Paul for the years 1887–91:—

| | Dollars. |
|---|---|
| 1887 | 37,251,600 |
| 1888 | 39,114,180 |
| 1889 | 49,598,894 |
| 1890 | 61,720,595 |
| 1891 | 64,584,923 |

**Banks.** St. Paul is a strong financial centre. There are 23 banks, of which 4 are national, 12 State, 5 savings, and 1 private bank. Their aggregate capital and surplus is over 10,000,000 dol. and their clearings over 200,000,000 dol. per annum.

The St. Paul clearing-house records for the years 1887-91 are:—

|      | Dollars. | c. |
|------|----------|----|
| 1887 | 205,012,122 | 78 |
| 1888 | 192,811,776 | 00 |
| 1889 | 209,409,381 | 03 |
| 1890 | 225,564,896 | 84 |
| 1891 | 242,075,278 | 10 |

*Assessed values.* The assessed valuation in reality is made once in two years, *i.e.*, every even numbered year. The following table shows the assessed real and personal valuation of St. Paul for five years:—

| Year. | Valuation. Real Estate. | Valuation. Personal Property. | Total Taxation. |
|-------|-------------|-------------------|-----------------|
|       | Dollars.    | Dollars.          | Dollars.        |
| 1887  | 72,479,471  | 17,296,371        | 89,775,842      |
| 1888  | 99,474,750  | 18,926,884        | 118,401,634     |
| 1889  | 101,183,826 | 19,373,093        | 120,556,919     |
| 1890  | 105,320,045 | 16,119,885        | 121,439,930     |
| 1891  | 106,576,329 | 16,322,047        | 122,898,374     |

*Tax assessments.* The tax assessments of St. Paul are made in the spirit of conservatism. The assessed value on real estate does not exceed 50 per cent. of the actual value, and on personal property the average is about 20 per cent. Total tax levy for five years:—

*Total levy for five years.*

|      | Dollars. | c. |
|------|----------|----|
| 1887 | 1,816,984 | 90 |
| 1888 | 2,170,125 | 25 |
| 1889 | 2,187,796 | 25 |
| 1890 | 2,473,875 | 61 |
| 1891 | 2,534,936 | 54 |

*Taxation last year.* The taxation last year was 20 mills on 1 dol.

*Public improvements.* The public improvements on the city of St. Paul for the year 1891, from the official records are:—

|  | Distance. | Cost. |
|---|---|---|
|  | Miles. | Dollars. c. |
| Streets graded | 20·5 | 264,808 54 |
| Streets paved | 1·2 | 53,767 02 |
| Sewers constructed | 6·6 | 71,838 00 |
| Sidewalks constructed | 6·3 | 9,782 00 |
| Streets sprinkled | 98 | 36,357 37 |
| Streets opened, widened, and extended | 6·9 | 16,135 28 |
| Street grades changed, costing | .. | 13,148 10 |
| Condemnation of slopes, costing | .. | 3,052 10 |
| Bridges constructed, costing | .. | 173,701 80 |
| Total | .. | 642,590 11 |

## CHICAGO.

Of the total cost of public improvements for 1891, 73,312 dol. 95 c. was paid from bond funds, and the balance, 569,277 dol. 16c. was assessed on the property specially benefited.

### Public Works.

|  | Total Miles. |
|---|---|
| Paved streets | 42 |
| Graded streets | 373 |
| Wooden sidewalks | 418 |
| Stone and cement | 40 |
| Sewers | 130 |

Building permits are issued in St. Paul on the fee system, and the cost of many, if not all, buildings exceed by a liberal percentage the sum named in the permit. During the year 1890, 3,174 permits were issued, and the value on which they were issued was 970,944,580 dol., and during the year 1891, 2,408 permits were issued, and the value 318,441,000 dol. The large decrease was caused by the fact that during the past year no buildings were erected for speculative purposes only, and the year 1891 was not, on the whole, a very bright one in the history of the city. The general depression existing throughout the country naturally affecting the north-west. *Building during the year.*

The St. Paul City Railway Company owns and operates all the street car lines in St. Paul, there are nearly 100 miles of street railway track. Two lines, one to the St. Anthony Hill district (west) and the other on the Seventh Street to the Daytons' Bluff district (east) are operated by cable. All the rest are electric lines. The cars on all the lines are large, new, and handsomely finished. So comprehensive is the system that nowhere in any part of the city that is fairly well built can you get more than five squares from a street car. Even the most distant and thinly built suburbs have their electric roads. The inter-urban line runs electric trains from the business centre of St. Paul to the business centre in Minneapolis in 45 minutes. Fare, 10 c., including transfer in either city. *Street railways.*

Transfer tickets are given in St. Paul for a continuous trip to any part of the city, for the single fare of 5 c.; transfers are given between cable and electric cars where the lines cross. All electric cars go on the loop, which is on Fifth Street, Robert Street, Eighth Street, and Walasha Street. The speed of the cable lines is 8 miles per hour, the electric lines run from 10 to 15 miles per hour. The central power plant is situated on Hill Street, near West Third Street, and cost, including machinery and electrical appliances, 265,000 dol. The plant contains three engines of 800 horse-power each, and each engine operates four dynamos of 200 horse-power each.

The different railroad companies owning roads which centre in St. Paul, with the mileage of each, are as follows:— *Railroads.*

## UNITED STATES.

|  | Miles. |
|---|---|
| Chicago, Milwaukee, and St. Paul | 5,656·83 |
| Northern Pacific | 4,230·55 |
| Great Northern | 3,425·86 |
| Chicago, St. Paul, Minneapolis, and Omaha | 1,372·90 |
| Chicago, St. Paul, and Kansas City | 930·68 |
| Wisconsin Central | 867·07 |
| Minneapolis, St. Paul, and Sault Ste Marie | 792·00 |
| Minneapolis and St. Louis | 579·00 |
| Chicago, Burlington, and Northern | 370·00 |
| St. Paul and Duluth | 274·75 |
|  | 18,472·64 |

**Business men's union.** The business men's union is an organisation formed to aid the growth of St. Paul as a manufacturing centre, in practical ways and particularly by efforts to secure the establishment here of certain definite industries for which there are special opportunities. Tangible and important results of the union's efforts have already been accomplished. All their meetings are executive, and only work completed is made public.

**Commercial club.** The Commercial Club was formed late in the fall of 1891. The idea was conceived by J. J. Corcoran, Esq., manager of the well-known commercial agency of R. G. Dean and Co., and Mr. Corcoran is the president of the club. It is rather early to judge of the good accomplished by the organisation, but the objects are amongst other things " to take aggressive action upon every movement concerning the welfare of St. Paul and her citizens. To encourage and promote the commercial and manufacturing interests of the city in every way possible, to advertise to the world the diversified advantages of the city and State, to ascertain the needs of the city, and assist in removing impediments to her progress; to foster and encourage, through social intercourse, a public spirit and a feeling of loyality which will inurue to the benefit of the city, and to teach that, whatever promotes the business interest of any class of citizens is for the benefit of all, and that, whatever injures business in any line is against the interest of all." The club has over 1,000 members. It is governed by a president, two vice-presidents, and 26 directors.

**Custom-house.**

|  | 1890. | 1891. |
|---|---|---|
|  | Dollars. c. | Dollars. c. |
| Value of dutiable goods | 675,345 53 | 612,759 00 |
| Total duties collected | 305,878 60 | 295,144 89 |
| Value of free goods | 434,895 28 | 261,398 00 |
| Value of domestic exports | 1,733,907 00 | 452,251 00 |

The apparent decrease in domestic exports is the result of the formation of the new customs district of North Dakota and South Dakota, the territory included in which formerly belonged to this district, and consequently as the bulk of these exports from Minnesota, and points south and east, pass out of the United

## CHICAGO.

States over the Northern Pacific Railway at Pembina, and the Great Northern Railway at Neche, North Dakota, the statistics are tabulated in the new district, and hence the St. Paul office can only give statistical information of such efforts as passed out at the sub-ports of St. Vincent and Rainy River (Lake of the Woods) in the State of Minnesota, which comprise a very small part of the exports formerly included in the reports of the office.

RETURN of Collections for the Years ending December 31, 1890-91. — Internal revenue.

| Description. | Internal Revenue. 1890. | Internal Revenue. 1891. |
|---|---|---|
| | Dollars. c. | Dollars. c. |
| Spirits | 2,080,835 50 | 2,035,447 70 |
| Tobacco, snuff, and cigars | 142,131 11 | 143,188 01 |
| Fermented liquors | 329,238 33 | 349,672 20 |
| Penalties | 1,948 25 | 3,048 23 |
| Special taxes | 126,084 71 | 123,023 86 |
| Total | 2,680,237 90 | 2,654,380 00 |

The city of Minneapolis, with a population of about 170,000, lies about ten miles from St. Paul, and the cities are connected by the electric line. — Minneapolis.

Minneapolis has been brought into great prominence this year because the National Republican Convention will be held there early next month, for the purpose of selecting a republican candidate for the presidency. — Republican national convention to be held.

The growth of this city has been wonderful, especially when one calls to mind the fact that 40 years ago the site was part of an Indian reservation. — Formerly an Indian reservation.

The assessed valuation of Minneapolis, as equalised by the State Board of Equalisation, 1891, is as follows:— — Assessed valuation.

| | Dollars. |
|---|---|
| Real estate | 120,093,423 |
| Personal property | 18,351,139 |
| Total | 138,444,562 |

During the past year 3,036 building permits were issued, and buildings to the cost of over 4,000,000 dol. erected. — Buildings erected during 1891.

The total number of manufacturing establishments in Minneapolis at the close of 1891 was 775, and of these 50 were organised during the past year. — Manufacturing establishments.

The third important city in the State of Minnesota is Duluth. The city is situated at the head of Lake Superior, the most — Duluth.

*At the head of Lake Superior.*

westerly of the great chain of lakes which reaches from this point to the eastern outlet of Ontario, north of New York, forming with the St. Lawrence River and the Gulf, a continuous navigable waterway from the State of Minnesota to the Atlantic Ocean.

*Fine residence sites.*

The topography of Duluth gives her a peculiar advantage in the way of fine residence sites. In all of the residence localities numerous fine and attractive houses have been built during the past year.

*Iron fields and iron mines.*

This city has near by, some of the richest iron mines in the world. Few other ranges compare with the Vermillion or Mesabi. The former, 90 miles from Duluth, was first developed in 1883, shipping 63,000 tons that year from the Minnesota Mine. The output of the Vermillion in 1891 was as follows, in long tons:—

|  | Long Tons. |
|---|---|
| Minnesota mine | 518,025 |
| Chandler mine | 373,177 |
| Pioneer mine | 3,079 |
| Total | 894,281 |
| ,, 1890 | 880,014 |
| Increase | 14,267 |
| Total output to date | 4,117,186 |

The year 1891 was a poor year for the iron trade, and all other ranges of the Lake Superior country showed a decrease in output, save the Vermillion, the total decrease being 2,000,000 tons.

*Recent discoveries: The Mesabi.*

Recent discoveries on the Mesabi range, 60 miles north of Duluth, show that range to be even richer in ore than the Vermillion, and the developments promise that it will become an immense iron-producing region.

*Duluth in 1891.*

The following figures show the position of this city in 1891:—

## CHICAGO.

| Description. | | Quantity. | Value. |
|---|---|---|---|
| | | | Dollars. |
| Vessels, arrivals and departures | Number | 2,895 | .. |
| ,, tonnage, Duluth | Tons .. | 3,268,031 | .. |
| ,, ,, head of the lake .. | ,, .. | 5,332,494 | .. |
| Coal receipts .. | ,, .. | 1,900,000 | .. |
| Flour, manufactured .. | Barrels | 684,000 | .. |
| ,, receipts .. | ,, .. | 2,783,494 | .. |
| ,, shipment | ,, .. | 3,452,494 | .. |
| Wheat, receipt.. | Bushels | 40,501,106 | .. |
| ,, shipment | ,, | 34,659,368 | .. |
| Lumber, manufactured, city mill .. | Feet .. | 98,730,000 | .. |
| Lumber, manufactured, Duluth district | ,, .. | 259,230,000 | .. |
| Iron ore, output | Tons .. | 894,281 | .. |
| Wholesale business | .. | .. | 22,334,000 |
| Retail ,, | .. | .. | 54,000,000 |
| Banking, capital and surplus.. | .. | .. | 3,578,340 |
| ,, business for the year | .. | .. | 716,384,525 |
| Bank clearings .. | .. | .. | 106,824,144 |
| Business of loan agents | .. | .. | 3,500,000 |
| Building improvements | .. | .. | 3,855,664 |
| Street and other public improvements .. | .. | .. | 1,465,201 |
| Total improvements .. | .. | .. | 7,014,331 |
| Railroad freight handled | Tons .. | 2,500,000 | |
| Output of manufactures | .. | .. | 8,510,000 |
| Tax assessments, city, suburbs | .. | .. | 84,155,808 |
| Postal business.. | .. | .. | 66,205 |
| Population .. | Number | 50,000 | .. |

## COLORADO.

Mr. Vice-Consul Pearce reports as follows:—

The trade and commerce of Denver and the State of Colorado for the year 1891 shows a falling-off from 1890, but is regarded as very fair when the monetary depression which has existed throughout the whole country, is taken into consideration.

Population.
The population of Denver and suburban towns is claimed by local authorities to be 154,000, although the Government census taken in 1890 placed it at 126,000. It is said the census was not thorough.

Value of new buildings.
The value of new buildings erected in Denver and suburban towns for the year 1891 was 2,100,796l., showing a decrease of 1,207,529l. A great many of the large business blocks, the construction of which was commenced in 1890, were completed during the year.

Clearing-house records.
The records of the Denver clearing-house for the year show a total of 45,760,000l., a decrease of 10·3 per cent. from 1890. The clearing-house is composed of 11 national banks with a capital aggregating 1,060,000l.

Transactions in real estate.
The transactions in real estate for the year were 9,503,157l., as against 13,155,985l. in 1890, a decrease of 3,652,828l. It is

## UNITED STATES.

**Taxable property.** claimed there has been very little shrinkage in values, and that the large decrease is mainly due to the stringency of the money market.

The value of taxable property in the whole State shows an increase of 2,172,246*l*. over 1890.

**Cable and electric railways.** The Cable and Electric Street Railway Company have added 42 miles of electric lines to their extensive system of street railways during the year, making a total of 142 miles of rapid transit lines in the city and its suburbs.

**Manufacturing.** The value of the products of the manufacturing interests of Denver for the year 1891 amounted to the sum of 10,186,262*l*., an increase over the previous year of 1,400,000*l*. The average number of persons employed during the year was 12,890*l*., and they received in wages 1,660,143*l*., an increase of 2,843 employés and an increase in wages of 243,151*l*. 251 establishments were added during the year, embracing almost every known industry.

**Mining.** The mining industry of Colorado for the year has made greater proportional progress than during any preceding year. The production of the mines has been larger, the number of paying properties increased, the mining area enlarged, transportation cheapened, smelting, milling, and concentration facilities multiplied, and railways have been extended to hitherto isolated districts.

There has been a gain in the gross value of the output from the mines of 714,822*l*., notwithstanding the low price of silver and lead which prevailed during the year.

The most notable of the new mining discoveries during the year is the Creede district, in the southern part of the State. The importance of this new mining camp was soon appreciated by the Denver and Rio Grande Railway Company, and in July a branch line was extended to this new district.

A new town has been started which is called Creede, with a population at this date of about 6,000.

The mines in the district are silver-bearing, and from the developments already made, it is estimated that the new field will largely increase the production of silver in the State.

The total value of the products from the mines in Colorado for the year is as follows:—

|  | £ |
|---|---|
| Silver | 4,553,474 |
| Gold | 899,773 |
| Lead | 1,094,645 |
| Copper | 146,730 |
| Total | 6,694,622 |

**Coal.** Mr. John McNeil, the State Inspector of Coal Mines, has kindly furnished me with the following statement of the coal production of the State for 1890 and 1891. It will be seen from this statement that there was an increase of 436,851 tons in 1891 over 1890. There has been no change in the price of coal since my last report.

## CHICAGO.

RETURN of Production of Coal by Counties in Colorado during the Years 1890-91, showing Increase and Decrease.

| Counties. | Quantity. 1890. | Quantity. 1891. | Increase. | Decrease. |
|---|---|---|---|---|
|  | Tons of 2,000 Lbs. | Tons of 2,000 Lbs. |  |  |
| Arapahoe | 681 | 1,273 | 592 | .. |
| Boulder.. | 409,130 | 498,494 | 89,364 | .. |
| Dolores.. | .. | 3,475 | 3,475 | .. |
| El Paso.. | 26,847 | 34,364 | 7,517 | .. |
| Fremont | 392,570 | 545,789 | 153,219 | .. |
| Gunnison | 238,139 | 261,350 | 23,211 | .. |
| Garfield.. | 198,086 | 191,994 | .. | 6,092 |
| Huerfano | 425,606 | 494,466 | 68,860 | .. |
| Jefferson | 12,334 | 17,910 | 5,576 | .. |
| Las Animas | 1,134,845 | 1,219,224 | 84,379 | .. |
| La Plata | 33,045 | 72,471 | 39,426 | .. |
| Mesa | 4,200 | 5,000 | 800 | .. |
| Park | 67,203 | 52,626 | .. | 14,577 |
| Pitkin | 74,362 | 91,642 | 17,280 | .. |
| Weld | 42,603 | 22,554 | .. | 20,049 |
| Estimated | 16,130 | .. | .. | 16,130 |
| Total | 3,075,781 | 3,512,632 | .. | .. |

SUMMARY of the Coal Statistics during the Years 1873-91.

Tons of 2,000 Lbs.

| | |
|---|---|
| 1873 | 69,977 |
| 1874 | 87,372 |
| 1875 | 98,838 |
| 1876 | 117,666 |
| 1877 | 160,000 |
| 1878 | 200,630 |
| 1879 | 322,732 |
| 1880 | 375,000 |
| 1881 | 706,744 |
| 1882 | 1,061,479 |
| 1883 | 1,220,593 |
| 1884 | 1,130,024 |
| 1885 | 1,398,796 |
| 1886 | 1,436,211 |
| 1887 | 1,791,735 |
| 1888 | 2,185,477 |
| 1889 | 2,373,954 |
| 1890 | 3,075,781 |
| 1891 | 3,512,632 |

(1372)

## UNITED STATES.

RETURN of Production of Coke in Colorado during the Years 1890-91, showing Increase and Decrease.

| Counties. | Quantity. 1890. | Quantity. 1891. | Increase. | Decrease. |
|---|---|---|---|---|
| | Tons of 2,000 Lbs. | Tons of 2,000 Lbs. | | |
| Las Animas | 149,503 | 184,047 | 34,544 | .. |
| Gunnison | 44,521 | 43,910 | .. | 611 |
| Pitkin | 34,463 | 47,014 | 12,551 | .. |
| Total | 228,487 | 274,971 | .. | .. |

*Imports.*

I have been able to obtain a statement of the value of imports from Great Britain for the year through the kindness of Mr. Heffron, the Surveyor of Customs of this city. From this statement we find a falling-off in the value of imports from last year to the amount of 6,503*l.* 8*s.*

STATEMENT of Value of Imports from Great Britain Entered at the Port of Denver during the Year 1891.

| | £ | s. | d. |
|---|---|---|---|
| Ale and stout | 240 | 8 | 0 |
| Bicycles | 72 | 12 | 0 |
| Carpets | 125 | 4 | 0 |
| Cement (Portland) | 328 | 8 | 0 |
| Chemicals and drugs | 686 | 4 | 0 |
| Clocks | 120 | 0 | 0 |
| Corticine | 377 | 12 | 0 |
| Earthenware chinaware, &c. | 1,391 | 0 | 0 |
| Gelatine | 189 | 4 | 0 |
| Household and personal effects | 192 | 16 | 0 |
| Lead in pigs | 243 | 0 | 0 |
| Manufactured cotton | 640 | 0 | 0 |
| ,,  metal | 564 | 0 | 0 |
| ,,  silk | 550 | 8 | 0 |
| ,,  wool clothing | 156 | 16 | 0 |
| ,,  ,, cloths | 2,347 | 4 | 0 |
| Miscellaneous articles | 232 | 4 | 0 |
| Oil paintings | 57 | 4 | 0 |
| Precious stones | 9,006 | 8 | 0 |
| Scientific apparatus and books for colleges | 270 | 4 | 0 |
| Seeds | 277 | 8 | 0 |
| Shot guns | 81 | 4 | 0 |
| Spirits, distilled— | | | |
| Brandy | 140 | 4 | 0 |
| Gin | 39 | 0 | 0 |
| Rum | 14 | 12 | 0 |
| Whisky | 204 | 0 | 0 |
| Sponges | 103 | 8 | 0 |
| Tin plates and terne plates | 4,676 | 12 | 0 |
| Varnish | 277 | 12 | 0 |
| Wine— | | | |
| Champagne | 2,242 | 8 | 0 |
| Still wine | 161 | 12 | 0 |
| Total | 26,008 | 16 | 0 |

## CHICAGO.

The following is a record of imports from Great Britain for the past six years :—

|  | 1886. | 1887. | 1888. | 1889. | 1890. | 1891. |
|---|---|---|---|---|---|---|
|  | £ s. | £ s. | £ s. | £ s. | £ s. | £ s. |
| Total value... | 3,201 0 | 5,043 12 | 8,109 12 | 17,585 7 | 32,512 4 | 26,008 16 |

## KANSAS CITY.

Mr. Vice-Consul Chandler reports as follows :—

There has been an increase in the volume of trade during the year 1891 in the two Kansas cities over any previous year, the total amount of trade being estimated at upwards of 100,000,000 dol. {Volume of trade.}

The livestock interests are the largest single industry, and extensive additions have been made to the stockyards and to the packing-house plants. {Live stock.}

The receipts of all food animals during the year were less than for the year 1890, but the condition of the market showed a decided improvement. {Food animals.}

The receipts of horses and mules for the year 1891 were not as large as for the year 1890, but the average range of prices was higher, indicating a continued improvement in prices as well as in grain. {Horses and mules.}

The following is a comparative table showing the receipts of all kinds for the years 1890 and 1891, together with the number of car-loads and the aggregate values :— {Live stock trade.}

| Description. | 1890. Quantity. | 1890. Value. | 1891. Quantity. | 1891. Value. |
|---|---|---|---|---|
|  | Number. | Dollars. | Number. | Dollars. |
| Cattle | 1,472,229 | .. | 1,280,839 | .. |
| Calves | 76,568 | .. | 83,500 | .. |
| Hogs | 2,865,171 | .. | 2,616,749 | .. |
| Sheep | 535,869 | .. | 388,034 | .. |
| Horses and mules | 37,118 | .. | 32,209 | .. |
| Cars | 108,160 | .. | 92,488 | .. |
| Total | .. | 75,503,119 | .. | 66,504,631 |

The table below shows the total receipts and shipments and the number of animals driven out for packers and city use for the year :—

(1372)

UNITED STATES.

| Description. | Receipts. | Shipments. | Driven out 1891. | Driven out 1890. |
|---|---|---|---|---|
| | Number. | Number. | Number. | Number. |
| Cattle | 1,280,839 | 734,620 | 546,219 | } 493,000 |
| Calves | 83,500 | 46,020 | 37,480 | |
| Hogs | 2,616,749 | 607,835 | 2,008,914 | 2,269,000 |
| Sheep | 388,034 | 178,168 | 209,866 | 152,000 |
| Horses and Mules | 32,209 | 23,278 | 8,931 | No report. |
| Total | 4,401,331 | 1,589,921 | 2,814,410 | 2,914,000 |

*Banking.* — Capital decreased from 11,617,300 dol. in 1890 to 9,308,000 dol. in 1891, and the surplus funds increased from 1,063,000 dol. to 1,555,000 dol. in the same period. The bank clearings for the year reached 461,000,000 dol., a decrease of 30,000,000 over the previous year. One national bank went into the hands of a receiver, one into voluntary liquidation, and one reduced its capital 25 per cent. Deposits amounting to 24,000,000 dol. were in the banks at the close of business, December 31, 1891.

*Grain trade.* — The Kansas grain inspection laws went into effect April 1, 1891; before that date no official reports were obtainable for Kansas inspection. The official reports for Kansas City, Mo., are obtainable for the first six months of the year 1891 only. The following table shows the inspection at both points in carload lots:—

| | Wheat. | Corn. | Oats. | Rye. | Barley. |
|---|---|---|---|---|---|
| | Number. | Number. | Number. | Number. | Number. |
| Kansas City, Kansas— April 1 to December 31 | 24,126 | 10,506 | 3,323 | 2,346 | 25 |
| Kansas City, Mo.— January 1 to June 30 | 4,221 | 6,959 | 1,749 | 67 | 2 |

*Meat inspection.* — Under the United States Meat Inspection Act of March 3, 1891, the law was put into effect in June at two of the packing-houses in Kansas City, Kansas, Armour's and Swift's.

*Inspection staff.* — All the meat intended for foreign export is inspected under the charge of 2 chief veterinary inspectors, assisted by a staff of 7 assistant inspectors, 23 microscopists, and 36 taggers.

*Cattle inspection.* — Cattle are subjected to an ante and post mortem examination, especial attention being given to the intestines; after inspection and approval each quarter is tagged with a seal and tag indicating that the particular quarter has been examined and passed by the United States Department of Agricultural Bureau of Animal Industry.

*Hog inspection.* — The inspection of hogs is conducted as follows: two specimens of meat are taken from each animal, one from the foot of the diaphragm, the other from the region of the dorsal vertebra; these are marked with distinctive numbers, and corresponding numbers are attached to the animal; each specimen is then subjected to a careful microscopical examination, and if trichinæ are discovered the animal is condemned and thrown out. Subsequently the animals passed are shipped in packages and each package is officially stamped and sealed. All consignments are accompanied by a certificate of inspection, signed by the Chief Veterinary Inspector.

The daily inspection at this point amounts from 500 to 1,400 head of cattle and 1,500 head of hogs. *Daily inspection.*

The system has been carefully examined by the representatives of foreign Governments, sent here for that purpose, and has met with their unqualified approval.

## Kansas.

Kansas is an agricultural State; there is no city in its limits with a population exceeding 45,000 inhabitants, and the prosperity of the people mainly depends upon the success of field crops. The year 1891 was one of the most prosperous in the history of the State; nearly every section of the State was favoured with one or more large crops; good prices have prevailed and several millions of mortgage indebtedness, incurred in the purchase and improvement of the farms, have been paid off. *General remarks.*

The fruit industry is assuming large proportions, and the crops have been universally good and remunerative. *Fruit industry.*

The following table shows the number of fruit trees in bearing and the number not yet in bearing in the entire State:—

| Variety. | In bearing. | Not in bearing. |
|---|---|---|
|  | Number. | Number. |
| Apple | 5,758,907 | 5,478,284 |
| Pear | 150,531 | 229,152 |
| Peach | 5,395,700 | 1,255,087 |
| Plum | 663,838 | 400,806 |
| Cherry | 1,263,857 | 562,317 |

The following table shows the number of acres in small fruits, nurseries, and vineyards:—

|  | Acres. |
|---|---|
| Nurseries | 4,991 |
| Raspberries | 3,015 |
| Blackberries | 4,140 |
| Strawberries | 2,286 |
| Vineyards | 7,035 |

## UNITED STATES.

State Summary showing the Total Acreage, Amount, and Value of Farm Products for the Year 1891.

| Description. | | Number of Acres. | Amount of Product. | Value. |
|---|---|---|---|---|
| | | | | Dol. c. |
| Winter wheat | Bushels | 3,582,006 | 56,170,694 | 40,997,417 02 |
| Spring „ | „ | 151,922 | 2,379,959 | 1,599,342 07 |
| Corn | „ | 5,209,234 | 139,363,991 | 48,057,978 93 |
| Oats | „ | 1,298,745 | 39,904,443 | 10,594,457 48 |
| Rye | „ | 332,673 | 5,443,030 | 3,528,680 23 |
| Barley | „ | 36,484 | 1,006,380 | 411,909 72 |
| Buckwheat | „ | 3,405 | 44,874 | 40,386 60 |
| Irish potatoes | „ | 69,542 | 5,483,900 | 2,689,637 39 |
| Sweet potatoes | „ | 3,939 | 404,442 | 343,775 70 |
| Castor beans | „ | 16,428 | 114,644 | 143,305 00 |
| Sorghum | | 195,758 | .. | *2,060,423 00 |
| Cotton | Lbs. | 1,782 | 445,500 | 35,640 00 |
| Flax | Bushels | 388,184 | 2,049,055 | 1,639,244 00 |
| Hemp | Lbs. | 247 | 172,500 | 8,225 00 |
| Tobacco | „ | 366 | 219,600 | 21,960 00 |
| Broom corn | „ | 58,225 | 28,261,450 | 918,497 12 |
| Millet and Hungarian | Tons | 308,093 | 633,405 | 2,533,620 00 |
| Timothy | „ | 498,854 | | |
| Clover | „ | 158,589 | | |
| Blue grass | „ | 101,869 | | |
| Alfalfa | „ | 34,384 | 401,640 | 2,008,200 00 |
| Orchard grass | „ | 5,701 | | |
| Other tame grasses | „ | 63,702 | | |
| Prairie grass under fence | „ | 4,997,886 | 1,369,945 | 4,062,546 50 |
| Wool | Lbs. | .. | 1,578,993 | 284,218 74 |
| Cheese | „ | .. | 613,772 | 67,514 92 |
| Butter | „ | .. | 29,084,837 | 4,362,725 55 |
| Animals slaughtered, or sold for slaughter | .. | .. | .. | 37,922,192 00 |
| Milk sold, other than that sold for butter and cheese | .. | .. | .. | 528,761 00 |
| Poultry and eggs sold | .. | .. | .. | 2,559,297 00 |
| Garden products marketed | .. | .. | .. | 818,958 00 |
| Horticultural products marketed | .. | .. | .. | 1,199,468 00 |
| Wine | Gallons | .. | 170,369 | 170,369 00 |
| Honey and wax produced | Lbs. | .. | 365,221 | 73,944 20 |
| Wood marketed | | .. | .. | 128,678 00 |
| Total | | 17,518,018 | .. | 169,811,372 17 |

* Syrup and forage.

## CHICAGO.

RETURN showing the Number of Live Stock as Returned by the Assessors and Value for the Year 1891.

| Description. | Quantity. | Value. |
|---|---|---|
|  | Head. | Dol.      c. |
| Horses | 776,533 | 54,357,310  00 |
| Mules and asses | 77,170 | 6,173,600  00 |
| Milch cows | 690,611 | 13,812,220  00 |
| Other cattle | 1,770,591 | 30,100,047  00 |
| Sheep | 260,558 | 716,534  50 |
| Swine | 2,085,875 | 12,515,250  00 |
| Total | .. | 117,674,961  50 |

Coal. The total output of coal, as reported by the State Inspector of Mines, amounts to 60,000,000 bushels of 80 lbs. each, valued at 3,000,000 dol.

Lead and zinc. The lead and zinc output from the Kansas mines is slightly less for the past year than for the year 1890, due to the low prices prevailing for these products. The following table shows the comparative output, in lbs., for the two years:—

| Articles. | Quantity. | |
|---|---|---|
|  | 1890. | 1891. |
|  | Lbs. | Lbs. |
| Lead | 7,985,000 | 7,204,420 |
| Zinc | 65,900,000 | 41,283,551 |

Large additions have been made during the past year to the capacity for smelting zinc ores. The Kansas production of zinc amounts to one-fourth of the total production of the United States.

LONDON:
Printed for Her Majesty's Stationery Office,
By HARRISON AND SONS,
Printers in Ordinary to Her Majesty.
(75  7 | 92—H & S  1372)

# FOREIGN OFFICE.
## 1893.
## ANNUAL SERIES.

### No. 1157.

### DIPLOMATIC AND CONSULAR REPORTS ON TRADE AND FINANCE.

# UNITED STATES.

### REPORT FOR THE YEAR 1892

ON THE

### FOREIGN COMMERCE OF THE UNITED STATES.

*Presented to both Houses of Parliament by Command of Her Majesty,*
*MARCH, 1893.*

LONDON:
PRINTED FOR HER MAJESTY'S STATIONERY OFFICE,
BY HARRISON AND SONS, ST. MARTIN'S LANE,
PRINTERS IN ORDINARY TO HER MAJESTY.

And to be purchased, either directly or through any Bookseller, from
EYRE & SPOTTISWOODE, East Harding Street, Fleet Street, E.C., and
32, Abingdon Street, Westminster, S.W.; or
JOHN MENZIES & Co., 12, Hanover Street, Edinburgh, and
90, West Nile Street, Glasgow; or
HODGES, FIGGIS, & Co., Limited, 104, Grafton Street, Dublin.

1893.

[C. 6855—44.]     *Price Twopence.*

# New Series of Reports.

Reports of the Annual Series have been issued from Her Majesty's Diplomatic and Consular Officers at the following places, and may be obtained from the sources indicated on the title-page:—

| No. | | Price. | No. | | Price. |
|---|---|---|---|---|---|
| 1039. | Brest | 1d. | 1098. | Nagasaki | 1d. |
| 1040. | Madeira | ½d. | 1099. | Constantinople | 2d. |
| 1041. | Antwerp | 1½d. | 1100. | Buenos Ayres | ½d. |
| 1042. | Taganrog | 2½d. | 1101. | Shanghai | 2d. |
| 1043. | Algiers | 2½d. | 1102. | Jeddah | ½d. |
| 1044. | Hankow | 1½d. | 1103. | Chicago | 3d. |
| 1045. | Nantes | 1½d. | 1104. | Erzeroum | ½d. |
| 1046. | Belgrade | 2d. | 1105. | Loanda | 3d. |
| 1047. | Fiume | 1d. | 1106. | Macao | ½d. |
| 1048. | Wuhu | 1d. | 1107. | Canton | 1d. |
| 1049. | Cagliari | 1d. | 1108. | Paramaribo | 1½d. |
| 1050. | Erzeroum | 1d. | 1109. | Tunis | 1½d. |
| 1051. | Syra | 1d. | 1110. | Sofia | 3d. |
| 1052. | Cherbourg | 1d. | 1111. | Brunei | 1½d. |
| 1053. | Lima | 1d. | 1112. | Athens | 2½d. |
| 1054. | Bilbao | 1½d. | 1113. | Alexandria | 2d. |
| 1055. | Cadiz | 2d. | 1114. | Vienna | 1d. |
| 1056. | Corunna | 2½d. | 1115. | Stettin | 2½d. |
| 1057. | Saigon | 1d. | 1116. | Berne | 1d. |
| 1058. | Port-au-Prince | 1d. | 1117. | Palermo | 2½d. |
| 1059. | Trebizond | 1d. | 1118. | Tokio | 1½d. |
| 1060. | Barcelona | 1½d. | 1119. | St. Petersburg | 3d. |
| 1061. | Tainan | 1d. | 1120. | Teneriffe | 1d. |
| 1062. | Smyrna | 1½d. | 1121. | Damascus | 1d. |
| 1063. | Old Calabar | ½d. | 1122. | Naples | 2d. |
| 1064. | Samoa | ½d. | 1123. | Hakodate | 1d. |
| 1065. | Tahiti | 1d. | 1124. | Montevideo | 2½d. |
| 1066. | Chefoo | 6d. | 1125. | Stockholm | 1½d. |
| 1067. | Gothenburg | 2d. | 1126. | Dantzig | 2d. |
| 1068. | Buenos Ayres | 1½d. | 1127. | The Hague | 1½d. |
| 1069. | Loanda | 1½d. | 1128. | Odessa | 1d. |
| 1070. | Guatemala | 1d. | 1129. | Berne | 1½d. |
| 1071. | Zanzibar | 1d. | 1130. | Malaga | 3d. |
| 1072. | Charleston | 2½d. | 1131. | Rome | 2½d. |
| 1073. | Nice | 1d. | 1132. | St. Jago de Cuba | 4½d. |
| 1074. | Caracas | 1d. | 1133. | Munich | 1½d. |
| 1075. | Lisbon | 2d. | 1134. | Meshed | 1d. |
| 1076. | Calais | 2d. | 1135. | Guayaquil | ½d. |
| 1077. | Rio Grande do Sul | 5½d. | 1136. | Rio de Janeiro | 4½d. |
| 1078. | Philadelphia | 2½d. | 1137. | Tonga | 1d. |
| 1079. | Brindisi | 2d. | 1138. | Copenhagen | 1d. |
| 1080. | New York | 2d. | 1139. | Tangier | 1½d. |
| 1081. | San Francisco | 1½d. | 1140. | Buenos Ayres | 2½d. |
| 1082. | Frankfort | 4d. | 1141. | Para | 1d. |
| 1083. | Hiogo | 1½d. | 1142. | Baghdad and Bussorah | 1½d. |
| 1084. | Tokio | 1½d. | 1143. | Christiania | 5½d. |
| 1085. | Amsterdam | 1d. | 1144. | Old Calabar | 2d. |
| 1086. | San Francisco | 3d. | 1145. | Trieste | 1½d. |
| 1087. | Bangkok | ½d. | 1146. | Quito | 1d. |
| 1088. | Sŏul | 1½d. | 1147. | Buenos Ayres | 6d. |
| 1089. | Chiengmai | 1d. | 1148. | Bogotá | 1d. |
| 1090. | Copenhagen | ½d. | 1149. | The Hague | 2d. |
| 1091. | New Caledonia | ½d. | 1150. | Mexico | 2½d. |
| 1092. | Bushire | 2d. | 1151. | Florence | 1d. |
| 1093. | Tamsui | 1d. | 1152. | Calais | 1d. |
| 1094. | Dunkirk | 1d. | 1153. | Lorenzo Marques | 1½d. |
| 1095. | Port Said | 1d. | 1154. | Patras | 1d. |
| 1096. | Guatemala | ½d. | 1155. | Taganrog | 1d. |
| 1097. | Chungking | 9d. | 1156. | Stockholm | 1d. |

# No. 1157.

# UNITED STATES.

## WASHINGTON.

*Sir J. Pauncefote to the Earl of Rosebery.*

My Lord,                        *Washington, February* 9, 1893.

I HAVE the honour to enclose a letter which I have received from Mr. Michael Herbert, First Secretary in this Legation, transmitting a Report which he has drawn up on the Foreign Commerce of the United States for the Fiscal Year ending June 30, 1892, and for the Calendar Year ending December 31, 1892.

I have, &c.
(Signed)     JULIAN PAUNCEFOTE.

---

*Mr. Herbert to Sir J. Pauncefote.*

Dear Sir,                        *Washington, February* 8, 1893.

I HAVE the honour to transmit herewith a Report, which I have drawn up, on the Foreign Commerce of the United States for the Fiscal Year ending June 30, 1892, and for the Calendar Year 1892.

The Tables and Figures given in this Report have been taken from various publications issued by the Bureau of Statistics.

I have, &c.
(Signed)     MICHAEL H. HERBERT.

---

*Report on the Foreign Commerce of the United States for the Fiscal Year ending June* 30, 1892, *and for the last Calendar Year.*

### ABSTRACT of Contents.

| | Page |
|---|---|
| Exports and imports for the year ending June 30, 1892 | 3 |
| „ for the year ending June 30, 1892 | 6 |
| Imports „ „ | 12 |
| Imports and exports for the calendar year ending December 31, 1892 | 22 |
| Remarks | 23 |

(1465)

## UNITED STATES.

**Value of exports and imports.**
The total value of the imports and exports of the United States during the fiscal year ending June 30, 1892, was 1,857,680,610 dol. (371,536,122*l.*) against 1,729,397,006 dol. (345,879,401*l.*) in 1891, an increase of 128,283,604 dol. (25,656,720*l.*).

**Value of imports.**
The value of the imports during the same period amounted to 827,402,462 dol. (165,480,492*l.*) against 844,916,196 dol. (168,983,239*l.*) in 1891, a decrease of 17,513,734 dol. (3,502,746*l.*).

**Value of exports.**
The value of the exports during the same period amounted to 1,030,278,148 dol. (206,055,629*l.*) against 884,480,810 dol. (176,896,160*l.*), an increase of 145,797,338 dol. (29,159,467*l.*).

**Large exports.**
The value of the exports during this period was the largest of any year in the history of the United States, as was also the aggregate value of imports and exports.

## WASHINGTON.

TABLE showing the Imports and Exports for each Fiscal Year from 1881 to 1892 inclusive, and the Increase or Decrease in the Imports, Exports, and the Total Values thereof respectively.

| Year ending June 30. | Value of Imports. | Yearly Increase (+) or Decrease (−) from 1881. | Value of Exports. | Yearly Increase (+) or Decrease (−) from 1881. | Total Value of Imports and Exports. | Yearly Increase (+) or Decrease (−) from 1881. | Excess of Exports. |
|---|---|---|---|---|---|---|---|
| | Dollars. | Dollars. | Dollars. | Dollars. | Dollars. | Dollars. | Dollars. |
| 1881 | 642,664,628 | .. | 902,377,346 | .. | 1,545,041,974 | .. | 259,712,718 |
| 1882 | 724,639,574 | + 81,974,946 | 750,542,257 | − 151,835,089 | 1,475,181,831 | − 69,860,143 | 25,902,683 |
| 1883 | 723,180,914 | + 80,516,286 | 823,839,402 | − 78,537,944 | 1,547,020,316 | + 1,978,342 | 100,658,488 |
| 1884 | 667,697,693 | + 25,033,065 | 740,513,609 | − 161,863,737 | 1,408,211,302 | − 136,830,672 | 72,815,916 |
| 1885 | 577,527,329 | − 65,137,299 | 742,189,755 | − 160,187,591 | 1,319,717,084 | − 225,324,890 | 164,662,426 |
| 1886 | 635,436,136 | − 7,228,492 | 679,524,830 | − 222,852,516 | 1,314,960,966 | − 230,081,008 | 44,088,694 |
| 1887 | 692,319,768 | + 49,655,140 | 716,183,211 | − 186,194,135 | 1,408,502,979 | − 136,538,995 | 23,863,443 |
| 1888 | 723,957,114 | + 81,292,486 | 695,954,507 | − 206,422,839 | 1,419,911,621 | − 125,130,353 | 28,002,607* |
| 1889 | 745,131,652 | + 102,467,024 | 742,401,375 | − 159,975,971 | 1,487,533,027 | − 57,508,947 | 2,730,277* |
| 1890 | 789,310,409 | + 146,645,781 | 857,828,684 | − 44,548,662 | 1,647,139,093 | + 102,097,119 | 68,518,275 |
| 1891 | 844,916,196 | + 202,251,568 | 884,480,810 | − 17,895,536 | 1,729,397,006 | + 184,355,032 | 39,564,614 |
| 1892 | 827,402,462 | + 184,737,834 | 1,030,278,148 | + 127,900,802 | 1,857,680,610 | + 312,638,636 | 202,875,686 |

\* Excess of imports.

## UNITED STATES.

TABLE showing the Condition of the Commerce of the United States with the Leading Countries and Grand Divisions of the World during the Year ending June 30, 1892.

| Grand Divisions. COUNTRIES. | Exports. Domestic. Dollars. | Exports. Foreign. Dollars. | Exports. Total. Dollars. | Imports. Dollars. | Total Exports and Imports. Dollars. | Excess of Exports (+) or of Imports (−). Dollars. |
|---|---|---|---|---|---|---|
| United Kingdom | 493,957,868 | 5,357,464 | 499,315,332 | 156,300,881 | 655,616,213 | + 343,014,451 |
| Germany | 104,180,732 | 1,340,826 | 105,521,558 | 82,907,553 | 188,429,111 | + 22,614,005 |
| France | 97,896,132 | 1,230,575 | 99,126,707 | 68,554,793 | 167,681,500 | + 30,571,914 |
| Belgium | 47,713,121 | 1,071,996 | 48,785,117 | 10,273,061 | 59,058,178 | + 38,512,056 |
| Netherlands | 43,556,865 | 361,119 | 43,917,984 | 10,886,802 | 54,804,786 | + 33,034,182 |
| Italy | 14,223,947 | 93,835 | 14,317,782 | 22,161,617 | 36,479,399 | − 7,843,835 |
| British North American possessions | 42,580,578* | 2,305,410 | 44,885,938 | 35,334,547 | 80,220,535 | + 9,551,441 |
| Mexico | 13,696,531* | 597,468 | 14,293,999 | 28,107,525 | 42,401,524 | − 13,813,526 |
| West Indies | 37,600,708 | 907,595 | 38,508,303 | 99,606,305 | 138,114,608 | − 61,698,002 |
| Brazil | 14,240,009 | 51,864 | 14,291,873 | 118,633,604 | 132,925,477 | − 104,341,731 |
| China | 5,663,471 | 26 | 5,663,497 | 20,488,291 | 26,151,788 | − 14,824,794 |
| British India and East Indies | 3,674,141 | 166 | 3,674,307 | 24,773,107 | 28,447,404 | − 21,098,800 |
| Japan | 3,288,282 | 1,829 | 3,290,111 | 23,790,202 | 27,080,313 | − 20,500,091 |
| All other countries | 93,459,626 | 1,225,964 | 94,685,590 | 125,584,174 | 220,269,764 | − 30,898,584 |
| Total | 1,015,732,011 | 14,546,137 | 1,030,278,148 | 827,402,462 | 1,857,680,610 | + 202,875,686 |

TABLE showing the Condition of the Commerce of the United States with the Leading Countries and Grand Divisions of the World during the Year ending June 30, 1892—continued.

| Grand Divisions. | Exports. Domestic. Dollars. | Exports. Foreign. Dollars. | Total. Dollars. | Imports. Dollars. | Total Exports and Imports. Dollars. | Excess of Exports (+), or of Imports (−). Dollars. |
|---|---|---|---|---|---|---|
| GRAND DIVISIONS. | | | | | | |
| Europe | 841,087,922 | 9,535,228 | 850,623,150 | 391,628,469 | 1,242,251,619 | + 458,994,681 |
| North America | 101,463,351* | 4,102,833 | 105,566,184 | 174,054,181 | 279,620,365 | − 68,487,997 |
| South America | 32,573,922 | 573,692 | 33,147,614 | 150,727,759 | 183,875,373 | − 117,580,145 |
| Asia | 19,581,056 | 9,294 | 19,590,350 | 80,138,251 | 99,728,601 | − 60,547,901 |
| Oceania | 15,274,896 | 297,871 | 15,572,767 | 23,133,062 | 38,705,829 | − 7,560,295 |
| Africa | 5,035,162 | 26,103 | 5,061,265 | 5,318,052 | 10,379,317 | − 256,787 |
| All other countries | 715,702 | 1,116 | 716,818 | 2,402,688 | 3,119,506 | − 1,685,870 |
| Total | 1,015,732,011 | 14,546,137 | 1,030,278,148 | 827,402,462 | 1,357,680,610 | + 202,875,686 |

* Exports by railways are incomplete.

## UNITED STATES.

**Large trade with Great Britain.**

It will be seen from this table that the total value of the trade of the United States with Great Britain amounted to 655,616,213 dol. (131,103,242*l.*), forming about 35 per cent. of the trade of the United States with all nations, and about 53 per cent. of the trade of the United States with all Europe.

### Exports.

**Exports.**

The great increase in the value of domestic exports from the United States was principally in breadstuffs, the result of the extraordinary wheat crop of 1891.

**Increase or decrease in exports.**

The material increase or decrease in the values of the principal articles of domestic export was during the last fiscal year as follows:—

#### INCREASE.

| Articles. | Value. |
|---|---|
| | Dollars. |
| Breadstuffs | 171,241,461 |
| Cattle | 4,653,846 |
| Fruits, including nuts | 4,191,352 |
| Seeds | 3,751,383 |
| Beef, fresh | 2,731,678 |
| Copper, manufactures of | 2,611,795 |
| Oil-cake and oil-cake meal | 2,261,110 |
| Bacon | 1,929,944 |
| Oleomargarine | 1,092,322 |
| Vegetable oils | 1,032,019 |

#### DECREASE.

| Articles. | Value. |
|---|---|
| | Dollars. |
| Cotton, unmanufactured | 32,251,657 |
| Mineral oils | 7,220,742 |
| Sugar, refined | 5,473,269 |
| Beef, salted, pickled, and other cured | 3,383,824 |
| Hog products, except bacon | 1,722,076 |
| Carriages, horse cars, and cars for steam railroads | 1,636,685 |
| Copper ore | 1,224,116 |
| Leather, and manufactures of | 1,194,066 |

Comparing the exports of the year 1890, the year prior to the change in the tariff (the McKinley Act became law in October, 1890), there was an increase in the value of domestic exports to—

| Country. | Value. |
|---|---|
| | Dollars. |
| United Kingdom | 49,498,859 |
| France | 48,883,128 |
| Belgium | 21,572,744 |
| Netherlands | 21,069,277 |
| Germany | 19,865,517 |
| Spanish West Indies | 5,513,833 |
| China | 2,719,681 |
| Brazil | 2,337,513 |

DECREASE.

| Country. | Value. |
|---|---|
| | Dollars. |
| Argentine Republic | 5,679,302 |
| Russia in Europe | 3,840,170 |
| Japan | 1,938,904 |
| Spain | 1,214,123 |
| British India and East Indies | 981,115 |
| Hawaiian Islands | 944,882 |

TABLE showing the Exports of the Domestic Merchandise of the United States during the last Three Fiscal Years Classified by Groups according to Sources of Production. *Different classes of exports.*

| Groups. | 1890. | 1891. | 1892. | Per cent., 1892. |
|---|---|---|---|---|
| | Dollars. | Dollars. | Dollars. | |
| Products of agriculture | 629,820,808 | 642,751,344 | 799,328,232 | 78·69 |
| ,, manufacture | 151,102,376 | 168,927,315 | 158,510,937 | 15·61 |
| ,, mining | 22,297,755 | 22,054,970 | 20,692,885 | 2·04 |
| ,, the forest | 29,473,084 | 28,715,713 | 27,957,423 | 2·75 |
| ,, the fisheries | 7,458,385 | 6,208,577 | 5,403,587 | 0·53 |
| Other products | 5,141,420 | 3,612,364 | 3,838,947 | 0·38 |
| Total | 845,293,828 | 872,270,283 | 1,015,732,011 | 100·00 |

Table showing the values of the various articles of merchandise of domestic product and manufacture exported from the United States during the fiscal year ending June 30, 1892:— *Value of various articles of export.*

## UNITED STATES.

| Order. | Articles. | 1892. | Per Cent. of Total for 1892. |
|---|---|---|---|
| | | Dollars. | |
| 1 | Breadstuffs | 299,363,117 | 29·47 |
| 2 | Cotton, unmanufactured | 258,461,241 | 25·44 |
| 3 | Provisions, including meat and dairy products | 140,362,159 | 13·83 |
| 4 | Mineral oils | 44,805,992 | 4·41 |
| 5 | Animals | 36,498,221 | 3·59 |
| 6 | Iron and steel, and manufactures of | 28,800,930 | 2·84 |
| 7 | Wood, and manufactures of | 25,788,967 | 2·54 |
| 8 | Tobacco, and manufactures of | 24,739,425 | 2·45 |
| 9 | Cotton, manufactures of | 13,266,277 | 1·30 |
| 10 | Leather, and manufactures of | 12,084,781 | 1·19 |
| 11 | Oil-cake and oil-cake meal | 9,713,204 | 0·97 |
| 12 | Coal | 8,649,158 | 0·85 |
| 13 | Naval stores (resin, tar, turpentine, pitch, and spirits of turpentine) | 7,989,923 | 0·79 |
| 14 | Copper, manufactures of | 7,226,392 | 0·71 |
| 15 | Chemicals, drugs, dyes, and medicines | 6,693,855 | 0·66 |
| 16 | Fruits, including nuts | 6,626,145 | 0·65 |
| 17 | Seeds | 6,252,282 | 0·61 |
| 18 | Copper ore | 6,036,777 | 0·60 |
| 19 | Vegetable oils | 5,334,955 | 0·52 |
| 20 | Fish | 4,522,763 | 0·45 |
| 21 | Paraffin and paraffin wax | 3,965,263 | 0·39 |
| 22 | Agricultural implements | 3,794,983 | 0·37 |
| 23 | Furs and fur skins | 3,586,339 | 0·35 |
| 24 | Fertilisers | 2,657,120 | 0·26 |
| 25 | Hops | 2,420,502 | 0·24 |
| 26 | Spirits, distilled | 2,401,117 | 0·24 |
| 27 | Glucose and grape sugar | 2,272,779 | 0·22 |
| 28 | Flax, hemp, and jute, manufactures of | 1,998,663 | 0·20 |
| 29 | Carriages and horse cars, and parts of | 1,944,170 | 0·19 |
| 30 | Books, maps, engravings, etchings, and other printed matter | 1,943,228 | 0·19 |
| 31 | Sugar and molasses | 1,935,984 | 0·19 |
| 32 | Vegetables | 1,898,145 | 0·18 |
| 33 | Indiarubber and gutta-percha, and manufactures of | 1,416,067 | 0·14 |
| 34 | Instruments and apparatus for scientific purposes | 1,388,117 | 0·14 |
| 35 | Paper, and manufactures of | 1,382,251 | 0·14 |
| 36 | Cars, passenger and freight, for steam railroads | 1,320,265 | 0·13 |
| 37 | Grease, grease scraps, and all soap stocks | 1,293,598 | 0·13 |
| 38 | Clocks and watches, and parts of | 1,239,616 | 0·12 |
| 39 | Hides and skins, other than furs | 1,223,896 | 0·12 |
| 40 | Musical instruments | 1,164,656 | 0·11 |
| 41 | Soap | 1,063,207 | 0·10 |
| 42 | Jewellery, and manufactures of gold and silver | 1,026,188 | 0·10 |
| 43 | Animal oils | 978,688 | 0·10 |
| 44 | Glass and glassware | 942,302 | 0·09 |
| 45 | Casings for sausages | 878,675 | 0·09 |
| 46 | Gunpowder and other explosives | 860,355 | 0·08 |
| 47 | Zinc, manufactures of | 765,507 | 0·07 |
| 48 | Paints and painters' colours | 709,857 | 0·07 |
| 49 | Marble and stone, and manufactures of | 707,536 | 0·07 |
| 50 | Malt liquors | 657,934 | 0·06 |
| 51 | Starch | 612,531 | 0·06 |
| | All other articles | 12,110,849 | 1·19 |
| | Total | 1,015,732,011 | 100·00 |

## WASHINGTON.

TABLE showing the Value of the Domestic Exports of the United States for 1892 to Foreign Countries in order of magnitude.

| Order | Countries to which Exported. | 1892. | Per Cent. of Total for 1892. |
|---|---|---|---|
|  |  | Dollars. |  |
| 1 | United Kingdom | 493,957,868 | 48·62 |
| 2 | Germany | 104,180,732 | 10·25 |
| 3 | France | 97,899,132 | 9·63 |
| 4 | Belgium | 47,713,121 | 4·69 |
| 5 | Netherlands | 43,556,865 | 4·27 |
| 6 | British North American Possessions | 42,580,578 | 4·19 |
| 7 | West Indies, including Bermuda | 38,491,660 | 3·79 |
| 8 | Brazil | 14,240,009 | 1·41 |
| 9 | Italy | 14,223,947 | 1·40 |
| 10 | Mexico | 13,696,531 | 1·35 |
| 11 | Spain | 11,522,150 | 1·12 |
| 12 | British Australasia | 11,246,474 | 1·10 |
| 13 | Denmark | 8,358,881 | 0·83 |
| 14 | Russia in Europe | 6,693,095 | 0·65 |
| 15 | Sweden and Norway | 6,578,857 | 0·64 |
| 16 | Central American States | 5,872,029 | 0·58 |
| 17 | China | 5,663,471 | 0·56 |
| 18 | Hong-Kong | 4,887,350 | 0·48 |
| 19 | Portugal | 4,081,453 | 0·40 |
| 20 | Venezuela | 3,991,908 | 0·39 |
| 21 | British East Indies | 3,674,141 | 0·36 |
| 22 | Hawaiian Islands | 3,662,018 | 0·36 |
| 23 | Chile | 3,533,342 | 0·35 |
| 24 | British Africa | 3,453,700 | 0·35 |
| 25 | Japan | 3,288,282 | 0·33 |
| 26 | Colombia | 3,065,466 | 0·30 |
| 27 | Argentine Republic | 2,643,325 | 0·26 |
| 28 | Guiana | 2,363,326 | 0·23 |
| 29 | Austria-Hungary | 1,485,233 | 0·15 |
| 30 | Dutch East Indies | 1,372,035 | 0·14 |
| 31 | Peru | 1,002,977 | 0·10 |
| 32 | Uruguay | 907,067 | 0·09 |
| 33 | Ecuador and Bolivia | 826,502 | 0·08 |
|  | All other countries | 5,021,486 | 0·55 |
|  | Total | 1,015,732,011 | 100·00 |

### RECAPITULATION.

| Geographical Divisions. | 1892. | Per Cent. of Total Export. |
|---|---|---|
|  | Dollars. |  |
| Europe | 841,087,922 | 82·82 |
| North America | 101,463,351 | 9·98 |
| South America | 32,573,922 | 3·21 |
| Asia | 19,581,056 | 1·93 |
| Oceania | 15,274,896 | 1·50 |
| Africa | 5,035,162 | 0·49 |
| All other countries | 715,702 | 0·07 |
| Total | 1,015,732,011 | 100·00 |

TABLE showing the Increase or Decrease of the Domestic Exports of the United States by Articles for the Fiscal Year ending June 30, 1892, as compared with the Fiscal Year ending June 30, 1891.

| Articles. | 1891. | 1892. | Increase. | Decrease. |
|---|---|---|---|---|
| | Dollars. | Dollars. | Dollars. | Dollars. |
| Agricultural implements | 3,219,130 | 3,794,983 | 575,853 | ... |
| Animals— | | | | |
|   Cattle | 30,445,249 | 35,099,095 | 4,653,846 | ... |
|   All other | 2,489,837 | 1,399,126 | ... | 1,090,711 |
|     Total | 32,935,086 | 36,498,221 | 3,563,135 | ... |
| Breadstuffs— | | | | |
|   Corn | 17,652,687 | 41,590,460 | 23,937,773 | ... |
|   Oats | 405,708 | 3,842,559 | 3,436,851 | ... |
|   Rye | 212,161 | 11,432,160 | 11,219,999 | ... |
|   Wheat and wheat flour | 106,125,888 | 236,761,415 | 130,635,527 | ... |
|   All other | 3,725,212 | 5,736,523 | 2,011,311 | ... |
|     Total | 128,121,656 | 299,363,117 | 171,241,461 | ... |
| Carriages, horse cars, and cars for steam railroads | 4,901,120 | 3,264,435 | ... | 1,636,685 |
| Copper, and manufactures of— | | | | |
|   Ore | 7,260,893 | 6,036,777 | ... | 1,224,116 |
|   Manufactures of | 4,614,597 | 7,226,392 | 2,611,795 | ... |
| Cotton— | | | | |
|   Unmanufactured | 290,712,898 | 258,461,241 | ... | 32,251,657 |
|   Manufactures | 13,604,857 | 13,226,277 | ... | 378,580 |
| Fruits, including nuts | 2,434,793 | 6,626,145 | 4,191,352 | ... |
| Glucose or grape sugar | 1,394,131 | 2,272,779 | 878,648 | ... |
| Leather, manufactures of | 13,278,847 | 12,084,781 | ... | 1,194,066 |
| Oil-cake and oil-cake meal | 7,452,094 | 9,713,204 | 2,261,110 | ... |
| Oils— | | | | |
|   Animal | 1,281,783 | 978,688 | ... | 303,095 |
|   Mineral, crude | 5,876,452 | 5,101,840 | ... | 774,612 |
|     „ refined, or manufactured | 46,150,282 | 39,704,152 | ... | 6,446,130 |
|   Vegetable | 4,302,936 | 5,334,955 | 1,032,019 | ... |
| Provisions— | | | | |
|   Beef products— | | | | |
|     Beef, fresh | 15,322,054 | 18,053,732 | 2,731,678 | ... |
|     All other beef | 19,766,261 | 16,382,437 | ... | 3,383,824 |
|   Hog products— | | | | |
|     Bacon | 37,404,989 | 39,334,933 | 1,929,944 | ... |
|     All other | 47,503,709 | 45,781,633 | ... | 1,722,076 |
|   Oleomargarine | 8,114,154 | 9,207,476 | 1,093,322 | ... |
|   Dairy products | 9,863,780 | 10,358,893 | 495,113 | ... |
| Seeds | 2,500,809 | 6,252,282 | 3,751,383 | ... |
| Spirits | 1,887,431 | 2,401,117 | 513,686 | ... |
| Sugar, refined | 6,138,746 | 665,477 | ... | 5,473,269 |
| Vegetables | 1,335,975 | 1,898,145 | 562,170 | ... |
| Wood, and manufactures of, not including firewood | 26,263,014 | 25,788,967 | ... | 474,047 |
| Zinc, manufactures of | 131,732 | 765,567 | 633,835 | ... |
| All other articles | 128,495,984 | 129,153,365 | 657,381 | ... |
|     Total | 872,270,286 | 1,015,732,011 | 143,461,728 | ... |

TABLE showing the Values of the Exports of the United States Sub-divided under the Headings "Domestic Merchandise other than Manufactures" and "Manufactures" during the Years 1875-92 inclusive.

| Date. | Domestic Merchandise other than Manufactures. ||||||||||| Domestic Manufactures. || Total Exports of Domestic Merchandise. |
|---|---|---|---|---|---|---|---|---|---|---|---|---|---|---|
| | Agriculture. || Mining. || Forest. || Fisheries. || Miscellaneous. || Total. || | | |
| | Value. | Per Cent. | Value. | Per Cent. | Value. | Per Cent. | Value. | Per Cent. | Value. | Per Cent. | Value. | Per Cent. | Value. | Per Cent. | Value. |
| | Dollars. | | Dollars. | | Dollars. | | Dollars. | | Dollars. | | Dollars. | | Dollars. | | Dollars. |
| Year ending June 30— | | | | | | | | | | | | | | | |
| 1875 | 430,306,570 | 76·95 | 6,469,181 | 1·15 | 19,165,907 | 3·43 | 4,874,660 | 0·87 | 5,742,506 | 1·03 | 466,558,824 | 83·43 | 92,678,814 | 16·57 | 559,237,638 |
| 1876 | 456,113,515 | 76·67 | 7,122,989 | 1·20 | 18,076,668 | 3·04 | 5,806,445 | 0·98 | 6,160,550 | 1·03 | 493,280,167 | 82·92 | 101,637,548 | 17·08 | 594,917,715 |
| 1877 | 459,734,148 | 72·63 | 8,770,769 | 1·39 | 19,943,290 | 3·14 | 5,737,879 | 0·91 | 4,861,219 | 0·77 | 499,047,305 | 78·84 | 133,933,549 | 21·16 | 632,980,854 |
| 1878 | 536,192,873 | 77·07 | 6,732,119 | 0·97 | 17,750,396 | 2·55 | 6,434,182 | 0·92 | 4,833,164 | 0·70 | 571,942,734 | 82·21 | 123,807,196 | 17·79 | 695,749,930 |
| 1879 | 546,476,703 | 78·12 | 6,405,813 | 0·92 | 16,336,943 | 2·34 | 6,282,368 | 0·90 | 7,021,186 | 1·00 | 582,523,013 | 83·28 | 117,015,729 | 16·72 | 699,538,742 |
| 1880 | 685,961,091 | 83·25 | 5,863,232 | 0·71 | 17,321,268 | 2·11 | 5,255,402 | 0·64 | 6,689,345 | 0·81 | 721,090,338 | 87·52 | 102,856,015 | 12·48 | 823,946,353 |
| 1881 | 730,394,943 | 82·63 | 7,401,82 | 0·84 | 19,486,051 | 2·20 | 5,556,459 | 0·63 | 6,854,013 | 0·78 | 763,692,728 | 87·08 | 114,233,219 | 12·92 | 883,925,947 |
| 1882 | 552,219,819 | 75·31 | 8,175,692 | 1·11 | 25,580,264 | 3·50 | 6,197,752 | 0·85 | 6,276,859 | 0·85 | 598,445,386 | 81·62 | 134,794,346 | 18·38 | 733,239,732 |
| 1883 | 619,269,449 | 77·00 | 10,446,719 | 1·30 | 28,636,199 | 3·56 | 6,276,375 | 0·78 | 5,366,807 | 0·67 | 669,995,519 | 83·31 | 134,228,083 | 16·69 | 804,223,632 |
| 1884 | 536,315,318 | 73·98 | 15,022,255 | 2·07 | 26,222,059 | 3·62 | 5,614,111 | 0·77 | 5,417,322 | 0·75 | 588,591,965 | 81·19 | 136,372,887 | 18·81 | 724,964,852 |
| 1885 | 530,172,366 | 72·96 | 15,797,885 | 2·18 | 22,014,839 | 3·03 | 5,955,122 | 0·82 | 5,554,607 | 0·76 | 579,495,419 | 79·75 | 147,187,527 | 20·25 | 726,682,946 |
| 1886 | 484,054,595 | 72·82 | 13,654,286 | 2·05 | 20,961,708 | 3·15 | 5,133,806 | 0·77 | 4,718,156 | 0·71 | 529,422,551 | 79·50 | 136,541,978 | 20·50 | 665,964,529 |
| 1887 | 523,073,798 | 74·41 | 11,758,662 | 1·67 | 21,126,273 | 3·01 | 5,155,775 | 0·73 | 5,173,310 | 0·73 | 566,287,818 | 80·55 | 136,735,105 | 19·45 | 703,022,923 |
| 1888 | 500,840,086 | 72·23 | 17,993,895 | 2·63 | 23,991,082 | 3·51 | 5,513,552 | 0·82 | 5,218,392 | 0·76 | 553,562,017 | 80·95 | 130,300,087 | 19·05 | 684,862,104 |
| 1889 | 532,141,490 | 72·87 | 19,947,518 | 2·73 | 26,997,127 | 3·70 | 7,106,388 | 0·97 | 5,414,579 | 0·74 | 531,667,102 | 81·01 | 133,615,507 | 18·99 | 730,282,609 |
| 1890 | 629,820,808 | 74·51 | 22,297,755 | 2·64 | 29,478,084 | 3·49 | 7,438,345 | 0·88 | 5,141,420 | 0·61 | 694,191,452 | 82·13 | 151,102,376 | 17·87 | 845,293,828 |
| 1891 | 642,751,344 | 73·69 | 22,054,970 | 2·53 | 28,715,713 | 3·29 | 6,208,577 | 0·71 | 3,612,364 | 0·41 | 703,342,968 | 80·63 | 168,927,315 | 19·37 | 872,270,283 |
| 1892 | 799,328,232 | 78·69 | 20,692,885 | 2·04 | 27,957,423 | 2·75 | 5,403,587 | 0·53 | 3,838,947 | 0·38 | 857,221,074 | 84·39 | 158,510,937 | 15·61 | 1,015,732,011 |

## UNITED STATES.

**Falling-off in manufactures.**
It will be seen from this table that although the exports of agricultural merchandise increased so largely during the last fiscal year, that the exports of manufactures fell off about 10,000,000 dol.

### Imports.

**Imports.**
As has before been stated the value of the imports into the United States for 1892 amounted to 827,402,462 dol. (165,480,492*l*.), showing a decrease of 17,513,734 dol. (3,502,746*l*.). The value of free merchandise imported was 457,999,658 dol. (91,599,931*l*.), and of dutiable 369,402,804 dol. (73,880,560*l*.), an increase in the value of free merchandise of 91,758,306 dol. (18,351,661*l*.), and a decrease in the value of dutiable goods of 109,272,040 dol. (21,854,408*l*.), caused mainly by the transfer of sugar from the dutiable to the free list by the new tariff.

**Increase or decrease in free and dutiable imports.**
The material increase or decrease in the value of the principal classes of free and dutiable imports during the year ending June 30, 1892, as compared with 1891, was as follows:—

INCREASE.

| Articles. | Value. |
| --- | --- |
|  | Dollars. |
| Free of duty— |  |
| Sugar and molasses | 61,386,453 |
| Coffee | 30,677,830 |
| Indiarubber and gutta-percha, crude | 1,812,280 |
| Textile grasses and fibrous vegetable substances | 1,172,423 |
| Dutiable— |  |
| Flax, hemp, and jute, manufactures of | 2,269,123 |
| Tobacco, leaf, suitable for cigar wrappers | 2,166,058 |

## WASHINGTON.

### Decrease.

| Articles. | Value. |
|---|---|
| | Dollars. |
| Free of duty— | |
|   Hides and skins other than fur skins | 1,272,626 |
|   Eggs | 1,053,964 |
|   Animals | 789,307 |
|   Fruits, including nuts | 773,236 |
| Dutiable— | |
|   Sugar and molasses | 52,128,440 |
|   Iron and steel, and manufactures | 24,820,275 |
|   Silk, manufactures of | 6,707,249 |
|   Wool, manufactures of | 5,494,201 |
|   Tobacco, leaf, other than suitable for cigar wrappers | 5,117,797 |
|   Fruits, including nuts | 4,265,994 |
|   Vegetables | 4,193,147 |
|   Flax, hemp, and jute, unmanufactured | 3,335,034 |
|   Barley | 1,630,553 |
|   Seeds | 1,606,133 |
|   Rice | 1,480,560 |
|   Cotton, manufactures of | 1,388,783 |
|   Chemicals, drugs, dyes, and medicines | 1,244,009 |
|   Wines | 1,062,557 |

Comparing the imports of the year 1890, the last complete year prior to the new tariff Act, with the imports of the year 1892 there was an increase in the value of imports from—

| Country. | Value. |
|---|---|
| | Dollars. |
| Brazil | 59,314,848 |
| Spanish West Indies | 23,324,461 |
| Mexico | 5,416,610 |
| China | 4,227,820 |
| British Australasia | 4,214,630 |
| British India and East Indies | 3,968,788 |
| Japan | 2,686,878 |
| Central American States | 2,167,344 |
| Italy | 1,831,566 |

And a decrease in the value of imports from—

| Country. | Value. |
|---|---|
| | Dollars. |
| United Kingdom | 30,188,075 |
| Germany | 15,930,130 |
| France | 9,117,518 |
| Netherlands | 6,142,431 |
| Philippine Islands | 5,283,973 |
| Hawaiian Islands | 4,238,026 |
| British North American Possessions | 4,062,433 |

## UNITED STATES.

Comparing the imports of the year 1891 with those of the year 1892 there was an increase in the value of imports from—

| Country. | Value. |
|---|---|
|  | Dollars. |
| Brazil | 35,403,009 |
| Spanish West Indies | 16,301,173 |
| Japan | 4,481,004 |
| British Australasia | 2,253,285 |
| British East Indies | 1,416,118 |

And a decrease in the value of imports from—

| Country. | Value. |
|---|---|
|  | Dollars. |
| United Kingdom | 38,422,381 |
| Germany | 14,408,830 |
| France | 8,134,202 |
| Hawaiian Islands | 5,819,715 |
| Austria-Hungary | 3,876,745 |
| British West Indies | 3,853,052 |
| Quebec, &c. | 2,681,385 |
| Venezuela | 1,753,203 |
| Nova Scotia, New Brunswick, &c. | 1,640,417 |
| Netherlands | 1,535,372 |

**Imports during last 7 years.**

The values of the imports of merchandise into the United States during the last 7 fiscal years, classified by groups according to degree of manufacture or uses, were as follows :—

| Year ending June 30. | Of Food and Live Animals. | | In a crude condition, which enter into the Various Processes of Domestic Industry. | | Wholly or Partially Manufactured for use as Materials in the Manufactures and Mechanic Arts. | |
|---|---|---|---|---|---|---|
|  | Value. | Per Cent. | Value. | Per Cent. | Value. | Per Cent. |
|  | Dollars. |  | Dollars. |  | Dollars. |  |
| 1886 | 199,176,405 | 31·35 | 148,146,022 | 23·31 | 78,843,160 | 12·41 |
| 1887 | 213,973,334 | 30·92 | 168,199,431 | 24·30 | 80,328,760 | 11·60 |
| 1888 | 220,786,451 | 30·50 | 174,270,070 | 24·07 | 84,932,085 | 11·73 |
| 1889 | 239,140,245 | 32·10 | 178,646,235 | 23·96 | 83,979,997 | 11·27 |
| 1890 | 251,944,708 | 31·92 | 180,846,654 | 22·91 | 84,746,767 | 10·74 |
| 1891 | 284,715,737 | 33·72 | 196,393,669 | 23·27 | 107,024,423 | 12·91 |
| 1892 | 303,158,928 | 36·64 | 204,093,996 | 24·67 | 83,206,471 | 10·06 |

## WASHINGTON.

| Year ending June 30. | Articles— Manufactured, Ready for Consumption. Value. | Per Cent. | Of Voluntary use, Luxuries, &c. Value. | Per Cent. | Total. Value. |
|---|---|---|---|---|---|
| | Dollars. | | Dollars. | | Dollars. |
| 1886 | 127,975,118 | 20·14 | 81,295,431 | 12·79 | 635,436,136 |
| 1887 | 139,969,453 | 20·21 | 89,848,790 | 12·97 | 692,319,768 |
| 1888 | 147,988,782 | 20·44 | 95,979,726 | 13·26 | 723,957,114 |
| 1889 | 140,080,553 | 19·61 | 97,284,622 | 13·06 | 745,131,652 |
| 1890 | 157,943,573 | 20·01 | 113,828,707 | 14·42 | 789,310,409 |
| 1891 | 138,469,966 | 16·21 | 118,312,401 | 13·89 | 844,916,196 |
| 1892 | 132,178,815 | 15·97 | 104,764,252 | 12·66 | 827,402,462 |

## UNITED STATES.

**Leading articles of imports.**

TABLE showing the Values of Merchandise Imported into the United States during the Years ending June 30, 1890, 1891, and 1892, respectively, with the Percentage of the Aggregate Value for 1892 of the Imports of each Class of Merchandise.

| Number. | Articles. | 1890. | 1891. | 1892. | Per Cent. of Total, 1892. |
|---|---|---|---|---|---|
| | | Dollars. | Dollars. | Dollars. | |
| 1 | Coffee | 78,267,432 | 96,123,777 | 128,041,930 | 15·48 |
| 2 | Sugar, molasses, sugar candy, and confectionery— | | | | |
| | Molasses | 5,168,795 | 2,659,172 | 2,877,744 | ... |
| | Sugar, sugar candy, and confectionery | 96,125,031 | 105,799,449 | 104,506,554 | ... |
| | Total | 101,293,826 | 108,458,621 | 107,384,298 | 12·98 |
| 3 | Silk, and manufactures of— | | | | |
| | Unmanufactured | 24,325,531 | 19,077,366 | 25,059,325 | ... |
| | Manufactures of | 38,686,374 | 37,880,143 | 31,172,894 | ... |
| | Total | 63,011,905 | 56,957,509 | 56,232,219 | 6·80 |
| 4 | Wools, hair of the alpaca, &c., and manufactures of— | | | | |
| | Unmanufactured | 15,264,083 | 18,231,372 | 19,688,108 | ... |
| | Manufactures of | 56,582,432 | 41,060,080 | 35,565,879 | ... |
| | Total | 71,846,515 | 59,291,452 | 55,253,987 | 6·68 |
| 5 | Chemicals, drugs, dyes, and medicines | 41,602,078 | 47,317,031 | 45,961,639 | 5·55 |
| 6 | Textile grasses or fibrous vegetable substances— | | | | |
| | Unmanufactured | 20,541,767 | 21,286,705 | 19,124,094 | ... |
| | Manufactures of | 28,514,200 | 24,191,546 | 26,454,666 | ... |
| | Total | 49,055,967 | 45,478,251 | 45,578,760 | 5·51 |
| 7 | Cotton, and manufactures of— | | | | |
| | Unmanufactured | 1,392,728 | 2,825,004 | 3,217,521 | ... |
| | Manufactures of | 29,918,055 | 29,712,624 | 28,323,841 | ... |
| | Total | 31,310,783 | 32,537,628 | 31,541,362 | 3·81 |
| 8 | Iron and steel, and manufactures of— | | | | |
| | Ores | 2,415,714 | 2,430,159 | 2,592,461 | ... |
| | Manufactures of | 41,679,501 | 53,544,372 | 28,928,103 | ... |
| | Total | 44,095,215 | 55,974,531 | 31,520,564 | 3·81 |
| 9 | Hides and skins, other than fur skins | 21,881,886 | 27,930,759 | 26,850,218 | 3·25 |
| 10 | Fruits, including nuts | 20,746,471 | 25,983,136 | 20,943,906 | 2·53 |
| 11 | Indiarubber and gutta-percha, and manufactures of— | | | | |
| | Crude | 14,854,512 | 18,020,804 | 19,833,090 | ... |
| | Manufactures of | 367,647 | 354,645 | 432,856 | ... |
| | Total | 15,222,159 | 18,375,449 | 20,265,946 | 2·45 |
| 12 | Wood, and manufactures of— | | | | |
| | Unmanufactured | 4,266,689 | 5,360,611 | 5,682,967 | ... |
| | Manufactured | 12,975,227 | 14,527,575 | 14,163,471 | ... |
| | Total | 17,241,916 | 19,888,186 | 19,846,438 | 2·40 |
| 13 | Tea | 12,317,493 | 13,828,993 | 14,373,222 | 1·74 |
| 14 | Distilled spirits, malt liquors, and wines— | | | | |
| | Malt liquors | 1,427,608 | 1,765,702 | 1,709,960 | ... |
| | Spirits, distilled | 3,312,746 | 4,254,661 | 2,950,495 | ... |
| | Wines | 8,859,956 | 10,007,060 | 8,944,503 | ... |
| | Total | 13,600,310 | 16,027,423 | 13,604,958 | 1·64 |

TABLE showing the Values of Merchandise Imported into the United States during the Years ending June 30, 1890, 1891, and 1892, respectively, with the Percentage of the Aggregate Value for 1892 of the Imports of each Class of Merchandise—continued.

| Number. | Articles. | 1890. | 1891. | 1892. | Per Cent. of Total, 1892. |
|---|---|---|---|---|---|
|  |  | Dollars. | Dollars. | Dollars. |  |
| 15 | Precious stones, not set, including diamonds, rough or uncut | 12,383,335 | 13,271,602 | 13,451,007 | 1·63 |
| 16 | Leather, and manufactures of | 12,436,080 | 12,683,303 | 13,300,321 | 1·61 |
| 17 | Tobacco, and manufactures of— |  |  |  |  |
|  | Leaf | 17,605,192 | 13,284,162 | 10,332,423 | ... |
|  | Manufactures of | 4,105,262 | 3,478,979 | 2,926,051 | ... |
|  | Total | 21,710,454 | 16,763,141 | 13,258,474 | 1·60 |
| 18 | Furs dressed and undressed, and manufactures of | 7,553,816 | 9,828,849 | 10,197,131 | 1·23 |
| 19 | Ore, silver-bearing | 7,748,572 | 8,953,608 | 9,656,761 | 1·17 |
| 20 | Glass and glassware | 7,352,513 | 8,364,312 | 8,758,964 | 1·06 |
| 21 | Earthen, stone, and china ware | 7,030,301 | 8,381,388 | 8,708,598 | 1·05 |
| 22 | Tin, bars, blocks, or pigs | 6,898,909 | 7,977,545 | 8,667,870 | 1·05 |
| 23 | Metals, metal compositions, and manufactures of, not otherwise specified | 4,234,082 | 7,222,670 | 6,574,483 | 0·79 |
| 24 | Feathers; flowers, artificial; perfumery, pipes, toys, &c. | 5,412,887 | 6,196,262 | 6,097,221 | 0·73 |
| 25 | Paper stock, crude | 5,261,448 | 5,018,248 | 5,418,263 | 0·66 |
| 26 | Breadstuffs and other farinaceous substances | 7,142,998 | 5,028,209 | 4,889,147 | 0·59 |
| 27 | Fish, not elsewhere specified | 4,590,585 | 5,044,628 | 4,585,450 | 0·55 |
| 28 | Coal, bituminous | 3,087,760 | 3,588,273 | 4,373,079 | 0·53 |
| 29 | Animals | 6,766,932 | 4,915,365 | 4,251,616 | 0·51 |
| 30 | Books, maps, engravings, and other printed matter | 3,994,070 | 4,227,403 | 3,996,085 | 0·48 |
| 31 | Cement | 2,172,952 | 4,021,998 | 3,855,572 | 0·47 |
| 32 | Lead, and manufactures of | 657,658 | 2,560,886 | 3,653,378 | 0·44 |
| 33 | Paper | 2,816,860 | 3,031,454 | 3,342,304 | 0·40 |
| 34 | Articles, the growth, produce, &c., of the United States, returned, except distilled spirits | 3,133,406 | 2,421,354 | 3,268,535 | 0·40 |
| 35 | Cocoa, crude, and leaves and shells of | 2,312,781 | 2,817,168 | 3,221,041 | 0·39 |
| 36 | Spices | 3,223,071 | 3,151,833 | 3,047,825 | 0·37 |
| 37 | Rice | 2,540,674 | 4,559,540 | 3,030,883 | 0·37 |
| 38 | Vegetables | 4,455,374 | 7,076,374 | 2,883,227 | 0·35 |
| 39 | Art works: paintings and statuary | 2,196,500 | 2,410,368 | 2,336,668 | 0·28 |
| 40 | Seeds, not medicinal | 4,089,814 | 3,266,230 | 2,264,837 | 0·27 |
| 41 | Clocks and watches, and parts of | 2,114,284 | 2,884,906 | 1,930,538 | 0·23 |
| 42 | Hats, bonnets, and hoods, and materials for | 3,398,657 | 2,222,660 | 1,897,190 | 0·23 |
| 43 | Hair, and manufactures of | 3,026,566 | 2,408,733 | 1,799,664 | 0·22 |
|  | All other articles | 48,073,114 | 51,015,140 | 47,256,883 | 5·71 |
|  | Total value of imports of merchandise | 789,310,409 | 844,916,196 | 827,402,462 | 100·00 |

(1465)

## UNITED STATES.

**Imports from different countries.**

TABLE showing the Values of Imports into the United States from Foreign Countries during the Years ending June 30, 1890 and 1892 respectively, with the Percentage of the Aggregate Value of Imports from each Country during 1892.

| Order. | Countries from which Imported. | 1890. | 1892. | Per Cent of total for 1892. |
|---|---|---|---|---|
| | | Dollars. | Dollars. | |
| 1 | United Kingdom | 186,488,956 | 156,300,881 | 18·89 |
| 2 | Brazil | 59,318,756 | 118,633,604 | 14·34 |
| 3 | West Indies, including Bermuda | 78,004,241 | 100,158,620 | 12·11 |
| 4 | Germany | 98,837,683 | 82,907,553 | 10·02 |
| 5 | France | 77,672,311 | 68,554,793 | 8·29 |
| 6 | British North American Possessions | 39,396,980 | 35,334,547 | 4·27 |
| 7 | Mexico | 22,690,915 | 28,107,525 | 3·40 |
| 8 | British India and East Indies | 20,804,319 | 24,773,107 | 3·00 |
| 9 | Japan | 21,103,324 | 23,790,202 | 2·89 |
| 10 | Italy | 20,330,051 | 22,161,617 | 2·68 |
| 11 | China | 16,260,471 | 20,488,291 | 2·46 |
| 12 | Switzerland | 14,441,950 | 13,196,469 | 1·60 |
| 13 | Netherlands | 17,029,233 | 10,886,802 | 1·32 |
| 14 | Central American States and British Honduras | 8,239,275 | 10,453,313 | 1·26 |
| 15 | Venezuela | 10,966,765 | 10,325,338 | 1·25 |
| 16 | Belgium | 9,336,482 | 10,273,061 | 1·24 |
| 17 | British Australasia | 4,277,676 | 8,492,306 | 1·03 |
| 18 | Hawaiian Islands | 12,313,908 | 8,075,882 | ·98 |
| 19 | Austria-Hungary | 9,331,378 | 7,718,565 | ·93 |
| 20 | Dutch East Indies | 5,791,250 | 6,914,743 | ·84 |
| 21 | Philippine Islands | 11,592,626 | 6,308,653 | ·75 |
| 22 | Argentine Republic | 5,401,697 | 5,343,798 | ·64 |
| 23 | Spain | 5,288,537 | 5,207,861 | ·63 |
| 24 | British Guiana | 4,326,975 | 4,363,204 | ·53 |
| 25 | Colombia | 3,575,253 | 4,116,886 | ·50 |
| 26 | Sweden and Norway | 3,534,890 | 3,754,932 | ·45 |
| 27 | Chile | 3,183,249 | 3,487,159 | ·42 |
| 28 | Russia on the Baltic and White Seas | 2,002,179 | 3,001,912 | ·36 |
| 29 | Turkey in Asia | 2,437,108 | 2,898,833 | ·35 |
| 30 | Uruguay | 1,754,903 | 2,480,596 | ·30 |
| 31 | British Possessions, all other | 1,711,630 | 2,307,444 | ·28 |
| 32 | Turkey in Africa | 759,122 | 2,330,639 | ·28 |
| 33 | Turkey in Europe | 1,426,549 | 2,028,208 | ·25 |
| 34 | Portugal | 1,418,309 | 1,966,369 | ·24 |
| 35 | Russia on the Black Sea | 1,304,442 | 1,914,718 | ·23 |
| 36 | Greece | 1,125,098 | 1,300,449 | ·15 |
| 37 | All other countries in Africa | 1,061,317 | 1,191,140 | ·14 |
| 38 | British Africa | 957,321 | 816,597 | ·10 |
| 39 | Ecuador | 535,060 | 809,831 | ·10 |
| 40 | Hong-Kong | 969,745 | 763,323 | ·09 |
| | All other countries | 2,290,475 | 3,452,691 | ·41 |
| | Total | 789,310,409 | 827,402,462 | 100·00 |

TABLE showing the Value of Free and Dutiable Merchandise Imported into the United States from each Country and Grand Division of the Globe during the Fiscal Year ending June 30, 1892.

*Free and dutiable imports from each country.*

| Countries. | Free of Duty. | Dutiable. | Total. | Free. | Dutiable. |
|---|---|---|---|---|---|
| | Dollars. | Dollars. | Dollars. | Per cent. | Per cent. |
| Europe— | | | | | |
| Austria-Hungary | 2,616,472 | 5,102,093 | 7,718,565 | 33·90 | 66·10 |
| Azores, and Madeira Islands | 9,553 | 25,118 | 34,671 | 27·61 | 72·39 |
| Belgium | 2,781,858 | 7,491,203 | 10,273,061 | 27·08 | 72·92 |
| Denmark | 126,595 | 101,950 | 228,545 | 55·39 | 44·61 |
| France | 8,068,044 | 60,486,749 | 68,554,793 | 11·77 | 88·23 |
| Germany | 18,869,832 | 64,037,721 | 82,907,553 | 22·75 | 77·25 |
| Gibraltar | 76,314 | 10,617 | 86,931 | 87·71 | 12·29 |
| Greece | 1,183,243 | 117,206 | 1,300,449 | 91·00 | 9·00 |
| Greenland, Iceland, and the Faroe Islands | 76,350 | 29 | 76,379 | 99·96 | 0·04 |
| Italy | 10,901,745 | 11,259,872 | 22,161,617 | 49·19 | 50·81 |
| Netherlands | 2,652,139 | 8,234,663 | 10,886,802 | 24·36 | 75·64 |
| Portugal | 1,575,880 | 390,489 | 1,966,369 | 80·16 | 19·84 |
| Russia on the Baltic and White Seas | 832,976 | 2,178,936 | 3,011,912 | 27·64 | 72·36 |
| Russia on the Black Sea | 625,368 | 1,289,350 | 1,914,718 | 32·64 | 67·36 |
| Servia | 17,753 | ... | 17,753 | 100·00 | ... |
| Spain | 1,234,284 | 3,973,577 | 5,207,861 | 23·60 | 76·40 |
| Sweden and Norway | 139,238 | 3,615,694 | 3,754,932 | 3·58 | 96·42 |
| Switzerland | 929,170 | 12,267,299 | 13,196,469 | 7·08 | 92·92 |
| Turkey in Europe | 1,055,392 | 972,816 | 2,028,208 | 51·99 | 48·01 |
| United Kingdom | 35,367,178 | 120,933,703 | 156,300,881 | 22·63 | 77·37 |
| Total | 89,139,384 | 302,489,085 | 391,628,469 | 22·76 | 77·24 |
| North America— | | | | | |
| Bermuda | 155,411 | 396,904 | 552,315 | 28·10 | 71·90 |
| British Honduras | 233,149 | 376 | 233,525 | 99·85 | 0·15 |
| British North American possessions | 9,923,299 | 25,411,248 | 35,334,547 | 25·18 | 74·82 |
| Central American States | 10,215,187 | 4,601 | 10,219,788 | 99·96 | 0·04 |
| Mexico | 23,702,496 | 4,405,029 | 29,107,525 | 84·35 | 15·65 |
| Miquelon, Langley and St. Pierre Islands | ... | 176 | 176 | ... | 100·00 |
| West Indies— | | | | | |
| British West Indies | 11,897,999 | 542,133 | 12,440,132 | 95·64 | 4·36 |
| Spanish West Indies | 69,377,172 | 11,802,506 | 81,179,678 | 85·44 | 14·56 |
| All other West Indies | 5,894,681 | 91,814 | 5,986,495 | 98·47 | 1·53 |
| Total | 131,399,394 | 42,654,787 | 174,054,181 | 75·51 | 24·49 |
| South America— | | | | | |
| Argentine Republic | 3,921,623 | 1,422,175 | 5,343,798 | 73·40 | 26·60 |
| Brazil | 118,428,158 | 205,446 | 118,633,604 | 99·86 | 0·14 |
| Chile | 3,179,638 | 207,521 | 3,487,159 | 91·18 | 8·82 |
| Colombia | 3,641,957 | 474,929 | 4,116,886 | 88·48 | 11·52 |
| Ecuador | 807,187 | 2,644 | 809,831 | 99·64 | 0·36 |
| Guiana | 4,938,979 | 268 | 4,939,247 | 99·98 | 0·02 |
| Peru | 555,959 | 35,341 | 591,300 | 94·07 | 5·93 |
| Uruguay | 1,883,927 | 596,669 | 2,480,596 | 75·96 | 24·04 |
| Venezuela | 9,174,816 | 1,150,522 | 10,325,338 | 88·84 | 11·16 |
| Total | 146,532,244 | 4,195,515 | 150,727,759 | 97·23 | 2·77 |
| Asia— | | | | | |
| China | 15,936,431 | 4,551,860 | 20,488,291 | 77·74 | 22·26 |
| East Indies— | | | | | |
| British | 19,741,725 | 5,031,382 | 24,773,107 | 78·60 | 21·40 |
| Dutch | 6,856,585 | 58,158 | 6,914,743 | 99·17 | 0·83 |
| Hong-Kong | 376,483 | 386,840 | 763,323 | 49·30 | 50·70 |
| Japan | 20,134,718 | 3,655,484 | 23,790,202 | 84·60 | 15·40 |
| Corea | 608 | ... | 608 | 100·00 | ... |
| Russia, Asiatic | 319,901 | 266 | 320,167 | 99·97 | 0·03 |
| Turkey in Asia | 1,374,013 | 1,524,820 | 2,898,833 | 47·38 | 52·62 |
| All other countries in Asia | 161,593 | 2,384 | 188,977 | 85·50 | 14·50 |
| Total | 64,902,057 | 15,236,194 | 80,138,251 | 81·03 | 18·97 |
| Oceania— | | | | | |
| British Australasia | 4,441,496 | 4,050,810 | 8,492,306 | 52·31 | 47·69 |
| French possessions in Oceania | 248,979 | 7,242 | 256,221 | 97·65 | 2·35 |
| Hawaiian Islands | 8,062,076 | 13,806 | 8,075,882 | 99·83 | 0·17 |
| Philippine Islands | 6,239,642 | 69,011 | 6,308,653 | 98·92 | 1·08 |
| Total | 18,992,193 | 4,140,869 | 23,133,062 | 82·10 | 17·90 |

TABLE showing the Value of Free and Dutiable Merchandise Imported into the United States from each Country and Grand Division of the Globe during the Fiscal Year ending June 30, 1892—continued.

| Countries. | Free of Duty. | Dutiable. | Total. | Free. | Dutiable. |
|---|---|---|---|---|---|
| | Dollars. | Dollars. | Dollars. | Per cent. | Per cent. |
| Africa— | | | | | |
| British Africa | 545,141 | 271,456 | 816,597 | 66·76 | 33·24 |
| Canary Islands | 32,467 | 29,003 | 61,470 | 52·87 | 47·13 |
| French Africa | 356,253 | 274,452 | 630,705 | 56·54 | 43·46 |
| Liberia | 21,271 | ... | 21,271 | 100·00 | ... |
| Madagascar | 252,650 | ... | 252,650 | 100·00 | ... |
| Turkey in Africa: Egypt and Tripoli | 2,249,003 | 81,636 | 2,330,639 | 96·52 | 3·48 |
| All other countries in Africa | 1,199,426 | 5,294 | 1,204,720 | 99·62 | 0·38 |
| Total | 4,656,211 | 661,841 | 5,318,052 | 87·56 | 12·44 |
| All other countries— | | | | | |
| British possessions, all other | 2,306,053 | 1,391 | 2,307,444 | 99·85 | 0·15 |
| All other islands and ports | 72,122 | 23,122 | 95,244 | 75·76 | 24·24 |
| Total | 2,378,175 | 24,513 | 2,402,688 | 99·00 | 1·00 |
| Grand total | 457,999,658 | 369,402,804 | 827,402,462 | 55·35 | 44·65 |

RECAPITULATION.

| Grand Divisions. | Free of Duty. | Dutiable. | Total. | Free. | Dutiable. |
|---|---|---|---|---|---|
| | Dollars. | Dollars. | Dollars. | Per cent. | Per cent. |
| Europe | 89,139,384 | 302,489,085 | 391,628,469 | 22·76 | 77·24 |
| North America | 131,399,394 | 42,654,787 | 174,054,181 | 75·51 | 24·49 |
| South America | 146,532,244 | 4,195,515 | 150,727,759 | 97·23 | 2·77 |
| Asia | 64,902,057 | 15,236,194 | 80,138,251 | 81·03 | 18·97 |
| Oceania | 18,992,193 | 4,140,869 | 23,133,062 | 82·10 | 17·90 |
| Africa | 4,656,211 | 661,841 | 5,318,052 | 87·56 | 12·44 |
| All other countries | 2,378,175 | 24,513 | 2,402,688 | 90·00 | 1·00 |
| Total | 457,999,658 | 369,402,804 | 827,402,462 | 55·35 | 44·65 |

*Imports and Exports.*

**Imports and exports for calendar year 1892.** The total value of the exports and imports of the United States for the calendar year 1892 was 1,814,618,072 dol. (362,923,614*l.*), a decrease of 43,062,538 dol. (8,612,507*l.*) compared with the fiscal year ending June 30, 1892.

**Imports.** The value of the imports of the United States for the same period amounted to 876,198,179 dol. (175,239,635*l.*), an increase of 48,795,717 dol. (9,759,143*l.*) over the fiscal year ending June 30, 1892.

**Exports.** The value of the exports of the United States for the same period amounted to 938,419,893 dol. (187,683,978*l.*), a decrease of 91,858,255 dol. (18,371,651*l.*) as compared with the fiscal year ending June 30, 1892.

**Value of domestic exports.** The following is a statement of the principal and all other articles of domestic exports for the calendar year 1892, and their values:—

## WASHINGTON.

| Classes of Articles. | 1892. |
|---|---|
| | Dollars. |
| Food animals and their products— | |
|    Hogs | 449,741 |
|    Hog products | 90,938,556 |
|    Cattle | 35,351,664 |
|    Beef products | 35,377,461 |
|    Dairy products | 10,053,158 |
|    All other meat products | 11,038,884* |
|    Sheep | 145,680* |
|       Total | 183,355,144 |
| Breadstuffs | 247,573,791 |
| Cotton, raw | 216,787,714 |
| Mineral oils | 42,696,701 |
| All other articles | 232,822,962 |
|       Total domestic exports | 923,236,312 |

\* Eleven months ending November 30.

The following table shows the values of the imports and exports of merchandise during each calendar year from 1870 to 1892 inclusive; also the annual excess of imports or of exports:—

*Value of imports and exports from 1870-92.*

## UNITED STATES.

### TABLE showing Imports and Exports of Merchandise.

| Year ending December 31. | Exports. Domestic. | Exports. Foreign. | Total Exports. | Imports. | Total Exports and Imports. | Excess of Exports over Imports. | Excess of Imports over Exports. |
|---|---|---|---|---|---|---|---|
| | Dollars. | Dollars. | Dollars. | Dollars. | Dollars. | Dollars. | Dollars. |
| 1870 | 387,780,302 | 15,805,708 | 403,586,010 | 461,132,058 | 864,718,068 | | 57,546,048 |
| 1871 | 445,563,259 | 14,788,829 | 460,352,088 | 573,111,099 | 1,033,463,187 | | 112,759,011 |
| 1872 | 452,143,553 | 16,694,395 | 468,837,948 | 655,964,699 | 1,124,802,647 | | 187,126,751 |
| 1873 | 550,098,492 | 17,659,375 | 567,757,867 | 595,248,048 | 1,163,005,915 | | 27,490,181 |
| 1874 | 553,929,342 | 15,943,211 | 569,872,553 | 562,115,907 | 1,131,988,460 | 7,756,646 | |
| 1875 | 497,263,737 | 13,683,685 | 510,947,422 | 503,152,936 | 1,014,100,358 | 7,794,486 | |
| 1876 | 575,735,804 | 14,930,825 | 590,666,629 | 427,347,165 | 1,018,013,794 | 163,319,464 | |
| 1877 | 607,566,495 | 12,735,917 | 620,302,412 | 480,246,300 | 1,100,548,712 | 140,056,112 | |
| 1878 | 723,286,821 | 13,805,252 | 737,092,073 | 431,812,483 | 1,168,904,556 | 305,279,590 | |
| 1879 | 754,656,755 | 10,503,070 | 765,159,825 | 513,602,796 | 1,278,762,621 | 251,557,029 | |
| 1880 | 875,564,075 | 14,119,347 | 889,683,422 | 696,807,176 | 1,586,490,598 | 192,876,246 | |
| 1881 | 814,162,951 | 19,386,176 | 833,549,127 | 670,209,448 | 1,503,758,575 | 163,339,679 | |
| 1882 | 749,911,309 | 18,070,637 | 767,981,946 | 752,843,507 | 1,520,825,453 | 15,138,439 | |
| 1883 | 777,523,718 | 17,685,598 | 795,209,316 | 687,066,216 | 1,482,275,532 | 108,143,100 | |
| 1884 | 733,768,764 | 15,597,664 | 749,366,428 | 629,261,860 | 1,378,628,288 | 120,104,568 | |
| 1885 | 673,593,506 | 14,656,292 | 688,249,798 | 587,868,673 | 1,276,118,471 | 100,381,125 | |
| 1886 | 699,519,430 | 13,884,591 | 713,404,021 | 663,429,189 | 1,376,833,210 | 49,974,832 | |
| 1887 | 703,319,692 | 11,981,352 | 715,301,044 | 708,818,478 | 1,424,119,522 | 6,482,566 | |
| 1888 | 679,597,477 | 12,163,266 | 691,760,743 | 725,202,714 | 1,416,963,457 | | 33,441,971 |
| 1889 | 814,154,864 | 12,951,483 | 827,106,347 | 770,526,484 | 1,597,632,831 | 56,579,863 | |
| 1890 | 845,999,603 | 11,502,945 | 857,502,548 | 823,397,726 | 1,680,900,274 | 34,104,822 | |
| 1891 | 957,333,551 | 13,176,095 | 970,509,646 | 828,330,943 | 1,798,830,589 | 142,188,703 | |
| 1892 | 923,226,312 | 15,193,581 | 938,419,893 | 876,198,179 | 1,814,618,072 | 62,221,714 | |

It will be seen from this table that the excess of exports over imports for the calendar year 1892 amounted to only 62,221,714 dol. (12,444,342), while the excess of exports over imports for the fiscal year ending June 30, 1892, amounted to 202,875,686 dol. (40,575,137*l*.), a difference of 140,653,972 dol. (28,130,794*l*.).

*Excess of exports compared with fiscal year.*

The enormous excess of exports over imports for the fiscal year ending June 30, 1892, has been widely quoted by the Protectionists in this country as evidence of the beneficial effect of the McKinley Act. But in reality this excess was caused by the large increase of exports of agricultural produce the result of the extraordinary crops of 1891, and had nothing whatever to do with the tariff. In relation to this point, the comparisons given above between the excess of exports over imports for the fiscal year ending June 30, 1892, and the calendar year ending December 31, 1892, will be found interesting.

*Remarks.*

In examining the various tables which I have given in this report, it is impossible not to be struck with the importance and magnitude of the trade of Great Britain with the United States. In 1860 the export trade of the United States to Great Britain amounted to about 166,000,000 dol. During the fiscal year ending June 30, 1892, it reached a total of no less than 474,000,000 dol., or nearly half the total exports of domestic merchandise from the United States to all countries. When it is considered that nearly the whole of these exports consisted of agricultural produce it will be seen how great a factor in the agricultural industries of the United States is the demand of the British market.

*Magnitude of commerce with Great Britain.*

LONDON:
Printed for Her Majesty's Stationery Office,
By HARRISON AND SONS,
Printers in Ordinary to Her Majesty.
(75  3 | 93—H & S  1465)

# FOREIGN OFFICE.
## 1893.
### ANNUAL SERIES.

### No. 1164.

### DIPLOMATIC AND CONSULAR REPORTS ON TRADE AND FINANCE.

# UNITED STATES.

### REPORT FOR THE YEAR 1892

ON THE

### TRADE OF THE CONSULAR DISTRICT OF GALVESTON.

REFERENCE TO PREVIOUS REPORT, Annual Series No. 989.

*Presented to both Houses of Parliament by Command of Her Majesty,*
*APRIL, 1893.*

LONDON:
PRINTED FOR HER MAJESTY'S STATIONERY OFFICE,
BY HARRISON AND SONS, ST. MARTIN'S LANE,
PRINTERS IN ORDINARY TO HER MAJESTY.

And to be purchased, either directly or through any Bookseller, from
EYRE & SPOTTISWOODE, EAST HARDING STREET, FLEET STREET, E.C., and
32, ABINGDON STREET, WESTMINSTER, S.W.; or
JOHN MENZIES & Co., 12, HANOVER STREET, EDINBURGH, and
90, WEST NILE STREET, GLASGOW; or
HODGES, FIGGIS, & Co., Limited, 104, GRAFTON STREET, DUBLIN.

1893.

[C. 6855—51.]   *Price Three Halfpence.*

# New Series of Reports.

Reports of the Annual Series have been issued from Her Majesty's Diplomatic and Consular Officers at the following places, and may be obtained from the sources indicated on the title-page:—

| No. | | Price. | No. | | Price. |
|---|---|---|---|---|---|
| 1042. | Taganrog | 2½d. | 1103. | Chicago | 3d. |
| 1043. | Algiers | 2½d. | 1104. | Erzeroum | ½d. |
| 1044. | Hankow | 1½d. | 1105. | Loanda | 3d. |
| 1045. | Nantes | 1½d. | 1106. | Macao | ½d. |
| 1046. | Belgrade | 2d. | 1107. | Canton | 1d. |
| 1047. | Fiume | 1d. | 1108. | Paramaribo | 1½d. |
| 1048. | Wuhu | 1d. | 1109. | Tunis | 1½d. |
| 1049. | Cagliari | 1d. | 1110. | Sofia | 3d. |
| 1050. | Erzeroum | 1d. | 1111. | Brunei | 1½d. |
| 1051. | Syra | 1d. | 1112. | Athens | 2½d. |
| 1052. | Cherbourg | 1d. | 1113. | Alexandria | 2d. |
| 1053. | Lima | 1d. | 1114. | Vienna | 1d. |
| 1054. | Bilbao | 1½d. | 1115. | Stettin | 2½d. |
| 1055. | Cadiz | 2d. | 1116. | Berne | 1d. |
| 1056. | Corunna | 2½d. | 1117. | Palermo | 2½d. |
| 1057. | Saigon | 1d. | 1118. | Tokio | 1½d. |
| 1058. | Port-au-Prince | 1d. | 1119. | St. Petersburg | 3d. |
| 1059. | Trebizond | 1d. | 1120. | Teneriffe | 1d. |
| 1060. | Barcelona | 1½d. | 1121. | Damascus | 1d. |
| 1061. | Tainan | 1d. | 1122. | Naples | 2d. |
| 1062. | Smyrna | 1½d. | 1123. | Hakodate | 1d. |
| 1063. | Old Calabar | ½d. | 1124. | Montevideo | 2½d. |
| 1064. | Samoa | ½d. | 1125. | Stockholm | 1½d. |
| 1065. | Tahiti | 1d. | 1126. | Dantzig | 2d. |
| 1066. | Chefoo | 6d. | 1127. | The Hague | 1½d. |
| 1067. | Gothenburg | 2d. | 1128. | Odessa | 1d. |
| 1068. | Buenos Ayres | 1½d. | 1129. | Berne | 1½d. |
| 1069. | Loanda | 1½d. | 1130. | Malaga | 3d. |
| 1070. | Guatemala | 1d. | 1131. | Rome | 2½d. |
| 1071. | Zanzibar | 1d. | 1132. | St. Jago de Cuba | 4½d. |
| 1072. | Charleston | 2½d. | 1133. | Munich | 1½d. |
| 1073. | Nice | 1d. | 1134. | Meshed | 1d. |
| 1074. | Caracas | 1d. | 1135. | Guayaquil | ½d. |
| 1075. | Lisbon | 2d. | 1136. | Rio de Janeiro | 4½d. |
| 1076. | Calais | 2d. | 1137. | Tonga | 1d. |
| 1077. | Rio Grande do Sul | 5½d. | 1138. | Copenhagen | 1d. |
| 1078. | Philadelphia | 2½d. | 1139. | Tangier | 1½d. |
| 1079. | Brindisi | 2d. | 1140. | Buenos Ayres | 2½d. |
| 1080. | New York | 2d. | 1141. | Para | 1d. |
| 1081. | San Francisco | 1½d. | 1142. | Baghdad and Bussorah | 1½d. |
| 1082. | Frankfort | 4d. | 1143. | Christiania | 5½d. |
| 1083. | Hiogo | 1½d. | 1144. | Old Calabar | 2d. |
| 1084. | Tokio | 1½d. | 1145. | Trieste | 1½d. |
| 1085. | Amsterdam | 1d. | 1146. | Quito | 1d. |
| 1086. | San Francisco | 3d. | 1147. | Buenos Ayres | 6d. |
| 1087. | Bangkok | ½d. | 1148. | Bogotá | 1d. |
| 1088. | Söul | 1½d. | 1149. | The Hague | 2d. |
| 1089. | Chiengmai | 1d. | 1150. | Mexico | 2½d. |
| 1090. | Copenhagen | ½d. | 1151. | Florence | 1d. |
| 1091. | New Caledonia | ½d. | 1152. | Calais | 1d. |
| 1092. | Bushire | 2d. | 1153. | Lorenzo Marques | 1½d. |
| 1093. | Tamsui | 1d. | 1154. | Patras | 1d. |
| 1094. | Dunkirk | 1d. | 1155. | Taganrog | 1d. |
| 1095. | Port Said | 1d. | 1156. | Stockholm | 1d. |
| 1096. | Guatemala | ½d. | 1157. | Washington | 2d. |
| 1097. | Chungking | 9d. | 1158. | Paris | 1½d. |
| 1098. | Nagasaki | 1d. | 1159. | Bengazi | 1d. |
| 1099. | Constantinople | 2d. | 1160. | Santos | 2½d. |
| 1100. | Buenos Ayres | ½d. | 1161. | Buenos Ayres | 1½d. |
| 1101. | Shanghai | 2d. | 1162. | Nantes | 1d. |
| 1102. | Jeddah | ½d. | 1163. | Beira | 5d. |

# No. 1164.

*Reference to previous Report, Annual Series No. 989.*

## UNITED STATES.

### GALVESTON.

*Consul Nugent to the Earl of Rosebery.*

My Lord,                    *Galveston, February* 25, 1893.

I HAVE the honour to transmit herewith enclosed my Annual Report on the Trade and Commerce of my Consular District for the year 1892.

I have, &c.
(Signed)     HORACE D. NUGENT.

---

*Report on the Trade and Commerce of the Consular District of Galveston for the Year* 1892.

ABSTRACT of Contents.

| | PAGE |
|---|---|
| **Texas—** | |
| Introductory remarks.. | 2 |
| Message of the Governor; condition of the State .. | 2 |
| Land Corporations .. | 2 |
| Imports .. | 3 |
| Exports.. | 3 |
| Cotton trade; freights; cotton-fires .. | 4 |
| Grain trade .. | 4 |
| Galveston Harbour Works .. | 4 |
| Manufactures .. | 5 |
| Agriculture .. | 5 |
| Fisheries .. | 6 |
| Railroads .. | 6 |
| Crime; criminal statistics .. | 6–7 |
| **New Mexico—** | |
| Land Court .. | 7 |
| Population .. | 7 |
| Finances .. | 8 |
| Public surveys.. | 8 |
| Irrigation .. | 8 |
| Climate .. | 8 |
| Agriculture and horticulture.. | 9 |
| Stock raising; cattle; sheep; wool.. | 9 |
| Mining; coal .. | 9 |
| New industries .. | 9 |
| Railroads .. | 10 |
| Tables .. | 11–20 |

(1483)

## UNITED STATES.

**Introductory remarks.**

The year 1892, and especially the latter half, has been on the whole a very prosperous one for the State of Texas, in particular have the farmers been fortunate. Crops were produced more cheaply than at any time in the history of the State. They planted cotton, expecting to receive 6 c. for it and received nearly 9 c.; they raised maize both for home consumption and for export. The stock-raising industry has been prosperous, and on the whole it is estimated that the producers in Texas are some 10,000,000*l.* better off than was expected 6 months ago. The prospects, too, are good, and the coming year promises to be a bountiful one. It all remains with the farmer to say whether his crops shall be remunerative or not. If he plants cotton alone, over-production and less remuneration must naturally follow: and the wise man will make a point of diversifying his crop. The danger is that the farmers may take last year as an index of what they should do not making allowance for the accidents that assisted the planters then.

As a consequence of the prosperity of the farmer, business in general has been brisk and remunerative, especially during the last few months. Collections have everywhere been promptly met, and the general feeling has been good. Business has been generally successful, as is shown by the number of failures, which are given as 457, amounting to 1,040,800*l.*, as against 539, amounting to 1,792,000*l.* in 1891.

**Message of the Governor.**

I may here appropriately quote from the message of Governor Hogg to the Legislature, presented on January 13 last:—

**Condition of the State.**

"As to law and order, except in two or three cities, Texas is taking first rank in the American Union. In material development she has been second to none of the Southern States within the past 2 years. Official reports show that within this time over 16,000,000 dol. have been invested in new material industries, and 323 miles of railroad constructed, equipped, and put and running operations in the State. To-day she presents the example of a free Government without a pool, a trust, or a combination to stifle competition in trade, and the criminal element convinced that no part of her territory is an asylum for them. Taxes have been decreased 25 per cent., so that they are now lower than in any other Southern State; the rate of interest has been reduced 2 per cent., the Public Debt paid when due, the charitable and all public institutions efficiently maintained without extravagance or scandal, the public health protected from infectious or epidemic diseases, and the people generally are prosperous. There have been less failures in mercantile circles and more universal prosperity diffused throughout every avenue and circle among the masses than the State has witnessed in many years before."

**Land corporations.**

The alien land law, mentioned by my predecessor in his report for 1892 as having caused much discussion, was, subsequent to its passage, declared unconstitutional. Although it has never been repealed it has been suffered to fall into desuetude.

The subject of the perpetuity of title in land caused by corporate ownership was, however, not allowed to drop entirely and Governor Hogg made a strong appeal in his message to the Legislature, which is now in session, to enact a law making such corporate ownership terminable after a given term. The lands now held by such corporations for grazing or other purposes, or that shall be acquired hereafter by them legally in settlement of claims for debt, &c., to revert to natural persons and the corporations to wind up their affairs and quit the State.

Should such a law pass it would naturally materially affect the large British interests in stock-raising and mortgage companies in this State, but although a somewhat emasculated form of such a Bill has been introduced into and passed the Senate it is extremely doubtful whether it will reach the lower House this session, much less become law.

There has been a decrease of about 20 per cent. in the total imports at Galveston during the year, the figures showing 863,981 dol., as against 1,082,151 dol. This is no doubt due to the effect of the McKinley tariff and the large stocks purchased prior to the passing of that Act. The chief decrease is in imports from Germany, Great Britain, and France. The imports from Brazil are about 100,000 dol. more than last year, all in coffee, which is duty free. *Imports: Annex A.*

As regards the chief imports from Great Britain cement has decreased from 86,230 dol. to 51,701 dol.; sheep dip remains about the same; coal has decreased from 20,184 dol. to 8,308 dol.; crockery increased from 9,033 dol. to 11,903 dol.; cotton manufactures have almost been nil; malt liquors have increased from 13,803 dol. to 24,366 dol.; salt has decreased from 32,391 dol. to 15,800 dol.; tin has decreased from 86,726 dol. to 16,483 dol.; new imports of note are burlaps, 16,483 dol., and coal tar oil, 16,818 dol. The total figures as regards Great Britain are 304,314 dol. in 1892, as against 394,483 dol. in 1891. The total imports in transit to Mexico show a decrease from 371,273 dol. to 101,977 dol.

The total exports from the district of Galveston show 35,097,002 dol. in 1892, as against 35,964,460 dol. in 1891, a slight decrease. Exports of cotton have increased in quantity, but owing to the lower prices obtainable have decreased in value. 808,628 bales were exported last year, valued at 32,610,901 dol., as against 774,826 bales in 1891, valued at 34,217,492 dol. The exports of oil cakes have increased from 43,196 tons, valued at 1,008,541 dol., in 1891, to 79,088 tons, valued at 1,867,441 dol., in 1892. The wheat exported in 1892 was 377,985 bushels, value 335,240 dol., as against 587,395 bushels, value 588,058 dol., in 1891. Exports of flour increased from 11,929 barrels to 21,296 barrels. *Exports: Annex B.*

The exports to France and Germany have increased, and those to Great Britain decreased. As regards cotton, in 1891 Great Britain took 668,353 bales, value 29,747,951 dol.; during 1892 she received only 529,795 bales, value 21,008,705 dol., whereas Germany received 143,626 bales, as against 44,269 bales, and France 126,177 bales, as against 45,240 bales. The export of oil cake shows a large increase to Great Britain and Germany over 1891. Great Britain received 23,141 tons, value 549,599 dol., as against 21,105 tons, valued at 470,302 dol. in 1891. Germany 50,466 tons, value 1,217,382 dol., as against 16,670 tons, value 415,791 dol., in 1891.

All the wheat exported was shipped to British ports.

*Cotton trade.* The cotton business has been one of a peculiar character in 1892-93, marked by a gradual steady rise in prices all along. This increase of value has been beneficial to the planter, but not to the exporter, whose business has been by no means remunerative this season.

*Freights.* The season for ship brokers and freight brokers has been most disastrous, and much money has been lost; the large gains of last year being completely upset, and in many instances swept away, owing to the excessively low rates of freight.

*Cotton fires.* These have been very numerous here this season, so much so as to excite the suspicion in some cases of incendiarism. In consequence of these fires insurance rates have ruled very high upon cotton. Steps will be taken next season, it is hoped, for a still more thorough inspection of cotton on arrival and during loading.

*Grain trade.* In the last month or two the grain trade has taken a surprising step forward, and bids fair to develop into a very important business. From November 24, 1892, the date on which reduced rates went into force on the Santa Fé Railway, to and including January 20, 1893, there have been bought 1,233,500 bushels of wheat for Galveston, of this amount 975,000 bushels are for export. As the total amount of wheat exported in 1892 was but 377,985 bushels, a large development of the grain-carrying trade is looked for in 1893. Several vessels are shortly expected here to load with grain, and the grain elevator is in constant use.

Galveston, as an export point for grain, has only been known to exist, one may say, for the past two or three months, nor has she been able to receive and handle large quantities of grain continuously for a longer period. But now with her modern handling facilities and the doing away with unnecessary expense of interior handling and commissions, her exporters buying direct, she has been able to buy within a short period, chiefly from Kansas, more grain than the railroads leading here could handle; and they are now increasing their facilities expressly for this business.

*Galveston harbour works.* The work for deepening the bar of Galveston harbour, alluded to in my predecessor's report, has made fair progress during 1892. 12,422 cars of stone, amounting to 226,594 tons, were delivered to the contractors during the year. Nearly 2 miles of jetty were completed, that is to say, 9,120 lineal feet of railroad and trestle at an average cost of 4 dol. per foot. During the last month the water has been exceptionally low, causing great inconvenience and cost to ship brokers and merchants. So much has this been felt that recently permission has been granted by the United States War Department for private enterprise to attempt to hasten the work of obtaining deep water by dredging or otherwise moving the sand on the bar. As the question of deep water is felt to be one affecting the vital interests of Galveston there is no doubt that some such attempt will be made shortly by private capitalists. The supposed beneficial effect of the jetties cannot presumably be fully felt till the completion of the entire enterprise, probably not earlier than 3 years from now.

*Manufactures.* The manufacturing statistics of Galveston taken at the last census have recently been published. Only such establishments as show a product of 500 dol. or more in value in the census year have been considered.

In 1880 there were 39 industries reported, with 170 establishments, with a capital of 871,350 dol., and employing 684 hands. In 1890 55 industries were reported, with capital invested of 4,831,345 dol., and 1,916 hands were engaged. Chief amongst the industries are 3 clothing establishments, 8 confectioneries, 6 foundry and machine shops, 5 newspaper and periodical printing offices, and 5 book and job printing establishments. Besides the above, a cotton mill employing a large number of hands, a well-known flour mill, and a bagging factory are prominent enterprises in Galveston. The latter employs 225, and the output is 6,000,000 yards of bagging, which covers about half the cotton crop of Texas, and nearly all the baling twine used. In connection with the bagging factory a rope factory has just been started to employ 80 to 100 hands.

*Agriculture.* The cotton crop in Texas for 1892–93 is estimated at about 2,000,000 bales, nearly 30 per cent. of the total crop of the United States. This is not as large as that of 1891–92, which aggregated 2,200,000 bales, the heaviest ever known. The present crop, no doubt, would have been larger, considering the area planted, had not bad weather materially interfered with its growth. This, however, was greatly in favour of the farmer, as I have noted in my introductory remarks, as a much better price was obtained than was anticipated.

The wheat crop of 1892 was about the same as that of 1891, viz., 8,000,000 bushels. Here again the crop realised was much below that expected, which was figured at 12,000,000 bushels.

Sugar was produced to the extent of 15,000,000 lbs., as against 18,000,000 lbs. to 19,000,000 lbs. in 1891.

The maize crop was heavier in the past year than in 1891, 75,000,000 bushels to 80,000,000 bushels, as against 71,000,000 bushels.

Oats were about the same, 15,000,000 bushels.

*Fruit* Besides the above, the industry of fruit growing is largely on the increase, and very favourable results have been had. Oranges, pears, peaches, plums, apricots, strawberries, and grapes of excellent quality can all be cultivated with but little expense and care, and it is not uncommon to find two crops of fruit and three of vegetables produced on the same land in one year. The industry is yet too young for any reliable statistics to be obtained, yet it is undoubtedly most successful, as also vegetable farming.

The corrected figures taken by the census officers in 1889 show that in that year there were 3,963,360 acres under cultivation in cereals, as compared with 3,089,068 acres in 1879, an increase of 874,292 acres, or 28 per cent. to 30 per cent. There was an increase of 606,279 acres in the area of maize, 290,845 acres in that of oats, and 1,904 acres in rye, while the area of land under cultivation of wheat decreased 22,004 acres, and of 2,783 acres in that of barley. At the same rate of increase mentioned above the area now under cultivation in cereals in 1892 in Texas would be 4,225,637 acres.

**Fisheries.** The fisheries in the Gulf States are of interest, and remarkable for their recent growth, and for the possibilities of greater future advancement. It is noteworthy that in recent years they have surpassed, both in extent and value, the fisheries of the South Atlantic region. As regards Texas, the coast line of the State is 2,010 miles, including indentations, affording ample scope for the fishing industries. The chief drawback is the want of good transportation facilities. In 1890, the date of the last report issued, 1,277 persons found employment in connection with the Texas fisheries, an increase of 112 per cent. since 1880. The capital invested in the various branches of the industry was, in 1890, 319,122 dol., an increase of not less than 652 per cent. since 1880. The product of the Texas fisheries in 1890 was 7,959,400 lbs., valued at 313,832 dol. More than two-fifths of the value of the catch represented oysters. Sea trout, channel bass, and sheephead together were worth nearly as much as oysters. Over 1,000,000 lbs. of each of the two first-named fish were taken, and nearly 800,000 lbs. of the latter, the catch of these species being larger than in any other State.

In connection with the fisheries are wholesale oyster and fish houses and turtle canning industries. There were 13 of these firms in 1890, owning property valued at 107,500 dol., and with a cash capital of 53,500 dol. 130,900 barrels of oysters were handled, 3,320,000 lbs. of fish, and 243,000 lbs. of turtle.

**Railroads.** There were in 1892 10,107 miles of railway in Texas, of which 8,978 miles were main line and branches, and 1,129 miles sidings, &c. The increase of mileage during the year was 211 miles. The earnings of these various lines for freight amounted to 26,473,838 dol. in the year ending June 30, 1892, compared with 25,777,374 dol. in the year ending June 30, 1891, a net increase of 696,463 dol.

The passenger revenue in Texas for the two years ending June 30, 1891, and June 30, 1892, shows 7,739,136 dol., compared with 7,581,970 dol., a net decrease for the year of 154,166 dol.

The Railway Commission mentioned in my predecessor's report for 1891 is still carrying on its labours, and the above figures are extracted from a report of that body recently issued. A good deal of dissatisfaction exists regarding this Commission, and it is not thought to be beneficial towards building new lines or extending those already built.

**Crime.** Governor Hogg, in that portion of his message quoted by me in my opening remarks, says:—"As to law and order, except in two or three cities, Texas is taking first rank in the American

Union." This view is probably slightly optimistic, for there is no doubt that there is a great deal of lawlessness in Texas, but better things are hoped for in the near future. The dilatory execution of the law, and the fear of a miscarriage of justice through legal quibbles, as well as the disinclination of some communities to relinquish their own execution of what they deem a proper penalty for certain heinous offences, often give rise to lynchings, and these mob-law executions are at times accompanied by shocking barbarities. It is only a few weeks ago that a negro who had outraged and murdered a white child, four years old, was put to death at Paris, in this State, by being burnt with red hot irons, in the presence of 15,000 people, his agony being prolonged for 50 minutes. It is only fair to say that such barbarities are discountenanced by the great majority of the more educated Texans.

Governor Hogg seems to recognise the necessity for stricter enforcement of the laws when he says :—

"It may not be inappropriate here to state that when from a maudlin sentiment, or other less commendable spirit, the people of any country permit offenders against the gaming or other misdemeanour laws, including those regulating the liquor traffic, to go unpunished in their open and defiant criminal course, they must expect to be prepared to submit to the frequent shock of their feelings of humanity by the crack of the assassin's gun. It is as necessary to enforce one law as another. Reform in the suppression of crime, like that of all other reform movements, must begin at the bottom."

On October 31 last there were in the State 3,375 persons undergoing punishment for penitentiary offences, of whom only 57 were women. Of these convicts, 3,073 were born in the United States (1,516 in Texas, 1,556 in other States), and only 502 in foreign countries. *Criminal statistics.*

Of these 3,375 convicts, only 61 came from the county of Galveston, a good testimony to the strict enforcement of the law; arrest and punishment of criminals being probably more certain here than elsewhere in the State.

## New Mexico.

Much satisfaction has been caused by the organisation of the Land Court, where a large number of claims, covering enormous tracts of land claimed under Spanish and Mexican grants, have been presented and a number confirmed. Some amendments of importance have, however, been suggested, and the subject will no doubt be brought before Congress at its present session. *Land court.*

There is a healthy growth in population. The census of 1880 gave 119,565 as the number of inhabitants, while that of 1890, the last available return, showed 153,593, of which number 142,719 were white and 10,874 coloured. The proportion of foreign population is only 8 per cent., or 11,259. *Population.*

**Finances.**

The real population of the territory is now estimated at over 185,000.

There are eight towns of over 1,000 inhabitants, Santa Fé, the capital, having about 7,000.

The assessed valuation of property has remained somewhat stationary during the last 5 years. In 1890 it was 45,199,847 dol., and in 1891 45,329,563 dol.

There has been a large and steady increase in the assessed value of the cattle during the last 5 years, but this has been counterbalanced by the increase of value in other kind.

The indebtedness of New Mexico at the close of the forty-second fiscal year, March 6 last, was 864,806 dol. 12 c., as against 866,433 dol. 3 c. in 1891.

The indebtedness is made up as follows :—

| Description. | Amount. |
| --- | --- |
|  | Dollars c. |
| Capitol Building Bonds, due 1904 | 100,000 00 |
| Capitol Building Bonds, due 1905 | 100,000 00 |
| Penitentiary Building Bonds, due 1894 | 109,000 00 |
| Current Expense Bonds | 150,000 00 |
| Provisional Indebtedness Bonds | 200,000 00 |
| Capitol Contingent Bonds, due 1903 | 50,000 00 |
| Insane Asylums Bonds | 25,000 00 |
| Outstanding warrants | 130,806 12 |
| Total | 864,806 12 |

The expenditures during the fiscal year were 270,923 dol.

**Public surveys.**

During the year ending June 30, 1892, the total number of Government lines established was 1,462. The number of township and mineral plats made in the Surveyor-General's office was 264, and 42 mineral surveys were approved.

The boundary line between New Mexico on the west and Texas and Oklahoma is still unsettled, and gives rise to much difficulty.

**Irrigation.**

The enterprises connected with irrigation in San Juan county have been carried forward, and the admirable systems in Pecos Valley extended. The important work of the Rio Grande Irrigation and Colonisation Company has been unfortunately delayed owing to litigation.

A new company has been formed to increase the water supply of the neighbourhood of Santa Fé, and the prospects are excellent for an extension of the agricultural area in the vicinity of that town. Another company has undertaken an important irrigation enterprise in the Puerco Valley. On the whole, the prospects of the various irrigation enterprises, which are of the utmost importance to New Mexico, are very good.

**Climate.**

New Mexico keeps up its reputation of having one of the finest climates in the world. Public attention throughout the United States and Europe has been more than ever directed to the territory as a sanitorium, and it is hoped by those interested that it may ere long compete with Florida and California as a health resort owing to the equable temperature and the dryness of the atmosphere.

In both agriculture and horticulture there has been both increase and improvement. The area of land employed has been greatly enlarged for grain, vegetables, and especially grasses and alfalfa. *Agriculture and horticulture.*

In horticulture the advance is said to be marvellous, and it is visible everywhere.

The planting of fruit trees at each recurring season is almost universal, and it is not possible even to approximate the number added last year. Off one peach orchard alone 500,000 lbs. of fruit were shipped prior to September 1, 1892.

The cattle business has been by no means prosperous. The number of cattle returned for taxation in 1891 was 1,041,237, as against 1,129,088 in 1890. A great many steers have been shipped and driven to northern ranges and pastures in Kansas and Nebraska during the year at prices varying from an average of 9 dol. for a yearling to 12 dol. for a 2-year-old, and 15 dol. for a 3-year-old and upwards. The total number shipped out of the territory during 1891 was 156,819. *Stock-raising: Cattle.*

The sheep industry continues to be very prosperous and profitable, New Mexico being specially adapted by nature to sheep-raising. Upwards of 200,000 sheep were shipped out to Nebraska and Kansas. Nearly all were wethers, and brought 1 dol. 25 c. to 1 dol. 75 c. for yearlings, and from 2 dol. to 3 dol. for 2 years and upwards per head. *Sheep.*

The wool product during the year 1891 was about 12,000,000 lbs., realising about 2,000,000 dol. For 1892 the product is estimated at 16,000,000 lbs. *Wool.*

The mining industry has fluctuated as usual, but on the whole has been in a flourishing condition during the year. The miners, owing to the McKinley tariff, have been able to secure better compensation, and are relieved from the competition of the cheaply-paid Mexican labourer. *Mining.*

Coal mining is one of the most important industries of New Mexico. It is chiefly carried on at Blossburg, at Amargo, at Gallup, and at Cerrillos. The last-named place has become the most important coal point in the south-western States. The owners of the great coal tracts in the vicinity have combined all interests, and in connection with the Atcheson, Topeka, and Santa Fé Railroad Company are building a number of branches to connect the various mines with the main line. *Coal.*

No exact figures are to be obtained as to the total output of coal in the territory, but the mines at Gallup alone produced 258,500 tons in 1891, and from January 1, 1892, to July 31, 1892, there were sold from these mines 156,200 tons.

Two notable new industries have been introduced lately into New Mexico—(1) the preparation of an extract of canaigre for tanning; (2) the manufacture of firebricks, tiling, &c., at Socorro. *New industries.*

## UNITED STATES.

**Railroads.**

No completed railroads have been added during 1892. The total length existing is 1,445·45 miles. The Atcheson, Topeka, and Santa Fé Railroad is building an extensive system of short roads into the coal region south of Cerillos; these will be over 70 miles in length when completed.

Two projected railroads are attracting some attention, namely, the Denver and El Paso short line, and a road from Durango, through San Juan county, to connect with the Atcheson, Topeka, and Santa Fé Railroad at either Albuquerque or Bernalillo.

The most important enterprise awaiting realisation is known as the Denver and El Paso independent line, which proposes to build a railroad from Trinidad, Colorada, to El Paso, Texas, viâ Las Vegas and White Oaks, with branches and telephone and telegraph lines.

## Annex A.—STATEMENT of Imports subject to Duty at the Port of Galveston for the Year 1892.

GALVESTON.

| Articles. | Germany. | Great Britain. | France. | Netherlands. | Mexico. | Nicaragua. | Porto Rico. | Turkey. | Spain. |
|---|---|---|---|---|---|---|---|---|---|
|  | Dollars. | Dollars. | Dollars. | Dollars. | Dollars. | Dollars. | Dollars. | Dollars. | Dollars. |
| Books and all other printed matter | ... | 1,225 | ... | ... | ... | ... | ... | ... | ... |
| Burlaps (Dundee) | ... | 16,483 | ... | ... | ... | ... | ... | ... | ... |
| Cement in barrrels | 6,099 | 51,701 | ... | 21,122 | ... | ... | 450 | ... | ... |
| Coal, bituminous | ... | 8,308 | ... | ... | ... | ... | ... | ... | ... |
| Coke | ... | 5,240 | ... | ... | ... | ... | ... | ... | ... |
| Chemicals and preparations of— |  |  |  |  |  |  |  |  |  |
| Sheep dip | ... | 57,990 | ... | ... | ... | ... | ... | ... | ... |
| Soda ash | ... | 3,599 | ... | ... | ... | ... | ... | ... | ... |
| ,, caustic | ... | 3,862 | ... | ... | ... | ... | ... | ... | ... |
| Coal tar oil (dead oil) | ... | 16,818 | ... | ... | ... | ... | ... | ... | ... |
| Soda sal | ... | 561 | ... | ... | ... | ... | ... | ... | ... |
| Crockery | 127 | 11,903 | 84 | ... | ... | ... | ... | ... | ... |
| Cotton, manufactures of | ... | 111 | ... | ... | ... | ... | ... | 43 | ... |
| Fish in oil | ... | ... | 5,846 | ... | ... | ... | ... | ... | ... |
| Fruits and vegetables, preserved | ... | 861 | 2,794 | ... | ... | ... | 251 | ... | ... |
| Oranges in bulk and boxes | ... | ... | ... | ... | ... | ... | ... | 312 | ... |
| Firebrick and tiles unglazed | ... | 2,233 | ... | ... | ... | ... | ... | ... | ... |
| Leather, manufactures of | ... | 24,366 | ... | ... | ... | ... | ... | ... | ... |
| Malt liquors | ... | 880 | ... | ... | ... | ... | ... | ... | ... |
| Ginger ale and soda water | ... | 15,800 | ... | ... | ... | ... | ... | ... | ... |
| Salt in bags | ... | 1,892 | ... | 1,123 | ... | ... | ... | ... | ... |
| Pickles and sauces | ... | ... | ... | ... | ... | ... | ... | ... | ... |
| Window glass | ... | 3,586 | ... | ... | ... | ... | 71 | ... | ... |
| Iron furniture | ... | 2,246 | 569 | ... | ... | ... | ... | ... | ... |
| ,, all other manufactures | ... | 722 | ... | ... | ... | ... | ... | ... | ... |
| ,, pig | ... | 687 | ... | ... | ... | ... | ... | ... | ... |
| Spirits, distilled | 168 | ... | 1,250 | ... | ... | ... | ... | ... | ... |
| Olive oil | ... | ... | 1,530 | ... | ... | ... | ... | ... | ... |
| Still wine in casks | ... | ... | 84 | ... | ... | ... | ... | ... | ... |
| ,, in bottles | 1,073 | ... | ... | ... | ... | ... | ... | ... | ... |
| Glass bottles and demijohns | ... | 16,483 | ... | ... | ... | ... | ... | ... | ... |
| Tin and terne plates | ... | 680 | ... | ... | ... | ... | ... | ... | ... |
| Woollens and manufactures thereof | ... | ... | ... | ... | ... | ... | ... | ... | ... |
| Tobacco and manufactures thereof | ... | ... | ... | ... | 1,876 | ... | ... | ... | ... |
| Wood (cedar logs) | 342 | ... | ... | ... | ... | ... | ... | ... | ... |
| Wood, manufactures of | ... | 1,248 | ... | ... | 136 | ... | ... | ... | ... |
| Cigars | 862 | ... | ... | ... | 115 | ... | ... | ... | ... |
| Whiskey, American re-imported | 644 | 1,954 | 262 | 329 | ... | ... | ... | ... | ... |
| Miscellaneous |  |  |  |  |  |  |  |  |  |
| Total, 1892 | 9,315 | 251,439 | 12,419 | 22,574 | 2,127 | ... | 772 | 355 | ... |
| ,, free, 1892 | 2,003 | 52,875 | 725 | 4,730 | 3,477 | ... | 10,857 | ... | ... |
| Grand total, 1892 | 11,318 | 304,314 | 13,144 | 27,304 | 5,604 | ... | 11,629 | 355 | ... |
| ,, 1891 | 77,438 | 394,483 | 18,023 | 42,148 | 44,637 | 163,403 | ... | 399 | 99 |

STATEMENT of Imports subject to Duty at the Port of Galveston for the Year 1892—continued.

## 12     UNITED STATES.

| Articles. | Italy. | Brazil. | Japan. | British West Indies. | Colombia. | Cuba. | Total, 1892. | Total, 1891. |
|---|---|---|---|---|---|---|---|---|
|  | Dollars. | Dollars. | Dollars. | Dollars. | Dollars. | Dollars. | Dollars. | Dollars. |
| Books and all other printed matter | ... | ... | ... | ... | ... | ... | 1,225 | 1,300 |
| Burlaps (Dundee) | ... | ... | ... | ... | ... | ... | 16,483 | ... |
| Cement in barrels | ... | ... | ... | ... | ... | ... | 78,922 | 124,503 |
| Coal, bituminous | ... | ... | ... | ... | ... | ... | 8,758 | 20,184 |
| Coke | ... | ... | ... | ... | ... | ... | 5,240 | ... |
| Chemicals and preparations of— |  |  |  |  |  |  |  |  |
| Sheep dip | ... | ... | ... | ... | ... | ... | 57,990 | 56,459 |
| Soda ash | ... | ... | ... | ... | ... | ... | 3,599 | 2,923 |
| Soda, caustic | ... | ... | ... | ... | ... | ... | 3,862 | 2,037 |
| Coal tar oil (dead oil) | ... | ... | ... | ... | ... | ... | 16,818 | 43,091 |
| Soda sal | ... | ... | ... | ... | ... | ... | 561 | ... |
| Crockery | ... | ... | ... | ... | ... | ... | 12,114 | 9,818 |
| Cotton, manufactures of | ... | ... | ... | ... | ... | ... | 154 | 3,272 |
| Fish in oil | ... | ... | ... | ... | ... | ... | 5,846 | 6,882 |
| Fruits and vegetables, preserved | ... | ... | ... | ... | ... | ... | 3,655 | 12,321 |
| Oranges in bulk and boxes | ... | ... | ... | ... | ... | ... | 251 | ... |
| Firebrick and tiles unglazed | ... | ... | ... | ... | ... | ... | 2,233 | 1,272 |
| Leather, manufactures of | ... | ... | ... | ... | ... | ... | 312 | ... |
| Malt liquors | ... | ... | ... | ... | ... | ... | 24,366 | 13,803 |
| Ginger ale and soda water | ... | ... | ... | 519 | ... | ... | 880 | ... |
| Salt in bags | ... | ... | ... | ... | ... | ... | 16,319 | 32,391 |
| Pickles and sauces | ... | ... | ... | ... | ... | ... | 1,892 | 4,881 |
| Window glass | ... | ... | ... | ... | ... | ... | 1,123 | ... |
| Iron furniture | 421 | ... | ... | ... | ... | ... | 3,586 | 3,639 |
| ,, all other manufactures | ... | ... | ... | ... | ... | ... | 2,667 | 1,351 |
| ,, pig | ... | ... | ... | ... | ... | ... | 793 | 238 |
| Spirits, distilled | 462 | ... | ... | ... | ... | ... | 1,256 | ... |
| Olive oil | 55 | ... | ... | ... | ... | ... | 462 | ... |
| Still wine in casks | ... | ... | ... | ... | ... | ... | 1,305 | 3,176 |
| ,, in bottles | ... | ... | ... | ... | ... | ... | 1,698 | ... |
| Glass bottles and demijohns | ... | ... | ... | ... | ... | ... | 1,157 | ... |
| Tin and terne plates | ... | ... | ... | ... | ... | ... | 16,483 | 86,726 |
| Woollens and manufactures thereof | ... | ... | ... | ... | ... | 396 | 680 | ... |
| Tobacco and manufactures thereof | ... | ... | ... | ... | ... | ... | 396 | 1,674 |
| Wood (cedar logs) | ... | ... | ... | ... | ... | ... | 1,876 | ... |
| Wood, manufactures of | ... | ... | ... | ... | ... | ... | 1,590 | ... |
| Cigars | ... | ... | ... | ... | ... | 136 | 272 | ... |
| Whiskey, American re-imported | ... | ... | ... | ... | ... | ... | 862 | 29,858 |
| Miscellaneous | 122 | ... | ... | ... | ... | ... | 3,426 | 16,470 |
| Total, 1892 | 1,060 | 439,723 | ... | 519 | ... | 532 | 301,112 | ... |
| ,, free, 1892 | 158 | ... | 432 | 2,578 | ... | 45,743 | 562,869 | ... |
| Grand total, 1892 | 1,218 | 439,723 | 432 | 3,097 | 10,120 | 46,275 | 863,981 | ... |
| ,, 1891 | 75 | 329,442 | ... | ... | ... | 1,452 | 1,082,151 | ... |

Annex B.—STATEMENT of Exports of Commodities of Domestic Manufacture and Growth from the Customs District of Galveston for the Year ending December 31, 1892.

| Destination. | Cotton. Quantity. | Cotton. Value. | Oilcake. Quantity. | Oilcake. Value. | Grain. Wheat. Quantity. | Grain. Wheat. Value. | Grain. Maize. Quantity. | Grain. Maize. Value. | Wheat Flour. Quantity. | Wheat Flour. Value. |
|---|---|---|---|---|---|---|---|---|---|---|
|  | Bales. | Dollars. | Tons. | Dollars. | Bushels. | Dollars. | Bushels. | Dollars. | Barrels. | Dollars. |
| Great Britain— |  |  |  |  |  |  |  |  |  |  |
| From Port of Galveston | 515,792 | 20,439,758 | 16,199 | 387,606 | 377,685 | 335,001 | 17,528 | 8,635 | 5,033 | 28,621 |
| ,, ,, Velasco | 14,003 | 568,947 | 6,942 | 161,993 | .. | .. | .. | .. | .. | .. |
| Germany— |  |  |  |  |  |  |  |  |  |  |
| From Port of Galveston | 143,626 | 6,146,648 | 44,629 | 1,050,268 | .. | .. | 24,000 | 12,000 | 2,641 | 9,784 |
| ,, ,, Velasco | .. | .. | 6,837 | 162,114 | .. | .. | .. | .. | .. | .. |
| France— |  |  |  |  |  |  |  |  |  |  |
| From Port of Galveston | 126,177 | 5,142,810 | .. | .. | .. | .. | .. | .. | .. | .. |
| Denmark— |  |  |  |  |  |  |  |  |  |  |
| From Port of Galveston | .. | .. | 2,420 | 58,080 | .. | .. | .. | .. | .. | .. |
| ,, ,, Velasco | .. | .. | 2,061 | 47,380 | .. | .. | .. | .. | .. | .. |
| Belgium— |  |  |  |  |  |  |  |  |  |  |
| From Port of Galveston | 2,360 | 95,523 | .. | .. | .. | .. | .. | .. | .. | .. |
| Italy— |  |  |  |  |  |  |  |  |  |  |
| From Port of Galveston | 1,000 | 39,516 | .. | .. | .. | .. | .. | .. | .. | .. |
| Cuba— |  |  |  |  |  |  |  |  |  |  |
| From Port of Galveston | .. | .. | .. | .. | .. | .. | 2,345 | 1,289 | 3,822 | 17,018 |
| Spain— |  |  |  |  |  |  |  |  |  |  |
| From Port of Galveston | 100 | 3,980 | .. | .. | .. | .. | .. | .. | .. | .. |
| Mexico— |  |  |  |  |  |  |  |  |  |  |
| From Port of Galveston | 420 | 15,500 | .. | .. | .. | .. | 89,452 | 67,625 | 5 | 23 |
| ,, ,, Sabine | .. | .. | .. | .. | .. | .. | .. | .. | .. | .. |

## UNITED STATES.

Statement of Exports of Commodities of Domestic Manufacture and Growth from the Customs District of Galveston for the Year ending December 31, 1892—continued.

| Destination. | Cotton. || Oilcake. || Grain. |||| Wheat Flour. ||
| | Quantity. | Value. | Quantity. | Value. | Wheat. || Maize. || Quantity. | Value. |
| | | | | | Quantity. | Value. | Quantity. | Value. | | |
| | Bales. | Dollars. | Tons. | Dollars. | Bushels. | Dollars. | Bushels. | Dollars. | Barrels. | Dollars. |
| British West Indies— | | | | | | | | | | |
| From Port of Galveston | .. | .. | .. | .. | 300 | 239 | 3,910 | 2,044 | 1,950 | 8,850 |
| Porto Rico— | | | | | | | | | | |
| From Port of Galveston | .. | .. | .. | .. | .. | .. | 7,540 | 4,332 | 7,845 | 33,927 |
| Brazil— | | | | | | | | | | |
| From Port of Sabine | .. | .. | .. | .. | .. | .. | .. | .. | .. | .. |
| Russia— | | | | | | | | | | |
| From Port of Galveston | 5,150 | 160,219 | .. | .. | .. | .. | .. | .. | .. | .. |
| Total for 1892 | 808,628 | 32,610,901 | 79,088 | 1,867,441 | 377,985 | 335,240 | 144,775 | 95,925 | 21,296 | 98,226 |
| ,, 1891 | 774,826 | 34,217,492 | 43,196 | 1,008,541 | 587,395 | 588,058 | 12,741 | 7,251 | 11,929 | 51,320 |

STATEMENT of Exports of Commodities of Domestic Manufacture and Growth from the Customs District of Galveston for the Year ending December 31, 1892—continued.

## GALVESTON.

| Destination. | Lumber. Quantity. Feet. | Lumber. Value. Dollars. | Cotton-seed Oil. Quantity. Gallons. | Cotton-seed Oil. Value. Dollars. | Walnut Logs. Value. Dollars. | Sundries. Value. Dollars. | Total Value. 1892. Dollars. | Total Value. 1891. Dollars. |
|---|---|---|---|---|---|---|---|---|
| Great Britain— | | | | | | | | |
| From Port of Galveston.. | .. | .. | .. | .. | .. | 2,401 | 21,262,022 | } 30,466,339 |
| ,, Velasco .. | .. | .. | .. | .. | .. | .. | 730,940 | |
| Germany— | | | | | | | | |
| From Port of Galveston.. | .. | .. | 10,915 | 4,100 | .. | 725 | 7,219,425 | } 2,417,382 |
| ,, Velasco .. | .. | .. | .. | .. | .. | .. | 166,214 | |
| France— | | | | | | | | |
| From Port of Galveston.. | .. | .. | 30,348 | 11,539 | .. | 2,080 | 5,156,429 | 2,149,871 |
| Denmark— | | | | | | | | |
| From Port of Galveston.. | .. | .. | .. | .. | .. | 750 | 58,830 | 93,656 |
| ,, Velasco .. | .. | .. | .. | .. | .. | .. | 47,380 | .. |
| Belgium— | | | | | | | | |
| From Port of Galveston. | .. | .. | .. | .. | 47,000 | .. | 140,523 | .. |
| Italy— | | | | | | | | |
| From Port of Galveston.. | .. | .. | .. | .. | .. | .. | 39,516 | 58,649 |
| Cuba— | | | | | | | | |
| From Port of Galveston.. | 13 | 179 | .. | .. | .. | 148 | 18,634 | 8,105 |
| Spain— | | | | | | | | |
| From Port of Galveston.. | .. | .. | .. | .. | .. | .. | 3,980 | .. |
| Mexico— | | | | | | | | |
| From Port of Galveston.. | 129 | 1,163 | .. | .. | .. | 2,783 | 87,037 | 306,712 |
| ,, Sabine .. | 675 | 7,004 | .. | .. | .. | .. | 7,004 | .. |

(1483)

STATEMENT of Exports of Commodities of Domestic Manufacture and Growth from the Customs District of Galveston for the Year ending December 31, 1892—continued.

| Destination. | Lumber. Quantity. Feet. | Lumber. Value. Dollars. | Cotton-seed Oil. Quantity. Gallons. | Cotton-seed Oil. Value. Dollars. | Walnut Logs. Value. Dollars. | Sundries. Value. Dollars. | Total Value. 1892. Dollars. | Total Value. 1891. Dollars. |
|---|---|---|---|---|---|---|---|---|
| British West Indies— From Port of Galveston.. | .. | .. | .. | .. | .. | .. | 11,133 | .. |
| Porto Rico— From Port of Galveston.. | 40 | 574 | .. | .. | .. | 1,017 | 39,850 | .. |
| Brazil— From Port of Sabine .. | 477 | 7,866 | .. | .. | .. | .. | 7,866 | .. |
| Russia— From Port of Galveston.. | .. | .. | .. | .. | .. | .. | 16,219 | 407,366 |
| Total for 1892 .. | 1,334 | 16,726 | 41,263 | 15,639 | 47,000 | 9,904 | 35,097,002 | 35,964,460* |
| ,, 1891 .. | .. | 16,883 | .. | 2,250 | .. | .. | 35,964,460 | .. |

\* Netherlands ..    Dollars. 24,042  
  Nicaragua ..    32,338

## GALVESTON.

RETURN of Shipping Engaged in the Foreign Trade in the District of Galveston during the Year ended December 31, 1892.

ENTERED.

| Nationality. | Galveston. ||||  Velasco. ||||  Sabine Pass. ||||
|  | In Ballast. || With Cargo. || In Ballast. || With Cargo. || In Ballast. || With Cargo. ||
|  | Number of Vessels. | Tons. | Number of Vessels. | Tons. | Number of Vessels. | Tons. | Number of Vessels. | Tons. | Number of Vessels. | Tons. | Number of Vessels. | Tons. |
| American | 3 | 435 | 8 | 1,688 | .. | .. | 1 | 116 | 2 | 645 | .. | .. |
| British* | 104 | 178,036 | 27 | 34,867 | 7 | 7,912 | .. | .. | .. | .. | .. | .. |
| German | 1 | 429 | .. | .. | .. | .. | .. | .. | .. | .. | .. | .. |
| Mexican | 1 | 107 | 1 | 107 | .. | .. | .. | .. | .. | .. | .. | .. |
| Norwegian | 5 | 4,475 | 1 | 915 | 1 | 2,189 | .. | .. | .. | .. | .. | .. |
| Spanish | 3 | 3,608 | 4 | 5,018 | 1 | 1,396 | .. | .. | .. | .. | .. | .. |
| Swedish | .. | .. | .. | .. | .. | .. | .. | .. | .. | .. | .. | .. |
| Total for 1892 | 117 | 187,090 | 41 | 42,595 | 9 | 11,497 | 1 | 116 | 2 | 645 | .. | .. |

\* Exclusive of 23 vessels arriving from ports in the United States.

## UNITED STATES.

Return of Shipping Engaged in the Foreign Trade in the District of Galveston during the Year ended December 31, 1892—continued.

### CLEARED.

| Nationality. | Galveston. In Ballast. Number of Vessels. | Tons. | With Cargo. Number of Vessels. | Tons. | Velasco. In Ballast. Number of Vessels. | Tons. | With Cargo. Number of Vessels. | Tons. | Sabine Pass. In Ballast. Number of Vessels. | Tons. | With Cargo. Number of Vessels. | Tons. |
|---|---|---|---|---|---|---|---|---|---|---|---|---|
| American | 7 | 3,493 | 8 | 1,830 | .. | .. | .. | .. | 3 | 1,078 | 2 | 801 |
| British | .. | .. | 156 | 223,799 | .. | .. | 8 | 9,044 | .. | .. | .. | .. |
| German | .. | .. | 1 | 429 | .. | .. | .. | .. | .. | .. | .. | .. |
| Mexican | .. | .. | 1 | 107 | .. | .. | .. | .. | .. | .. | .. | .. |
| Norwegian | .. | .. | 7 | 5,262 | .. | .. | 1 | 915 | .. | .. | .. | .. |
| Spanish | .. | .. | 8 | 9,734 | .. | .. | 1 | 1,396 | .. | .. | .. | .. |
| Swedish | .. | .. | 1 | 356 | .. | .. | .. | .. | .. | .. | .. | .. |
| Total for 1892 | 7 | 3,493 | 182 | 246,517 | .. | .. | 10 | 11,355 | 3 | 1,078 | 2 | 801 |

## GALVESTON.

STATEMENT of Imports Free of Duty at the Port of Galveston for the Year 1892.

| Articles. | Germany. | Great Britain. | France. | Netherlands. | Mexico. | Porto Rico. | Turkey. | Spain. | Italy. | Brazil. | British West Indies. | Cuba. | Total, 1892. | Total, 1891. |
|---|---|---|---|---|---|---|---|---|---|---|---|---|---|---|
| | Dollars. | Dollars. | Dollars. | Dollars. | Dollars. | Dollars. | Dollars. | Dollars. | Dollars. | Dollars. | Dollars. | Dollars. | Dollars. | Dollars. |
| Coffee | ... | ... | ... | ... | 2,208 | 4,604 | ... | ... | ... | 439,723 | 577 | ... | 447,112 | 368,458 |
| Sugar | ... | ... | ... | ... | ... | 5,763 | ... | ... | ... | ... | ... | 45,743 | 51,506 | ... |
| Jute butts | ... | 33,682 | ... | ... | ... | ... | ... | ... | ... | ... | ... | ... | 33,682 | 121,473 |
| Fruit and nuts | ... | ... | ... | ... | 290 | 490 | ... | ... | ... | ... | 2,001 | ... | 2,781 | ... |
| Petroleum barrels | ... | 18,048 | ... | ... | ... | ... | ... | ... | ... | ... | ... | ... | 18,048 | ... |
| Mineral waters | ... | ... | ... | 1,663 | ... | ... | ... | ... | ... | ... | ... | ... | 1,663 | ... |
| Wood, unmanufactured | ... | ... | ... | ... | 750 | ... | ... | ... | ... | ... | ... | ... | 750 | ... |
| Philosophical and scientific instruments, specimens of anatomy and chemical preparations | 1,787 | 415 | 407 | ... | ... | ... | ... | ... | ... | ... | ... | ... | 2,609 | ... |
| Church vestments, oil paintings for church | 190 | ... | 318 | ... | ... | ... | ... | ... | ... | ... | ... | ... | 508 | ... |
| Household and personal effects, books, &c. | ... | 507 | ... | 3,067 | ... | ... | ... | ... | ... | ... | ... | ... | 3,574 | ... |
| Gums | ... | ... | ... | ... | 209 | ... | ... | ... | ... | ... | ... | ... | 209 | ... |
| Birds, live | ... | ... | ... | ... | 20 | ... | ... | ... | ... | ... | ... | ... | 20 | ... |
| Miscellaneous free goods | 26 | 223 | ... | ... | ... | ... | ... | ... | 158 | ... | ... | ... | 407 | 68,050 |
| Total | 2,003 | 52,875 | 725 | 4,730 | 3,477 | 10,857 | ... | ... | 158 | 439,723 | 2,578 | 45,743 | 562,869 | 557,981 |

(1483)

## UNITED STATES.

### In Transit to Mexico viâ Port of Galveston for the Year 1892.

| Countries. | January. | February. | March. | April. | May. | June. | July. | August. | September. | October. | November. | December. | Total. |
|---|---|---|---|---|---|---|---|---|---|---|---|---|---|
| | Dollars. | Dollars. | Dollars. | Dollars. | Dollars. | Dollars. | Dollars. | Dollars. | Dollars. | Dollars. | Dollars. | Dollars. | Dollars. |
| Belgium | ... | ... | ... | ... | ... | ... | ... | ... | ... | ... | ... | ... | ... |
| France | ... | ... | ... | 1,011 | ... | ... | ... | ... | ... | ... | ... | ... | 1,011 |
| Germany | ... | ... | ... | ... | ... | ... | 250 | ... | ... | ... | ... | ... | 250 |
| England | 18,320 | 1,994 | 2,292 | 5,417 | ... | ... | 680 | ... | 7,019 | 2,122 | 38,164 | 24,568 | 100,566 |
| Mexico | 150 | ... | ... | ... | ... | ... | ... | ... | ... | ... | ... | ... | 150 |
| Total, 1892 | 18,470 | 1,994 | 2,292 | 6,428 | ... | ... | 980 | ... | 7,019 | 2,122 | 38,164 | 24,558 | 101,977 |
| „ 1891 | 41,053 | 73,589 | 26,132 | 3,468 | 299 | 56,085 | 21 | 33,304 | 38,236 | 17,274 | 44,551 | 37,261 | 371,273 |

### Transported into Mexico viâ the following Frontier Ports for the Year 1892.

| Ports. | January. | February. | March. | April. | May. | June. | July. | August. | September. | October. | November. | December. | Total. |
|---|---|---|---|---|---|---|---|---|---|---|---|---|---|
| | Dollars. | Dollars. | Dollars. | Dollars. | Dollars. | Dollars. | Dollars. | Dollars. | Dollars. | Dollars. | Dollars. | Dollars. | Dollars. |
| Brownsville | 150 | ... | ... | 1,011 | ... | ... | ... | ... | ... | ... | ... | ... | 1,161 |
| Eagle Pass | 50 | 249 | ... | 2,092 | ... | ... | 522 | ... | ... | 796 | 1,838 | ... | 5,547 |
| El Paso | 559 | ... | ... | ... | ... | ... | ... | ... | ... | ... | ... | ... | 559 |
| Laredo | 17,711 | 1,496 | 2,292 | 3,325 | ... | ... | 408 | ... | 7,019 | 1,326 | 85,426 | 14,391 | 88,394 |
| Nogales | ... | 249 | ... | ... | ... | ... | ... | ... | ... | ... | 900 | 5,167 | 6,316 |
| Total | 18,470 | 1,994 | 2,292 | 6,428 | ... | ... | 930 | ... | 7,019 | 2,122 | 38,164 | 24,558 | 101,977 |

# FOREIGN OFFICE.
# 1893.
## ANNUAL SERIES.

---

### No. 1176.

### DIPLOMATIC AND CONSULAR REPORTS ON TRADE AND FINANCE.

---

# UNITED STATES.

---

REPORT FOR THE YEAR 1892

ON THE

### TRADE OF BALTIMORE AND DISTRICT.

===

*Presented to both Houses of Parliament by Command of Her Majesty,*
APRIL, 1893.

===

**LONDON:**
PRINTED FOR HER MAJESTY'S STATIONERY OFFICE
BY HARRISON AND SONS, ST. MARTIN'S LANE,
PRINTERS IN ORDINARY TO HER MAJESTY.

---

And to be purchased, either directly or through any Bookseller, from
EYRE & SPOTTISWOODE, EAST HARDING STREET, FLEET STREET, E.C., and
32, ABINGDON STREET, WESTMINSTER, S.W.; or
JOHN MENZIES & Co., 12, HANOVER STREET, EDINBURGH, and
90, WEST NILE STREET, GLASGOW; or
HODGES, FIGGIS, & Co., Limited, 104, GRAFTON STREET, DUBLIN.

---

1893.

[C. 6855—63.] *Price Three Halfpence.*

# New Series of Reports.

Reports of the Annual Series have been issued from Her Majesty's Diplomatic and Consular Officers at the following places, and may be obtained from the sources indicated on the title-page:—

| No. | | Price |
|---|---|---|
| 1054. | Bilbao | 1½d. |
| 1055. | Cadiz | 2d. |
| 1056. | Corunna | 2½d. |
| 1057. | Saigon | 1d. |
| 1058. | Port-au-Prince | 1d. |
| 1059. | Trebizond | 1d. |
| 1060. | Barcelona | 1½d. |
| 1061. | Tainan | 1d. |
| 1062. | Smyrna | 1½d. |
| 1063. | Old Calabar | ½d. |
| 1064. | Samoa | ½d. |
| 1065. | Tahiti | 1d. |
| 1066. | Chefoo | 6d. |
| 1067. | Gothenburg | 2d. |
| 1068. | Buenos Ayres | 1½d. |
| 1069. | Loanda | 1½d. |
| 1070. | Guatemala | 1d. |
| 1071. | Zanzibar | 1d. |
| 1072. | Charleston | 2½d. |
| 1073. | Nice | 1d. |
| 1074. | Caracas | 1d. |
| 1075. | Lisbon | 2d. |
| 1076. | Calais | 2d. |
| 1077. | Rio Grande do Sul | 5½d. |
| 1078. | Philadelphia | 2½d. |
| 1079. | Brindisi | 2d. |
| 1080. | New York | 2d. |
| 1081. | San Francisco | 1½d. |
| 1082. | Frankfort | 4d. |
| 1083. | Hiogo | 1½d. |
| 1084. | Tokio | 1½d. |
| 1085. | Amsterdam | 1d. |
| 1086. | San Francisco | 3d. |
| 1087. | Bangkok | ½d. |
| 1088. | Söul | 1½d. |
| 1089. | Chiengmai | 1d. |
| 1090. | Copenhagen | ½d. |
| 1091. | New Caledonia | ½d. |
| 1092. | Bushire | 2d. |
| 1093. | Tamsui | 1d. |
| 1094. | Dunkirk | 1d. |
| 1095. | Port Said | 1d. |
| 1096. | Guatemala | ½d. |
| 1097. | Chungking | 9d. |
| 1098. | Nagasaki | 1d. |
| 1099. | Constantinople | 2d. |
| 1100. | Buenos Ayres | ½d. |
| 1101. | Shanghai | 2d. |
| 1102. | Jeddah | ½d. |
| 1103. | Chicago | 3d. |
| 1104. | Erzeroum | ½d. |
| 1105. | Loanda | 3d. |
| 1106. | Macao | ½d. |
| 1107. | Canton | 1d. |
| 1108. | Paramaribo | 1½d. |
| 1109. | Tunis | 1½d. |
| 1110. | Sofia | 3d. |
| 1111. | Brunei | 1½d. |
| 1112. | Athens | 2½d. |
| 1113. | Alexandria | 2d. |
| 1114. | Vienna | 1d. |

| No. | | Price |
|---|---|---|
| 1115. | Stettin | 2½d. |
| 1116. | Berne | 1d. |
| 1117. | Palermo | 2½d. |
| 1118. | Tokio | 1½d. |
| 1119. | St. Petersburg | 3d. |
| 1120. | Teneriffe | 1d. |
| 1121. | Damascus | 1d. |
| 1122. | Naples | 2d. |
| 1123. | Hakodate | 1d. |
| 1124. | Montevideo | 2½d. |
| 1125. | Stockholm | 1½d. |
| 1126. | Dantzig | 2d. |
| 1127. | The Hague | 1½d. |
| 1128. | Odessa | 1d. |
| 1129. | Berne | 1½d. |
| 1130. | Malaga | 3d. |
| 1131. | Rome | 2½d. |
| 1132. | St. Jago de Cuba | 4½d. |
| 1133. | Munich | 1½d. |
| 1134. | Meshed | 1d. |
| 1135. | Guayaquil | ½d. |
| 1136. | Rio de Janeiro | 4½d. |
| 1137. | Tonga | 1d. |
| 1138. | Copenhagen | 1d. |
| 1139. | Tangier | 1½d. |
| 1140. | Buenos Ayres | 2½d. |
| 1141. | Para | 1d. |
| 1142. | Baghdad and Bussorah | 1½d. |
| 1143. | Christiania | 5½d. |
| 1144. | Old Calabar | 2d. |
| 1145. | Trieste | 1½d. |
| 1146. | Quito | 1d. |
| 1147. | Buenos Ayres | 6d. |
| 1148. | Bogotá | 1d. |
| 1149. | The Hague | 2d. |
| 1150. | Mexico | 2½d. |
| 1151. | Florence | 2d. |
| 1152. | Calais | 1d. |
| 1153. | Lorenzo Marques | 1½d. |
| 1154. | Patras | 1d. |
| 1155. | Taganrog | 1d. |
| 1156. | Stockholm | 1d. |
| 1157. | Washington | 2d. |
| 1158. | Paris | 1½d. |
| 1159. | Bengazi | 1d. |
| 1160. | Santos | 2½d. |
| 1161. | Buenos Ayres | 1¼d. |
| 1162. | Nantes | 1d. |
| 1163. | Beira | 5d. |
| 1164. | Galveston | 1½d. |
| 1165. | Berlin | 1d. |
| 1166. | Bordeaux | 2½d. |
| 1167. | Calais | 2½d. |
| 1168. | The Hague | 2d. |
| 1169. | Athens | 1s. 0d. |
| 1170. | Galatz | 1½d. |
| 1171. | Guayaquil | 1d. |
| 1172. | Riga | 2d. |
| 1173. | Trebizond | 1d. |
| 1174. | Havre | 2½d. |
| 1175. | Saigon | ½d. |

## No. 1176.

# UNITED STATES.

## BALTIMORE.

*Consul Segrave to the Earl of Rosebery.*

My Lord,                                *Baltimore, March 7, 1893.*

I HAVE the honour to transmit herewith, to your Lordship, Reports on the Trade and Commerce of Baltimore, Norfolk, and Richmond for the year 1892.

I have, &c.
(Signed)      W. F. SEGRAVE.

---

*Report on the Trade and Commerce of the Consular District of Baltimore for the Year 1892.*

### ABSTRACT of Contents.

| | PAGE |
|---|---|
| Condition of the year's trade | 2 |
| Prospects of future trade | 2 |
| Currency: effects of legislation on | 3 |
| Immigration: restrictions upon | 4 |
| Quarantine | 4 |
| Port | 5 |
| Labour | 5 |
| Residents in Maryland: financial position of | 5 |
| Immigrants and their nationality | 6 |
| Exports: approximate value of | 7 |
| Vessels: rapid loading of | 7 |
| Trade: details of | 7 |
| Ship-building, wrecks, &c. | 8 |
| Marriages | 8 |
| Divorces | 9 |
| Tables | 9-12 |
| Trade of Norfolk | 12 |
|   ,,    Richmond | 15 |

(1496)

## UNITED STATES.

**State of trade.**

The condition of trade at Baltimore during the year 1892, presents fair grounds for congratulation.

The increase in exports was very large, to counterbalance which, however, there was a considerable contraction in imports.

The past crop year, as well as the year previous, was very prosperous for local trade, the more especially for exporters. Money was easy, and there was no such scarcity as existed three years back.

The president of the Corn and Flour Exchange reports the receipts of grain as unprecedented, and the export as exceeding that of the former year by some 15,000,000 bushels.

**Fall in prices.**

On the other hand, there was a very sharp decline in value. Wheat fell from 105 c. to 70 c.; in fact, at the close of the year it was only 3 c. dearer in Liverpool than in Baltimore.

Corn (maize) fell from 59 c. to 45 c., a shrinkage which might have produced disastrous results on other markets; but that there were neither defaults nor failures here is good evidence of the soundness of Baltimore trade.

The export of flour exceeded that of 1891 by about 1,000,000 barrels, and as in the case of wheat there was a serious depreciation of prices, to the extent of something like 1 dol. 50 c. per barrel.

Railway rates advanced on October 10, but ocean freights were very much depressed.

Inland freights have received the benefit of enhanced value at the seaboard, whilst prices of grain delivered abroad have not changed.

Freights to Liverpool closed at $2\frac{1}{2}$ c. a bushel, and was at one time as low as $1\frac{3}{4}$ c.

**Transport.**

Complaints are made that flour is sent direct from the west to Europe on through rates, which are much lower than those granted for inland transport.

Serious complaints are also made of the failure of the railways to provide sufficient rolling stock to accommodate the traffic, and it is proposed to test before the Courts the liability of the companies to damages for undue delay in transit.

**Anti-option: its evil influence on speculation.**

Speculation has been somewhat restricted owing to apprehensions of the passing of the "Anti-Option" Bill, as traders dread legislation the effects of which cannot possibly be foreseen.

Very little option business is done in this market, so that the Bill would have less effect here than in other centres. 75 per cent. of the business done in Baltimore is against the account of grain purchased in the West from country dealers, a sale for future delivery being made against the same.

**Decrease of imports and increase of customs revenue.**

The local statistician reports that the decrease in imports was to the value of 4,000,000 dol., but as the increase in the customs revenue amounted to 736,000 dol., it is manifest that here at least the new tariff works to the advantage of the revenue at the cost of the consumer.

**Future prospects.**

Whilst the fate of the present tariff is assumed to be in the balance, any extension of the foreign import trade of the country cannot be expected. Indeed, the contrary may be anticipated.

Importers naturally do not care to be overstocked with goods paying heavy import duties, at the risk that Congress may at any moment abrogate the present tariff law, when they would find themselves subject to ruinous competition with goods entering under different conditions and lower rates of duties.

Of course it is only reasonable to assume that sufficient time would be allowed for trade to settle down into the new order of things, if not in the interest of the importer, then in that of the local manufacturer, who would otherwise find himself on the road to ruin by being suddenly forced to compete with cheap goods from Europe, not to mention that vast numbers of working men would be thrown out of employment.

This is a contingency which no Government would care to meet, and least of all the Government of this country. For these reasons, although there may be a risk, which no business man may care to incur, it may be safely assumed that any change in the tariff will be gradual, and that in all probability it will not be by any means as radical as sanguine traders have been led to hope.

Another reason why the change may not be so speedy and thorough lies in the fact that the two bountiful harvests with which this country has been blessed have brought prosperity to all classes of the people, with the result that, in spite of the high tariff, the import of certain classes of goods has largely increased. A clear proof that the American now has money in his pocket, and that, when so circumstanced, he buys what he takes a fancy to irrespective of increase in customs duties.

*Who pays the import duty?* — One of the most frequently repeated and successful arguments in favour of the high tariff was the claim of its supporters that the import duties would be paid, not by the consumer, but by the producer.

A year's experience has somewhat modified that assertion, and it is now more generally allowed that any duty on non-competing products is paid directly by the consumer, but, in the case of competing articles, the incidence of the tax, whether on consumer or producer, would entirely depend on the capacity or strength of the home market to compete with the foreign market. Thus in the case of tin-plate, it was persistently asserted that the home product would throw the cost of the protective duty on the producer. The result has not so far realised these anticipations, and it is now conceded that the weakness and incapacity of the home market has thrown the import tax on the consumer.

*Silver Act: its effect on the currency.* — The Bill introduced into Congress to repeal what is termed the "Sherman Silver Act" is of much interest to Baltimore finance, for, unless the currency is placed upon a sound basis, success in business is unattainable.

It is argued, on the one hand, that the wealth of this country is so great and its credit so stable that the mere stamping on a piece of paper "This is a dollar" is sufficient to give it currency and that the people in general are satisfied with the kind of money that is in circulation.

But that the financial houses do not share the public confidence is shown by the fact that the silver currency is discriminated against, and that not only gold-notes but greenbacks are hoarded to such an extent that little but silver-notes are in circulation.

The reason assigned is that greenbacks are payable in gold.

It is therefore the gold value of the greenback which makes it more desirable than coin-notes, which the Government now indeed redeem in gold, but which it has the option of paying in silver.

But as the country has an external commerce and owes debts abroad, such debts must be paid in a currency which will be received.

Now the silver policy causes distrust abroad and so induces the withdrawal of capital lest perchance creditors may not receive payment in gold, and no one can deny that the result of the silver policy would afford justification for such distrust.

The foreign demand for gold has so depleted the Treasury that but little remains beyond what is required to reduce the legal tender greenback issue.

The dilemma is such that there are but two courses to pursue.

Either that the Government sell bonds to replenish the gold reserve, which is considered a most underisable expedient, or that Congress repeal the Silver Act, which the concensus of public opinion declares to be in every sense the preferable course.

*Anti-option Bill.* The so-called Anti-option Bill now before Congress is another measure about which considerable diversity of opinion prevails.

The general idea, however, is that, if passed, it will work much mischief, and that no one will suffer more than the farmer, in whose interest the Bill was supposed to have originated.

*Restriction on immigration.* A third Bill, which, however, unlike the former ones, meets with general assent, is that to restrict immigration.

Medical scientists and sanitary experts have plainly warned the people that if the epidemic diseases now or recently raging in parts of Europe were to obtain a foothold in this country it would be extremely difficult to eradicate them in consequence of the neglect of sanitary precautions which prevails, and that if unrestricted immigration were to be tolerated they must promptly put their houses in order, sweep and garnish their highways, and see to the purity of their water supply.

*Quarantine.* Loud complaints are made of the system of quarantine which was established during the prevalence of the cholera epidemic in Europe.

It is averred that the national quarantine, as distinct from the State quarantine, which was established at the entrance of Chesapeake Bay, the water highway to Washington and Baltimore, against vessels bound to this port, resulted in serious and expensive delays and was manifestly unjust, inasmuch as it was not enforced against most of the neighbouring and competing ports.

Vessels for Baltimore were subjected to a double detention, once at Cape Charles, the Government station which is in the State of Virginia, and again at the local quarantine station.

The establishment of a national quarantine as distinct from a

State quarantine is loudly called for and would receive general approval, as it would place every port and the whole Canadian frontier alike under federal supervision.

Port.
The water approaches to Baltimore have been much improved during the past year.

The channel as completed is nowhere less than 600 feet wide, whilst at angles and points where it may be necessary to change the ship's direction it is much wider. It is 27 feet deep at ordinary low-water and 28½ feet deep at high-water, so that ships of the heaviest burthen can now pass in and out. It is objected that it is badly lighted and buoyed, and great improvements are required under these heads.

Labour.
The efforts of labour agitators in Baltimore produced during the past year two prolonged strikes and eight others of less extent and duration. This is, no doubt, a considerable improvement on former years. About 3,000 men and women were involved in these strikes, but only about 600 were out for a longer period than 3 weeks.

It is estimated that the loss in wages to the strikers amounted to about 30,000*l*., whilst the town also suffered considerably through stagnation in business.

The two principal strikes were those of the carpenters, who demanded an 8-hour day, and the journeymen tailors. On May 2 600 carpenters were out of work, but by the end of the month so many had obtained employment elsewhere that their union was only paying about 250 men the strike pay of 9 dol. a week.

It speaks volumes for the strength of the union that it can afford to pay 5s. 6d. a day to its idle members.

Financial condition of residents.
There are in the State of Maryland 204,000 families, of which 39 per cent. are owners of their lands or tenements and 61 per cent. are tenants.

Of the owners 27 per cent. are encumbered and 73 per cent. free from encumbrance.

Of these families 41,372, or 20·50 per cent., are agricultural, 63 per cent. of whom are owners and 27 per cent. tenants.

30 per cent. of these latter have encumbrances on their properties and 70 per cent. are free from encumbrance.

Urban residents are in a larger proportion tenants than residents in the country.

The city of Baltimore is said to contain 86,457 families, of which 74 per cent. are tenants and 26 per cent. owners of their tenements.

75 per cent. of the owners are not encumbered and 25 per cent. have encumbrances on their property.

The aggregate value of house and land property in this State which is encumbered is 64,000,000 dol. and the ratio of debt to value is, for agricultural property, 38·50 per cent., and for urban property 40 per cent.

The official rate of interest in Maryland is 6 per cent. This rate is paid on 79 per cent. of encumbered rural property and on 73 per cent. of urban property.

(1496)

# UNITED STATES.

Although this is the regular and usual rate of interest there are some 4 per cent. of house owners who pay as high as 12 per cent., and in one instance 30 per cent. is paid on a small loan on mortgage.

**Local finance.** Bank clearances during the year amounted to 769,000,000 dol., against 739,000,000 dol. in the previous year, showing an increase of 34,000,000 dol.

They show further an increase of 15,500,000 dol. over the clearances for 1890, which, up to that time, had been the heaviest since the foundation of the clearing-house.

The 27 national banks of Baltimore had a—

|  | Amount. |
|---|---|
|  | Dollars. |
| Paid-up capital | 13,243,000 |
| Surplus | 4,477,000 |
| Deposits | 24,826,000 |
| Loans and discounts | 31,565,000 |

The eight savings banks in the city had on the last day of December, 1892, on deposit 41,877,000 dol., an increase of 3,000,000 dol. during the year.

**Immigrants whence arrived.** In 1892 immigrants to the number of 48,559 were landed at this port.

They came from the following countries:—

| Country. | Number of Immigrants. |
|---|---|
| England | 153 |
| Ireland | 43 |
| Scotland | 8 |
| West Indies | 7 |
|  | 211 |
| Austria | 2,499 |
| Belgium | 3 |
| Bohemia | 1,181 |
| Denmark | 7 |
| France | 11 |
| Germany | 15,870 |
| Hungary | 1,929 |
| Netherlands | 60 |
| Norway and Sweden | 243 |
| Russia and Poland | 5,334 |
| Roumania | 5 |
| Switzerland | 6 |

Of these there were—

|  | Number. |
|---|---|
| Males | 27,419 |
| Females | 21,140 |

## BALTIMORE.

Baltimore stands as the third city in the United States in the value of its exports.

The approximate value of the chief articles is shown below—

*Exports: approximate value of.*

| Articles. | Value. |
|---|---|
|  | Millions of dollars. |
| Wheat | 22½ |
| Flour | 17 |
| Corn | 9½ |
| Cattle | 6 |
| Beef | 4 |
| Lard and tallow | 7 |
| Cotton | 12 |
| Tobacco | 8 |
| Timber | 1½ |

The export of copper has become an important element in the trade of Baltimore, whose merchants control the output of the famous Montana mines, which they refine here, and last year exported the product in the shape of copper matte to the value of 2,750,000 dol.

Copper matte consists of 60 per cent. of pure copper, 35 ounces of pure silver, and $\frac{14}{100}$ of an ounce of pure gold per ton.

A large amount of seeds have also been exported, with a prospect of considerable future increase in the trade. Seeds to the value of 1,250,000 dol. were exported in the past year.

Baltimore is amply provided with means for the rapid loading of ships, and possesses elevators with a storage capacity of 5,800,000 bushels of grain.

*Ships: rapid loading of.*

An instance of rapid loading is worthy of record.

The steamship "Tynedale" commenced loading at No. 3 Elevator at 1.15 P.M. on October 31 last, and had completed her cargo at 7.20 the same day. During the 6 hours and 5 minutes that had elapsed she had shipped 106,200 bushels of wheat, of which 94,000 bushels were in bulk and 12,200 bushels in bags.

The exports from Baltimore during the past year were valued at 93,000,000 dol., showing an increase of 13,500,000 dol. over the previous year.

*Details of trade.*

The imports amounted in value to 14,238,571 dol., being a decrease of 4,000,000 dol.

The trade in canned goods was, during the year, active and profitable. There was a decrease of 1,000,000 cans of peaches, but vegetables and fruit were preserved in large quantities, and with sensible increases in demand and price.

*Canned goods.*

Since the opening of the oyster season in September there has been an increase of 25 per cent. as compared with 1891.

Cotton opened dull in 1892, but a reaction shortly took place, and the trade was larger during the year than in 1891. The price advanced 2 c. per lb. owing to a decrease in the crop estimate of 25 per cent.

*Cotton.*

## UNITED STATES.

On this basis the crop for 1892–3 will be about 6,500,000 bales, as against 9,000,000 bales last year. Receipts were 389,268 bales and the exports 271,159 bales.

**Coffee.** The coffee trade was more profitable and satisfactory than for many years past, though there was but little variation in the import. The demand was brisk and prices were maintained throughout the year.

**Tobacco.** The Maryland crop of leaf tobacco was of better colour and quality than for many years past. The quantity was, however, unfortunately much below the average. Only about 21,000 hogsheads were received, to the value of 1,250,000 dol. France contracted for about 13,000 hogsheads Maryland, and 15,000 hogsheads Ohio, but it is doubtful whether her demand can be met.

The market was very active during the year, and better prices were obtainable than during former years.

Only about 200 hogsheads were left over at the commencement of the present year, being the smallest stock left in the warehouses for the past 50 years.

**Cattle.** Live stock were shipped in large quantities during the early part of the year, but the small demand and low prices obtainable in Europe caused the trade to fall away speedily, and the export showed considerable shrinkage over that of former years.

**Tin-plates.** The manufacture of tin-plate, which is being attempted in this country, has hitherto proved unsatisfactory, if not a failure; nevertheless, the glut in the import of this article the previous year, and such competition as exists in this country, has reduced the import by about 8 per cent.

**Customs.** The customs receipts for the past year amounted to—

|  | Amount. |
|---|---|
|  | Dollars. |
| In 1892 | 4,003,993 |
| Against, in 1891 | 3,267,034 |
| Showing an increase in 1892 of | 736,959 |

**Shipbuilding.** Shipbuilding in Baltimore and its immediate vicinity shows considerable increase during the past 12 months, as well in the number of vessels launched as in the aggregate net tonnage.

During the year 67 vessels have been launched with tonnage amounting to 12,000 tons.

Including the amount paid by Government on the two cruisers "Detroit" and "Montgomery," at present under construction here, over 1,500,000 dol. have been invested in shipbuilding during the year.

**Wrecks.** There were 73 reports of wrecks received, involving the loss of 33 lives and 144,000 dol. worth of property.

**Marriages.** There were 4,502 marriage licenses issued during the year, a decrease of 58 from the previous year.

## BALTIMORE.

287 applications for divorce were filed in the Court and 159 divorces were granted. The rates of applications for divorce to the number of marriages was as one of the former to 15 of the latter.

**Divorces.**

### Annex A.—RETURN of all Shipping at the Port of Baltimore in the Year 1892.

#### ENTERED.

| Nationality. | Sailing. Number of Vessels. | Sailing. Tons. | Steam. Number of Vessels. | Steam. Tons. | Total. Number of Vessels. | Total. Tons. |
|---|---|---|---|---|---|---|
| British* | 53 | 20,139 | 558 | 968,678 | 611 | 988,817 |
| American, foreign | 149 | 45,063 | 7 | 1,736 | 156 | 46,799 |
| German | 2 | 900 | 91 | 351,076† | 93 | 351,976 |
| Italian | 13 | 9,941 | 1 | 1,324 | 14 | 11,265 |
| Swedish and Norwegian | 2 | 895 | 56 | 31,130 | 58 | 32,025 |
| Dutch | ... | ... | 27 | 56,874 | 27 | 56,874 |
| Spanish | ... | ... | 11 | 19,773 | 11 | 19,773 |
| All others | ... | ... | 1 | 1,198 | 1 | 1,198 |
| Total | 219 | 76,938 | 752 | 1,431,789 | 971 | 1,508,727 |
| ,, for the year preceding | 222 | 82,925 | 701 | 1,221,199 | 923 | 1,304,124 |

\* British increase, vessels, 41; tonnage, 124,516.
† German tonnage is evidently gross tonnage.

#### CLEARED.

| Nationality. | Sailing. Number of Vessels. | Sailing. Tons. | Steam. Number of Vessels. | Steam. Tons. | Total. Number of Vessels. | Total. Tons. |
|---|---|---|---|---|---|---|
| British* | 54 | 21,491 | 567 | 988,775 | 621 | 1,010,266 |
| American, foreign | 147 | 51,817 | 7 | 1,714 | 154 | 52,531 |
| German | 2 | 900 | 91 | 351,076 | 93 | 351,976 |
| Italian | 13 | 9,941 | 1 | 1,324 | 14 | 11,265 |
| Swedish and Norwegian | 2 | 895 | 56 | 31,130 | 58 | 32,025 |
| Dutch | ... | ... | 27 | 56,874 | 27 | 56,874 |
| Spanish | ... | ... | 11 | 19,773 | 11 | 19,773 |
| All others | ... | ... | 1 | 1,198 | 1 | 1,198 |
| Total | 218 | 85,044 | 761 | 1,451,864 | 979 | 1,536,908 |
| ,, for the year preceding | 214 | 75,497 | 687 | 1,176,877 | 901 | 1,252,374 |

\* British increase, vessels, 32; tonnage, 165,553.

## UNITED STATES.

### Annex B.—Return of the Principal Articles of Export from Baltimore, 1891-92.

| Articles. | | 1892. Quantity. | 1892. Value. | 1891. Quantity. | 1891. Value. |
|---|---|---|---|---|---|
| **Grain and bread stuffs—** | | | | | |
| Wheat | Quarters | 2,046,017 | | 2,095,912 | |
| Flour | Barrels | 727,107 | | 539,709 | |
| Corn, maize | Cwts. | 1,064,655 | | 239,460 | |
| ,, meal | Tons | 4,716 | | 2,276 | |
| Rye | Bushels | 749,892 | | 754,826 | |
| **Provisions—** | | | | | |
| Cattle, live | Head | 54,932 | | 65,399 | |
| Beef, various | Tons | 20,196 | | 20,648 | |
| Pork, hams, and bacon | ,, | 10,328 | | 13,285 | |
| Canned goods | Cases | 38,420 | | 65,656 | |
| Lard, tallow, and grease | Tons | 49,923 | | 41,941 | |
| **Oils—** | | | | | |
| Illuminating | Barrels | 419,913 | | 270,000 | |
| Vegetable and animal | ,, | 245,000 | Total, 93,000,000 dol. = 19,175,257*l*., at 4 dol. 85 c. per *l*. | 170,450 | Total, 79,365,959 dol. = 13,193,199*l*., at 4 dol. 85 c. per *l*. |
| Oil cake | Tons | 33,889 | | 27,978 | |
| **Minerals—** | | | | | |
| Copper, various | Tons | 34,139 | | 17,317 | |
| Zinc | ,, | 1,184 | | 1,217 | |
| Coals | ,, | 101,929 | | 115,290 | |
| **Timber—** | | | | | |
| Lumber | M. feet | 29,055 | | 31,318 | |
| Staves | Thousands | 1,216 | | 1,735 | |
| **Various—** | | | | | |
| Apples, dried | Tons | 2,796 | | 3,578 | |
| Bark | Bags | 36,689 | | 29,389 | |
| ,, extract | Barrels | 13,486 | | 16,329 | |
| Cotton | Bales | 271,159 | | 190,827 | |
| Resin | Barrels | 78,648 | | 111,414 | |
| Seeds | Tons | 3,361 | | 6,879 | |
| Sugar and glucose | ,, | 1,034 | | 1,215 | |
| Starch | ,, | 2,061 | | 1,927 | |
| Tobacco | Hogsheads | 62,010 | | 55,808 | |
| Wax | Tons | 927 | | 1,419 | |
| Whisky | Barrels | 33,863 | | 7,136 | |

## BALTIMORE.

Annex C.—RETURN of the Principal Articles of Import into Baltimore during 1891-92.

| Articles. | | 1892. Quantity. | 1892. Value. | 1891. Quantity. | 1891. Value. |
|---|---|---|---|---|---|
| Minerals, metals— | | | | | |
| Iron ore | Tons | 284,959 | | 418,833 | |
| ,, manganese | ,, | 44,424 | | 12,780 | |
| ,, speigle | ,, | 9,478 | | 3,150 | |
| ,, purple ore | ,, | 25,960 | | 19,351 | |
| ,, various | ,, | 1,971 | | 1,560 | |
| Steel, various | ,, | 1,392 | | 1,240 | |
| Tin-plate | Boxes | 876,173 | | 976,647 | |
| Various and taggers | ,, | 12,055 | | ... | |
| Chemicals and fertilizers— | | | | | |
| Salt, manure | Bags | 95,554 | | 62,166 | |
| ,, cake | Casks | 13,771 | | 6,982 | |
| Soda ash | ,, | 63,507 | | 39,929 | |
| ,, caustic | ,, | 9,877 | | 2,120 | |
| Sulphur | Tons | 15,077 | | 14,995 | |
| Bleaching powder | Tierces | 8,825 | | 5,102 | |
| Fertilizers, other | Bags | 84,906 | | 152,366 | |
| Clay— | | | | | |
| Various | Tons | 26,158 | Total, 14,238,571 dol. = 2,935,787*l*., at 4 dol. 85 c. per 1*l*. | 25,043 | Total, 18,193,199 dol. = 3,638,639*l*., at 4 dol. 85 c. per 1*l*. |
| Cement | Casks | 221,066 | | 125,607 | |
| Earthenware and china | Crates | 35,827 | | 24,099 | |
| Drink— | | | | | |
| Beer | Barrels | 3,471 | | 3,067 | |
| Mineral waters | Cases | 6,811 | | 6,611 | |
| Whisky | Barrels | 5,601 | | 14,081 | |
| Wines and liquors | Cases | 13,720 | | 7,237 | |
| Fruit— | | | | | |
| Bananas | Bunches | 585,593 | | 590,624 | |
| Cocoanuts | Thousands | 4,329 | | 1,425 | |
| Pine-apples | Dozens | 492,901 | | 375,277 | |
| Lemons and oranges | Cases | 27,276 | | 44,956 | |
| Fruit, dried | ,, | 25,739 | | 22,212 | |
| Various— | | | | | |
| Coffee | Tons | 41,649 | | 41,454 | |
| Fish, salt | Barrels | 33,879 | | 30,287 | |
| Rice | Tons | 9,416 | | 12,399 | |
| Salt | ,, | 11,315 | | 17,749 | |
| Tags | Cases | 10,389 | | 10,433 | |
| Pepper and spices | Bags | 5,055 | | 3,876 | |
| Tar, gas, and coal | Casks | 9,870 | | 17,083 | |
| Hides | Bales | 2,322 | | 19,203 | |
| Paints | Tubs | 6,729 | | 8,542 | |
| Pickles and preserves | Cases | 2,239 | | 6,383 | |

12    UNITED STATES.

Annex D.—Table showing the Total Value of all Articles Exported from or Imported into Baltimore in the Years 1891-92.

| Country. | Exports. 1892. | Exports. 1891. | Imports. 1892. | Imports. 1891. |
|---|---|---|---|---|
|  | £ | £ | £ | £ |
| Great Britain | 10,750,000 | 10,500,000 | 1,350,000 | 1,850,000 |
| Belgium | 1,200,000 | 1,000,000 | 130,000 | 50,000 |
| Brazil | 450,000 | 600,000 | 350,000 | 400,000 |
| Cuba and Spain | 120,000 | 100,000 | 250,000 | 350,000 |
| France | 1,200,000 | 950,000 | 15,000 | 100,000 |
| Germany | 2,650,000 | 2,500,000 | 255,000 | 275,000 |
| Netherlands | 2,150,000 | 1,750,000 | 240,000 | 150,000 |
| Italy | .. | .. | 30,000 | 125,000 |
| Portugal | .. | .. | 12,000 | .. |
| Scandinavia | 250,000 | 250,000 | .. | .. |
| Other countries | 450,000 | 540,000 | 250,000 | 300,000 |
| Total | 19,220,000 | 18,190,000 | 2,882,000 | 3,600,000 |

## NORFOLK.

Mr. Vice-Consul Myers reports as follows:—

While the trade of Norfolk for the last year shows an increase in some of its branches, and especially in the matter of yellow pine lumber, there has been a very decided falling-off in its receipts and exports of cotton, which has been largely due to the reduced crop in the Atlantic States.

A comparative statement is appended hereto showing the increase of business in certain lines during the last 4 years, to which special attention is directed.

Table showing the Movement of Shipping at this Port (not including the Coasting Trade in American Vessels, representing the Entries and Clearances to and from Foreign Ports only.

ENTERED.

| Nationality. | Sailing. Number of Vessels. | Sailing. Tons. | Steam. Number of Vessels. | Steam. Tons. | Total. Number of Vessels. | Total. Tons. |
|---|---|---|---|---|---|---|
| British | 2 | 2,499 | 449 | 633,146 | 451 | 635,645 |
| American | 6 | 1,641 | 2 | 244 | 8 | 1,885 |
| Spanish | ... | ... | 3 | 5,326 | 3 | 5,326 |
| Italian | 1 | 465 | ... | ... | 1 | 465 |
| Norwegian | 1 | 656 | ... | ... | 1 | 656 |
| Total | 10 | 5,261 | 454 | 638,716 | 464 | 643,977 |

## BALTIMORE.

### Cleared.

| Nationality. | Sailing. Number of Vessels. | Tons. | Steam. Number of Vessels. | Tons. | Total. Number of Vessels. | Tons. |
|---|---|---|---|---|---|---|
| British | 7 | 5,169 | 423 | 602,316 | 430 | 607,485 |
| American | 41 | 15,538 | 1 | 161 | 42 | 15,699 |
| Spanish | ... | ... | 33 | 53,570 | 33 | 53,570 |
| Italian | 12 | 6,770 | ... | ... | 12 | 6,770 |
| Norwegian | ... | ... | 8 | 8,507 | 8 | 8,507 |
| German | ... | ... | 3 | 4,186 | 3 | 4,186 |
| Total | 60 | 27,477 | 468 | 668,740 | 528 | 696,217 |

TABLE showing the Principal Articles of Export and Import at this Port during the past Year, value calculated at 5 dol. to the 1*l*.

### Exports.

| Articles. | | Quantity. | Value. £ |
|---|---|---|---|
| Cotton | Bales | 125,406 | .. |
| Coal | Tons | 148,451 | .. |
| Flour | Barrels | 78,918 | .. |
| Corn | Bushels | 598,552 | .. |
| Wheat | ,, | 628,247 | .. |
| Oats | ,, | 148,000 | .. |
| Rye | ,, | 149,919 | .. |
| Corn meal | Barrels | 214 | .. |
| Cotton-seed meal | Pounds | 8,904,840 | .. |
| ,, oil | Gallons | 1,397,643 | .. |
| Tobacco | Pounds | 4,620,074 | .. |
| Staves | .. | .. | 58,516 |
| Logs | .. | .. | 80,888 |
| Bark | Bags | 13,379 | .. |
| Resin | Barrels | 3,017 | .. |
| Boat oars | .. | .. | 388 |
| Fence | Bundles | 195 | .. |
| Cattle | Head | 1,380 | .. |
| Hay | .. | .. | 169 |
| Canned goods | Cases | 750 | .. |
| Tallow | Barrels | 57 | .. |
| Mineral water | Cases | 80 | .. |
| Peas | Bushels | 100 | .. |
| Total | .. | .. | 1,676,482 |

# UNITED STATES.

IMPORTS.

| Articles. | | Quantity. | Value. |
|---|---|---:|---:|
| | | | £ |
| Oil of tar | Barrels | 3,390 | .. |
| Sperm oil | Gallons | 34,843 | .. |
| Salt | Pounds | 2,894,000 | .. |
| Kainit | Tons | 1,976 | .. |
| Grain sacks | ,, | 7,425 | .. |
| Wine | Packages | 94 | .. |
| Manufactures of bone and horn | .. | .. | 260 |
| Manufactures of paper | .. | .. | 104 |
| ,, metal | .. | .. | 365 |
| ,, wood | .. | .. | 120 |
| ,, wool | .. | .. | 37 |
| ,, glass | .. | .. | 58 |
| ,, leather | .. | .. | 35 |
| ,, shell | .. | .. | 13 |
| Pearl beads | .. | .. | 18 |
| Jewellery | .. | .. | 69 |
| Lithographic prints | .. | .. | 27 |
| Chromos | .. | .. | 12 |
| Brushes | .. | .. | 29 |
| China vases | .. | .. | 42 |
| Dry goods | .. | .. | 76 |
| Smokers' articles | .. | .. | 18 |
| Pocket knives | Dozen | 274 | .. |
| Razors | ,, | 525 | .. |
| Total | .. | .. | 10,794 |

## BALTIMORE.

COMPARATIVE Statement showing the Increase in Several Branches of the Trade and Industry of Norfolk for the 4 Years ending December 1, 1892.

| Articles. | | Quantity 1888. | Quantity 1892. | Increase Quantity. | Increase Per Cent. |
|---|---|---|---|---|---|
| **LUMBER.** | | | | | |
| Lumber | Feet | 138,625,263 | 293,725,122 | ... | 112 |
| Logs | ,, | 105,637,554 | 114,386,459 | ... | 8 |
| Staves | Mille | 5,843,966 | 8,798,917 | ... | 52 |
| Shingles | ,, | 30,714,540 | 47,790,696 | ... | 55 |
| Railroad ties | ,, | 185,173 | 631,425 | ... | 241 |
| **GRAIN.** | | | | | |
| Hay | Tons | 7,709 | 14,017 | ... | 82 |
| Corn | Bushels | 736,858 | 1,206,691 | ... | 61 |
| Oats | ,, | 247,970 | 424,543 | ... | 71 |
| Meal | ,, | 183,924 | 313,388 | ... | 70 |
| Rough rice | ,, | 6,168 | 37,434 | ... | 513 |
| Bran | ,, | 103,442 | 169,182 | ... | 64 |
| Rye | ,, | 1,181 | 124,500 | ... | 955 |
| Wheat | ,, | 138,338 | 552,101 | 413,763 | ... |
| Peanuts | Bags of 4 bushels each | 289,162 | 404,514 | 115,352 | .. |
| **GROCERIES.** | | | | | |
| Coffee | Bags | 10,024 | 10,807 | 559 | ... |
| Sugar | Barrels | 30,154 | 49,277 | 19,123 | ... |
| Cheese | Boxes | 14,168 | 22,108 | 7,940 | ... |
| Butter | Tubs | 20,185 | 23,413 | 3,228 | ... |
| Flour | Barrels | 181,798 | 228,721 | 46,923 | ... |
| ,, | Bags | 2,300 | 381,583 | 379,283 | ... |
| **PROVISIONS.** | | | | | |
| Pork | Barrels | 11,080 | 13,852 | 2,772 | ... |
| Fish | Barrels and boxes | 23,939 | 47,617 | 23,678 | ... |
| Meat | Lbs. | 13,819,075 | 19,779,783 | 5,960,708 | ... |
| **MISCELLANEOUS.** | | | | | |
| Cotton-seed oil | Barrels | 5,799 | 31,560 | 25,761 | ... |
| ,, meal | Bushels | 61,539 | 91,657 | 30,127 | ... |
| Horses | Head | 922 | 3,364 | 2,422 | ... |
| Cattle | ,, | 2,949 | 11,635 | 8,686 | ... |
| Naval stores | Barrels | 14,198 | 55,906 | 41,708 | ... |
| Coal | Tons | 938,369 | 1,802,385 | ... | 100 |
| Pig-iron | ,, | 38,545 | 127,455 | ... | 231 |
| Coke | ,, | 168 | 4,159 | ... | ... |

## RICHMOND.

Mr. Vice-Consul Marshall reports as follows:—

General trade.
Trade everywhere appears to have been fairly active during the past year. Several new industries have sprung up, viz., electro-plating works, preserving establishment, varnish manufactory, bag and twine factory, &c., besides which others have increased their plants. The bad effect of the land-booms of two years ago is wearing off and public confidence re-establishing.

(1496)

## UNITED STATES.

**Tobacco.**

In the tobacco industry the leading firms are well satisfied with the results of their trade for 1892. They have more or less increased their business, and for various reasons look to the current year for a large increment in their out-turn.

The system of loose sales of tobacco mentioned in last report is said to be working wonders. Five large warehouses are now engaged in this branch where two years ago there were practically none, and during the past few months fresh capital, amounting to 100,000 dol., has been invested in several warehouses to meet this growing business.

As an example of this increase, from January 1, 1892, to January 1, 1893, 5,000,000 lbs. of bright tobacco were sold, against 1,207,916 lbs. in the preceding year, while the sale of loose dark tobacco has increased correspondingly.

The bright tobacco crop of 1892 was not up to expectation.

This tobacco is reported as short, rich, and dark, suitable for "fillers," and deficient in weight, about 25 per cent., fine black wrappers being scarce, also "fine English stripping."

The sale of western (Burley) tobacco has increased during the year, much having been put up for shipment to the United Kingdom.

The manufacture of cigars and cigarettes continues to improve. The use of the Bohl cigarette machine which has been acquired by one of the companies here proves to be a high success.

**Jobbing trade.**

The jobbing trade of this city for 1892 is ahead of the previous year, with an increase in the sales of 241,800 dol., and in capital invested of 36,500 dol. This business is a most important one, Richmond being, so to speak, the feeder of an immense area of country.

The over-production of cotton in the south created a great depression in price of the raw material during the early part of the year. Business consequently declined until the autumn, owing, it is said, to the system of "overstrained credits." A change for the better then took place, followed by the increase in the value of sales above shown.

**The James River improvement.**

The authorities have decided to make an effort to secure if possible for Richmond some of the sea-borne trade which the more convenient ports of Newport News, Norfolk, and even West Point are in a better position to control.

A contract has been entered into—to be completed in two years' time, with effect from December 1, 1892—to deepen the James River so as to secure a mean draught of water of 20 feet at high tide, with a width of 100 feet, from Richmond Docks to the mouth of the river.

This work has hitherto been carried on in a desultory fashion, owing to want of funds, which have been supplied by the State and the United States Government from time to time by grants.

As a draught of 20 feet will be insufficient to permit of large steamers ascending to Richmond, it is contemplated to deepen the channel of the James to $25\frac{1}{2}$ feet eventually.

**The State Debt of Virginia.**

The projected settlement of the State Debt of Virginia was noticed in last year's report.

In view of the large amount of these bonds, which are held in England, some information regarding the funding of the debt may be found of interest.

The terms of the Act, dated February 20, 1892, passed by the State Legislature, provide that the committee appointed by the bondholders shall surrender to the Commissioners of the sinking fund not less than 23,000,000 dol. of the obligations of the State, and that new bonds in lieu be issued in the proportion of 19,000 dol. for every 28,000 dol. of the obligations surrendered. The time allowed for this arrangement to be to June 30, 1892, the State Commissioners being permitted to make one extension of time not exceeding six months. This extension was accordingly made to December 31, 1892.

The new bonds to be dated July 1, 1891, and payable July 1, 1891, with the option of payment at par at any time after that. The interest to be 2 per cent. for 10 years from July 1, 1891, and 3 per cent. thereafter for the balance of 90 years. This is to be payable on January 1 and July 1 of each year at the office of the treasurer of the State or at certain agencies in New York.

Securities not deposited with the Bondholders' Committee for funding to be deposited for that purpose with the Commissioners of the Sinking Fund, who will fund them on the same terms as provided by the Bondholders' Committee.

The interest on the new bonds for the three half-years from July 1, 1891, has been fully paid to the Bondholders' Committee. The bondholders as yet have received none of it, owing, through unavoidable delay, to the distribution of the bonds not being settled.

As to the fulfilment by the State of its obligations. The railways and other taxable interests of Virginia have so immensely improved of late years the public finances that no apprehension exists of the State's future ability to meet its creditors fully and regularly.

The following statement abridged from the report of the second auditor of the Commonwealth of Virginia names the securities which, up to October 15, 1892, had been presented by the Bondholders' Committee to the Commissioners of the Sinking Fund for verification in accordance with the Act, viz. :—

# UNITED STATES.

| Description. | Amount. |
|---|---|
| | Dollars c. |
| Bonds and certificates under Act of March 30, 1871 | 16,488,085 12 |
| " " " " amended by Act of March 7, 1872 | 296,821 27 |
| Bonds and certificates under Act of March 28, 1879 | 6,220,013 50 |
| " " Acts prior to April 17, 1861, and under Act of March 2, 1866, also sterling (English currency) certificates issued under Act of March 30, 1871 | 1,653,115 66 |
| Total presented | 24,658,035 55 |
| Deduct* West Virginia's portion of the old debt | 551,842 66 |
| Total amount to be redeemed by Virginia in the proportion of 19 to 28 | 24,106,192 89 |
| New bonds will be issued therefore to the amount of | 16,357,773 74 |

\* West Virginia, now a separate State of the Union, was prior to June 20, 1863, a part of Virginia, and therefore takes a share of the old debt.

## Statistics of the Port of Richmond for the Year 1892.

### Imports.

| Articles. | Value. |
|---|---|
| | Dollars. |
| Guano | 24,000 |
| Farm and garden seeds | 12,202 |
| Hair and hides | 6,956 |
| Dry goods and woollens | 4,692 |
| Wines and ale | 3,431 |
| Metal goods and cutlery | 2,999 |
| Plaster | 1,600 |
| Fresh fruit | 1,480 |
| Cigarette paper | 1,105 |
| Painted windows (stained glass) | 487 |
| Olive oil | 264 |
| Miscellaneous | 12,185 |
| Total | 71,401 |

### Exports.

| Articles. | Value. |
|---|---|
| | Dollars. |
| Cotton (in bales) | 3,334,813 |
| Flour | 112,706 |
| Cotton-seed oil | 73,085 |
| Tobacco (hogsheads and tierces) | 32,224 |
| Cotton-seed meal | 20,360 |
| Shuttle blocks (cases) | 7,665 |
| Bark | 3,945 |
| Lard | 712 |
| Miscellaneous | 1,037 |
| Total | 3,586,547 |

## BALTIMORE.

| Country. | Imports. | Exports. |
|---|---|---|
|  | Dollars. | Dollars. |
| Great Britain | 22,076 | 2,947,450 |
| British possessions | 6,062 | 888 |
| France | 4,404 | .. |
| Germany | 3,281 | 244,252 |
| Belgium | 1,842 | 212,700 |
| Italy | 770 | 68,085 |
| Austria | 2,010 | .. |
| Brazil | 6,956 | 113,172 |
| Orchilla, West Indies | 24,000 | .. |
| Total | 71,401 | 3,586,547 |

RETURN of Vessels Entered and Cleared from the Port of Richmond, Va., and Sub-Port of West Point in 1892.

### ENTERED.

| Nationality. | Steam. Number of Vessels. | Steam. Tons. | Sailing. Number of Vessels. | Sailing. Tons. |
|---|---|---|---|---|
| British | 17 | 27,349 | 5 | 1,147 |
| Foreign | 1 | 1,396 | 4 | 1,065 |
| United States | .. | .. | 5 | 1,438 |
| Total | 18 | 28,745 | 14 | 3,650 |

### CLEARED.

| Nationality. | Steam. Number of Vessels. | Steam. Tons. | Sailing. Number of Vessels. | Sailing. Tons. |
|---|---|---|---|---|
| British | 17 | 27,349 | 3 | 603 |
| Foreign | 1 | 1,396 | 5 | 1,812 |
| United States | .. | .. | 1 | 428 |
| Total | 18 | 28,745 | 9 | 2,843 |

(1496)

LONDON:
Printed for Her Majesty's Stationery Office,
By HARRISON AND SONS,
Printers in Ordinary to Her Majesty.
(75  4 | 93—H & S  1496)

# FOREIGN OFFICE.
## 1893.
## ANNUAL SERIES.

### Nº 1181.
### DIPLOMATIC AND CONSULAR REPORTS ON TRADE AND FINANCE.

# UNITED STATES.

### REPORT FOR THE YEAR 1892
#### ON THE
### TRADE OF THE CONSULAR DISTRICT OF BOSTON (MASS.).

REFERENCE TO PREVIOUS REPORT, Annual Series No. 1015.

*Presented to both Houses of Parliament by Command of Her Majesty,*
*MAY, 1893.*

LONDON:
PRINTED FOR HER MAJESTY'S STATIONERY OFFICE,
BY HARRISON AND SONS, ST. MARTIN'S LANE,
PRINTERS IN ORDINARY TO HER MAJESTY.

And to be purchased, either directly or through any Bookseller, from
EYRE & SPOTTISWOODE, EAST HARDING STREET, FLEET STREET, E.C., and
32, ABINGDON STREET, WESTMINSTER, S.W.; or
JOHN MENZIES & Co., 12, HANOVER STREET, EDINBURGH, and
90, WEST NILE STREET, GLASGOW; or
HODGES, FIGGIS, & Co., Limited, 104, GRAFTON STREET, DUBLIN.

1893.

[C. 6855 –68.]     *Price One Penny.*

# New Series of Reports.

Reports of the Annual Series have been issued from Her Majesty's Diplomatic and Consular Officers at the following places, and may be obtained from the sources indicated on the title-page:—

| No. | | Price. | No. | | Price. |
|---|---|---|---|---|---|
| 1061. | Tainan | 1d. | 1121. | Damascus | 1d. |
| 1062. | Smyrna | 1½d. | 1122. | Naples | 2d. |
| 1063. | Old Calabar | ½d. | 1123. | Hakodate | 1d. |
| 1064. | Samoa | ½d. | 1124. | Montevideo | 2½d. |
| 1065. | Tahiti | 1d. | 1125. | Stockholm | 1½d. |
| 1066. | Chefoo | 6d. | 1126. | Dantzig | 2d. |
| 1067. | Gothenburg | 2d. | 1127. | The Hague | 1½d. |
| 1068. | Buenos Ayres | 1½d. | 1128. | Odessa | 1d. |
| 1069. | Loanda | 1½d. | 1129. | Berne | 1½d. |
| 1070. | Guatemala | 1d. | 1130. | Malaga | 3d. |
| 1071. | Zanzibar | 1d. | 1131. | Rome | 2½d. |
| 1072. | Charleston | 2½d. | 1132. | St. Jago de Cuba | 4½d. |
| 1073. | Nice | 1d. | 1133. | Munich | 1½d. |
| 1074. | Caracas | 1d. | 1134. | Meshed | 1d. |
| 1075. | Lisbon | 2d. | 1135. | Guayaquil | ½d. |
| 1076. | Calais | 2d. | 1136. | Rio de Janeiro | 4½d. |
| 1077. | Rio Grande do Sul | 5½d. | 1137. | Tonga | 1d. |
| 1078. | Philadelphia | 2½d. | 1138. | Copenhagen | 1d. |
| 1079. | Brindisi | 2d. | 1139. | Tangier | 1½d. |
| 1080. | New York | 2d. | 1140. | Buenos Ayres | 2½d. |
| 1081. | San Francisco | 1½d. | 1141. | Para | 1d. |
| 1082. | Frankfort | 4d. | 1142. | Bagbdad and Bussorah | 1½d. |
| 1083. | Hiogo | 1½d. | 1143. | Christiania | 5½d. |
| 1084. | Tokio | 1½d. | 1144. | Old Calabar | 2d. |
| 1085. | Amsterdam | 1d. | 1145. | Trieste | 1½d. |
| 1086. | San Francisco | 3d. | 1146. | Quito | 1d. |
| 1087. | Bangkok | ½d. | 1147. | Buenos Ayres | 6d. |
| 1088. | Söul | 1½d. | 1148. | Bogotá | 1d. |
| 1089. | Chiengmai | 1d. | 1149. | The Hague | 2d. |
| 1090. | Copenhagen | ½d. | 1150. | Mexico | 2½d. |
| 1091. | New Caledonia | ½d. | 1151. | Florence | 2d. |
| 1092. | Bushire | 2d. | 1152. | Calais | 1d. |
| 1093. | Tamsui | 1d. | 1153. | Lorenzo Marques | 1½d. |
| 1094. | Dunkirk | 1d. | 1154. | Patras | 1d. |
| 1095. | Port Said | 1d. | 1155. | Taganrog | 1d. |
| 1096. | Guatemala | ½d. | 1156. | Stockholm | 1d. |
| 1097. | Chungking | 9d. | 1157. | Washington | 2d. |
| 1098. | Nagasaki | 1d. | 1158. | Paris | 1½d. |
| 1099. | Constantinople | 2d. | 1159. | Bengazi | 1d. |
| 1100. | Buenos Ayres | ½d. | 1160. | Santos | 2½d. |
| 1101. | Shanghai | 2d. | 1161. | Buenos Ayres | 1½d. |
| 1102. | Jeddah | ½d. | 1162. | Nantes | 1d. |
| 1103. | Chicago | 3d. | 1163. | Beira | 5d. |
| 1104. | Erzeroum | ½d. | 1164. | Galveston | 1½d. |
| 1105. | Loanda | 3d. | 1165. | Berlin | 1d. |
| 1106. | Macao | ½d. | 1166. | Bordeaux | 2½d. |
| 1107. | Canton | 1d. | 1167. | Calais | 2½d. |
| 1108. | Paramaribo | 1½d. | 1168. | The Hague | 2d. |
| 1109. | Tunis | 1½d. | 1119. | Athens | 12d. |
| 1110. | Sofia | 3d. | 1170. | Galatz | 1½d. |
| 1111. | Brunei | 1½d. | 1171. | Guayaquil | 1d. |
| 1112. | Athens | 2½d. | 1172. | Riga | 2d. |
| 1113. | Alexandria | 2d. | 1173. | Trebizond | 1d. |
| 1114. | Vienna | 1d. | 1174. | Havre | 2½d. |
| 1115. | Stettin | 2½d. | 1175. | Saigon | ½d. |
| 1116. | Berne | 1d. | 1176. | Baltimore | 1½d. |
| 1117. | Palermo | 2½d. | 1177. | Brest | 1d. |
| 1118. | Tokio | 1½d. | 1178. | Buenos Ayres | ½d. |
| 1119. | St. Petersburg | 3d. | 1179. | Adrianople | ½d. |
| 1120. | Teneriffe | 1d. | 1180. | Algiers | 2½d. |

# No. 1181.

*Reference to previous Report, Annual Series No. 1015.*

## UNITED STATES.

### BOSTON.

*Acting-Consul Stuart to the Earl of Rosebery.*

My Lord,   Boston, *March* 24, 1893.

I HAVE the honour to enclose a Report on the Trade and Commerce of Boston and the Boston Consular District for the year 1892.

I have, &c.
(Signed)   W. H. STUART.

---

*Report on the Trade and Commerce of the Consular District of Boston for the Year* 1892.

#### ABSTRACT of Contents.

|   | PAGE |
|---|---|
| Condition of trade | 1 |
| Foreign exports and imports at Boston | 4 |
| Foreign maritime trade at Boston | 4 |
| Rates of exchange | 5 |
| Mercantile failures in district | 5 |
| Statistics of manufactures in Massachusetts | 5 |
| Statistics of labour in Massachusetts | 5 |
| Statistics of labour in Maine | 7 |
| Tables | 8–9 |

The past year has shown a decided improvement in business over the year 1891, and chiefly owing to that year's bounteous harvests which, together with deficient harvests abroad, increased the means of producers as also consumers in this country, and enlarged the demand for manufactured goods and wares. *(General condition of trade.)*

In this Consular District this demand has given labour for the masses, which has given them power to spend and thereby help all lines of trade.

NOTE.—Sterling amounts in this report are given at 5 dol. to the 1*l.*

(1506)

## UNITED STATES.

In the first part of 1892 dulness prevailed, making merchandise low, and, owing to a surplus of goods on hand, depressed trade.

This surplus, however, being got rid of by curtailment of production and a large consumption setting in, caused during the last half of the year a steady but sure and increasing improvement in all kinds of business.

Operators, however, were cautious and, following the tactics of 1891, did not buy ahead of actual wants, but after the first part of the year a steady and general demand caught up with production, and manufacturers were able to keep their machinery busy.

The tendency of the trade in all probability will be to continue a hand-to-mouth policy, owing to the nearing change of administration, and thus be in position to meet any changes that may be made hereafter.

In general the business of the past year can be best stated as steady without speculative features and with a general strengthening at the close.

**Cotton and cotton goods.**
The year opened with raw cotton and cotton fabrics on a low basis, but small profits were generally made, as raw cotton declined to a very low price, owing to the pressure to sell the large crop of 1891.

The low price for raw cotton discouraged growers, which brought about a lighter acreage for 1892, which, as demand increased, caused a shortage and a mark-up of about $1\frac{1}{2}d.$ per lb. in a few weeks' time, as also a decided mark-up in the price of manufactured goods in sympathy. Dealers being bare of goods, the prices ran still higher, and the year ended leaving mills with unexecuted orders for months to come.

The advance on the higher grades of cotton fabrics was from $\frac{1}{4}d.$ per yard to $\frac{1}{2}d.$ per yard.

**Wool and woollens.**
Owing to the sharp competition of foreign wools the wool market, although showing a large business, has brought low prices.

The year closed with a healthier demand and Ohio fleeces show an advance of $\frac{1}{2}d.$ over prices 2 months ago.

Manufacturers of woollens have found no boom in any kind of goods but sufficient demand to absorb all the production of their mills at a profit.

Worsteds sold well, but cheviots yet hold their place at the top.

Cassimeres dragged. The mills altogether have done a profitable business, and the year closes with orders ahead.

**Iron, steel and copper, &c.**
The market has shown a steady consumption, but owing to large production values have ruled low.

Values of steel have been easy, with more or less fluctuations in price.

Copper has been very low during most of the year, but under the influence of speculation values advanced $1d.$ per lb. in the fall, and the market closes firm.

Tin and other metals have ruled quiet with values low.

**Hides and leather.**
During the first half of the year a good demand for leather

prevailed, but accumulated supplies kept values on a very low basis.

Dealers, therefore, decided to stop production for 2 months, during which time no hides were to be "wet in," which put the market on a healthy basis.

Sales of Buenos Ayres' hides were made below 6d. Domestic hides closed dull.

Business has been very good during the year, the shipments having been the largest of any year, being 278,000 cases in excess of 1891, and 162,000 cases more than in 1890. *Boots and shoes.*

The situation has been remarkable for the evenness and steadiness of trade as also of prices. *Lumber trade.*

Building operations took all the spruce produced.

Shingles and clap-boards have ruled dull, while laths have been high all the year.

Hard woods have sold steadily and brought fair prices.

The New England fish trade had a fairly active and prosperous year, with, however, some sharp fluctuations in supply and demand. *Fish trade.*

The codfish catch by the New England fleet was very successful and lasted from March to November.

Owing to a well-stocked market in the early part of the season, prices fell considerably until June, when they gradually advanced to the highest point in October, and continued firm to the end of the year.

Mackerel were in good supply and of good quality off Cape Cod in May, and subsequently along the coast of Massachusetts and Maine up to the early part of September, when they almost entirely disappeared.

The total native catch, in addition to about an equal quantity imported from Canada, Newfoundland, the United Kingdom, France, Norway, and Sweden, amounted to 62,000 barrels.

Imports from Ireland were not as large as in 1891, but the quality and condition of the fish showed a marked improvement on former shipments. Norwegian mackerel, however, are awarded the palm for quality, careful curing and excellent packing.

The shore catch of herring was above the average in quantity, quality, and size, and together with importations from Newfoundland, Scotland, Norway, and Holland, kept the market well stocked, and though not in excess of the demand, produced a sensible fall in price.

Bloaters, formerly received from England, are now extensively prepared in this country from herrings imported from Newfoundland.

The receipts of fish in the Boston market in 1892 were:—

(1506)

## UNITED STATES.

| Articles. | | Quantity. | |
|---|---|---|---|
| | | Domestic. | Foreign. |
| Codfish | Quintals | 91,505 | 41,481 |
| Mackerel, fresh and salted | Barrels | 22,787 | 54,180 |
| Frozen herring | ,, | 21,343 | 32,136 |
| Smoked herring and bloaters | Boxes | 831,208 | 189,805 |
| All other kinds of fish | Quintals | 76,452 | 1,151 |
| | Barrels | 14,977 | 9,495 |
| | Boxes | 13,744 | 17,877 |

**Foreign imports and exports.**

The Boston custom-house returns for 1892 show imports (including 5,000*l.* in coin and bullion) to the value of 15,118,712*l.*, and exports (including 100,110*l.* in coin and bullion) to the value of 17,761,041*l.*

The increase of imports over the previous year was 957,788*l.*, and that of exports was 1,409,110*l.*

The value of free goods imported was 7,572,598*l.*, and that of dutiable goods was 7,546,114*l.*, being an increase in the value of free goods of 940,861*l.*, and of dutiable goods of 16,927*l.*

Of exports 17,648,306*l.* represented domestic goods, and 112,735*l.* foreign goods.

**Foreign maritime trade.**

The number of vessels of all nationalities which entered the port of Boston from foreign ports in 1892 was, according to the custom-house returns, 2,396 vessels of 1,705,492 tons, or an increase of 54 vessels and 151,892 tons over the previous year.

Of these, 1,884 vessels of 1,379,636 tons were British, 370 vessels of 201,045 tons were American, and 142 vessels of 124,811 tons were of other nationalities.

This shows an increase over the previous year of 78 British vessels of 146,537 tons, an increase of 28 American vessels of 43,080 tons, and a decrease of 52 vessels of 37,725 tons of other nationalities.

The number of British vessels from all ports, including United States ports, entered at the Consulate, was 1,933 vessels of 1,377,327 net tons, of which 729 vessels of 1,214,002 tons were steamships and 1,204 vessels of 163,325 tons were sailing vessels, the increase over the previous year in steamers being 89 vessels of 133,232 tons, and the decrease in sailing vessels of 4, with an increase, nevertheless, of 6,393 tons, making a total increase of 85 British vessels of 132,625 net tons.

**Ocean freights.**

Inward freights from Boston to the United Kingdom have been most unsatisfactorily low, and, it is stated, giving no return to capital invested, the same can be said of outward freights, which to the United Kingdom fell-off considerably during the year, with but a small and only partial recovery towards its close.

Thus grain ranged from 4*d.* to 6*d.* in January, 1*d.* to $2\frac{3}{5}d.$ in September, $2\frac{1}{2}d.$ to 3*d.* in December.

Provisions declined from 1*l.* to 1*l.* 10*s.* in January, from 7*s.* 6*d.* to 16*s.* 3*d.* in October, and 8*s.* to 17*s.* 6*d.* in December.

Flour from 12s. to 1l. in January, from 7s. to 10s. in June, and 8s. to 12s. 6d. in December.

Cotton from $\frac{3}{16}d.$ to $\frac{3}{32}d.$ and recovered to $\frac{5}{32}d.$ Cattle from 2l. 15s. in January to 1l. 10s. in September, and 1l. 15s. in December. Apples from 2s. 3d. in January to 1s. 6d. in December.

Sole leather from 1l. 12s. 6d. to 1l. 15s. in January, and 17s. 6d. to 1l. in December.

Bankers' sight bills were in January 4 dol. 85 c. per 1l.; in April, 4 dol. 84¾ c.; in June, 4 dol. 88¾ c.; in September, 4 dol. 87¼ c.; in October, 4 dol. 86½ c.; and in December, 4 dol. 88 c. with very slight fluctuations between these dates. *Sterling exchange.*

The number of firms in business in this Consular District in the year 1892 was 81,047, or an increase of 819 over the preceding year, and the number of failures and amount of liabilities 804 and 2,040,891l., or a decrease of 88 and 984,812l. respectively. *Mercantile failures.*

In continuation of the fifth annual report on manufactures for the year 1890, of which an abstract was given in the last commercial report of this Consulate, the Bureau of Statistics of Labour has since published its sixth annual report on manufactures in 1891. *Statistics of Massachusetts manufactures.*

Of the 25,000 industrial establishments assumed to be in operation in Massachusetts, only 3,745 furnished sufficiently complete data for comparison between 1890 and 1891.

As, however, these establishments comprise the most important industries, their returns enable a fairly correct estimate to be made of the relative extent and value of the industries of the State in these two years.

Some of these 3,745 establishments were amalgamated, and some were transferred from private firms to corporations.

| Description. | 1890. Number. | 1890. Amount. | 1891. Number. | 1891. Amount. |
|---|---|---|---|---|
| | | £ | | £ |
| Thus the number of private firms was | 2,987 | ... | 2,952 | ... |
| The number of corporations | 730 | ... | 762 | ... |
| The amount of capital invested | ... | 84,944,762 | ... | 86,931,220 |
| Value of stock used | ... | 70,487,135 | ... | 72,444,074 |
| ,, product | ... | 121,006,533 | ... | 122,620,143 |
| Average number of persons employed | 287,900 | ... | 292,866 | ... |
| Smallest number of persons employed | 261,107 | ... | 258,771 | ... |
| Greatest number of persons employed | 322,288 | ... | 329,634 | ... |
| Amount of wages paid | ... | 25,216,061 | ... | 25,883,249 |

It thus appears there was an increase in 1891 over 1890, in these 3,745 establishments, of 2·34 per cent. in the value of stock used, of 1·33 per cent. in the value of produce, of 1·72 per cent. in the average number of persons employed, and of 2·65 per cent. in the amount of wages paid.

In accordance with a legislative resolution of the year 1891, the 22nd annual report of the Massachusetts Bureau of Statistics of Labour, published in 1892, deals with the question of rented tenements in the City of Boston. *Statistics of labour.*

Rented tenements, as defined in the report, applies to "places of residences hired or leased, without distinction of the class of persons occupying them, but not to hotels, boarding-houses, or tenements exclusively occupied by their owners."

The first of three sections into which that subject is divided, and which gives the number of houses, tenements, and rooms, hired or leased as residences, the number of families or persons occupying them, and the rents paid, is the only one published in this report; Sec. 2 and Sec. 3, treating respectively of the sanitary condition of tenements, and the nationality, place of birth, and occupation of occupiers, being reserved for future publication.

This Sec. 1 contains detailed returns for each of the 205 precincts, comprised in the 25 wards into which the city is divided, and abstracts of these returns for the whole city.

From these abstracts it appears, at the time of enquiry, the number of tenement houses (besides 14,788 houses occupied by owners, and 3,131 boarding and unoccupied houses) was 36,223, that the number of rented tenements (besides 5,483 unoccupied) was 71,665, containing 342,544 rooms, and occupied by 71,665 families, aggregating 311,396 persons.

It is thus shown that the relative average of tenements ranging from 1 to 47 to each tenement house was 1·98, the average of rooms ranging from 1 to 32, to each tenement 4·78, the average number of persons to each rented house 8·60, the average number of persons to each tenement as well as to each family 4·78, and the average of persons to each room (the highest percentage in the case of nine persons living in two rooms being 4·50, and the lowest in that of nine persons in 32 rooms being 0·28) was 0·91.

It is further stated that the total population of Boston being 464,751 and the total number of families 92,950, those living in rented tenements constituted 67 per cent. of the total population and 77·10 of the total number of families.

From a comparative table for the years 1875 and 1891 it appears moreover that the increase in the number of dwelling-houses in the latter year was 26·65 per cent. and that of population 35·92 per cent.

As regards rents, which range from 50 c. (2s.) to 144 dol. 17 c. (28*l.* 16s.), the average rent paid by 71,665 families in 1891 was 17 dol. 26 c. (3*l.* 9s.) per month.

Whilst not directly connected with the foregoing subject, the report contains, as a sequel to former publications, the following labour laws passed by the Legislature of Massachusetts in 1891.

Chapter 270 of the Massachusetts Statutes gives to persons to whom a debt is due for having performed labour on public works owned by a city or town, under contract with any person having authority from or rightfully acting for such city or town, a right of action against such city or town to recover such debt with costs.

Chapter 330 enacts that any person or corporation, or agent or officer on behalf of such person or corporation, who shall hereafter coerce or compel any person or persons to enter into an agreement, either written or verbal, not to join or become a member of any labour organisation, as a condition of such person or persons securing employment or continuing in the employment of any such person, or corporation, shall be punished by a fine of not more than 100 dol.

Chapter 375 enacts that from July 1, 1892, no minor under 18 years of age and no woman shall be employed in any manufacturing or mechanical establishment more than 58 hours in a week.

Chapter 410 provides that the system, now or anytime hereafter, employed by manufactories of grading their work shall in no way affect or lessen the wages of a weaver, except for imperfections in his own work; and in no case shall the wages of those engaged in weaving be affected by fines or otherwise, unless the imperfections complained of are first exhibited and pointed out to the person or persons whose wages are to be affected, and no fine or fines shall be imposed upon any person for imperfect weaving, unless the provisions of this section are first complied with and the amount of the fines are agreed upon by both parties.

The second section of this chapter imposes on any employer who shall violate the provisions of this Act a fine of not more than 100 dol., and for a second or subsequent violation thereof a fine of not more than 300 dol.

In the State of Maine the granite industry has been seriously affected by protracted strikes and lock-outs.

*Statistics of labour in Maine.*

These strikes have but recently been settled, otherwise labour has been employed on full time and at fair wages, if we except the encroachments of women, in fields of labour formerly occupied by men, in which case wages have been kept down.

From the pay-rolls of seven mills, employing 3,531 hands, engaged in the manufacture of cotton goods, it appears that the average wages paid per day is, in the carding department, 4s. 7d.; in the ring spinning department, 3s. 2½d.; mule spinners, 4s. 7d.; weaving, 5s. 2¾d.; dressing, pooling, &c., 4s. 2½d.; cloth finishing, 4s. 5d.; selt and roll, 5s. 2¼d.; and repair, 7s. 5d.; average wages paid being 4s. 10¼d.

In the corn factories in this State there are employed 4,709 men, 2,165 women, 637 boys, and 489 girls; the average daily wages paid being for men, 6s. 5½d.; women, 3s. 7½d.; boys, 3s. 2d.; girls, 2s. 3½d.; average wages of all being 3s. 10½d.

*Indian corn.*

There were 9,312 acres planted with corn, which allowed the packing of 13,161,028 cans.

The largest number of cans packed per acre was 2,333, but the poor land produced but 480 cans to the acre.

The total value of the plants is 76,000l., and the average pack per acre was 26l.

During the past year this State has been successful in the manufacture of silk goods, the Westbrook Mills alone producing 350,000 yards.

The average number of days worked by all in Maine is 220 in a year.

The smallness of this average is to be accounted for by the

severity and length of the winter, which prevents the employment of many artisans, &c., during that period.

Annex A.—RETURN of Shipping in the Foreign Trade at the Ports in the Boston Consular District in the Fiscal Year ended June 30, 1892.

ENTERED.

| Nationality. | Sailing. || Steam. || Total. ||
| | Number of Vessels. | Tons. | Number of Vessels. | Tons. | Number of Vessels. | Tons. |
| --- | --- | --- | --- | --- | --- | --- |
| British and other foreign | 2,682 | 19,065 | 1,305 | 1,487,944 | 3,987 | 1,807,009 |
| American | 558 | 170,008 | 280 | 274,930 | 838 | 444,938 |
| Total | 3,240 | 489,073 | 1,585 | 1,762,874 | 4,825 | 2,251,947 |
| ,, for the year preceding | 3,803 | 564,855 | 1,269 | 1,487,899 | 5,072 | 2,052,754 |

CLEARED.

| Nationality. | Sailing. || Steam. || Total. ||
| | Number of Vessels. | Tons. | Number of Vessels. | Tons. | Number of Vessels. | Tons. |
| --- | --- | --- | --- | --- | --- | --- |
| British and other foreign | 2,789 | 306,170 | 1,156 | 1,251,599 | 3,945 | 1,557,769 |
| American | 1,019 | 257,286 | 282 | 273,613 | 1,301 | 530,899 |
| Total | 3,808 | 563,456 | 1,438 | 1,525,212 | 5,246 | 2,088,668 |
| ,, for the year preceding | 4,250 | 621,406 | 1,090 | 1,237,446 | 5,340 | 1,858,852 |

Annex B.—RETURN of Principal Articles of Export from and Imports to Ports in the Boston Consular District during the Fiscal Years ended June 30, 1892–91.

EXPORTS.

| Articles. | Value. ||
| | 1892. | 1891. |
| --- | --- | --- |
| | £ | £ |
| Meat and dairy products | 6,653,217 | 6,426,522 |
| Horned cattle | 2,367,293 | 1,879,359 |
| Corn, flour, and other bread-stuffs | 3,381,166 | 2,056,091 |
| Raw cotton | 2,565,501 | 2,463,655 |
| Leather, and manufactures of | 846,994 | 1,033,307 |
| Cotton manufactures | 252,497 | 211,922 |
| Tobacco in leaf and manufactured | 105,694 | 219,941 |
| Iron, steel, and manufactures of | 422,355 | 375,229 |
| Sugar and molasses | 206,197 | 102,787 |
| All other domestic merchandise | 1,988,063 | 1,980,275 |
| Foreign imports re-exported | 169,074 | 86,149 |
| Coin and bullion | 4,848 | 251,989 |
| Total | 18,962,899 | 17,087,226 |

## BOSTON.

Imports.

| Articles. | Value. 1892. | Value. 1891. |
|---|---|---|
| | £ | £ |
| Sugar and molasses | 2,714,648 | 2,694,017 |
| Wool | 743,080 | 1,819,498 |
| Woollen goods | 365,242 | 436,987 |
| Hides, goat and fur skins, and furs.. | 958,562 | 1,076,457 |
| Iron ore, iron, steel, and manufactures of | 922,877 | 1,142,406 |
| Chemicals, drugs, dyewood and dyes | 1,039,442 | 1,024,795 |
| Flax, hemp, jute, and manufactures of | 684,888 | 1,369,834 |
| Cotton goods | 280,423 | 286,965 |
| Fish | 279,063 | 363,805 |
| All other imported merchandise (including 97,391l., value of domestic exports reimported) | 8,015,913 | 5,800,778 |
| Coin and bullion | 12,879 | 6,547 |
| Total | 16,017,017 | 16,022,089 |

Annex C.—Tables showing the Value of all Articles Exported from and Imported to Ports in the Boston Consular District during the Fiscal Years 1892–91.

| Country. | Exports. 1892. | Exports. 1891. | Imports. 1892. | Imports. 1891. |
|---|---|---|---|---|
| | £ | £ | £ | £ |
| United Kingdom and colonies | 17,106,749 | 15,960,875 | 8,974,339 | 9,758,789 |
| Germany | 536,175 | 238,852 | 804,254 | 857,963 |
| France and colonies | 129,100 | 195,170 | 514,971 | 487,429 |
| Spain and colonies | 45,208 | 29,938 | 2,724,534 | 2,257,796 |
| Austria-Hungary | 664 | .. | 158,790 | 81,395 |
| Netherlands and colonies | 274,660 | 34,276 | 429,377 | 280,468 |
| Belgium | 488,985 | 309,537 | 274,556 | 300,539 |
| Sweden and Norway | 20,043 | .. | 161,326 | 185,208 |
| Italy | 10,901 | 15,916 | 321,345 | 315,468 |
| Russia | 10,569 | .. | 140,856 | 101,329 |
| Turkey | 30,241 | 16,568 | 223,548 | 144,050 |
| Argentine Republic | 104,248 | 28,427 | 643,624 | 639,054 |
| Uruguay | 8,663 | 13,776 | 104,462 | 94,888 |
| Brazil | 2,159 | 2,156 | 2,828 | 73,104 |
| Chile | 48,283 | 56,715 | 63,835 | 60,439 |
| Mexico | 69 | .. | 389,793 | 138,682 |
| Hayti | 8,179 | 19,868 | 41,663 | 65,329 |
| All other countries | 138,003 | 165,152 | 42,916 | 180,159 |
| Total | 18,962,899 | 17,087,226 | 16,017,017 | 16,022,089 |

LONDON:
Printed for Her Majesty's Stationery Office,
By HARRISON AND SONS,
Printers in Ordinary to Her Majesty.
(75  5 | 93—H & S  1506)

# FOREIGN OFFICE.
## 1893.
## ANNUAL SERIES.

### No. 1203.

### DIPLOMATIC AND CONSULAR REPORTS ON TRADE AND FINANCE.

# UNITED STATES.

### REPORT FOR THE YEAR 1892
ON THE
### TRADE OF THE CONSULAR DISTRICT OF CHARLESTON, S.C.

REFERENCE TO PREVIOUS REPORT, Annual Series No. 1072.

*Presented to both Houses of Parliament by Command of Her Majesty,*
*MAY, 1893.*

LONDON:
PRINTED FOR HER MAJESTY'S STATIONERY OFFICE
BY HARRISON AND SONS, ST. MARTIN'S LANE,
PRINTERS IN ORDINARY TO HER MAJESTY.

And to be purchased, either directly or through any Bookseller, from
EYRE & SPOTTISWOODE, EAST HARDING STREET, FLEET STREET, E.C., and
32, ABINGDON STREET, WESTMINSTER, S.W.; or
JOHN MENZIES & Co., 12, HANOVER STREET, EDINBURGH, and
90, WEST NILE STREET, GLASGOW; or
HODGES, FIGGIS, & Co., Limited, 104, GRAFTON STREET, DUBLIN.

1893.

[C. 6855—90.] *Price Twopence Halfpenny.*

# New Series of Reports.

Reports of the Annual Series have been issued from Her Majesty's Diplomatic and Consular Officers at the following places, and may be obtained from the sources indicated on the title-page:—

| No. |  | Price. | No. |  | Price. |
|---|---|---|---|---|---|
| 1081. | San Francisco | 1½d. | 1142. | Baghdad and Bussorah | 1½d. |
| 1082. | Frankfort | 4d. | 1143. | Christiania | 5½d. |
| 1083. | Hiogo | 1½d. | 1144. | Old Calabar | 2d. |
| 1084. | Tokio | 1½d. | 1145. | Trieste | 1½d. |
| 1085. | Amsterdam | 1d. | 1146. | Quito | 1d. |
| 1086. | San Francisco | 3d. | 1147. | Buenos Ayres | 6d. |
| 1087. | Bangkok | ½d. | 1148. | Bogotá | 1d. |
| 1088. | Söul | 1½d. | 1149. | The Hague | 2d. |
| 1089. | Chiengmai | 1d. | 1150. | Mexico | 2½d. |
| 1090. | Copenhagen | ½d. | 1151. | Florence | 2d. |
| 1091. | New Caledonia | ½d. | 1152. | Calais | 1d. |
| 1092. | Bushire | 2d. | 1153. | Lorenzo Marques | 1½d. |
| 1093. | Tamsui | 1d. | 1154. | Patras | 1d. |
| 1094. | Dunkirk | 1d. | 1155. | Taganrog | 1d. |
| 1095. | Port Said | 1d. | 1156. | Stockholm | 1d. |
| 1096. | Guatemala | ½d. | 1157. | Washington | 2d. |
| 1097. | Chungking | 9d. | 1158. | Paris | 1½d. |
| 1098. | Nagasaki | 1d. | 1159. | Bengazi | 1d. |
| 1099. | Constantinople | 2d. | 1160. | Santos | 2½d. |
| 1100. | Buenos Ayres | ½d. | 1161. | Buenos Ayres | 1½d. |
| 1101. | Shanghai | 2d. | 1162. | Nantes | 1d. |
| 1102. | Jeddah | ½d. | 1163. | Beira | 5d. |
| 1103. | Chicago | 3d. | 1164. | Galveston | 1½d. |
| 1104. | Erzeroum | ½d. | 1165. | Berlin | 1d. |
| 1105. | Loanda | 3d. | 1166. | Bordeaux | 2½d. |
| 1106. | Macao | ½d. | 1167. | Calais | 2½d. |
| 1107. | Canton | 1d. | 1168. | The Hague | 2d. |
| 1108. | Paramaribo | 1½d. | 1169. | Athens | 12d. |
| 1109. | Tunis | 1½d. | 1170. | Galatz | 1½d. |
| 1110. | Sofia | 3d. | 1171. | Guayaquil | 1d. |
| 1111. | Brunei | 1½d. | 1172. | Riga | 2d. |
| 1112. | Athens | 2½d. | 1173. | Trebizond | 1d. |
| 1113. | Alexandria | 2d. | 1174. | Havre | 2½d. |
| 1114. | Vienna | 1d. | 1175. | Saigon | ½d. |
| 1115. | Stettin | 2½d. | 1176. | Baltimore | 1½d. |
| 1116. | Berne | 1d. | 1177. | Brest | 1d. |
| 1117. | Palermo | 2½d. | 1178. | Buenos Ayres | ½d. |
| 1118. | Tokio | 1½d. | 1179. | Adrianople | ½d. |
| 1119. | St. Petersburg | 3d. | 1180. | Algiers | 2½d. |
| 1120. | Teneriffe | 1d. | 1181. | Boston | 1d. |
| 1121. | Damascus | 1d. | 1182. | Marseilles | 1½d. |
| 1122. | Naples | 2d. | 1183. | Warsaw | 1d. |
| 1123. | Hakodate | 1d. | 1184. | Piræus | 1½d. |
| 1124. | Montevideo | 2½d. | 1185. | Callao | 1d. |
| 1125. | Stockholm | 1½d. | 1186. | Jerusalem | ½d. |
| 1126. | Dantzig | 2d. | 1187. | Chefoo | 1½d. |
| 1127. | The Hague | 1½d. | 1188. | Munich | 2d. |
| 1128. | Odessa | 1d. | 1189. | Resht | 1d. |
| 1129. | Berne | 1½d. | 1190. | Batavia | 1½d. |
| 1130. | Malaga | 3d. | 1191. | Batoum | 1½d. |
| 1131. | Rome | 2½d. | 1192. | Tainan | 1d. |
| 1132. | St. Jago de Cuba | 4½d. | 1193. | Amoy | 1d. |
| 1133. | Munich | 1½d. | 1194. | Zanzibar | 4d. |
| 1134. | Meshed | 1d. | 1195. | Corunna | 2d. |
| 1135. | Guayaquil | ½d. | 1196. | Algiers | 15½d. |
| 1136. | Rio de Janeiro | 4½d. | 1197. | Pakhoi | 1d. |
| 1137. | Tonga | 1d. | 1198. | Nice | 1½d. |
| 1138. | Copenhagen | 1d. | 1199. | Kiungchow | 1½d. |
| 1139. | Tangier | 1½d. | 1200. | Aleppo | 1d. |
| 1140. | Buenos Ayres | 2½d. | 1201. | Stettin | 4½d. |
| 1141. | Para | 1d. | 1202. | Swatow | 1d. |

# No. 1203.

*Reference to previous Report, Annual Series No. 1072.*

# UNITED STATES.

## CHARLESTON.

*Acting-Consul Harkness to the Earl of Rosebery.*

My Lord,  Charleston, April 22, 1893.

I HAVE the honour to transmit herewith the Annual Trade Reports for Charleston, Brunswick, and Wilmington for the year 1892.

I regret that I am not able to obtain a Report also from Savannah, as Mr. Vice-Consul Robertson reports that he is unable to prepare the same in consequence of an accident.

I have, &c.
(Signed) A. HARKNESS.

---

*Report on the Trade and Commerce of the Consular District of Charleston for the Year 1892.*

ABSTRACT of Contents.

| | Page |
|---|---|
| General trade | 1 |
| Cotton | 6 |
| Phosphates and fertilisers | 8, 9 |
| Chemicals | 10 |
| Rice | 11 |
| Naval stores and lumber | 14, 15 |
| Shipping and navigation | 15 |
| Freights; new channel | 16 |
| Miscellaneous | 19 |
| Brunswick Vice-Consulate | 20 |
| Wilmington " | 25 |

*General Trade.*

During the year 1892 a great and very general business depression prevailed at Charleston and throughout the State of South Carolina. This depression was also experienced over the entire cotton-growing section of the American Union. Low prices at the beginning of the year caused great distress among southern farmers and producers, and the ill-effects were sorely felt

*Marginal note:* General depression.

(1544)

at most of the commercial centres. The unfavourable conditions in the country were naturally reflected in the towns, and Charleston's total trade for the year, compared with the previous season, is estimated to have fallen off about 14,000,000 dol. (nearly 3,000,000*l.*). The official figures of the whole amount of business done in 1892 were a little over 83,000,000 dol. (17,000,000*l.*), against 98,000,000 dol. (20,000,000*l.*) for the year before. It is believed that fully one-half of the above-mentioned decrease in the trade of this port for the past year is attributable to the falling-off in cotton values. Low prices for this staple also had a most unfavourable effect upon the phosphate and fertiliser business, the demand for commercial manures having been largely decreased by the inability of cotton planters to buy so freely as in former seasons.

Shipping.

A reference to the return of British shipping for 1892, attached elsewhere to this Report, will show that the shipping trade also suffered severely from the bad business in cotton and fertilisers. The total number of arrivals of vessels flying the English flag were only 51 for last year, against 96 for the year before, a falling-off of 45 vessels, or nearly 50 per cent. There was also, unfortunately, a considerable amount of inconvenience, together with loss of time and money, sustained by a number of British steamers that took cotton cargoes at this port last fall, in consequence of the unwillingness of cotton dealers to ship this product at the low prices prevailing and the inability on the part of several charterers to load vessels according to the terms agreed upon in charter parties, or to meet claims for demurrage incurred thereunder. These cases appear to have been purely instances of business misfortune, the result of an exceptionally depressed cotton trade, and insufficient financial strength to weather the storm on the part of the charterers.

The unpleasant facts in the condition of British shipping trade at Charleston this year, however, have been, to a certain extent, offset and compensated for by the large exports of Carolina phosphate rock from Port Royal, Beaufort, Coosaw, and Bull River. About 65 British steamers having taken cargoes from the Beaufort Custom-house District (which includes the four places named) during 1892, the indications at the close of the year being that, for the incoming year, there is likely to be a considerable increase in the amount of British tonnage that will be required for the carrying trade in this branch of business next season. As most of the Carolina phosphate industries are managed or controlled from Charleston, much of the business done at other places in this State is beneficial, in a measure, to the commercial interests of this port, and contributes, in this sense of the word, directly or indirectly to its welfare.

General trade of the year.

But taking the general trade for the whole year in cotton, phosphates, and fertilisers there seems to be no doubt that the past season was one of the most unsatisfactory ever known in these industries. Matters were aggravated, moreover, by the fact that trade depression was not confined to Charleston nor to this State or country. During the early part of 1892 there was a general collapse in cotton values and a stagnation of trade almost to the point of congestion in nearly all of the markets of the world. The depression also almost ruined the mining of apatite in Canada; and the principal French and German phosphate mines were unable to sell half of the quantity of rock in 1892 that they had mined in 1891, and sales were made at far less remunerative prices. The same depressed condition also existed in fertilisers both here and abroad, and nearly all other branches of trade sympathised with and were unfavourably affected by the bad state of affairs in the three above-stated leading industries of this section. One conspicuous exception, however, was that of the cotton spinners, the Carolina mills doing a good business during the year, owing to the exceptionally low prices at which they were able to buy the raw cotton early in the season.

It may also be stated, in reviewing the past year's trade, that the principal industries have been characterised by a marked absence of over-production, being in striking contrast, in this respect, with the previous season.

The total American cotton crop receipts for the four months of September, October, November, and December, 1892, were about 2,000,000 bales short of the crop for the same period in 1891, and in phosphate mining and fertiliser manufacturing but few of the companies worked up to their full capacity, the acid chambers of several of the largest fertiliser establishments only working for a short time.

It has, unfortunately, been the case that a number of misleading articles have, from time to time of late, been published in various industrial trade journals throughout this country with reference to the phosphate business. While these articles may not, perhaps, have been purposely intended to deceive the public, they have, nevertheless, been calculated to give wrong impressions, their tone being too optimistic and the colour too rosy to give correct ideas as to the facts connected with this subject. The plain truth, plainly stated, appears to be that during the past year there was, not only a great shrinkage in value of phosphates and fertilisers, but that a considerable reduction was also sustained in the volume of business done. It must, however, be stated that there was a material improvement towards the close of the year, the general trade conditions, as the year closes, showing very much better prices prevailing, a brisker demand for cotton and phosphates, and a favourable outlook for an improvement in general trade conditions next season.

Reports received from all sections of the State of South Carolina show that farmers and business men entered upon the year just closed with many misgivings as to the outcome of the year's work, owing to the low prices for cotton and the large stocks remaining on hand unsold from the previous season and unsaleable at remunerative figures. The acreage planted in cotton was reduced by at least 25 per cent., and there was a

*Misgivings.*

corresponding, or even greater, reduction in the orders for commercial fertilisers. More land, however, was devoted to wheat and other small grains than ever before and with highly satisfactory results.

The cotton crop produced was only fairly good, but better prices were obtained for it, the price for middling having advanced from 6 c. per lb. at the beginning of the year to 9½ c. for the same grade of cotton on the last day of December, 1892. It is estimated that more smoke-houses in this State have this year been filled with South Carolina raised meat than has ever been the case before, the bills for commercial fertilisers were never so light, and store accounts, as a rule, represent only purchases that were strictly necessary. Economy has been the watchword, and, although the past year was a most trying one for the merchants, they have generally been able to meet their obligations and overcome their difficulties.

Business was done more on a cash basis than heretofore and the records of Bradstreet's and Dun's commercial agencies show a gratifying smallness in the percentage of business failures officially recorded during the year, in view of the exceptionally bad trade conditions experienced.

In spite, however, of the exceptionally bad season that Charleston experienced, there has been a considerable addition made to the Terminal Railway facilities since the last Consular Report from this office was sent home.

During the autumn months the East Shore Terminal Railway Company extended their tracks from a point opposite Broad Street to the southern wharves, the limit of the dock system here on the ocean side of the town, thus practically completing a system of Terminal Railway tracks which places every wharf on the eastern side in direct communication with the entire network of railways on the North American continent. Steps have also been taken, during the past year, by parties interested in the terminal facilities of this port to secure, jointly with the other South Atlantic seaport towns, such a reduction in the railway rates on grain from the West as would enable these ports to compete on equal terms with Baltimore, Newport News, and New Orleans for a fair proportion of the enormous quantities of Western-grown grain which are now annually shipped from the last-named places to Europe.

The importance of this matter will be understood from the fact that the only port south of Cape Hatteras that exported grain last year to foreign countries was New Orleans, and, according to official figures, over 21,000,000 bushels were shipped last year from that place to all parts of Europe, the principal shipments going to France and Germany, although Great Britain also enjoyed a large portion of the trade.

The grain exports from New Orleans the year before last were only 7,000,000 bushels, thus showing an excess in favour of the past season of 14,000,000 bushels, and, at the same time, clearly establishing the fact that this business is both a large and a growing one.

At the time this report is written it is understood that a satisfactory readjustment of railway rates has been secured, and that hereafter the South Atlantic ports, including Charleston, Port Royal, Savannah, and Brunswick, will be on an equal footing in the matter of grain rates with the Gulf ports and exporting points north of Cape Hatteras. With the doing away of prohibitive freight rates, the principal difficulty has been removed, and concerted action on the part of the respective ports interested, through their representative commercial bodies, will, it is expected, soon secure charters for the formation of grain-exporting companies to inaugurate and develop this business. There is ample capital in Charleston to handle a grain-exporting trade, and although there are no grain elevators here as yet they will be built when grain shipments make them necessary. *Railway rates.*

In addition to the extension and improvements made on the east side of the town last year there was also a spur or branch line built by the Charleston and Savannah Railway Company on the west, or Ashley River side, connecting the main line about 7 miles north with nearly all the principal phosphate establishments along the Western River frontage for a distance of about 7 miles. British and other vessels are now able to discharge cargoes of pyrites, nitrate, kainit, or sulphur, of which there are numerous arrivals, on either the east or the west sides of the town, as may be most convenient or desirable, the railway facilities being equally good in the way of direct through connections and track accommodation for the handling and distribution of these cargoes to interior points. *Extension and improvement.*

With reference to other matters connected with the improvement of Charleston Harbour, which took place during the past year, perhaps the most important one to be mentioned was the passage last summer by the American National Congress of a Bill authorising the Secretary of War to contract, for a sum not exceeding 2,175,000 dol., for continuous work upon and the completion thereof of the system of jetties now in progress for deepening the water on Charleston Bar. Irregular and inadequate appropriations have seriously retarded this work during recent years, but by the action of Congress in passing the above-named measure, the improvement of the bar is now placed beyond the contingencies which affect river and harbour bills in Congress, and there is no further danger of the work being suspended by reason of the failure of such appropriation bills henceforward. Although the jetties are not likely to be completed for several years, there has already been a marked increase in the depth of water on the north or jetty channel across the bar. Up to last year 12 feet of water was about the maximum through this channel, but now there is obtainable by this passage way to the sea a depth of 15 feet, according to soundings made by the United States revenue cutter, "Morrill," and numerous vessels went to sea by this channel last year that could not have used it before. *Harbour.*

It is also gratifying to be able to report that no cotton fires occurred on board British or other vessels at Charleston during *Cotton fires.*

(1544)

## UNITED STATES.

the year 1892, and so far as known, no fires were reported on ships taking cargoes here as having developed after leaving this port. The record for 1892 being even better in this respect than for the year before, although it must be stated that the number of ships taking cotton cargoes last season was considerably reduced.

*Trade.* Fuller details and figures in regard to the principal branches of trade for the past year are set forth as follows under their respective headings, an effort being made to avoid unnecessary elaboration in treating the different subjects, and minimising, so far as it could well be done, the use of figures and tabulated statistics.

### Cotton.

*Cotton.* The total receipts of cotton at Charleston for the commercial year ending August 31, 1892, were 511,273 bales, against 557,744 bales in 1891, and 349,828 bales in 1890, showing a decrease the past season of 46,471 bales, compared with 1891, and increase as compared with the previous year of 161,445 bales.

The receipts last year, while not so large as for the year before, have nevertheless shown that the comparative decrease here was less than at any of the other South Atlantic cotton ports.

In some respects the season was a remarkable one in the cotton trade, over 9,000,000 bales were produced during 1891–92 by American cotton-growers—the largest crop of the staple ever made in this country, and prices for middlings went down to the lowest point recorded for 40 years, the quotations during January, February, March, and April, 1892, ranging from $6\frac{1}{4}$ c. to $6\frac{3}{4}$ c. per lb.

*Rise in prices.* In May, however, prices commenced to rise, and cotton sold for $7\frac{1}{8}$ c. on August 31, and at the end of December the closing quotations for middlings were $9\frac{5}{8}$ c., after reaching 10 c. during the middle of the month.

*Exports.* The total exports of cotton from Charleston from September 1, 1891, to August 31, 1892, inclusive, were 478,079 bales as compared with 534,921 bales for the same period the year before. Of the amount exported last year 158,102 bales went to Liverpool, 5,550 bales to Havre, 184,632 bales to other Continental ports, and 129,795 bales to New York and interior points of the United States.

From September 1, 1892, to December 31, 1892, the receipts of cotton at Charleston were 245,813 bales, as compared with 410,473 bales received during the last 4 months of 1891, a decrease last year of 164,660 bales. The exports from September 1, 1892, to December 31, 1892, amounted to 204,747 bales, against 333,208 bales for the corresponding period in 1891. Leaving the stock on hand and on shipboard on the last day of the year of 48,763 bales, against 74,367 bales for the same day a year ago. Of the cotton exported during the last 4 months of

1892, the shipments to Liverpool were 76,369 bales; Havre, 7,900 bales; Continental ports, 71,692 bales; and to New York, 53,676 bales.

According to general expectation the crop of Sea Island cotton produced last year was smaller than that of the preceding season, and if the number of bags brought forward from the year before be deducted from last year's receipts it will be seen that the actual growth of the past season was less than 55,000 bags.

*Sea Island cotton.*

The market opened in October, 1891, at 19 c. per lb. for medium fine Carolinas and 17½ c. per lb. for fine Floridas, but prices speedily declined, and in January, 1892, the quotations for medium fine Carolinas were 16 c. per lb. and fine Floridas 14½ c. per lb.

The demand, however, for extra fine Carolinas was very good, and prices for this quality were about the same as last year.

After the month of May unfavourable crop reports caused prices to advance, and by September 1 the quotations were 24 c. per lb. for medium fine Carolinas and 17½ c. per lb. for fine Floridas.

In September the reports from the new crop were bad, and the indications from South Carolina, Georgia, and Florida gave promise of a smaller crop for the coming year; the greatest falling off was reported from Florida, in consequence of reduced acreage and bad crop conditions prevailing in that State.

The receipts and exports of South Carolina, Georgia, and Florida Sea Island cotton at Charleston, for the cotton year ending August 31, 1892, compared with the year before, were as follows:—

*Receipts and exports.*

RECEIPTS.

|  | Quantity. | |
|---|---|---|
|  | 1892. | 1891. |
|  | Bags. | Bags. |
| Receipts of Islands | 9,218 | 13,241 |
| Georgias and Floridas | 31 | 173 |
| Old Stock | 564 | 67 |
| Total | 9,813 | 13,481 |

EXPORTS.

|  | Quantity. | |
|---|---|---|
|  | 1892. | 1891. |
|  | Bags. | Bags. |
| Exports of Islands | 9,664 | 12,744 |
| Georgias and Floridas | 30 | 173 |
| Stock, Islands | 119 | 564 |
| Total | 9,813 | 13,481 |

# UNITED STATES.

**Exports.**

Of the exports from this port of Sea Islands during last year 2,557 bags were shipped to Liverpool, 241 bags to Havre, and 6,896 bags went coastwise to New York; making a grand total of 9,694 bags exported, against 12,917 bags for the previous season, leaving a stock on hand, September 1, 1892, of 119 bags to be carried forward to next year's crop statement.

According to official figures, the total amount of the Sea Island cotton crop produced in the United States last season was 59,232 bags, as compared with 68,063 bags for the year before. Of last season's crop, Savannah received 33,084 bags; Charleston, 9,249 bags; Fernandina, 4,113 bags; Brunswick, 3,456 bags; and Jacksonville, 330 bags.

**The total cotton crop for 1891-92.**

The following is the estimate made of the total American cotton crop, including Uplands and Sea Islands, for the season of 1891-92, made up to August 31, 1892:—

|  | Quantity. |
| --- | --- |
|  | Bales. |
| Receipts at the ports.. | 7,102,145 |
| Net overland movement | 1,262,110 |
| Southern consumption | 651,715 |
| Total cotton crop for 1891-92 | 9,015,970 |

### Phosphates and Fertilisers.

The Carolina phosphate and fertiliser business last year was severely affected by the disastrous collapse in the cotton trade and the large surplus stock of 1,500,000 bales on hand on January 1, for which no remunerative market could be found. The low price of cotton appears to have been the principal cause for the depression which prevailed in the values of rock, acid phosphate, and fertilisers; but, in addition to this, there were several other causes which contributed to unfavourably affect the market. The heavy and continuous rains which prevailed during the mining season greatly retarded work and reduced profits, and the legal decision adverse to the Coosaw Mining Company, which was the final result of the litigation between that company and the State, caused the shutting down of its extensive machinery and the closing of the Coosaw Mines to all mining operations for more than a year, entailing considerable loss to the State Treasury in diminished royalties, and also offering advantages to Florida competitors in marketing their phosphate products, river rock particularly, which they would not otherwise have enjoyed. The manufacturers of Great Britain and the Continent, who used river rock, were willing to use the Florida article because the well and favourably known Coosaw rock could not be obtained. The Coosaw River is now open again, however, to all miners, and with its good machinery and management is once more making large returns. It has always been a favourite rock abroad, being of high grade, uniform quality, and well prepared. Its good reputation, together with the low prevailing prices, has attracted the attention of foreign buyers again, and large shipments of Carolina-mined rock are expected to be made during the next season.

For the past 23 years South Carolina produced more phosphate rock than any other section, and the State still holds her place in this industry, notwithstanding the serious competition of the Florida rock for the last two or three years. There are 14 or 15 companies manufacturing phosphate fertilisers around Charleston, and these, together with the Coosaw Company and the manufacturing companies near Beaufort and Savannah, will greatly aid this State in its efforts to maintain its position of supremacy as a phosphate market. It is probable that for many years to come the Charleston manufacturers will require from 150,000 to 200,000 tons of rock annually to supply their wants, and this demand alone will give employment to a dozen or more companies mining rock, as few of them produce more than 25,000 tons yearly.

In addition to the Coosaw territory and the many large and prosperous land companies in this State, there is also good mining in the Edisto, Ashepoo, Wando, Stono, and Ashley Rivers.

The total shipments of Carolina phosphate rock from January 1, 1892, to December 31, 1892, amounted to 516,786 tons. The shipments from Charleston were 2,475 tons to foreign countries, 134,132 tons to domestic ports, and 125,000 tons consumed here, the shipments from Beaufort being as follows:—132,234 tons to foreign ports, 56,277 tons to domestic ports and interior places by rail and 15,000 tons consumed.

The total shipment of Florida phosphate rock for the year 1892 was 314,399 tons; of this amount 229,383 tons were shipped to foreign ports, and 85,016 tons were sent to domestic points or consumed. The principal foreign shipments of Florida rock last year were from the ports of Fernandina, 118,678 tons; Punta Gorda, 41,365 tons; Port Tampa, 40,459 tons; and Brunswick, 15,469 tons. The smaller shipments from Savannah and Tampa were 7,412 tons and 6,000 tons respectively.

*Fertilisers.*

The older companies manufacturing fertilisers in this State had a fairly prosperous season during the commercial year ending August 31, 1892; they manufactured large supplies, and sales were made at moderately remunerative prices, collections were good, and they were able to pay large and regular dividends, making their stocks favourite ones for investment, many persons preferring them for this purpose to the mining companies. *Prosperous season.*

Notwithstanding the check which was placed upon the

manufacture of commercial manures and fertilisers last year by the low prices of cotton, it is believed that this business will inevitably grow, and small reverses will not long retard its future development.

Large sums of money have been invested in the manufacture of fertilisers, and the facility with which money has been raised from banks, together with the intelligent and trustworthy character of the men managing the business, gives the public confidence, and appears to justify the belief that the fertiliser industry is not likely to suffer more than temporary depression from the bad cotton year just passed.

There was manufactured in the United States in 1892 1,365,000 tons of fertilisers, compared with 1,360,000 tons in 1891 and 1,250,000 tons for the year before.

*Shipments.* The shipment of fertilisers from Charleston for 1892 were 214,338 tons, against 287,975 tons for 1891; shipments from Port Royal, 30,000 tons last year, against 33,000 tons in 1891; and from Savannah, 108,119 tons in 1892 and 112,000 tons the year before.

The total sales for the same periods were: at Charleston, 214,338 tons in 1892, against 287,975 tons in 1891; Savannah, 108,119 tons, against 112,000 tons; and Port Royal, 30,000 tons, against 33,000 tons.

Of the shipments of fertilisers last season from this port 208,175 tons were shipped to interior points by rail, and the remaining 6,163 tons went forward by steamer, mostly to northern ports.

*Prices.* The prevailing prices for fertilisers at the close of the year were as follows:—

Fertilisers—Kainit, 12 dol. 50 c. per ton; acid phosphate, 13 per cent., 9 dol. 50 c.; dissolved bone, 9 dol. 50 c.; ammoniated fertiliser, 2 per cent., 18 dol. to 18 dol. 50 c.; ammoniated fertiliser, 2½ per cent., 19 dol. to 19 dol. 50 c.

Phosphate rock—Land rock, crude, 4 dol. per ton.; land rock, hot air dried, 4 dol. 80 c. to 5 dol.; river rock, crude, 3 dol. 75 c.; river rock, hot air dried, 4 dol. 75 c.; ground rock, 7 dol. 50 c.

### *Chemicals Imported into Charleston.*

The following table will show the quantities of chemicals, used in the manufacture of fertilisers, imported into Charleston during the last two commercial years, ending August 31, 1892 and 1891, respectively:—

## CHARLESTON.

| Articles. | 1890-91. | | 1891-92. | |
|---|---|---|---|---|
| | Quantity. | Value. | Quantity. | Value. |
| | Tons. | Dollars. | Tons. | Dollars. |
| Kainit | 19,164 | 133,713 | 40,301 | 195,018 |
| Sulphur | 25,243 | 436,808 | 24,316 | 580,344 |
| Muriate of potash | 3,306 | 111,770 | 2,506 | 88,915 |
| Pyrites | .. | .. | 17,071 | 62,047 |
| Fertilisers | 548 | 5,489 | 1,577 | 11,797 |
| Nitrate of soda | 1,966 | 63,046 | 3,035 | 74,939 |
| Total | 50,227 | 750,826 | 88,806 | 1,013,060 |

It is believed that next year the quantity of pyrites likely to be used here will be very much larger, and the amount of kainit required considerably smaller than last year, unless the price of sulphur should fall greatly below present quotations.

### Rice.

The harvest season during the autumn of 1891 was an unfavourable one for the rice interests. Harvest.

Long continued rains and frequent heavy showers during the first weeks of the season retarded work in the fields and also delayed the cutting of much rice after it was ready for the sickle. Great waste and injury was sustained, too, by that part of the crop which had been cut and stacked up in the fields, it having suffered greatly, both as to quantity and quality.

It was found when the rice was brought to the threshing mills that calculations that had been made, by experienced planters, as to the yield per acre, were greatly overestimated. The straw was abundant enough, but the grain was missing, and the fact was established that, on most plantations, the average yield to the acre was much below the figures for the last few years, while the expenses necessary for harvesting were considerably increased.

The result shows that there was a shortage in the rice crop of this State last season of 63,438 bushels, as compared with the year before; and that the total shortage, the past year, in the Atlantic coast rice growing States of North Carolina, South Carolina and Georgia amounted to 154,105 bushels.

The rice crop of the Gulf State of Louisiana fared better at the critical period of harvest time, and this, together with the larger acreage planted, resulted in an increase of 1,001,402 bushels of Louisiana rice marketed.

The total rice crop produced in the United States during the season of 1891-92 is estimated at 5,883,629 bushels, as compared with 5,036,332 bushels for the year before; showing an increase in the American rice crop last year of 847,297 bushels.

The first new Carolina rice reached this port on September 11,

1891, and was sold on the following day for 5 c. per lb. This shipment, which came from Georgetown County, was quickly followed by others from all the rice growing sections of the State. Many of these shipments bore evidence of the injury which the grain had received, and some of the rice was in such bad condition that it had to be turned out and dried at the city mills before it could be properly cleaned and milled for market. The receipts in September, were unusually light, but increased in volume during October and prices gradually receded to $4\frac{1}{2}$ c. and $4\frac{5}{8}$ c. per lb. for good grades. Choice grades were scarce and brought full prices throughout the season and in some instances as high a figure as $5\frac{1}{2}$ c. to $5\frac{3}{4}$ c. was paid for the light offerings of this quality. During November and December there was no great change in quotations, and the market was generally in buyer's favour.

There was a slight reaction, however, late in December, that continued throughout the greater part of January, and prices were $\frac{1}{4}$ c. to $\frac{3}{8}$ c. better for fair to good grades, but as the season advanced the market became quiet and the advance could not be maintained, and as spring and summer approached sellers were obliged to meet the views of buyers and accept lower prices in order to market their stocks. On September 1, 1892, all of the old crop had been disposed of and the new rice season of 1892-93 opened with no old rice in first hands. At this time reports as to the new crop, then being harvested, were favourable, and the crop indications gave planters reason to hope that, if the weather continued good, the crop would be gathered under more advantageous conditions than for several preceding seasons.

Up to the year 1884 rice was packed in tierces averaging 600 lbs. each, net weight; but since that year it has been sent to market in barrels containing 300 lbs. net. The following figures are, therefore, in barrels, and represent cleaned or milled rice as distinguished from uncleaned or rough rice, given in bushels as above:—

## CHARLESTON.

### RICE Crop—Season of 1891-92.

| Rice Crop of— | Quantity. | |
|---|---:|---:|
| | Barrels. | Barrels. |
| **SOUTH CAROLINA.** | | |
| Milled at Charleston | 58,936 | |
| ,, Georgetown | 31,677 | |
| | | 90,613 |
| **GEORGIA.** | | |
| Milled at Savannah | .. | 40,019 |
| **NORTH CAROLINA.** | | |
| Milled at Wilmington, Newberne, and Washington | .. | 22,326 |
| **LOUISIANA.** | | |
| Milled at Louisiana | .. | 344,533 |
| Grand total crop for United States (including Gulf and Coast crops) | .. | 497,491 |

Receipts of rice at Charleston from September 1, 1891, to August 31, 1892, amounted to 82,923 barrels as compared with 87,657 barrels for the year before. There were no exports to foreign countries, but the shipments to New York and to interior places by rail were 58,923 barrels last season and 66,457 barrels the year before.

The quantity of rice that was consumed at Charleston during 1891-92 was 24,000 barrels against 20,000 barrels for the year before, and there was no stock remaining on hand on September 1, 1892, the beginning of the new season of 1892-93.

In addition to the above information respecting the rice trade at this port, the following facts are given in order to show the amount of business done during the last 4 months of last year— that is, from September 1, 1892, to January 1, 1893. During this period the total receipts of rice were 31,478 barrels, against 24,391 barrels for the corresponding time a year ago. The total exports for this year were 18,948 barrels, and for last year 16,754 barrels, leaving a stock remaining on hand and on shipboard on January 1, 1893, of 8,430 barrels, against 4,862 barrels for January 1, 1892. Of the 18,948 barrels exported, the shipments to New York were 9,150 barrels, and to interior places by railway 9,798 barrels.

*Supplementary rice figures.*

## UNITED STATES.

The Charleston rice market closed December 31, 1892, ruling easy; the quotations for prime were 4½ c. to 4¾ c. per lb.; for good, 4 c. to 4¼ c.; fair, 3⅝ c. to 3⅞ c.; and for common grades, 3 c. to 3¼ c., with small sales for the last week of the year, and a moderate demand prevailing.

### Naval Stores and Lumber.

There was a considerable falling-off in the receipts of naval stores at this port during the last commercial year, owing in a great measure to the reduced territory now sending resin, turpentine, &c., to this market; a territory that is being steadily curtailed in consequence of the gradual exhaustion of the yellow pine forests in the section of country tributary to Charleston, and also to the low prices prevailing, making manufacturers unable to prepare the products of the pine for market with any profit to themselves. While prices for resin were tolerably well maintained, spirits of turpentine declined throughout the year, and on September 1, 1892, had reached the lowest price recorded for several years, namely, 26 c. per gallon, against 34½ c., the price quoted on the same date for the year before.

*Receipts, export, and stock of naval stores.* The following comparative statement shows the receipts, exports, and stock of resin and spirits of turpentine at this port during the year ended August 31, 1892, and also for the same period of the year before:—

|  | 1891–92. || 1890–91. ||
|---|---|---|---|---|
|  | Spirits. | Resin. | Spirits. | Resin. |
|  | Casks. | Barrels. | Casks. | Barrels. |
| Stock on hand | 3,282 | 9,011 | 3,710 | 19,774 |
| Receipts | 25,969 | 127,262 | 35,414 | 163,816 |
| Total | 29,251 | 136,273 | 39,124 | 183,590 |

The total exports for the year 1891–92 were 27,798 casks of spirits and 120,299 barrels of resin, against 35,845 casks of spirits and 174,579 barrels of resin for the previous year.

Of the exports last year, 11,382 casks of spirits and 97,821 barrels of resin were shipped to foreign countries, and 16,446 casks of spirits and 22,470 barrels of resin went coastwise or by rail to domestic ports.

*Prices.* The prices quoted for the leading grades of resin on September 1, 1892, were as follows:—For "C" resin, 1 dol. per barrel; "G" resin, 1 dol. 10 c. per barrel; "H" resin, 1 dol. 15 c. per barrel; "I" resin, 1 dol. 35 c. per barrel; "K" resin, 1 dol. 50 c. per barrel; "M" resin, 1 dol. 70 c. per barrel; "N" resin, 2 dol. per barrel. The closing quotations for spirits of turpentine in regular packages (casks) was 26 c. per gallon as compared with 34½ c. for the same day the year before.

A review of the Charleston naval stores market for the past 30 years show that this business underwent a steady increase from the season of 1865-66, when the total receipts in barrels and casks were 32,136, until the year 1882-83, when the receipts amounted to 366,471 packages in all, the highest figures recorded since the American Civil War. For the last 10 years, however, there has been an average rate of decrease in the receipts of about 20,000 casks and barrels per year. The decadence in the naval stores trade of this port having naturally resulted, as already stated, from the gradual working out of the Carolina pine forests.

### Lumber.

There has been no very material change in the general condition of the lumber market during the past year, although the increased facilities now existing enable Charleston lumber dealers to handle and execute orders more promptly than in former years. Low prices last season had a discouraging effect on manufacturers, and the business done was mainly due to the easier and less expensive handling now possible. With new railways tapping the lumber territory, and direct transfer of shipments from railway trucks to vessels, the competition of rival ports was met, and better supply of lumber has been obtainable. *Low prices*

The manufacture and shipment of kiln-dried lumber has become an important addition to the trade of Charleston, and it is expected that this branch of trade will add considerably to the business of this market in the near future.

There were but few transactions last season in large hewn or ranging timber for foreign shipping purposes, and the railway cross-tie business was neither brisk nor satisfactory, in consequence of the general depression that prevailed throughout the greater part of the year. *Depression.*

The exports of lumber, timber, and railway cross-ties from the port of Charleston for the year ending August 31, 1893, amounted in round numbers to 56,000,000 feet, as compared with 53,000,000 feet for the year before. Of last year's exports, 45,500,000 feet were shipped to domestic ports of the United States, and 5,500,000 to foreign ports, principally to the West Indies and South America. Very little lumber or timber is now shipped from here to Europe. *Exports of lumber, &c.*

### Shipping and Navigation.

The total number of arrivals of vessels at this port last year, registering 100 tons or over, was 839, as compared with 967 for the previous year. Of last year's arrivals 709 were American vessels, and 130 foreign, 51 of the last-named being British, nearly all steamers of large carrying capacity. (For full particulars of

## UNITED STATES.

British shipping, see return of British shipping at Charleston for 1892, herewith attached.) The total net tonnage of this port last year was—

|  | Tons. |
|---|---|
| Total tonnage, American | 752,667 |
| " British | 61,247 |
| Other foreign nations | 46,078 |
| Total | 859,992 |

against 938,259 tons the year before.

### Freights.

Steamer freight rates during the past year were poor, and as there was little demand for grain vessels, too many ships sought cotton cargoes to make paying rates for shipowners for whom the season was on the whole a hard one.

Coastwise freights were also very low during the year just closed. The depressed condition of business throughout the country, together with the greatly decreased demand for phosphates and fertilisers, reduced rates for freights so greatly that shipowners have not found the past year profitable.

This condition of affairs, however, was not confined to Charleston, as freights were everywhere inactive, and business generally in a state of depression.

### The New Jetties Channel.

*Progression.*

During the past year the work on the new jetties channel entrance to Charleston harbour has progressed steadily, and it is expected, by the United States engineer in charge, that, within the next 3 years, a channel will be afforded of 21 feet straight away from Fort Sumter to the sea, and that eventually this depth will be increased to 25 feet, or more, on ordinary high tides. With a channel way of, say, 21 feet at mean low water, this port would afford accommodation for merchant vessels drawing 25 feet, when loaded. This would enable Charleston to compete with New York and other northern ports for the grain and mineral products of the south-west. At the present time the first deep water port to the southward of Cape Hatteras is Port Royal, South Carolina, with a depth of 26 feet on the bar, but the rival interests of Charleston and Savannah have, hitherto, prevented the development of the advantages Port Royal undoubtedly possesses for the export of grain and cotton.

The entrance to the present main ship channel approach to Charleston harbour is 3 miles southward of the entrance to the new jetties channel. The course steered in crossing the bar by the channel now used is, for the greater part of the distance, north-west by west, while the course of crossing the new jetties channel bar will be south-east by east half east.

The advantages of the new channel entrance will be especially felt during the winter time, when most of the foreign shipping comes to this port. During the winter months the prevalent winds on this coast approach from the northward and eastward. A north-east flow would make a fair wind for a vessel coming up the proposed new channel; whereas, by the present channel, northerly to north-easterly winds range abeam to broad on to an incoming ship's bow.

In addition to this the new channel will afford vessels coming from Europe and the northward the further advantage of saving them a run of 3 miles down the coast and back, which they are obliged to make by the present route. Besides, the new channel run will be 2 miles or 3 miles shorter than the old one, thus saving, in all, about 8 miles. Even this small gain is something not to be despised when it is considered that the bulk of the shipping that comes to this port approaches the harbour entrance from the northward.

The following is a "return of British shipping" at the port of Charleston for the year 1892, which shows, in detail, the proportion of last season's shipping business by vessels flying the British flag:—

## RETURN of British Shipping at the Port of Charleston, South Carolina, in the Year 1892.

### Direct Trade in British Vessels from and to Great Britain and British Colonies.

#### Entered.

| Total Number of Vessels. || | Total Tonnage. || | Total Number of Crews. | Total Value of Cargoes. |
|---|---|---|---|---|---|---|
| With Cargoes. | In Ballast. | Total. | With Cargoes. | In Ballast. | Total. | | |
| 4 | 6 | 10 | 1,457 | 8,593 | 10,050 | 204 | £ 17,150 |

#### Cleared.

| Total Number of Vessels. || | Total Tonnage. || | Total Number of Crews. | Total Value of Cargoes. |
|---|---|---|---|---|---|---|
| With Cargoes. | In Ballast. | Total. | With Cargoes. | In Ballast. | Total. | | |
| 20 | ... | 20 | 20,969 | ... | 20,969 | 394 | £ 987,000 |

### Indirect or Carrying Trade in British Vessels from and to other Countries.

#### Entered.

| Countries whence Arrived. | Number of Vessels. ||| Tonnage. ||| Number of Crews. | Value of Cargoes. |
|---|---|---|---|---|---|---|---|---|
| | With Cargoes. | In Ballast. | Total. | With Cargoes. | In Ballast. | Total. | | |
| France ... | ... | 1 | 1 | ... | 1,530 | 1,530 | 25 | £ ... |
| Germany ... | 3 | 1 | 4 | 4,174 | 1,625 | 5,799 | 92 | 14,500 |
| Italy ... | 1 | 1 | 2 | 1,580 | 1,417 | 2,997 | 51 | 9,000 |
| Portugal ... | 2 | 3 | 5 | 2,395 | 4,351 | 6,746 | 115 | 4,500 |
| Spain ... | 7 | ... | 7 | 8,816 | ... | 8,816 | 156 | 21,000 |
| United States ... | ... | 22 | 22 | ... | 25,309 | 25,309 | 432 | ... |
| Total ... | 13 | 28 | 41 | 16,965 | 34,232 | 51,197 | 871 | 49,000 |

#### Cleared.

| Countries to which Departed. | Number of Vessels. ||| Tonnage. ||| Number of Crews. | Value of Cargoes. |
|---|---|---|---|---|---|---|---|---|
| | With Cargoes. | In Ballast. | Total. | With Cargoes. | In Ballast. | Total. | | |
| France ... | 1 | ... | 1 | 1,417 | ... | 1,417 | 26 | £ 43,000 |
| Germany ... | 16 | ... | 16 | 20,436 | ... | 20,436 | 352 | 655,000 |
| Italy ... | 1 | ... | 1 | 1,108 | ... | 1,108 | 23 | 2,000 |
| Spain ... | 3 | ... | 3 | 2,446 | ... | 2,446 | 67 | 76,000 |
| United States ... | ... | 13 | 13 | ... | 15,135 | 15,135 | 259 | ... |
| Total ... | 24 | 13 | 34 | 25,407 | 15,135 | 40,542 | 727 | 776,000 |

## Miscellaneous.

*Manufactures.*

After several years of almost uninterrupted prosperity Charleston's manufacturing establishments, together with most of the other branches of trade in this section, had to contend with the depressing influences of a large cotton crop sold at the lowest prices since the war.

The depression in agricultural interests was keenly felt in Charleston's principal industrial pursuit, the manufacture of commercial fertilisers. As compared with the previous year, prices declined about 10½ per cent. on acid phosphate and 10 per cent. on ammoniated goods. At the same time the price of chemicals advanced from 40 per cent. to 50 per cent. The farmers were unable to buy as largely as in former years, and the companies curtailed their line of credit business, the result being that 16 of the Charleston manufacturing companies carried over in stock about 75,000 tons of fertilisers, whereas in preceding years warehouse floors were usually swept clean by the end of the season. The burning of the Berkeley Mills in November decreased, somewhat, the production, but the organisation and operation of the Bowker Mill (formerly the Pacific) added about 15,000 tons to the total.

The number of hands employed in the different fertiliser works during the past year was 1,675, against 1,703 the preceding year. The capital employed was 5,428,000 dol. (about 1,000,000*l.*), against 5,323,000 dol. the year before, and the value of the annual product, including stock carried over, 4,679,007 dol. last year, as compared with 5,280,000 dol. for the season of 1891.

In consequence of the rise in the price of brimstone many mills have changed their furnaces so as to make the sulphuric acid required from pyrites, saving, by this method, about 33 per cent. in the cost of the acid, and, it is believed, that with a revival in general business the phosphate mills will once more enjoy their former prosperity.

The Charleston Cotton Mill last year turned out more goods than ever before in its history, but the decline in the prices of cloth and yarns caused some reduction in the value of the annual product, which, for last year, amounted to 625,000 dol. (125,000*l.*).

The bagging factory figures for last year shows that the production had slightly decreased as compared with the previous season, but prices were higher, and the cost of raw materials higher also.

The barrel manufacturing business was prosperous. The Palmer Manufacturing Company added new machinery to their plant, and did a business fully as large as in 1891. A fine business was also done the past season by the Tidewater and Ventilated Barrel Company.

In the bag manufacturing industry a good year was also experienced. The product exceeded the output for the previous year, and, notwithstanding lower prices, the total value of the year's product was fully equal to that of the season of 1890–91.

(1544)

## UNITED STATES.

Among the new manufacturing companies established at Charleston are the following: the Bowker Fertiliser Factory, the Mutual Oil Refinery, and the Charleston Lead Company. The Bowker Company is the successor of the old Pacific Guano Company, and turned out last year 15,000 tons of fertilisers.

The oil refinery also had a good start the past season, the company employs 25 hands, uses 40,000 dol. capital, and turns out an annual product valued at 140,000 dol. (28,000*l.*).

The total number of manufactories now in operation at Charleston are 387, employing 6,714 hands, and having a capital altogether of 11,562,500 dol., equal in sterling to about 2,312,500*l*. The estimated value of the annual product is reported to be 15,838,000 dol., or about 3,167,600*l*.

*Railways.* The railway situation, so far as the interests of this port are concerned, has not materially changed since last year's report was made. No permanent organisation has been, as yet, made in the affairs of the South Carolina Railway, Charleston's principal feeder; and no final settlement of the road is likely to be made for another year at least. This railway continues to be under the temporary control of Receiver D. H. Chamberlain, appointed by the United States Court, whose management of the property during the past very adverse business year has been able. It is impossible to state, at this time, what the eventual outcome will be, but when a permanent adjustment is effected of the roads' affairs there is no doubt but what strong and, it is believed, successful efforts will be made to make sure that this railway shall, hereafter, be conducted in a manner in harmony with and conducive to the commercial interests of the port of Charleston.

This matter is regarded here as of vital importance in view of the fact that, within 3 years, there is a prospect that the jetties will be completed, and with their completion it is hoped that deep water on Charleston bar will be an accomplished fact.

## BRUNSWICK.

*Cotton exports.* The exports of cotton to foreign countries from the port of Brunswick during the year 1892, as compared with that of 1891, show a decrease of about 10,000 bales. The exports of pitch-pine lumber and timber have somewhat increased. The exports of naval stores have greatly increased, and the exports of phosphate rock have increased from about 4,000 tons shipped in 1891 to about 22,000 tons shipped in 1892, or about 18,000 tons more than the year previous. This is entirely a new business here, and the port of Brunswick is deeply interested in its promotion and growth, and will do all in its power to attract it this way and make this a big shipping point in future.

*Pitch-pine lumber and timber exports.*
*Naval stores exports.*
*Phosphate rock exports.*

*Prices of Georgia exports.* The prices of the principal Georgian exports to foreign countries have not increased during the twelvemonth in question, but, on the contrary, have shown, in some instances, a falling-off, and whilst the rates of freight on steam and sailing vessels have not increased, it has been more steady than during the year 1891.

<small>Rates of freight.</small>

The oyster industry has during last year developed considerably. Two large factories have in the winter season worked to their full capacity canning oysters, and furnishing employment in the factories to about 100 men and 75 women, besides about 50 men engaged in gathering and planting this bivalve, which seems to thrive remarkably in these waters. The number of factories or the capacity of the present ones will undoubtedly be increased in the near future unless something unexpected occurs to prevent it. It is asserted that both factories pay handsome dividends to their stockholders.

<small>Oyster industry.</small>

<small>Number of hands employed.</small>

In August of 1892 the Congress of the United States of America granted a contract to deepen the channel across the outer, or St. Simon's, bar to a depth of 26 feet of water at mean high-water by the use of dynamite only, to one of Brunswick's enterprising and energetic lawyers, Mr. C. P. Goodyear, who proposed to undertake the task on results, payable as follows: 10,000 dol. (2,080l.) for 22 feet, 10,000 dol. for 23 feet, 10,000 dol. for 24 feet, 10,000 dol. for 25 feet, 10,000 dol. for 26 feet, and 50,000 dol. (10,400l.) for maintaining a depth of 26 feet for 2 years following. Under the terms of the contract Mr. Goodyear was to have a depth of 23 feet of water in the channel by January 1, 1893, and the United States' engineers are now taking soundings to ascertain the true depth through the channel, the result of which is not yet known.

<small>Contract for deepening the channel across the bar.</small>

The annexed tables show the commerce of Brunswick with other countries during the year 1892.

COMPARATIVE Statement of all the Shipping from the Port of Brunswick, Ga., in the Years 1890–92.

| Year. | Tonnage. | Exports. |
|---|---|---|
|  |  | Dollars. |
| 1890.. | 360,974 | 10,878,699 |
| 1891.. | 326,963 | 9,137,335 |
| 1892.. | 392,570 | 14,430,986 |

REPORT on the Rates of Freight having prevailed at the Port of Brunswick, Ga., for the Year 1892.

| Countries. | Pitch Pine Lumber. Per Standard. | Pitch Pine Lumber. Per 1,000 feet. | Pitch Pine Timber. Per Standard. | Turpentine. Per Barrel of 40 Gallons. | Turpentine. Per Case of 10 Gallons. | Resin. Per Barrel of 310 Lbs. | Cotton. Per Lb. | Phosphate Rock. Per Ton. |
|---|---|---|---|---|---|---|---|---|
| | £ s. | Dol. c. | £ s. | s. d. | s. d. | s. d. | d. | s. d. |
| Great Britain | 4 5 | .. | 4 5 | 3 9 | .. | 2 3 | $\frac{5}{16}$ | 17 6 |
| North of France | 4 5 | .. | 4 5 | .. | .. | .. | $\frac{5}{16}$ | 17 6 |
| Germany | .. | .. | .. | 3 9 | .. | 2 3 | $\frac{5}{16}$ | 17 6 |
| Holland | 4 5 | .. | 4 5 | .. | .. | 2 3 | $\frac{5}{16}$ | .. |
| Russia | .. | .. | .. | .. | 0 8 | 2 6 | .. | .. |
| South of France | .. | .. | .. | .. | 0 8 | 2 9 | .. | .. |
| Italy | .. | .. | .. | .. | 0 9 | 2 9 | .. | .. |
| Austria | .. | .. | .. | .. | .. | 2 9 | .. | .. |
| Spain | .. | 11 0 | .. | .. | .. | 3 0 | .. | .. |
| Brazil | .. | 14 50 | .. | .. | .. | .. | .. | .. |
| River Plate | .. | 14 0 | .. | .. | .. | .. | .. | .. |
| W. I. Islands | .. | 7 0 | .. | .. | .. | .. | .. | .. |

CHARLESTON.

Return of all Shipping to Foreign Ports at the Port of Brunswick, Ga., for the Year 1892.

| Country. | Cotton. Quantity. | Cotton. Quantity. | Cotton. Value. | Resin. Quantity. | Resin. Value. | Turpentine. Quantity. | Turpentine. Value. | Boards, Deals, and Planks. Quantity. | Boards, Deals, and Planks. Value. | Joists and Scantlings. Quantity. | Joists and Scantlings. Value. |
|---|---|---|---|---|---|---|---|---|---|---|---|
| | Bales. | Lbs. | Dollars. | Barrels. | Dollars. | Gallons. | Dollars. | M. feet. | Dollars. | M. feet. | Dollars. |
| Great Britain | 81,874 | 39,356,154 | 3,056,793 | 68,404 | 160,321 | 800,627 | 221,956 | 1,723 | 21,154 | 48 | 622 |
| Scotland | 2,408 | 1,199,138 | 107,922 | .. | .. | .. | .. | 336 | 4,841 | .. | .. |
| Ireland | .. | .. | .. | .. | .. | .. | .. | 539 | 6,541 | .. | .. |
| Nova Scotia | .. | .. | .. | .. | .. | .. | .. | 702 | 8,763 | .501 | 6,437 |
| British West Indies | .. | .. | .. | 4 | 6 | .. | .. | 563 | 7,474 | 303 | 3,600 |
| British Guiana | .. | .. | .. | 30,022 | 42,465 | .. | .. | .. | .. | .. | .. |
| Austria | .. | .. | .. | .. | .. | .. | .. | 5,250 | 66,584 | 432 | 5,610 |
| Brazil | .. | .. | .. | .. | .. | .. | .. | 80 | 1,204 | 1 | 11 |
| Colombia | .. | .. | .. | .. | .. | .. | .. | 1,195 | 15,205 | 577 | 8,661 |
| France | 13,474 | 6,615,575 | 537,954 | 75,455 | 101,312 | 268,713 | 77,922 | .. | .. | .. | .. |
| Germany | .. | .. | .. | 19,155 | 22,230 | 40,000 | 14,000 | 1,118 | 15,627 | 8 | 105 |
| Italy | .. | .. | .. | 69,040 | 10,629 | 835,465 | 250,958 | 236 | 3,169 | 134 | 1,337 |
| Netherlands | .. | .. | .. | .. | .. | .. | .. | 123 | 1,262 | 81 | 808 |
| Azores Islands | .. | .. | .. | .. | .. | .. | .. | .. | .. | .. | .. |
| Cape Verde Islands | .. | .. | .. | 11,221 | 16,190 | .. | .. | 2,816 | 35,102 | 692 | 9,426 |
| Russia | .. | .. | .. | 149 | 271 | .. | .. | 253 | 3,916 | 256 | .. |
| Spain | .. | .. | .. | .. | .. | .. | .. | 599 | 8,270 | 181 | 2,715 |
| Cuba | .. | .. | .. | 34 | 43 | 514 | 151 | 231 | 3,296 | 66 | 858 |
| Puerto Rico | .. | .. | .. | .. | .. | .. | .. | .. | .. | .. | 3,141 |
| Canary Islands | .. | .. | .. | .. | .. | .. | .. | 136 | 1,362 | 250 | 3,141 |
| Sweden and Norway | .. | .. | .. | .. | .. | .. | .. | .. | .. | .. | .. |
| Uruguay | .. | .. | .. | .. | .. | .. | .. | .. | .. | .. | .. |
| Total | 97,756 | 47,170,867 | 3,702,669 | 273,484 | 423,467 | 1,945,319 | 564,987 | 15,900 | 203,770 | 3,530 | 46,872 |

## UNITED STATES.

Return of all Shipping to Foreign Ports at the Port of Brunswick, Ga., for the Year 1892—continued.

| Country. | Sawn Timber. Quantity. | Sawn Timber. Value. | Hewn Timber. Quantity. | Hewn Timber. Value. | Cotton Seed. Quantity. | Cotton Seed. Value. | Phosphate. Quantity. | Phosphate. Value. | All other Articles. Value. | Total Value. |
|---|---|---|---|---|---|---|---|---|---|---|
|  | M. feet. | Dollars. | Cubic feet. | Dollars. | Tons. | Dollars. | Tons. | Dollars. | Dollars. | Dollars. |
| Great Britain | 4,534 | 46,109 | 105,643 | 13,017 | 1,609 | 24,710 | 17,176 | 189,028 | 5,225 | 3,738,935 |
| Scotland | 1,656 | 16,061 |  |  |  |  |  |  |  | 128,824 |
| Ireland | 1,880 | 19,464 | 49,520 | 6,097 |  |  |  |  |  | 32,102 |
| Nova Scotia |  |  | 513 | 86 |  |  |  |  |  | 8,849 |
| British West Indies | 50 | 742 |  |  |  |  |  |  | 4,067 | 18,726 |
| British Guiana |  |  |  |  |  |  |  |  |  | 3,600 |
| Austria | 57 | 750 |  |  |  |  |  |  |  | 42,465 |
| Brazil |  |  |  |  |  |  |  |  |  | 72,944 |
| Colombia | 16 | 233 |  |  |  |  |  |  | 1,200 | 2,648 |
| France | 304 | 3,119 | 23,062 | 3,044 |  |  |  |  |  | 30,029 |
| Germany |  |  |  |  |  |  | 2,460 | 22,800 | 240 | 740,228 |
| Italy |  |  |  |  |  |  |  |  |  | 36,230 |
| Netherlands | 1,430 | 14,366 | 40,232 | 5,077 |  |  |  |  |  | 366,762 |
| Azores Islands | 70 | 1,020 |  |  |  |  |  |  |  | 5,526 |
| Cape Verde Islands |  |  |  |  |  |  |  |  |  | 2,070 |
| Russia |  |  |  |  |  |  |  |  |  | 16,190 |
| Spain | 1,753 | 22,337 | 292 | 42 |  |  |  |  | 208 | 67,386 |
| Cuba |  |  |  |  |  |  |  |  | 2,500 | 9,957 |
| Puerto Rico | 48 | 714 |  |  |  |  |  |  |  | 11,699 |
| Canary Islands |  |  |  |  |  |  |  |  |  | 4,348 |
| Sweden and Norway |  |  |  |  |  |  | 2,000 | 20,000 |  | 20,000 |
| Uruguay |  |  |  |  |  |  |  |  | 222 | 4,725 |
| Total |  11,798 | 124,915 | 219,262 | 27,363 | 1,609 | 24,710 | 21,636 | 231,828 | 13,662 | 5,364,243 |

## WILMINGTON.

The following tables, compiled at the Vice-Consulate of Wilmington, show the direct foreign trade and commerce of Wilmington, North Carolina, during the year 1892, viz.:—

| Table. | Exports of— | | Quantity. | Value. | |
|---|---|---|---|---|---|
| | | | | Dollars | c. |
| A | Cotton | Bales | 125,182 | 5,082,689 | 0 |
| B | Resin | Barrels | 258,248 | 358,952 | 33 |
| C | Spirits turpentine | ,, | 19,664 | 284,876 | 55 |
| D | Tar | ,, | 10,522 | 17,085 | 77 |
| E | Pitch | ,, | 253 | 406 | 50 |
| F | Timber and lumber | Feet | 13,108,872 | 181,224 | 47 |
| G | Shingles | Number | 2,856,344 | 15,403 | 27 |
| H | Sundries | .. | .. | 1,738 | 0 |
| | Total | .. | .. | 5,942,375 | 89 |

The following table shows the receipts at Wilmington for the year ending December 31, 1891, to be as follows :—

| Articles. | | Quantity. |
|---|---|---|
| Cotton | Bales.. | 169,005 |
| Spirits turpentine | Casks.. | 58,444 |
| Resin | Barrels | 267,506 |
| Tar | ,, | 71,836 |
| Crude turpentine | ,, | 15,183 |

The improvement of the Cape Fear River and bar, which was begun by the United States Government in the year 1870, has progressed steadily and most favourably up to the present time; the total expenditure by the Government being 2,276,000 dol. to date, resulting in the entire closure of New Inlet and the deepening of the river and bar fully 5 feet. Vessels can now cross Cape Fear Bar in safety on an ordinary tide drawing 19 feet to Southport, a small town at the mouth of the river, and can proceed thence to Wilmington, 25 miles further up the river, drawing 18 feet. On full tides there is now 21 feet on the bar 19 feet in the river all the way to Wilmington.

The British steamer "Holyrood" loaded in Wilmington in December last at the Champion Compress Docks to 18 feet 3 inches and proceeded to Southport, where she loaded with coal to a depth of 20 feet 3 inches, and proceeded to sea without difficulty.

The class of steamers employed in the cotton trade of Wilmington during the last 10 years and up to 1892 ranged in registered net tonnage from 1,000 tons to 1,500 tons. During this season, however, a much larger class of steamers has been employed with safety, several over 2,000 tons net register having loaded full at Wilmington without difficulty. The largest cargo, and the most valuable that has ever been cleared from Wilmington, was taken out recently by the British steamer "Huntcliffe," being 10,000 bales of cotton valued at nearly 100,000*l*. It is confidently expected by the United States engineers that there will be a safe channel all the way from the bar of Wilmington of 20 feet at low water, within the next few years.

Major W. S. Stanton, of the Corps of Engineers, U.S. Army, in charge of this important work, has supplied the following official report. It will be noted that the reports of the engineers have reference to depth of water at mean low-water, and that there is a rise of the tide averaging $3\frac{1}{2}$ feet from Wilmington to sea :—

The Cape Fear River is under improvement by the United States from the ocean bar, 145 miles, to Fayetteville, the appropriations being made separately for the part above, and for the part at and below Wilmington.

From Point Peter, between the Cape Fear and its northeast branch, and at their confluence opposite Wilmington, the distance by river to the ocean bar (2 miles seaward from its mouth) is 30 miles, nearly south.

Its width is 1,200 feet at Point Peter, 640 feet where narrowest at Wilmington, increasing to 1,400 feet in its upper 4 miles to near the mouth of Brunswick River, which is a branch of the Cape Fear, $5\frac{3}{4}$ miles long, and leaving it $4\frac{1}{2}$ miles above Point Peter.

Below the mouth of Brunswick River, the ultimate junction of the Upper Cape Fear, the river is a broad and shallow estuary, its width in the next 9 miles varying from 1 to $1\frac{1}{4}$ miles, below which it is $1\frac{1}{8}$ to $2\frac{1}{4}$ miles.

Its right bank for the upper 12 miles is low and swampy and the land adaptable to the culture of rice, which is grown to some extent along the river. The rest of its right bank and its left bank are generally higher and sandy.

The range of tides is 4·5 feet on the bar and 2·5 feet at Wilmington, and although perceptibly is not materially increased at Wilmington by freshets.

Between the years 1823 and 1829 the State of North Carolina made an unsuccessful attempt to improve the river, principally by closing Brunswick River and Campbell's Island, 5 miles below, upon which at that time there was only $7\frac{1}{2}$ feet of water at low-water.

The United States commenced the work of improving the river between Wilmington and the bar in 1829, and began the improvement of the bar in 1853, at which dates their condition was as follows :—

In 1829 the navigation of the river was so obstructed as to

prevent the approach of all vessels drawing more than 10 feet water; that vessels of that description cannot approach the town, and are obliged to anchor 14 miles below it and discharge part of their cargoes into lighters.

In 1853 there was in the channel on the bar, by the survey of 1852, at low water 7½ feet of water in the eastern channel and 7 feet in the western channel at the main outlet at the mouth of the river, and 8 feet at the New Inlet, about 7 miles above the mouth, cut through the narrow beach and the ocean by a violent storm in 1761.

The work of the fiscal year, ending June 30, 1892, is as follows:—Dredging to obtain a channel 20 feet deep at mean low water and 270 feet wide was in progress under contract with Mr. P. Sandford Ross, of December 24, 1890, from July 1, 1891, to June 2, 1892, during which time a channel 20 feet deep was finished to the full width of 270 feet through the shoal at Wilmington, and cut to the width of 148 feet through the shoal at Alligator Creek, and entirely through the shoal 7,700 feet in length at Brunswick River, 37 feet wide for a length of 3,464 feet and 74 feet wide for a length of 4,236 feet.

This project of increasing the depth of the channel from Wilmington to the bar 4 feet (from a depth of 16 feet to a depth of 20 feet) and to a depth of 270 feet involved dredging through 10 shoals, aggregating 17·2 miles in length, and its completion would involve dredging, subsequent to June, 1892, amounting at the present contract price of 13¼ c. per cubic yard, with allowance for contingent and engineering expenses, to 791,947 dol., and at the rate at which appropriations have hitherto been made would occupy at least 10 years, or until 1902, until which date vessels could not reach Wilmington drawing any more water than at present, and the commerce of the port derive no appreciable benefit from the money meantime applied.

If restricted to a depth of 18 feet at mean low water the dredging of a channel 270 feet wide could be completed through all the shoals between Wilmington and the bar at an estimated cost of about 440,000 dol., while with 240,000 dol. a channel 18 feet deep and 150 feet wide could be cut through them within two years after the money became available, permitting vessels of 2 feet greater draft than at present to reach Wilmington, and permitting the commerce of the port within a comparatively short time to realise the benefit of the money appropriated.

Several steamers of 1,800 to 2,500 tons net register, with a capacity of 9,000 to 12,000 bales of cotton on a draft of 18 feet of water, are now building for the Wilmington trade. A channel with a normal depth of 18 feet at mean low water, with the excess usually dredged to insure that minimum, together with the tidal range of 2½ and 4½ feet respectively at Wilmington and on the bar, will give vessels of the above class almost unrestricted ingress and egress, and is believed to be what the immediate interests of the port of Wilmington require.

On May 25, 1892, it was, therefore, recommended by the district engineer that the dredging should be restricted to the depth of 18 feet, and that the United States suction dredge "Woodbury" should be employed, as at present, toward securing 18 feet at mean low water on the bar, working in Snows Marsh Channel when the sea prevents work upon the bar.

The recommendation was concurred in by the division engineer, who thought it "judicious to restrict the depth of dredging to 18 feet at low water from the bar to Wilmington with such funds as are now available, or are likely to be in the next two years," and who recommend that the dredge "Woodbury" be worked on the bar when she can, to obtain as great depth as she can, not to exceed 18 feet at low water; elsewhere, when not on the bar, where her operations may be most advantageous; and that a channel 18 feet deep and as wide as the funds will allow be dredged from the bar to Wilmington, in order that the navigation be improved to that extent as soon as possible, it being left to the experience of the next few years to decide whether it be necessary or expedient to work for a greater depth.

The recommendation was approved by the chief of engineers, June 9, 1892.

A survey made in May, 1892, at New Snows Marsh Channel revealed shoaling to the extent of about 94,000 cubic yards, the depth on the crest of the shoal at the south-easterly side being about 7·1 feet, in the middle about 13 feet, and along the north-westerly side 13·7 feet, but with a somewhat tortuous channel across the shoal not less than 14 feet deep at mean low water. An agreement with the contractor, supplemental to the contract, was entered into on May 16 and approved by the Secretary of War on May 20, 1892, providing for the transfer of one of the contractor's dredges to this shoal at 15 dol. 79 c. per hour, being the average earnings of the dredge for the preceding three months under the contract upon the shoals in the river above. The dredging commenced May 20, and to June 30, 39,443 cubic yards had been removed from the shoal, and re-dredging was still in progress, one cut 14 feet wide having been made through it to the depth of 18 feet, and another cut of the same width well advanced.

This new cut at Snows Marsh Channel had previously shoaled, and from February 23 to March 14, 1891, 8,808 cubic yards were redredged from it, making a channel 111 feet wide.

The United States suction dredge "Woodbury" has been engaged throughout the year in dredging in Baldhead Channel on the bar, and when the sea was too rough to work there upon the shoal in New Snows Marsh Channel, and has removed from the two channels during the fiscal year 150,645 cubic yards.

At the date of this report there is a depth at mean low water on the bar in the Baldhead Channel of not less than 17 feet, and of not less than 16 feet thence to Wilmington for a width of 270 feet, excepting upon the shoal in New Snows

Marsh Channel, at which the minimum depth is 16 feet and the minimum width 40 feet, and excepting at Lilliput Shoal, 11 miles below Wilmington, where for a distance of 300 feet the minimum depth is 15 feet.

The minimum mid-channel depth is, therefore, on the bar 17 feet, and between the bar and Wilmington 15 feet.

## UNITED STATES.

### Annex A.—Exports of Cotton for the Year ended December 31, 1892.

| Nationality. | Description of Vessel. | Names of Vessels. | Destination. | Quantity. Bales. | Quantity. Lbs. | Value. Dollars. |
|---|---|---|---|---|---|---|
| German | Barque | C. L. Weyer | Ghent | 1,533 | 734,546 | 53,255 |
| German | ,, | Stella | ,, | 1,855 | 893,997 | 64,815 |
| British | Steamship | Bertie | Bremen | 4,700 | 2,257,813 | 158,050 |
| German | Barque | Farewell | ,, | 2,000 | 978,143 | 66,100 |
| British | Steamship | Pencalenick | Liverpool | 5,715 | 2,796,318 | 188,750 |
| British | ,, | Torgorm | Ghent | 5,338 | 2,639,020 | 178,135 |
| German | Brig | Dr. Witte | Bremen | 1,077 | 513,932 | 33,400 |
| British | Steamship | Sneaton Tower | Liverpool | 4,000 | 1,961,487 | 142,200 |
| British | ,, | Southwold | ,, | 5,150 | 2,622,920 | 196,720 |
| British | ,, | Leander | ,, | 9,600 | 4,773,768 | 381,900 |
| British | ,, | Maltby | ,, | 9,000 | 4,364,159 | 349,130 |
| British | ,, | Sturworth | Bremen | 7,150 | 3,450,217 | 276,000 |
| British | ,, | Urania | Liverpool | 7,781 | 3,745,559 | 319,021 |
| British | ,, | Calliope | Bremen | 9,000 | 4,307,983 | 371,500 |
| British | ,, | Headlands | Liverpool | 9,710 | 4,623,900 | 427,700 |
| British | ,, | Ormesby | Bremen | 9,180 | 4,400,027 | 407,000 |
| British | ,, | Dean | Hango | 4,400 | 2,123,001 | 196,370 |
| British | ,, | Cape Colonna | Liverpool | 8,921 | 4,211,846 | 383,600 |
| British | ,, | Picton | Bremen | 7,562 | 3,591,742 | 350,195 |
| British | ,, | Holyrood | ,, | 5,450 | 2,575,275 | 247,870 |
| British | ,, | Sandhill | Liverpool | 6,060 | 2,818,092 | 290,978 |
| Total | | | | 125,182 | 60,383,745 | 5,082,689 |

Annex B.—EXPORTS of Resin for the Year ended December 31, 1892.

CHARLSTON.

| Nationality. | Description of Vessel. | Names of Vessels. | Destination. | Quantity. Barrels. | Quantity. Lbs. | Value. Dol. c. |
|---|---|---|---|---|---|---|
| German | Barque | Ceres | Newcastle | 3,550 | 1,214,575 | 5,400 0 |
| Russian | Schooner | Zeriba | Liverpool | 838 | 296,015 | 1,721 86 |
| Norwegian | Barque | Bellona | Newcastle | 4,635 | 1,567,085 | 6,954 0 |
| German | Brig | Diana | Rostock, Germany | 2,769 | 917,310 | 4,300 0 |
| Norwegian | Barque | Emma Parker | Bristol | 3,961 | 1,389,885 | 6,701 23 |
| Norwegian | ,, | Girgen Lorentzen | London | 3,743 | 1,191,705 | 5,586 0 |
| Norwegian | ,, | ,, | ,, | 1,000 | 334,710 | 1,554 0 |
| Norwegian | ,, | Bayard | Hamburg | 4,500 | 1,517,745 | 7,115 46 |
| German | Brig | Clara | Liverpool | 3,140 | 1,090,755 | 5,259 0 |
| German | Barque | Burgermeister Kerstein | Stettin | 3,463 | 1,114,120 | 5,211 90 |
| Norwegian | ,, | Hooding | Bristol | 3,771 | 1,298,380 | 6,086 15 |
| German | ,, | Hestia | Antwerp | 4,532 | 1,621,775 | 6,950 50 |
| Norwegian | ,, | Valkyrien | London | 5,458 | 1,640,175 | 7,500 0 |
| British | ,, | Celurca | Hamburg | 3,560 | 1,049,730 | 5,500 0 |
| Danish | ,, | Jorgensen | London | 5,309 | 1,674,080 | 7,391 38 |
| Swedish | ,, | Carin | Belfast | 3,827 | 1,201,435 | 6,007 15 |
| German | ,, | Lucy and Paul | Harburg | 3,444 | 1,059,930 | 4,245 44 |
| German | ,, | Albert Newman Berlin | Bristol | 4,410 | 1,490,775 | 6,988 0 |
| German | ,, | Demetra | Harburg | 4,042 | 1,290,940 | 6,051 27 |
| Norwegian | ,, | Candeur | Glasgow | 3,877 | 1,267,400 | 7,000 0 |
| Norwegian | ,, | Princessen | Newcastle | 4,160 | 1,275,315 | 7,200 0 |
| German | ,, | Patria | Garston | 3,307 | 1,049,170 | 4,918 92 |
| German | ,, | Sirene | Liverpool | 1,500 | 481,860 | 2,400 0 |
| Russian | ,, | Pollux | Fleetwood | 1,739 | 864,160 | 2,519 80 |
| Norwegian | ,, | Jury | Garston | 2,780 | 965,245 | 4,524 12 |
| Norwegian | ,, | Artemis | Hamburg | 4,867 | 1,698,290 | 7,600 0 |
| German | ,, | Friedrich Wilhelm Jebens | Antwerp | 3,958 | 1,204,495 | 5,646 9 |

(1544)

## UNITED STATES.

Exports of Resin for the Year ended December 31, 1892—continued.

| Nationality. | Description of Vessel. | Names of Vessels. | Destination. | Quantity. | Quantity. | Value. |
|---|---|---|---|---|---|---|
| | | | | Barrels. | Lbs. | Dol. c. |
| Norwegian | Barque | Skjoldmoer | Fleetwood | 3,705 | 1,232,200 | 5,500 88 |
| Norwegian | ,, | Dagmal | London | 4,091 | 1,291,840 | 5,800 0 |
| Norwegian | ,, | Trygoe | Harburg | 4,205 | 1,340,715 | 6,285 35 |
| British | Schooner | Gamma | Halifax | 125 | 46,125 | 335 0 |
| British | | | St. Johns | 500 | 177,090 | 1,340 0 |
| Norwegian | Barque | Constance | Granton | 6,044 | 2,005,695 | 9,302 15 |
| German | Brig | Atlantic | London | 2,897 | 915,750 | 4,088 16 |
| Norwegian | Barque | Prosit | ,, | 3,850 | 1,247,770 | 5,848 90 |
| Norwegian | ,, | Bayard | Bristol | 5,118 | 1,591,505 | 7,161 74 |
| Norwegian | ,, | Louise | Copenhagen | 4,300 | 1,420,500 | 6,087 85 |
| American | Schooner | Wm. F. Green | Port-au-Prince | 12 | 3,420 | 1,527 0 |
| German | Barque | Toni | London | 4,400 | 1,401,980 | 6,008 50 |
| Norwegian | ,, | Swalen | ,, | 3,006 | 946,115 | 4,175 40 |
| Norwegian | ,, | Ole Bull | Antwerp | 5,150 | 1,585,445 | 6,160 0 |
| Swedish | ,, | Alfhild | Stettin | 3,613 | 1,117,940 | 4,192 23 |
| Danish | ,, | Jorgensen | Garston | 4,666 | 1,486,330 | 6,867 93 |
| Norwegian | ,, | Adela | Riga | 4,184 | 1,372,210 | 5,145 76 |
| Norwegian | ,, | Skjoldmoer | London | 3,810 | 1,205,980 | 4,572 0 |
| Norwegian | ,, | Erna | Hamburg | 4,850 | 1,450,680 | 5,300 0 |
| Norwegian | ,, | Alfred Gibbs | London | 3,113 | 1,033,805 | 3,876 76 |
| Norwegian | ,, | Skjold | ,, | 2,100 | 656,780 | 2,462 92 |
| Norwegian | ,, | Elpida | ,, | 4,806 | 1,504,895 | 5,010 0 |
| Norwegian | Brig | Caroline | Bristol | 1,050 | 317,530 | 1,070 75 |
| Swedish | Barque | Aurelia | ,, | 2,700 | 867,120 | 2,926 53 |
| Norwegian | ,, | Bayard | Antwerp | 5,365 | 1,836,350 | 6,541 61 |
| British | ,, | Gler | Hull | 577 | 203,910 | 838 0 |
| Norwegian | ,, | Statsminister Stang | Bristol | 2,030 | 703,870 | 2,388 12 |

EXPORTS of Resin for the Year ended December 31, 1892—continued.

CHARLESTON.

| Nationality. | Description of Vessel. | Names of Vessels. | Destination. | Quantity. Barrels. | Quantity. Lbs. | Value. Dol. c. |
|---|---|---|---|---|---|---|
| Norwegian | Barque | Freidig | Bristol | 3,570 | 1,144,540 | 4,077 40 |
| Norwegian | ,, | Argo | Garston | 5,269 | 1,718,485 | 7,865 5 |
| German | ,, | Oscar Wendt | London | 4,811 | 1,503,580 | 5,906 0 |
| German | ,, | Catalina | Bowling | 4,584 | 1,431,385 | 4,887 0 |
| Norwegian | ,, | Johan Hansen | London | 5,236 | 1,702,850 | 6,082 0 |
| British | ,, | Augusta | Garston | 4,281 | 1,458,530 | 6,772 0 |
| Norwegian | ,, | Hieronymus | Hull | 3,857 | 1,177,795 | 4,627 0 |
| Russian | ,, | Austra | ,, | 826 | 250,110 | 983 0 |
| Norwegian | ,, | Agur | London | 3,844 | 1,291,700 | 4,843 87 |
| Norwegian | ,, | Victoria | Antwerp | 3,429 | 1,095,345 | 4,303 15 |
| Norwegian | ,, | Try | Saltport | 4,463 | 1,430,635 | 5,557 40 |
| Norwegian | ,, | Espeland | London | 3,730 | 1,210,870 | 4,973 20 |
| Norwegian | ,, | Walle | Bristol | 4,872 | 1,693,475 | 6,048 12 |
| German | ,, | Stella | Stettin | 3,860 | 1,190,955 | 4,253 41 |
| Norwegian | ,, | Artemis | Garston | 5,060 | 1,675,950 | 6,284 81 |
| British | ,, | Belle Flower | London | 2,648 | 861,315 | 4,367 39 |
| Norwegian | ,, | Krageroe | Swansea | 4,076 | 1,314,935 | 6,396 50 |
| German | ,, | Clara | | 3,485 | 1,090,920 | 4,090 95 |
| Total | | | | 258,248 | 83,674,285 | 358,952 33 |

(1544)

## UNITED STATES.

### Annex C.—Exports of Spirits Turpentine for the Year ended December 31, 1892.

| Nationality. | Description of Vessel. | Names of Vessels. | Destination. | Quantity. Casks. | Quantity. Gallons. | Value. Dol. c. |
|---|---|---|---|---|---|---|
| American | Schooner | Nettie Shipman | Hayti | 4 | 203 | 57 75 |
| German | Brig | Clara | Fleetwood | 2,090 | 104,533 | 31,360 0 |
| Norwegian | Barque | Jirgen Lorentzen | London | 250 | 12,340½ | 3,887 0 |
| Norwegian | ,, | Bayard | Hamburg | 600 | 29,823 | 9,394 24 |
| Swedish | ,, | Carin | Belfast | 275 | 13,731 | 5,492 40 |
| Russian | ,, | Pollux | Fleetwood | 1,650 | 81,789·2 | 29,444 22 |
| British | Schooner | Gamma | Halifax | 75 | 3,800 | 1,254 0 |
| British | ,, | ,, | St. Johns | 75 | 3,650·2 | 1,204 67 |
| Norwegian | Barque | Bayard | Bristol | 500 | 24,905·2 | 7,596 0 |
| American | Schooner | Wm. F. Green | Port-au-Prince | 3 | 145 | 43 50 |
| German | Barque | Toni | London | 50 | 2,471 | 815 40 |
| Norwegian | ,, | Svalen | ,, | 1,500 | 75,761 | 20,375 72 |
| Danish | ,, | Jorgensen | Garston | 417 | 21,230 | 6,273 90 |
| Norwegian | ,, | Skjold | London | 1,278 | 62,874·2 | 16,288 0 |
| Norwegian | ,, | Elpida | ,, | 500 | 25,331·2 | 6,525 0 |
| American | Schooner | Wm. F. Green | Port-au-Prince | 3 | 151 | 40 2 |
| Norwegian | Brig | Caroline | Bristol | 1,017 | 50,739 | 13,585 84 |
| Swedish | Barque | Aurelia | ,, | 969 | 48,167 | 12,041 75 |
| British | ,, | Gler | Hull | 2,200 | 110,226 | 30,864 0 |
| Norwegian | ,, | Statsminister Stang | Bristol | 1,110 | 55,971 | 15,280 0 |
| Norwegian | ,, | Freidig | ,, | 1,716 | 85,619·2 | 23,375 0 |
| Norwegian | ,, | Argo | Garston | 300 | 14,906 | 4,068 75 |
| Norwegian | ,, | Johan Hansen | London | 145 | 7,280·2 | 2,140 0 |
| Russian | ,, | Austra | Hull | 1,650 | 81,922 | 24,576 50 |
| Norwegian | ,, | Krageroe | London | 400 | 19,898 | 5,969 50 |
| German | ,, | Stella | Bristol | 500 | 24,841 | 7,203 89 |
| British | ,, | Belle Flower | Garston | 397 | 19,717 | 5,720 0 |
| Total | | | | 19,664 | 983,027 | 284,876 55 |

## CHARLESTON.

### Annex D.—Exports of Tar for the Year ended December 31, 1892.

| Nationality. | Description of Vessel. | Names of Vessels. | Destination. | Quantity. | Value. |
|---|---|---|---|---|---|
| | | | | Barrels. | Dol. c. |
| American | Schooner | Nettie Shipman | Hayti | 15 | 64 17 |
| Russian | ,, | Zeriba | Liverpool | 2,515 | 4,500 0 |
| American | ,, | Orlando | Port-au-Prince | 12 | 19 20 |
| German | Barque | Sirene | Liverpool | 3,200 | 5,120 0 |
| British | Schooner | Gamma | Halifax | 850 | 1,445 0 |
| British | ,, | | St. Johns | 300 | 510 0 |
| German | Barque | Titan | Liverpool | 3,474 | 5,080 0 |
| American | Schooner | Wm. F. Green | Port-au-Prince | 12 | 19 20 |
| American | ,, | | ,, | 12 | 20 40 |
| American | ,, | Jessie W. Starr | Antigua | 5 | 8 0 |
| American | ,, | Max | Port-au-Prince | 12 | 19 80 |
| British | ,, | Julia Elizabeth | Nassau | 6 | 8 0 |
| American | ,, | John H. Cannon | Mayaguez | 55 | 137 0 |
| American | ,, | Ann L. Lockwood | Ponce | 54 | 135 0 |
| Total | | | | 10,522 | 17,085 77 |

## UNITED STATES.

**Annex E.—Exports of Pitch for the Year ended December 31, 1892.**

| Nationality. | Description of Vessel. | Names of Vessels. | Destination. | Quantity. | Value. |
|---|---|---|---|---|---|
| | | | | Barrels. | Dol. c. |
| American | Schooner | Nettie Shipman | Hayti | 15 | 27 50 |
| British | ,, | Edwin Janet | Nassau | 2 | 3 20 |
| British | ,, | Gamma | Halifax | 100 | 150 0 |
| British | ,, | Wm. F. Green | St. Johns | 100 | 150 0 |
| American | ,, | Wm. F. Green | Port-au-Prince | 6 | 9 0 |
| American | ,, | Jessie W. Starr | Antigua | 5 | 9 0 |
| British | ,, | Julia Elizabeth | Nassau | 5 | 7 80 |
| American | ,, | John W. Cannon | Mayaguez | 10 | 25 0 |
| American | ,, | Ann L. Lockwood | Ponce | 10 | 25 0 |
| Total | | | | 253 | 406 50 |

## CHARLESTON.

### Annex F.—Exports of Timber and Lumber for the Year ended December 31, 1892.

| Nationality | Description of Vessel | Names of Vessels | Destination | Quantity | Value |
|---|---|---|---|---|---|
| | | | | Feet. | Dol. c. |
| American | Schooner | Nettie Shipman | Hayti | 104,311 | 1,520 70 |
| American | " | Thos. N. Stone | Kingston (Jamaica) | 251,471 | 3,862 59 |
| American | " | Ella M. Watts | Barbadoes | 326,411 | 4,896 0 |
| American | " | J. G. Morse, jr. | Petit Goave (Hayti) | 51,775 | 722 37 |
| American | " | Roger Moore | Mayaguez (P.R.) | 256,464 | 3,431 0 |
| American | " | Jas. E. Kelsey | Macoris (San Domingo) | 82,704 | 1,150 90 |
| American | Brig | Mary C. Mariner | Kingston (Jamaica) | 496,730 | 3,252 0 |
| American | Schooner | Maggie Todd | St. Johns (P.R.) | 148,477 | 1,953 0 |
| American | " | Seth M. Todd | Aguadilla (P.R.) | 193,513 | 2,472 0 |
| British | " | Carrie Easler | Barbadoes | 75,170 | 1,252 0 |
| American | " | Orlando | Port-au-Prince | 98,000 | 2,504 92 |
| British | " | Julia Elizabeth | Nassau | 600 | 8 0 |
| American | " | Milford | San Domingo City (San Domingo) | 220,347 | 3,824 58 |
| American | " | Maggie Todd | Port-au-Prince (Hayti) | 134,970 | 1,759 33 |
| American | " | Alice J. Crabtree | Santiago (Cuba) | 310,515 | 3,992 72 |
| American | " | G. H. Holden | Port-au-Prince (Hayti) | 185,830 | 2,296 0 |
| American | " | James E. Kelsey | Macoris (San Domingo) | 67,769 | 677 0 |
| British | " | Mabel Darling | Nassau (N.P.) | 24,000 | 447 0 |
| American | " | Wm. F. Green | Port-au-Prince (Hayti) | 175,213 | 2,285 30 |
| American | " | Seth M. Todd | St. Pierre (Martinique) | 216,883 | 3,017 0 |
| American | " | Louisa A. Grout | Cape Hayti (Hayti) | 119,502 | 1,537 7 |
| British | Brig | Moss Glen | Petit Goave " | 55,000 | 725 0 |
| American | Schooner | Lula Everett | Cape Haytien (Hayti) | 181,283 | 2,515 54 |
| American | " | Maggie Todd | St. George (Grenada) | 139,300 | 1,951 0 |
| American | " | M. A. Achorn | Santiago de Cuba (Cuba) | 15,205 | 3,878 85 |
| British | " | Edwin Janet | Nassau (N.P.) | 33,430 | 545 31 |
| German | Barque | Fortuna | Walgash (Germany) | 351,843 | 5,465 0 |

## UNITED STATES.

Exports of Timber and Lumber for the Year ended December 31, 1892—continued.

| Nationality. | Description of Vessel. | Names of Vessels. | Destination. | Quantity. | Value. | |
|---|---|---|---|---|---|---|
| | | | | Feet. | Dol. | c. |
| American | Schooner | Orlando | Port-au-Prince (Hayti) | 193,710 | 2,519 | 16 |
| American | ,, | E. H. Harriman | Jacmel (Hayti) | 169,067 | 2,169 | 1 |
| American | ,, | Daisy E. Parkhurst | Demerara | 357,273 | 4,710 | 0 |
| British | Brig | Julia A. Merritt | Port-au-Prince (Hayti) | 85,575 | 1,112 | 35 |
| American | Schooner | Seth M. Todd | St. Pierre (Martinique) | 181,351 | 2,627 | 0 |
| American | ,, | Maggie Todd | Barbadoes | 36,988 | 560 | 0 |
| American | Brig | Enoma | Port of Spain (Trinidad) | 347,170 | 4,964 | 0 |
| American | Schooner | Addie E. Snow | Cape Haytien (Hayti) | 130,272 | 1,642 | 72 |
| American | Brig | Edith | Port-au-Prince (Hayti) | 194,923 | 2,594 | 44 |
| American | Schooner | Wm. F. Green | ,, | 196,740 | 2,708 | 89 |
| American | ,, | De Mary Gray | St. Thomas | 286,195 | 4,545 | 0 |
| American | ,, | Norman | Mayaguez (P.R.) | 265,591 | 3,302 | 0 |
| American | ,, | Nettie Langdon | Guantanamo (Cuba) | 251,740 | 3,209 | 55 |
| American | ,, | Orlando | Port-au-Prince (Hayti) | 187,524 | 2,414 | 96 |
| American | ,, | Margaret A. Gregory | Cape Haytien (Hayti) | 182,690 | 2,432 | 28 |
| American | ,, | Gertie M. Rickerson | Jacmel (Hayti) | 110,971 | 1,575 | 12 |
| American | ,, | Roger Moore | Ponce (P.R.) | 261,581 | 3,923 | 71 |
| British | Brig | Kathleen | Port-au-Prince (Hayti) | 152,742 | 1,963 | 46 |
| American | Schooner | Martin E. Ebel | St. Thomas | 364,333 | 4,435 | 0 |
| British | ,, | Julien | Gonaives (Hayti) | 69,968 | 883 | 82 |
| American | ,, | Wm. F. Green | Port-au-Prince (Hayti) | 165,958 | 2,179 | 88 |
| British | Brig | Julia A. Merritt | ,, | 84,948 | 1,044 | 63 |
| American | ,, | Sullivan | St. Kitts | 241,000 | 3,615 | 0 |
| American | Schooner | Norman | Guadeloupe | 275,000 | 4,125 | 0 |
| American | ,, | Julia Fowler | Port-au-Prince (Hayti) | 239,279 | 3,454 | 56 |
| American | ,, | George Bird | Jacmel (Hayti) | 183,827 | 2,436 | 1 |
| American | ,, | Mary Sanford | Santiago (Cuba) | 325,745 | 4,205 | 59 |

## CHARLESTON.

Exports of Timber and Lumber for the Year ended December 31, 1892—continued.

| Nationality. | Description of Vessel. | Names of Vessels. | Destination. | Quantity. | Value. |
|---|---|---|---|---|---|
| | | | | Feet. | Dol. c. |
| American | Schooner | Ella M. Watts | St. Pierre (Martinique) | 300,787 | 4,511 0 |
| American | ,, | Seth M. Todd | Humacao (P.R.) | 179,627 | 2,179 0 |
| American | ,, | Margaret A. Gregory | Cape Hayti (Hayti) | 191,227 | 2,374 65 |
| American | ,, | Orlando | Port-au-Prince (Hayti) | 185,855 | 2,419 1 |
| American | ,, | Annie E. Rickerson | ,, | 146,892 | 1,800 96 |
| American | Brig | Fairfield | ,, | 80,199 | 972 63 |
| American | Schooner | Jessie W. Starr | Antigua | 266,036 | 3,990 0 |
| American | ,, | Roger Moore | Ponce (P.R.) | 270,651 | 3,560 0 |
| British | ,, | Mineola | St. Johns (P.R.) | 165,012 | 2,236 28 |
| American | ,, | Max | Port-au-Prince (Hayti) | 135,706 | 1,776 26 |
| American | ,, | Willis S. Shepard | Barbadoes | 170,000 | 2,210 0 |
| American | ,, | Edna | Samana (S.D.) | 290,181 | 3,707 50 |
| British | ,, | Onora | Kingston (Jamaica) | 123,587 | 1,827 82 |
| American | ,, | Leila Smith | Macoris (S.D.) | 230,320 | 3,454 80 |
| British | Brig | Julia A. Merritt | Aux Cayes (Hayti) | 69,808 | 1,038 4 |
| British | Schooner | Julia Elizabeth | Nassau (N.P.) | 12,123 | 210 20 |
| American | ,, | John H. Cannon | Mayaguez (P.R.) | 194,597 | 2,496 0 |
| American | ,, | Ann L. Lockwood | Ponce (P.R.) | 237,387 | 3,135 0 |
| Total | | | | 13,108,872 | 181,224 47 |

(1544)

## UNITED STATES.

### Annex G.—Exports of Shingles for the Year ended December 31, 1892.

| Nationality. | Description of Vessel. | Names of Vessels. | Destination. | Quantity. | Value. |
|---|---|---|---|---|---|
| | | | | | Dol. c. |
| American | Schooner | Nettie Shipman | Hayti | 40,000 | 260 0 |
| American | ,, | Thos. N. Stone | Kingston (Jamaica) | 155,000 | 775 0 |
| British | ,, | Carrie Easler | Barbadoes | 228,650 | 1,420 0 |
| British | ,, | Julia Elizabeth | Nassau (N.P.) | 231,000 | 1,236 0 |
| American | ,, | Alice J. Crabtree | Santiago (Cuba) | 50,000 | 282 50 |
| British | ,, | Mabel Darling | Nassau (N.P.) | 192,000 | 1,152 0 |
| American | ,, | Maggie Todd | St. George (Grenada) | 50,000 | 268 0 |
| American | ,, | M. A. Achorn | Santiago de Cuba (Cuba) | 39,300 | 222 4 |
| British | ,, | Edwin Janet | Nassau (N.P.) | 85,200 | 483 15 |
| British | Brig | Julia A. Merritt | Port-au-Prince (Hayti) | 16,000 | 104 0 |
| British | Schooner | Seth M. Todd | St. Pierre (Martinique) | 53,750 | 120 0 |
| American | ,, | Maggie Todd | Barbadoes | 440,050 | 2,110 0 |
| American | ,, | Orlando | Port-au-Prince (Hayti) | 10,000 | 65 0 |
| American | ,, | Margaret A. Gregory | Cape Hayti (Hayti) | 50,000 | 300 0 |
| British | Brig | Julia A. Merritt | Port-au-Prince (Hayti) | 10,000 | 65 0 |
| American | ,, | Sullivan | St. Kitts | 79,000 | 287 0 |
| American | Schooner | George Bird | Jacmel (Hayti) | 50,000 | 300 0 |
| American | ,, | Mary Sanford | Santiago (Cuba) | 51,900 | 311 40 |
| American | ,, | Annie E. Rickerson | Port-au-Prince (Hayti) | 25,000 | 100 0 |
| American | ,, | Max | ,, | 10,000 | 112 0 |
| American | ,, | Willis T. Shepard | Barbadoes | 625,000 | 3,125 0 |
| British | ,, | Roberts and Russel | Nassau (N.P.) | 109,494 | 1,000 18 |
| British | ,, | Onora | Kingston (Jamaica) | 50,000 | 300 0 |
| British | Brig | Julia A. Merritt | Aux Cayes (Hayti) | 60,000 | 420 0 |
| British | Schooner | Julia Elizabeth | Nassau (N.P.) | 145,000 | 585 0 |
| Total | | | | 2,856,344 | 15,403 27 |

## CHARLESTON.

### Annex H.—SUNDRY Exports for the Year ended December 31, 1892.

| Nationality. | Description of Vessel. | Names of Vessels. | Destination. | | Quantity. | Value. |
|---|---|---|---|---|---|---|
| | | | | | | Dol. c. |
| American | Schooner | Thos. N. Stone | Kingston (Jamaica) | Laths | 10,000 | 15 0 |
| British | ,, | Julia Elizabeth | Nassau | 2 barrels oil | .. | 25 0 |
| British | ,, | ,, | ,, | 10 sacks peas | .. | 15 0 |
| Norwegian | Barque | Jirgen Lorentzen | London | 200 barrels gum thus | 51,992 | 650 0 |
| British | Schooner | Gamma | Cardenas | 500 hogsheads, puncheons, &c. | .. | 539 0 |
| American | ,, | M. A. Achorn | Santiago de Cuba | 100 doors | .. | 114 0 |
| American | ,, | ,, | ,, | 5 bundles blinds | .. | 22 50 |
| British | ,, | Edwin Janet | Nassau | 500 laths | .. | 7 50 |
| Norwegian | Barque | Walle | London | 150 G. thus | .. | 350 0 |
| Total | | | | | .. | 1,738 0 |

## UNITED STATES.

**Annex I.**—EXPORTS, Domestic and Foreign, from Wilmington, N.C., for Year ended December 31, 1892.

| Articles. | | Quantity. |
|---|---|---|
| Cotton | Bales | 151,520 |
| Spirits, turpentine | Casks | 58,034 |
| Resin | Barrels | 273,291 |
| Tar | ,, | 69,091 |
| Crude turpentine | ,, | 16,216 |
| Pitch | ,, | 5,202 |
| Spirits, turpentine | Cases | 21 |
| Tar | ,, | 2,629 |
| Timber and lumber | Feet | 25,874,331 |
| Peanuts | Bushels | 102,291 |
| Shingles | | 10,274,329 |
| Cotton goods | Bales | 1,818 |
| Yarns | ,, | 218 |
| Paper stock | ,, | 662 |

**Annex K.**—RECEIPTS for Year ending December 31, 1892.

| Articles. | | Quantity. |
|---|---|---|
| Cotton | Bales | 169,005 |
| Spirits, turpentine | Casks | 58,444 |
| Resin | Barrels | 267,506 |
| Tar | ,, | 71,836 |
| Crude turpentine | ,, | 15,183 |

LONDON:
Printed for Her Majesty's Stationery Office,
By HARRISON AND SONS,
Printers in Ordinary to Her Majesty.
(75  5 | 93—H & S  1544)

# FOREIGN OFFICE.
## 1893.
## ANNUAL SERIES.

### No. 1205.

### DIPLOMATIC AND CONSULAR REPORTS ON TRADE AND FINANCE.

# UNITED STATES.

### REPORT FOR THE YEAR 1892

ON THE

### TRADE OF THE CONSULAR DISTRICT OF NEW ORLEANS.

REFERENCE TO PREVIOUS REPORT, Annual Series No. 986.

*Presented to both Houses of Parliament by Command of Her Majesty,*
*MAY, 1893.*

LONDON:
PRINTED FOR HER MAJESTY'S STATIONERY OFFICE,
BY HARRISON AND SONS, ST. MARTIN'S LANE,
PRINTERS IN ORDINARY TO HER MAJESTY.

And to be purchased, either directly or through any Bookseller, from
EYRE & SPOTTISWOODE, EAST HARDING STREET, FLEET STREET, E.C., and
32, ABINGDON STREET, WESTMINSTER, S.W.; or
JOHN MENZIES & Co., 12, HANOVER STREET, EDINBURGH, and
90, WEST NILE STREET, GLASGOW; or
HODGES, FIGGIS, & Co., Limited, 104, GRAFTON STREET, DUBLIN.

1893.

[C. 6855—92.]   *Price Twopence Halfpenny.*

# New Series of Reports.

Reports of the Annual Series have been issued from Her Majesty's Diplomatic and Consular Officers at the following places, and may be obtained from the sources indicated on the title-page:—

| No. | | Price. | No. | | Price. |
|---|---|---|---|---|---|
| 1089. | Chiengmai | 1d. | 1147. | Buenos Ayres | 6d. |
| 1090. | Copenhagen | ½d. | 1148. | Bogotá | 1d. |
| 1091. | New Caledonia | ½d. | 1149. | The Hague | 2d. |
| 1092. | Bushire | 2d. | 1150. | Mexico | 2½d. |
| 1093. | Tamsui | 1d. | 1151. | Florence | 2d. |
| 1094. | Dunkirk | 1d. | 1152. | Calais | 1d. |
| 1095. | Port Said | 1d. | 1153. | Lorenzo Marques | 1½d. |
| 1096. | Guatemala | ½d. | 1154. | Patras | 1d. |
| 1097. | Chungking | 9d. | 1155. | Taganrog | 1d. |
| 1098. | Nagasaki | 1d. | 1156. | Stockholm | 1d. |
| 1099. | Constantinople | 2d. | 1157. | Washington | 2d. |
| 1100. | Buenos Ayres | ½d. | 1158. | Paris | 1½d. |
| 1101. | Shanghai | 2d. | 1159. | Bengazi | 1d. |
| 1102. | Jeddah | ½d. | 1160. | Santos | 2½d. |
| 1103. | Chicago | 3d. | 1161. | Buenos Ayres | 1½d. |
| 1104. | Erzeroum | ½d. | 1162. | Nantes | 1d. |
| 1105. | Loanda | 3d. | 1163. | Beira | 5d. |
| 1106. | Macao | ½d. | 1164. | Galveston | 1½d. |
| 1107. | Canton | 1d. | 1165. | Berlin | 1d. |
| 1108. | Paramaribo | 1½d. | 1166. | Bordeaux | 2½d. |
| 1109. | Tunis | 1½d. | 1167. | Calais | 2½d. |
| 1110. | Sofia | 3d. | 1168. | The Hague | 2d. |
| 1111. | Brunei | 1½d. | 1169. | Athens | 12d. |
| 1112. | Athens | 2½d. | 1170. | Galatz | 1½d. |
| 1113. | Alexandria | 2d. | 1171. | Guayaquil | 1d. |
| 1114. | Vienna | 1d. | 1172. | Riga | 2d. |
| 1115. | Stettin | 2½d. | 1173. | Trebizond | 1d. |
| 1116. | Berne | 1d. | 1174. | Havre | 2½d. |
| 1117. | Palermo | 2½d. | 1175. | Saigon | ½d. |
| 1118. | Tokio | 1½d. | 1176. | Baltimore | 1½d. |
| 1119. | St. Petersburg | 3d. | 1177. | Brest | 1d. |
| 1120. | Teneriffe | 1d. | 1178. | Buenos Ayres | ½d. |
| 1121. | Damascus | 1d. | 1179. | Adrianople | ½d. |
| 1122. | Naples | 2d. | 1180. | Algiers | 2½d. |
| 1123. | Hakodate | 1d. | 1181. | Boston | 1d. |
| 1124. | Montevideo | 2½d. | 1182. | Marseilles | 1½d. |
| 1125. | Stockholm | 1½d. | 1183. | Warsaw | 1d. |
| 1126. | Dantzig | 2d. | 1184. | Piræus | 1½d. |
| 1127. | The Hague | 1½d. | 1185. | Callao | 1d. |
| 1128. | Odessa | 1d. | 1186. | Jerusalem | ½d. |
| 1129. | Berne | 1½d. | 1187. | Chefoo | 1½d. |
| 1130. | Malaga | 3d. | 1188. | Munich | 2d. |
| 1131. | Rome | 2½d. | 1189. | Resht | 1d. |
| 1132. | St. Jago de Cuba | 4½d. | 1190. | Batavia | 1½d. |
| 1133. | Munich | 1½d. | 1191. | Batoum | 1½d. |
| 1134. | Meshed | 1d. | 1192. | Tainan | 1d. |
| 1135. | Guayaquil | ½d. | 1193. | Amoy | 1d. |
| 1136. | Rio de Janeiro | 4½d. | 1194. | Zanzibar | 4d. |
| 1137. | Tonga | 1d. | 1195. | Corunna | 2d. |
| 1138. | Copenhagen | 1d. | 1196. | Algiers | 15½d. |
| 1139. | Tangier | 1½d. | 1197. | Pakhoi | 1d. |
| 1140. | Buenos Ayres | 2½d. | 1198. | Nice | 1½d. |
| 1141. | Para | 1d. | 1199. | Kiungchow | 1½d. |
| 1142. | Baghdad and Bussorah | 1½d. | 1200. | Aleppo | 1d. |
| 1143. | Christiania | 5½d. | 1201. | Stettin | 4½d. |
| 1144. | Old Calabar | 2d. | 1202. | Swatow | 1d. |
| 1145. | Trieste | 1½d. | 1203. | Charleston | 2½d. |
| 1146. | Quito | 1d. | 1204. | Syra | 1d. |

# No. 1205.

*Reference to previous Report, Annual Series No. 986.*

# UNITED STATES.

## NEW ORLEANS.

*Consul St. John to the Earl of Rosebery.*

My Lord,              *New Orleans, March* 29, 1893.

I HAVE the honour to transmit herewith my Annual Trade Report for 1892, as well as those from Mr. Howe, H.M. Vice-Consul at Pensacola, and Mr. Taylor, British Vice-Consul at Mobile.

I have, &c.
(Signed)     C. L. ST. JOHN.

---

*Report on the Trade and Commerce of the Consular District of New Orleans for the Year* 1892.

### ABSTRACT of Contents

| | PAGE |
|---|---|
| New Orleans— | |
| Principal crops | 3 |
| Cotton | 3 |
| Sugar | 5 |
| Rice | 6 |
| Grain | 7 |
| Shipping | 8 |
| Wharves | 9 |
| Levees and crevasses | 9 |
| Bridge over Mississippi | 10 |
| Nicaragua Canal | 10 |
| Finances | 11 |
| Real estate | 11 |
| Timber | 11 |
| Oak staves | 11 |
| Population of New Orleans | 12 |

## UNITED STATES.

### Abstract of Contents—continued.

| | PAGE |
|---|---|
| **Pensacola—** | |
| Business of Pensacola in pitch-pine wood | 12 |
| Probable time that pitch-pine forests will last | 12 |
| British vessels taking cargoes of pitch-pine | 12 |
| Imports from abroad limited | 13 |
| Manufactory at Pensacola, supported in Ireland | 13 |
| British steam tonnage at Pensacola, increased | 13 |
| British sailing vessels falling off in arrivals | 13 |
| Hints to builders of steamers in Pensacola trade | 14 |
| Pensacola, as regards cotton shipments | 14 |
| New exporting business from Pensacola | 15 |
| Coal shipments | 15 |
| British steamers chartered to carry coal | 15 |
| People of Pensacola prosperous | 16 |
| No strikes in labour market at Pensacola | 16 |
| Banking houses—English capital | 16 |
| Pensacola, free of epidemic last year | 16 |
| Return of articles of export | 16 |
| Return of articles of import | 17 |
| Return of countries to which shipments were made, and values | 18 |
| Return of shipping entered and cleared at Pensacola, during the year | 18 |
| Return of shipments of pitch-pine to ports in the United Kingdom | 20 |
| Return of shipments of pitch-pine to ports on the Continent and elsewhere | 21 |
| **Agriculture—** | |
| Pitch-pine wood | 22 |
| Information to dealers in the United Kingdom | 22 |
| Growth and probable continued supply | 22 |
| Ten species of merchantable pine | 23 |
| Department of agriculture of United States on supply | 24 |
| Strength of pitch-pine | 25 |
| General uses | 25 |
| Tobacco | 26 |
| Railroad officials interested in growth of tobacco | 26 |
| Oranges | 29 |
| **Mobile—** | |
| Cotton, receipts and prices | 30 |
| „ exports | 30 |
| Lumber and timber | 30 |
| Hard woods | 31 |
| Vegetables | 31 |
| Harbour improvements | 32 |
| Shipping up and down channel | 32 |
| Annex A.—Return of all shipping entered and cleared at the port of Mobile during the year 1892 | 33 |
| Annex B.—Return of principal articles of import | 34 |
| „ C.—Value of exports and imports to and from foreign countries | 34 |
| Return of principal articles of export | 35 |
| **Alabama—** | |
| Agriculture | 35 |
| Wheat | 36 |
| Cotton | 36 |
| Truck farming | 36 |
| Fruits, &c. | 36 |
| Tobacco | 36 |
| Grasses | 37 |
| Stock | 38 |
| Sheep | 38 |
| Hogs | 39 |
| Climate | 39 |

## NEW ORLEANS.

The principal crops heretofore handled in the New Orleans market, or exported through its port, have been cotton, sugar, and rice. Now grain has to be added to the list. During the past year great changes have taken place in the production, prices, and handling of these great crops, so much so that each merit an extended note in this report.

The cotton crop of the United States for the year ending August 31, 1892 (according to the statistics of the New Orleans Cotton Exchange), amounts to 9,035,379 bales (498·44 lbs. to the bale), exceeding the crop of 1890–91 by 382,782 bales, and that of 1889–90 by 1,724,057 bales. Of this great crop, of over 9,000,000 bales, the largest ever produced, there were exported through New Orleans 2,162,859 bales against 1,955,540 bales during 1890. Of the bales exported in 1892, 986,551 bales were shipped to Great Britain, 513,417 bales to France, and 662,891 bales to the Continental ports.

*Cotton.*

Two years ago when the price of Indian corn was the lowest ever known, as the result of the production of more than 2,000,000,000 bushels, and the price of wheat had become lower than the assumed cost of producing it, the value of cotton was well sustained in the markets of the world, and made the planters and cotton men in general believe, to a great extent, that cotton was an exceptional crop not to be affected by over-production.

Large crops of cotton were planted, under favourable conditions the yield was great. The enormous production as well as other influences caused the price of middling to drop in March, 1892, to $6\frac{1}{4}$ c. ($3\frac{1}{8}d.$) per lb., which was the lowest price since 1848 when it fell to 5 c. ($2\frac{1}{2}d.$) per lb. The result of these low prices has caused planters to decrease their planting acreage and to abandon from necessity the credit system. This change cannot fail in the future to be of benefit to the country, although less cotton may be produced.

The following table shows the acreage of cotton grown in this Consular District for the year 1891–92:—

| States. | Acreage. |
| --- | --- |
| Arkansas | 1,325,335 |
| Mississippi | 2,374,170 |
| Louisiana | 927,238 |
| Alabama | 2,271,634 |
| Florida | 187,798 |
| Total | 7,086,175 |

Whereas during the year 1890–91, in the same district, the acreage amounted to 8,504,625 acres; showing a decrease during the last season of 1,418,450 acres.

New Orleans, it is stated, has handled, during the season 1891–92, over 2,500,000 bales net, and more than 2,700,000 bales

# UNITED STATES.

gross, exceeding her largest net receipts before or since the war by nearly 350,000 bales.

*Cotton consumption in the States.*

The total number of bales consumed in the Southern States during 1891-92 amounted to 686,080 bales against 604,661 bales for the season of 1890-91. This shows an increase over last year of about 13½ per cent., and over the season before of 25 per cent., that is to say, one-fourth greater than it was 2 years ago.

There are at present 305 mills in operation against 287 in 1891.

### Southern Cotton Mills in 1891-92.

| States. | Total. | In Operation. | Idle. | New, not Completed. |
|---|---|---|---|---|
| Alabama | 29 | 21 | 6 | 2 |
| Arkansas | 4 | 2 | 2 | .. |
| Georgia | 64 | 57 | 5 | 2 |
| Kentucky | 6 | 6 | .. | .. |
| Louisiana | 4 | 4 | .. | .. |
| Mississippi | 11 | 7 | 4 | .. |
| Missouri | 2 | 1 | 1 | .. |
| North Carolina | 127 | 118 | 3 | 6 |
| South Carolina | 56 | 49 | 1 | 6 |
| Tennessee | 32 | 24 | 7 | 1 |
| Texas | 7 | 4 | 3 | .. |
| Virginia | 14 | 12 | 1 | 1 |
| Total | 356 | 305 | 33 | 18 |

### Spindles in Operation.

| States. | Number. |
|---|---|
| Alabama | 115,158 |
| Arkansas | 6,000 |
| Georgia | 474,271 |
| Kentucky | 51,800 |
| Louisiana | 50,700 |
| Mississippi | 53,024 |
| Missouri | 10,500 |
| North Carolina | 475,194 |
| South Carolina | 477,386 |
| Tennessee | 112,347 |
| Texas | 35,720 |
| Virginia | 99,472 |
| Total | 1,961,572 |

The Southern cotton consumption for the above-named States amounted in 1891 to 604,661 bales against 686,080 bales in 1892, showing an increase last year of 81,419 bales.

Owing to the overgrowing of cotton in the Southern States, by which the planters sustained heavy losses, the question is again mooted as to the absolute necessity of reducing the acreage. At the solicitation of numerous farmers and merchants a convention is being called to take such action as may seem best for that purpose. Though nothing can be done by the convention that would be binding on the planter, yet their attention can be drawn to the folly of pursuing the old methods of planting mostly cotton, to the exclusion of cereals and other crops, so necessary for support to home and family. Only sufficient cotton, it is proposed, should be planted to furnish the actual luxuries of life.

The crop of sugar of Louisiana, which is entirely made from cane, is the most important to the prosperity of the residents of New Orleans. The sugar plantations extend to a distance of 150 miles from the city, and the supply for these estates of implements and machinery all come from New Orleans, as also skilled workmen to repair the machinery and to convert the crop into sugar. Therefore a good sugar harvest favourably affects the prosperity of the town. *Sugar.*

Since April 1, 1891, sugar has been admitted free of duty and the sugar bounty law, in operation.

Each year planters are improving their machinery, using more fertilizers, and endeavouring to increase the yield. They maintain that under the bounty law there is more profit in making refined sugars than that of a low grade by the old open-kettle process.

The sugar crop of Louisiana of 1890-91 was 220,000 tons (of 2,240 lbs.), of which 123,430 tons were marketed through New Orleans. The crop of 1891-92 was estimated at 200,000 tons. The tendency, since the operation of the bounty law, is towards the central factory system, and each year advances are made in that direction.

THE following are Receipts and Sales at this Port of Sugar and Molasses.

|  |  | Quantity. |  |
|---|---|---|---|
|  |  | 1891-92. | 1890-91. |
| Receipts— |  |  |  |
| Sugar.. | Hogsheads .. | 65,978 | 110,185 |
| ,, .. | Barrels .. | 782,932 | 948,320 |
| Molasses | ,, .. | 274,222 | 422,461 |
| Sales— |  |  |  |
| Sugar.. | Hogsheads .. | 65,926 | 110,161 |
| ,, .. | Barrels .. | 782,932 | 948,760 |
| Molasses .. | ,, .. | 273,455 | 423,247 |

Genuine molasses, says the "Times Democrat," of September 1, 1892, to which I am indebted for much information, continue to gradually lessen as years roll on; at least as an article of consumption. Most of it passes into the hands of re-boilers, who manipulate it under various names. The deterioration in quality is attributed to the greater use of centrifugal machinery. These machines separate the sugar from the cane juice more effectually than formerly, but reduces the quality.

The refineries at this port consist of the American Sugar Refining Company's houses, and one owned by Mr. W. Henderson.

The capacity of the former is about 2,000,000 lbs. daily, and the capacity of the latter about 100,000 lbs.

During the crop season they work on Louisiana sugar only, but later on are obliged to import, principally from Cuba.

Nice.

The development of the rice culture in Louisiana shows an almost phenomenal advance. Ten years ago the Atlantic coast was the leading rice producing section of the United States; but Louisiana has so increased her rice planting area that of late years she has produced more than all the Atlantic States put together. The lands of the prairies of Louisiana, heretofore used for grazing, seem well adapted to the raising of rice, of which more is actually raised west of the Mississippi River than east of it. The crop of 1890-91 was 1,000,000 sacks (162 lbs. each); the crop of 1891-92 was estimated at 2,000,000 sacks.

Nearly 275,000 acres were planted with rice in Louisiana during the year 1892, and it was supposed that they would yield a crop of nearly 9,000,000 bushels. This doubles any crop raised since the war, and is nearly three times as much as raised before it.

The large quantity of rice planted last year in this State (Louisiana) is, in a great measure, due to the determination of the farmers not to plant exclusively, as heretofore, cotton or cane.

This port handled the entire Louisiana rice crop, amounting to twice as much as that of all the other States combined.

The first receipts of new rice in 1892 were on August 13, in 1891 on August 31, and in 1890 on July 30.

Rice Season's Movement.

|  | Rough. | Clean. |
|---|---|---|
|  | Sacks. | Barrels. |
| Receipts since August 1, 1891 | 947,634 | 5,604 |
| Same time year before | 826,761 | 4,115 |
| Sales since August 1, 1891 | 937,006 | 257,536 |

This statement does not include country mills, which are estimated to have consumed at least 75,000 sacks of rough rice, hence this added to the seed rice, say 75,000 sacks, and the receipts here, would make the late rice crop, at least, 1,100,000 sacks rough rice.

The following were the average local prices during the year: good, 4¾ c. to 4⅝ c.; head, 4½ c. to 4¾ c.

The increase in the receipts and exports of grain has been Grain. exceedingly great, and far more so than predicted in the last report. It is estimated that 25,000,000 bushels were exported from this place in 1892. Wheat is received here from all parts of the country by rail and by barge on the Mississippi River. The fear of a hot and moist climate affecting wheat shipped in bulk no longer existing has assured New Orleans a valuable trade for the future. Texas conveys by rail to this port mainly what is called "Mediterranean" wheat, so called from its origin. Red wheat comes from Missouri. From Kansas large quantities of fine wheat are received by barges and transferred by floating elevators to the holds of the vessels.

There are three large elevators, that of Southport having a capacity of 150,000 bushels, the "New Orleans" elevator of 200,000 bushels capacity, the Westwego elevator of 300,000 bushels capacity. A fourth and a much larger elevator is to be erected by the Illinois Central Railroad Company.

Notwithstanding all this increased elevator capacity more is needed, as grain has often to remain some weeks in the trucks for want of storage room. As the railway lines to this port are more perfected the receipts of grain for export will greatly increase, especially as ships of largest draught pass in and out of the Mississippi without detention.

But better and larger accommodation for the stowage of wheat is now being seriously felt at New Orleans, when last year 24,000,000 bushels were handled, and a considerable quantity refused for want of available facilities. There is no doubt that business men are now fully alive to the wants of this port, and that before long improvements will be made in this direction.

The following are the exports of flour from this port to different countries during the last three years:—

| Year. | Quantity. |
| --- | --- |
|  | Barrels. |
| 1892.. | 213,016 |
| 1891.. | 29,544 |
| 1890.. | 47,805 |

There can be no doubt of the rapid growth of the grain traffic at New Orleans. It appears that during February of the presen year (1893) nearly 2,000,000 bushels were exported from this port, showing an increase of over 400,000 bushels over the same month last year, and this at a time when wheat exports from the country, as a whole, fell off nearly 750,000 bushels.

New Orleans, it is said, shipped more wheat abroad during last February than New York, where the export was 1,941,871 bushels, though New York shipped more flour. Taking the exports for the eight months of the Government's fiscal year from July 1, 1892, there have been aggregate shipments from New Orleans of over 10,000,000 bushels, against nearly 12,000,000 bushels in the corresponding period of last year, being a decrease of only about 2,000,000 bushels, whereas from the whole country the decrease was 34,000,000 bushels. While the wheat shipments in February (as has been above stated) amounted to nearly 2,000,000 bushels in the whole of the calendar year 1890 there were only 1,301,710 bushels; in 1889 but 982,215 bushels, and in 1888, 1,027,332 bushels.

*Shipping.* Owing to the increased amount of grain to be exported ocean freights during 1891-92 ruled higher. Eads' jetties at the mouth of the Mississippi have stood all violent storms, and a good depth of water has been maintained in the channel enabling at all seasons the largest draught ships to cross the bar without detention.

The records of this Consulate show that from January 1 to December 31, 1892, the total number of British vessels entered was 483 (of which 464 were steam and 19 were sail), having a tonnage of 713,134, and crews numbering 14,817. The clearances for the same period were 494 vessels (of which 473 were steam and 21 sail), with a tonnage of 731,258, and crews numbering 14,050.

Annex A contains a return of British and foreign shipping at this port during 1892.

RETURN of the Principal Exports carried in British Ships during the Year 1892.

| Articles. | | Quantity. |
|---|---|---|
| Cotton | Bales | 1,28*,332 |
| „ seed | Sacks | 21,759 |
| „ „ oil | Barrels | 24,*85 |
| „ „ cakes | Sacks | 357,390 |
| „ „ meal | „ | 910,654 |
| „ „ soap stock | Barrels | 11,814 |
| Corn (in bulk) | Bushels | 6,872,641 |
| „ | Sacks | 10,536 |
| Wheat (in bulk) | Bushels | 11,786,046 |
| „ | Sacks | 72,625 |
| Rye | „ | 371,888 |
| Flour | „ | 167,367 |
| Staves | Pieces | 1,199,715 |
| Timber | Logs | 3,658 |
| „ | Pieces | 50,681 |
| „ | Feet | 10,000 |
| Lumber | Logs | 11,215 |
| „ | Pieces | 56,325 |
| „ | Feet | 364,000 |
| Lead | Pigs and bars | 52,264 |
| Copper and silver ore | Sacks | 25,195 |
| Tallow | Tierces | 6,045 |
| Rice polish and rice bran | Sacks | 26,319 |
| Molasses | Barrels | 39,733 |
| Tanning root | Sacks | 14,876 |
| Phosphates | Tons | 11,137 |

Annex A.—RETURN of all Shipping at the Port of New Orleans during the Year 1892.

ENTERED.

| Nationality. | Sailing. Number of Vessels. | Sailing. Tons. | Steam. Number of Vessels. | Steam. Tons. | Total. Number of Vessels. | Total. Tons. |
| --- | --- | --- | --- | --- | --- | --- |
| British | 19 | 5,330 | 464 | 707,804 | 483 | 713,134 |
| American | 30 | 9,601 | 218 | 136,203 | 248 | 145,804 |
| Spanish | 17 | 10,939 | 64 | 118,319 | 81 | 129,358 |
| Italian | 29 | 15,915 | 21 | 14,631 | 50 | 30,546 |
| German | 14 | 25,087 | 33 | 79,518 | 47 | 104,605 |
| French | 1 | 475 | 13 | 33,877 | 14 | 34,352 |
| Swedish | 5 | 3,412 | 21 | 17,346 | 26 | 20,758 |
| Norwegian | 5 | 3,412 | 130 | 56,321 | 135 | 59,733 |
| Total | ... | ... | ... | ... | 1,084 | 1,238,290 |
| ,, for the year preceding | ... | ... | ... | ... | 959 | 1,065,681 |

CLEARED.

| Nationality. | Sailing. Number of Vessels. | Sailing. Tons. | Steam. Number of Vessels. | Steam. Tons. | Total. Number of Vessels. | Total. Tons. |
| --- | --- | --- | --- | --- | --- | --- |
| British | 21 | 6,513 | 473 | 724,745 | 494 | 731,258 |
| American | 15 | 6,421 | 190 | 118,192 | 205 | 124,613 |
| Spanish | 17 | 10,939 | 66 | 119,419 | 83 | 120,358 |
| Italian | 35 | 19,261 | 20 | 13,989 | 55 | 33,250 |
| German | 12 | 21,648 | 31 | 74,119 | 44 | 95,767 |
| French | 1 | 475 | 13 | 33,877 | 14 | 34,352 |
| Swedish | ... | ... | 21 | 17,346 | 21 | 17,346 |
| Norwegian | 8 | 6,178 | 130 | 56,755 | 138 | 62,933 |
| Total | ... | ... | ... | ... | 1,054 | 1,219,877 |
| ,, for the year preceding | ... | ... | ... | ... | 894 | 1,016,177 |

During the past year the wharves and landings of New Orleans have been leased for a period of 10 years. The lessees are now building new wharves higher and better than the old ones, the approaches being improved so as to give all conveniences to shipping. *Wharves*

In the spring of 1892 many levees could not stand the extraordinary rise of the Mississippi, and several disastrous overflows, called locally "crevasses," took place. The most destructive was that of Belmont, about 60 miles above the city, which ruined many fine sugar estates. *Levees and crevasses.*

The national Government has made very liberal appropriations for levees, and the State several levee taxing districts. With the means derived from these two sources the engineers are endeavouring to control the Mississippi River current by constructing higher and stronger levees. Ten years ago levees cost 60 c. (2s. 6d.) per cubic yard to build, but to-day contracts are let as low as 15 c. (7½d.) per cubic yard. Even at this low price contractors, with the aid of horse scrappers and other modern inventions, make money. As yet no steam levee building machine has been invented.

It is fortunate, therefore, that the low prices exist and have enabled the engineers to do a great deal of work. Some of the crevasses have been stopped a few hours after the break, but the big break, even with the expenditure of 20,000 dol. (4,000*l*.), have not. In such cases engineers merely secure the ends from washing away by tarpaulins and cribwork, and wait till the flood subsides.

*Bridge over the Mississippi.* Congress at its recent session passed the Act authorising the bridging of the Mississippi River at any point above the limits of the City of New Orleans within five miles. At first it was suggested by some to place the bridge below or opposite the town; but it was found that such a structure in the stream would be not only inconvenient but dangerous to shipping. Above the city the river is about one-half mile wide and 100 feet deep at high water in the deepest part, and its current is about 6 feet per second—four miles per hour. The river carries a volume of about 1,250,000 cubic feet per second. The bed of the river is, to a great depth, composed of alternate strata of sand and clay, being the silt which the river itself has brought down in past ages to fill up what was formerly a great estuary of the Gulf of Mexico. The land on each side is very low, probably 10 feet below the flood level of the river. The country on each side is protected by embankments called levees. The banks are continually washing away or making as the direction of the current changes, so that the exact situation for a bridge where the banks are stationary is difficult to find. According to the Act of Congress there can be but two piers placed in the river, and the main channel span must be at least 1,000 feet in the clear at low water level, and the entire bridge at least 85 feet above extreme high water mark. The foundations will probably need to go at least 150 feet below low water in order to find a stratum of material sufficiently compact for supporting the immense weight of the piers, &c. The superstructure will not be less than 100 feet in height, and the probable entire height from the foundation to the top will be 350 feet. The grade descending from the bridge on either side to the level of the present railway tracks will probably be $1\frac{1}{2}$ per cent., or about 80 feet to the mile. The steel structure will extend on either side until a height of about 40 feet above the land is reached. This will give a continuous steel structure of about 11,000 feet long. The length of the bridge at Cairo, Illinois, over the Ohio comes next. The longest river span in any railroad bridge in the United States is the 790-foot channel span at Memphis, Tenessee, over the Mississippi; but this New Orleans bridge is to have secondary spans of 800 feet, while the central span will be nearly 1,100 feet. This great bridge will cost about 3,000,000 dol. (600,000*l*.), and three years will be required for its construction. It is designed for a railway bridge only, and is being built by capital furnished by several railways that are to use it to form connections east and west.

*Nicaragua Canal.* The proximity of New Orleans to Nicaragua has created here a great interest in that canal project. In January, 1892, a convention of delegates from all parts of the United States was held here, and resolutions highly commending the project were adopted and Congress was asked to give substantial aid.

There is no doubt that the opening of the canal on the Tehuantepec Railway route will greatly benefit this port and extend its commerce with the Pacific slope. It is claimed that such a canal would open a route for raw cotton to be delivered to mills in China and Japan, where cotton cloths formed the raiment of the majority of their inhabitants.

Finance. The financial prosperity of New Orleans and the state of Louisiana has improved in a remarkable manner. Money has been plentiful and the rates of money on call have been as low as 3 per cent. in banks and on the street.

The city of New Orleans was authorised by the Legislature to issue a new 4 Per Cent. Loan to fund all outstanding bonds that were presented. This 4 Per Cent. Loan was taken at par and at the present date is selling at nearly 102. This, it is claimed, shows a confidence of capitalists in the city's ability and integrity to pay its debts, and at the same time it indicates that money is plentiful and investors are obliged to take a city of New Orleans bond that pays less than 4 per cent. interest.

The last State Legislature decided to issue a new State 4 Per cent. bond in exchange of the old State 7 per cent. bond, which had the reduction of interest, 4 per cent., stamped on its face, making the bond an unsightly evidence of indebtedness. The issue of this new clean bond has been accomplished and has served to strengthen the credit of the State of Louisiana in this market.

All bonds, stocks, and shares have felt the impulse of the prosperity that has dawned on this city and have advanced in value. The city railway charters in many instances have been extended with a view of adopting electricity as a motive power, and syndicates of northern capitalists have purchased these roads.

Real estate. Real estate has advanced in value, especially in the suburbs, where new lines of tramway have been built or converted into electric roads. Capitalists, who formerly would not touch real estate as an investment, are now buying, as they find it more remunerative than 4 per cent. bonds.

Taxation is not high and it is probable that it will be reduced in the future. The sound financial basis of New Orleans is guarantee to the real estate investor.

Timber. The value of timber lands has greatly increased during the past year. Englishmen as well as northern men are buying them in the south.

The yellow pine is considered most valuable for building purposes, having great strength and durability. Cypress is one of the most valuable woods known, and every year is increasing in demand for fine woodwork, and stands exposure. Red gum, sweet gum, and other varieties are coming into the market as valuable for furniture manufacturing.

Oak staves. The receipt of oak staves at this port for the season ending

## UNITED STATES.

August 31, 1892, was about 4,000,000 pieces, valued at about 500,000 dol. (100,000*l.*).

Export of Staves.

| Country. | Quantity. |
|---|---|
|  | Pieces. |
| To United Kingdom | 863,325 |
| France | 226,568 |
| Spain | 1,642,318 |
| Portugal | 663,630 |
| Germany and Holland | 222,877 |
| Belgium | 19,870 |
| Italy | 100,000 |

*Population.* According to the census of 1880 the total population for that year was 250,000, whereas at present it is estimated at 265,000.

### PENSACOLA.

Mr. Vice-Consul Howe reports as follows:—

*Trade in 1892.* This report on the trade of Pensacola for the year 1892 will show that the business of the port in its chief export, pitch pine-wood, was not below its average activity in comparison with years past, and I again remark that most of the shipments of pitch-pine go to ports in the United Kingdom.

*Mostly with United Kingdom.*

*Pitch-pine forests.* I have embodied in my agricultural report for this year, some particulars respecting the present supply and probable duration of time that the pitch-pine forests about here will hold out. I have no doubt that this information will be of interest to those in the United Kingdom dealing in this great article of trade.

*Satisfactory trade.* In considering the vast quantities of pitch-pine wood shipped yearly from Pensacola to the United Kingdom, it appears that this trade continues to be satisfactory, in the average, to all concerned in it. Some of the timber merchants in the United Kingdom dealing in pitch-pine wood from Pensacola are also shipowners, and it may be observed that they, or some of them, very often work in their own vessels in this trade when it appears more profitable to do so for the respective ledger accounts.

*British shipowners in timber trade send their vessels to be loaded here.*

*To Pensacola in ballast to load timber.* There are some sailing vessels of certain lines in the United Kingdom which have taken cargoes of pitch-pine wood from Pensacola for many years past on account of the owners, timber dealers, principally in Scotland and Wales. In some of these cases the vessels were loaded at home for ports in South America, principally proceeding from the latter ports to Pensacola in ballast to load timber cargoes. Lately, some of these vessels have been sent out direct to Pensacola in ballast to load pitch-pine. This new plan has been adopted, no doubt, in some cases in order to avoid the risk to which owners and others have been lately subjected in the summer trade at South American ports in respect of yellow fever epidemic there; and, again, the additional loss of time to the vessels here by quarantine restrictions when arriving from those parts. And, really, I suppose that a calculation, figured for probable best results in these voyages, taking into consideration the serious drawbacks above referred to, would nearly always, when there is business offering at Pensacola in the summer months, leave it more desirable for the direct run out and back home as the best business to be more surely reckoned upon. *Avoids risk at ports in South America. Lessens detention at quarantine.*

The imports direct from foreign ports to Pensacola, as frequently remarked in these yearly reports, are quite limited. These imports are confined to salt from Liverpool, some fertilisers from the United Kingdom and Germany, superphosphates to be used in making up manures, and, lastly, a cargo of iron ore from Huelva, Spain, which article went forward to towns in Alabama, where foundries have been established for smithing purposes. A British steamer left Dublin, Ireland, at about the end of the year loaded with fertilisers for Pensacola, to be used in a fertiliser factory here (the "Goulding Fertiliser Company"), a concern established at Pensacola by parties in Dublin at a large cost, and having its headquarters in Dublin. I have, in my former reports, referred to this large concern. *Imports from foreign ports not large. Fertilisers from Dublin.*

Cargoes of West Indian fruits come here frequently from the West Indian Islands in small British vessels. The bulk of everything, however, principally in the chief articles for everyday use, are brought to Pensacola from the large cities of the northern and western States, and amount to several millions of dollars per year, to supply this town and the smaller places which draw their supplies of everyday necessaries of life from Pensacola. *Fruit from British West Indies. Chief articles come from large cities in Western States.*

The shipping table annexed to this report will show that British vessels arriving at Pensacola during the year were, in number and tonnage, beyond such arrivals of the year preceding. In tonnage they were equal to one-third of that of other foreign vessels entering the port. The number of British steamers was beyond the largest number of such arrivals in any year before at Pensacola, and in tonnage these vessels went beyond the average of such steamers in former years. They averaged nearly 1,600 tons net each and they took cargoes averaging about $1\frac{3}{4}$ tons in dead weight to their tonnage; therefore, these British steamers alone took away from Pensacola a very large proportion of the entire shipments which went in foreign bottoms, and British tonnage altogether carried from Pensacola about one-third of the cargoes of pitch-pine wood exported during the year to foreign ports. *British shipping at Pensacola good in 1892. Average in tons of British steamers.*

It will be seen that, as regards sailing vessels under the British flag coming to Pensacola now, the comparison with such arrivals to what they were 10 years or 12 years ago is very different. I have frequently before, in the last few years in these reports, when *British sailing vessels fall off.*

writing on shipping at Pensacola, explained that a very large number of British vessels which used to ply here formerly have passed into the hands of foreign shipowners, particularly those of Norway and Sweden, and that many of these vessels come here now under the flags of these countries.

*Sold to foreign people.*

During the past year the number and tonnage of British sailing vessels were beyond the number and tonnage of this class of vessels for the past several years arriving at Pensacola.

*Steam will hereafter do most of carrying trade.*

I will remark again, as I have before stated in these reports, that I believe, sooner or later, the entire or nearly all of the export trade of Pensacola will be done by steamers, and, of course, in such case British steamers would be, I think, largely in the majority.

*Timber supply.*

If my report on the prospective timber supply of these parts can be taken as correct, and I have mainly followed an official report on this subject from a publication on the question by the Department of Agriculture in the United States (see my agricultural report for 1892), it will be observed that tonnage will be required for this timber trade for many years to come, and, in view of this apparent fact, I advise British shipowners to adopt, so far as they can, when building steamers which may be made applicable for this trade, such construction as will suit these timber cargoes. I need not attempt to advise as to how such construction should be, for the owners of steamers who have experienced inconvenience and loss to their vessels at Pensacola in the taking down of compartments in loading their vessels with timber, will know as to what an improved construction of the vessels for this trade should be.

*Tonnage required for many years to move it.*

*Construction of steamers.*

*Pensacola a cotton port.*

For many years past it has been endeavoured to make Pensacola a cotton shipping port; but after a shipment or two yearly the business ceases. At the end of the year a British steamer was loaded at Pensacola with cotton for Liverpool. Her net tonnage was 1,359 tons, and she took 7,619 bales of cotton, averaging 500 lbs. to the bale. I am informed that the quantity of cotton taken to the tonnage of this vessel was exceptional. The cotton, however, had been compressed at Montgomery, Alabama—the great centre for purchase and compress of cotton for European shipments—by an improved press. The stevedoring was also most excellent in loading the vessel, when it is considered that the Pensacola stevedores have so few opportunities to load such cargoes.

*Late shipment on British steamer.*

*Well compressed.*

*New start in cotton exports from Pensacola.*

I hear that a fresh impetus is in view in this cotton exporting business from Pensacola. I hope it will be properly inaugurated, and continued hereafter without interruption. I am sure that this business can be well established if all of the interests concerned would combine to make this trade, from this port, a success.

In connection with the Louisville and Nashville Railroad an eminent shipping firm at Pensacola (they are also established at New Orleans and other cities) have put on a steamer to ply between Pensacola and the Cuban ports. At present the runs are made semi-monthly, but I am informed that more tonnage will be

*Trade between Pensacola and Cuba.*

put on, and the business this way increased as fast as it is developed.

**Will add to Pensacola business.**
This new trade will no doubt add greatly to the business of Pensacola. The arrangements made to carry on this business have much in their favour and stability by the countenance and encouragement given in every way toward the development of the trade by this great railroad company at its back.

**Supplies of goods shipped.**
As I understand it, the merchants in Cuba have orders continually in the hands of their agents at Louisville, St. Louis, and such western markets for the supplies required—flour, corn, oats, hay, bran, butter, hams, cheese, corn-meal, peas, lard, liquors, &c. The time is calculated for the arrival of the steamer at Pensacola, and the goods are in transfer to meet her, and thus the business goes on. 

**Arrangements for payments.**
The money arrangements for payment of these cargoes are, I am informed, by letter of credit on New York, in some instances, and in other ways by drafts on Cuba. 

**Goods through by rail from western cities.**
Through bills of lading are signed at the western shipping points immediately as the goods are received by the railroad. I am informed that very soon, in addition to the freight business, a well arranged plan will be put in effect also by the projectors above alluded to, for the carriage of passengers who may be desirous of visiting the Cuban ports. Particularly will this be a very accommodating arrangement for the visitors who come to Pensacola in large numbers during the winter to escape the severe cold of the northern and western ports of the country. No doubt many of them, with their families, will avail themselves of the opportunity to visit that very interesting, and, in winter particularly, most genial island. The bill of fare, and all attention otherwise for the comfort of passengers, will be, I am told, of the very best getting up.

**Coal exports.**
Referring to the table of exports, in respect to shipments of coal from Pensacola, I must remark that two British steamers were chartered during the year for the carriage of coal hence to ports in Mexico, and other places, perhaps, in Central America. One of these steamers, the "Scotsman," was taken for nine of these trips, and she started on her first trip in December. 

**British steamers chartered to carry coal.**
The other steamer, the "Austerlitz," was taken at first for one voyage, but the charter was altered to three voyages, with the privilege, to the shipper of coal, of three more voyages. The rates of freight to these vessels have, no doubt, suited the owners, and perhaps this trade may be increased to the benefit of British steamer tonnage, as only this class of vessel will answer in this coal export trade. 

**Coal mines in Alabama.**
The coal for these shipments, as I have stated in some of my former reports, is brought here by railroad from the coal mines in Alabama, and the vessels are loaded in coal elevators right at the coal company's wharf. The facilities for the business are admirably arranged, and I think this export trade in coal through Pensacola is going to increase to very large dimensions. While on this subject I may add that a British steamer en route from New Orleans to a Florida port to load phosphate called at the close of the year at Pensacola to coal; no doubt this may also, to some extent, become a coaling port of call.

(1525)

## UNITED STATES.

### General Remarks.

**General remarks.**
**All people here contented.**

In referring to the welfare generally of the inhabitants of this most pleasant town, I must again remark that the even tenour of their way from year to year never seems to vary. Each class appear to be well contented and prosperous in their calling. The merchants, those in the timber shipping business, as well as those in so many other branches of trade here, never appear to be embarrassed, and failures in trade are seldom heard of, at least none of any importance; and as I have also before remarked, from time to time in these reports, there is no apparent poverty here.

**No strikes.**

There are no strikes at Pensacola in the labour market—it is a long time since I have heard of any—any little differences in the labour market, which have been mostly in the loading of timber ships, are quickly adjusted.

**Banking business and British capital.**

The banking business at Pensacola has been increased by an establishment termed the British-American Banking and Trust Company. I believe that much of the capital of this bank is from England. Another bank, I am told, will also soon be established here.

The average business of Pensacola for the year past, as I remarked above, in this report, may be looked for, in my opinion, for many years to come.

I give, according to the tables annexed, the statistics of exports, imports, shipping, &c., in connection with this report.

**Pensacola healthy.**

Pensacola was free from epidemics of any kind during the year. I am also glad to be able to observe that quarantine restrictions against vessels arriving at this port were carried out in the minimum, I think, in comparison with like administration in years past.

Annex A.—RETURN of Principal Articles of Export from Pensacola during the Years 1892-91.

| Articles. | | 1892. Quantity. | 1892. Value. £ s. d. | 1891. Quantity. | 1891. Value. £ s. d. |
|---|---|---|---|---|---|
| Pitch-pine lumber | Super. feet | 135,439,000 | 338,597 10 0 | 113,569,000 | 283,890 0 0 |
| Sawn pitch-pine timber | Cubic ,, | 15,544,482 | 388,612 1 0 | 11,179,576 | 279,419 8 0 |
| Hewn pitch-pine timber | ,, ,, | 431,717 | 9,893 10 3 | 539,930 | 12,373 7 11 |
| Cotton | Bales | 7,619 | 71,428 2 6 | ... | ... |
| Coal | Tons | 41,611 | 26,006 17 6 | 48,191 | 32,627 11 4 |
| Resin | Barrels | 1,534 | 767 0 0 | ... | ... |
| Cedar | Cubic feet | 1,550 | 118 2 6 | 2,400 | 175 0 0 |
| Flour | Barrels | 6,696 | 4,887 3 4 | ... | ... |
| Bran | Sacks | 2,000 | 500 0 0 | ... | ... |
| Corn | ,, | 3,916 | 979 0 0 | ... | ... |
| Other articles | ... | ... | 1,999 19 0 | ... | 25,000 0 0 |
| Total | ... | ... | 843,789 6 1 | ... | 611,055 7 3 |

The values of the articles in the above given table are: lumber at 12 dol. (2l. 10s.) per 1,000 superficial feet, board measure; sawn timber at 12 c. (6d.) per cubic foot, basis 40 feet average; hewn timber at 11 c. (5½d.) per cubic foot, basis 100 feet average; cotton at 9 c. (4½d.) per lb., in bales of 500 lbs. average weight each bale; coal at 3 dol. (12s. 6d.) per ton, in 1892; cedar at 36 c. (1s. 6d.) per cubic foot; resin at 2 dol. 40 c. (10s.) per barrel; flour at 3 dol. 50 c. (14s. 7d.) per barrel; bran at 1 dol. 20 c. (5s.) per sack; corn at 1 dol. 20 c. (5s.) per sack. Sterling is at the rate of 4 dol. 80 c. per 1l. in the above values

Annex B.—RETURN of Principal Articles of Import to Pensacola during the Years 1892–91.

| Articles. | Value. | |
|---|---|---|
| | 1892. | 1891. |
| | £ | £ |
| Chief articles | .. | .. |
| Other  „ | 4,346 | 12,302 |

NOTE.—The chief articles brought to Pensacola are from the Northern and Western States of this country, and comprise the every day requirements of the community. These supplies amount to several millions of dollars yearly. I have referred to these chief articles in another part of this report.

(1523)

# UNITED STATES.

Annex C.—TABLE showing the Total Value of all Articles Exported from Pensacola and Imported to Pensacola from and to Foreign Countries during the Years 1892–91.

| Country. | Exports. 1892. £ s. d. | Exports. 1891. £ s. d. | Imports. 1892. £ | Imports. 1891. £ |
|---|---|---|---|---|
| United Kingdom | 439,934 9 2 | 235,412 10 6 | 1,314 | 6,052 |
| South Africa | .. | 4,316 11 8 | .. | .. |
| British West Indies | .. | 602 10 0 | .. | .. |
| Netherlands | 57,381 18 8 | 33,540 8 9 | .. | .. |
| Argentine Republic | 44,810 16 0 | 17,830 0 0 | .. | .. |
| France | 41,305 11 1 | 94,397 7 4 | .. | .. |
| Spain and Colonies | 45,946 16 7 | 25,139 15 3 | 1,283 | 2,750 |
| Italy | 38,289 6 4 | 43,421 2 8 | 111 | .. |
| Brazil | 32,471 10 0 | 35,356 7 0 | .. | .. |
| Germany | 28,324 1 1 | 14,182 13 0 | 1,638 | 3,500 |
| Belgium | 21,806 10 10 | 20,581 8 5 | .. | .. |
| Mexico | 12,669 10 0 | 4,983 7 11 | .. | .. |
| Central America | 7,468 10 0 | 4,579 15 10 | .. | .. |
| Costa Rica | .. | 3,749 13 9 | .. | .. |
| Portugal | 5,271 3 1 | 5,928 2 6 | .. | .. |
| Uruguay | 3,460 0 0 | 3,402 0 0 | .. | .. |
| Austria | 2,646 18 3 | 650 12 10 | .. | .. |
| Nicaragua | .. | 2,903 6 8 | .. | .. |
| Tunis | 616 5 0 | .. | .. | .. |
| Other countries | .. | 594 10 0 | .. | .. |
| Total to foreign countries | 782,403 6 1 | 551,582 4 1 | 4,346 | 12,302 |
| Total to ports in the United States | 61,386 0 0 | 59,473 3 2 | .. | .. |
| Total | 843,789 6 1 | 611,055 7 3 | 4,346 | 12,302 |

Annex D.—RETURN of all Shipping at the Port of Pensacola in the Year 1892.

ENTERED.

| Nationality. | Sailing. Number of Vessels. | Sailing. Tons. | Steam. Number of Vessels. | Steam. Tons. | Total. Number of Vessels. | Total. Tons. |
|---|---|---|---|---|---|---|
| British | 50 | 34,532 | 55 | 84,368 | 105 | 118,900 |
| American | 148 | 77,354 | 1 | 661 | 149 | 78,015 |
| Swedish and Norwegian | 184 | 160,700 | 12 | 14,287 | 196 | 174,987 |
| Italian | 61 | 41,693 | ... | ... | 61 | 41,693 |
| Russian | 37 | 26,462 | ... | ... | 37 | 26.462 |
| Austrian | 16 | 11,732 | ... | ... | 16 | 11,732 |
| German | 7 | 6,649 | ... | ... | 7 | 6,649 |
| French | 10 | 5,543 | ... | ... | 10 | 5,543 |
| Spanish | 2 | 2,132 | 2 | 3,308 | 4 | 5,440 |
| Dutch | 2 | 2,051 | ... | ... | 2 | 2,051 |
| Danish | 1 | 577 | ... | ... | 1 | 577 |
| Portuguese | 1 | 560 | ... | ... | 1 | 560 |
| Total | 519 | 369,985 | 70 | 102,624 | 589 | 472,609 |
| ,, for the year preceding | 467 | 309,753 | 74 | 88,804 | 541 | 398,617 |

## NEW ORLEANS.

CLEARED.

| Nationality. | Sailing. Number of Vessels. | Sailing. Tons. | Steam. Number of Vessels. | Steam. Tons. | Total. Number of Vessels. | Total. Tons. |
|---|---|---|---|---|---|---|
| British | 44 | 30,580 | 54 | 83,292 | 98 | 113,872 |
| American | 155 | 78,059 | 1 | 661 | 156 | 79,620 |
| Swedish and Norwegian | 185 | 159,551 | 12 | 14,287 | 197 | 173,838 |
| Italian | 62 | 43,157 | ... | ... | 62 | 43,157 |
| Russian | 38 | 27,909 | ... | ... | 35 | 27,909 |
| Austrian | 16 | 11,644 | ... | ... | 16 | 11,644 |
| German | 9 | 8,392 | ... | ... | 9 | 8,392 |
| French | 10 | 5,795 | ... | ... | 10 | 5,795 |
| Spanish | 1 | 1,137 | 2 | 3,608 | 3 | 4,745 |
| Dutch | 3 | 2,547 | ... | ... | 3 | 2,547 |
| Danish | 1 | 577 | ... | ... | 1 | 577 |
| Portuguese | 1 | 560 | ... | ... | 1 | 560 |
| Total | 525 | 370,808 | 69 | 101,848 | 594 | 472,656 |
| ,, for the year preceding | 460 | 309,132 | 74 | 88,804 | 534 | 397,936 |

(1523)

Annex E.—TABLE showing the Quantities, Assortment, and Value of Pitch-pine Wood Shipped from Pensacola to Ports and Places in the United Kingdom and British Colonies during the Year 1892.

| Ports and Places. | Sawn Timber. | Hewn Timber. | Deals, Lumber, &c. | Value. |
|---|---|---|---|---|
| | Cubic feet. | Cubic feet. | Super. feet. | £ s. d. |
| Liverpool | 1,512,663 | 50,354 | 4,475,488 | .. |
| London | 1,046,619 | .. | 5,757,633 | .. |
| Cardiff | 834,546 | 27,036 | 401,765 | .. |
| Greenock | 1,691,843 | 28,962 | 1,340,575 | .. |
| West Hartlepool | 623,922 | 11,368 | 749,751 | .. |
| Fleetwood | 402,599 | 18,515 | 350,779 | .. |
| The Tyne | 190,916 | .. | 57,000 | .. |
| Hull | 501,813 | .. | 1,228,822 | .. |
| Barrow | 569,849 | .. | 271,755 | .. |
| Troon | 187,500 | 3,425 | 520,000 | .. |
| Sutton Bridge | 91,836 | .. | 560,000 | .. |
| Newcastle | 156,500 | .. | 60,000 | .. |
| Bristol | 257,712 | .. | 881,000 | .. |
| Grimsby | 428,639 | 4,380 | 209,064 | .. |
| Queenstown | 663,855 | 116 | 1,098,694 | .. |
| Swansea | 128,666 | 9,799 | 85,000 | .. |
| Sunderland | 180,083 | .. | 265,000 | .. |
| Harwich | 152,000 | .. | 93,000 | .. |
| Garston | 42,666 | .. | 25,000 | .. |
| Southampton | 30,083 | .. | 97,000 | .. |
| Dublin | 8,083 | .. | 260,000 | .. |
| Glasgow | 5,333 | .. | 295,000 | .. |
| Penarth | 65,416 | .. | 14,000 | .. |
| Granton | 125,500 | .. | 57,000 | .. |
| Newport | 161,333 | .. | 108,000 | .. |
| Lynn | 154,018 | .. | 643,807 | .. |
| Whitehaven | 52,270 | 5,137 | 21,131 | .. |
| Grangemouth | 209,893 | .. | 196,308 | .. |
| Queensborough | 171,326 | .. | 253,863 | .. |
| Dundee | 252,198 | .. | 360,813 | .. |
| Perth | 25,500 | .. | 61,000 | .. |
| Chatham | 28,083 | .. | 12,000 | .. |
| Leith | 78,333 | .. | 40,000 | .. |
| Newry | 26,833 | 10,606 | 36,000 | .. |
| South Shields | 41,333 | 2,734 | 19,000 | .. |
| Middlesborough | 84,333 | .. | 39,000 | .. |
| Barry Dock | 70,833 | .. | 23,000 | .. |
| Sharpness | 101,250 | 19,331 | 162,250 | .. |
| Plymouth | .. | .. | 115,000 | .. |
| Poole | 5,333 | .. | 272,000 | .. |
| Cork | 28,000 | 5,228 | 26,000 | .. |
| Belfast | 23,416 | .. | 800,000 | .. |
| Ayr | 42,183 | .. | 22,000 | .. |
| Elsfleth | 3,500 | .. | 237,000 | .. |
| Cape Town | 83,000 | .. | 107,000 | .. |
| Port Natal | .. | .. | 273,000 | .. |
| Barbadoes | .. | .. | 241,204 | .. |
| Lagos | .. | .. | 223,000 | .. |
| Algoa Bay | 83,666 | .. | 33,000 | .. |
| Belize | .. | .. | 541,668 | .. |
| Manchester Canal | 130,400 | .. | 87,000 | .. |
| East London | 22,045 | .. | 15,348 | .. |
| Nassau | .. | .. | 75,025 | .. |
| Total | 11,777,721 | 197,031 | 24,212,818 | 359,448 13 5 |

Annex F.—TABLE showing the Quantities, Assortment, and Value of Pitch-pine Wood shipped from Pensacola to Ports and Places in Countries abroad, other than the United Kingdom, during the Year 1892.

| Ports and Places. | Sawn Timber. | Hewn Timber. | Deals, Lumber, &c. | Value. |
|---|---|---|---|---|
|  | Cubic feet. | Cubic feet. | Super. feet. | £  s.  d. |
| France— |  |  |  |  |
| Marseilles | 59,333 | 5,270 | 1,227,000 | .. |
| Fécamp | 137,050 | .. | 70,713 | .. |
| Trouville | .. | .. | 189,000 | .. |
| Dunkirk | 159,250 | 19,037 | 237,000 | .. |
| Cherbourg | 28,333 | 7,106 | 1,397,000 | .. |
| St. Nazaire | 46,500 | 27,198 | 210,000 | .. |
| Boulogne | 10,000 | 12,914 | 652,000 | .. |
| Havre | 71,869 | 22,069 | 324,600 | .. |
| Caen | 26,666 | 2,154 | 216,000 | .. |
| Honfleur | 110,895 | .. | 580,600 | .. |
| Nice | 28,833 | 925 | 80,000 | .. |
| Dieppe | .. | .. | 220,000 | .. |
| Nantes | 6,333 | .. | 230,000 | .. |
| Calais | .. | .. | 588,000 | .. |
| Rochefort | 30,165 | 2,337 | 1,735,765 | .. |
| Bordeaux | 17,916 | .. | 258,000 | .. |
| Italy— |  |  |  |  |
| Genoa | 589,282 | 33,548 | 6,032,000 | .. |
| Venice | 2,333 | 21,074 | 41,000 | .. |
| Palermo | 11,000 | 1,910 | 219,000 | .. |
| Naples | 60,333 | 15,878 | 585,000 | .. |
| Savona | 37,333 | .. | 281,000 | .. |
| Cagliari | 2,016 | .. | 471,000 | .. |
| Netherlands— |  |  |  |  |
| Zaandam | 99,649 | .. | 592,000 | .. |
| Amsterdam | 377,619 | 4,863 | 2,446,573 | .. |
| Dordrecht | 295,738 | 17,315 | 5,650,105 | .. |
| Delfzijl | 218,750 | 10,422 | 121,981 | .. |
| Rotterdam | 105,666 | .. | 2,091,250 | .. |
| Terneuzen | 82,000 | .. | 48,000 | .. |
| Harlingen | 24,583 | 5,831 | 8,000 | .. |
| Germany— |  |  |  |  |
| Braake | 2,091 | .. | 1,683,000 | .. |
| Hamburg | 59,583 | .. | 2,742,000 | .. |
| River Maas | 1,583 | 1,304 | 472,000 | .. |
| Geestemunde | 45,826 | .. | 860,000 | .. |
| Lubeck | .. | .. | 917,000 | .. |
| Bremmerhaven | 2,000 | .. | 236,000 | .. |
| Emden | 37,250 | 4,757 | 100,000 | .. |
| Bremen | .. | .. | 709,000 | .. |
| Belgium— |  |  |  |  |
| Ghent | 59,718 | 16,187 | 2,058,867 | .. |
| Antwerp | 47,103 | 3,250 | 6,288,319 | .. |
| Ostend | 1,916 | .. | 976,000 | .. |
| Spain— |  |  |  |  |
| Bilbao | 12,833 | .. | 1,671,000 | .. |
| Mazarron | .. | .. | 337,000 | .. |
| Carthagena | 2,500 | 11,008 | 1,370,000 | .. |
| Havana | .. | .. | 3,996,678 | .. |
| Cienfuegos | .. | .. | 2,839,000 | .. |
| Matanzas | .. | .. | 220,000 | .. |
| Caibairen | .. | .. | 104,000 | .. |
| Huelva | .. | .. | 994,635 | .. |
| Cadiz | 7,000 | .. | 242,000 | .. |

(1523)

## UNITED STATES.

Annex F.—TABLE showing the Quantities, Assortment, and Value of Pitch-pine Wood Shipped from Pensacola to Ports and Places in Countries abroad, other than the United Kingdom, during the Year 1892—continued.

| Ports and Places. | Sawn Timber. | Hewn Timber. | Deals, Lumber, &c. | Value. |
|---|---|---|---|---|
| | Cubic Feet. | Cubic Feet. | Super. Feet. | £   s.   d. |
| Austria— | | | | |
|   Lussinpicoli | 61,366 | 2,346 | 71,000 | .. |
|   Trieste | 33,000 | .. | 21,000 | .. |
| Brazil— | | | | |
|   Rio de Janeiro | 3,333 | .. | 12,592,528 | .. |
|   Ceara | 8,333 | .. | 298,000 | .. |
| Argentine Republic— | | | | |
|   Buenos Ayres | 108,333 | .. | 17,741,324 | .. |
| Uruguay— | | | | |
|   Monte Video | .. | .. | 1,383,818 | .. |
| Central America— | | | | |
|   La Guayra | .. | .. | 325,000 | .. |
|   Port of America | .. | .. | 53,000 | .. |
|   Colon | .. | .. | 351,000 | .. |
|   Port Simon | .. | .. | 692,000 | .. |
| Portugal— | | | | |
|   Lisbon | 192,416 | 7,799 | 125,000 | .. |
| Tunis | 26,750 | .. | 17,000 | .. |
| Mexico— | | | | |
|   Tampico | .. | .. | 265,000 | .. |
|   Coatzocolas | .. | .. | 300,000 | .. |
| Total | 3,352,379 | 256,502 | 89,254,776 | 312,814  0  5 |

NOTE.—See table Annex A for value of each description of the assortment of pitch-pine wood, given in the two tables above, which, if figured up, would show the total value as given in the tables.

### Agriculture.

**Pitch-pine timber.** The Forestry Bureau of the Department of Agriculture in the United States has lately issued a statement respecting southern pitch-pine wood.

The immense quantities of pitch-pine wood, hewn, sawn, and manufactured, which have been shipped from Pensacola to so many countries in the world (notably in greater proportions to the United Kingdom) for so many years past, and which is still being shipped without any diminution, leaves it apparent that information on this subject, generally, and particularly on the **Probable duration.** probable length of time that these pitch-pine forests will hold out will be of value and interest to the principal dealers abroad in this great article of trade. (See my trade report on Pensacola for the year 1892.)

**Growth.** It will be understood that the pitch-pine tree of these Southern States is of spontaneous growth, and especially indigenous to these sandy soils near to the water of the Gulf and

Atlantic coasts, and therefore hardly any attention is given to the culture of these trees, so far as I am aware. Nevertheless it may be that the pitch-pine tree of these Southern States, in some or all of its varieties, might grow in climates and soils abroad, if the seeds of these trees were there sown; still the result would, I think, be very doubtful as regards propagation—at least in such a way as to be available in quantity and size for the purposes of trade. {Might be sown abroad; but propagation doubtful.}

It is believed that the pine wood of these Southern States is coming more and more to the front, and that it is the most valuable wood of this country for mercantile purposes; and that as the white-pine wood of the Western and Eastern States becomes exhausted, that the Southern States will, necessarily, be fallen back on. {Valuable wood.}

In writing on this wood trade—the growth of the timber and its present and possible continued supply—I am, of course, having in view its connection with Pensacola, my post, the largest pitch-pine exporting place in the world, I believe. But to arrive at my main desire, to show that Pensacola's average exports yearly of this wood will not soon diminish, I must be allowed to refer to and remark upon the statistics of other wood producing and exporting places in this country, beyond these Southern States; much of the pitch-pine timber of the adjacent States of Alabama is received at and shipped from Pensacola. {Pensacola largest exporting port. Will not decrease.}

The New Orleans "Times Democrat," when recently reviewing the report of the Forestry Bureau of Agriculture on Southern pine timber, the same referred to above by me, contained an article on "Southern pine," and among other things written on at length on this subject, remarked that, "As the white pine of Michigan, Wisconsin, and Minnesota is exhausted the people are compelled to fall back on its southern brother. Some 7 years or 8 years ago the attention of the northern lumbermen was turned in this direction. The pine here was investigated by them, and its quality found to be excellent, suitable for almost any purpose for which lumber can be used, while not as pretty a timber for certain purposes as western white pine, the southern product was more durable, stronger, and adapted to more uses. Large purchases of pine lands were made by western capitalists and speculators in the south—purchases which, by-the-bye, have resulted most favourably, improving in value from 250 per cent. to 400 per cent.—and there was a large increase in the production and consumption of both the long and short-leaf pines. A great deal of information was published on the subject at the time; but each year more has been learned of southern forestry, and the publication of the Department of Agriculture in this matter just now is most timely and interesting, especially as the southern pine is evidently destined to become the chief lumber wood of the United States, and that within a very few years; and is attracting more attention to-day than any other." {Information about Southern pine. Suitable for all building purposes. Southern forestry.}

There are, it is stated officially, about ten species of merchantable pine in these southern States—the white-pine, and pitch-pine, {The several species.}

**Principal species.**

the scrub or spruce-pine, the sand-pine, the pond-pine, small and of no value; but the five distinctive growths for commercial purposes are, the cedar pine, which seldom reaches the market, and the long-leaf, short-leaf, loblolly, and Cuban pines, which are the principal ones in general use.

**Local names of pine timber, long-leaf pine.**

There is a great deal of confusion, it appears, from the indiscriminate use of local names for these timbers. Thus, the long-leaf pine is called yellow pine, hard pine, pitch-pine, and various other names; but the settled name of this species of wood for commercial purposes at Pensacola is pitch-pine; and this quality of wood forms the largest, if not the entire bulk of the shipments of pine wood from Pensacola. The short-leaf is called the old field and spruce-pine, the loblolly, bull swamp, sap pine and Virginia pine. The most important of these woods—the long-leaf pine—grows in the Atlantic and Gulf States, at some distance from the coast, covering a belt of about 125 miles in width. I am informed that in Florida the belt of long-leaf pine of the Atlantic coast may be traced as far south as St. Augustine, being thence, southward, largely replaced by the Cuban pine. On the Gulf side more important long-leaf growth is found further southward, until the savannas and everglades are reached, where again the Cuban pine replaces it. In Western Florida, Pensacola's position in the State, large areas of pine timber are comparatively exhausted. The Gulf Coast pine belt, covering some 40,000 square miles to the Mississippi River basin, shows no difference from the Atlantic forest.

**Area of pine forests.**

**Short leaf pine.**

Next in importance to the long-leaf pine—pitch-pine—is the short-leaf pine, and this is more widely distributed than any of the other growths of pine.

**Covers large areas.**

It is the predominating growth in some of these Southern States. It covers immense areas to the exclusion of almost every other tree, I am informed.

**Grows in Western Florida.**

In Florida the short-leaf pine is found along the northern border of the State. In Western Florida, nearer to Pensacola, it approaches the Gulf within 25 miles.

**Quantity per acre.**

It is said that the short-leaf pine gives from 3,500 feet to 4,000 feet, board measure, per acre. A rough guess places the possible standing timber of this species, distributed through the Southern States, at about 160,000,000,000 feet board measure.

**Loblolly pine.**

The loblolly pine is found, I believe, only in the northern part of Florida, none of this latter wood goes forward from Pensacola that I know of.

**Cuban pine.**

The Cuban pine is found principally in Florida, and along the Gulf Coast. It grows mainly on the so-called pine flats, or pine meadows. It is indiscriminately cut and made into timber together with the long-leaf pine, without distinction, and really is about the same in quality, I believe.

**Maps issued by Department of Agriculture.**

The Department of Agriculture has issued complete maps of the several pine districts in these Southern States, and from which publications the amount of merchantable pine now in sight, according to a published computation by the New Orleans "Times Democrat," is as follows:—

| Description. | Feet, Board Measure. | |
|---|---|---|
| Long-leaf and Cuban pine | 232,000,000,000 | Quantities of best species standing. |
| Short-leaf pine | 160,000,000,000 | |
| Loblolly pine | 102,000,000,000 | |
| Total | 494,000,000,000 | |

About 12 years ago, the official estimates of the merchantable pine timber standing in the Southern States, gave a probable quantity of 225,000,000,000 feet, board measure. There has been an enormous quantity of timber cut since that time, still the amount standing now, as will be seen by the table above, is estimated at over twice what it was 12 years ago. *Estimate of quantities 12 years ago.*

If the last estimates and maps given by the Department of Agriculture be correct, the estimates in 1880 must have been far below the mark as to the amount of timber then standing. Under any circumstances, however, as regards estimates of the timber now standing, I think that a very long time will elapse, many decades of years, before the southern forests will be bare of pine timber for commercial purposes. *Double quantity now standing. Will last a long time.*

The long-leaf pine is known to be superior to all the other species in strength and durability. In textile strength it is said to approach, and perhaps surpass cast-iron. In cross-breaking strength it rivals the oak, it is believed, requiring 10,000 lbs. pressure per square inch to break it. In stiffness it is superior to oak wood by 50 per cent. to 100 per cent. It is best adapted and much used for the construction of heavy work in shipbuilding; the inside and outside planking of vessels taking the deals and planks of the best quality. For house-building it is used almost entirely in these parts; and in buildings for railroads, railroad cross-ties, viaducts, and trestles, this wood is foremost. The finer grades and the "curly" wood are very much used for the nicer and unpainted wood in the best dwellings. The hardness of this wood especially fits it for planks and flooring. The finer grades of curly pine are used for the manufacture of furniture, and it is said that for bedsteads it is admirably adapted, as the resinous wood is a preventative to inroads of insects and such pests. The resinous products of pine wood supply many parts of the world with pitch, resin, and turpentine. And contrary to opinion formerly held in this respect, it is said that the tapping of the pine tree for turpentine strengthens instead of weakening the wood. It may be that the tapping of the trees for the substances yielded by them does not weaken the wood, but I think so as to counteract the idea that the wood was thereby deteriorated those concerned in the sale of the timber after being tapped agreed to set aside any doubts or question in such respect, and thus arose the statement that the wood was strengthened by being tapped. I do not see how it can be strengthened, even if it is not weakened by the tapping. *Strength of long-leaf pine. Uses put to. House building. Railroad cross-ties, &c. Finer grades. Curly pine used in furniture. Resinous products of pine. Tapping the pine.*

The Cuban pine is like the long-leaf pine, and it is used in trade to a large extent. I think there is no difference made in the specifications of these species of pine when brought to market for sale by the timber getters here.

*Cuban pine like long-leaf pine.*

The short-leaf pine is a softer wood, I am informed and is more easily worked perhaps. This wood is admirable for house work also, and is largely used by builders and cabinet makers. It is used for various other purposes, and is a splendid wood, not comparable, however, in many ways to the long-leaf pine. For strength it is not equal to the long-leaf pine.

*Short-leaf pine softer wood.*

*Not as strong as long-leaf.*

The loblolly pine is suited for rougher work than the other two species given. It is not as strong, I learn, and will not last as long as the others. I believe that a good deal of this inferior grade of pine finds large markets in some of the northern and western markets of this country, manufactured there into timber of small dimensions for certain purposes. The above are some of "the new facts" brought out by the investigation of the Department of Agriculture of the United States, in respect of the pine forests of the Southern States, and it is said that the supply is good for 50 years to come, and "it is to be hoped," following the investigation and publications made about the pine tree, "that an intelligent system of forestry will prevail in this country, that will prevent the exhaustion of our pine forests" in these Southern States.

*Loblolly suited to rough work.*

*Sells in northern and western markets. New facts.*

*Supply good for fifty years.*

## Tobacco.

A most interesting, and from a money point of view, an exceedingly important gathering took place in Pensacola during the latter part of the year of the tobacco growers about here and elsewhere in the State of Florida.

*Meeting of tobacco growers.*

The "Tobacco Fair," as the meeting was termed, was brought about by leading gentlemen of Pensacola and other parts of the State of Florida. Notably among the promoters of the movement were prominent officials of the railroad lines running in and out of Pensacola.

*Arranged by leading railroad officials.*

Some time ago the foremost officials of these railroad companies, in order to stimulate the people towards the purchase and cultivation of some of the large tracts of waste railroad lands in their possession, in Florida, as well, no doubt, for general extensive good, pointed out the large benefit that would be derived from the increased cultivation of tobacco in Florida. Scientific and experienced agriculturists in this especial department were enlisted to write upon the subject, and the fullest and most practical information for entering into the culture of the tobacco plant was prepared and circulated broadcast throughout many portions of the State of Florida, and, besides, every possible assistance was tendered to those already working in that direction; and to others who would also embark in this comparatively new but promising industry in these parts. The best qualities of tobacco seed were secured, and offered by the railroad companies to persons

*Cultivation of railroad lands.*

*Cultivation of tobacco beneficial.*

*Information as regards culture. Growers assisted.*

*Seed supplied.*

desiring to be so supplied, and many more facilities were tendered and made use of. The result of this original movement appears to be that a small army of tobacco growers are now in the field in Florida, and the time being ripe to bring forward the first fruits of their most important crops, the meeting referred to was called to assemble at Pensacola, and it was very largely attended by agriculturists and others from afar and near. Among those who were actually engaged in the cultivation of tobacco under the recent impetus given, and who had good samples to exhibit, were some agriculturists of the coloured population. Large and small samples of the tobacco grown within the last planting season were exhibited, and the meeting and exhibition continued for several days. *Result of movement. Meeting largely attended. Samples exhibited.*

The meeting was from time to time addressed by experienced persons on the subjects. It was stated and shown that in comparison with other growths of this plant the tobacco of Florida was of very good quality, and that samples of it had been tested in many ways in the tobacco manufactories of the northern States, and pronounced as good enough to compete with Cuban grown tobacco. Examples were given of the increased tillage of the land in Florida within the past few years for tobacco growing, and the money results to those engaged in the business. *Florida tobacco good quality. Increased tillage.*

A paper was read at the meeting, showing that the planting of tobacco in Florida was no new enterprise, for it was successfully pursued in the State before the late civil war, and that many of the citizens of the counties in which the industry was followed became wealthy, and that the industry ceased owing to the war. That in the year 1888, about the recommencement of the tobacco business in one of the tobacco counties in Florida, the merchants of that town did a business in the tobacco product of that place amounting to 246,702 dol. In 1891 it had increased there to 545,957 dol., and in the present year estimated to reach 896,820 dol., an increase of over 650,000 dol. in the 4 years. *Not a new enterprise. Ceased on breaking out of war. Statistics of new business.*

Continuing to show the warranted good results expected to be derived in future from the tobacco industry, lately vigorously entered into in Florida, I give some extracts of information from a written paper before the meeting of the tobacco growers at Pensacola. *Future good results.*

"We never had a bank here (County of Quincy, Florida), until August 29, 1889, when the Quincy State Bank commenced with a paid up capital of 60,000 dol., on that day its deposit account was 2,281 dol. and its loan account 1,535 dol. The same date in 1891 the deposit account was 48,000 dol. and loan account 104,000 dol. On June 12, 1892, the deposit account was 100,000 dol., the loan account 102 000 dol., with a surplus of 12,000 dol. There was paid for tobacco alone over the counters of this bank in 1892, 300,000 dol., and they pay a semi-annual dividend of 3 per cent. These are figures that show prosperity and speak for themselves, as well as the small number of mortgages now on record in our clerk's office as compared with 1888.

"In 1890 there was grown by Gadsden county farmers (not including the Owl Cigar Company, Schroder and Bond, and Carl Voght), 650 acres of tobacco, ranging in acreage from 1 acre to 20 acres in a crop. The average yield was 392 lbs. to the acre, and sold for an average price of 25 c. per lb. The total number 254,800 lbs. Amount received by the farmers 63,700 dol. or 98 dol. per acre, with a cost not to exceed 48 dol. per acre.

"In 1891 the acreage increased to 2,000 acres, with an average of 430 lbs. to the acre, and brought the farmers an average price of 31 c. per 1 lb., making a total of 308,700 dol., or an average of 133 dol. 30 c. per acre, with a cost not to exceed 50 dol. per acre. This year there is every reason to expect as good prices as in 1891, and as good weights as last year. This being the case, the resources will be 500,000 dol. this year from tobacco for the farmers of this country alone.

"There appears to be a timidity on the part of some about growing much tobacco for fear of over-stocking the market. If every available foot of land for tobacco had grown a crop this season there would not have been enough to supply the demand for good tobacco. The amount of tobacco grown in Florida cuts no figure in the market. To show you, careful gathered statistics show there are 600,000 smokers in New York City every night, and a small average is three cigars to a smoker—that is, 1,800,000 cigars each night, at 25 lbs. tobacco to the thousand, and we have 450,000 lbs. smoked in New York alone in one night, or each night."

**Sowing of crop for 1893.** Information was given to the meeting by an experienced tobacco grower as to the sowing of the crop for 1893. He offered some statements and advice, giving the last two crops as follows:—"1891: January 20, first sowing of beds; March 27, first setting plants; May 5, last setting plants; June 22, first cutting plants; August 10, last cutting; July 20, commenced handling; September 15, finished handling. 1892: January 30, first sowing of beds; February 3, second sowing of beds; February 22, finished sowing of beds; April 12, first setting; June 1, last setting; July 8, first cutting; August 6, first tying; August 10, last cutting; September 8, last handling and tying."

It was stated at the meeting that a tea-spoonful of seed would sow 20 square feet of land, and that as much as 3 acres had been sown from 1 square.

**Prizes to successful exhibitors.** Valuable prizes were distributed to the successful exhibitors of tobacco at the "fair." In the contest between the West Florida counties for a 40-acre tract of land to the exhibitors of the best 100 lbs. from each county the judges reported seven counties as winning, and each successful exhibitor was presented with a deed for the prize won. One of the contestants, and winner, was a lady of Pensacola, who has lately gone largely into agricultural pursuits, her extensive lands being a few miles from Pensacola.

**Second prizes.** Many valuable second prizes were also given to successful exhibitors.

## Orange Tree Blight.

For the benefit of those in the British possessions, particularly where oranges are cultivated, and the export of them made a business, I give the following, extracted from an agricultural paper here on the cause of orange tree blight:—

"Many persons who have hitherto taken pride in their orange trees have been grieved to see them sicken and gradually die without apparent cause.

"Close examination will disclose the fact that the bodies of the tree, their branches, and even many of the leaves are covered with a brownish substance which might be mistaken for dust. Attempt to brush it off, and it will be found to adhere closely in the form of minute scales. When hatched the young insects move about for awhile, then attach themselves to the tree and form the scale over the bodies, and literally suck the life from the tree, attacking the lower branches first.

"Twice a year (spring and fall) they send forth broods of young, when the old insect dies, and at such times the scale is found dry, loose, and easily washes off. Then the young insect can be seen by good eyes, but an ordinary microscope will show scores, if not hundreds, of the young to each square inch, actively running about.

"While the insect when encased under the scale is hard to kill by any safe application, when young and exposed they may be easily destroyed by the following simple emulsion, which was first recommended by Professor Riley, the Government entomologist:—

"The remedy is: One bar of soap dissolved in one gallon of boiling water, to which add while yet hot two gallons of coal-oil. Immediately churn by violent agitation in a demijohn, or, better still, by a hand-force pump in an open vessel, and in a few minutes it will become thoroughly mixed and assume a creamy consistency. Test it on a pane of glass, and if it adheres without being oily it is ready for use as soon as cold, but (do not forget this) before applying to the tree it should be diluted with nine parts of water to one part of the emulsion. After thoroughly slaking it may be applied with a brush to every part of the tree which can be reached, but a better plan is to attach a spraying nozzle to the force-pump (often used in gardens), and thoroughly spray body, branches, and leaves.

"The young insects are now moving about, and one application will kill most of them. However, as a matter of precaution, the trees should be sprayed with this emulsion two or three times, a few days apart."

In writing about oranges, I see it stated that the orange crop of Florida has reached such large proportions that for some time past the growers have been looking elsewhere for new markets. Last year the State produced 3,500,000 boxes; this year's crop is 3,000,000 boxes. It is said that the Florida orange has driven, or is driving, the Spanish and Italian product out of the American market; and that, besides this, a large trade has been commenced in Europe.

**Shipments of oranges. Shipment in British steamer to Liverpool. Line of steamers to be put on.**

A short time ago a shipment of oranges, amounting to 9,566 boxes, was made to Liverpool. The shipment was made in a British steamer. The vessel had a stormy voyage, which caused the fruit to reach England in a more or less damaged condition. The said fruit, however, sold at such good prices as left the shippers a handsome profit. The shippers of this cargo propose to put on a regular line of fruit carriers, I learn, from Florida to England, and ports on the Continent. It is thought that from 100,000 to 300,000 boxes will be shipped to Europe next year.

## Mobile.

Mr. Vice-Consul Barnwall reports as follows:—

The commercial year commences on September 1, 1891, and ends on August 31, 1892.

**Cotton receipts and prices.**

Cotton receipts were 287,971 bales, valued at 10,607,852 dol., against 311,673 bales, valued at 13,779,063 dol., of the year preceding; average price per 1 lb., 7·40 c., against 8·78 c. the year previous.

**Exports.**

There has been a decrease in the direct exports to Liverpool of 14,788 bales, and a decrease to other points of 529 bales.

**Lumber.**

The shipments of lumber from this port during the past 12 months were the largest in the history of the city, being about 8,000,000 feet more than the largest previous year (1890), when they reached nearly 53,000,000 feet. This does not include local consumption, shipments to the interior by steamboats and railroads, nor by small vessels under coasting license and not clearing through the custom-house. From the best information obtainable it is estimated that the local consumption and shipments by the latter routes will reach 15,000,000 feet, which, added to the previous total, gives a grand total of 76,000,000 feet. This large increase is not attributable altogether to a better demand in the markets of the world, but is due mainly to the fact, which has become generally known, that Mobile is a far more accessible port than it was last year. During the past winter and spring dredges have been at work deepening the channel, and have succeeded in obtaining a depth of water nearly sufficient to permit vessels of 1,500 tons burden to load to their full capacity at the city. The shipment of creosoted lumber piling, &c., has become quite a feature at this port, not less than 10 cargoes having been shipped this year to Carthagena, Republic of Colombia, for the construction of wharves, docks, &c., and as the countries of Mexico Central and South America are opened up to civilisation the demand will increase. All of this lumber is creosoted at Pascagoula and brought to Mobile by rail to be transferred to vessels, which adds an additional expense to an already very expensive article.

Our rich forests continue to add greatly to the wealth of Mobile and South Alabama, and the following statement, the timber being reduced to superficial feet, gives the trade of this port:—

| Description. | Quantity. |
|---|---|
| | Super. Feet. |
| Lumber, coastwise in vessels | 22,780,789 |
|   ,, foreign ,, | 38,318,106 |
|   ,, railroad shipments | 8,200,000 |
|   ,, towed to the islands | 38,000 |
| Timber, direct in vessels— | |
|   Hewn | 33,645,960 |
|   Sawn | 27,219,096 |
| Amount towed from Mobile to Horn and Ship Islands— | |
|   Sawn | 2,900,694 |
|   Hewn | 1,190,784 |
| Lumber, local consumption, steamboat shipments, &c. | 7,500,000 |
| Total | 141,793,429 |
|   ,, for the year preceding | 122,235,200 |
| Increase | 19,558,229 |

**Hard woods.** The consumption of these woods, oak, cedar, ash, poplar, and walnut, is gradually increasing, and in the course of a few years will occupy a very prominent place in the timber trade of Mobile, for it is said the old sources of supply are failing and new ones must be obtained. Mobile has an inexhaustible supply of these valuable woods within 50 miles of her which are easily reached, either by rail or river, the shipments to Europe the past year have been as follows: oak, 193,480 cubic feet hewn; assorted cedar, ash, walnut, poplar, &c., 88,971 cubic feet hewn.

**Vegetables.** The vegetable trade continues to be an important factor in the general trade of Mobile; the acreage is being increased annually and bids fair in the near future to reach such proportions as will entitle it to rank among our largest items of export. The total value of the yield is 251,463 dol. against 267,808 dol. the previous year, being a decrease of 16,345 dol.

(1523)

## 32 UNITED STATES.

**Harbour improvements.**

CONDITION of the Dredged Channel in Mobile River and Bay on August 1, 1892.

| Mean Low Water. | | Length of that Portion of the Channel having a Minimum Central Depth of at— | |
|---|---|---|---|
| From— | To— | Mobile River. | Mobile Bay. |
| Feet. | Feet. | Feet. | Feet. |
| 23 and over | .. | 23,535 | 96,409 |
| 22 | 23 | 1,885 | 7,400 |
| 21 | 22 | 70 | 20,089 |
| 20 | 21 | .. | 16,041 |
| 19 | 20 | .. | 2,739 |
| 18 | 19 | .. | .. |
| 17 | 18 | .. | .. |
| 16 | 17 | .. | .. |
| 15 | 16 | .. | .. |
| Total | .. | 25,490 | 142,678 |

**Shipping up and down channel.**

List of vessels that have arrived and departed from this port beginning September 1, 1891, and ending August 31, 1892, these vessels being all large vessels of their respective rigs and drawing up to and including 17 feet 6 inches up and 19 feet 10 inches down channel.

| Description. | Drawing up to and Including. | | Number. | |
|---|---|---|---|---|
| | Up. | Down. | Up. | Down. |
| | Ft. in. | Ft. in. | | |
| Steamships | 16 6 | 18 10 | 86 | 86 |
| Ships and barks | 17 6 | 19 10 | 139 | 139 |
| Brigs | 12 0 | 15 6 | 11 | 11 |
| Schooners, which include four, three, and two masters | 15 6 | 17 6 | 160 | 160 |
| Total | .. | .. | 396 | 396 |
| ,, up and down | .. | .. | 792 | |

These vessels have with their respective draughts passed up and down the channel without material detention. The deepest draught that passed up and down the year previous was 17 feet 6 inches, whereas in this year's report the deepest draught is 19 feet 10 inches, a difference of 2 feet 4 inches.

# NEW ORLEANS.

**Annex A.**—RETURN of all Shipping at the Port of Mobile during the Year 1892.

ENTERED.

| Nationality. | Sailing. Number of Vessels. | Sailing. Tons. | Steam. Number of Vessels. | Steam. Tons. | Total. Number of Vessels. | Total. Tons. |
|---|---|---|---|---|---|---|
| British | 65 | 27,180 | 22 | 22,605 | 87 | 49,785 |
| American | 90 | 32,833 | ... | ... | 90 | 32,833 |
| Norwegian | 69 | 62,466 | 18 | 9,623 | 87 | 72,089 |
| Swedish | 8 | 5,818 | 1 | 479 | 9 | 6,297 |
| French | 1 | 256 | ... | ... | 1 | 256 |
| Russian | 11 | 7,966 | ... | ... | 11 | 7,966 |
| German | 4 | 3,057 | ... | ... | 4 | 3,057 |
| Spanish | 3 | 2,418 | ... | ... | 3 | 2,418 |
| Dutch | 4 | 4,531 | ... | ... | 4 | 4,531 |
| Italian | 3 | 1,858 | ... | ... | 3 | 1,858 |
| Mexican | 2 | 401 | ... | ... | 2 | 401 |
| Portuguese | 1 | 393 | ... | ... | 1 | 393 |
| Total | 261 | 149,177 | 41 | 32,707 | 302 | 181,884 |
| Coastwise | ... | ... | ... | ... | 129 | 101,021 |
| Grand total | ... | ... | ... | ... | 431 | 282,905 |
| Total for the year preceding | ... | ... | ... | ... | 333 | 190,865 |

CLEARED.

| Nationality. | Sailing. Number of Vessels. | Sailing. Tons. | Steam. Number of Vessels. | Steam. Tons. | Total. Number of Vessels. | Total. Tons. |
|---|---|---|---|---|---|---|
| British | 61 | 26,512 | 19 | 18,522 | 80 | 45,034 |
| American | 88 | 29,495 | 1 | 428 | 89 | 29,923 |
| Norwegian | 69 | 64,823 | 22 | 11,583 | 91 | 76,406 |
| Swedish | 6 | 2,674 | 1 | 478 | 7 | 3,152 |
| French | 1 | 256 | ... | ... | 1 | 256 |
| Russian | 11 | 7,582 | ... | ... | 11 | 7,582 |
| German | 4 | 3,330 | ... | ... | 4 | 3,330 |
| Spanish | 3 | 2,228 | ... | ... | 3 | 2,228 |
| Dutch | 6 | 6,872 | ... | ... | 6 | 6,872 |
| Italian | 6 | 3,894 | ... | ... | 6 | 3,894 |
| Mexican | 2 | 420 | ... | ... | 2 | 420 |
| Portuguese | 1 | 399 | ... | ... | 1 | 399 |
| Total | 258 | 148,485 | 43 | 31,011 | 301 | 179,496 |
| Coastwise | ... | ... | ... | ... | 129 | 88,446 |
| Grand total | ... | ... | ... | ... | 430 | 267,942 |
| Total for the year preceding | ... | ... | ... | ... | 319 | 173,044 |

(1523)

### Annex B.—RETURN of Principal Articles of Import to Mobile during the Years 1891–92 and 1890–91.

| Articles. | | 1891–92. Quantity. | 1891–92. Value.* | 1890–91. Quantity. | 1890–91. Value. |
|---|---|---|---|---|---|
| | | | £ s. d. | | £ s. d. |
| Bagging | Pieces | 23,030 | ... | 20,973 | ... |
| Iron ties | Bundles | 34,740 | ... | 32,315 | ... |
| Bacon | Hogsheads | 15,393 | ... | 15,705 | ... |
| Cotton | Bales | 287,971 | 2,209,969 3 4 | 311,673 | 2,870,638 2 6 |
| Coffee | Sacks | 14,392 | ... | 12,633 | ... |
| Corn | ,, | 357,917 | ... | 426,525 | ... |
| Flour | Barrels | 130,349 | ... | 154,341 | ... |
| Fertilisers | Sacks | 163,728 | ... | 286,898 | ... |
| Hay | Bales | 40,936 | ... | 72,731 | ... |
| Lard | Tierces | 5,870 | ... | 5,361 | ... |
| Molasses | Barrels | 3,007 | ... | 2,251 | ... |
| Oats | Sacks | 117,283 | ... | 85,737 | ... |
| Potatoes | Barrels | 20,156 | ... | 16,341 | ... |
| Pork | ,, | 3,021 | ... | 1,520 | ... |
| Rice | ,, | 6,110 | ... | 6,330 | ... |
| Salt | Sacks | 14,983 | ... | 16,212 | ... |
| Soap | Boxes | 18,192 | ... | 19,835 | ... |
| Sugar | Barrels | 17,607 | ... | 14,561 | ... |
| Tobacco | Boxes | 19,223 | ... | 25,796 | ... |
| Whiskey | Barrels | 6,982 | ... | 6,923 | ... |
| Coal | Tons | 70,098 | ... | 53,042 | ... |
| Wool | Lbs. | 775,000 | 36,328 2 6 | 973,100 | 47,641 7 1 |

\* 4 dol. 80 c. = 1*l*.

NOTE.—I cannot enumerate articles imported from foreign countries, nor give the value of above enumerated articles, with the exception of cotton and wool.

### Annex C.—TABLE showing the Total Value of all Articles Exported from Mobile and Imported to Mobile from and to Foreign Countries during the Years 1890–91, and 1891–92.

EXPORTS.*

| Year. | Value. |
|---|---|
| | £ s. d. |
| 1890–91 | 670,638 5 2 |
| 1891–92 | 582,701 8 9 |

IMPORTS.

| Year. | Value. |
|---|---|
| | £ s. d. |
| 1890–91 | 18,164 15 10 |
| 1891–92 | 34,538 6 8 |

\* I have no means of dividing the above exports as to countries except as regards cotton, included in above:—

| Year. | Value. |
|---|---|
| | £ s. d. |
| 1890–91 | 484,965 5 7 |
| 1891–92 | 290,621 11 0 |

## NEW ORLEANS.

RETURN of Principal Articles of Export from Mobile during the Years 1891–92 and 1890–91.

| Articles. | | 1891–92.* | | 1890–91. | |
|---|---|---|---|---|---|
| | | Quantity. | Value.* | Quantity. | Value. |
| | | | £ s. d. | | £ s. d. |
| Cotton | Bales | 283,985 | 2,179,584 17 8 | 299,852 | 2,761,761 17 2 |
| Timber | Cubic feet | 5,072,088 | 135,018 17 0 | 3,592,924 | 99,635 12 8 |
| Lumber | Feet | 61,098,895 | 185,938 7 11 | 50,892,805 | 125,382 9 7 |
| Staves, foreign | Mille | 147,000 | 4,583 6 10 | 68,168 | 1,738 10 10 |
| ,, coastwise | ,, | 156,000 | 4,863 19 2 | ... | ... |
| Shingles | 1,000 | 1,369,302 | 1,231 0 4 | 895,100 | 896 13 5 |
| Merchandise | ... | ... | 3,464 1 6 | ... | 1,969 15 2 |
| Vegetables | ... | ... | 52,388 2 6 | ... | 74,391 0 10 |
| Machinery | ... | ... | 12,475 0 0 | ... | ... |
| Total | ... | ... | 2,579,547 12 11 | ... | 3,065,775 19 8 |

* 4 dol. 80 c. = 1l.

### ALABAMA.

Mr. Vice-Consul Wm. Barnwall reports as follows:—

I hereby submit my report for the year 1892, and there are many encouraging features which may be noticed, especially that of diversified farming, stock development, and fruit culture. There are many excellent opportunities for the investment of capital in the lands of this county when the price is considered with the value of what they may be made to produce and for which there is always a market at good prices. In her fisheries she has a resource which has not been developed as it should be, as no waters can produce better fish or in more abundant quantities than the waters of the Gulf of Mexico and tributary waters. The oyster-beds are more extensive than elsewhere, and hundreds of thousands of acres of these beds are still unoccupied. As the southern oyster reaches maturity in 3 years, when it takes the oyster on the Atlantic coast 5 years, the advantage in favour of the southern product may be easily seen. The oyster laws are liberal, yet tend to the proper propagation of this valuable bivalve.

The past year has seen an almost new departure in Alabama agricultural life, owing to low prices of cotton for several years and the farmer was bound to do something else so as to pay for the tilling of the soil, and it has been of inestimable value to him, as he has begun diversified farming, which to the south means much more than to any other country which has not such a climate as this. For years his only crop was cotton, he had to pay the very highest price for every article of food, had to have his cotton crop mortgaged for these supplies before a seed was in the ground, and his labour was not remunerative. This he is changing. He is now raising his own corn, wheat, oats, potatoes, and everything else required, and in a year or two will become an exporter of them; so it is with his stock. He is, as

*Agriculture.*

**Wheat.**

rapidly as possible raising cattle, horses, sheep, mules, and hogs, and as there are millions of acres of unoccupied lands in nearly every section of the State they cost but little.

The Agricultural Department of the State the past year has done much towards the introduction of wheat in the southern section, and distributed seed which has been obtained, not only from this country, but also from London, England. Although test was made, and the yield was certainly favourable, large red, 23 bushels per acre, purple straw; $17\frac{29}{30}$ bushels per acre; Anglo-Canadian, $16\frac{17}{30}$ bushels per acre; earlier of all, $14\frac{14}{15}$ bushels per acre, and white chaff, $13\frac{3}{10}$ bushels per acre. As soon as these are acclimated the yield will largely increase. The berry was plump and showed the adaptability of even the light soils of the south for wheat raising. Corn is a large producer, while roots, vegetables, and fruits add to the profits of the farmer.

**Cotton.**

The past year was a disastrous one for the cotton grower, as, in addition to a less acreage planted, the season was most unfavourable, and a short crop has been the result. In fact, so short that the surplus of last year is wiped out and a deficit stares the cotton dealers of the world. The price, however, has advanced, so that if even a crop of 9,000,000 bales are raised in 1893 it would do no more than supply the demand. The planter can raise it much more cheaply than he has done, as he finds the advantage in raising his own supplies, and in his cotton seed he has much of the fertiliser required.

**Truck farming.**

Truck farming, or market gardening, has become one of the most important industries throughout this State and adjoining ones, and is of no mean value. The shipments from Mobile district shows the following during 1892: 135,000 crates of cabbages, 52,300 barrels of potatoes, 45 cars of potatoes in bulk, each car containing 150 barrels, 24,500 boxes of beans, and 2,800 boxes of peas. As a sample of profit from truck-farming at the experimental farm of the Mobile and Ohio Railway at Buckatunna, 80 miles north from Mobile, 5 acres of cabbage yielded a net profit of 663 dol. 73 c. The strawberry crop is even still more profitable, while sweet potatoes, Irish potatoes, beans, peas, and small vegetables swell the list. Artificial manures, or those that give quick results, are the best, as products are grown for the earliest markets. For future results, however, the regular barnyard manures are preferable, as the excellent clay subsoils everywhere found keep the full strength of whatever is put in the soil.

**Fruits, &c.**

This southern portion of the United States is particularly noted for the excellence and variety of fruits which grow to perfection, and which are not subject to blight or disease as in less favourable sections. As a pear country it is unexcelled, while peaches, oranges, olives, figs, pecans, grapes, strawberries, blackberries, and raspberries, persimons, plums, apples, and a host of others are profitably cultivated, and as there is an abundance of suitable lands still unoccupied, there is no limit to the amount which may be produced.

**Tobacco.**

Owing to glauconite, or marl of a peculiar kind, many parts of

Alabama can produce a tobacco equal to the famed Havana, or Spanish tobacco, and as the area is much larger, the supply can be made unlimited. That which has been grown is acknowledged by experts in Cuba to be equal, if not superior, to any grown there. The whole of this district is suitable for the growth of all kinds, and capital during the past year has been drawn in that direction. The light pine lands are equal producers with the river bottoms or the more rolling mixed woodlands and tobacco will be largely produced in the near future for export.

The State of Alabama is certainly not deficient in the most nutritious grasses, and those, too, which produce the most abundantly, the growth being especially vigorous owing to the large precipitation. No country produces any better grasses as the list of the foreign kind vie with the native grasses, becoming easily acclimated. Every section has those suitable to it whether in the piney region, with its light sandy soil, the stiff clay of the prairie hardwood lands, or the rich alluvial river bottoms, each and all have the requisite grasses for stock of all kinds. Besides, the seasons are so favourable that many of the grasses will bear mowing two to four times in a season, some yielding as high as 6 tons per acre.   *Grasses.*

The principal grasses are : red clover, Bermuda grass, orchard grass, crab grass, Kentucky blue grass, Johnson grass, cow peas, Japan clover, alfalfa, melilotus, ferrel grass, rescue grass, red tops, smooth brome, Australian blue grass, Indian beard grass, water grass, carpet grass, Texas millet, speeding prarie, Texas blue grass, Mexican clover, crimson clover, burr clover, winter vetch, the sorgums, Timothy and a few other local grasses. Crab grass is found everywhere, and as it comes up spontaneously after other crops are removed, it is a most valuabe grass, yielding sometimes as high as 6 tons per acre : thus showing its rapid growth.

It is impossible to find any one forage plant which continues in growth throughout the year. For this reason a mixture of two or three kinds will usually prove to be better than either one where planted alone, and, when possible, one planted in the mixture should belong to the clover family. No one, two or three varieties will succeed best in all parts of this State, and the choice for each farm must depend on local conditions. Most of the true grasses are affected more by moisture than by any other difference in the soil, while most of the cloves are affected more by the amount of lime.

For general cultivation, Bermuda, Japan. or lapediza melilotus, red clover, and Johnson grass are the best five species for this State, and are in value in the order named. For hay alone, Bermuda, lapediza, and Johnson grass are the best, while for pasture none are found better than Bermuda, orchard grass and run clover for the light and more sandy soils of the pine woods region. When a fertilizer crop is wanted for immediate effect there is nothing equal to the cow pea, and when the land is to remain without cultivation for a year or more, melilotus, red clover, and lapediza is the best crop that can be sown.

Nearly every species which are now in general cultivation have

**Stock.**

come to this State from the cooler climate of the Northern States or of Europe. Bermuda, Johnson grass, and lapediza are almost the only ones which have come to us from countries having a similar climate to our own, and they are the ones which grow best here, yet the others improve rapidly as they become acclimated.

For a State with such a variety of the best grasses, and being well watered throughout, stock of all kinds do specially well. The climate being also favourable, there being but little winter, so that most stock may shift for themselves, although those who put up hay, which costs only the cutting, for winter use, find them in much better condition in spring.

Cattle do well, and this industry is being rapidly developed. The common cattle of the country are being crossed with some of the best-blooded stock, especially Jerseys, Holsteins, Devons, short-horns, and Brahma. The latter shows the best offspring for slaughter and they are superior range animals, owing to their activity. The Jerseys and Holsteins are good dairy cattle, while the Devons and short-horns are more for beef, but they are too heavy for good foragers, especially on light sandy lands. In sugar-cane bottoms they are the most profitable breeds.

The breeding of horses of especially fine breeds for market is engaging the attention of capitalists throughout the South, and such is carried on under vary favourable climatic conditions, as lung troubles but seldom affect horses, especially when bred in or near the Gulf counties, as the largest stables in the county move their whole stables to Southern Alabama during the winter months. Racehorses and roadsters are those principally bred and they show qualities equal to the Kentucky breeds. Large amounts have been invested in this the past year.

The breeding of mules in this State has had a successful beginning, and as the best Jacks have been imported and the surroundings most favourable, the young mules show superior quality.

**Sheep.**

The sheep industry is making greater strides than that of any other stock raising in the South, and not only the climate but the excellent ranges for such, give advantages possessed by no other section of this county. Breeders of sheep, not only from the North and Western States, but also from Europe, are taking a lively interest in sheep-farming and are investing largely. These ranges can be purchased now at about 4s. 3d. per acre, and of these dry highlands hundreds of thousands of acres may be secured. Disease is unknown, as the flocks roaming the country have always a dry, clean ground on which to lie, and, therefore, foot rot, scab, and other diseases of sheep do not decimate the southern flocks. When the native sheep, hardy, and of good sized bone, are crossed with either South Down, Leicester, or merinos, the offspring is a valuable sheep, with a wool cut averaging as high as 6 lbs. each, although half-bred wethers clip over 10 lbs. to the fleece. There are no burrs or anything else to injure the fleece. It requires no washing, and is in demand, not only in the American woollen factories, but in those of Britain. There is a field open here for a profitable development of the sheep industry.

The native hogs, in derision "the razor back," when crossed by Hogs. the Berkshire and others, prove themselves exceedingly profitable, and as they can always shift for themselves, they are no cost to raise. Some corn, sweet potatoes, and peanuts will always make them ready for market in two weeks' time. Their flesh is so firm, tender, and mixed with fat and lean, that they command a higher price in market than the large hogs from the West. The breed is being improved.

The climate of this and other Southern States is certainly Climate. uniform, as the following table from the Weather Signal Service of Mobile district shows:—

| Months. | Temperature. ||| Precipitation. |
|---|---|---|---|---|
| | Mean. | Maximum. | Minimum. | |
| | Degrees. | Degrees. | Degrees. | Inches. |
| 1891— | | | | |
| December | 53·4 | 60·9 | 46·0 | 6·81 |
| 1892— | | | | |
| January | 47·0 | 55·5 | 38·5 | 9·97 |
| February | 56·8 | 65·1 | 48·6 | 2·09 |
| March | 55·5 | 64·7 | 46·3 | 8·52 |
| April | 66·2 | 72·8 | 59·5 | 3·10 |
| May | 72·4 | 80·0 | 64·8 | 1·49 |
| June | 78·8 | 86·8 | 70·7 | 4·09 |
| July | 79·0 | 85·6 | 72·4 | 14·43 |
| August | 79·8 | 87·4 | 72·3 | 13·47 |
| September | 75·2 | 83·9 | 66·6 | 4·93 |
| October | 69·1 | 78·3 | 59·9 | 3·03 |
| November | 58·4 | 67·8 | 49·1 | 1·93 |
| Average | 66·0 | 74·1 | 57·9 | .. |

The total precipitation for the year is 73·86 inches, much heavier than usual, and the principal cause of the short cotton crop. July and August flooding the plantations and interfering with their cultivation.

(1523)

LONDON:
Printed for Her Majesty's Stationery Office,
By HARRISON AND SONS,
Printers in Ordinary to Her Majesty.
(75  5 | 93—H & S  1523)

# FOREIGN OFFICE.
## 1893.
## ANNUAL SERIES.

### No. 1233.

### DIPLOMATIC AND CONSULAR REPORTS ON TRADE AND FINANCE.

# UNITED STATES.

### REPORT FOR THE YEAR 1892
#### ON THE
### TRADE OF THE CONSULAR DISTRICT OF CHICAGO.

REFERENCE TO PREVIOUS REPORT, Annual Series No. 1103.

*Presented to both Houses of Parliament by Command of Her Majesty,*
*JUNE, 1893.*

LONDON:
PRINTED FOR HER MAJESTY'S STATIONERY OFFICE,
BY HARRISON AND SONS, ST. MARTIN'S LANE,
PRINTERS IN ORDINARY TO HER MAJESTY.

And to be purchased, either directly or through any Bookseller, from
EYRE & SPOTTISWOODE, EAST HARDING STREET, FLEET STREET, E.C., and
32, ABINGDON STREET, WESTMINSTER, S.W.; or
JOHN MENZIES & Co., 12, HANOVER STREET, EDINBURGH, and
90, WEST NILE STREET, GLASGOW; or
HODGES, FIGGIS, & Co., Limited, 104, GRAFTON STREET, DUBLIN.

1893.

[C. 6855—120.] *Price Threepence.*

# New Series of Reports.

Reports of the Annual Series have been issued from Her Majesty's Diplomatic and Consular Officers at the following places, and may be obtained from the sources indicated on the title-page:—

| No. | | Price. |
|---|---|---|
| 1111. | Brunei | 1½d. |
| 1112. | Athens | 2½d. |
| 1113. | Alexandria | 2d. |
| 1114. | Vienna | 1d. |
| 1115. | Stettin | 2½d. |
| 1116. | Berne | 1d. |
| 1117. | Palermo | 2½d. |
| 1118. | Tokio | 1½d. |
| 1119. | St. Petersburg | 3d. |
| 1120. | Teneriffe | 1d. |
| 1121. | Damascus | 1d. |
| 1122. | Naples | 2d. |
| 1123. | Hakodate | 1d. |
| 1124. | Montevideo | 2½d. |
| 1125. | Stockholm | 1½d. |
| 1126. | Dantzig | 2d. |
| 1127. | The Hague | 1½d. |
| 1128. | Odessa | 1d. |
| 1129. | Berne | 1½d. |
| 1130. | Malaga | 3d. |
| 1131. | Rome | 2½d. |
| 1132. | St. Jago de Cuba | 4½d. |
| 1133. | Munich | 1½d. |
| 1134. | Meshed | 1d. |
| 1135. | Guayaquil | ½d. |
| 1136. | Rio de Janeiro | 4½d. |
| 1137. | Tonga | 1d. |
| 1138. | Copenhagen | 1d. |
| 1139. | Tangier | 1½d. |
| 1140. | Buenos Ayres | 2½d. |
| 1141. | Para | 1d. |
| 1142. | Baghdad and Bussorah | 1½d. |
| 1143. | Christiania | 5½d. |
| 1144. | Old Calabar | 2d. |
| 1145. | Trieste | 1½d. |
| 1146. | Quito | 1d. |
| 1147. | Buenos Ayres | 6d. |
| 1148. | Bogotá | 1d. |
| 1149. | The Hague | 2d. |
| 1150. | Mexico | 2½d. |
| 1151. | Florence | 2d. |
| 1152. | Calais | 1d. |
| 1153. | Lorenzo Marques | 1½d. |
| 1154. | Patras | 1d. |
| 1155. | Taganrog | 1d. |
| 1156. | Stockholm | 1d. |
| 1157. | Washington | 2d. |
| 1158. | Paris | 1½d. |
| 1159. | Bengazi | 1d. |
| 1160. | Santos | 2½d. |
| 1161. | Buenos Ayres | 1½d. |
| 1162. | Nantes | 1d. |
| 1163. | Beira | 5d. |
| 1164. | Galveston | 1½d. |
| 1165. | Berlin | 1d. |
| 1166. | Bordeaux | 2½d. |
| 1167. | Calais | 2½d. |
| 1168. | The Hague | 2d. |
| 1169. | Athens | 12d. |
| 1170. | Galatz | 1½d. |
| 1171. | Guayaquil | 1d. |

| No. | | Price. |
|---|---|---|
| 1172. | Riga | 2d. |
| 1173. | Trebizond | 1d. |
| 1174. | Havre | 2½d. |
| 1175. | Saigon | ½d. |
| 1176. | Baltimore | 1½d. |
| 1177. | Brest | 1d. |
| 1178. | Buenos Ayres | ½d. |
| 1179. | Adrianople | ½d. |
| 1180. | Algiers | 2½d. |
| 1181. | Boston | 1d. |
| 1182. | Marseilles | 1½d. |
| 1183. | Warsaw | 1d. |
| 1184. | Piræus | 1½d. |
| 1185. | Callao | 1d. |
| 1186. | Jerusalem | ½d. |
| 1187. | Chefoo | 1½d. |
| 1188. | Munich | 2d. |
| 1189. | Resht | 1d. |
| 1190. | Batavia | 1½d. |
| 1191. | Batoum | 1½d. |
| 1192. | Tainan | 1d. |
| 1193. | Amoy | 1d. |
| 1194. | Zanzibar | 4d. |
| 1195. | Corunna | 2d. |
| 1196. | Algiers | 15½d. |
| 1197. | Pahoi | 1d. |
| 1198. | Nice | 1½d. |
| 1199. | Kiungchow | 1½d. |
| 1200. | Aleppo | 1d. |
| 1201. | Stettin | 4½d. |
| 1202. | Swatow | 1d. |
| 1203. | Charleston | 2½d. |
| 1204. | Syra | 1d. |
| 1205. | New Orleans | 2½d. |
| 1206. | Suakin | 1½d. |
| 1207. | Caracas | 1d. |
| 1208. | Somali Coast | 1d. |
| 1209. | Nantes | 1d. |
| 1210. | Tahiti | 2d. |
| 1211. | Ichang | 3½d. |
| 1212. | Wênchow | 1d. |
| 1213. | Havana | 2d. |
| 1214. | Cagliari | 1d. |
| 1215. | Old Calabar | ½d. |
| 1216. | Foochow | 1d. |
| 1217. | Wuhu | 1d. |
| 1218. | Vera Cruz | 1½d. |
| 1219. | San José | 1d. |
| 1220. | Antwerp | 1d. |
| 1221. | Mogador | 2½d. |
| 1222. | Berlin | 1½d. |
| 1223. | Rome | 1d. |
| 1224. | Constantinople | 6½d. |
| 1225. | Barcelona | 2½d. |
| 1226. | Madeira | 5½d. |
| 1227. | Söul | 1½d. |
| 1228. | Chinkiang | 1d. |
| 1229. | Newchwang | 1d. |
| 1230. | Chungking | 1½d. |
| 1231. | Hankow | 1d. |
| 1232. | Odessa | 2d. |

# No. 1233.

*Reference to previous Report, Annual Series No. 1103.*

# UNITED STATES.

## CHICAGO.

*Consul Hayes Sadler to the Earl of Rosebery.*

My Lord,                            *Chicago, May* 13, 1893.

I HAVE the honour to transmit herewith a Report on the Trade of Chicago for the year 1892, together with the Annual Reports of the British Vice-Consuls at St. Louis, St. Paul, Kansas City, and Denver.

I have, &c.
(Signed)      J. HAYES SADLER.

---

*Report on the Trade and Commerce of the Consular District of Chicago for the Year* 1892.

### ABSTRACT of Contents.

| | PAGE |
|---|---|
| Chicago— | |
|     Trade of | 2 |
|     Produce trade | 4 |
|     Wholesale trade | 7 |
|     Manufactures | 9 |
|     Real estate and building | 12 |
|     Shipping | 17 |
|     Exports and imports | 18 |
|     Notes on the West | 21 |
| St. Louis | 26 |
| St. Paul | 37 |
| Kansas | 39 |
| Denver | 41 |

(1562)

## UNITED STATES.

### Introductory.

It is proposed to give a summary of those matters connected with trade which appear to have the widest range of interest, collected from the most reliable authority, although in a limited report it is impossible to furnish more than a general view of so large a district, where development has been and is progressing at so rapid a rate. There may be many subjects of economic and commercial interest left unnoticed, which might well be looked for in the scope of an annual review of this part of the United States, and many parts of this district, regarding which it is regretted that either space allows of little mention to be made or special information is not at hand. Progress, looking to the future, is the important question here; there seems little time for record of the past. The great features of the year are undoubtedly the marvellous prosperity of the city of Chicago, and the preparations for the World's Columbian Exposition. A report* on the inauguration and condition of the Exhibition on May 1, 1893, has recently been transmitted, and no further mention will be made here. The other subject matters treated, together with the reports of the Vice-Consuls in the district, will be found under separate heads.

### The Trade of Chicago.

As far as the city of Chicago is concerned, the record of the year 1892 has proved an exception to the general rule that a Presidential Election year is a dull one. Besides the impetus given by preparations for the Exhibition the bountiful harvest of 1891 assisted much in causing unusual prosperity. It placed a large amount of money at the disposal of the farmers in this neighbourhood and all through the West; it provided them with means to renew their stock of implements and necessaries, to pay part of their mortgages or debts, and to purchase many articles of luxury, thus directly benefiting the trade of this city, which is still the great centre from which they derive their supplies. The Exhibition created abnormal activity in the building and other trades; an immense number of people have been attracted to the city, causing increased demand for accommodation and a considerable rise in prices; the large amount of money thus circulated added to the general prosperity, which was reflected on all branches of trade. Almost all industries improved their position in the course of the year, with, perhaps, the sole exception of the packing business.

The record, however, though showing very great prosperity, is said scarcely to have equalled expectations. The volume of business was carried on quietly, with no speculative transactions. The dealings in real estate were not so large as in the preceding year, but it is thought by many that the increase in value of real estate has not greatly depended on the selection of Chicago for the

* See Report No. 292, Miscellaneous Series.

Exhibition, but has been a natural growth, and in the same manner it is considered, with perhaps greater force, that the increase in trade is natural, and has been dependent on no outside circumstances.

The increase in volume of trade was compensated by lower prices in grain and some other produce, consequent on abundant supply, though the demand caused by the bad harvest in Europe enabled producers to secure a fair price, and prevented any great fall in value; cotton and wool were extremely low in price; there was not much done in railway building nor any great demand for rails, and the iron trade was not in a satisfactory condition. The only real exception to prosperity, however, was shown in fire insurance business, the losses of the various companies having been as great as those in 1891, which was a disastrous year. The fires in this city were not extensive, and a fair profit was made on that business, but an extraordinary number of conflagrations, giving strong grounds for belief in incendiarism, occurred in many other localities. The numerous fires at Milwaukee absorbed twice over the premiums of the whole State of Wisconsin; the city of St. Louis consumed all the profits of the Missouri business, and the premiums of the State of Nebraska were used up by fires at Omaha, while losses elsewhere were heavy.

After allowing for duplications in the different trades in the same manner as the estimate has been made in previous years, for which the sum of 26,600,000*l*. has been deducted, the total trade of the city of Chicago in 1892 is calculated at 317,113,400*l*., against 300,825,000*l*. in 1891. The increase in produce trade is calculated at 2 per cent. over the preceding year, the wholesale trade is estimated to have increased $10\frac{7}{8}$ per cent., and the manufacturing trade $3\frac{3}{8}$ per cent. This estimate, which is irrespective of the value of real estate business, includes only such transactions as have been followed by delivery from producer to consumer, and is calculated on the first selling value of goods received, except the precious metals, with the additional value they may have acquired by local manufacture. It does not reach to one-third the amount of the clearings of the associated banks, which indicate the prosperity which has existed; in 1891 the clearings amounted to 918,944,000*l*., and in 1892 to 1,058,921,900*l*., or an increase of 139,977,900*l*., while 6 years ago they reached the sum of 537,944,000*l*. only. Thus the bank clearings of Chicago have now surpassed in magnitude those of Boston, and are only exceeded in the United States by those of New York. The total trade may not seem to bear a very large percentage of increase over that of 1891, but it must be borne in mind that every year has shown an increase in the volume of business done, notably the year 1890, when the increase was $17\frac{1}{2}$ per cent., and that all these gains have been maintained, and an additional increase of $5\frac{3}{8}$ per cent. has been secured. It is an increase of as nearly as possible 50 per cent. in 10 years, and of 300 per cent. compared with the trade of 20 years ago; in 1860, 32 years ago, the whole volume of trade was scarcely 20,000,000*l*., and in 1850 it only amounted to

(1562)

4,000,000*l*., or about one-seventy-seventh of the expansion it has developed in 42 years. The substantial gain in value and the large increase in volume of trade, together with the continued rise in the value of real estate, has sufficed, without mention of the Exhibition, to make Chicago at the present time the most prosperous city in the most prosperous country in the world, and, perhaps, nowhere has such an extraordinary scene of activity prevailed during any year as at Chicago in 1892.

*Produce Trade.*

The receipts and shipments of the principal articles of produce, according to statements of the Board of Trade and other sources, were as follows compared with the year 1891.

RETURN of the Principal Articles Received and Shipped at and from Chicago during the Years 1892–91.

| Articles. | | 1892. Received. | 1892. Shipped. | 1891. Received. | 1891. Shipped. |
|---|---|---|---|---|---|
| Flour | Barrels | 5,919,343 | 5,710,629 | 4,516,617 | 4,048,129 |
| Wheat | Bushels | 50,234,555 | 43,833,795 | 42,931,258 | 38,990,169 |
| Corn | ,, | 78,510,385 | 66,104,220 | 72,770,304 | 66,758,300 |
| Oats | ,, | 78,827,985 | 67,332,322 | 74,402,413 | 68,771,614 |
| Rye | ,, | 3,633,308 | 2,775,600 | 9,164,198 | 7,572,991 |
| Barley | ,, | 16,989,278 | 10,438,281 | 12,228,480 | 7,858,108 |
| Grass seeds | Lbs. | 53,228,779 | 60,670,835 | 66,166,230 | 55,152,971 |
| Flax seed | Bushels | 9,473,824 | 8,802,220 | 11,120,138 | 9,990,798 |
| Cured meats | Lbs. | 179,965,327 | 743,859,554 | 206,898,958 | 751,684,862 |
| Canned meats | Cases | 92,998 | 1,428,331 | 41,744 | 1,253,480 |
| Dressed beef | Lbs. | 149,496,436 | 1,212,344,343 | 105,061,775 | 877,295,883 |
| Pork | Barrels | 16,934 | 294,781 | 13,970 | 278,553 |
| Lard | Lbs. | 68,371,502 | 398,915,558 | 74,021,945 | 362,109,099 |
| Cheese | ,, | 64,396,960 | 48,504,956 | 63,922,939 | 50,204,235 |
| Butter | ,, | 154,128,700 | 139,118,655 | 127,765,048 | 140,737,620 |
| Live hogs | Number | 7,714,435 | 2,926,945 | 8,600,805 | 2,962,514 |
| Cattle | ,, | 3,511,796 | 1,121,675 | 3,250,359 | 1,066,264 |
| Sheep | ,, | 2,145,079 | 483,368 | 2,153,537 | 688,205 |
| Calves | ,, | 197,576 | 31,004 | 205,383 | 48,331 |
| Horses | ,, | 86,998 | 74,368 | 94,396 | 87,273 |
| Hides | Lbs. | 110,082,233 | 229,711,358 | 110,981,894 | 198,571,824 |
| Wool | ,, | 28,388,364 | 44,396,698 | 35,049,664 | 57,189,677 |
| Lumber | Met. feet | 2,203,874 | 1,060,117 | 2,045,418 | 865,949 |
| Potatoes | Bushels | 5,563,950 | 897,590 | 2,250,000 | ...* |
| Eggs | Cases | 2,153,032 | 1,653,118 | 1,508,477 | ... |
| Piped oil | Barrels | 4,500,000 | ... | 4,062,500 | ... |

\* Unknown.

Cereals.

The total receipts of flour and grain in bushels amounted to 255,832,554 bushels, against 232,821,429 bushels in 1891, and the quantity shipped was 216,182,008 bushels, compared with about 212,000,000 bushels in 1891. The harvest was nearly 25 per cent. less in 1892 than in the preceding year, but the great difficulty which was experienced by the railways in providing means for transportation threw the shipments of grain largely into last year, and with regard to corn the movement scarcely ever begins before quite the end of the year in which it is produced. The receipts of cereals were therefore larger, but on account of lower prices the value is estimated at 2,020,620*l.* less than in 1891, or a total of 26,020,620*l.*

Arising from various causes, amongst which may be mentioned an improved supply from other producing countries for the European markets, there was an almost gradual and continued fall in the price of wheat. No. 2 spring wheat fell from 3*s.* 7*d.* in January to 2*s.* 11*d.* in December, the average price having been 3*s.* 3¼*d.*, against 4*s.* 1*d.* in 1891 and 3*s.* 8*d.* in 1890. The 50,234,555 bushels received were only valued at 7,608,247*l.*, or 185,567*l.* more than the 42,931,258 bushels received in 1891. It was the same with flour, and the 5,919,333 barrels were valued at very little in excess of the 4,516,617 barrels received in 1891.

Wheat.

Corn, on the contrary, rose from 1*s.* 7*d.* in January to 2*s.* 2*d.* in May, when after some fluctuations there was a gradual fall to 1*s.* 8½*d.* in December, the average value of No. 2 corn having been 1*s.* 10*d.*, against 2*s.* 5*d.* in 1891 and 1*s.* 7½*d.* in 1890.

Corn.

The market for oats showed nothing remarkable beyond a rise in the summer, which was fairly maintained to the close of the year. Prices, however, were lower than in 1891, when they averaged 1*s.* 7¼*d.*, while in 1892 the average was 1*s.* 3½*d.* The total value of receipts of oats is estimated at 5,101,030*l.*, or about the same as those of the preceding year. Rye showed a decided decline from the beginning to the end of the year, the average price having been 2*s.* 9½*d.*, against 3*s.* 5*d.* in 1891. The market was affected by the large surplus quantity of low-grade wheat, and the value of the receipts, which were four-ninths of those of 1891, was only about one-third of that of the year before. The crop of barley was indifferent in many parts of this district, and the price varied from 2*s.* to 2*s.* 8*d.*

Other grain.

The supply of hogs was short, and when the fact was fully realised prices rose to a high figure. Early in the year the value per 100 lbs. varied from 17*s.* to 1*l.* 0*s.* 7*d.*; during the last 4 months the price was abnormal, as high as 1*l.* 8*s.* having been paid. The rise was in contradiction to the general turn of the market, as it is usual that when the winter packing season comes on, and large quantities are shipped for sale, the value falls; the price was 8*s.* to 10*s.* higher than at the same period in 1891. The products consequently experienced a considerable rise in the summer, when the prospect of a short supply of animals was confirmed. Lard especially was affected, and, though the summer rise was not maintained during the time of the cholera scare, the late autumn showed a further increase in price, and at one time in November lard fetched 5¼*d.* per lb. Cash pork also rose to 3*l.* 2*s.* 1*d.* per 100 lbs., the average price was 2*l.* 6*s.* 7*d.*, against 2*l.* 2*s.* 1*d.* in 1891; and the average price of lard was 1*l.* 10*s.* 4*d.*, against 1*l.* 5*s.* 9*d.* in the preceding year. The number of hogs received was 7,714,435, nearly 900,000 short of the number in 1891, but the price being higher, the valuation was but little short of that of the 8,600,805 received in 1891.

Live stock. Hogs.

Chicago has for a long time been the central market for all that

Cattle.

(1562)

## UNITED STATES.

great territory which extends westward across the Mississippi and Missouri Valleys to the Rocky Mountains, and largely absorbs the cattle growing resources of that immense district from the ranch State of Texas to the frontier of Canada. Though many animals are bought for the smaller packing establishments in other cities west of Chicago, at no place can the same number be consumed, nor in any other cities are buyers so generally represented as at this great centre of distribution. For the last few years the beef packing business has taken a wide expansion, and the year 1892 shows the largest number of cattle yet received, surpassing that of 1890, when 3,484,280 reached the city. In 1892 the receipts were 3,511,796, and in 1891 3,250,359. The price paid for half-fed cattle was low, but good animals sold fairly well, although on account of the large number marketed the price was at no time high, nor did the bulk of the supply consist of well-fed farm animals. The value ranged from about 18s. 6d. to 1l. 3s. 6d. per 100 lbs.

*Sheep.* The arrivals of sheep were much about the same as in each of the last two years, but the shipments were nearly one-third less. There were 2,145,079 received and 483,368 shipped, leaving 1,661,711 consumed in the city or used in the packing establishments.

*Horses.* Good horses were in great demand for the East at good prices, but the number received was not equal to the receipts in 1891. About 74,368 were shipped, out of 86,998 received.

The expansion which Chicago has developed as a live-stock market will be seen by the following comparison with 10 years ago :—

| Year. | Cattle and Calves. | Hogs. | Sheep. | Horses. | Aggregate Value. |
|---|---|---|---|---|---|
|  | Number. | Number. | Number. | Number. | £ |
| 1882 | 1,607,495 | 5,817,504 | 620,887 | 13,856 | 40,550,560 |
| 1891 | 3,455,742 | 8,600,805 | 2,153,537 | 94,396 | 49,368,600 |
| 1892 | 3,709,372 | 7,714,435 | 2,145,079 | 86,995 | 52,337,320 |

*Dairy products.* The receipts of butter were unusually large, 154,280,000 lbs., representing a value of 6,366,700l., and the shipments amounted to 139,118,655 lbs. The average price of good cream butter was 1s., and including the lower grades the average price was 10d. which shows that the proportion of poor butter was less than usual.

There was a less demand for cheese for export, and a greater demand for home consumption. The average market price of all cheese received was 4½d. Of the 94,397,000 lbs. received 48,505,000 lbs. were shipped.

*Fruits.* The fruit season in this part of the country was unfavourable but large quantities continue to arrive from California, Florida, and other localities, and prices were higher than usual. The value of fruit received from California alone was about 824,750l. against 655,700l. in 1891.

The egg trade has immensely increased; in round numbers 2,153,000 cases of 30 dozen were received against 1,508,000 cases in 1891, and 1,653,000 cases were shipped. The average price was 9*d*. per dozen. The total value was 2,398,000*l*. compared with 1,565,000*l*. in 1891.

*Eggs.*

## Wholesale Trade.

The wholesale trade was in an eminently prosperous condition, and the increase of 11 per cent. in the estimated value of business done is considered, by no means, to represent the full advance made. Throughout the year there was a tendency towards lower prices, which had a general character, except in some branches of the dry good business; the increase in volume of trade is said to have greatly exceeded the advance represented by the money value, and there is scarcely a branch of the wholesale business which does not show an increase in volume of business done. Prosperity seems to have ruled throughout and in certain articles of luxury, in jewellery, musical instruments, furs, and carriages the increase was especially remarkable. As previously observed this may be greatly accounted for by the large amount of ready money available from the harvest returns of 1891, but it may also in some measure be owing to increase of population and the impetus given by preparations for the Exhibition; the influence of the latter is distinctly observable in the brick, stone, marble, terra cotta and other industries connected with the building trade, in some of which the advance is valued at 50 per cent.

The dry goods and carpet business shows an advance in value of about 1,628,900*l*. Carpets improved about 1½*d*. per lb. in price towards the close of the year, but the demand, which is doubtless being since made for fitting up many of the new hotels and buildings on account of the Exhibition, had scarcely begun to be felt before the year was over. Cottons have risen in price, especially bleached cottons, and some goods have increased 15 per cent. in value. Fine cotton satines are much imported for printing here. Clothing, boots and shoes, millinery and business of that nature show a large advance in business done. The total sales in the dry goods and carpet trade amounted in round numbers to 21,917,500*l*.

*Dry goods and carpets.*

The volume of business done in the grocery trade is estimated at a value of 12,845,400*l*., or about 10 per cent. more than in 1891. A feature in the trade was the increased consumption of tea, and a tendency towards a preference of Ceylon and Indian teas over those of China and Japan, which were formerly the only varieties consumed or known in these parts.

*Groceries.*

The furniture trade has been unusually active in consequence of preparations to accommodate visitors to the Exhibition, and the great influx of strangers. This city has for some time been a great centre for the manufacture of furniture, and the great demand for new hotels and other buildings has greatly increased the business

*Furniture.*

## UNITED STATES.

**Lumber.**

done. Sales of local manufactured goods, valued at about 5,000,000*l.*, were supplemented by the less fine productions of factories outside the city to the estimated extent of 2,000,000*l.*

The vast quantity of lumber required in the construction of the Exhibition buildings and other erections caused an exhaustion of stocks, and an increase in the market sales of about 200,000,000 feet is greatly owing to this cause. The total quantity sold in the Chicago market is estimated at 2,300,000,000 feet, and at advanced prices.

**Other goods.**

Increase in trade in furs, musical instruments, as well as in jewellery is especially noticable, but there is no branch of wholesale trade which does not show some increase in the value of business done in 1892 as will be seen in the following comparison with the three preceding years :—

| Articles. | 1889. £ | 1890. £ | 1891. £ | 1892. £ |
|---|---|---|---|---|
| Dry goods and carpets | 18,062,000 | 19,326,000 | 20,292,000 | 21,175,000 |
| Groceries | 11,134,000 | 11,691,000 | 11,691,000 | 12,860,000 |
| Lumber | 7,423,000 | 7,601,000 | 8,041,000 | 8,866,000 |
| Manufactured iron | 3,202,000 | 3,202,000 | 3,504,000 | 4,115,000 |
| Clothing | 4,433,000 | 4,433,000 | 4,742,000 | 5,366,000 |
| Boots and shoes | 4,742,000 | 5,340,000 | 5,670,000 | 6,237,000 |
| Drugs and chemicals | 1,402,000 | 1,464,000 | 1,567,000 | 1,711,000 |
| Crockery and glassware | 1,051,000 | 1,132,000 | 1,237,000 | 1,340,000 |
| Hats and caps | 1,237,000 | 1,443,000 | 1,650,000 | 1,814,000 |
| Millinery | 1,340,000 | 1,443,000 | 1,443,000 | 1,568,000 |
| Tobacco and cigars | 2,778,000 | 2,237,000 | 2,371,000 | 2,608,000 |
| Fresh and salt fish and oysters | 1,060,000 | 1,126,000 | 1,134,000 | 1,247,000 |
| Oils | 825,000 | 825,000 | 928,000 | 1,030,000 |
| Dried fruits | 722,000 | 887,000 | 887,000 | 969,000 |
| Building materials | 765,000 | 919,000 | 928,000 | 1,670,000 |
| Furs | 309,000 | 309,000 | 361,000 | 449,000 |
| Carriages | 338,000 | 382,000 | 413,000 | 474,000 |
| Pianos and musical instruments | 1,366,000 | 1,485,000 | 1,608,000 | 1,850,000 |
| Music books, sheet music | 107,000 | 119,000 | 129,000 | 148,000 |
| Books, stationery, wall paper | 4,268,00 | 4,536,000 | 4,536,000 | 5,155,000 |
| Pig-iron | 3,340,000 | 4,131,000 | 4,227,000 | 4,804,000 |
| Coal | 4,792,000 | 5,170,000 | 5,361,000 | 6,185,000 |
| Hardware, cutlery | .. | 3,608,000 | 3,984,000 | 4,536,000 |
| Wooden, willow-ware | 592,000 | 652,000 | 722,000 | 783,000 |
| Liquors | 2,371,000 | 2,845,000 | 3,093,000 | 3,402,000 |
| Jewellery, watches, diamonds | 3,505,000 | 4,206,000 | 5,155,000 | 5,928,000 |
| Leather and findings | 495,000 | 520,000 | 567,000 | 619,000 |
| Pig-lead, copper | 775,000 | 1,168,000 | 1,237,000 | 1,312,000 |
| Miscellaneous | 1,587,000 | 1,883,000 | 2,287,000 | 1,670,000 |
| Total | 91,959,000 | 100,372,000 | 106,631,000 | 118,351,000 |

## Manufactures.

Owing to the falling-off in the supply of hogs and consequently a diminution in the product of that branch, the whole manufacturing business of the city shows a comparatively small percentage of increase, when the advance made in previous years is referred to. The manufacturing trade in general, however, is continually and largely extending, and in some branches, especially that of building materials, the year shows a great advance. Altogether the decrease in the packing business has been made up in other industries, and an increase of 3½ per cent. in the value of manufactured goods has been made. The number of manufacturing firms is now 3,433 against 3,307 in 1891. The capital employed increased during the year from 43,361,000*l*. to 47,260,000*l*., chiefly owing to investments in the iron and steel, packing, brass and copper, textile and provision industries. The number of hands employed rose from 180,870 to 186,085 and the wages paid from 21,588,000*l*. to 23,575,000*l*. For the reason already stated, and lower prices in some goods, the whole value of product only increased from 116,910,000*l*. to 120,894,000*l*., or 3,984,000*l*.

Packing.
The packing business was in the least satisfactory condition last year of any of the manufacturing trades. The hog product, owing to the short supply of hogs, was valued at 11,402,000*l*. against 12,371,000*l*. in 1891, and consequent on larger shipments of cattle, the beef packing product decreased in value from 11,340,000*l*. to 8,927,600*l*. There were 2,600 fewer hands employed and the total sum of wages paid was about 200,000*l*. less, and amounted to 2,882,000*l*. The value of the whole products, including lard, stearine, butterine, &c., fell off more than 3,000,000*l*. notwithstanding higher prices, and is estimated at 24,478,000*l*. against 27,600,000*l*. in 1891 and 28,304,000*l*. in 1890. There are in this city 20 pork packing, and 12 beef packing establishments, 20 lard and stearine, 5 butterine, and 18 sausage factories.

Iron and steel.
With regard to the iron and steel trade there has been great demand for building purposes, but rails have been in little request on account of the small mileage of new road constructed. The Illinois Steel Company, which employs about 9,000 hands, pays about 1,300,000*l*. yearly in wages, consumes 85 per cent. of the iron ore which is delivered here, and has recently extended its immense works, does not produce the girders and architectural steel which are so much used in the framework and construction of tall buildings; some arrangement has apparently been made by which this work is done in Pennsylvania, and to Chicago is left the manufacture of all steel rails required; the probability is that materials for construction thus cost the builders considerably more than was necessary. The demand for architectural iron has

lately been in excess of supply, and delay in delivery, partly caused by the strike at the Homestead works in Pennsylvania, has in many instances caused inconvenience to contractors in this city. The different branches of the iron and steel industry in Chicago are of great importance and yearly increasing, about 30,000 hands being employed. The tonnage of pig-iron made last year was the largest ever turned out, and notwithstanding that increased consumption reduced the stocks in hand prices were lower than in 1891. Steel rails were maintained at nearly 6*l*. 8*s*. per ton first quality. The six rolling mills in Chicago turned out a product last year valued at 5,005,150*l*., and the 62 foundries a value of 2,309,280*l*. There are 78 machinery and malleable ironworks, which produced a value of 1,958,800*l*., and the five car-wheel works a value of 1,000,000*l*. The whole number of establishments in the iron and steel industry, counting boiler, steam-fitting, stove, barbed-wire and other works, is now 340 against 316 in 1891, and the aggregate product last year was valued at 14,934,000*l*. against 14,577,000*l*. in 1891; the capital employed in these works increased by 1,150,000*l*. and amounted to 10,244,000*l*. The production of iron from the Lake Superior district, which is the great source of supply for a large part of the United States, is now so numerous, and so many new mines have been opened, that prices cannot be so easily manipulated. The total lake shipments from the mining regions of Marquette, Menominee, Gogebec, and Vermillion are said to have numbered 8,475,675 long tons, and the total production to have been more than 9,000,000 tons. Some portion of this, however, is believed to have remained unsold at the ports of consignment. The production of ore from the whole Lake Superior district up to the present time is stated to have been 73,660,873 tons, of which 13,053,923 tons were produced from the Gogebec, and 5,272,676 tons from the Vermillion mines in Minnesota, the other mines being in the State of Michigan. The Gogebec district increased its output last year by nearly 1,000,000 tons, and the Vermillion mines by nearly 250,000 tons. The lately discovered Messaba mines, 60 miles west of Duluth, from which the first shipment was made late in last year, promise to be extremely productive.

**Brass and copper, &c.**
The 155 establishments, engaged in the manufacture of brass and copper and other metals, turned out a value of 10,785,000*l*. against 9,390,000*l*. in 1891, of which the four smelting and refining works produced 5,724,000*l*. The jewellery manufacturers turned out a product valued at 567,000*l*. against 500,000*l*. in 1891. The 34 tin, stamped and sheet metalware industries produced a value of 1,546,000*l*. against 1,541,000*l*. in the preceding year. The manufacture of wagons and carriages, which has largely increased, was valued last year at 850,000*l*. and of agricultural implements at 4,082,500*l*. The total output of the manufactures of wood and iron was about 8,950,000*l*. against 8,495,000*l*. in 1891.

**Wood.**
There are 477 establishments in the wood-working industry, of which 260 are furniture manufactories. These latter turned out a value of 5,152,600*l*., an increase of about 822,600*l*. compared

with those of the preceding year, owing to the demand for equipment of new buildings; the chief specialities of Chicago manufacture are upholstered goods, which were made to the value of 1,237,000*l*., and folding beds now so greatly used in hotels and boarding houses, and even in private houses. The production of the planing mills, sash, door and staircase factories increased 15 per cent. owing to the same demand, and was valued at 2,371,000*l*. The piano and organ works factories continue to augment their works, and the output last year was estimated at 1,546,000*l*., or an increase of 103,600*l*. over the value in 1891. It was last year mentioned what marvellous development has taken place in the manufacture of these articles in so short a time. The total manufactures of wood are estimated at a value of 10,684,000*l*., or an increase of 1,191,000*l*. over that of the preceding year. There was a corresponding increase in the number of hands employed, and the wages paid are calculated at 3,587,000*l*., or an addition of 800,000*l*. to the sum paid in 1891.

**Brick and stone.** The industries in brick and stone profited enormously from the demand caused by the large number of new buildings erected, and produced a value of about 3,267,000*l*., being nearly 50 per cent. more in value than was turned out the year before. The number of bricks made is said to have been 725,000,000; the average price was 1*l*. 9*s*. per 1,000 against 1*l*. 2*s*. 2*d*. per 1,000 in 1891. Pressed bricks sold for 3*l*. 14*s*. 3*d*. per 1,000, and 40,000,000 bricks were produced, being nearly double the quantity made in 1891, and prices were higher. The demand could not be wholly supplied by local manufacture. Stained glass was also in increased request for the more expensive buildings erected, and in consequence of great demand elsewhere. There were 233 establishments in the brick and stone industries in 1892 and 212 in 1891; the total sum paid in wages is said to have been 50 per cent. more than in the latter year.

**Other manufactures.** All other branches of manufacture show increased production except distilleries. The clothing industries produced an increased value of about 10 per cent. The stationery and book-publishing business and all industries connected with printing had a prosperous year.

The capital employed in the entire manufacturing industries of Chicago has almost doubled in the last 4 years, and the product has increased by about 45 per cent. There seems every prospect of further development; the vast railway system and the great lakes afford peculiar and unlimited facilities for transportation, which are ever attracting the attention of manufacturers, and the home market is continually expanding. As the value of real estate in the centre of the city has already risen to so high a point there seems much probability of fresh enterprises eventually finding location along the lines of railway in the environs, where the same advantages of distribution almost equally exist within easy reach of the heart of Chicago. There are indications that before many years are over Chicago will become the leading manufacturing city in the United States, which is and has for some years been the greatest manufacturing country in the world. The increase in value of manufactured products of the works, according to the last census, was 148¾ per cent. in 10 years. During that period from 1880 to 1890 the amount of capital invested in manufacturing industries increased 313¾ per cent., the number of establishments by 155½ per cent., the number of hands employed by 143½ per cent., and the wages paid by 228½ per cent., while the population increased 118½ per cent. The population of the city is now about 1,500,000, or about 300,000 more than in 1890.

### Real Estate and Building.

The great boom in real estate, which commenced in the course of 1889, has continued and been well maintained, though the number of transfers last year scarcely equalled that of either of the preceding ones. The real estate sales, which 5 years ago amounted, in round numbers, to 19,150,000*l.*, rose to 28,000,000*l.* in 1889, and 42,400,000*l.* in 1890. In 1891 they amounted to 40,950,000*l.*, and in 1892 to 36,700,000*l.* In 1891 there were 20,800 transfers of real estate of the value of 200*l.* and upwards for an aggregate consideration of about 29,000,000*l.*, and in 1892 the number was 19,283, and the consideration 31,581,000*l.* The value of property in the central business part of the city, which does not extend much above a half mile square, may be judged from the actual sales during the past year; the transactions have been bonâ fide, and not speculations. The highest rate paid was for a small lot at the corner of Madison Street and Dearborn Street, for which 51*l.* 11*s.* was given per square foot for an area of 40 feet by 20 feet; this was an exceptional transaction. The next highest price paid was 27*l.* 8*s.* 5*d.* per square foot for a lot in a good situation, and several transfers ranged between that price and 10*l.* per square foot, while prior to last year the rate of 20*l.* per square foot had never been exceeded. In these valuations the building standing on the ground practically counts for nothing, as the purchases are made with a view to improvement and removal of the building. A still higher standard of value seems to have been established since last year, and very high rates for real estate in the heart of the city are now being realised. Leases of business property for 99 years were last year occasionally made, and are now becoming not uncommon. A 99 years' lease has lately been concluded for a building 90 feet by 91½ feet at the corner of Washington Street and State Street, on a basis at 5 per cent. of 3,200*l.* a front foot, or about 37*l.* 18*s.* 9*d.* a square foot; another, in not quite so prominent a situation, on a basis of 2,000*l.* a front foot. As above mentioned, in these cases the building, even if appraised at a value of 4,000*l.*, is not considered, and the price is practically a ground value. The sale of lease of an improved modern structure is very rare; the new office building, however, the Phoenix building, was sold last year for 309,280*l.*; **and another** improved corner building, diagonally opposite, 90 feet by 100 feet, the sum of 500,000*l.* is said to have been refused. A property leased 4 years ago at 5,000*l.* a year has been re-leased this year for the balance of the 99 years for 8,000*l.* a year, and the lessee will pull down the building and erect a new one at a cost of over 200,000*l.* In other parts of the city real estate has been well maintained in value, and in most cases transferred at increased prices. The demand, at advanced rates, for good residential property in the environs and beyond the business quarter, with a view to the erection of private mansions, indicates the vast wealth accumulated, and there seems to be an opinion that the advance is of a permanent character, and will go still further. Little fear is entertained of a fall in the value of real estate or house property after the Exhibition is over. Even on the south side, in the vicinity of Jackson Park, where property rose during the last 2 or 3 years 300 per cent. or 400 per cent. in value, and in some cases more, from proximity to the Exhibition, it is thought that there may be a temporary lull when the Exhibition is closed, and a possible difficulty of realising, but the great facilities of transportation which the Exhibition has given to the neighbourhood are considered to have permanently and greatly increased the value of property.

In the central business part of the city the erection of office Building. and store buildings has continued with fully the same activity as in the two preceding years. More than 2,000,000*l.* were thus expended in 1892, chiefly in office and wholesale constructions, the steel frame system being universally adopted. Those which were contracted for and built during the year in this part of Chicago at a cost exceeding 100,000*l.* each are as follows:—The Illinois Central Railway Depôt, 1,000,000 dol.; the annex to the Auditorium Hotel, 1,000,000 dol.; addition to Marshall Field's dry goods retail house, 800,000 dol.; the Columbus Building, 800,000 dol.; addition to Monadnock Building, 800,000 dol.; the Old Colony Building, 600,000 dol.; the Hartford Building, 600,000 dol.; and the Young Men's Christian Association Building, 600,000 dol. The great value of property in this limited area caused the present tall buildings, rendered possible by the adaptation of the elevator or lift, to be erected. No new permits are now issued for these very lofty constructions, and the city ordinance, lately passed, will probably be put in force limiting the height to 130 feet.

The total constructions of the year 1892 in the whole city numbered 13,194, with a frontage of 327,573 feet, at a cost of 16,686,000*l.*, to which must be added about 20 per cent. above contract price. In 1891 11,805 buildings were erected, with frontage of 282,672 feet, and the sum expended was 11,414,000*l.*; thus, roughly speaking, in the last 2 years more than 28,000,000*l.* have been spent in constructing 25,000 buildings, with a frontage extending 115½ miles. In 1890 the buildings erected cost, at contract price, 9,757,000*l.*, and in 1889 5,168,000*l.*, before which time the annual cost of constructions had not exceeded 4,000,000*l.*

On the north and west sides of the city building was extensively carried on, and on the latter 3,620 constructions, with a frontage of 92,664 feet, were erected, at a cost of 3,000,000*l*. The largest amount of money was, however, expended on the south side, and in the Hyde Park district alone, adjacent to the Exhibition grounds, 3,204 buildings were constructed, with frontage of 85,366 feet, at a cost of 4,787,000*l*. A number of hotels and apartment houses have sprung up in all parts of the city, but it is in the above district, which includes the environs of Jackson Park, that this class of construction has taken the widest expansion, with a view to accommodate visitors to the Exhibition. Over 100 large hotels have been built, or are nearly completed, in that neighbourhood, a few of them capable of accommodating 1,000 visitors each; some are only temporary constructions, and will not be used for hotel purposes after the year is over, but some are permanent, well-constructed buildings. Counting the smaller hotels and apartment houses capable of holding about 50 people each, the total number built near Jackson Park is 278.

*Cost of living.* Some are arranged to meet the requirements of the working class, with rooms at about 4*s.* a night, others at varying prices up to 1*l.* per day on the American principle, or less where no objection is felt to share the accommodation of a room with others, while the charge at first-class hotels varies from 16*s.* to 1*l.* 10*s.* per day on the American system, and at a few still higher prices are asked per head. It may be doubted if high prices will be maintained after the opening of the Exhibition. It is quite unusual for so many furnished houses to be available for rent as at present, but rates are extremely high, and it is very questionable whether, except in the case of a large family, housekeeping is more reasonable than hotel life. The cost of living is different to what it was even a few years ago, and servant's wages have greatly risen, and now vary from 1*l.* to 1*l.* 15*s.* per week, with all found. Rents, which had been gradually increasing for the last few years, have again risen in all parts of the city, and even at the extreme opposite direction to the Exhibition grounds the rise is at least 25 per cent. In anticipation of these extra prices, leases were not entered into beyond the end of April this year, and notice of increase has been almost universal. Articles of food have been also rising in price for some time, and it is difficult to calculate a less increase in general cost of living than from 25 per cent. to 30 per cent. above the cost of 1 year or 2 years ago, while many articles have increased in higher proportion.

*Public buildings.* The new public library, which is in course of construction in the central part of the city, will be a very large and important construction; the foundations are laid and the superstructure commenced. The library at present contains more than 187,000 volumes.

A new court-house is being constructed on the north side of the city.

*Newberry library.* Among the quasi public buildings may be mentioned the Newberry Library, which is nearly completed, and will be open this year, and has been erected from funds bequeathed by the late

Mr. Newberry. The reading rooms are open to the public in their temporary quarters from 9 A.M. to 5 P.M. and 7 P.M. to 10 P.M. every week day, and, besides current periodicals and journals, the library contains about 100,000 volumes.

The art institute on the lake front in the heart of the city, a permanent building of limestone, with base of granite, is now finished. It is 320 feet long, with a mean depth of 175 feet, and two stories high, with two central courts. Temporary arrangements are added in these interior courts, with main and gallery floors for the accommodation of the Congress Auxiliary of the World's Columbian Exposition, the two halls being capable of holding 3,000 persons each, and here the meetings of the Congress will be held. The building has cost 130,000*l*., of which 40,000*l*. was subscribed by the Exhibition. After the Exhibition is closed the Institute will contain the galleries and school of arts, which now numbers 600 students. *Art institute.*

Five years ago the University of Chicago was not thought of, and now there are 12 fine buildings of English Gothic architecture, either finished and occupied or in course of construction, on 25 acres of land owned by the University in the neighbourhood of Jackson Park near the Exhibition grounds, where 3 years ago was a marsh. The University has now a large staff of professors, selected from other institutions in the country and Europe, and about 1,000 students. Its origin and rapid growth are greatly owing to the generosity of Mr. Rockefeller, who in 1889 offered an endowment of 120,000*l*. if a committee could raise the sum of 80,000*l*.; this sum was quickly raised, and about the same time a merchant of Chicago presented the University with 12 acres of the ground on which the buildings now stand. Further gifts came in, and up to the present time the total donations amount to 1,284,000*l*., of which Mr. Rockefeller alone has contributed 754,000*l*. The sums given in 1892 amounted to 711,500*l*., and among the gifts was the offer of a telescope, to be the largest and most powerful in the world, which, with the observatory in which it will be placed, will cost more than 150,000*l*. The University was opened last October with a faculty of 115 professors, men and women. One of the features of its regular work will be university extension and a system for the education of the masses. *University.*

A magnificent gift was last year presented to the city, and entitled the Armour Institute, after the patriotic and public benefactor of that name. It consists of a large and handsome building already completed, and fitted interiorly with marble wainscoting on every floor, marble arches, and marble bath-rooms, and the gift was accompanied with an endowment of 289,000*l*. It is to be used as a manual training school and an institute for every branch of science and art; it is fitted with laboratories, forges, gymnasium, and library, and contains electrical, lecture, and other rooms for domestic sciences. It is intended as a benefit to young men and women of every class, to be within the range of the poorest, and is taking the form of a school of technology. *Armour Institute.*

**Water supply.** The condition of the water supplied to the city has been much talked about, and there is little doubt that it is far from what it ought to be, considering the vast expanse of perfectly pure water from Lake Michigan so close at hand. The trouble is that the Chicago River is an open sewer, flowing sluggishly sometimes up stream and sometimes down stream according as the pumping-power exceeds the natural flow; and in the spring particularly, when heavy rains are most frequent, the present power is inadequate to cope with the flush, and to pump the river water into the canal, from whence it should find its way down the Illinois River to the Mississippi, and consequently the flow is into the Lake. At that season it is especially necessary to boil and filter the water for drinking purposes, as pollution reaches some distance into the Lake. An important work has been completed in the new tunnel and crib four miles distant from the shore which was opened at the close of the year, but still some of the supply of water to the city is derived from the old two-mile crib, and it is prudent at all times to boil and filter the water before drinking. The tunnel on the south side which is to supply Jackson Park is not yet finished, but the Exhibition authorities have prohibited the supply of drinking water inside the grounds which is not filtered, and a large number of fountains of filtered water are provided for the public. The quantity of water supplied to the city last year was 71,035,000,000 gallons.

**Other works.** Amongst other improvements conducted by the Public Works Department during the year may be mentioned 104 miles of new sewers constructed, 799 miles of new sidewalk constructed, and 134 miles repaired, and 108 miles of streets paved, making 878 miles of streets paved, while the total length of streets in the city is 2,370 miles. Crematories are in course of erection for the destruction of garbage and refuse, which will probably be in operation in the course of the summer, and be of great benefit to the city in a sanitary point of view. The system is already at work in the Exhibition grounds.

**Health.** The general healthfulness of the city showed a great improvement over the condition in 1891, when the death-rate was 22·02 per 1,000, and typhoid fever was prevalent. Last year the death rate was 18·23, or from natural causes 17·4 per 1,000, and stood probably lower proportionately than in any other large city. Of special diseases pneumonia carried off the largest number of victims, 2,370, against 2,898 in 1891; phthisis, 2,157, against 2,120; and typhoid, 1,479, against 1,997 in 1891. The deaths from the different diseases under which they are classed were as follows:—Zymotic, 7,084; constitutional, 3,693; local, 12,519; development, 1,148; and violence, 1,565. Under the head of violence there were 1,242 deaths from accidents, against 1,158 in 1891, 79 from homicide, and 244 from suicide. The climate is undoubtedly healthy, though the sudden changes and extreme range of temperature render it trying to Europeans and natives of southern climes. In the month of January this year the mean temperature was 12 deg. Fahr., ranging as low as 18 deg. below zero, and a change of 30 deg. or 40 deg. in a few hours is not uncommon. It was reported that one day this winter the change of temperature at Dodge City, Kansas, in 24 hours was 82 deg., at Kansas City 65 deg., and at other parts of that State a change of similar character, though less remarkable.

### Shipping.

The customs district of Chicago includes the two adjacent ports of South Chicago and Michigan City, the former of which has quadrupled the tonnage entered during the last 10 years. To show the enormous traffic on the Lake system it may be mentioned that Chicago takes the fourth place among the ports of the world in importance as regards tonnage entered and cleared, the aggregate being nearly 12,000,000 tons, far exceeding any port in the United Kingdom, except London and Liverpool, and exceeds New York in the number, 21,123, of vessels entered and cleared; at the port of Milwaukee, 90 miles north on Lake Michigan, the number of vessels entered is nearly the same as at Chicago.

The following is a return of shipping at Chicago in 1892 compared with the three preceding years:—

| Nationality. | Entered. Number of Vessels. | Entered. Tons. | Cleared. Number of Vessels. | Cleared. Tons. | Total. Number of Vessels. | Total. Tons. |
|---|---|---|---|---|---|---|
| Coasting trade | 10,411 | 5,903,387 | 10,263 | 5,809,249 | 20,674 | 11,712,636 |
| Foreign trade— | | | | | | |
| Canadian | 61 | 35,257 | 62 | 38,463 | 124 | 76,720 |
| American | 84 | 27,982 | 241 | 120,625 | 325 | 148,607 |
| Total, 1892 | 10,556 | 5,966,626 | 10,567 | 5,968,337 | 21,123 | 11,934,963 |
| ,, 1891 | 10,224 | 5,524,852 | 10,394 | 5,506,700 | 20,618 | 11,021,552 |
| ,, 1890 | 10,507 | 5,136,253 | 10,547 | 5,150,615 | 21,054 | 10,286,868 |
| ,, 1889 | 9,802 | 4,521,886 | 10,023 | 4,629,184 | 19,825 | 9,151,070 |

Lake freights were not so high as was anticipated would be the case, in consequence of the bountiful harvests of 1891, and fell 25 per cent. below expectations, though a large increase in shipments of iron ore was certain. Freights on corn to Buffalo varied from $\frac{1}{2}d.$ to $1\frac{5}{8}d.$ per bushel, the average being just under $1d.$ Both the number and tonnage of vessels frequenting the port is yearly increasing, so that even should, as is thought, the iron and grain trade take still larger proportions, there seems little probability of any considerable rise in rates. The movement of produce by rail was so great that at times the railway lines, especially in the west, met with much difficulty in providing sufficient cars to supply demands. The freight on grain to New York varied from $10d.$ to $1s.$ $0\frac{1}{2}d.$ per 100 lbs. (the latter rate having been maintained late in the autumn, and $1s.$ $3d.$ for provisions. A certain allowance of $1\frac{1}{2}d.$ on freight eastward has been in force for the last year for cartage, which was formerly paid by the shipper.

(1562)

## UNITED STATES.

### Imports and Exports.

**Imports.**

The following return, from information furnished by the customs authorities, shows the nature and value of the different articles of merchandise imported in bond at Chicago, compared with the three preceding years, thus covering a period before the McKinley Act came into force. It represents only a portion of the imports, as the majority of goods received for consumption here are entered and pay duty at the customs ports on the seaboard:—

| Articles. | Value. | | | |
|---|---|---|---|---|
| | 1889. | 1890. | 1891. | 1892. |
| | £ | £ | £ | £ |
| Free goods | 496,257 | 702,121 | 672,482 | 827,816 |
| Ale, beer, porter | 8,312 | 10,377 | 9,747 | 12,889 |
| Art materials | 13,369 | 15,248 | 9,650 | 12,119 |
| Books, printed | 9,220 | 10,624 | 8,192 | 7,867 |
| Brushes | 4,322 | 5,600 | 7,187 | 6,465 |
| Chemicals | 6,681 | 3,871 | 5,772 | 2,200 |
| China, glassware | 106,836 | 115,710 | 171,765 | 173,445 |
| Caustic soda | 13,280 | 18,888 | 11,998 | 13,769 |
| Cigars, tobacco, manufactured | 102,309 | 136,744 | 61,842 | 62,695 |
| Cutlery | 6,181 | 4,907 | 4,880 | 6,808 |
| Diamonds, precious stones | 66,103 | 74,486 | 25,853 | 51,906 |
| Dressed furs | 26,621 | 32,240 | 49,405 | 24,355 |
| Dried fruits, nuts | 70,003 | 113,050 | 66,050 | 67,700 |
| Drug sundries | 9,625 | 9,006 | 8,836 | 15,322 |
| Dry goods | 933,980 | 991,231 | 832,262 | 1,101,031 |
| Fish, all kinds | 40,117 | 31,371 | 48,501 | 54,919 |
| Guns | 9,506 | 8,940 | 4,414 | 1,261 |
| Iron manufactures, wire | 22,656 | 37,961 | 78,605 | 127,796 |
| Jewellery | 3,915 | 3,160 | 11,361 | 2,293 |
| Leaf tobacco | 41,273 | 34,326 | 42,298 | 79,739 |
| Leather manufactures | 61,285 | 52,115 | 50,320 | 59,442 |
| Looking-glass plates | 2,000 | 3,455 | 11,950 | 18,172 |
| Metal manufactures | 32,422 | 45,222 | 57,530 | 71,483 |
| Millinery goods | 17,346 | 18,284 | 18,801 | 23,166 |
| Musical instruments | 39,704 | 43,216 | 43,890 | 41,739 |
| Needles | 2,445 | 2,328 | 272 | 275 |
| Paintings, statuary | 12,066 | 15,069 | 11,619 | 18,168 |
| Paper manufactures | 4,266 | 4,504 | 12,589 | 17,377 |
| Paperhangings | 924 | 459 | 1,082 | 2,311 |
| Pickles and sauces | 3,250 | 2,968 | 5,264 | 6,785 |
| Plate window glass | 16,534 | 12,214 | 8,509 | 7,380 |
| Smoker's articles | 1,818 | 2,616 | 5,559 | 4,308 |
| Stone, marble | 2,458 | 7,681 | 8,618 | 12,251 |
| Tin-plates | 296,925 | 336,599 | 328,094 | 270,042 |
| Toys, fancy articles | 25,532 | 24,796 | 15,802 | 31,785 |
| Varnish | 757 | 866 | 1,055 | 712 |
| Wines, liquors | 67,381 | 76,178 | 88,567 | 106,057 |
| Wood manufactures | 13,203 | 12,104 | 38,956 | 35,561 |
| Total including a few other articles | 2,785,018 | 3,174,617 | 3,116,653 | 3,585,257 |
| Duties | 1,040,984 | 1,069,582 | 1,233,730 | 1,544,035 |

From the above it will be seen that, so far as goods imported in bond to Chicago are concerned, there was an increase in value of 468,604*l.* over the value in 1891, in which year, on account of the quantity of merchandise imported in view of the McKinley tariff, the imports were slightly less than in 1890. The increase in value compared with the year 1889 was 800,239*l.*, nearly half of which must be put down to free goods. Of the 468,604*l.* above mentioned 155,334*l.* is owing to larger quantities of free goods, but it is presumable, as prices have been generally lower, that the increase in quantity of dutiable goods imported was relatively greater than the increased value.

Dry goods were imported to the increased value of 268,769*l.*, but the customs returns do not enable a comparison to be made as to the share British goods had in that amount. The import of millinery goods was also greater than in 1891. Cutlery recovered from the check caused by the McKinley Act, and was imported in greater quantity than before the Act, but the value of guns received has again decreased, and amounts to scarcely one-eighth of what it was four years ago. Manufactures of iron and metal largely increased, while tin-plate decreased in value of import by 58,052*l.* The value of drugs imported increased about 90 per cent. The import of diamonds and precious stones doubled in value, and amounted to 51,906*l.*, but does not come up to what it was before the Act, while jewellery was imported in less quantity, greatly owing to increased local manufacture. For the same reasons musical instruments show a falling off. Paintings and statuary were imported to more than 50 per cent. increased value, and all articles of luxury are in demand to meet the growing refinement of taste which accumulated wealth gives unlimited power to gratify.

Comparing the year 1889, before the McKinley Act came in force, with last year, it appears that the import of free goods increased from 496,257*l.* to 827,816*l.*, or 331,559*l.* The increase of dutiable goods from 2,288,761*l.* to 2,757,441*l.*, or 468,680*l.*, was not relatively equal to the increased population of the city in the three years, but taking last year, and especially during the first three months of this year, the increase in quantity of merchandise imported has proportionately exceeded the increase of population.

*The McKinley Act.*

No very great value, however, can be given to these comparisons, the customs returns here, as already stated, representing but a small proportion of the goods imported, but, as far as they lead to any conclusion, and according to local opinion, there is but little to be said regarding the McKinley Act. A check occurred after the new duties came into force, surplus stocks having been purchased in anticipation of the duty. When these surplus stocks were exhausted prices rose for a time, but prices now are as low as before the Act, and imports are greater than ever. Whether the increase in imports would have been more pronounced had the Bill not passed is a question, but the effect seems to have been almost entirely confined to a few particular articles, notably pearl buttons, which are now entirely made in the country.

(1562)

Manufactures are unquestionably extending; the United States has become the greatest manufacturing country in the world; but demand is ever on the increase, and there are many articles which cannot be, or are not yet, made in this country to the same perfection as in Europe. The demand for such articles is still increasing. Inquiries have been lately more frequent for the names and addresses of manufacturers in Great Britain of certain articles, and if a good commercial directory were periodically supplied to this Consular office it would probably be of public service in enabling a ready response to be given, so that parties here might place themselves in communication with houses in England, where the particular goods they require could be obtained.

*Exports.*

No record is obtainable of the exports from Chicago to Europe on through bills of lading. The exports to Canada consisted chiefly of grain, and amounted to 8,638,659 bushels.

*Drawbacks. Tin-plate.*

The following table gives the amount of drawback on tin-plate to which the canned goods exported were entitled, together with the quantity of tin-plate so exported, compared with that of the preceding year:—

|  | Entitled to Drawback. |  | Amount of Drawback. |  |
| --- | --- | --- | --- | --- |
|  | 1891. | 1892. | 1891. | 1892. |
| Tin-plate .. .. | Lbs. 8,735,992 | Lbs. 7,333,187 | £ 18,542 | £ 32,008 |

With regard to this drawback on exported canned goods, it would seem to act as a premium on imported plate, home-made plates being entitled to no drawback, and to raise the price of such canned goods to the home consumer in a degree equivalent to 99 per cent. of the duty. Tin-plate can at the present time be purchased, delivered at Chicago, at the same general cost (1*l.* 2*s.* 3*d.*) as before the McKinley Act, or even a few pence cheaper, the lower price of the English manufacture being about equivalent to the duty. The increased tariff appears to have no effect here beyond giving a start to local manufacture, and it is thought that if the duty were now taken off, the enterprise is so firmly established that it would suffer but a temporary check. A strong opinion seems entertained that eventually the market will be supplied by home manufacture, though at present there is not sufficient made, and for many years there may not be much more made than to keep pace with increased demand. There are so many circumstances which influence a market that the price of an article in any one year can scarcely be judged on any one principle in comparison with that of another year, but it is a fact that the canners are now selling cans cheaper than before the McKinley Act was thought of. Omitting the years when anticipation or uncertainty of the extra duty acted on the market and imports, the great canning houses here were selling in February, 1888, their 2-lbs. and 3-lbs. cans for fruit packing at 9s. 1d. per 100 cans, in 1892 at 7s. 10d. per 100 cans, and in 1893 at 8s. 0½d. at the same time of the year when large orders for the season are generally received.

With regard to the factories in operation in this district, Messrs. Norton, of Chicago, who consume about 1,000 boxes per day in their canning trade, are now turning out 800,000 lbs. of tin-plate a quarter from their new works and are preparing to make their own black plates; the St. Louis Stamping Company in Missouri, where the steel-plate is also made, turn out about 1,000 or 1,200 boxes a day; the Canning Steel Company of Chicago, and the Joliet Tin-plate Company have started their works, and the International Tin-plate and Refining Company of Chicago are prepared to do so. The total number of establishments in the United States in September, 1892, was 46, of which 32 were in operation and 10 were making or preparing to make their own black plates. The production of tin-plates or terne-plates from these factories for the year ended September 30, 1892, was, according to official reports, 13,646,719 lbs., and for the quarter ended the same day, 10,952,725 lbs. It is estimated that the production for the year ended September 30, 1893, will be 100,000,000 lbs., and for the quarter ended that day that the production will be at an annual rate of 200,000,000 lbs. The report for the last quarter of 1892 is not at hand, but it is stated that the 32 firms in operation in the United States now making tin-plates and terne-plates produced during that quarter 19,756,491 lbs. against the 10,952,725 lbs. produced in the September quarter.*

## Notes on the West.

Though for many years attention has been drawn to the West, a true knowledge of its marvellous development has been limited, and even the wonderful progress of Chicago in enterprise and civilisation has scarcely entered within the scope of general observation. Within the last two years the name of this city, since it was decided that the international exhibition should be held here, has been brought prominently to the notice of every community, and every commercial interest in the world. It is the type of the western city, the type of advancement and activity, and perhaps at no period in the world's history can an example be shown of such increase of wealth, or such marvellous results accomplished in so short a time. It has outstripped the older cities East except New York; St. Louis has been left far behind, though an older city and greatly increased in wealth and resources, with a present population of 500,000. It has far outstripped Milwaukee, which has similar advantages in its situation on the Lake and had the start of Chicago in the race for supremacy. Milwaukee has now a population of 250,000 inhabitants. But Chicago is only the

* For fuller particulars with regard to this industry see Foreign Office Report, Miscellaneous Series No. 280.—ED.

type of western progress; numerous other cities have since risen up which for the time of their existence have shown almost equally rapid development. 20 years ago St. Paul, Minneapolis, Kansas City, Omaha, and Denver were scarcely known, and now contain from 100,000 inhabitants to 200,000 inhabitants each, while numerous smaller cities have sprung up like mushrooms in a field, with this difference that their growth is permanent and continual. It is but 50 years ago since the whole of this district, west to the Rocky Mountains, was practically unexplored, except a few points along the line of, or adjacent to, the Mississippi, or occupied as military posts, and was considered worthless in an agricultural point of view. It is little more than 40 years ago since the first pioneers, crossing the vast extent of prairie in search of gold in California, encountered no human being but the wild Indian, no serviceable animal but the buffalo, and these two were in joint possession of the country. All this is changed since then. The Indian is gradually disappearing, those that remain are confined to reservations which are from time to time bought back and opened to occupation, the buffalo has entirely vanished except where a small herd or two are kept in public preserves, and, as if in sympathy, the buffalo grass which formerly covered so vast an area is vanishing too. Where the Indian and buffalo formerly roamed are now seen not only all the cities above-mentioned, but thousands of smaller cities, towns, and villages; a great part of the land is cultivated and dotted with farms and buildings, or in the wilder parts occupied as ranches for raising cattle and horses. Even that wide belt of territory which, till recently, was considered arid and impracticable for cultivation is gradually, with the aid of irrigation, becoming a profitable occupation from the richness of the soil, which needed but that assistance.

Agricultural enterprise and cattle-raising were the first phases of this rapid change, and in proportion as population increased, so land became more distributed; higher cultivation and smaller holdings followed, and less extended ranches are a continual and marked feature in the condition of the country at the present time. As cultivation developed so necessities arose, means of transportation increased, towns sprung up, requirements multiplied, mining enterprises were opened out, and one of the great origins of the prosperity of the city of Chicago was its ability to seize the position, for which its situation eminently qualified it, of becoming the source of supply as well as the centre of distribution and communication between the east and the west. Enterprises gradually attracted capital from all parts, and as they multiplied and stretched over this vast district so the value of land, originally of no account, increased, and fortunes were made with no effort. The mere increase in the value of real estate over such an extent of country, especially in city sites and more particularly at Chicago, accounts for much of the enormous wealth which has been accumulated and the general prosperity of the country.

This development of the West has, however, been of far more than local interest. Its effect has been widespread; to its influence may be traced the depreciation in the value of agricultural land, not only in Great Britain and particularly in Ireland, but also in the Eastern States of the Union, as well as the comparative non-recovery of prosperity in the South. The West, with its great advantage of an almost unlimited area of land at a low value, with the aid of economic changes, rapid and cheap transportation, and labour-saving machinery seems to have absorbed the agricultural prosperity of the world, and to have levelled the value of product almost to the cost and profit of production. While working out these changes it sought for its growing wants the assistance of the manufacturers of the East and of other countries, which it tended to support, till it has now entered on another phase, which promises an equally rapid and prosperous development.

The latest phase is manufacture. Each year accumulated wealth is seeking fresh outlet, fresh enterprises are opened out, and manufactures increase. Many demands are now wholly supplied by local factories; some manufactured goods already find their way to the East, from whence they used to be derived. Chicago has become a great manufacturing city, and is being followed by other cities further West. The one thing which keeps the balance now with regard to many articles is the enormous and ever-increasing demand, arising from increased wealth, luxury, and population; at present it is as much as this increased demand can be met by local manufacture, and it may be many years yet before much more can be accomplished, but there is little room for doubt that this district will eventually become entirely independent of the East, and supply with many goods those parts of this and other countries on which it formerly depended. Every natural resource is abundant; the question is that of labour.

The State of Wyoming is the slowest to develop of any in this district, though some progress is being made. By far the greater part can only be utilised for pasturage purposes, and the continued predominance of ranch industries, so many still devoting themselves to the utilisation of free grazing lands, checks the development of agriculture. Canals must be constructed before settlers can occupy much of the land for agricultural enterprise, being dependent on irrigation in the arid belt, and the cost of canals is beyond the reach of the settler. The capital invested in ditches to water public lands has been practically a failure, as success depends on all the land being used. As this water supply enhances the value of the land, and it is not necessary under the homestead law for a settler to be a user of water, temptation is offered to speculative holders to secure unoccupied land, and thus benefit by the increased value, with no intention of cultivating it. Again, markets are far removed, from a lack of transportation facilities.

A comparison between the assessed valuation of different kinds of property in this mountainous State in 1891 and 1892 shows a decrease of 150,000*l*. in cattle, 35,000*l*. in horses, and 90,000*l*. in capital in merchandise and manufactures, while there is an increase of 55,000l. in sheep, and a considerable increase in value of railroad property, town lots, moneys, and credits. The whole property valuation, which has remained about stationary for the last 7 years, shows a slight net loss last year. The number of cattle in the State is now 428,823, valued at 2l. 4s. 9d. per head, against 898,121 in 1886, when the valuation per head was 3l. 7s. 3d.; therefore the valuation of the cattle in Wyoming is less than one-third what it was 7 years ago. On the other hand, sheep show a large increase. The resources of the State are undeveloped; the mineral wealth is great, but unopened; the oil region very extensive, but needing better transportation.

**North Dakota.** In the agricultural State of North Dakota remarkable results have in many instances been secured from the cultivation of grain, and the last 2 years have been profitable for the farmer. Livestock raising, however, is found to be very remunerative in conjunction with grain-growing, and sheep are receiving particular attention. In 1889 there were only 43,664 sheep in the State, and in 1891 the number was 231,355, or 430 per cent. increase. Cattle during those 2 years increased 50 per cent., and horses 28 per cent. The number of cattle in North Dakota in 1892 was 269,607, of horses 155,491, and of sheep 317,647.

**South Dakota.** The same general remarks apply to South Dakota, but here other enterprises are more developed. From inquiries made it has been found that nearly all the farmers own the land they till. Some till their own land and rent of others, and some till part of their own land and rent a part to others. It has been found that the average number of acres in a farm is 365, of which about 138 acres are under cultivation, and that the present value is about 4l. 15s. per acre, against a value of 12s. 6d. at the time of taking possession. This indicates prosperity, and promises well for more newly-settled districts. About 69 per cent. of the farms are mortgaged to an average extent of one-fifth of their value, and the rate of interest averages 8·44 per cent. Many families from different parts are reported to have lately immigrated to this State and settled on farms. Mining operations seem progressing satisfactorily, though no signs of product from the tin mines in the Black Hills are yet visible. Advancement has been made in the treatment of refractory gold-bearing ores, and some mills are in successful operation; the ores, after perfect trituration and roasting, are subject to a chemical treatment of chlorine in iron retorts, which carries off the precious metal with profitable result. It is said that 2,000,000l. have been invested in mining property during last year, and that the output will this year reach 1,000,000l. The Yankton cement mines are steadily developing, and the product acquiring a front rank in the commercial market.

**Nebraska.** The great material progress made of late years in the State of Nebraska was treated at some length in the report for the year 1891. Wheat and oats are extensively raised, but corn is the great agricultural crop, and the average cost of raising it is 1l. 6s. 5d. per acre. A considerable quantity of flax is grown, as well as sugar beet for local factories, and tobacco and chicory are new industries. The number of cattle in the State in 1891 was 1,699,854. The shipments of surplus commodities, exclusive of silver (2,459,000*l*.), gold, lead, and sulphate of copper, amounted in value to 24,226,000*l*., or nearly equal to those of the older State of Missouri. The bank clearings of the city of Omaha increased nearly 40 per cent. in 1892, and trade throughout the State was in a flourishing condition.

Montana.

There has been a steady growth in almost every line of business in the State of Montana, and stock and agricultural industries advanced, but a certain depression has existed owing to the low price of silver; though most mines have been worked to their full capacity, there has been no great activity, and wages have fallen.

Other States.

In the older States of this district the customary annual progress has been made. Great advance in general prosperity has ruled on account of the abundant harvests of the last 2 years, and the price of land is well maintained. The State of Kansas, from the abundance of the late crops, is again attracting the attention of farmers.

Illinois.

The State of Illinois has an extended area of 385 miles from north to south, and conditions are liable to be influenced by climate, soil, storms, and other causes, so that crops vary in different divisions. Corn is grown chiefly in the northern portion, and winter wheat in the central and southern districts. The total area in wheat in this State in 1892 was 1,568,285 acres, and in corn 5,188,432 acres. The profit on the latter grain in 1891 is put down at 6,670,000*l*., the largest since 1864; in 1892 the profit was about 450,000*l*., the product value having been as nearly as possible 1*l*. 18*s*. 11*d*. per acre, and the cost of production 1*l*. 17*s*. 1*d*. per acre. In the last 30 years losses on the cultivation of corn have been as frequent as profits and nearly as heavy. There has been a tendency lately towards a slight decrease in area of wheat and corn, while rye, timothy seed, buckwheat, and sorghum are grown on scarcely one-fourth of the area of 15 years ago. The cultivation of tobacco has also greatly decreased, though the profit has been heavy, and amounted to nearly 700,000*l*. for the last 2 years. With regard to animal industry, there has scarcely ever been a time when the price of beef and dairy breeds of cattle has been so low as last year, and the same may be said of draft and coach horses, which, though greatly improved in quality, have decreased in number. The stock of hogs has been low, and the supply on hand is below the average, while there has been a slight increase in the number of sheep. The dairy interests are very extensive; the amount of milk sold (101,000,000 gallons) nearly double the quantity and value of 5 years ago, the smaller quantity made and the higher price of butter, and a great falling-off in the production of cheese, may be remarked. The increased demand for all farm produce caused by the Exhibition at Chicago is now creating a rise in prices all round. At no period has more material advancement or greater industrial progress prevailed, or labour been employed at better wages, or farmers had more money in hand than last year. Never has advance in the price of average good farm land been so rapid. In some parts of the State the advance in 1891 was 25 per cent., and a further advance took place this year. General prosperity seems everywhere to prevail.

## St. Louis.

Mr. Vice-Consul Bascome reports as follows:—

The year has been one of progress and profit, as demonstrated by the details of different lines of business given on succeeding pages.

In nearly all departments of business an increase is shown, and the advance is remarkable in the erection of new buildings for mercantile and manufacturing purposes, as well as in dwellings.

Tonnage. The increased tonnage handled by rail and river shows an increased traffic, and the records of the clearing-house and post-office are sure indications of the city's activity.

Manufactures. The year closed was marked by many evidences of prosperity in which no leading industry shows any falling-off. The manufactured product of the city reached an estimated value of 54,000,000*l*.

Clearings. The transactions of the clearing-house increased 18,400,000*l*. over the previous year.

New buildings. The value of new buildings erected and improvements made during the year is estimated at 6,000,000*l*., and the sales of real estate aggregate 12,494,000*l*.

Spring floods. Operations in some departments of trade were partially impaired by the floods in the west and south during the spring of 1892, which were made up by an increased business in the fall caused by an advance in cotton of 2*l*. to 3*l*. per bale, or nearly 18,000,000*l*. to the value of the estimated crop of 7,000,000 bales.

Advance in cotton.

St. Louis fifth as a manufacturing city. St. Louis now stands as the fifth manufacturing city of the United States; New York, Chicago, Philadelphia, and Brooklyn alone outranking it.

The increase in manufactured product the past decade to 1890 was for St. Louis 100 per cent., and was only exceeded by Chicago, which was 149 per cent. during the same period.

Brick. The annual output of bricks in the city was 300,000,000, worth 420,000*l*., which falls short of meeting the demand for building purposes.

Sewer pipe and retorts. The other manufactures of clay, such as sewer-pipe, fire-brick, retort furnaces and terra-cotta, keeps pace with the building brick. The sales of sewer-pipe shows an increase of 15 per cent., and the whole output from all the factories is estimated at 50,000 tons annually.

Cut stone. The product of cut stone was for the year about 200,000*l*.

Lumber. The receipts of lumber for the year were 62,121 car loads, equal to 745,452,009 feet by railway and 115,491,163 feet by river, and 7,852,880 superficial feet of logs, making an aggregate of 883,943,163 feet, an increase of 18,545,152 feet over 1891. The shipments aggregated 409,260,000 feet, an increase of 103,776,000 feet over 1891. Over one-half the receipts were required for consumption by the manufactories of the city.

The product of the planing mills was nearly 400,000*l*., and the jobbing trade aggregated about 800,000*l*. There was a strike among the operatives which decreased the output. Planing mills.

There was an addition of two new factories during the year, bringing the number up to 59, and an increase of capital of 100,000*l*. Furniture.

The year's output of manufactured goods was about 1,200,000*l*., the hands employed, about 4,500, adding the jobbing and retail trade, the result will reach an aggregate of 4,000,000*l*. for the year.

Although wooden and willow-ware is not numbered among the leading manufactures of the city, it is claimed by many that St. Louis sells one-half of all the wooden-ware used in the United States, and the larger portion distributed is made at factories owned by the dealers of the city, the increase over last year is claimed to be 15 per cent. Wooden and willow ware.

The manufacture of paints and oils is reported to be growing and prosperous, and the output for 1892 is reported at 1,200,000*l*. Paints and oils.

St. Louis ranks at the head of the tobacco manufacturing points in the United States, as shown by the statistics of the Internal Revenue Bureau. The whole product of manufactured tobacco in the United States for the fiscal year ending January 30, 1892, was 253,962,372 lbs., of which the factories produced 21½ per cent., more than one-fifth. The product of 1892 was 260,218,401 lbs., of which St. Louis produced 57,863,876 lbs., or 22¼ per cent., of the value of 3,600,000*l*., and at the same time there were manufactured 56,964,376 cigars, worth 360,000*l*., an increase over the previous year of 14 per cent. Tobacco.

Brewing maintains the high position among St. Louis industries it has long held. Brewing.

The quantity of beer made in 1892 was 60,804,919 gallons, worth 2,400,000*l*. Towards the end of the year a sharp competition between the united breweries controlled by British capital and some of the American breweries, which forced the price of beer down from 1*l*. 12*s*. to half that price per keg.

The clothing industry continues to grow. The increase in 1892 over the previous year is estimated at 12½ per cent., and the value of the product at 1,400,000*l*. Clothing.

The manufacture of cars of all kinds for electric cable and steam railways shows a vigorous growth, and the value of the product for 1892 is estimated at 2,000,000*l*., exclusive of a very large plant at Madison, east of the river, owned and operated by St. Louis parties. Cars.

Some of the crude and heavy iron manufactures, chiefly iron making, have fallen off, and one large firm transferred its iron pipe department to Birmingham, Alabama, where the conditions are more favourable. This loss has been made up in the increased product of architectural iron, in which has been noted an increase of 15 per cent. The product being about 1,400,000*l*. for iron goods, Iron manufactures.

and in connection with other metal goods manufactured the total product is estimated at 3,600,000*l.*

**Stoves and ranges.** The manufacture of stoves and ranges remains steady, but does not seem to increase. The output in 1892 was about 400,000*l.*

**Whitelead.** St. Louis has held a prominent position in this manufacture for many years, and it is claimed to be the largest manufacturer of white-lead in the United States. The output in 1892 was 20,000 tons, of the value of 500,000*l.*

**Saddlery and harness.** The leather manufactured here was valued at 360,000*l.* in 1892, and the amount sold was 700,000*l.*, a great deal being used in the manufacture of saddlery and harness, which trade shows the general prosperity, and an increase of from 7 per cent. to 10 per cent. The output being estimated at 700,000*l.* in 1892, to which may be added 150,000*l.* in trunks and valises.

**Electrical goods.** There has been an increased manufacture of electrical supplies. During the year 1892 these manufactures were sent to Pittsburg, New York, Costa Rica, Panama, and even to London, the output being estimated at 280,000*l.*

**Agricultural machinery.** The demand for agricultural machinery was somewhat lessened in 1892, there are about 25 manufactories and jobbing houses whose united business amounted to 2,400,000*l.*

**Carriages and wagons.** This business has been good, and has kept the factories steadily at work. The value of carriages turned out is estimated at 1,500,000*l.* The value of waggons manufactured was over 100,000*l.*, and the total output 1,600,000*l.*

### Boots and Shoes.

**Boots and shoes.** The "Shoe and Leather Gazette" gives the following review of the business of 1892: "The shoe trade of St. Louis may be justly first considered as supreme to the other industries, and of paramount interest. Her jobbing houses have increased in number, in size, and in importance year after year, until now the city is recognised as the principal shoe jobbing point in the country."

The Merchants' Exchange reports 828,071 cases of shoes received, as compared with 577,630 cases in 1891, showing a gain of 250,441 cases, or over 40 per cent. The average value per case has diminished from 7*l.* to 5*l.* per case.

**Shoe shipments.** St. Louis leads, the shoe shipments in 1892 being 323,927 cases, against 310,489 for 1891, and was the only city of the six leading cities which increased its shipments.

**Shoes manufactured.** A careful canvas of the shoe manufactories by the Merchants' Exchange shows that during 1892 full 5,000,000 pairs of shoes were made in the city of St. Louis, at an average valuation of 7*s.* 6*d.* making a total yield of 1,800,000*l.*, or a gain over 1891 of 10 per cent. in the product of its 25 factories.

**Soap and candles.** The product of soap and candles is estimated at 600,000*l.* for 1892, but was not quite up to that of 1891.

## CHICAGO.

**Dry goods.** The dry goods trade closed with satisfaction to those engaged in it, there being no failures, and a promising outlook. The sales are estimated at 8,000,000*l.*, an increase of 1,000,000*l.* over 1891.

**Groceries.** The "Interstate Grocer" reports the business in a flourishing condition. The sales being 17,000,000*l.*, an increase of about 12½ per cent. over 1891, there being a slight decrease in the handling of sugar.

**Coffee.** The receipts of coffee in sacks is reported at 265,096 in 1892, against 253,154 in 1891.

**Rice.** There is a heavy stock of rice in St. Louis at present, the receipts for 1892 being reported at 110,250 barrels, against 87,192 barrels received in 1891.

**Drugs.** The business in drugs seems to maintain its prominence, the total trade for the year 1892 was reported at 2,400,000*l.*

**Hardware.** The hardware trade is reported in a prosperous condition, the sales for the year 1892 being placed at 3,700,000*l.*, and an increase of 10 per cent. over 1891.

**Population.** The population does not exhibit the annual increase that many north-western cities do, but it is steady and healthy, not influenced by any particular booms in business.

In 1890 the United States census gave the population of the city as 451,770, and it is estimated that the population at the close of 1892 was 585,000.

**Street car service.** There are 124½ miles of street railway in St. Louis, 72½ miles are traversed by electric cars, 39½ miles by cable cars, and 12½ miles by horse cars, and arrangements are made for discontinuing the horse car service very soon.

The number of passengers carried in 1892 was 91,685,555, an increase of 10,687,000 over 1891 or over 13 per cent.

### Grain Trade.

**Grain trade.** The grain trade of St. Louis shows an increase of 11,000,000 bushels of 1892 handled over the previous year.

The receipts for 1892 were:—

| Articles. | Quantity. |
|---|---|
| | Bushels. |
| Wheat | 27,483,855 |
| Corn | 32,030,030 |
| Oats | 10,604,810 |
| Rye | 1,189,153 |
| Barley | 2,691,249 |
| Total | 73,999,097 |

The total receipts of wheat and flour reduced to wheat was 80,548,136 bushels.

**Wheat.** Of the receipts of wheat there was exported, viâ New Orleans, 6,662,799 bushels, and 1,536,166 bushels, viâ railways to the

## UNITED STATES.

Atlantic seaboard cities, making a total of 8,198,965 bushels exported, and 7,711,013 bushels were ground in city mills. The year was noted for very low values. At the close of the year the stock in public elevators and private hands was 7,545,050 bushels.

**Corn.** The crop of 1892 was an average one, the receipts in St. Louis being 32,030,030 bushels against 21,530,940 bushels the previous year. The yield was 23 bushels to the acre, and the State of Missouri takes fourth rank among corn-producing States.

**Oats.** The crop of oats in Missouri in 1892 was 24,093,000 bushels, a falling-off from the crop of 1891 of 3,500,000 bushels.

The receipts in St. Louis were 10,604,810 bushels in 1892.

**Rye.** The receipts of rye were 1,189,153 bushels, about the same as the previous year, and the shipments were 1,032,374 bushels.

**Barley.** The receipts of barley show a considerable increase, being 2,691,049 bushels in 1892 against 2,108,546 bushels the previous year, of which only 29,851 bushels were imported from Canada.

### Cotton.

**Cotton.** The gross receipts of cotton for the year ending August 31, 1892, were 723,028 bales, the largest ever reported against 706,469 bales the previous year. The local receipts show a slight decrease being 297,891 bales against 306,015 bales the previous year. The price declined to $6\frac{5}{16}$ c. per lb. in March, 1892.

The shipments were 685,789 bales, of which 195,678 bales were exported direct to Europe, 176,494 bales going to England. The city consumption amounted to 2,788 bales, and 1,180 bales were consumed by fire.

**Cotton bagging.** The trade in this line is of about the usual proportions. The manufacture reached 13,000,000 yards, most of which has been consumed, prices ruling at a moderate scale.

**Iron ties.** Those of domestic manufacture are used exclusively at present and prevailing prices were low.

### Livestock.

**Cattle.** The total cattle receipts of St. Louis for 1892 were 801,111 head, the largest on record, nearly all of which were sold here, when in previous years only 60 per cent. or 70 per cent were marketed here.

**Hogs.** There was a slight decrease in the hog trade of 1892 occasioned by high water overflows, the values were, however, much higher in 1892.

**Sheep.** The sheep trade exhibited a declining market and receipts declined correspondingly.

**Wool.** The receipts of wool in this city in 1892 were 25,850,690 lbs. against 21,975,954 lbs. in 1891. The shipments in 1892 were 27,450,379 lbs. against 21,464,552 lbs. in 1891.

**Provisions.** The business of 1892 in fresh beef indicates a growing trade, the receipts from western points were 25,580,464 lbs. and the total shipments 68,071,698 lbs. A new establishment will be opened the current year which will largely increase the business.

The business in hog products shows a slight decrease from the previous year, due to the decreased supply of hogs.

**Hog products.**

The Government inspection of meats destined for Europe was established in October, 1892, and has proved very satisfactory. The receipts for 1892 were 264,341,960 lbs. and shipments 369,411,500 lbs.

COMPARATIVE Business in Leading Articles at St. Louis during the Years 1891-92.

|  | Articles. |  | Quantity. 1891. | Quantity. 1892. |
|---|---|---|---|---|
| Flour, amount manufactured | | Barrels | 1,748,190 | 1,455,342 |
| „ handled | | „ | 4,932,464 | 4,870,852 |
| Wheat, total receipts | | Bushels | 25,523,183 | 27,483,855 |
| Corn „ | | „ | 21,530,940 | 32,030,030 |
| Oats „ | | „ | 12,432,215 | 10,604,810 |
| Rye „ | | „ | 1,149,490 | 1,189,153 |
| Barley „ | | „ | 2,108,546 | 2,291,249 |
| All grain received, including flour reduced to wheat | | „ | 68,835,754 | 80,548,136 |
| Cotton, receipts | | Bales | 765,784 | 506,037 |
| Bagging, manufactured | | Yards | 15,000,000 | 13,000,000 |
| Hay, receipts | | Tons | 141,398 | 131,148 |
| Tobacco „ | | Hogsheads | 41,042 | 41,936 |
| Lead „ in pigs of 80 lbs. | | Pigs | 1,739,977 | 1,526,484 |
| Hog product, total shipments | | Lbs. | 358,595,516 | 369,411,500 |
| Cattle, receipts | | Head | 779,499 | 801,111 |
| Sheep „ | | „ | 402,989 | 376,922 |
| Hogs „ | | „ | 1,380,569 | 1,310,311 |
| Horses and mules, receipts | | „ | 55,975 | 45,759 |
| Lumber and logs | | Feet | 865,398,011 | 883,913,163 |
| Shingles | | Pieces | 73,980,750 | 171,942,500 |
| Lath | | „ | 20,231,050 | 22,205,300 |
| Wool, total receipts | | Lbs. | 21,975,954 | 25,850,690 |
| Hides „ | | „ | 34,744,949 | 38,412,854 |
| Sugar, received | | „ | 253,960,132 | 250,950,264 |
| Molasses (including glucose) received | | Gallons | 2,657,990 | 3,029,050 |
| Coffee, received | | Bags | 253,154 | 265,096 |
| Rice, receipts | | Packages | 87,192 | 110,250 |
| Coal „ | | Bushels | 72,078,225 | 82,302,228 |
| Nails „ | | Kegs | 440,697 | 581,278 |
| Potatoes „ | | Bushels | 1,832,137 | 1,686,641 |
| Salt „ | | Barrels | 381,671 | 290,487 |
| „ „ | | Sacks | 42,478 | 48,963 |
| „ „ (in bulk) | | Bushels | 388,440 | 473,200 |
| Butter | | Lbs. | 13,791,258 | 13,401,788 |
| Freight of all kinds received and shipped | | Tons | 16,420,027 | 18,388,174 |

## St. Louis Commerce and Industries during the Year 1892.

| Articles. | | 1892. Quantity. | 1892. Value. |
|---|---|---|---|
| | | | £ |
| Bank clearings | .. | .. | 246,314,393 |
| Banking capital—Banks and Trust Companies | .. | .. | 6,100,000 |
| Real estate sales | .. | .. | 12,494,865 |
| New buildings erected | Number | 5,472 | 6,000,000 |
| Total manufactures | .. | .. | 54,000,000 |
| Manufactured— | | | |
| Tobacco | Lbs. | 57,863,876 | 3,600,000 |
| Iron and metal goods | .. | .. | 3,600,000 |
| Boots and shoes | .. | .. | 1,875,000 |
| Carriages and waggons | .. | .. | 1,600,000 |
| Furniture | .. | .. | 1,200,000 |
| Clothing | .. | .. | 1,400,000 |
| Cars, railroad and street | .. | .. | 2,000,000 |
| Planing mill product | .. | .. | 400,000 |
| Beer | Gallons | 60,804,919 | 2,400,000 |
| Stoves and ranges | .. | .. | 400,000 |
| Electrical goods | .. | .. | 280,000 |
| Coffee and spices, roasted and ground | .. | .. | 560,000 |
| Soap and candles | .. | .. | 600,000 |
| Whitelead | Tons | 20,000 | 500,000 |
| Flour | .. | .. | 1,500,000 |
| Bricks | Number | 300,000,000 | 420,000 |
| Sewer pipe | .. | .. | 120,000 |
| Stonework | .. | .. | 200,000 |
| Cigars | Number | 56,964,376 | 360,000 |
| Architectural iron | .. | .. | 500,000 |
| Leather | .. | .. | 360,000 |
| Cornmeal, hominy and grits | .. | .. | 270,000 |
| Sales— | | | |
| Groceries | .. | .. | 17,000,000 |
| Dry goods | .. | .. | 8,000,000 |
| Furniture | .. | .. | 4,000,000 |
| Hardware | .. | .. | 3,500,000 |
| Wooden and willow-ware | .. | .. | * |
| Paints and oils | .. | .. | 1,200,000 |
| Saddlery and harness | .. | .. | 680,000 |
| Agricultural machinery | .. | .. | 1,400,000 |
| Boots and shoes | .. | .. | 2,030,000 |
| Hats and caps | .. | .. | 900,000 |
| Drugs | .. | .. | 1,400,000 |
| Planing mill product | .. | .. | 800,000 |
| Leather goods | .. | .. | 850,000 |
| Tonnage, total tons handled | Tons | 18,388,174 | .. |
| Coal, received | Bushels | 82,302,228 | .. |
| Lumber „ | Feet | 883,943,163 | .. |
| Bullion „ | .. | .. | 1,200,000 |
| Grain „ | Bushels | 73,999,097 | .. |
| Pork products distributed | Lbs. | 369,411,500 | .. |

\* Not obtained.

## CHICAGO.

Custom-house Transactions for 1892. Condensed Classification of Commodities Imported into St. Louis during the Year 1892, showing Foreign Value and Duty Paid.

| Articles. | Value. | Duty. |
|---|---:|---:|
|  | £ s. | £ s. |
| Ale and beer .. | 3,974 16 | 1,436 12 |
| Anvils .. | 14,069 0 | 1,587 11 |
| Art works .. | 11,563 16 | 1,735 1 |
| Books and printed matter .. | 2,436 16 | 654 12 |
| Bricks and tiles .. | 836 4 | 185 2 |
| Barley .. | 3,058 0 | 1,791 2 |
| Brushes .. | 2,453 8 | 981 7 |
| Carpets and carpeting .. | 878 16 | 570 1 |
| Cement (15,904,241 lbs.) .. | 12,339 8 | 2,547 18 |
| Chemicals and drugs .. | 24,199 12 | 3,622 12 |
| China and earthenware .. | 28,912 0 | 16,265 8 |
| Corks and manufacture of corks .. | 6,702 0 | 1,510 6 |
| Cutlery .. | 5,946 9 | 4,747 7 |
| Diamonds and precious stones .. | 9,967 0 | 1,003 2 |
| Fancy goods .. | 6,977 16 | 2,871 16 |
| Fish .. | 7,209 16 | 1,630 1 |
| Free goods .. | 75,530 4 | .. |
| Glassware .. | 5,980 16 | 4,330 10 |
| Guns and firearms .. | 9,800 12 | 5,024 5 |
| Hops .. | 13,926 16 | 5,697 15 |
| Jewellery merchandise .. | 5,778 2 | 1,508 15 |
| Marble .. | 3,163 4 | 1,812 19 |
| Manufactures of cotton .. | 69,959 4 | 41,444 14 |
| ,, linen .. | 23,139 8 | 9,476 10 |
| ,, iron sheets, bars, &c. .. | 8,749 0 | 4,639 5 |
| ,, leather .. | 5,254 1 | 1,192 0 |
| ,, metals .. | 16,812 16 | 7,565 7 |
| ,, paper .. | 5,699 16 | 1,699 14 |
| ,, silk .. | 12,375 15 | 5,740 18 |
| ,, wood .. | 2,521 0 | 906 14 |
| ,, wool .. | 15,628 0 | 13,416 8 |
| Musical instruments .. | 540 12 | 254 0 |
| Nuts and fruits .. | 1,686 0 | 1,125 14 |
| Paints and colours .. | 4,104 8 | 1,057 2 |
| Rice, granulated .. | 46,135 8 | 6,067 11 |
| Seeds, &c. .. | 1,417 0 | 272 5 |
| Steel bars .. | 2,348 4 | 731 1 |
| ,, wire .. | 14,202 8 | 6,863 2 |
| Tin-plate (B O., No. 63 ; 239,282) .. | 16,181 4 | 13,070 19 |
| ,, (O., No. 63 ; 86,160) .. | 541 12 | 3,379 2 |
| Terne-plate (N.O., No. 63 ; 939,282) .. | 4,999 12 | 4,168 1 |
| Tobacco and cigars .. | 31,852 8 | 31,530 4 |
| Varnishes .. | 321 16 | 112 4 |
| Wines, sparkling, &c. .. | 29,634 16 | 15,183 13 |
| Window glass .. | 39,620 12 | 10,702 1 |
| Woollen dress goods .. | 5,175 16 | 4,836 5 |
| Spirituous liquors .. | 7,366 4 | 7,523 10 |
| Miscellaneous merchandise .. | 8,438 0 | 2,577 6 |
| Total .. | 630,429 4 | 257,049 7 |

Note.—The collections from all other sources amounted to 8,538*l*. 13*s*.

(1562)

## 34 UNITED STATES.

RETURN of Merchandise brought into the Port of St. Louis in Bond from the following Ports of Entry during the Year 1892, showing Foreign Value and Duties.

| Ports. | Value. | Duty. |
|---|---|---|
|  | £ s. | £ s. |
| Baltimore | 52,032 12 | 18,816 4 |
| Boston | 5,352 0 | 2,161 8 |
| Detroit | 527 0 | 210 16 |
| Newport News | 9,737 0 | 5,854 16 |
| New Orleans | 79,974 16 | 32,369 16 |
| New York | 217,824 16 | 135,129 16 |
| Philadelphia | 29,900 12 | 11,960 0 |
| Port Huron | 59,480 16 | 25,792 4 |
| Portland, Maine | 45,669 4 | 18,267 12 |
| San Francisco | 3,187 16 | 1,275 0 |
| Tacoma | 1,665 16 | 666 4 |
| Direct to St. Louis | 3,260 16 | 1,304 4 |
| Total | 507,513 4 | 243,808 0 |
| In warehouse, December 31, 1892 | 27,394 12 | 15,996 16 |

STATEMENT showing Bank Clearing-house Business for the Year 1892 compared with 1891.

| Months. | Clearings. 1892. | Clearings. 1891. | Balances. 1892. | Balances. 1891. |
|---|---|---|---|---|
|  | £ | £ | £ | £ |
| January | 19,651,048 | 19,524,149 | 2,697,663 | 2,450,951 |
| February | 19,474,002 | 16,403,608 | 2,418,822 | 1,775,223 |
| March | 19,837,332 | 17,928,729 | 2,398,779 | 1,854,768 |
| April | 20,676.325 | 17,990,916 | 3,192,671 | 1,999,644 |
| May | 18,819,728 | 18,121,168 | 2,298,265 | 1,997,294 |
| June | 19,819,728 | 17,424,063 | 3,062,021 | 2,239,409 |
| July | 20,005,459 | 19,137,733 | 2,572,319 | 2,225,767 |
| August | 21,057.826 | 19,500,840 | 2,758,353 | 2,517,006 |
| September | 20,340,937 | 19,482,320 | 2,313,842 | 2,055,244 |
| October | 21,385,916 | 20,886,748 | 1,990,517 | 2,103,332 |
| November | 21,618,198 | 19,561,692 | 2,396,580 | 2.049,199 |
| December | 23,532,519 | 22,047,944 | 2,462,274 | 2,681,342 |
| Aggregate | 246,220,018 | 227,919,910 | 30,562,406 | 25,959,179 |
| Increase, 1892 | 18,200,108 | .. | 4,603,227 | .. |

CHICAGO.

UNITED STATES Internal Revenue collected in St. Louis during the Years 1891–92.

| Description. | Amount. 1891. | | | Amount. 1892. | | |
|---|---:|---:|---:|---:|---:|---:|
| | £ | s. | d. | £ | s. | d. |
| Lists (penalties, &c.) | 2,812 | 6 | 6 | 2,383 | 7 | 0 |
| Spirit stamps | 381,851 | 0 | 0 | 669,369 | 15 | 0 |
| Tobacco stamps | 603,624 | 1 | 5 | 692,328 | 13 | 0 |
| Cigar " | 31,964 | 19 | 5 | 34,190 | 12 | 0 |
| Snuff " | 380 | 0 | 7 | 368 | 18 | 0 |
| Beer " | 334,944 | 14 | 5 | 362,868 | 0 | 0 |
| Special tax | 32,860 | 19 | 0 | 32,531 | 1 | 0 |
| Total | 1,389,438 | 1 | 7 | 1,794,040 | 6 | 0 |
| Increase, 1892 | | | | 404,602 | 4 | 5 |

DISTRIBUTION and Dispatch of Mails during the Years 1891–92.

| Description. | Quantity. 1892. | Quantity. 1891. | Increase. |
|---|---:|---:|---:|
| | Lbs. | Lbs. | Lbs. |
| First class mail matter— | | | |
| Letters originating in St. Louis | 1,065,357 | 940,190 | 125,167 |
| Postal cards originating in St. Louis | 48,555 | 38,322 | 10,233 |
| Second class matter, newspapers from St. Louis | 11,855,552 | 9,011,137 | 2,844,415 |
| Third class and transient newspapers | 3,901,410 | 3,376,786 | 524,624 |
| Fourth class matter, merchandise from St. Louis | 1,137,222 | 569,033 | 568,189 |
| Total | 18,008,096 | 13,935,468 | 4,072,628 |

AVERAGE Rates of Freight on Wheat per Bushel in Cents by Steamer from St. Louis to Liverpool viâ New Orleans for the Years 1892–91.

| Months. | St. Louis to New Orleans. | | New Orleans to Liverpool. | | Total, St. Louis to Liverpool. | |
|---|---|---|---|---|---|---|
| | 1892. | 1891. | 1892. | 1891. | 1892. | 1891. |
| | Cents. | Cents. | Cents. | Cents. | Cents. | Cents. |
| January ... ... | 7 | 7½ | 10½ | 8½ | 17¼ | 16 |
| February ... ... | 7 | 7½ | 9¾ | 8 | 16¾ | 15½ |
| March ... ... | 6½ | 6½ | 8¾ | 7½ | 15½ | 14 |
| April... ... ... | 5½ | 6 | 9 | 6½ | 14½ | 12½ |
| May ... ... ... | 5 | 6½ | 5 | 6 | 10 | 11½ |
| June... ... ... | 5 | 5½ | 7 | 5½ | 12 | 11 |
| July ... ... ... | 5 | 6 | 5 | 6 | 10 | 12 |
| August ... ... | 5½ | 6½ | 6¾ | 8½ | 12¼ | 15 |
| September ... ... | 6 | 7½ | 8½ | 9½ | 14½ | 17 |
| October ... ... | 6½ | 8 | 9 | 11 | 15½ | 19 |
| November ... ... | 6½ | 8 | 8¾ | 12 | 15¼ | 20 |
| December ... ... | 6½ | 8 | 8 | 12 | 14½ | 20 |

RETURN of Foreign Shipments of Flour from St. Louis viâ Atlantic and Gulf Seaports during the Years 1891–92.

| Destination. | Quantity. | |
|---|---|---|
| | 1891. | 1892. |
| | Barrels. | Barrels. |
| Europe .. .. .. .. | 327,045 | 540,340 |
| Central and South America .. | 238 | 435 |
| Newfoundland .. .. .. | 1,775 | .. |
| Canada .. .. .. .. | 12,490 | 37,900 |
| Cuba .. .. .. .. | 2,958 | 70,710 |
| Total .. .. .. | 344,506 | 649,385 |

NOTE.—Nearly all was shipped in sacks and is reduced to barrels in calculation.

## CHICAGO.

**RETURN of the Surplus Commodities Marketed in the State, as shown in my last Report for the Year 1892.**

| Description. | | Quantity. | Value. | Total Value. |
|---|---|---|---|---|
| | | | Dol. c. | Dollars. |
| Cattle | Head | 629,438 | Per head ... 40 00 | 25,177,520 |
| Hogs | ,, | 2,006,444 | ,, 8 00 | 16,051,552 |
| Horses and mules | ,, | 65,927 | ,, 100 00 | 6,592,700 |
| Sheep | ,, | 190,631 | ,, 4 00 | 762,524 |
| Wheat | Bushels | 21,635,458 | Per bushel 0 80 | 17,308,306 |
| Corn | ,, | 9,652,938 | ,, 0 35 | 3,378,528 |
| Oats | ,, | 5,152,701 | ,, 0 25 | 1,288,175 |
| Wool | Lbs. | 3,235,685 | Per lb. 0 20 | 647,137 |
| Poultry | ,, | 28,049,177 | ,, 0 10 | 2,804,918 |
| Butter | ,, | 2,949,537 | ,, 0 15 | 442,431 |
| Eggs | Dozens | 14,090,426 | Per dozen 0 10 | 1,409,043 |
| Railway ties | Each | 2,314,806 | Each 0 30 | 694,442 |
| Dried fruit | Lbs. | 1,564,162 | Per lb. 0 04 | 62,566 |
| Flour | Barrels | 2,295,746 | Per barrel 3 50 | 8,035,111 |
| Apples | ,, | 544,914 | ,, 1 75 | 953,599 |
| Mixed livestock | Cars | 5,415 | Per car 500 00 | 2,707,500 |
| Hay | ,, | 8,284 | ,, 260 00 | 2,153,840 |
| Wood | Cords | 119,873 | Per cord 3 00 | 359,619 |
| Lumber | Cars | 34,445 | Per car 185 00 | 6,372,325 |
| Hoops | ,, | 2,152 | ,, 190 00 | 408,880 |
| Timothy seed | Bushels | 37,770 | Per bushel 1 27 | 45,428 |
| Game | Lbs. | 321,007 | Per lb. 0 20 | 64,201 |
| Fish | ,, | 88,625 | ,, 0 05 | 4,431 |
| Hides | ,, | 1,689,994 | ,, 0 05 | 84,500 |
| Stone | Cars | 7,250 | Per car 125 00 | 906,250 |
| Lime | Barrels | 921,407 | Per barrel 0 52 | 479,132 |
| Cheese | Lbs. | 160,576 | Per lb. 0 06 | 9,635 |
| Rye | Bushels | 30,156 | Per bushel 0 75 | 22,617 |
| Potatoes | Barrels | 13,743 | Per barrel 0 96 | 13,193 |
| Sewer pipes and tiles | Cars | 5,387 | Per car 195 00 | 1,050,465 |
| Bricks | ,, | 16,482 | ,, 73 68 | 1,214,394 |
| Ice | ,, | 1,408 | ,, 61 50 | 86,592 |
| Coal | Tons | 2,655,882 | Per ton 1 31 | 3,488,058 |
| Lead and zinc | ,, | 144,550 | ,, 32 80 | 4,740,912 |
| Iron | ,, | 123,571 | ,, 2 39 | 295,335 |
| Flax | Cars | 862 | Per car 400 00 | 344,800 |
| Onions | Bushels | 89,481 | Per bushel 0 80 | 71,585 |
| Tobacco | Cars | 178 | Per car 1,000 08 | 179,424 |
| Canned goods | ,, | 46 | ,, 650 00 | 29,900 |
| Cotton | Bales | 29,652 | Per bale 35 00 | 1,037,820 |
| Cotton-seed products | Lbs. | 23,763,133 | Per ton 7 00 | 83,169 |
| Melons | Cars | 1,761 | Per car 75 00 | 132,075 |
| Grass seeds | ,, | 72 | ,, 1,260 00 | 90,750 |
| Meat | Lbs. | 402,643 | Per lb. 0 10 | 40,264 |
| Shipstuffs | Cars | 1,115 | Per car 240 00 | 277,200 |
| Mixed grain | ,, | 1,677 | ,, 343 00 | 554,631 |
| Other shipments | ,, | 46,779 | ,, 250 00 | 11,694,750 |
| Small fruit | Crates | 264,720 | Per crate 1 50 | 397,080 |
| Total | ... | ... | ... | 125,049,335 |

## ST. PAUL.

Mr. Acting Vice-Consul Gilbert reports as follows:—

Owing to the absence of the Vice-Consul, Mr. Morphy, and the fact that statistics, concerning the commercial and industrial business of the past year, have not been tabulated by any of the organisations that usually attend to such matters, such as the Chamber of Commerce, Board of Trade, &c., it is quite impossible for this office to furnish a report containing more than a very general statement of the condition of affairs in its jurisdiction.

Probably the most noticeable feature of commercial and industrial life in the north-west is the same one which is reported to exist generally all over the United States, that is, the great scarcity of money.

The lack of circulating medium necessarily reduces the volume of trade, and to a large extent prevents the inauguration of new enterprises. Nevertheless, some very noticeable enterprises calculated to materially increase the prosperity of St. Paul and Minneapolis have been commenced and completed during the past year, among them the North-Western Cordage Company's Works and the Wood Harvester Works, both large and substantial concerns backed with ample means and under the control of experienced business men.

The completion of the Great Northern Railroad to Puget Sound is an event materially affecting and increasing the prosperity of these cities. So much do the people of St. Paul appreciate the advantages to be derived from the completion of this magnificent undertaking that in June a public celebration of the event is to take place.

Other railroads centering in these cities are also extending their lines, and some new roads are proposed which will give better and short communication with the country south-west of here; that country being the best in the State, and being also naturally tributary to St. Paul, Minneapolis, and Duluth, but its trade is now diverted to Chicago, as there is no direct communication by rail with the north-western cities.

Another scheme about the practibility of which there seems to be a difference of opinion has recently been inaugurated with headquarters at Duluth. This is the proposed canal to connect the head waters of the Mississippi with Lake Superior. A company with a capital of 2,000,000 dol. has been organised, and those having it in charge are very enthusiastic, but as yet no work has been done beyond making surveys.

In spite of the fact that money is scarce the country is far from a bad financial condition. The lack of money, as before stated, limits present operations, but excellent crops and consequent excellent trade of 1891 and 1892 have enabled the debtor class to largely reduce their indebtedness, so that they are much better able to stand the effects of the present stringency than they would have been two years ago. Another fact that is of great help to this country at the present time, is that the country no longer depends so entirely on the wheat crop for its prosperity. The amount of stock raised, not on ranges but on the farm, has very greatly increased. This is especially true of sheep.

The outlook for the coming season is generally regarded as favourable.

The past winter has been more than usually severe, with many violent storms and a most unusual precipitation of snow. While this has been most disagreeable to the individual, its effect has been to thoroughly saturate the ground with that moisture, the lack of which has been the cause and the only cause of the failure of crops.

The excessively wet, cold and backward spring may have the effect of limiting the acreage sown, but the return from what is sown is likely to be much greater than in an early but dry season.

## CHICAGO.

The biennial session of the State Legislature closed on April 18. An effort was made to reduce the rate of interest allowed, but the effort failed. An attempt was also made to pass a law authorising the payment of gold contracts in silver, but this also failed.

### Kansas.

There has been a satisfactory gain in the volume of trade in the two Kansas Cities during the year 1892. The real estate depression, which has been existing here since 1889, is fast disappearing; the process of liquidating the debts and obligations incurred during the boom has almost been completed, and a marked recovery and increase in all lines of business is noticeable. *Trade and business.*

The livestock interests continue to be the largest single industry, and during the year 1892 extensive additions were made to the various plants, involving an expenditure of upwards of 2,000,000 dol. *Livestock.*

The past year was the best year in the history of the cattle business. More cattle and calves were put on the market than in any previous year; these were of a better average grade, and values were steadier and considerably improved over 1891. *Cattle.*

There was an immense shortage in the supply of hogs in all parts of the country during 1892, and prices have been higher and the demand greater than ever before. *Hogs.*

The sheep market has been good, the supply up to the demand, and the prices received by both growers and packers were considered remunerative. *Sheep.*

The horse and mule trade shows an increase over previous years, and the prices realised have been satisfactory. *Horses and mules.*

The following is a comparative table showing the receipts of all kinds for the years 1891 and 1892, together with the number of car-loads, and the aggregate values:— *Livestock trade.*

| Description. | 1891. Quantity. | 1891. Value. | 1892. Quantity. | 1892. Value. |
| --- | --- | --- | --- | --- |
|  | Number. | Dollars. | Number. | Dollars. |
| Cattle | 1,280,839 | .. | 1,492,765 | .. |
| Calves | 83,500 | .. | 97,810 | .. |
| Hogs | 2,616,749 | .. | 2,437,884 | .. |
| Sheep | 388,034 | .. | 441,822 | .. |
| Horses and mules | 32,209 | .. | 32,831 | .. |
| Cars | 92,488 | .. | 98,282 | .. |
| Total | .. | 66,504,631 | .. | 76,600,000 |

The table below shows the total receipts and shipments and

the number of animals driven out for packers and city use for the year:—

| Description. | Receipts. | Shipments. | Driven out, 1891. | Driven out, 1892. |
|---|---|---|---|---|
| | Number. | Number. | Number. | Number. |
| Cattle | 1,492,765 | 792,369 | 546,219 | 700,396 |
| Calves | 97,810 | 44,401 | 37,480 | 53,409 |
| Hogs | 2,437,884 | 593,291 | 2,008,914 | 1,844,593 |
| Sheep | 441,822 | 209,838 | 209,866 | 231,984 |
| Horses and mules | 32,831 | 22,233 | 8,931 | 10,598 |
| Total | 4,503,112 | 1,662,132 | 2,811,410 | 2,840,980 |

**Meat inspection.** The United States Meat Inspection Department at this point has been extended, and the daily inspection has largely increased in volume. The system has proven itself a success, and of great advantage to the packers and buyers.

**Banking.** No material changes have occurred in the amount of capital invested in the banking interest. Surplus and undivided profits have been increased from 1,063,000 dol. for 1891 to 1,420,000 dol. for 1892. Deposits to the amount of 26,855,000 dol. were in the banks at the close of business, December 31, 1892, as against 24,000,000 dol. at the corresponding date the previous year. The bank clearings amounted to 510,186,611 dol. for 1892, as against 460,471,785 dol. for 1891.

**Grain trade.** The following table shows the amount of grain received and inspected during 1892 as compared with the preceding year:—

| | Wheat. | Corn. | Oats. | Rye. | Barley. |
|---|---|---|---|---|---|
| | Cars. | Cars. | Cars. | Cars. | Cars. |
| Kansas City, Kansas— | | | | | |
| 1891 | 24,126 | 10,506 | 3,323 | 2,346 | 25 |
| 1892 | 51,832 | 13,905 | 2,318 | 1,917 | 144 |
| Kansas City, Mo.— | | | | | |
| 1891* | 4,221 | 6,959 | 1,749 | 1,962 | .. |
| 1892 | 18,386 | 8,252 | 1,601 | 583 | 11 |

\* For January to June inclusive, 1891.

### Kansas State.

**General remarks.** The condition of the State has been generally satisfactory. The past season was favourable to the farming class, and business of all kinds throughout the State has been satisfactory. The inhabitants of the State are essentially an agricultural community, and their main dependence is upon farm products.

**Field crops.** The acreage devoted to field crops is reported to have been 18,360,240 acres, a slight increase over the previous year, and the value of all farm products was placed at 164,648,955 dol. as compared with 169,811,372 dol. for 1891.

## CHICAGO.

RETURN showing the Number of Livestock, as returned by the Assessors, and Value for the Year 1892.

| Description. | Quantity. | Value. |
|---|---|---|
| | Head. | Dollars. |
| Horses | 804,923 | 52,319,995 |
| Mules and asses | 79,262 | 5,944,650 |
| Milch cows | 631,386 | 11,364,948 |
| Other cattle | 1,708,368 | 29,042,256 |
| Sheep | 240,568 | 721,704 |
| Swine | 1,605,098 | 9,630,588 |
| Total | .. | 109,024,141 |

*Mining and smelting coal.* The output from the Kansas coal mines shows a small increase over the output for the previous year, and the production has found a ready and remunerative sale within the limits of the State.

*Lead and zinc.* The lead and zinc mines show an increased production, and the smelting facilities have been increased in the mining district.

## DENVER.

Mr. Vice-Consul Pearse reports as follows:—

The condition of the trade and commerce of the city of Denver and the State of Colorado for the year 1892 has been fairly satisfactory.

Transactions in real estate and building operations show a considerable falling-off as compared with last year. It is claimed, however, that there has been no very material decrease in values, and that the business of the city has settled down on a substantial basis, free from the excitement which prevailed in the two previous years.

*Value of new buildings.* The value of new buildings erected during the year was 1,552,663*l.*, the greater part of which was expended in the construction of residences; this shows a decrease of 548,163*l.* in comparison with 1891.

*Real estate.* Transactions in real estate for the year were 8,350,140*l.*, as against 9,503,197*l.* in 1891. The largest proportion of the transactions for the year was in residence property.

During the year 5,158,850*l.* was loaned on real estate, the average rate of interest being 7·22 per cent.

The paving of the streets in the business section of the city during the year has enhanced the real estate values considerably, and added greatly to the appearance of the city and comfort of the inhabitants.

*Value of taxable property.* The total assessed valuation of taxable property in the whole

State for the year was 47,576,440*l.*, an increase of 1,095,830*l.* over the assessment of 1891.

**Clearing-house records.** The records of the Denver clearing-house for the year show a total of 53,169,959*l.*, an increase over 1891 of 7,409,959*l.*

The total resources of the 11 national banks of the city at the close of the year were 5,843,487*l.*, an increase over 1891 of 711,395*l.* The deposits were 4,095,173*l.*, an increase of 631,531*l.*; loans, 3,543,844*l.*—increase, 460,934*l.*

**Manufacturing.** The value of the manufactured products of the various manufacturing establishments in the city, including the output of the ore smelting companies for the year, was 9,114,323*l.*, a decrease from 1891 of 1,071,939*l.* Total number of employés, 12,135. Amount paid in wages, 1,707,333*l.* The falling-off in value is said to be due to the low price of silver which prevailed during the year.

Two important enterprises have been added to the manufacturing industries during the past two years, viz., paper-making and the manufacture of cotton goods. The paper is prepared from the pulp obtained from the white spruce wood of the Rocky Mountains, grown at an elevation of from 8,000 to 11,000 feet; it is said to produce a very superior paper.

The raw cotton for the cotton mills comes from the south over the Denver, Texas, and Fortworth Railroad, which extends from Denver to the Gulf of Mexico. The amount of capital invested in these two enterprises is 160,000*l.*

**Wholesale merchandise.** Denver is rapidly becoming a distributing point for the various articles of merchandise in this and neighbouring States, and the wholesale merchants report a satisfactory year's business, there being comparatively few failures. The total sales of the mercantile houses for 1892 were 9,529,400*l.*, as against 8,702,100*l.* in 1891.

**Street railways.** The street railway companies have added 14 miles of electric and cable lines to their extensive system of street railways during the year, making a total of 156 miles now in operation. The pay-roll is about 20,000*l.* per month. Over 30,000,000 passengers were carried during the year.

**Railways.** The 19 railway systems of Colorado embrace 5,271 miles of road in actual operation, an increase of 969 miles since my report of 1888. The number of railway employés is 13,000, and the disbursement of wages for 1892 amounted to 2,100,000*l.* The total number of car-loads of all the principal articles of industry received in Denver during the year was 122,775; the total for 1891 was 163,508. It is claimed that this decrease is due to the fact that a great many articles formerly brought from the East are now being manufactured in Denver.

**Agriculture.** 1,488,000 acres of farming and fruit land were irrigated during the year by the various irrigating ditches throughout the State, and the value of the crops from these lands is shown as follows:—

| Articles. | Value. |
|---|---|
| | £ |
| Alfalfa | 976,690 |
| Tame grasses | 248,076 |
| Native ,, | 1,794,268 |
| Grains | 3,267,795 |
| Vegetables and fruits | 2,200,000 |
| Total | 8,486,829 |

Filings and final entries were made on 733,000 acres of Government land by settlers during the year.

The low price of silver which prevailed throughout the year had the effect of retarding progress in mining, the chief industry of the State. A number of the low-grade silver mines were compelled to suspend operations and development work was brought to a standstill in hundreds of mining properties. The average price of silver for 1892 was ·868 c. per oz., as against ·9855 c. per oz. in 1891. The figures which I have been able to obtain show a decrease in value of the metal product, as compared with 1891, of 224,069*l*.

The following is the estimated value of the output for 1892 :—

| Articles. | Value. |
|---|---|
| | £ |
| Silver | 4,405,714 |
| Gold | 945,519 |
| Lead | 997,466 |
| Copper | 121,854 |
| Total | 6,470,553 |

During the past year more coal was mined in Colorado than during any year in the history of the State. The output was 3,771,234 tons, the value of which at the mines was 1,267,134*l*.

## UNITED STATES

### SUMMARY of the Coal Statistics during the undermentioned Years.

| Year. | Quantity. |
|---|---|
| | Tons (of 2,000 lbs.). |
| 1874 | 87,372 |
| 1875 | 98,838 |
| 1876 | 117,666 |
| 1877 | 160,000 |
| 1878 | 200,630 |
| 1879 | 322,732 |
| 1880 | 375,000 |
| 1881 | 706,744 |
| 1882 | 1,061,479 |
| 1883 | 1,220,593 |
| 1884 | 1,130,024 |
| 1885 | 1,398,796 |
| 1886 | 1,436.211 |
| 1887 | 1,791,735 |
| 1888 | 2,185,477 |
| 1889 | 2,400,629 |
| 1890 | 3,075,781 |
| 1891 | 3,512,632 |
| 1892 | 3,771,234 |

### RETURN of Production of Coal by Countries during the Years 1891-92, showing Increase and Decrease.

| Countries. | Quantity. 1891. | Quantity. 1892. | Increase. | Decrease. |
|---|---|---|---|---|
| | Tons (of 2,000 lbs.). | Tons (of 2,000 lbs.). | Tons (of 2,000 lbs.). | Tons (of 2,000 lbs.). |
| Arapahoe | 1,273 | 654 | .. | 619 |
| Boulder | 498,494 | 569,326 | 70,832 | .. |
| Dolores | 3.475 | 3,475 | .. | .. |
| El Paso | 34,364 | 35,788 | 1,424 | .. |
| Fremont | 545,789 | 497,382 | .. | 48,407 |
| Gunnnison | 261,350 | 198,483 | .. | 62,867 |
| Garfield | 191,994 | 285,550 | 93,556 | .. |
| Huerfano | 494,466 | 541,596 | 47,130 | .. |
| Jefferson | 17,910 | 23,556 | 5,646 | .. |
| Las Animas | 1,219,224 | 1,329,178 | 109,954 | .. |
| La Plata | 72,471 | 89,612 | 17,141 | .. |
| Mesa | 5,000 | 7,300 | 2,300 | .. |
| Montezuma | .. | 675 | 675 | .. |
| Park | 52,626 | 87,949 | 35,323 | .. |
| Pitkin | 91,642 | 77,526 | .. | 14,116 |
| Weld | 22,554 | 13,184 | .. | 9,370 |
| Small mines not reported | .. | 10,000 | 10,000 | .. |
| Totals | 3,512,632 | 3,771,234 | .. | .. |

RETURN of Coke Production during the Year 1891-92.

| Counties. | Quantity. 1891. | Quantity. 1892. | Increase. |
|---|---|---|---|
| | Tons (of 2,000 lbs.). | Tons (of 2,000 lbs.). | Tons (of 2,000 lbs.). |
| Las Animas | 184,047 | 240,177 | 56,130 |
| Gunnison | 43,910 | 51,879 | 7,969 |
| Pitkin | 47,014 | 53,019 | 6,005 |
| La Plata | 5,548 | 10,000 | 4,452 |
| Mesa | .. | 20 | 20 |
| Total | 280,519 | 355,095 | 74,576 |

The oil-fields at Florence, the only developed oil region in the State, produced during the year 730,000 barrels of crude oil. *Petroleum.*

The following is a record of imports from Great Britain for the past 6 years:— *Imports.*

| Year. | Value. |
|---|---|
| | £ s. |
| 1887 | 5,043 12 |
| 1888 | 8,109 12 |
| 1889 | 17,585 7 |
| 1890 | 32,512 4 |
| 1891 | 26,008 16 |
| 1892 | 9,357 4 |

## UNITED STATES.

STATEMENT of Values of Imports from Great Britain entered at the Port of Denver during the Year 1892.

| Articles. | Value. |
|---|---|
| | £ s. |
| Antiquities and curios | 76 4 |
| Carpets | 68 16 |
| Confectionery | 31 4 |
| Cotton, manufactures of— | |
|    Clothing | 20 16 |
|    Cloths | 84 16 |
|    Other | 11 8 |
| Earthenware, stoneware, chinaware, &c. | 2,135 0 |
| Gelatine | 378 8 |
| Household and personal effects | 531 12 |
| Laces | 154 12 |
| Metals, manufactures of— | |
|    Brass balances | 84 16 |
|    Iron bedsteads | 717 8 |
|    Sheep shears | 73 8 |
|    Other | 172 12 |
| Miscellaneous articles | 119 0 |
| Olive oil | 37 8 |
| Shot guns | 72 16 |
| Silk, manufactures of— | |
|    Wearing apparel and handkerchiefs | 541 0 |
|    Other | 12 8 |
| Spirits, distilled— | |
|    Brandy | 99 16 |
|    Gin | 3 0 |
|    Rum | 3 16 |
|    Whiskey | 218 4 |
| Tin-plates | 2,316 12 |
| Varnish | 140 0 |
| Wines | 345 12 |
| Wool, manufactures of— | |
|    Clothing | 122 0 |
|    Cloths and dress goods | 784 12 |
| Total | 9,357 4 |

**Internal revenue.**

The United States Internal Revenue Collector's District, having Denver for its headquarters, embraces Colorado and Wyoming.

The receipts of the office for the year just closed were 71,200*l.* as compared with 65,472*l.* for 1891. The district has in operation 115 cigar factories, 22 tobacco factories, 28 breweries (of which 5 are in Denver), 5 rectifying establishments, and 1 oleomargarine factory.

There were 200,000 barrels of beer manufactured in the breweries during the year.

**Education.**

Increase in population has made it necessary to increase the educational facilities of the public schools in the State during the year.

According to the report of the State Superintendent of Schools, 93 new school-houses were erected at a cost of 72,427*l.* There are 23 new school districts, with an increase of 3,256 scholars. The valuation of public school buildings and property in the State is 1,197,033*l.*

The sanitary condition of Denver shows a marked improvement for the past year, under the efficient Health Commissioner and his inspectors, the death-rate being 14·48 per 1,000 people which is the lowest mortality record in the history of the city.

Health.

LONDON:
Printed for Her Majesty's Stationery Office,
By HARRISON AND SONS,
Printers in Ordinary to Her Majesty.
(75  6 | 93—H & S   1562)

WITHDRAWN